F.R. LEAVIS:

A Life in Criticism

Robert Austin's drawing of F.R. Leavis, one of the pictures of leading men of letters in the *Bookman*, Christmas 1934.

Ian MacKillop

F.R. LEAVIS:

A Life in Criticism

ALLEN LANE
THE PENGUIN PRESS

ALLEN LANE
THE PENGUIN PRESS

Published by the Penguin Group
Penguin Books Ltd, 27 Wrights Lane, London w8 5tz, England
Penguin Books USA Inc., 375 Hudson Street, New York, New York 10014, USA
Penguin Books Australia Ltd, Ringwood, Victoria, Australia
Penguin Books Canada Ltd, 10 Alcorn Avenue, Toronto, Ontario, Canada m4v 3b2
Penguin Books (NZ) Ltd, 182–190 Wairau Road, Auckland 10, New Zealand

Penguin Books Ltd, Registered Offices: Harmondsworth, Middlesex, England

First published 1995
1 3 5 7 9 10 8 6 4 2
First Edition

Filmset by Datix International Limited, Bungay, Suffolk
Printed in Great Britain by
Clays Ltd, St Ives plc
Set in 11/13.5 pt Monophoto Bembo

A CIP catalogue record for this book is available from the British Library
ISBN 0–713–99062–7

To the memory of Maurice B. Kinch
13 July 1928 to 14 February 1993

Is not the pastness of the past the profounder, the completer, the more legendary, the more immediately before the present it falls?

– Thomas Mann, The Magic Mountain

'Art in the blood is liable to take the strangest forms.'

– Arthur Conan Doyle, 'The Greek Interpreter',
The Memoirs of Sherlock Holmes

CONTENTS

CONTENTS

PART FOUR
NEW SHIPS 1963–1975

CHAPTER TEN
THE END OF CAMBRIDGE 1963–1965

CHAPTER ELEVEN
NEW UNIVERSITIES 1965–1975

PART FIVE
EPILOGUE 1975–1978

LIST OF ILLUSTRATIONS

═══

Frontispiece: Robert Austin's drawing of Leavis, one of the illustrations of leading men of letters, *Bookman*, Christmas 1934 (National Portrait Gallery)

★

Harry Leavis, F.R. Leavis's father (by courtesy of Kate Leavis)

Kate Sarah Moore Leavis, F.R. Leavis's mother (Cambridgeshire Collection, Cambridgeshire Libraries & Heritage Service)

The Leavis piano business, opposite Downing College (Cambridgeshire Collection, Cambridgeshire Libraries & Heritage Service)

Leavis at the Perse School (by courtesy of Kate Leavis)

Leavis in the Friends' Ambulance Unit (by courtesy of Kate Leavis)

Queenie Dorothy Roth during her first term at Cambridge, October 1925 (The Mistress and Fellows of Girton College, Cambridge)

Queenie Leavis with her son Ralph, aged one, January 1935 (by courtesy of Kate Leavis)

F.R. Leavis with Ralph, January 1935 (by courtesy of Kate Leavis)

The Leavis family home in Chesterton Hall Crescent (by courtesy of Kate Leavis)

I.A. Richards (by courtesy of Kate Leavis)

Marius Bewley (by courtesy of Peter Dewes)

Queenie Leavis, Harold Mason, Kate and Robin Leavis (by courtesy of S. Betsky-Zweig)

Morris Shapira (by courtesy of Peter Sharrock)

F.R. and Queenie Leavis on the steps of West Lodge, Downing College, summer 1961 (by courtesy of Robert Fothergill)

F.R. Leavis in Bulstrode Gardens, November 1976 (John Cleave/Times Newspapers Ltd)

Text Illustrations

PREFACE

The aim of this book is to set on display the long career of Frank Raymond Leavis, a writer who, like Tennyson's Ulysses, has 'become a name'. So has his wife and collaborator, Queenie Dorothy Leavis. In the course of writing it my admiration for Q.D. Leavis has grown, but I have focused specifically on F.R. Leavis, partly in order to counteract a trend towards the melding of his identity with hers into a joint concept, 'The Leavises'.

For the life of F.R. Leavis there is a mass of material: the published bibliography (see below) runs to over five hundred pages. There are two volumes of his letters, and those of Q.D. Leavis, to the press, *Letters in Criticism* (1974), edited by John Tasker, and *More Letters in Criticism* (1992), edited and privately published by Maurice Kinch. I have used these sources and also studied much, but certainly not all, of his correspondence. Leavis wrote something like half a dozen letters a day, often 'in compulsory haste', as he called it, sometimes generous, sometimes hilariously scornful of the 'major pachyderms', sometimes obsessed, rarely dull. Besides letters supplied by his correspondents (noted below), I have used the main collections at the University of Texas at Austin, at Downing and Emmanuel Colleges, Cambridge, at the Brotherton Library, University of Leeds, and at the University of Reading, which has the care of the publishing papers of Chatto & Windus; these contain evidence of all Leavis's relations with his publisher from the early 1930s to the 1970s. Other collections exist in private hands, including family letters, and letters to L.C. Knights, Harold Mason and John Speirs. Apart from written sources, an oral tradition survives: I have had the benefit of a wealth of reminiscence.

Many people have helped me, in person and in correspondence, especially several generations of Leavis's pupils at Downing College, Cambridge, and former students of other colleges and institutions. I hope they will not be exasperated by the use I have made of their testimonies. Those who have allowed me to study and reproduce substantial material in their possession are listed in the Acknowledgements at the end of this book. Here I would like to single out other individuals who have given me advice, data or inspiration, sometimes all three: Marie Addyman, Tim Armstrong, Sir David Attenborough, Sarah Bendall, Sarah Betsky-Zweig, T.A.B. Birrell, Derek Brewer, Glen Cavaliero, Graham Chainey, Rupert Christiansen, Stefan Collini, Alistair Cooke, Hazel Eagle, David Hamilton Eddy, H.L. Elvin, D.J. Enright, Nancy Fraser, Gwendolen Freeman, Marjorie Glick, Jean Gooder, Richard Gooder, Damian Grant, Ronald Gray, Simon Gray, George Greenfield, Norman Guilding, Ian Hamilton, Bernard Harrison, A.D. Harvey, John Harvey, Ronald Hayman, Norman Henfrey, Colin Hill, John Holloway, Father P.C. Hunting, George Hyde, Fred Inglis, Peter Jackson, Howard Jacobson, Susan M. Jarratt, Robert Jefford, Arthur Johnston, Peggy Kinch, G. Klingopulos, L.C. Knights, William Roger Louis, Duncan McCallum, Fiona MacCarthy, Carla MacKillop, Edward MacKillop, James MacKillop, Alistair McLeery, David Matthews, Wilfrid Mellers, Karl Miller, Howard Mills, Lord Morris, Christopher Parry, Roger Poole, S. Gorley Putt, Clare Ratliff, Theodore Redpath, Neil Roberts, Colin Roth, G.H.W. Rylands, Rosalin Sadler, G.S. Singh, Sir Stephen Spender, Geoffrey Strickland, Frank Stubbings, Kevin Taylor, Etain Todds (*née* Kabraji), John Vice, Iris Walkland, Geoffrey Walton, Garry Watson, Frank Whitehead, Charles Winder and Michael Yudkin.

I have had the good fortune to receive funds or privileges from the British Academy, the Harry Ransom Humanities Research Center at the University of Texas at Austin, Clare Hall, Cambridge, and the University of Sheffield. At Penguin Books I have had continuous, imaginative support from Clare Alexander, Judith Flanders and especially Paul Keegan. The expert reading and copyediting of Donna Poppy has improved every inch of this book. I am indebted to David Bowron for the care and subtlety shown in his work on the index.

I am indebted to the consideration of the literary executors of F.R. Leavis (Robin Leavis and G.S. Singh) and the help of Kate Leavis for furnishing me with family photographs – but it must be stressed that representatives of the Leavis family are not responsible for 'authorizing' this book. I am grateful to Michael Black, Roger Gard, Patrick Harrison, Charles Page, Alison Platt and Richard Storer for work on my drafts, yielding many suggestions and the discovery of innumerable errors.

Specialist librarians and archivists have been particularly helpful, notably Sarah Bendall (Emmanuel College); Michael Bott (University of Reading); Graham Dalling (Edmonton Green Library); Cathy Henderson (Harry Ransom Humanities Research Center); Nick Lee (University of Bristol); David McKitterick (Wren Library, Trinity College, Cambridge, temporarily housing some Cambridge University Press manuscripts); Paul Millett (Downing College); Kate Perry (Girton College); Mike Petty (Cambridge City Libraries: Cambridgeshire Collection); and Christopher Stevenson (University of Leeds).

I wish to express my appreciation of the help of Rosie Ford, and of the late Maurice Kinch, joint author (with William Baker and John Kimber) of *F.R. Leavis and Q.D. Leavis: An Annotated Bibliography*, published by Garland Publishing, Inc., in 1989, originally conceived by William Baker with the encouragement of Q.D. Leavis. A formidable amount of research and editing was undertaken by Maurice Kinch. Without this work, his other publications and his personal assistance and hospitality, my book could not have been attempted. I would have liked the finished article to be subjected to his compassionate severity.

Finally, a note on nomenclature. The writing of a book about two persons called 'Leavis' (both, actually, '*Dr* Leavis') presents a problem to an author who feels uncomfortable with the familiar usage of their first names. I decided mostly to use 'Leavis', 'F.R.L.' and 'Q.D.L.'. I think it works.

PROLOGUE

1961

Back in England, Wordsworth eludes for a while the close confident knowledge aspired to by the modern biographer.
   – F.R. Leavis, 'Wordsworth: The Creative Conditions', 1971

John Forster, with his intimate personal knowledge of his friend (a friendship which survived storms), gives us the sense, as no other biographer does or now can, of being in the same room as Dickens, and even, more important, of being really inward with Dickens's personality and character, and without being concerned to make out a case by 'interpreting' his subject.
   – F.R. and Q.D. Leavis on John Forster's *The Life of Charles Dickens* from *Dickens the Novelist*, 1970

The Portrait

F.R. Leavis died on 14 April 1978. Nearly twenty years later, at the centenary of his birth, he is often mentioned, but not widely or carefully read. The case was different between the mid-1930s and 1970s, and then it was not only his writings that were current. The critic, whose thinking focused on an idea of 'impersonality', was known for a personal presence, appropriate for an indefatigable teacher.

The purpose of this Prologue is to evoke this presence at one moment in 1961, using the report of one who watched Leavis closely near the end of his official career at Cambridge. As he approached retirement, the Governing Body of Downing College, where Leavis was a fellow, arranged for his portrait to be painted. He would have liked the artist to be Lawrence Gowing, but he was pleased with the choice of Peter Greenham, who knew his family slightly. Leavis found Greenham a cordial companion during the thirty or forty hours of sitting that the painter required. Greenham was absorbed by Leavis's company, painting and over-painting until he feared the picture would be too dark for the college Hall. 'You look different from every point of view,' he said. 'I should have thought everybody did,' replied Leavis.[1]

Leavis quite liked the painting when it was done, though he considered he looked too benign in it. In a few years he was to fall out with Downing and said the college would best have its new picture hung in a dingy corner. There, perhaps on 'E' staircase, it could accompany the visages of long-forgotten college notorieties ('like Perkins'), with the legend EXORCIZED inscribed below. A passer-by would not have thought the Greenham portrait particularly diabolic.[2] He depicted a lively, hesitant man, unlike the austere Leavis of popular imagination. At that date Leavis had hardly ever been drawn or photographed for the press. When the portrait was exhibited at the Royal Academy exhibition in May 1962, people were surprised. Evelyn Waugh remarked to Greenham that he had actually made Leavis 'look *intelligent*'.

Peter Greenham died in 1992. Not long before his death he made notes about his experience of the sittings with Leavis; they are an excellent introduction to the critic and teacher. They give Leavis's manner, which matters for a writer who made such personal impact. Greenham shows what Leavis liked to quote, notably Thomas Hardy's poem 'After a Journey', of which he wrote a study in a neglected essay. It evokes Q.D. Leavis in the wings, so to speak; it was probably she who located and quoted the remark about John Forster at the head of this Prologue – that his life of Dickens gives a sense of 'being in the same room as Dickens'. Greenham certainly shows what it was like to be in the same room as Leavis.

When I was painting Leavis, he was beginning to like Dickens, especially the early chapters of *Dombey and Son*, though to the high life, the titled bosoms heaving with jewellery . . . he said, 'No, no!' All the same, he confirmed so many of my own tastes, that one morning I said boldly, 'I like Arnold Bennett's novels.' (I used to paint Leavis in the dining hall of Downing College. I sat on a table, and he sat below me. In those days I smoked one cigarette after another, but he never complained about the smoke or the ash.) He was so courteous that when he said, 'No – you don't,' I went on to say, 'Well, I used to like *some* of Bennett's novels,' and was rebutted with a stern 'No, Greenham.' I still stuck to it, but said, 'There was a time when I *thought* I liked *one* or *two* of Bennett's novels.' In the afternoon Leavis sat down with a book under his arm. Presently he read a passage from it, then shut it with a bang and said, '*That* is what Henry James says about the novels of Arnold Bennett, and I think you will agree,

Greenham, it is *final*.' But it wasn't, for I still love to read *Riceyman Steps*, and Leavis spoke later, if only in a footnote, of the 'shared quality of human experience' – I may have got the words wrong – to be found in Bennett. It was an indication of the loyalty which Leavis attracted that on the one or two occasions I repeated the incident, I thought I had betrayed his confidence. In the end (after he died) I wrote to Queenie and told her the story. She was delighted and said it was to go into the memoir. Did she ever live to write it?

I had less luck with Kipling. But he did tell me about an Indian who had complained that Forster had been unjust to one set of people in *A Passage to India*. 'You mean the Mohammedans?' 'No.' 'The Hindus?' 'No.' 'The Parsees?' 'No – the English.' There was a touch of the 'bull-dog breed' about him. He seemed to respect the admiral who had been the Master of Downing much more than the current Master: and once when a stray Alsatian came to the dining-hall window, Leavis (who used to feed it with scraps) said ferociously, 'Is he going to worry the Master's thin shanks?' He spoke with similar ferocity of other dons, and, of course, of C.P. Snow, about whom he used words I saw again in the famous pamphlet a few months later [in February 1962].

Sometimes he spoke more to himself than to me. I remember that he told me a publisher had asked him to bring out a selection of Hardy's poems, the best ones, but he said he couldn't. Often, in a low voice, he would say over the poem that begins 'Hereto I come to view a voiceless ghost.'* He had a smile of extraordinary sweetness.

He was not 'a man of the world'. He would tell me how much he had in the bank, why his wife wouldn't let him keep a dog, and of his visits (getting by heart a Shakespeare sonnet in the waiting room at Bletchley) to his son Ralph, of whom he spoke sadly yet proudly. One day he asked me if he could have a glance, no more, at the portrait, so that he could tell his wife he had seen it. She wanted news of it.

He often spoke of his admiration for Augustus John's portrait of Thomas Hardy, of its majestic subtlety; and he admired the John portrait of Bernard Shaw for its 'exposure of a charlatan'. The other painting in the Fitzwilliam that he spoke of with warmth – I think it was his favourite – was Pissarro's 'Farm Girl'. It struck me that he had a much surer taste in paintings than I am accustomed to meet in my sitters, commonly military, episcopalian or academic. He was pleased that George Eliot wrote warmly of Rubens.

So I sat in that dining hall, and waited for him to enter quickly, and quietly. He was never late and always sat still; the most courteous of sitters, much

* Hardy's 'After a Journey'. Leavis's distinctive speaking voice was often noted. BBC records at Caversham give an expert view in the report of a producer, R.E. Keen, on 20 September 1949: 'Quiet, rather flat voice with East Anglian vowels, which sounds somewhat monotonous and pleasant.'

ashamed of interruptions, especially one by an American who claimed to be a cousin of Henry James. On another occasion, he told me that the college butler had asked us to tea in his pantry, and would be hurt if the cakes were not eaten. 'You know I never eat anything, Greenham, so I count upon you to eat everything.' I did my best – jam tarts, sandwiches, fruit cake.

A magnificent face, a noble expression, to which no photograph has ever done any justice. A small tense body; the air of being of a different make from ordinary men, all made such an impression on me in the sunny dusty hall that when he asked me to give a paper to a group of his pupils I thought that if I failed the portrait would fail too. I had written about twelve pages on the paintings of D.H. Lawrence, but, noticing Leavis sitting with his eyes shut, I skipped page after page. While I was at breakfast next morning, Leavis walked into the room and remarked, 'Well, the *men* enjoyed it.' So when he asked me to give another talk, this time on 'Drawing' with slides, I was not unprepared to observe Leavis, Queenie and their daughter all sitting with their eyes shut.

He had the effect, almost more than any other sitter, of making a sitting not merely an occasion, but something exalted. Whether he was reciting a poem in a voice hardly audible, or remembering men he admired such as Wittgenstein, or, in an amused but affectionate way, Quiller-Couch, or mocking his enemies (with a sandalled jerking foot, as if about to kick them). His voice was low yet excited (and not in any way like his voice on the radio).

Though he looked older than most men of sixty-seven, and sometimes spoke of the respect now attached to him ('and now – this portrait'), he didn't speak of his coming retirement as far as I can remember. He was tanned by the sun; and that, together with the colour of his clothes (set off by a white shirt which looked fresh every day), gave him a russet glow. When I dropped one of my brushes, he stooped to pick it up. Not every sitter does so!

He told me that his father was for the Boers in 1900; and he used to tell with special pleasure of the Australian soldiers in the War who refused to be intimidated by the English officers. And yet there was something in the way he spoke of the tradition of a gentleman which is echoed in what he writes about Sir Leicester Dedlock, and the training of merchant seamen in the essay on *The Shadow-Line*.

All this is known, perhaps – what I think you want from me is the effect he had on me. Most courteous, tormented, kind, never trivial. He once said, 'They talk of the power of the atom bomb. There's enough energy in my wife to blow Europe to pieces.' His was another kind of energy: suppressed, but like a torrent, no outlet. Once, when he was describing somebody to me, he said, 'I am a novelist *manqué*.'

He had one of the most impressive heads I have ever seen: to compare with Einstein and Paderewski, both of whom I saw in the street in Oxford. I wish

Epstein could have done a bust of him . . . Later he wrote to me a letter to say that the sittings might have been a sorry trial, but were not.[3]

Greenham wrote to Q.D.L. after her husband's death in 1978, encouraging her with the memoir she planned to write. She replied, 'There are things that only he and I knew, and I can't bear to think of anyone else not getting it right. But then there's my own work — there's so much to do, and I'm seventy-one.' Q.D.L. was seriously depressed in bereavement and had been in poor health; understandably the memoir did not materialize, though she kept a drawer for her notes. She certainly wanted to set the record straight. When she encountered a howler about Leavis's life, she would expostulate, 'Why can't people check with the family?'[4] She solicited one of her Girton contemporaries for reminiscences, which would give 'great pleasure to my children who can remember us only as grey-haired and worn down with battling for survival in a hostile environment — in fact I can hardly remember myself that we (F.R.L. and I) were once gay, good-looking and hopeful'.[5]

Would Leavis himself have wanted a memoir? He was popularly associated with literary criticism of a purity that eschewed interest in authors' lives. He did not object, in theory, to the idea of writing his own memoirs, though in practice he thought the task was not for his temperament. In his eighties both Q.D.L. and his publisher urged Leavis towards autobiography ('A best-seller — and absolutely necessary'), but Leavis declared, 'I shall never write more than there is in my Clark Lectures.'[6] There were several reasons why Leavis would not embark on autobiography, apart from the obvious one that he was busy, to the end, with plans for more criticism. First, he thought autobiography would play into the hands of those who accused him of obsession, including 'persecution-mania'. Second, as he remarked to Greenham, he played with the idea of writing a novel, but, as he told a former pupil, he had more important things to do.[7] Third, he believed that his account could not satisfy Q.D.L.'s 'formidable sense' of the past. 'She is intensely — but intensely — indignant about the way Cambridge, and the academic and literary worlds in general, have treated us; with the result that we have now to live mainly on my royalty income.'[8] He could not risk the effect of published recollections on her health. 'There must be no intensities of that kind risked now: her illness has left her with a heart that requires a daily drug (her complex illness includes pericarditis).' And there was a temperamental disinclination, which on one occasion (to his pupil,

Geoffrey Walton) he identified as 'masculine'. He believed that his inner nature required him not to be diagnostically or descriptively explicit about the betrayals he had experienced.[9] His history was hardly secret; he revealed some of it, in talk and letters, to many contacts over the years, a discourse that virtually constituted an 'unwritten work', Raymond Williams remarked.[10]

As to an account of his life by someone outside his family, of this Leavis was distinctly dubious. Rather unwillingly he allowed a former pupil, William Walsh, to write a book about him. When, in 1976, Ronald Hayman published a straightforward life called *Leavis* the subject treated this offering with disdain, though he partly objected to it on an issue of literary politics: Hayman's work originally came out in the *New Review*, whose funding by the Arts Council Leavis despised. By the end of his life Leavis encouraged no one to act as his biographer and instructed his literary executors to discourage proposals. They have continued to respect Leavis's wishes. This book must not be construed as one authorized by the Leavis estate.

The present book is not an authorized biography, and perhaps hardly a biography at all in that it contains very little material of the 'two-days-and-a-failed-mackerel-fishing-trip-later' kind. But it seemed time for 'a life' for two reasons, at least. First, Leavis was a dynamic figure, handling challenges and circumstances as they presented themselves (and for Leavis a circumstance was often a reading of a work, new or familiar). In the coming pages Leavis will quite often be heard using military language, like 'liaison', 'field-performance'. His literary criticism was a series of life-activities, a *praxis*. This aspect of his work was well appreciated in a first-class study, Francis Mulhern's *The Moment of Scrutiny* (1979); it took the New Left to understand a political figure, a 'militant'. A 'life' also was required because Leavis was a teacher with charisma. This personal presence was not an incidental quality; he was not simply a teacher with a remarkably interesting personality. His teaching was a way of being a person – or not being another sort of academic person. It did not invite imitation. People *did* (and still do) mimic the manner, but this was a sign of his inimitableness, rather than the contrary; you could not 'do a Leavis' in real life. Leavis's demeanour as a teacher and in person became an emblem of seriousness, and that – embarrassing to admit it – is what a pupil wants. The matter is well put by one of Leavis's pupils (1951–4), Michael Baxandall, later an art historian of great distinction. 'I am sure he had a deeper effect on me than any other teacher I had; I would say that two others, art historians, had the same order of intellectual effect, but Leavis's was also what I have to call moral, for want of a more focused term.' Baxandall considered how Leavis affected people in other academic fields, or who moved to them. The effect was not necessarily a desire to apply *Scrutiny*-type methods elsewhere. More than that

it is a matter perhaps of modification by demands of the medium of the objects one addresses. For myself I know I set out partly to do Leavis on painting, so to speak, and that what emerged may not look like that. But I am sure a whole set of values and priorities I try to observe I owe to Leavis – belief in a sense of relevance, belief in valuation, admiration of complexity, belief in the detail texture as index of the quality of total order, liking for culture in touch with the vernacular, a sense of the morality of technique, and so on. There would be lots of other lists. The point is, though, that a thoroughly and consciously Leavisian anthropologist, say, might be doing things that did not look superficially Leavisian. I am not putting this very well.[11]

Leavis became a conscience for some pupils, by means of the person he was in his tutorial contacts. To give a sense of Leavis means giving a sense of him as a teacher.

There is another reason for attempting 'a life'. Modern biography favours detail, and detail appears to be an earnest of depth. A 'life' may have depth, but it must have width, and width is required, at this juncture, for the understanding of Leavis. In the fifteen years since his death 'Leavis' has become a coagulation of attitudes and beliefs, sometimes described well, sometimes barbarically. What is not yet generally clear is the sequence and scale, and the types, of his work. There were many Leavisian discoveries communicated to pupils that were little known to others: how often is the importance of *Hamlet* to Leavis noted? How often is his valuation of Wordsworth's 'The Ruined Cottage' recognized? 'A life' requires a wide-angle lens, something appropriate, now, for this author.

Also, the life was an unusual one conducted in circumstances that seem familiar, but call out to be specified. Wittgenstein once asked a pupil, Theodore Redpath, whether there had been any tragedies in his life. 'I asked him what he meant by "tragedy". "Well," he replied, "I don't mean the death of your old grandmother at the age of eighty-five, I mean *suicides, madness* or *quarrels*." I said that I had been fortunate enough not to have experienced any of these terrible things.' There were quarrels in Leavis's life, as well as suffering, resolution and bitterness. To know a little of the circumstances of his life and his professional predicaments, through two world wars, leads out to some of the lesser-known discoveries he made as a literary critic.

The Secret Sharers

Michael Baxandall was proud to have been a pupil of Leavis. I am myself, having been taught by him between 1957 and 1960, four mornings a week attending his seminars, with the rest of my year at Downing. I have a few memories of personal contact: principally being visited as a freshman when the college was laid low with 'flu. More interesting is the advice Leavis gave me when I wanted to do a Ph.D. A research subject, he said, must yield something concrete to be done on a Monday morning: literary critical thinking was too gruelling to be done more than a few hours a week; lesser tasks are necessary to prepare for greater, and to allow the student to feel that progress is being made. I have one inconsequential memory of a talk in the Downing court on a hot June day in 1961. Leavis chatted courteously, seating himself on the library steps. Clive Parry, professor of international law and the 'witty deep-revolving' college librarian, emerged into the sunlight. 'Ah, Leavis, like Socrates with his pupils,' he remarked. 'Socrates was not a very *handsome* man, Parry,' replied Leavis.

The community of pupils, sometimes collaborators (from his own wife onwards), was important to Leavis. Their significance is shown in an allegorical fashion in a lecture Leavis gave at the University of York in 1966, not long after his retirement, about Joseph Conrad's novella *The Secret Sharer*. Conrad's story is about a young merchant captain who conceals a fugitive, as young as he, on the ship of his command, one who has killed a seaman but whom the captain decides instinctively (acting 'on his full human judgement') must have the chance to escape. The fugitive is hidden from the crew in the captain's tiny quarters, indeed, in the captain's clothes. He has his vessel manoeuvred dangerously to accomplish the escape. In his lecture Leavis's theme was partly the 'relations between training, law, society and personal responsibility'. One of his aims was to validate the conception of 'reflex': experience and training make possible an *immediacy* of response and 'grasp', something shown in Leavis's own literary critical conduct. The idea that instinctive judgement has a validity certainly appealed to his pupils. It has been said that young people liked his criticism because his belief in knowing a few things well, or that life is too short for the usual 'Lit. Crit.' eclecticism, appealed to their indolence. The view discounts the passion of youth, its desire to do something serious and to realize that it is engaged with the difficult.

Leavis's lecture on *The Secret Sharer* had another interest in its dwelling on the relationship between the captain and his intimate fugitive, or 'double' as Leavis calls him. The captain says, 'I did not think of asking him for details and he told me the story in brusque, disconnected sentences. I needed no more. I saw it all going on as though I were myself inside that other sleeping-suit.' Throughout his life, Leavis had his own doubles. He saw Eliot as a 'double', believing in old age that Eliot identified Leavis himself as *his* double in 'Little Gidding', in the figure of the ghostly humanist who certainly had Leavis's countenance, for Eliot (or the interlocutor) was accosted by one in whose 'brown baked features' were

> The eyes of a familiar compound ghost
> Both intimate and unidentifiable.

Leavis had, for a time, a double in his former pupil, Denys Harding, who, on Leavis's suggestion, formed a definition of 'disinterestedness', on which Leavis relied and which he freely acknowledged. There was always, of course, Q.D.L., who had numerous connections with Leavis's thinking, one of which was seldom noted. Unlike Leavis, the great re-reader, she was omnivorous: his discipline matched her catholicity. Some doubles were at a remove from Leavis, at ease in another discipline, or from another culture, like the American Marius Bewley.

There was also a reverse side to doubling, a sense of belonging provoked in pupils who became conspirators. Leavis told them 'All's fair in love, war and examinations. Don't be afraid to say anything that suits you about me in the tripos.' These were the junior secret sharers – myself included. One way in which the Leavis position worked for them was ordinary but influential, and is illustrated by the testimony of one pupil of the 1940s. At school Geoffrey Lees was introduced to *Revaluation* (1936) by a former pupil, G.C. Greenfield. He found its 'analytical, factual, disciplined approach a great relief'. Once at Downing, Leavis exercised his influence personally on Lees in a way seemingly less serious but still educationally momentous. Leavis could seductively announce to a lecture audience that 'I don't, of course, approach Keats with enthusiasm', then shock it with a splendid analysis of the 'Ode to a Nightingale'. Back in college, over the tattered dating-sheets (taken in at the end of the hour in those days), Leavis would aphorize.

> – You can't get a First and go to heaven, you know.
> – One must ask the question: Is it realized?
> – It's just *not there*, you know.

Lees remembered sayings of what he called 'a different order'.

> – Mr X? Oh, he can wear a morning coat.
> – Mr Y has just written a book. He's a very ignorant man.
> – You won't learn anything from Dr Z. He looks like a pork butcher.

Lees confessed to being guilty at remembering these seeming trivialities, and enjoying them. He felt obliged to excuse the jibes as Leavis's compensation for 'dissatisfaction with the English Faculty'. They were not in awfully good taste, but they were part of a larger tendency: for Leavis was a critic by vignette. He enjoyed delivering the small grotes-queries of literary history: Baudelaire's upper lip coming away on the shaving razor; Thomas Hardy's heart, momentarily left on the kitchen table by Florence Emily, carried off by the cat. He relished E.J. Trelawny (a 'blackguard'), the author of *Records of Shelley, Byron, and the Author* (1858), who furtively flicked the shroud from Byron's corpse to authenti-cate his supposed club-foot. He liked Peacock's story of reassuring Shelley that it was not night, but his hat had fallen over his eyes. Leavis's taste for such tales was close to some of his literary critical enthusiasms for works of the grotesque, like Pope's *The Dunciad*, or some parts of his 'Elegy to the Memory of an Unfortunate Lady', or the poem by Thomas Gray that he put into currency, the 'Impromptu' about the last years of a disgraced eighteenth-century grandee, which ends with the wicked peer sighing, or howling, a lament for what might have been.

> Purged by the sword, and sanctified by fire,
>   Then had we seen proud London's hated walls;
> Owls would have hooted in St Peter's choir,
>   And foxes stunk and litter'd in St Paul's.

The man who enjoyed these lines worried a pupil by telling him he had no objection to a stray mongrel in Downing College: 'The master doesn't like the dog, but I feed it with bones.'[12]

Leavisian mischief was exciting and actually had a serious function.

Leavis liked to discount or undermine *gravitas*, especially his own. (He said to Greenham: 'And now – this portrait.') He could see himself as David to Goliath, the resolute mischief-maker. In late life he portrayed himself as tying tin-cans to the tail of the great and the good, like Noël Annan or, earlier, C.P. Snow. He did not see himself as little-man-against-the-world', though he would mention his 'eight stone, fighting weight'. He disliked Chaplin, preferring, but without Q.D.L.'s passion, Buster Keaton ('He was an athlete, you know'). Leavis's position was so serious that he did not want it deflected into solemnities. His thinking about literature was, indeed, underpinned by radical considerations about European culture, the considerations of *The Waste Land*. In the 1920s he would quote Oswald Spengler's apocalyptic *Der Untergang des Abendlandes* (*The Decline of the West*). He liked to remark of, and quote from, D.H. Lawrence: he wrote 'for the race, as it were'. Leavis, in obvious ways, occupied the space of a sage; he knew that for many young people he was a model of what being serious was like. But he was temperamentally uncomfortable with being sage-*like*. This was alien to his literary criticism with its principle of working by specificities, not rhetoric. Socially (perhaps psychologically) mischief defeated the large gesture. In some ways he was Victorian; but it was necessary for him to be not 'Victorian'. (Compare his commitment to specificity with that of another survivor of the First World War, Lewis Namier.) Once, at a student tea, Leavis overheard Q.D.L. say that in the Civil War 'my husband would have been one of Cromwell's generals'. 'No, my dear,' he called across the room: 'I would have been *Cromwell*.' The point of the joke is that he thought he would not have been.

Being a Critic

A written life need not be a complicated matter. A life ought, at least, to resemble a guidebook. Guidebooks, like lives, are often about the semi-known. What is semi-known about Leavis is that he was a literary critic, but possibly to many people, including academics, it is not altogether clear what a literary critic is, and if not, then it cannot be clear what Leavis's was a career *in*. The career was spent at Cambridge, but 'Cambridge' suggests pedagogy and authority, both somewhat misleadingly. Leavis may be seen the more clearly if he is imagined in other roles. Leavis was a don, but he behaved *like* a reviewer, he was a judging analyst, but he behaved *like* an artist.

The main point about a reviewer is regular responsiveness, weekly, monthly or quarterly. Some literary academics have reviewed a much greater range of books than Leavis, but, with his love of journals, Leavis was still of this kind, the commentator continuously coping with a flow. To see him thus serves better than seeing him as literary scholar with a responsibility to the fields of knowledge. (William Empson, though wonderfully lively, was actually less of a 'reviewer' than Leavis; and, though a poet, less of an 'artist-critic'.) Indeed, it is the lack of this kind of responsibility that sets Leavis in the category of artist-critic, doing criticism somewhat in the way the novelist does criticism. No one expects a creative writer to keep an open mind or be respectful of a syllabus, the range of the supposedly valuable, or what is just 'there'. The creative writer values what can be used and is not held responsible for what does not serve. One might regret that Philip Larkin wrote so few novels but hardly deplore it, as Leavis's dislike of Laurence Sterne has been deplored. The creative writer is responsible to his or her art. In *that* way Leavis was responsible, not to the art of his own composition, but to the new art he drank in on his return to England after the Armistice. His responsibility was 'vicarious', the word to be interpreted literally and intensely.

Leavis ran his own journal, *Scrutiny*, between 1932 and 1953. Many literary academics have been involved with literary critical journals. In observing the life of Leavis we have to consider how many did so in the *Scrutiny* period. The situation was quite different later. And it must be remembered that Leavis was working in Britain. In America there was, even in the early 1930s, much evidence of cross-over between journals run by literary 'men of letters' and literary academics; Leavis called it the 'higher journalism'. It is not that Leavis was doing something unique for his time in publishing *Scrutiny*. Nor did he think so: he was definite about its models. But there was a problem posed by the mixed provenance of *Scrutiny*, half in and half out of both literary world and university. Was it a 'Cambridge' journal, a university journal, or not? It boasted its origins, yet it had the push and bite of a literary-world production like the *Calendar of Modern Letters*, one of its models. Did it belong to academe? Journals that were institutionally mixed (partly academic, partly commercial) existed in America, like the *Hudson Review* or the *Sewanee*. But they did not really have British counterparts. The seemingly anomalous provenance of *Scrutiny* created some of the difficulties of Leavis's position, including semi-social difficulties. From Leavis's vantage-point T.S. Eliot was an authoritative figure, running the *Criterion* from an office in Faber and Faber, where he did indeed have secure backing. Yet Eliot's position was fragile, needy of contributions and contributors, running a journal as an American abroad in a time of economic slump. Leavis hardly seemed to grasp the insecurity. On the other side, Eliot may have envied Leavis his Cambridge position. It was not a strong one, as Eliot (the former academic) knew; I.A. Richards told him about the poverties of Cambridge life. None the less, to an outsider Leavis may have appeared a secure don, settled for life.

What Leavis did as a literary critic will emerge in the coming pages. Initially, some notes (indeed, personal ones) about his style of literary criticism may be helpful.

First, developing the suggestion that Leavis 'behaved like' an artist, he was a protector of species. He absorbed what he considered to be the founding modes of modern British writing and his life was one of standing by, and sometimes enlarging, these decisions. The life's work was one of loyalties.* Once again the circumstances of these loyalties must be remembered. We are accustomed to think, rightly, of the wealth of modern (or modernist) literature – partly because of the overall movement to which Leavis himself belonged, that is, the establishment of modern literature as an academic subject: academe has been a *producer* of literature in that it sets syllabuses and sales targets for the book trade. But, in the years in which he began, Leavis was loyal to some fragile growths. It is understandable that Leavis believed the modern was in danger, could be stunted (by academe, careerism or old tastes). In the early 1920s much of the modern, to which we are accustomed, did not yet exist. Even up to 1936, the year of Leavis's appointment as a tenured Lecturer in Cambridge, many works of the modern world had not, or had hardly, arrived. Their currency cannot be easily measured by the documents of the literary 'critical heritage'. International reviewing and academic response is well ahead of actual

---

* In 1934 Edith Sitwell teased Leavis as a 'gentleman who plays in the literary life of Mr T.S. Eliot, and in a lesser degree that of Mr Ezra Pound, much the same part as that played by the faithful Dr Watson in the life of Sherlock Holmes'. She was not so foolish: it was Leavis's *métier* to be the reliable assistant.

currency. For example, *The Great Gatsby* was published in 1925, yet in 1935 an exhilarating reference to it in a Cambridge lecture by I.A. Richards inspired a well-read undergraduate – who had never heard of the novel and had to ask a bookshop to order a copy from America. We must not presume that Leavis's circumstances were those of the *later* twentieth century.

The second feature of Leavis's criticism that can be briefly stated is that he was very much a commentator on *poetry*. He is known for his work on the novel and is supposed to be a propagandist for the realist novel and its allegedly 'transparent' prose. But the essays on the novel adapted into *The Great Tradition* (1948) were originally headed 'The Novel as Dramatic Poem'. (As to 'dramatic poems', he is not so well known for his work on Shakespeare, but there were important essays – and Shakespeare was *the* poet for Leavis.)

Another feature of Leavisian criticism, what he *did*, needs more explanation. He absorbed what moved him in the modern movement when he returned from the war in 1919. Some of what moved him fed into his own style. If *The Waste Land* is a tapestry of allusion, so Leavis worked to create a form of tapestry-criticism, favouring the clinching and epitomizing quotation of prose or verse. Hence the pregnant appendices to *Revaluation*, which are mostly quotation. Thus the astonishing amount of quotation in *D.H. Lawrence: Novelist* (1955). Leavis's use of quotation was not unlike the procedure recommended by Ezra Pound in *How to Read*. He argued that the history of poetry is best presented as anthology, a series of passages, like the glass picture-slides (today 'transparencies') used by a 'lantern Lecturer'. To show poetry by extracts enabled precision and evaluative comparison. Setting one such slide against another would make differences more manifest than verbiage of explanation. To change the simile to one not used by Pound, such comparison can be like placing a transparency of one Rorschach ink-blot over another, every difference thus being revealed. What Pound called the 'ideogrammatic method' was close to Leavis's procedure.

Leavis also favoured allusion to compressed, even gnomic statements with the virtues of immediacy. His citations may be semi-anecdotal, meant to capture a quality obliquely. At the end of an essay on Samuel Johnson, a quotation from Johnson on Swift's handling of his household affairs is used to characterize the satirist: 'To his domesticks he was naturally rough; and a man of rigorous temper, with that vigilance of minute attention which his works discover, must have been a master that few could bear.'[13] Leavis's use of quotation is not unlike Pound's use of detail in *Hugh Selwyn Mauberley*, a formative poem for Leavis. And he favoured the pregnancy of literary criticism in verse. No one taught by Leavis could forget how much he adored Shelley's lines about Wordsworth in *Peter Bell the Third*, voiced frequently with relish, dealing with a favourite writer and a favourite theme (sense and thought).

> He had as much imagination
>   As a pint-pot; – he never could
> Fancy another situation
> From which to dart his contemplation,
>   Than that wherein he stood.
>
> Yet his was individual mind,
>   And new created all he saw
> In a new manner, and refined
> Those new creations, and combined
>   Them, by a master-spirit's law.
>
> Thus – though unimaginative,
>   An apprehension clear, intense,
> Of his mind's work, had made alive
> The things it wrought on; I believe
>   Wakening a sort of thought in sense.

About Leavis as critic two axioms should be remembered. First, he was 'a critic', not an 'English Literature critic'. He did not profess English literature only. He worked for literature in English, but the point of literary study was, for him, that it was at the crossroads of other studies: English was the route to other disciplines – and so it was for some other twentieth-century critics, but not at all necessarily for each and every literary academic in the profession of 'Eng. Lit.'. Or, to put it another way and to avoid the implication that Leavis thought English literature was everything, English studies mattered as an example of the way in which the best studies at *large* mattered. Second, Leavis's was a *life* of criticism. 'Shows' are the events in the lives of painters or performers. What are the events in the life of a critic? One type of event in the life of Leavis occurred in 1920 when he purchased a book of essays, *The Sacred Wood*, just after it came out, but 'by some accident, I

had not come on Mr Eliot's name before'. For the next few years Leavis
read these essays by T.S. Eliot 'pencil in hand'. They showed him (in
summary, and the italics for key-words are mine, not Leavis's)

what the *disinterested* and effective application of *intelligence* to literature looks
like, what is the nature of *purity* of interest, and what is meant by the principle
(as Mr Eliot states it) that 'when you judge poetry it is as poetry you must
judge it, and not as another thing'.

The purchase of the essays, the event, encouraged Leavis to define for
himself the meaning of the italicized words. And this became a thread in
his life's work. If that work is to be evaluated, then what he meant by
'disinterested', 'intelligence' and 'purity' cannot be avoided. A historian
who returned repeatedly to Leavis (and was rather ill-used by him in
controversy) is Noël Annan. His reading of Leavis was critical but
ultimately lacked trenchancy because it had at bottom the conviction
that Leavis was merely a '*technical* critic'. He was not: his larger claims
call to be confronted, those claims to define, for example, 'intelligence',
'disinterestedness' and 'purity' − and, indeed, the nature of 'thought in
sense'.

   However, this aspect of the 'Eliot-event' is something that occurs in
any life of the mind. The essays had more specific effects. One of them,
'Tradition and the Individual Talent' (1919), illuminates Leavis's *type* of
activity as a critic.

What happens when a new work of art is created is something that happens
simultaneously to all the works of art which preceded it. The existing monu-
ments form an ideal order among themselves, which is modified by the
introduction of the new (the really new) work of art among them.

The 'new work' is absorbed into the bloodstream and nothing is the
same again. In the life of the critic the discovery of 'new works' and the
reckoning of their *consequences* are major events.[14]

The first chapter of *The Great Tradition* ends thus:

I have, then, given my hostages. What I think and judge I have stated as
responsibly and clearly as I can. Jane Austen, George Eliot, Henry James,
Conrad and D.H. Lawrence: the great tradition of the English novel is *there*.

Is it possible to be equally deliberate about Leavis himself? Of what can
one say, 'The best Leavis is *there*'? If asked by one who had heard more

of Leavis than read him I would make half a dozen suggestions. They would not embody the essential Leavis, but they would contest – 'dislodge' was the Leavisian word – some of the commonplace ideas about this critic. They would include some of Leavis's own preferences. One is an analysis by Leavis, written in 1953, of a seventeenth-century poem, Andrew Marvell's 'A Dialogue between the Soul and Body'. It is about one of his preoccupations: the way in which poems are and are not 'visual'. Another is a meditation on Wordsworth; another is a polemic about the elaborate *Encyclopaedia Britannica* publication, the 'Great Books', an ingeniously indexed home library. The first is called 'Wordsworth: The Creative Conditions' (1971). At the age of seventy Leavis said it was 'the best thing I've done'. When approaching sixty he called 'The "Great Books" and a Liberal Education' (1953) one of 'the best, wittiest and most unanswerable things I've ever done'. The essay on Wordsworth is partly about 'The Ruined Cottage'. Leavis's celebration of some literary works remains even now little known, and this is one of them. He describes the writer 'beginning to be a poet in his twenty-eighth year', almost the year in which Leavis became a literary critic. Like Wordsworth, Leavis returned from a European conflagration. He pointedly quoted a passage from 'The Ruined Cottage' about those hearts which, like that of *Hamlet*'s Horatio, no 'piteous revolutions' have felt or 'wild varieties of joy and grief'.★

There are three important essays on poetry in *The Living Principle: 'English' as a Discipline of Thought* (1975) called ' "Thought" and Emotional Quality', 'Imagery and Movement' and 'Reality and Sincerity', published in *Scrutiny* between 1944 and 1952 but probably written years earlier for lectures and a book on criticism Leavis never finished. Of Leavis's books I would recommend *Education and the University*, partly because in it Leavis reprinted his pamphlet *How to Teach Reading*, which debated with Ezra Pound and shows Leavis at his economical best. Then there is *D.H. Lawrence: Novelist*, which Leavis thought would be '*the* book' on Lawrence, though he blushed the next day to have boasted it. It forms a second volume of *The Great Tradition*, is written with more consistent drive and is on a major Leavis theme, 'The Novel as Dramatic Poem'. The book attempts to define a certain kind of art, as much

★ These essays are in two posthumous collections edited by G.S. Singh, *The Critic as Anti-Philosopher: Essays and Papers* (1982) and *Valuation in Criticism and Other Essays* (1986). The Marvell analysis is in the latter, in an essay called 'The Responsible Critic: or, The Function of Criticism at Any Time' (1953).

Dickensian as Lawrentian; it also dramatically addresses the values of the
cadre that Leavis believed rejected Lawrence. In *D.H. Lawrence: Novelist*
Leavis handles the mix of social and aesthetic values with the greatest
intensity.

If I had to show a page of Leavis to someone who wanted to know
what his writing and enthusiasm were like, my choice would be one first
published in 1963, written at the time of the Greenham portrait. He
returned frequently to its subject in tutorials and lectures. There is
hardly a pupil who did not hear Leavis read and comment upon the
passage by D.H. Lawrence. In it Lawrence gives his response to the
death of Rupert Brooke. The passage is from a letter to Lady Ottoline
Morrell written on 30 April 1915:*

The death of Rupert Brooke fills me more and more with the sense of the
fatuity of it all. He was slain by bright Phoebus's shaft – it was in keeping with
his general sunniness – it was the real climax of his pose. I first heard of him as a
Greek god under a Japanese sunshade, reading poetry in his pyjamas, at
Grantchester, – at Grantchester upon the lawns where the river goes. Bright
Phoebus smote him down. It is all in the saga.

O God, O God, it is all too much of a piece: it is like madness.

Leavis comments:

The passage really belongs in its epistolary context – it has been thrown off
with an unstudied spontaneity; but how marvellous is the living precision with
which the delicate complexity of the reaction, the wholeness of the characteristic
Laurentian response, is conveyed! And how few words he takes for it! The
appalled sense of tragic fatuity stated in the first sentence establishes the ground
tone. Without abrogating the prepotence of this, Lawrence can, in the next
sentence, move into the irony – which in another context would have been
satiric irony – 'he was slain by bright Phoebus's shaft'. It is satiric here only in
so far as it recalls the amused placing observation that had registered King's
Hellenism of Brooke's pre-war Cambridge. The irony of 'Bright Phoebus' can
produce with an inevitable ease of transition the 'sunniness' – a sympathetic
tribute; the 'pose' (the diagnosis becomes fully explicit in this word) is ridiculous,
but there was never any animus in Lawrence's amusement. And he can make

---

* About six weeks after Lawrence's meeting in Cambridge with J.M. Keynes, which had
an indirect but momentous effect on the life of Leavis. See Chapter Eight, No Common
Pursuit, 'Bloomsbury Again: Damned Humbug 1949–1951'. Leavis's account of Lawrence's letter is in ' "Lawrence Scholarship" and Lawrence' in *Anna Karenina and Other
Essays* (1967).

the development of 'pose' that follows, the piquant comedy evocation of that culture of affected attitudinizing, at the same time the expression of a poignant tragic sense ('I first heard of him . . .'). The comedy for Lawrence — I recall in contrast a sentence from Santayana's from a letter that is tucked away in a drawer somewhere: 'The dons, with their bevy of simpering prigs, I can only see as figures in a pleasant comedy' — yields the tragic irony of 'bright Phoebus smote him down', the tone and feeling of which resounds in the concluding protest (for the climax of this pose is death): 'O God, O God . . . it is like madness.'

Part One

CULTURE AND ENVIRONMENT

1895–1931

CHAPTER ONE

ORIGINS
1895–1919

Ils ont fondu dans une absence épaisse,
L'argile rouge a bu la blanche espèce,
Le don de vivre a passé dans les fleurs.
– Paul Valéry, 'Le Cimetière marin',

Into the City 1895–1910

Paul Valéry's lines about the dead could be freely translated thus:

They melted into cold obstruction:
The red clay drank their human white,
The gift of life went only into flowers.

They are moving, austere and artful. Leavis was haunted by them, thought of them as being about the dead of the Great War, and was exasperated by the austerity, or 'classicism', of their rendering of devastation. The Great War was the major experience of the first twenty-five years of Leavis's life, the years before he made a late start as an undergraduate studying English at Cambridge University.

In those early years he moved up through the Cambridge educational system, making progress unprecedented in a family only just come, in his father's generation, from the life of rural crafts people of the Fens into trade in the city of Cambridge. He was not 'educated out of his class'. His father, a flamboyant patriarch and prominent citizen, rose with him in the Cambridge social scene. Both father and son began in the Cambridge trades region, the New Town area. They made their social progress across the street-map of Cambridge.

The main highway through Cambridge runs south-east to north-west.

Under half a dozen successive street names, it is an urban section of the trunk road crossing Cambridgeshire from Essex into Huntingdonshire. This road is not prominent on the map, nor does it go anywhere in particular (with due respect to Huntingdon), but within the city it is a geographical marker. Town is to the right and gown to the left. On the town side there is some industry, an airport, the road to Newmarket, and the site of an ancient fair on Midsummer Common. On the gown side there is the academic sector bounded by the string of colleges compacted along the River Cam, on land ruthlessly acquired at the expense of the town. Rupert Brooke's Grantchester is on this side.

On a wider scale Ely is to the right of the thoroughfare, then the Fens, the Norfolk Broads, and the East Anglian seaside towns of which the more austere, like Southwold and Aldeburgh, are favoured for holidays by the academic classes. This is East Anglian waterland. Cambridge itself was once a port, serving barges that went up river through a series of locks; Ely still boasts a marina. The country to the left of the thoroughfare shades into the Home Counties.

To the visitor the academic sector appears varied but homogeneous. Each college has its fellowship, forming a Governing Body, chaired by a President, Master or Mistress, or, in the case of King's College, the Provost. The fellows run college business, also performing their professional duties for the federation of colleges that is the University of Cambridge.

A college is home for its senior and junior members. Undergraduates, like student lawyers at the London Inns, have to reside to qualify for their degrees. They must keep three 'Full Terms' a year (Michaelmas, Lent and Easter) of eight weeks each, during which all the teaching is done; the academic year begins in early October. The severest discipline of an undergraduate is 'rustication', a serious penalty because the offender is excluded from college, so must make up nights of residence at his inconvenience, and, worse, forbidden to reside within the city limits. Leavis himself had only one brush with the authorities, but the rustication rule had an indirect effect on him. In his early years as a university teacher he was delighted by the poetry of William Empson (still an undergraduate at Magdalene College) and analysed it in his lectures. Soon after his graduation, on the point of taking up a fellowship, Empson was sent down for possessing contraceptives. It turned out that the man whom Leavis thought was an intellectual leader of his generation was lost to Cambridge for good.

Despite similarities in structure Cambridge colleges are fiercely autonomous. They would be better understood if they were a chain of
institutions, like monasteries, miles distant from each other. In a sense
Cambridge provides its pupils with two educations, that of the university
and that of the college. The harshness of Leavis's life partly derived from
friction between the two modes.

The highway through Cambridge marks its entry and exit with
names to celebrate the tiny elevations characteristic of the county. It
comes in as Hills Road and goes out as Castle Hill. Hills Road passes a
junction at which stands the Church of Our Lady and the English
Martyrs, known locally as the Catholic Church. Its scale deceives visitors,
but there is no cathedral in Cambridge. Leavis attended his grammar
school a stone's throw from the Catholic Church. It overlooks Downing
College, where it was a high table joke that it was endowed by a
Belgian manufacturer of open-and-shut dolls' eyes. Its spire is nearly the
highest point in a city of low buildings. The sky is always evident.
Cambridge weather is intense, by turns sparkling cold and leaden damp
in winter, and sticky in summer. The climate of East Anglia is technically
continental, producing minuscule whirlwinds, funnels of wind that whip
up debris in late summer. Much of the domestic brickwork is grey,
known locally as 'corpse brick'.

Past the Catholic Church, Hills Road becomes Regent Street, whose
shops conceal a great grass oblong on each side. The right-hand one is
called Parker's Piece, on the far side of which Leavis attended elementary
school. The left-hand one is the quadrangle of Downing, where Leavis
was a fellow for twenty-five years. It looks more like an American
college in Virginia than a Cambridge one. Facing its gates is the shop
once owned by Leavis's father. Nearer the city centre, still in Regent
Street, is Emmanuel College, where Leavis studied for his bachelor's
degree and his doctorate. The thoroughfare now narrows, a couple of
lanes leading off to a typical East Anglian market square. The intersection
with St John Street is punctuated by a tiny circular Norman church.
Next to the Round Church is the students' Union Society building;
when Leavis was an undergraduate it had the only decent library of
contemporary writing. Next door is the site of the jobbing print-works
that produced Leavis's quarterly journal, *Scrutiny*.

The road crosses the river, at its narrowest passing Magdalene College,
where William Empson was taught by I.A. Richards, also an inspiration
for Leavis. The ground rises ever so slightly at a crossroads, leading to

suburbs right and left. To the right Leavis was brought up; to the left he retired in old age. The right-hand street follows the Cam, there workman-like with a lock, bordering the premises of light industry. By the left-hand road it is a collegiate river flowing through the Backs of the colleges. There are the university library and prosperous academic villas, said by town to be 'where the dons live'.

This is where Leavis spent his life. It takes about eight minutes to cross the central part of the city by bicycle.

Frank Raymond Leavis was born on 14 July 1895. He was aware of its revolutionary associations. His father, a great traveller, was in France with him for one of his boyhood birthdays, where he thought the *quatorze juillet* festivities were in his honour. In old age he told of his arrival in France for his war service in 1916. When he saw bunting from the lorry that was bumping him over the *pavé* to the French front, he wondered how the villagers knew it was his twenty-first birthday. 'Finally I realized it wasn't me, but the Fête Nationale.'[1]

Leavis was at ease in France. He would speak of ancestors among the Huguenots, the Protestant sect that fled France after the Edict of Nantes. A family legend claimed descent from François Gaston Pierre, Duc de Lévis, who succeeded Montcalm at Quebec. Leavis enjoyed the idea of possessing the 'hereditary Huguenot-ducal pride or ferocity' of the refugee 'marked down for clan slaughter'. An important fact in Leavis's ancestry is negative. He was not, as sometimes supposed, Jewish. A Cambridge don is said to have once remarked that the trouble with Leavis was that he was a Jew and didn't know it. Often Leavis was thought of as Jewish. In the post-war period an undergraduate who attended the lectures remarked 'his odd accent and the clothes that made him look like a member of the Knesset in its early days'. But Leavis was definitively gentile: his Jewish wife was disowned by her family for having 'married out'.[2]

The Leavis family came from the Fens. Its first known member in Britain was William, originally from the Leicester region, who settled as a gardener in East Anglia, in the village of Elm near Wisbech. Two of his three sons, John and William, were basket-makers. William's second marriage of three was socially distinctive, to Jane Witton, daughter of an Anglican clergyman who became a Methodist and was consequently rejected by his prosperous family. To prevent being impressed into the Navy during the Napoleonic wars, he went to the length of cutting off a finger. William had ten children, with three sons: Elihu, Frederick and a younger William. Frederick and William, both basket-makers by trade, emigrated to Canada and America. Elihu, the eldest, was Leavis's grandfather. His name was pronounced Elihu.[3]

Elihu Leavis's life was based on the Fen village of Denver, thirty miles from Cambridge. He was a piano-tuner, in the era in which the fireside recital was a regular family occasion and ownership of a piano a serious aspiration. The 'piano man' visited by bicycle twice a year. Elihu Leavis was the first of the extravagant-sounding male figures who surrounded Leavis in his youth, indeed for much of his life. Elihu died when Leavis was six years old, but he remembered him as 'an Arab sheik with his white hair, high cheek bones and fine nose'. During the Boer War his grandfather bicycled him out, on his cross-bar, to the thatched cottage at Denver.

Going with him down the village street, I remember a child calling out 'Kruger', then slipping into a cottage and slamming the door. My Grandfather got off his bicycle, and knocked on the door. 'Did you want to speak to me?' he asked. 'Oh, no sir,' said the frightened little face. Though he was only a piano-tuner, the village respected him and was desperately afraid of him.[4]

Elihu had three children, Frederick, Alice and Leavis's father, Harry. Elihu was widowed early, left to bring up the children. He appears to have moved between Denver, Elm and Cambridge. The 1871 census records the children as living with an uncle at Elm, although they are entered as born in Cambridge. Ten years later Elihu was lodging with Harry and Alice (aged eighteen and sixteen) in the New Town area, near Mill Road, half a mile to the town side of the main thoroughfare.[5] Alice was a draper's assistant and Harry a clerk. He went on to serve an apprenticeship in shop-keeping at a nearby emporium, Sturton's of Fitzroy Square, which advertised 'grocery, oil and paper-hanging materials'. His wife-to-be shared a house near by with her brother, a dentist in New Square. Kate Sarah Moore was originally from Mildenhall. Nine years older than her husband, she was a quiet woman, said to be 'dumpy', easily hurt by Harry's brisk scorn for religion. He was, said Leavis, 'a Victorian radical. There was a fierce, Protestant conscience there, but it was divorced from any religious outlet.' He approved of the Rationalist Press Association and spoke familiarly of 'Barney' Shaw (G.B.S.). He did not stay long at Sturton's: instead he went to Broadwood's in London to learn the piano business. He returned in 1890 to set up shop in Mill Road and was so successful that he moved through a series of premises down Mill Road, each coming closer into the city.

Harry and Kate Leavis brought up three children. The first, Ruth, was born in 1893. Frank Raymond Leavis was born at No. 64, Mill Road, in 1895. The youngest son, Ralph Moore, was born eighteen months later.*

In 1901 Harry Leavis moved again, finally away from Mill Road, leaving New Town behind. Fitzroy Street and Mill Road are on the same spoke of the town road, separated (still) from gown by Parker's Piece, the great square of green completely unembellished but for two diagonal footpaths and a lofty gas-standard at their intersection. At the corner one footpath arrives at Regent Street, by the University Arms Hotel, next to which is a long narrow shop to which Harry Leavis removed the piano and music business. The building has hardly changed in a hundred years, except that it now wears the livery of Pizza Hut. Harry Leavis bought it in 1901, leaving town for gown and making an entry into the Edwardian era, whose mood is expressed by the architecture of the University Arms Hotel, which is more typical of Bournemouth than Cambridge. There is still a seaside air about this corner of the town, as if the Leavis shop had been on a promenade, with Parker's Piece like a great beach with the tide out.

The shop was plain, elegant and one-storeyed, a narrow spit of building with long frontage suitable for display. Next to it was the house Henry Sidgwick had set up for female students. The glass-roofed entrance shelter of the University Arms was adjacent, stretched across the pavement matching the sign on the shop roof, LEAVIS: PIANOS. Directly opposite were the gates of Downing College. Harry Leavis soon opened a warehouse next to them, renting land from Downing. He was a leading supplier of beautiful pianos, remembered for their golden wood and candle-sconces. Leavis pianos survive.[6]

The young Leavis returned daily to the other side of Parker's Piece to attend Eden Street Infants' School. At the end of March 1903, four months before his eighth birthday, he was admitted to Paradise Street Higher Grade School, where he stayed until April 1910. In the Cambridge Local Examinations he took third-class honours, with distinctions

---

* Ralph went into the family business, until it was sold in the early 1930s. He remained unmarried, dying in 1980. Leavis's sister, Ruth, married an architect and had three daughters, one of whom, Mary Pitter, is author of the excellent memoir '6, Chesterton Hall Crescent, and the Early Years' in *The Leavises* (1984).

in English and Religious Knowledge. He was awarded 'Mr Starr's Prize for English' at the city Guildhall on 24 February 1910.[7]

Harry Leavis was a cultured man: a Liberal, a republican and a Rationalist. He played a major part in creating the New Chesterton Institute in Holland Street, originally the Old Chesterton Young Men's Club. It ran various societies, including a drama group for which he played Shylock and Serjeant Buzfuz in the play of *The Pickwick Papers*. Harry Leavis made a point of going up to London to hear Mark Twain read at the Savage Club. He was a traveller and met some of his relatives on a visit to America. He was President of the New Chesterton Cricket Club and on the Fen District Committee of the National Skating Association. He supported the Cambridge branch of the League of Nations Association. At home he was a man of views, requiring short hair of his eldest daughter, for hygienic reasons. He insisted on weekly family readings of Dickens. His ambition for his son was that he should play for England at Lord's and become Lord Chancellor. According to Leavis, his father had 'an un-English quickness of mind and of speech'. He was 'a man of a certain distinction, a dominating personality and an all-round ability. Intellectually he would have stood out in any company.'[8] His 'retiring disposition' disinclined him to take part in civic affairs. He was evidently respected by the dons. The son said that an 'acquaintance of my father's' was Sir Albert Seward, 'palaeo-botanist' and Master of Downing College.[9] Leavis was later to meet Seward in curious circumstances.

The move to Regent Street brought Harry Leavis closer to the university community. In 1907 he moved his family across the river to a new house between the city and the village of Chesterton: No. 6, Chesterton Hall Crescent. A recently built bridge over the Cam opened up for suburban development an area between Chesterton and the city. Leavis designed his new house himself. It was commodious, full of bric-à-brac, with the front door guarded by a statuette of a knight-in-armour. It was not old-fashioned but designed in Arts and Crafts movement, Voysey style, and built with carefully chosen materials: window-frame wood, for instance, which would weather without external house-painting. The garden was ample, planted well with trees, with a summer-house glazed in coloured panes. Inside, the rooms were designed to be sound-proofed from each other, and corridor corners rounded to make passage easier. There was plenty of evidence of nature-study collections, like shells and birds' nests.[10] Leavis liked butterflies. In a school essay he described the collection shown him by a diminutive elderly relative who made long collecting expeditions by tricycle. 'I can see him now, seated, pipe in mouth, in the armchair at the corner of the hearth, peering at the evening newspaper through (or was it under? I could never tell) his glasses.'[11] Sixty years later a freshman was surprised that the first subject aired by Leavis in a tutorial group was not literary at all but the decline of the butterfly population of East Anglia. 'They're killing them off with insecticide. You can see it everywhere: it's a truth, you know, a symbolic truth.'[12]

Leavis inherited the house and it became a centre for literary criticism, in tune with the ideals of a radical, socially mobile father. The other side of the family moved up socially but not into the same stratum of the middle class as Harry. The eldest son of Elihu was the handsome Frederick, Leavis's uncle, and at one time landlord of the Six Bells public house near Mill Road. Socially he remained on the town side of Parker's Piece. Of his children, one went into the motor trade, as did his son after him: Frederick Charles owned a tyre company. For some time he was involved with the Festival Theatre on Newmarket Road. His daughter Ida married a bookmaker and his other daughter, Doris, the owner of a charabanc company. The children of Elihu thus divided into two channels: in one direction there was the lower-middle-class business family of Frederick; in the other there was the vigorous gentility of Harry Leavis. One handled automobiles, the other sold musical instruments. About thirty years after Harry's move across the town, Queenie Dorothy Roth, who married his son, described the social history in which he played a part in her book *Fiction and the Reading Public*, concluding that 'The car has replaced the piano as the sign of social status.' In 1978 the son of Frederick Charles learned he had a famous relative in the city and telephoned the Leavis house. Q.D.L. told him Leavis was too ill to see anyone.[13]

Harry and Frederick took different paths. The rift was secured by F.R.L. himself, whose abilities took him to a school in an utterly different sphere from that of the other Leavises.

Sixth Form at the Perse, Freshman at Emmanuel 1910–1915

In the autumn of 1910 Leavis graduated from elementary school, at the age of fifteen, to the Cambridge and County School. He was made a prefect and was soon on the committee of the debating society, taking the Liberal position. He opposed the motion that 'for the welfare of the country every able-bodied man should by law be compelled to undergo a period of military training after the model of the continental countries'. He argued that the welfare of the country was best effected by improving conditions for both men and women. He was proposer of a motion in favour of state nationalization of railways and another on the abolition of the death penalty. In this debate he laid emphasis on the fallibility of judges and the finality of the death sentence. If all murderers were 'for the time being' lunatics, they should not be treated differently from other lunatics. He won the school essay prize for a piece about a diminutive butterfly-collector, 'Little-Boy-Man'. It was presented by the novelist H. Rider Haggard. He started reading poetry, imbibing what he later called the 'hypnoidal vagueness' of W.B. Yeats, 'incantatory' rhythms of a 'dim, dream-pale Celtic twilight'.[14] At home he ran *The Home Made Magazine*, price $1\frac{1}{2}$ d., for the family. Two issues (October 1907 and May 1908) survive.[15] Later (in 1910–11) the father, or perhaps the son, subscribed to the *English Review*, in which F.R.L. first read Lawrence.

In July 1911 Leavis took the local examinations and did well enough to win a scholarship to grammar school. The sixteen-year-old Leavis entered the Perse Grammar School, where he spent eight terms (two and a half years) through to the summer of 1914. He entered the school as a modern British boy might enter a sixth-form college. The Perse numbered two hundred, with a sixth form of thirty. After 1914 there was the steep drop in numbers caused by the war. The sixth form went down to eight boys.[16]

In 1912 the Perse School owed its character and prosperity to one of the great British headmasters. W.H.D. Rouse (1863–1950) was a prolific scholar, notable for his translations and editions of classical texts, and his general editorship of the Loeb Classical Library (original texts with literal translations *en face*). He was always 'Dr Rouse' or, to Leavis, 'Old Rouse'. At the Perse it was not unknown for a class discussion of Mark Twain's *Life on the Mississippi* to be conducted in Greek.

Rouse was appointed to the Perse in 1902, having previously taught at Rugby, at Cheltenham and at Bedford. Not the least of his contributions to the school was insistence on the use of the Direct Method of teaching classical languages, in which the language was used to teach the language itself. One of Leavis's favourite stories was about being late for school because his bicycle had a puncture: Rouse required him to explain in Greek, 'observing due accent and measure', how to mend a tyre. The Direct Method was so successful that the Board of Education made extra direct grants to the school, as well as the usual grant, made under Free Place regulations, payable when a quarter of its places were given to boys from elementary schools (as was Leavis). These funds were essential: when Rouse arrived numbers were declining, and the school was in competition with the new county school, administered by the local authority, which had been established in anticipation of the Education Act of 1902. The county school had a bias towards science, following government policy. In choosing the Perse for his son, Harry Leavis opted for humanist education, for he must have known the school's reputation for classics. The Perse under Rouse also pioneered new methods in the study of English, methods that spun off from the innovations in classics' teaching. 'We venture to hope,' wrote Rouse, 'that our work is beginning to produce an effect upon educational method: and in particular, we hope that the first steps have been taken towards an improvement in English teaching not unlike what we have tried to effect in classical teaching.' Most remarkable was the school's commitment to drama, under H. Caldwell Cook, establishing within very few years a school theatre, 'The Mummery', and a reputation that continued down to the 1960s. Leavis's time at the school coincided with Cook's main period of experimentation.

The Perse was socially progressive in its mix of students. It was one of the first schools to have a Hillel House for Jewish boys. Rouse encouraged enrolment from abroad, especially India: he had been born in Calcutta and was an expert Sanskritist. He knew the Aegean and its folklore, and that of India, where his parents had been Bengali-speaking missionaries. The emphasis on singing and dancing in the school showed these influences.

Rouse disliked public examinations ('quite misleading as a guide to comparative merit'), so Perse boys did not take the School Certificate. They were expected to make direct university entrance through college scholarship examinations; if they did not, Rouse believed that a report from himself (especially within the city of Cambridge) meant more than percentage ratings from an outside, probably meddling authority. Each year a booklet was published, giving school examination results, the reports of its visiting examiners and a review of the year from the headmaster. It specified holiday reading, ensuring this information was in the hands of parents. Erasmus's *The Praise of Folly* was a typical assignment.

Leavis went at the age of sixteen into the Special Remove class, equivalent to the lower sixth in present-day Britain. In the Remove he took history prizes. For Latin and English he scored higher percentages (in the nineties) than any other pupil. His leaving scores were equally impressive: higher than anyone else in Latin, Greek, French and German. His lowest mark was in Greek at 66 per cent. In the 1930s George Rylands of King's sat next to him at the annual Greek Play (performed in the original) and noticed how readily Leavis followed and commented on the language. One of Leavis's last public engagements was a lecture at the Perse, where he lectured on tragedy, quoting easily in Greek. The schoolmaster who most influenced Leavis was L.H.G. Greenwood, who took him for English and History. Leavis was in the rugby First Fifteen, and swam, taking two life-saving medals. In 1913 he won both five- and seven-mile cross-country races, doing the latter in 33 minutes, 59 seconds. In the following year in the same event he won and left for home long before the second runner crossed the finishing line. He disliked regimentation, like his father. He was a member of an élite of boys called the 'Squash Mob', who joined neither the Officer's Training Corps nor the Boy Scouts.[17]

In his last year at school Leavis played the title role in a scene of *Macbeth*. The local newspaper regretted his lack of 'an air of mystery and the supernatural'. However, he excelled in a part that combined the romantic and the down-to-earth, in a play to which he probably made a contribution as a writer.

The Wraggle Taggle Gypsies: A Dramatization of the Ballad by Members of the Sixth Form was devised because the ballad of the 'Wraggle Taggle Gypsies' was being taught in an English class of ten boys keen on folksong and dance. Three of them actually visited Cecil Sharp, the celebrated ballad collector, in Stratford-on-Avon. The boys wrote the play themselves. Caldwell Cook liked spontaneous composition, but the authors were sceptical, believing that improvisation was 'not suited to adult self-consciousness'. The finished product was mostly the work of one boy who preferred anonymity. Leavis had the leading part, as the Gypsy Man. This time the newspaper applauded: he 'expressed remarkably well everything in the rather fascinating part'.[18]

The Wraggle Taggle Gypsies was about a restless Lady of high degree who yearned for the simple life. She is wooed into the woods by strains of gypsy song, to the bewilderment of her faithful Lord, who wonders whether she is moonstruck. 'You are,' he puzzles, in a manner audibly schoolboy, 'unusually – er – well, *strange* . . .' The word 'natural' (for 'lunatic') is used throughout the play with youthful relish. In the woods the Lady meets the Gypsy Man, who behaves as one of nature's gentlemen – his wife is less cordial – considering her to be a kindred spirit, both having known imprisonment, he imprisoned as a sturdy beggar (and his ears removed), she mewed up with the tiresome Lord: 'He does not understand me, and he never will. The thought is appalling.' No good comes of it all. The Lady is disillusioned by gypsy life, not to mention the weather, but she is finally stuck with it because the long-suffering Lord is swept away from the search-party by a torrent.

Years later Leavis alluded to the old ballad in his essay on D.H. Lawrence's tale, 'The Virgin and the Gypsy', in which a rector's daughter longs for the gypsy life like the Lady of the school play and is very nearly swept away by a flood. She too meets a gypsy, an encounter that threatens her whole sense of self. The tale had 'nothing to do with Wraggle-taggle-gypsyism', remarked Leavis. In this tale the heroine is affected by an erotic passion of which *The Wraggle Taggle Gypsies* was properly innocent. None the less, there was a bridge between the play and Leavis's critique of the tale: its concern with the figure of the errant woman. Leavis was absorbed by the same theme in another tale by Lawrence, 'The Woman Who Rode Away'.[19]

Some of the principles of the Perse, or the general 'feel' of the school in Leavis's time, may have provided him with a model of education such as he later wanted at Downing College. Like Rouse, Leavis considered his own methods and judgement to be paramount within his own domain. In December 1913 Leavis made the first move towards university. He took the scholarship examination at Emmanuel College, consisting of an essay paper, a paper of general questions, one on Greek and Roman history, and one of Latin and French translation. Leavis's marks were sound; they were best in the essay paper (70 per cent), implying that he was something of a literary stylist. In this result he led the field of twenty-seven candidates. Overall Leavis took a good scholarship worth £60, but it was not the best. Scholarships of £80 were only awarded to alpha-plus candidates. Leavis was now ready to read for the Historical

Tripos at Emmanuel College, a few minutes further into the city from the Perse. He probably stayed on at school until the end of the summer term in 1914.

Leavis went down the road to read history, becoming one of fifty-eight Emmanuel College freshmen. Two months before he matriculated war was declared; of this fifty-eight, half a dozen were killed. His tutor – 'moral tutor', as opposed to academic supervisor – was E.B.C. Greenwood, a Greek scholar from King's and member of the J.T. Sheppard 'hedonist' circle. (A.C. Seward had also been a tutor and was appointed as Master of Downing College, soon after Leavis went up.) Leavis was allocated a room on 'P' staircase in a drab court across the road from the beautiful cloistered first court with its Wren chapel. Leavis's staircase was reached, then as now, by a white-tiled subterranean corridor in the mode of underground railway architecture.

Emmanuel was not an expensive college. One of Leavis's later friends, Muriel Bradbrook, called it 'a good college for a town boy'. It was an Elizabethan foundation, predominantly Puritan in orientation, a reputation enhanced later by its association with the Cambridge Platonists in the seventeenth century. In the twentieth century it took a fair number of men seeking orders.

When Leavis went up to university the city was not itself. Cambridge had recently become a garrison town, quartering the Welsh Division of the Territorials, full of artillery horses and mud. The small undergraduate population was now a handful of (cruelly called) 'infants, Indians and invalids'. Before the war there were over 120 candidates for the Historical Tripos taken in the second year, the first university, as opposed to college, examination in the subject. When Leavis took his first-year intercollegiate examination there were fewer than thirty candidates. (The diminishment of the university is well illustrated by the career of I.A. Richards, Leavis's later mentor: in 1915 he took his finals in philosophy – but was one of a total of only four candidates.) Leavis began his examinations on 19 June 1915. He performed satisfactorily. He did not take any history examinations at university level until after the war, when he changed to English.

During Leavis's second term at Emmanuel there was growing stir about military conscription, especially at meetings of the Union of Democratic Control that Leavis attended in March 1915. Conscription was soon to come. Leavis's future could well be decided for him. He decided to take the decision into his own hands. After completing his first year at Emmanuel, Leavis withdrew from the university before the next academic year began. He was accepted for training as a hospital orderly at a Quaker centre in York.

War 1915–1919

Participation in the First World War has always been associated with Leavis, more so than with his Cambridge peers. His pupils explained some mannerisms by his war service. The nasal speech and the preference for open-neck shirts were attributed to gas-poisoning. He had difficulty with digestion. The pupils saw him at high table toying with soup or a small fish course. 'I suffer from the digestive weakness which had established itself by 1915. (No! – not gas at Ypres, but the things I didn't say.)'[20] Leavis did not refuse to talk about the war but displayed severe reticence, so successfully that it was only occasionally apparent how few of his memories he was prepared to make public. This is illustrated by a curious incident in the late 1950s. A former pupil, Patrick Harrison, used often to visit York and mentioned how much he liked the city.[21] (It was long before Leavis went there as Visiting Professor.)

'Yes, I remember it well,' he said. 'That great curving station. I've only been there once – in 1915.' I went on to speak of the pleasures of the city when he suddenly cut me short. 'I shouldn't have mentioned that. It was very wrong of me to say what I did. Please forget it entirely.'[22]

To say that Leavis's experience of the war (and even pre-war, seemingly tangential incidents) was suppressed is perhaps misleading. But it is certainly true that Leavis believed that report on his experience should be controlled. With trusted friends he was able to be frank. With a pupil like Harrison he exercised self-censorship. In the 1970s he was exceptionally open about the subject to Michael Tanner, a Cambridge don with whom he had become friendly and whom he regarded as a collaborator. In a letter Leavis described to him his pathway to the Somme.

I was at school till the term before war was declared. I had refused to join the OTC and defied the Headmaster, old Rouse – but I was the school athlete. I wasn't sophisticated or articulate. My father's articulateness accounted for that – and the effect of his personality. He dominated every company he was in, though he wasn't overbearing. Simply a centre of human power. He said to me in the Kitchener days, 'You'll do as you decide, but I advise you not to join the army.' That's how I felt. I couldn't be a pacifist (that word came in then); I knew that the Germans mustn't be allowed to win. But . . . I worried about the 'ought'; the problem was insoluble. I joined the Friends' Ambulance Unit. Stinking blankets and lice, and always a job to do that was too much for me. But after the Bloody Somme there could be no question for *anyone* who knew what modern war was like of joining the army.

I didn't want to come home, and couldn't communicate with my father – whom I loved.[23]

The first practical step towards 'the blood deluge', as Leavis called it, had been taken in the autumn of 1915, when he decided not to return to Emmanuel but to serve in France in a non-military capacity, through the agency of the Quakers, the Religious Society of Friends.[24] His brother, Ralph, made the same decision. He became a driver and Leavis a medical orderly. The main route to active service for those who objected to the war on grounds of conscience was joining the Quakers' medical brigade, the Peace Service of the Society of Friends. The Peace Service manned two hospital ships, and administered the Queen Alexandra Hospital, medical convoys and the Services Sanitaires Anglais (SSA), which employed various types of vehicle, in most cases run in collaboration with the French forces. The convoys operated under military conditions, the work therefore affording an opportunity for the award of military honours. Several volunteers received the Croix de Guerre. The Quakers also ran the Friends' Ambulance Unit, and to this Leavis was assigned.

The Society of Friends had been quick to explore the practical implications of the war for conscientious objectors. In August 1914, before Leavis went up to college, Philip Noel Baker, a former President of the Cambridge Union Society and university athlete, appealed in the society's journal for the formation of a Friends' non-combatant medical brigade. In September 1914 a training-camp ('Jordans' in Buckinghamshire) was opened for sixty volunteers. Baker knew well the plight of the Belgians in defence of the Channel ports and received permission from the Joint War Committee of the British Red Cross Society and the Order of St John of Jerusalem to operate an Anglo-Belgian Ambulance Unit. On 30 October 1914 its first group went to France.[25]

The Friends' work expanded. In the summer of 1915 it opened a military hospital, the Settlement, in the dining-hall of a factory in York,

the premises provided by Rowntree's, the Quaker chocolate manufacturer. Soldiers from the Expeditionary Forces from France and the
Dardanelles were treated there, as well as men on home service. Leavis
was assigned to the Settlement in York for 1 October 1915, where he
was allowed to join the Friends' Ambulance Unit. Immediately he
began a two-week training course. On 16 November he reported for
duty as a mess orderly. He did not think much of the instruction: 'I had
no training with the FAU, though I had passed the British Red Cross
exam (whatever it's called).' In York, at Godfrey's bookshop in Stone-
gate, he bought a copy of Milton's English poems in the World's
Classics, which he remembered in 1974 as 'the only book I carried
steadily in my pocket between 1915 and 1919. I have the book, dirty
and stained, still.'[26]

Like many Quakers, the staff at the Friends' hospital were highly
educated, with representatives of fourteen universities. Arriving in November, Leavis was one of the early volunteers. At Christmas his status
changed, as it did for all young men over eighteen years old on 15
August 1915. They fell under the jurisdiction of the Military Service
Act, so liable for conscription. Conscientious objectors had to apply for
exemption to local tribunals, where exemption or exception could be
sought on religious grounds, or because of engagement in work of
national importance. The Friends were able to secure block exemptions
for its peace workers, including all those already on the staff. At York,
Leavis was successively a mess orderly, then a nursing orderly, for
periods of two months each, with a two-week spell as a guard. He had,
therefore, about five months as a hospital worker before he moved to
the more dangerous, but more temperamentally congenial, business of
active service.

In the summer of 1916 plans were ready for the catastrophic push along
the Somme. The number of men in the field increased. On 25 June
Leavis left York, having had his two inoculations, for Jordans, the transit
training camp, where he spent just over a week. On 8 July he sailed for
France and arrived the next day at the Friends' base camp. The Somme
offensive had been going for two weeks. On his birthday (14 July) he
joined an ambulance train at Boulogne. He was not sorry to leave the
hospital, preferring 'the rougher, more obviously wearing and tearing
and harrowing work of the "field" – or rather, the lines-of-communica-
tion – at which I spent the greater part of the war'. But 'by 1916 all

one's friends were dead'.[27] Leavis's war was to be spent on one of the Friends' ambulance trains, specifically Ambulance Train Number 5 or AT 5.

There were four ambulance trains by the time Leavis arrived in France, AT Numbers 5, 11, 16 and 17. In September 1916 the FAU had 187 personnel on these trains. Each one had a military commanding officer, two or three doctors and three nurses and about 50 non-commissioned officers and men appointed by the FAU. Each had a quartermaster sergeant, sergeant, cooks, nursing orderlies and general orderlies. Some of the trains, called 'khaki trains', were custom-designed in England, with 'lying wards' in which the central corridor of the carriage had three tiers of spring beds down each side of it. These trains also had fitted kitchens, store-rooms and living quarters. However, AT 5 was of an older type, a heterogeneous set of carriages roughly adapted for medical purposes. The main function of the trains was to bring the wounded back from casualty clearing stations to hospital, and sometimes on to the hospital ships. Much of the loading was done at night, with several stops, and, on arrival at base, there was usually no rest period before the train was sent onward to the port. There were interminable delays, as the heavy trains waited for passage on single-track lines. Crews had to tend serious injuries, provide regular meals and maintain records. The carriages had to be endlessly cleaned, and loaded with food and water. Apart from two Primus stoves, the only source of heat was the two kitchens. The train crews fell sick more than any other FAU men. There were other miseries. One feature of the war in France was that mail was quickly and reliably distributed, but not for trains on the move, to which even visits from headquarters were relatively rare.[28]

There were many types of war experience from August 1914. The nomadic experience of train life was perhaps in its own category, with some resemblance to that of prisoners-of-war. The crews formed small, almost collegiate groups, dealing with constantly changing patients, rarely seeing cure, and often only death. There were compensations. Sometimes a crew had time on its hands, during refitting or when the train seemed to have been forgotten by headquarters. It could even be delayed for a whole summer fortnight, at halt in a meadow of cow-parsley. The crews were readers: AT 17 had a library of a thousand books; they played football and cricket and explored the countryside. Each train had its own, or a succession of, home-made journals, sometimes set up in type by local French printers. There were concert parties, including, on AT 17, an 'Offensive Party' and a 'Hundredth Thousandth Patient Party'.

Leavis's train was the last to be put into commission. By January 1916 the British Red Cross was responsible for three ambulance trains, all run by FAU personnel. During the early months of the year there was a surplus of FAU men, so the society applied to the authorities for them to work at stretcher-bearing in the front line, in field ambulances or at casualty dressing-stations. The request was rejected because these volunteers were not enlisted soldiers. A further ambulance train was therefore put to work, taken over from the Royal Army Medical Corps in August 1916. It was a medley of twenty-one green-painted French pieces of rolling stock of assorted kinds and named Ambulance Train 5. The fact that the carriages were assorted had a significant consequence for those who lived and worked in them. No corridor linked the wagons, so the only way of passing along the train, even when in motion, was along the roof. ('I used to carry cocoa along the roofs of French trains to men who would have died without it. The trains had overhead wires, and it was very easy to get your head caught. Don't ever try it – it's an art.' The cocoa was carried in buckets, one to each hand.[29]) AT 5 saw some of the hardest train work of the war, in two or three periods carrying more patients than any other train.

Leavis was one of the 'bulge' of FAU personnel and was destined for the new train. When he first arrived, however, he remained for a month with the khaki train, AT 17, which from July to August 1916 worked a triangular route, inland to Blendecques, then north-west to Calais, then south back to Boulogne.[30] Leavis's service period was characteristic. A week after joining the train, he saw aircraft picked out by searchlights over St Omer, during a raid on Audruicq. At one casualty station nearly 400 Australians were set down in the lying ward. There was relief a week later with time during a hot day for bathing at a paper-mill at Blendecques and cricket.

On 16 August 1916 Leavis was moved to his permanent posting on AT 5, where he spent twenty-one months, first as one of four in the rank of Cook, then as Nursing Orderly. He joined AT 5 at the beginning of a six-week series of runs between Étaples and Calais, making as many as thirty trips, loading between 10 p.m. and 3 a.m., in forty days. There was a pause for refitting in October, then in November work was heavy as a result of fighting during the recapture of Beaumont Hamel by the

51st Highland Division, and at the Butte de Warlencourt, the final actions of the Somme offensive. Ten trips were made in November, with more gravely wounded men. At Christmas AT 5 worked between the Somme and the northern bases. All water pipes were frozen.[31] During the hard frost at the end of January 1917 the train went again to the repair workshops. It then returned to the Somme. In February there was a shock: 'I remember where I was on the Western Front when, at the railhead, we picked up accumulated mail, and I read the news of the Russian Revolution in Massingham's *Nation*.' Periodicals were fairly easily available in France, though less easy for train personnel. Leavis read Horatio Bottomley's serials in *John Bull* and 'one didn't want to come home'.[32]

At the beginning of April eleven men were withdrawn from the train (nearly a quarter of the crew) to work on a temporary ambulance train, increasing strain on the remaining orderlies. At this point the Germans were in retreat, and the train personnel saw the devastation left behind them. Fifteen base-to-base journeys were made in May. After a workshop withdrawal AT 5 made a series of trips to the Villers-Bretonneux and Péronne districts, carrying a wide variety of patients: British and colonial troops, civilians, Indians, Portuguese, Egyptians and three Germans. At the end of July 1917 the British offensive in Flanders began, and so the huge losses at Passchendaele. There were repeated journeys to the Ypres railhead. At Rémy on 17 August the train was attacked from the air. On 21 September it took its heaviest load ever, of 700 patients. The train worked the Ypres area till Leavis's second Christmas in France.

In January 1918 there were repairs in Paris. Back at the Cambrai front, American soldiers were seen for the first time. Cultural life aboard the train was active. There were bridge drives, debates on the Press and on the merits of boarding school education; there was a Social Reconstruction Study Circle, a literary reading circle, classes in French, Spanish and book-keeping. There were lectures on Whitman and on Edward Carpenter. 'I first met Ruskin early in the 1914 war.'[33] Once, when ill, Leavis read Charlotte Brontë's *Shirley*. Like the other trains, AT 5 had its own journal, called *La Vie sanitaire*. In April most of the train windows were shattered by bombing, and Leavis had three weeks away from the train in the Queen Alexandra Hospital, going there first for dental treatment, then staying on as a nursing orderly. In May he was back on AT 5. He encountered many Australians wounded in the defence of Amiens. In early June the train was sent into Champagne, where the British and French were fighting the Germans off Paris. It made no progress on the congested lines and was returned to Paris, within reach of the 'Grosse Bertha'. After repairs AT 5 was sent to a tiny village, Theil–Cérisiers in the Vannes valley near Sens – and was forgotten. No orders arrived and the crew enjoyed a summer idyll of three weeks. Work intensified in August, as a result of the British counter-offensive that began on 8 August east of Amiens, during which nearly 12,000 patients were carried. In October the train carried civilians who were ill with gas. (Medical staff suffered from combatants' clothing, soaked in the dark oily fluid of poison gas.) At the beginning of November AT 5 collided with a heavy goods train near St Pol, and was returned to the workshops in Paris. So Leavis was actually in the capital for the Armistice at the eleventh hour on the eleventh day of the eleventh month.[34]

Back home the man who was to be Leavis's mentor, I.A. Richards, climbed on the fountain in Cambridge market square. After midnight he stayed up with his friend C.K. Ogden and talked through the ideas of their book, *The Meaning of Meaning*.[35]

Leavis returned to Cambridge in a stunned condition. His digestion had gone by 1915. He did his 'quasi-Olympic times on the Ely road' in the 1920s, because a doctor suggested combating his insomnia by night-time running.[36] There was the tension of what he 'didn't say' (that he was against the war but not a 'pacifist') probably to his father during the period in which he decided to be a non-combatant. He suffered on his return to Cambridge from a general speech defect.

Leavis remained unwilling to promulgate his experience, as we have seen. A late incident of 1960 shows Leavis's unwillingness to be identified as a 'man of 1914', one who was fluently articulate about the trauma. In the course of an interview for the *Guardian* Leavis mentioned a copy of a Saturday issue of the *Westminster Gazette*, which was sent to him in France, when he was among 'the twenty miles of confluent shell-holes on the Somme'. On its competition page there was a German poem for translation, and Leavis duly sent in his version. After the interview was published, Leavis wrote off in some distress to the *Guardian* and to the interviewer, a former pupil. He was very anxious to explain that he mentioned the German poem competition in order to make a point about journalism and its high quality in the old days. Once upon a time it was not strange to find 'Latin verse, Greek verse, or niceties of French composition' set for competition in a weekly paper. Leavis wanted to remind the *Guardian* of the world that was lost. What he was not wanting was to tell war stories. In a private letter to the interviewer he said that he feared that, in his 'garrulity', he had spoken with too much facility. 'I can't bear to seem to have gone in for 1914 panache . . . (can't bear: I lost too many friends, etc.).'[37] Leavis did not scrutinize the political significance of the war. He admired the left-wing writer H.N. Brailsford and recommended his book *Shelley, Godwin and His Circle* to students. But he made no allusions to Brailsford's radical criticism of war as an arm of capitalism in, for instance, *Why Capitalism Means War*, though he would have known of this analysis from the meetings he attended of the Union of Democratic Control. Leavis allowed himself to be a critic of industrialism but somewhat less a critic of capitalism than Ruskin.

As a literary critic Leavis never gave priority to the poetry of the First World War. In 1932 he wrote as if the phenomenon of 'war poetry' was dead. He believed Wilfred Owen and Siegfried Sassoon had merit, but thought that, poetically, they were hardly modern, not strong enough to be able to dissolve and invalidate Edwardian romanticism. With one poet it was different. Leavis did not write much about Isaac Rosenberg, but he campaigned vigorously for his work. He read his verse aloud in public, with electrifying effect, especially 'Dead Man's Dump' (written in 1917).

> Here is one not long dead;
> His dark hearing caught our far wheels,
> And the choked soul stretched weak hands
> To reach the living word the far wheels said,
> The blood-dazed intelligence beating for light,
> Crying through the suspense of the far torturing wheels
> Swift for the end to break
> Or the wheels to break,
> Cried as the tide of the world broke over his sight.

These are not the wheels of an ambulance locomotive but limbers of barbed-wire that Rosenberg had to unreel during night-time maintenance in the Royal Engineers. But Leavis saw a procession of 'blood-dazed' men, and some women, on AT 5. What mattered to Leavis in Rosenberg was not so much the depiction of the unspeakable but a quality of psychological demeanour. Leavis knew well what Rosenberg once said: 'I will not leave a corner of my consciousness covered up, but

saturate myself with the strange and extraordinary new conditions of
this life, and it will refine itself into poetry later on.' Leavis admired a
manner 'matter-of-fact, unexcited and business-like' and in Rosenberg's
letters 'a quiet detachment . . . one aspect of the intensity, the intense
disinterestedness, of genius'.[38] Detachment and dispassionateness of a
soldierly kind were among the tones of voice that Leavis more than
relished. He found it in unexpected places: in the style of some Shakespearean speeches, like those of Posthumus in *Cymbeline*; he admired a
'soldierly' quality in the figure of the Moor in *Othello*.[39] In 1944 the
spiritual quality of detachment, or 'impersonality', was the subject of
one of Leavis's most sombre pieces of meditation, on tragedy.

Leavis's experience of the war never urged him to favour 'war
writing'. But it is hard not to associate his knowledge of twenty-one
months in France with his later respect for the literature of devastation,
like Gerard Manley Hopkins's 'The Wreck of the Deutschland', which
he read aloud as memorably as 'Dead Man's Dump'. In 1964, a couple
of years after his portrait was painted, Leavis wrote of the devastation he
experienced.

I see the faces of those boys who were with me at school as if it were last week
and hear their voices. They began to appear in the 'Roll of Honour' within a
few months: Festubert, Loos, and then the Somme, where they were reaped in
swathes. They were shot down over Ypres, and, having survived from the days
of Kitchener's first army to the 'victorious' battles of 1918, died of wounds –
and of sickness after the Armistice.[40]

An assessment must be attempted of how the war figured in Leavis's
life, to distinguish its place in *this* life.* Patrick Harrison, the pupil to
whom Leavis apologized for mentioning York railway station, came to
this conclusion about Leavis's war service:

His experiences in the Friends' Ambulance Unit obviously had a profound
effect upon him and possibly gave him, as an introverted and impressionable,
but not naturally sociable person, a forced diet of close contact with all sorts and
kinds of people that lasted him a lifetime. Left to himself he established in
marriage an essentially reclusive habit of life in which I suspect that outside
relations were seldom intimate. But the wartime experiences remained influential, not always in obvious ways. He seemed temperamentally rather than

---

* For an important recollection of the war by Leavis in late life, see Chapter Eleven,
New Universities, 'Dickens 1970'.

politically or ideologically pacifist and was by no means out of sympathy with the disciplines and traditions of army life as a long established variety of human experience. He must have been aware of some of the inanities of command in the war, but it was as if the enormity of the whole gigantic farce were altogether beyond individual responsibility or control at any level. I never heard him ridicule the military mind or military personalities and he would express in asides an almost reverential respect for the good humour, kindliness and forbearance of British soldiers towards one another in the appalling conditions of the Somme; qualities of comradeship probably only drawn out in war ... He once surprised me as I was telling him about a visit to Ulster: 'There's no country in the world whose soldiers could undertake the kind of duties we are asking of our boys in Northern Ireland.'

In estimating the effect of the 'emergency' (his word) on Leavis, it must be remembered that he left England with the Friends' Ambulance Unit not only for war but for *France*. A critic once rather sourly commented upon what he believed to be Leavis's 'twentyish fixation with France'. It went deeper. Leavis saw himself as a Huguenot. His daughter once recalled that 'when he was a young man Frenchmen in England, complete strangers, would pick him out in a crowd to speak to, believing him French'. Kate Leavis was relying either on Leavis's memory or that of her mother. It is clear there was some 'Frenchness' in Leavis's sense of himself. Throughout his career he insisted on his pupils' reading French literature, especially Benjamin Constant's *Adolphe* and Valéry's 'Le Cimetière marin' (with which this chapter began). In one of the rare references to his own wartime experiences, Leavis recalled 'the comrades, whose faces I can see' and quoted without attribution a phrase from Valéry on how the comrades' blood went into the earth to sustain the flowers: 'le don de vivre a passé dans les fleurs'. Leavis glossed his quotation with a translation, replacing Valéry's beautiful trope with the colloquialism, 'pushing up daisies'. This is a more gritty version of the idea of life passing into flowers, and a very English one. Arguably, the French tongue heightened Leavis's sense of the English language – a language he was hardly able to use when he came back with a stammer from France.[41]

CHAPTER TWO

ENGLISH AT CAMBRIDGE
1919–1924

A Greek was murdered at a Polish dance,
Another bank defaulter has confessed.
I keep my countenance,
I remain self-possessed
Except when a street piano, mechanical and tired
Reiterates some worn-out common song
With the smell of hyacinths across the garden
Recalling things that other people have desired.
Are these ideas right or wrong?
> – T.S. Eliot, 'Portrait of a Lady', 1917

The preparation depends less on teaching and more on the student's private reading than that required for any other honours examination.
> – 'English', *Cambridge University Student's Handbook*, 1921

Return to Cambridge 1919

Leavis was demobilized on 2 January 1919 and returned home 'a retarded and war-bedraggled youth'.[1] The appearance of Cambridge had recovered from the mess of wartime, helped by five inches of snow.

Back at Emmanuel College, Leavis set about completing work on his interrupted course in history. Having missed the previous term, he had five months to catch up. In the spring of 1919 he sat the Part One examinations of the Historical Tripos. There were only thirty-one candidates, of whom over twenty were women, who as yet had no constitutional place in the university. (The only candidate to take a First was a woman.) Before the war, in normal conditions, there had been 133 candidates.

In the summer Leavis decided to change from studying history to English. It may or may not have been evident to Leavis, but Emmanuel was a good college for English, not because it supplied particularly stimulating teaching in modern literature, which was Leavis's passion, but because it was part of a network of human contacts out of which was constructed the coming Cambridge English school. F.L. (Fred) Attenborough was in charge of English at Emmanuel, a young man whom a football injury had kept out of the war. (It was Attenborough who brought to the college another young man from the public education system, H.S. (Stanley) Bennett, who was for a few years at Leavis's side in English at Emmanuel.) After a false start at college education at Bangor, Attenborough had gone up to Emmanuel and studied English in the only tripos in which it could be done in wartime and before, the Modern and Medieval Languages Tripos. Originally Attenborough had been taught by one of the great schoolmasters, Samuel Clegg of the County School and Pupil–Teacher Centre at Long Eaton in Derbyshire. Clegg's specialism was the teaching of drawing and design, but as headmaster he developed a teaching space of beauty and aesthetic discipline. Attenborough, in Cambridge, happened to make known Clegg's genius for the visual to Mansfield Forbes, a young history don at Clare, a lively lecturer and social presence, who had become increasingly involved in English studies rather than history. Forbes was close to H.M. Chadwick, who held the university chair of Anglo-Saxon, and in due course Attenborough became a research assistant to Chadwick.[2] Though young, Attenborough was therefore close in to the plans for a new English course in which Chadwick and Forbes were involved during the war. And it was this course, the new English Tripos, for which Leavis registered in October 1919. As with history, the examinations had been taken by only a few candidates, three men and fourteen women; but in the aftermath of war Leavis was joining a course taken by more than a hundred students, in spite of its being called 'the novel-reading tripos' (or because of it). For Leavis the change from history to English did not mean leaving history behind.

Leavis changed to English, having become fascinated by new English poetry. He dated his 'continuous cultivated interest in modern poetry' to the year of his return from France. His first loves were in the poetry of 1917: the world of W.B. Yeats's 'The Wild Swans at Coole' and T.S. Eliot's 'Love Song of J. Alfred Prufrock', which he read in 'some

anthology of American verse'. One other poem was particularly important for him. He awoke from the war to the hesitant voice of Eliot's
'Portrait of a Lady':

> Now that lilacs are in bloom
> She has a bowl of lilacs in her room
> And twists one in her fingers while she talks . . .

Leavis did not begin with Eliot at the point of *The Waste Land* (1922),
the poem that, whatever else it is and does, actually shows Europe in
devastation. The earlier poems attracted Leavis at a visceral level, communicating rhythms. In two senses the earliest Eliot was not 'modern'. His
poetry had qualities that were recognizable in some of the new styles,
like *vers libre* or Imagism. But Leavis found in him a strange aural
quality, a rhythmic pulse that was not merely a 'threshold' quality of
sound whose function led the reader into a semantic sanctum. For Leavis
this sound *was* the poetry, the 'rhythmic life' was basic, not introductory,
a 'delicate play of shifting tone that is essential to the theme and
communication of the poem'. It freed the writing from Victorianism. It
appealed to the 'sense of how things go naturally'. Leavis was reading at
a time when little had gone 'naturally'. (One wonders how Harry Leavis
talked about the war when his son returned.)

While Leavis was completing his history studies in April 1919, a
leading journal, the *Athenaeum*, came under the control of a new editor,
John Middleton Murry. Edwardian taste had not been dispelled from
the literary scene at the death of Edward VII in 1910. Murry attacked
the popular Georgian verse in the fourth of a train of volumes, *Georgian
Poetry: 1911–1922*. He declared war on sentiment and on the robust,
bookishly manly journal, the *London Mercury*, whose editor, Sir John
Squire, he taught Leavis to hold in disdain.[3] Murry provided Leavis with
terms of reference for a critical reading of Yeats, who was, wrote
Murry, pitifully locked into a dream-world, 'worn out not with dreams,
but with the vain effort to master them and submit them to his own
creative energy. He has not subdued them nor built a new world for
them.'[4] Leavis liked Murry's reviews of D.H. Lawrence's *Aaron's Rod*
and *Women in Love*, of Robert Bridges's *Milton's Prosody* and Murry's
short book *The Problem of Style* (1922).[5] Eliot was also a critical guide,
notably in *The Sacred Wood: Essays in Poetry and Criticism* (1920).
Although he was not interested in poetry of the war, Leavis was aroused
by Eliot's praise of Isaac Rosenberg in 1920.[6]

The Original 'Cambridge English' 1919–1926

By changing to English Leavis could indulge a passion for poetry. The change enabled him to join a newly devised system or structure of study, one that he never disowned and that shaped his thought for many years. To explain the system it is best to begin with the Cambridge word 'tripos', archaically associated with an examiner's three-legged stool.

A Cambridge tripos is a collection of examinations under a broad subject heading, divided into two groups, Parts One and Two. For the degree of BA it is necessary to take two parts, but they do not have to be from the same tripos. Leavis could have taken a Part One and a Part Two tripos in history, but he opted to vary the diet. Part One is usually taken after the first two years of study and Part Two after the third. The first part is usually a survey course and the second part more specialized. A student could take two Part Ones, that is, two introductory courses; two Part Twos would not, understandably, be admissible.

The English Tripos was an innovation, fashioned in wartime and partly because of the war. Before 1919 students could take English studies, but (as we saw) only as one of the examinations set for the tripos in modern and medieval languages. After the efforts of Mansfield Forbes and several others, the English Tripos was devised. But, though the subject was no longer in the purlieus of modern languages, it had only one part. Students had therefore to take one part of another tripos to make up an honours degree. This one-part English Tripos was in two sections, students opting for one of them. They could take either 'English Literature: Modern and Medieval' or 'Early Literature and History'. When Leavis changed to English, he opted for 'English Literature: Modern and Medieval', beginning his studies in October 1919 at the age of twenty-four. He spent six years within this structure, as undergraduate and graduate student, until an important change in 1926. But it was in this six-year period, the years of the *original* English Tripos, that his attitudes were formed; to the end of his life he retained a pride in the original system of studying English.

Despite the foundation of a new course, English at Cambridge was an informal matter in the early 1920s. It was short on personnel, 'no plausible team', said Leavis, though there were glowing exceptions.[7]

There was no 'department' or 'faculty', let alone a building. An English library was slowly built up from donations, principally by A.C. Benson. There were college libraries and the university library (only open to undergraduates in the afternoons), but these had their limits for a new subject. It was in the Union Society library that Leavis found D.H. Lawrence's *The Prussian Officer* on the recommended shelves. (He 'registered that the author I had read six or seven years before [in the *English Review*] was D.H. Lawrence'.) The teaching establishment was small. The university furnished only three teaching officers, two of them professors. Sir Arthur Quiller-Couch was responsible for post-Renaissance literature and H.M. Chadwick was an Anglo-Saxonist. There was one University Lecturer, the medievalist G.G. Coulton. This is not to say there were no other teachers, but the bulk of the teaching (lecturing and tutoring) was done by men and women engaged by individual colleges. Students were usually tutored in their own college, and the college furnished lectures that could be attended by students from other colleges. Students had to make swift sorties around the city – bicycles are used in Cambridge not only because the city is flat. They gave their names as they went in to lectures so they could be billed. Two lectures could be attended before a student was committed to the fee of about one pound for the course. In their own college students had a Director of Studies, who taught small groups, or 'supervisions', very often one-to-one. The Director of Studies advised on which lectures to attend and appointed other supervisors where necessary, who did not have to be connected to the college. Despite the impressive title, a Director of Studies need not be a senior person. In a college that did not go in for English the office could be administered by a specialist in some other subject, a state of affairs that continued to the late 1960s. In effect the provision of individual teaching depended on a pool of young freelancers, relying on payment by the hour. ('Hand-to-mouth disease', I.A. Richards called it.) In vignette an Oxford tutorial would be don and pupil in a college room with strands of ivy seen through a mullioned window. Cambridge supervisions were frequently in scruffy college hostels or bed-sitting rooms off Mill Road.

Final examinations were centralized. The tripos examinations, taken in academical dress, were followed by the May Week festivities, usually in June. High-flying graduates aimed for a junior fellowship, which could be attained after a tripos First (preferably starred, showing performance 'with distinction') or after winning an essay prize, like the Le Bas for a short book-length monograph. There were also prizes for success in special non-curricular examinations, like those for the Charles Oldham Shakespeare Scholarship. This was the normal route into senior academe – the one that Leavis did *not* take.

With the founding of its tripos the institution of Cambridge English emerged. It was based on a curriculum, with syllabus, examinations, supervisions, lectures. But Cambridge English was also a literary world in its own right. Cambridge had a full cultural calendar. There was theatre, including the annual 'Greek Play' (that is, in Greek), and, after 1926, the modernist Festival Theatre on Newmarket Road. Ten years later there was the Arts Theatre, funded by the efforts of J.M. Keynes. Cambridge was keen on films, fostering at least one important documentary film-maker, Humphrey Jennings. For literature, there were series of public lectures, like the Clark Lectures at Trinity, at which poets, novelists and literary journalists could be heard in person. During the 1920s Leavis's favoured critics spoke: John Middleton Murry on Keats and T.S. Eliot on the metaphysical poets. E.M. Forster delivered the lectures that became *Aspects of the Novel*. There was Desmond MacCarthy on Byron, Herbert Read on Wordsworth, and lectures by André Maurois, Harley Granville-Barker and Edmund Blunden. At college clubs there were frequent papers and readings. Leavis later propagated his enthusiasm for the poetry of Ronald Bottrall by a whistle-stop tour of college societies, such as the Nashe or the Hesperides. At Downing, Leavis's college for many years, the Doughty Society was a centre for Leavisian visitors. There were papers and readings at the Literary Club, which had Walter de la Mare on Keats in December 1922; it was succeeded by the English Club. There were periodicals to which undergraduates contributed, as well as dons and aspirant dons working on prize essays. The glossiest was *The Granta*, somewhat like *Punch*, with review pages edited by 'The Skipper', a typically laid-back title. This position was occupied by some men (never women) who later became well-known literary figures. William Empson had a turn at 'The Skipper', as did James Smith and R.G. Cox, both of Leavisian persuasion. There were little magazines, ranging from the arty *Venture* of the 1920s to the austere *Delta* of the 1950s. All journals produced by junior members of the university had to be licensed by the university authorities, a rule not applicable to the *Cambridge Review*, run by and for dons, like a national quarterly of general interest but appearing weekly during university terms. Once it was edited by Ian Parsons, later London's main publisher of literary criticism (and Leavis's).

Leavis's attitudes were formed in the six-year period of the original Cambridge English. Although H.M. Chadwick, Mansfield Forbes and I.A. Richards were, for Leavis, at its intellectual heart, there was a flamboyant figure as its master of ceremonies. The public knew of Cambridge English through Sir Arthur Quiller-Couch, always known as 'Q', a *nom de plume* surviving from his student writings in Oxford in the 1880s.

Q was born in 1863, and was much too old for military service in 1914. But he was a war casualty in that he suffered the loss of his son, who died in 1919 on reconstruction duties in Germany. From 1912 Q was King Edward VII Professor of English Literature. Far from being endowed by the Crown, this chair was funded by the Fleet Street magnate Sir Harold Harmsworth (later Viscount Rothermere) in memory of the late King. The journalistic association was appropriate for Q, who had lived by his pen for twenty-five years, author of fiction, poetry, essays and anthologies, notably a celebration of Victorian taste, the *Oxford Book of English Verse*, which was bestowed upon the post-war world in a new edition in 1918. Q was knighted for his work for education in his beloved West Country. He was a progressive liberal, of the same persuasion as the Leavis family. When A.L. Rowse was proposed for a county scholarship, Q's support was certain when the committee muttered doubts about the supposed socialist leanings of Rowse. Q's politics were not favoured in the society of Tory Cambridge, nor was his appearance. A.C. Benson thought he was 'amiable but somehow common. He looks like a racing tout,' cruelly observing Q's distinctively red face. He was something of a 'man's man', showing perhaps an outer face of shyness. Q sailed on the Cornish coast as much as he could, an 'atavistic' passion, his biographer called it. Leavis was always amused at Q's pride in his appointment as Commodore of the Fowey Yacht Club.

Q was long-lived in an era in which there was no retirement age for professors. The man who had been a bright young Oxford writer of the 1880s remained at his Cambridge post until the spring of 1944, presiding over Cambridge English through two world wars. For some of these years he was dutiful to Cambridge English, but lukewarm about it. It should not be inferred that the faculty was damaged by lack of leadership.

THE PROFESSOR OF ENGLISH

Drawn by H. M. Brock

Sir Arthur Quiller-Couch, drawn by H.M. Brock for *The Granta*
in December 1923

In Cambridge professorial powers are limited. None the less, there was for many years a certain stasis. But after his appointment in 1912 Q was far from passive. In October 1916, when Leavis was in France, in his lectures he denounced the way in which 'statute and practice' had made proper reading of English literature 'all but impossible' in schools, colleges and universities, including (and especially) Cambridge. At that time English studies at Cambridge was merely 'Section A (English)' of the Modern Languages Tripos. The course required a knowledge of 500 years of literature, with specialization in the eighty-five years from 1700. On top of this, work had to be done on 'writings' ('the Statute discreetly avoids calling them literature') from 1200 to 1500 and Chaucer, not to mention the Wessex dialect, with possible questions on the cornet, flute and sackbut. Q remonstrated that 'the whole business of reading English literature in two years, to *know* it in any reputable sense of the word – let alone your learning to write English – is, in short, impossible'.[8]

Q worked with Chadwick and Forbes to cut away the undergrowth of so-called 'English', comprising so much peripheral material, let alone cornet, flute and sackbut. They devised a curriculum designed to encourage the student really to know a limited number of works. Q wanted a faculty of discrimination. He bluntly called one of his lecture courses 'The Art of Criticizing'.[9] The campaign of Q, Chadwick and Forbes created the new tripos, by means of which focus could be attained, or rather two triposes, two sets of examinations in the English field, so it was possible to take a whole degree in English, one part 'Modern and Medieval' and one part 'Early'. In the early part philology was diminished, and in the modern part critical discrimination encouraged. It was the Modern and Medieval Tripos that Leavis took. This course epitomized the Q generation. Leavis had to study for the following examinations.

ENGLISH LITERATURE: MODERN AND MEDIEVAL

1. Life, Literature and Thought (1350–1603)
2. History of English Literature (1603–   )
3. Shakespeare, including passages (some unattributed) for comment, and questions on language, metre, literary history and criticism
4. Special Period of Literature (1789–1870)
5. Special Subject: Tragedy
6. History of Literary Criticism[10]

For each there was a three-hour examination paper, five answers required, two more than was the norm in Britain from about 1970. The nature of Cambridge English was vividly shown in the examination questions Leavis had to answer in 1921. Some were perky, some plain. 'State what you know of *two* of the following: (a) the Oldcastle–Falstaff business . . .' Some were garrulous.

'Shakespeare is incarnated uncompromising Feudalism in Literature' (Walt Whitman). Criticize the validity of this judgement. May Shakespeare be said, of his sympathy with the feudal spirit, to incarnate in Coriolanus the vices of its virtues and in Falstaff the virtue of its vices?

'The story interest and the poetic interest are different things. The function of the poet is to blend them inextricably' (*Athenaeum*, 25 June 1920). Estimate how far any two . . . Give a brief account of the pre-Raphaelite movement in literature, stating the importance of three of the following writings in its history: *The Germ, Guinevere, Poems and Ballads* (vol. i), *The Fleshly School of Poetry, Goblin Market*.

Write short notes on any four of the following dramatists: Calderón, Lope de Vega, Racine, Voltaire, Otway, Kotzebue, Schiller, Alexandre Dumas (*fils*), Sardou, Shaw, Sudermann, Chekhov.

The last two questions show the contemporaneity of the curriculum, with living authors and an up-to-the-minute quotation from the *Nation and Athenaeum*. (In the late twentieth century it would be unusual to find questions framed round quotations from *The Times Literary Supplement* or the *New York Review of Books*.) These tripos papers were at the intersection of literary journalism and undergraduate writing.

In some respects the tripos was a course in world literature ('Write short notes on . . . Calderón, Lope de Vega . . .'), but its basic orientation was towards English literature, or rather 'England'. Its nationalism is indicated by a fictional dialogue that Q contributed to *The Granta*. He showed himself under interrogation by a fogey professor in the employ of Whitehall about the eccentricities of Cambridge English.

PROFESSOR: What, Sir, has a question on the styles of architecture to do with English Language and Literature?
Q (*wearily*): The Professor, Sir, mistakes the very name of our tripos. It is not a tripos of 'English Language and Literature'; but an English tripos. We think

that English architecture bears most importantly on English life and thought between 1350 and 1603.

PROFESSOR (*muttering*): Not a single question upon *Ferrex and Porrex* . . .

Q wanted 'his' tripos to school undergraduates in England, of which literature was a part. He wanted it to be a school of English in a literal sense. Whitehall could not understand the national–historical orientation of the course, nor did it realize that the English Tripos was meant to teach undergraduates to *write*. Q thought that the conventional professors were often deficient in 'the extremely difficult business of writing their mother tongue'. He wanted a school of lucidity in English, as well as of England, its graduates capable of exercising their skills in the literary reviews. Early on he remarked proudly that 'already the work of several of our few first-class men – work in criticism especially – is being eagerly taken by London editors'.[11] Q was a professor but also a professional author, and had been a Fleet Street man. He enjoyed his tripos being a school of serious journalism.

There is one question in the 'History of English Literature from 1603' that was of particular significance for Leavis. He returned to its quoted material several times in later lectures and writings. The question was elaborate, starting out with lines from a ballad in *The Heart of Mid-Lothian* by Sir Walter Scott.

> Proud Maisie is in the wood,
>   Walking so early;
> Sweet Robin sits on the bush,
>   Singing so rarely.
>
> 'Tell me, thou bonny bird,
>   When shall I marry me?'
> 'When six braw gentlemen
>   Kirkward shall carry ye.'

Then comes:

'Inexperienced critics have often named this, which may be called the Homeric manner, superficial, from its apparent simple facility: but [the] first-rate excellence in it is in truth one of the least common triumphs of poetry. This style should be compared with . . . the searching out of inner feeling, the expression of hidden meanings, the revelation of the heart of Nature and of the Soul within the Soul – the analytical method, in short – most completely represented by Wordsworth and by Shelley' (Palgrave).★

A long lead-in to the question: 'Compare it, giving instances in such plenty as time allows.' Two whole stanzas from Scott and six lines of Palgrave look more like a segment of an anthology than an examination question. In Britain there were in later years examination papers that were virtually portfolios of quotation, with questions appended, but these were generally examinations in literary analysis. The present example is from an examination in literary history and was characteristic of all the Cambridge literary history papers. In 1921 the '1789–1870' paper printed two elegiac poems in full. The '1350–1603' paper had a whole poem in old spelling, with the gruff command to 'write out lines 3 and 4 of the third stanza in their old spelling and indicate the scansion'. The questions displayed an interchange between textual study and history in the material chosen for comment. Cambridge English became a home for close reading, but from the beginning, even in the typographical look of the papers, its examinations urged an intimate connection between analysis and history. Ten years after taking his finals, Leavis reviewed Empson's *Seven Types of Ambiguity*, which was notorious for the intricate subjectivity of its analyses. Yet Leavis's accolade was that 'there is more of the history of English poetry in this book than in any others that I know'. For Leavis the distance was not so great from the old Historical Tripos to the new English Tripos.

The life of a university faculty is not usually identified with its examinations and regulations. Official documents do, however, have a crude power. The published or the spoken word is influential, but regulations and examination papers are usually obeyed. The spore of Cambridge English showed its imprint in the annual guide to the university, *The Student's Handbook*. It reminded students that preparation for the tripos depended to a high degree on *private* reading, and that

The student who means to take both sections of the English Tripos will do well not to limit his reading exclusively to the subjects directly required in the examination. He should give up some part of his time to the study of general literature and history, and more especially to reading good translations of Classical literature.

★ The quotation is from *The Golden Treasury*, which was, with *The Oxford Book of English Verse*, for Leavis an incarnation of Victorian taste. The quotation in the examination paper replaces 'A narrow criticism' with 'Inexperienced critics'.

Ten years into the life of Cambridge English, I.A. Richards in *Practical Criticism* (1929) analysed, fastidiously and correctly, the swashbuckling *simplesse* of judgements on poems by Cambridge English students. Later, two other English faculty dons exposed to print selections of English Tripos student howlers.[12] But it had been the faculty itself that invited undergraduates to speak out, with faith in their own responses. Did not *The Student's Handbook* state that the course was designed to encourage, then test, their actual experience? Post-war students were notably lacking in docility; Leavis, awkward in manner, passionate in preference, was representative of the new age. The men had come from the war or (as ominously) not come from the war. The women were experimenting with new sorts of education. (There was a high proportion of women in Cambridge English in the 1920s: this was not Cambridge of the 1950s.) These undergraduates were invited to be independent, and they were.

Leavis later put the principles of the *Handbook* into practice with disarming candour when he advised his pupils on which lectures to attend. 'There *is* the Master of Jesus . . .' (that is, Tillyard), he would murmur at the beginning of term, avoiding eye-contact. Leavis believed that attending too many lectures was irresponsible for a student with a workload of literary texts that required meditative reading. Pupils could be taken aback by his *lèse-majesté*. But, though the manner was conspiratorial, Leavis's attitude expressed the semi-official policy of Cambridge English. *The Student's Handbook* itself directed that the student need not attend many lectures.

On the structure of the English Tripos, *The Student's Handbook* makes a surprising remark, almost in passing, about the two parts of the tripos. Undergraduates who took both, modern and 'early', would have a comprehensive curriculum. However, taking both sections was not really what the designers of the tripos wanted. Each section could, just as well, be used as an alternative to a part from another tripos. The *Handbook* observed approvingly that 'the majority of students will probably take only one section'. The new sections were *meant* to go with other studies and the English Tripos to be a focus for them.[13] This was one of its special features, one thoroughly endorsed by Leavis. Although most academics prefer students to stay within their subject and cannot have them do too much of it, Leavis and Cambridge English were pleased for pupils to pass from one subject to another. It was in the original Cambridge English, in its first six years, that he learned English was an enhancement or even a meeting-point of other disciplines. This aspiration became part of the theory of English studies he developed in the early 1940s.

It is tempting to set Q against Leavis, old-guard against avant garde, but this does not work, and not only because Leavis referred affectionately to Q throughout his life. Q was right to be proprietorial about the new tripos; and, with its emphasis on personal response and 'criticizing', on nations and nationalisms, on writing, as well as its sympathy with the contemporary and with the life of the journals (not precisely 'journalism'), it was in tune with Leavis's practice over the years. Leavis did not go to Q for insight into contemporary writing or literature at large. And there was one conflict at a fundamental level. Q did not question the belief that 'to have taken the Classical Tripos with credit qualified you to teach the English'.[14] But Q did give English the *setting* in which Leavis grew up. The literary critical tool-box was elsewhere.

Two men junior to Q helped him make his dream of a new English course into reality. Both departed from their first academic disciplines to do so. They were Manny Forbes of Clare and I.A. Richards, whom Forbes recruited to the new group of English teachers. The lectures of both were remarkable in conception and content, and as performance. While Q was stately, lecturing in morning dress with a white slip above his waistcoat, Forbes was puckish. He gave, said one woman student, 'the most original, quirkish, unpredictable and exciting course of lectures'. Another woman, Queenie Roth, who married Leavis, described him as 'a mooncalf or an archangel'.[15] One of his most influential courses was on romanticism, defined very widely, from William Blake to Joseph Conrad. His lectures were liable to turn into seminars, or Forbes would not turn up for two or three weeks, after which he materialized to talk enchantingly about a poem, following its ramifications into music, painting and especially architecture, his first love. Forbes did not like formal supervisions, but many testified to his readiness to talk in all sorts of places. And he entertained students at 'Finella', the late-Victorian villa he leased over the river from King's, on which Forbes bestowed all his architectural imagination. The interior was revamped in modernist-glitz style, with full use of unusual materials, like black-mirror glass, so there were many unexpected visual entries to the rooms. Above the front door there was a wooden figure-head whose eyes lit up; there were fountains instead of fireplaces. Forbes liked a crowd, and devised elaborate games and contests. A bachelor, he was looked after by a loyal couple; party meals were brought over the Backs from Clare kitchens.

Forbes's bohemianism must not be exaggerated, though it must be given its due, remembering the solemn respectability of most of the English dons. For Leavis it was indispensable. The students could see in him what thinking was like:

They got from him what they couldn't have got from the server-up of Oliver Elton or of Bradley and Raleigh or from the belletristic product of Classics. Forbes at Cambridge had read History. It came between him and whatever he may have had of Public School Classics.

He was 'young, convinced, contagiously charged and irrepressible'. The History Tripos was his saving inoculation against classics and the public school ethos. Forbes's only published work was, indeed, historical. To say that it was a history of Clare College is misleading. His *Book of Clare* is an extraordinary mixture of aesthetic tribute and modern archaeology.[16]

If Forbes was Peter Pan to Cambridge English, I.A. Richards was its Wizard of Oz. The literary intellectuals made pilgrimages to him; like a wizard, at the very last resort he could give a disciple the slip. Richards was an eccentric college man. He disliked Cambridge, making it his business to travel whenever possible, lecturing or mountaineering. He was a spellbinding lecturer, filling the large Mill Lane lecture-room theatre for whole courses, unlike Forbes, who was popular for a couple of weeks, then having only a faithful following of about forty students. Richards did not improvise but, like Q, delivered himself elegantly in prose. He was blunter in his lectures than on the page: they had a 'fighting aspect'. He liked to 'take the guff out of the experts', giving the impression that he was with friends 'to whom he could tell things he dare not say in print'.[17] (Leavis may have learned his own confidentially rebellious teaching manner from Richards.) Forbes taught him analysis and how to be a personality in criticism, Richards supplied new, basic concepts for criticism, but also concepts of the social relations of literature to other subjects, of the place of poetry among other forms of knowledge and expression. He was eventually a god that failed. And one only two years older than Leavis, but longer established in Cambridge because he had been unfit for war service.

Forbes and Richards were part of Cambridge for a much shorter time than Q. In the mid-1930s Forbes died prematurely and Richards departed Cambridge for America. But the other teachers of Cambridge English had the longevity of Q. Leavis was taught by a group, some of whose members were war veterans like himself, which was in place when he returned from France (or he could have been taught by them, had he attended their lectures). The 1919 group was motley, casually appointed, earning hourly fees. The group hardened after 1926 when the Faculty system was introduced. It is interesting to observe the curriculum vitarum of this group, which proved to be Leavis's academic family for decades, the men whom he bitterly knew were always just a little ahead of himself (until the end of his career).

The personnel of early Cambridge English had its origins in the established professional classes. The English supervisor at Leavis's own college, Emmanuel, was probably the closest to him in terms of social class. Leavis's voice was Cambridgeshire; Stanley Bennett never lost his South Coast twang (sometimes called 'cockney' in Cambridge). The thirty-year-old Bennett was second-in-command in English at Emmanuel, strikingly handsome in the Rupert Brooke mould.[18] Son of a Hastings butcher, Bennett had been a pupil-teacher in London. He worked for a degree in English through King's College of the University of London, then went to the war in the infantry. Promoted captain, he was demobilized after losing a foot. Back in London, where he hated his unruly classes, he saw a notice about the new English Tripos in *The Times* and decided to try his luck. He successfully approached Emmanuel, which had a policy of encouraging working-class entrants. Bennett was on the 'Early Literature and History' side of Cambridge English.[19] Bennett did not proceed through the English Tripos. At that date it was possible for a graduate from outside Cambridge to take a BA degree by research, a system often used by foreign students. Having already part of a degree from London University, Bennett was urged by his mentor, the medieval historian G.G. Coulton, to take this route.* Coulton was the only university-appointed Lecturer in English and stimulated medieval studies, like Bennett's own, a chronicle of a fifteenth-century family, *The Pastons and Their England*, which became a minor classic, or the work of G.R. Owst, author of *Literature and Pulpit in Medieval England*, a

* Appointed in 1919 when over sixty, having settled in Cambridge as freelance coach. Apart from his work as a medieval social historian, he campaigned for compulsory military service in *The Case for Compulsory Military Service* (1917).

I. A. RICHARDS

" *If this young man expresses himself*
In terms too deep for me,
Why what a most particularly deep young man
This deep young man must be."

THE GRANTA

FEB. 8TH, 1929

I.A. Richards, drawn by Alistair Cooke for *The Granta* in February 1929

contemporary of Leavis at Emmanuel.[20] Leavis went out bicycling with Coulton and Bennett, and probably knew Owst, whose book he valued. He had moved across to English but was still in touch with social history, or a mode of medieval cultural studies.

Unlike Stanley Bennett, few of the English Tripos teachers had degrees in English. Most came from classics, like Aubrey Attwater, E.M.W. Tillyard and F.L. Lucas. Attwater was a respectable Tory and textual scholar; stout, limping and often in pain, having been badly wounded in the Royal Welch Fusiliers. Attwater is 'Brains' in Robert Graves's *Goodbye to All That* (1929). Leavis never complained about Attwater, and he liked Brian Downs of Christ's, a linguist who lectured on modern Scandinavian as well as English literature. (Each year his private system was to devote the twelve months to study of one decade of English literature.) Leavis thought Downs a 'nice man' who always 'looked as if he had come from his tailor'. Not so Lucas and Tillyard, towards whom his enmity grew.

Leavis's pupils became accustomed to scornful murmurings about E.M.W. Tillyard (1889–1962). Tillyard had been at the Perse and came from a well-known Cambridge family. His father was a literary man (journalist and law-coach) and a mayor of the borough. He was a Presbyterian. A colleague remarked of the son that, though liberal–agnostic, he had some of the 'apostolic ardour' of the 'escaped Puritan': had he been to public school rather than the progressive Perse, he would probably have been more rebellious or more conventional, which may have been true of Leavis too.[21] Tillyard was one schoolboy generation older than Leavis, having left school three years before him. Leavis's jibes, especially the intonation of Tillyard's elaborate Christian names, Eustace Mandeville Wetenhall, had a flavour of schoolyard sarcasm. He went up to Jesus in 1908, becoming Master of the college in 1945. He took Firsts in classics in his last year, from which followed a Craven Scholarship and a prize from the Cambridge University Peace Society for an essay on the Athenian empire (1911–13). He spent a year at the British School of Classical Archaeology in Athens, specializing in Greek ceramics, returning in 1912 to a two-year research fellowship at Jesus, where Q had now joined the fellowship. Tillyard served with the British Expeditionary Force and at Salonika.[22]

On leave during the war Tillyard encountered Forbes through their shared interest in archaeology. Forbes was excited by the prospect of an English Tripos and persuaded Tillyard to meet Chadwick, who enlisted

The Chairman of Examiners

Mr. E. M. W. Tillyard.

NEXT graceful Tillyard shall my numbers sing—
Of half the Arts School undisputed king;
Soft in rebuke, in judgment never hard,
Lover alike of builder and of bard;
Admirer of each form and school and style,
Cubist, Augustan, staid, or juvenile.
By Eliot charmed, to J. C. Squire resigned,
One bias only frets his peaceful mind—
Not even trial by fire or death by drowning
Could reconcile him to the works of Browning.

                                        HILAIR

E.M.W. Tillyard as seen by *The Granta* in June 1928

him for the lectures on literary criticism that he gave after the Armistice. Tillyard helped out with supervision at Jesus, where Q was in shock after the death of his son and preoccupied with literary work; he made himself indispensable. An all-year-round resident of Cambridge, Tillyard soon became the 'political factotum' at the centre of the casual web of Cambridge English. He was an indefatigable supervisor, teaching at his little house in New Square, near where the Leavis family established its first urban bridgehead in its progress from the Fens.

Tillyard was the administrator of Cambridge English from the beginning, and he was a member of the team of university Lecturers appointed in 1926 when the faculty system began, but his progress to college establishment was slow: he became a full fellow of Jesus in 1933, not so very long before Leavis's establishment at Downing. None the less, Tillyard's career, unlike Leavis's, had the standard honours: Firsts, prize essay, research fellowship, full fellowship.

A more glorious version of this route was taken by F.L. Lucas, an exact contemporary of Leavis. Lucas was the son of a South London schoolmaster. He went up from Rugby to Trinity (Porson Prize for Greek iambics) and had a good war.[23] A brilliant linguist, Lucas returned to take a First in Part One of the Classical Tripos, with Chancellor's Medal and immediate fellowship at King's College. He remained for the rest of his life, occupying the place that would have been taken by Rupert Brooke had he survived, for Brooke in 1914 had wanted to join the English lecturing team.[24] Brooke was elected to a fellowship at King's in 1912 on the strength of his fellowship dissertation on the Jacobean dramatist John Webster, published as *John Webster and the Elizabethan Drama* (1916), partly a work of textual scholarship. Lucas took over textual study of Webster, publishing his complete works in 1927. Lucas lectured variously, especially on tragedy; these lectures were published by the Hogarth Press. During the 1920s Lucas became its literary representative in Cambridge, helping to cement the connection between King's and Bloomsbury.

Lucas and Tillyard were immediate seniors to Leavis. There were two juniors who should be mentioned. Lucas was adopted by Bloomsbury, not with great enthusiasm: Virginia Woolf called him a 'bony rosy little austere priest'.[25] George Rylands, a key figure at King's and always known as 'Dadie' Rylands, worked for a short time for the Hogarth Press and was regarded with much more affection. When Leavis returned to Cambridge in 1919, Rylands was only seventeen years old. Like

Leavis, but unlike Lucas and Tillyard, he took one part of the English Tripos, a year after Leavis in 1922. (His other tripos was in classics, taken in 1924.) He belonged to the post-war generation, and the Eliot generation. Tillyard took time to get used to Eliot and Lucas mocked him, but Rylands, like Leavis, adored 'Portrait of a Lady' and attempted a homage to it in a poem that Eliot offered to publish in the *Criterion* but which came out as *Russet and Taffeta* from the Hogarth Press. The other junior, later prominent in Cambridge English, was Basil Willey. Son of a London businessman and Methodist, he was two years younger than Leavis and demobilized in 1919, having been wounded with the West Yorkshires. He took history in 1920. He was to remark that he was 'one of those whose pattern of life, fixed long before the Great War of 1914–18, has had to be unmade and remade again'.[26] Leavis could have said the same. It was Basil Willey, not Leavis, who succeeded Q in the King Edward VII Chair of English in 1946.

When Leavis changed to English the seniors were Q, Forbes and Richards, with Attwater an attendant lord. For medieval and Anglo-Saxon studies there was G.G. Coulton and H.M. Chadwick. The young men were F.L. Lucas, George Rylands and Stanley Bennett. In appearance the gangling Coulton and typically Yorkshire Chadwick were in the familiar style of tweedy academic, as was Tillyard. But the bearers of modern English studies were mostly eye-catching. Q dressed with theatrical correctness, Forbes was elfin, and Lucas affected always to wear blue. Rylands was ethereally handsome and the toast of undergraduate theatre. Leavis himself had a combination of sportiness and army-surplus, in an Emmanuel blazer and cricket shirts, his books in a rucksack.[27] They were a good-looking group in a city not averse to male admiration. The widely travelled wife of an American Leavisian remarked years later that only in Cambridge streets did people whistle at her husband.

Undergraduate and Postgraduate 1919–1924

Leavis studied English without event until he took his finals in the spring of 1921, at which point a catastrophe occurred. He had to take six examination papers at the end of May, within seven days, ending with the 'History of Literary Criticism' on the Friday afternoon.[28] A week earlier, on 13 May, while he was revising, his father was fatally injured.

Harry Leavis was riding out of Cambridge to Hauxton on his motor-cycle, a Lee-Francis. Another motorcyclist pulled out to overtake a lorry and collided with him. The machines were locked together, and Harry Leavis suffered severe head injuries, only recovering consciousness inter-mittently. The other rider survived, but could remember nothing of the accident. During the following days Leavis was at his bedside at Addenbrooke's Hospital, watching over his father as he had attended men in France. He told Denys Harding about it later. 'He said he drew on his wartime experience . . . of giving what care and attention was still possible for badly wounded men for whom no further medical treatment was useful or available.' A week after the accident Harry Leavis went into a coma; two days later he died, on the day of his son's first examination paper. The funeral took place during the afternoon of the day Leavis took the 'Tragedy' paper.[29] At Old Chesterton Church, it was attended by many citizens, including the Deputy Mayor and representa-tives of the Liberal Club and the League of Nations Union. Harry Leavis was fifty-nine years old. The piano and music business was left in the charge of Ralph Leavis, the younger son. As for Leavis himself, he appeared in the First Class in the tripos results that were published on 21 June.

In late life Leavis would talk fairly freely with relative strangers about some family matters (the gifts of his elder son, for instance). He was reticent about the death of his father. But he did jot an interesting note on his copy of D.H. Lawrence's *Fantasia of the Unconscious*, probably in the late 1960s. He was clearly alerted to a passage in which Lawrence wrote about families and how the connections between members of them are as intricate as those 'between the Marconi stations, two great wireless stations'. Leavis underlined one sentence:

It is a ripple of life through the many bodies as through one body. But all the time there is the jolt, the rupture of individualism, the individual asserting himself beyond all ties or claims. *The highest goal of every man is the goal of pure individual being.* But it is a goal you cannot reach by the mere rupture of all ties. A child isn't born by being torn from the womb.

In the margin, against his underlining, Leavis wrote: 'Yes! 13 May 1921.'

Leavis was now the head of the family. He was at the point of his career at which he could consider becoming a don. He had one excellent tripos result but a poor one in history. There was no likelihood of immediate election to a junior fellowship, for which there were few endowments at

Emmanuel anyway. He could have prepared a prize essay, but he needed an income. He therefore applied for a research studentship, taking a route rather like that of a young modern academic, a non-Cantabridgean route. Q wrote a letter of recommendation for him to the Director of Studies at Emmanuel, to be forwarded to the Governing Body, a sign that Leavis was not particularly well known in his college.

Leavis did quite well in the Tripos, especially in the earlier papers which were consistently good. There was quality in them too: and if they were, here and there, a trifle thin, one felt that the man had spent time in trying to express himself well. On the last (the Criticism) paper he collapsed, but knowing the circumstances, and finding on inquiry that in the Mays his Criticism paper had led the whole field, I hadn't the faintest compunction in signing him up for a First – even apart from the pluck of the whole performance, which was astonishing. (I lost my father in my last year at Oxford, and know what it means.) I suppose Leavis was too shy to worry me personally for advice: and you know that under pretty constant bombardment by those who are not shy I haven't the time to look up those who are. But I should be happy to make amends if given the chance of supervising his work for a research degree. He has suggested a very good subject, and I know enough of him to be pretty sure he would make a good fist of it.[30]

He was successful. Mansfield Forbes had also acted as referee, for which Leavis wrote a letter of thanks. It throws light on how Leavis pictured himself, and how he may have been seen by others:

I'm glad to be able to tell you that your exertions on my behalf have not been in vain: I've got the Emmanuel Research Studentship. What I owe to you for this result I cannot adequately acknowledge. My sense of obligation is the more overwhelming since I had no claim on your attention, and am, moreover, painfully aware that in our personal intercourse I've always displayed a singularly unprepossessing gaucherie. But please believe that I am fully sensible of your great kindness. The studentship means all the more to me since, owing to circumstances at home, I should in any case have been unable to take a job away from Cambridge. So you have done me a very great service indeed.[31]

The studentship was worth £150. Leavis was registered as a research student under the supervision of Q. He began work on a study of the relations between journalism and literature for the Ph.D. that was earned by submitting, within three years of registration, a long dissertation.

The title that appeared on Leavis's finished dissertation was 'The Relationship of Journalism to Literature: Studied in the Rise and Earlier Development of the Press in England'. It focused on the eighteenth century. But the original scope was wider, and there were difficulties. Q later explained to I.A. Richards that 'No small part of that job was steering him clear of nervous breakdown. Once – I think twice – I got the Board to abbreviate the scope of his thesis and consent to altering its title. I was extremely anxious about him, to the last moment.'[32] Leavis began by doing a study of journalism that encompassed nineteenth- and twentieth-century history, understandably, given his interest in new poetry. This is attested by the title that was originally registered: 'Journalism and Literature: A Historical Study of Relations between them in England'. Q petitioned a change in February 1924. The original broader subject may have dealt with fields closer to Q's expertise. As for scholarly influence from outside Cambridge, a French source should be mentioned. Alexandre Beljame's *Le Public et les hommes de lettres en Angleterre au dix-huitième siècle* was published in 1881, seven years before the death of Matthew Arnold, and not translated into English until 1949. This was a prime model for Leavis's literary sociology; its detail was unrivalled by any other study in English.[33]

The completed dissertation surveyed journalism from the Elizabethan period to that of the great reviews, the *Edinburgh* and the *Quarterly*, of the nineteenth century, with more general handling of the proliferation of printed matter in the era of the Harmsworth brothers (Alfred Harmsworth becoming Lord Northcliffe) who acquired the *Daily Mail*, the *Daily Mirror* and *The Times* between 1896 and 1908, and whose fortune funded Q's chair. Leavis had two themes that were to emerge later, in his own work and especially in that of his wife. One theme was sociological. With the growth of the print industries a complex variety of specialized markets was created: groups of readers found their niches and it became increasingly difficult to move, mentally, between the types of work designed for different readership groups. The taste of a *Daily Mail* reader would be locked on to a channel different from that of the *Blackwood's*. Markets became exclusive: thus emerged high-, low- and middle-brow niches. The second theme was artistic. When writers directed themselves to a market they tailored their arts to it. So *Robinson Crusoe* was vitiated by Defoe's deference to the shop-keeper mentality. He directed his artist's energy into enjoying the creation of down-to-earth resourcefulness, not capturing the anguish of solitude. (To which

Leavis was no stranger, on Ambulance Train 5.) When the writer designed to please, the attitudes or states of consciousness expressed were the less subtle. The evaluation of *attitude* was soon to become the mark of Leavis's literary criticism, with the help of writings by I.A. Richards that were appearing as he worked on his dissertation.

Leavis was to be accused of nostalgia for a lost world of rural, 'organic community'. In his Ph.D. dissertation the golden world is a brief urban one, that of the post-Restoration London of John Dryden and Roger L'Estrange, with the coffee-house a nerve-centre of communication in which writing was for group, not market.

To study for a doctorate now seems an inevitable procedure for an aspiring academic. It was not so in the odd world of 1920s Cambridge. Leavis took an unusual path by registering for a newly invented degree. An account of why it was unusual will help to explain some of the stresses of Leavis's position.

Cambridge had offered a doctorate since 1883 in the form of a Litt.D., awarded after assessment of a body of published work. A doctorate by thesis had been suggested, but it was thought to be a cheap option, window-dressing that would devalue the Litt.D. This situation was not satisfactory for outsiders coming to Cambridge who could only take a BA by research (as Stanley Bennett in Emmanuel had done), or a certificate attesting they had done high-level study. Foreign academics who needed Cambridge research and something more than a second BA found the procedure demeaning. There was demand for a degree that recognized scientific research. The need was felt by Ernest Rutherford, the great New Zealand scientist, who said that a new degree, the Ph.D., would be 'a real and very great departure in English education – the greatest revolution in my opinion in modern times'.[34] There was a vigorous campaign for the establishment of the Ph.D., led by the Master of Emmanuel, Peter Giles. The new degree was eventually approved in 1919, and students registered for it from May 1920.

So, as in changing from history to English, Leavis was also taking an unexpected or risky step in registering for the Ph.D. The degree may have been needed by scientists, but it was not necessarily a promising route for higher studies in the humanities. The ideal prospect after graduation was immediate election to a junior fellowship on the strength of tripos performance, something so much part of the examination system that the fellowship election of the best First-class men was signified by an asterisk in the result lists when printed in book form. This was the best possible move (that of F.L. Lucas). The next best was to move up by prizes and fellowship dissertation (the Tillyard route). But Leavis's First in English was not starred, and in Part One he had only a Lower Second in history. He was in a similar position to that of Lytton Strachey in 1902, who was also mortified by his Second in history, from which he tried to recover by writing a prize essay to secure a research studentship. Leavis was more fortunate. He received a research studentship, but it obliged him to take on a longer piece of work than a prize essay. He could have gone elsewhere, but in his circumstances, as he told Forbes, he wanted to stay with his mother. He decided on a Ph.D., the distinctively modern option with scientific overtones. It was not a prestigious course: to have a doctorate for which one had worked did not impress. Why had this 'Dr' gone in for thesis-writing at all? Ten years later Leavis was the only Ph.D.-holder teaching Cambridge English, though there were to be other doctors, like Richards and Tillyard, who owed their title to a set of publications. Leavis himself was slightly embarrassed by his higher academic qualification. He did not want 'Ph.D.' on the title-page of *New Bearings in English Poetry*: 'It would raise the worst suspicions, and, anyway, looks comic.' In later years much was made of *Dr* Leavis, sometimes as a Crippen-like, 'murdering-to-dissect' analyst. (He was also, of course, married to another Dr Leavis.)

That the doctorate was no guarantee of academic success is shown by the fact that while Leavis was preparing his thesis three other men, younger than himself, were working through the English Tripos, took the 'prize route' and were to move into established posts before Leavis himself. Like Leavis, each had taken one tripos in another subject, either classics or modern languages. L.J. Potts graduated in 1922 and went straight to a fellowship at Queens'. T.R. Henn, son of an Irish Protestant land-agent, graduated in 1923, took a post with an oil company in India and returned to teach freelance for the English Tripos while working on a prize essay. His Director of Studies was Tillyard, who taught him in the little house on New Square. And George Rylands, after graduating in 1924, began work on a fellowship dissertation on the speaking of poetry for King's. The trio overtook Leavis.

Despite Q's concern, Leavis completed his work on time. A doctoral thesis was assessed by a report from and interview with the Cambridge supervisor and an examiner from another institution. On this occasion the external examiner was George Saintsbury, the historian of criticism and prosody, as well as critic and translator of French literature. Among his other qualifications for assessing a thesis on journalism, he had been assistant editor of the *Saturday Review* from 1883 to 1894. In his seventies this old bon vivant was writing his *Notes on a Cellar-Book*. Leavis wrote ruefully that 'He (and I) still belonged to pre-1914 England.'[35] Saintsbury did not dispute the value of the work, and the degree was approved on 18 November 1924, to be conferred a week later. It became thesis No. 66 for the new degree.

Matters of Feeling: Forbes and Richards

Leavis had graduated as B A three years before his Ph.D. was conferred just before Christmas 1924. This did not mean he ceased going to university lectures that interested him, and in 1925 there was one course of undergraduate lectures to which Leavis gave intense attention. It was I.A. Richards's series 'Practical Criticism'. This series was as much about the analysis of responses to poetry as about analysis of poetry itself. Richards handed out printed sheets of poems (four poems at a time), inviting his audiences 'to comment freely in writing upon them'. He then took back the statements, which he called 'protocols', analysed them and lectured on the results. He wanted to know how people read poetry, but he had a larger project in mind. Poetry, he argued, belonged to the 'vast *corpus* of problems' that are addressed by subjective opinion, rather than scientific method or conventional rule of thumb: 'The whole world, in brief, of abstract opinion and disputation about *matters of feeling*.' Poetry invited subjectivity, so it was 'an eminently suitable *bait* for anyone who wishes to trap current opinions and responses'. His survey of the protocols was therefore 'a piece of fieldwork in comparative ideology'. Leavis attended, and went on attending, even when the course was repeated 'four or five years in a row, to the same ones'; to Richards, it was 'uncanny'.[36] Not so uncanny: the course was an extraordinary innovation in at least three ways. Richards offered new concepts for the analysis of poetry; he looked for the first time, it seemed, at what people, not authors or men of letters, really thought about what they read – and at the views of students. And his method, the use of the mass survey, was ground-breaking. (The use of the questionnaire became standard Leavisian practice, notably in Q.D.L.'s

preparation for her *Fiction and the Reading Public*.) The performance style
of the lectures was original as well, signifying a new means of interaction
between audience and Lecturer, with implications for the relations
between teacher and student. No wonder Leavis wanted to attend.
Mansfield Forbes was also often present. Both he and Leavis duly gave
in their (anonymous) protocols for analysis by Richards, and for eventual
publication when Richards wrote up the experiment in *Practical Criticism:
A Study of Literary Judgement* (1929).

The Forbes contributions to Richards's data-store illustrate the vivacity
that made him (Leavis thought) the soul of the new subject. Forbes and
Leavis were intrigued by Group II in Richards's sets of poems, a set of
four by Edna St Vincent Millay, Gerard Manley Hopkins, D.H. Lawrence – and J.D.C. Pellew, whose poem Richards meant to be the dud.[37]
Leavis very often used, and read plangently, the Millay poem in his own
later lectures. What Forbes had to say about it in 1924 illustrates a
concept that became basic to Leavis's criticism, the concept of a 'complex', even though he did not use that word.

> What's this of death, from you who will never die?
> Think you the wrist that fashioned you in clay,
> The thumb that set the hollow just that way
> In your full throat and lidded the long eye
> So roundly from the forehead, will let lie
> Broken, forgotten, under foot some day
> Your unimpeachable body, and so slay
> The work he most had been remembered by?
> I tell you this: whatever of dust to dust
> Goes down, whatever of ashes may return
> To its essential self in its own season,
> Loveliness such as yours will not be lost,
> But, cast in bronze upon his very urn,
> Make known him master, and for what good reason.

Forbes compared Millay's sonnet to the good Pellew's sentimental poem
in the same group:

This is a studied orgasm from a 'Shakespeare–R. Brooke' complex, as [Pellew's]
from a 'Marvell–Wordsworth–Drinkwater, etc., stark-simplicity' *complex*. [*my
italics*] Hollow at first reading, resoundingly hollow at second. A sort of
thermos vacuum, 'the very thing' for a dignified picnic in this sort of Two-
Seater sonnet. The 'Heroic-Hectoring' of line 1, the hearty quasi-stoical

button-holing of the unimpeachably equipped beloved, the magisterial finger-
wagging of 'I tell you this'!! Via such conduits magnanimity may soon be laid
on as an indispensable, if not obligatory, modern convenience.[38]

Forbes gave the name 'complex' to two stylistic amalgams, one a
mixture of elements from 'Shakespeare–R. Brooke' and the other from
'Marvell–Wordsworth–Drinkwater'. This method of defining style,
showing how it 'carried' and disseminated down through writer- and
readerships, was in Forbes's hands vivid and subtle. It also delivered a
mission to the literary critic, or potential critic in the case of Leavis.
Influential writers, said Foucault much later, create 'a possibility for
something other than their discourse, yet something belonging to what
they founded'. So Freud 'made possible a certain number of divergences
– with respect to his own texts, concepts, and hypotheses – that all arise
from the psychoanalytical discourse itself'. The Marxian or Freudian
becomes a complex of meaning. The mission of the commentator may
be to separate off the complex from the original. It was certainly the
mission of Leavis as literary critic to try to ensure that a writer's
originating style was not eclipsed by derivative mixtures, complexes that
occur beyond his or her responsibility. This critic's endeavour was to
protect Wordsworth from the Wordsworthian, to beware the stylistic
packages that form when an adhesiveness in one style cannot resist an
appealing surface shape in another. Leavis was much concerned with
authenticity. He liked to set examination questions challenging candidates
to distinguish Shakespeare from the Shakespeare-ish (something slightly
different from the Shakespearean).

Leavis's commentaries on the Group II poems appear alongside
Forbes's in *Practical Criticism*. (Of poor Pellew, he only wrote 'Uplift'.)
He wrote on Millay's sonnet.

It seems to me that these four poems have been chosen because they all play for
easily touched-off and full-volumed responses, and so are in danger of sentimentality and kindred vices. [This] offers cheap reassurance in what is to most men
a matter of deep and intimate concern. It opens with Browning's brisk no-
nonsense-about-me directness and goes on with a cocksure movement and
hearty alliteration. It contains (along with the appropriate 'dust to dust') echoes
of all the best people. It is full of vacuous resonances ('its essential self is its own
season') and the unctuously poetic.

He most favoured Gerard Manley Hopkins's 'Margaret':

I like this best of all. What looks like preciosity – 'Golden grove unleafing' and 'world of wanwood leafmeal lie' – is really a means of compression. I was puzzled at first reading because I took 'will' in 'and yet you will weep and know why' to be future. Wistfulness without sentimentality: the pang of transience well conveyed.

Of D.H. Lawrence's 'Piano' he wrote that

I have not been able to find a moment for this when I have not been too tired to trust my judgement. It runs an appalling risk of sentimentality and yet seems to have escaped all offensiveness; a considerable achievement. It is poignant, but not, I think, of very great value. The accent is familiar. D.H.L.?[39]

(This curious, intimate note of fatigue was voiced by Leavis throughout his life.)

The sound of poetry was important to Forbes. In his lectures on Romanticism there were enthusiastic readings-out of poetry. Forbes's rendering of Wordsworth's sonnet 'Surprised by Joy – Impatient as the Wind' issued in a diagram of its structure:

The architectonics of the poem consist of three sentences forming rhythmic groups with a vital unity of rhythm. The motor imagery with its minor suggestions of movement makes up for the lack of visual imagery. In words like 'tomb' and 'pang' there is something different from normal onomatopoeia – a sound echo of the *emotional* sense.[40]

This sonnet became a classic object of exposition for Leavis. Forbes's point about rhythm compensating for imagery, or sound echoing 'emotional sense', was valuable for him when he wanted to contest the common idea, partly promoted by the Imagist movement, that poetry is primarily visual. Richards also read out poetry. He would 'take breath and read it with the ears', not always having quite enough breath for Shelley or Hopkins. (Leavis said he could himself swim a hundred yards under water, but not manage a Swinburne stanza.) On one occasion Forbes collaborated with Richards in an aural experiment: both gave renderings to the lecture audience, but each stepped outside so as not to be influenced by the reading of the other. Richards especially admired C.K. Ogden's virtuoso reading of Hopkins's 'The Wreck of the Deutschland'. Some of Richards's lecture material appears in an essay he wrote on Hopkins in the American journal the *Dial*. He demonstrated that subtlety of rhythm was tied in with verbal intricacy, the thing that Cambridge criticism was popularly supposed to be about. Richards showed that difficult rhythms slowed down or paced attention, enabling the reader to catch hold of ambiguity, while blander modes of verse hurried on. Hopkins's rhythms were a preparation for his semantic complexities. Leavis took up these ideas in his lectures, and when he came to write on Hopkins in *New Bearings in English Poetry* (1932). He favoured too Richards's patrician scorn for the clumsiness and pretension of the prosodists' worries about the metrics of Hopkins.[41] For Leavis, it was *sound* that was at the heart of Cambridge. No longer was it 'the surge and thunder of the *Odyssey*' that mattered but a new pulse, 'the subtleties of living speech', some of it in T.S. Eliot:

> 'Ah, my friend, you do not know, you do not know
> What life is, you who hold it in your hands';
> (Slowly twisting the lilac stalks) . . .'[42]

CHAPTER THREE

EXCITING STRANGENESS
1925–1931

It is an event to have the response of a younger generation to the problems envisaged by Mr Eliot and Mr Richards, for Mr Empson is as alive as they to the exciting strangeness of the present phase of human history.

– F.R. Leavis, 'Intelligence and Sensibility', *Cambridge Review*, 1931

Freelance 1925–1926

Leavis got on well with Stanley Bennett at Emmanuel College and with the young woman he married. Joan Frankau was from a well-off Jewish family, and went up to Girton College from Wycombe Abbey School to do two years of French and Spanish for the Medieval and Modern Languages Tripos. She then changed to the new English Tripos, taking a First in its very first set of examinations in 1919. During her year of English she met Stanley Bennett; they fell in love and married in 1920. The Bennetts were part of the small group making up Cambridge English that lasted down to the early 1960s. Leavis was a regular visitor to the Bennetts through the 1920s, and would go on holiday with them to France, usually near Clermont-Ferrand. The friendship lasted until a couple of years after Leavis's own marriage.

There were many female students of the humanities in Cambridge, young women in tussore silk blouses and Liberty ties (and some still in gym-slips), much bicycling back and forth from Newnham, which had more English students, and Girton. Stanley Bennett was a supervisor at both and Leavis followed him into freelance supervising at the beginning of 1925, his doctorate now behind him. There was plenty of supervising to be done. At Girton the Director of Studies in languages was Hilda Murray, who inherited English students when the new tripos was formed. Daughter of Sir James Murray, editor of the great *Oxford English Dictionary*, much of her youth was spent in writing out word-quotation slips (at sixpence a thousand), which developed her formidable memory and a severe enthusiasm for medieval studies. Aware that the English Tripos made demands unsuited to her Oxford education, she engaged Leavis as supervisor and took a liking to him. At that date there was prospect of later employment, even though college fellowships were few and far between. Three years earlier the Royal Commission had reported on the organization (or disorganization) of the university, and the government proposed making an annual grant of £90,000 to the university itself, the federation of colleges, as opposed to any one college, so long as its central organization was rationalized. By this means the university itself would have greater administrative autonomy; it would have faculties and lectureships, fortified by the government funds. Previously the subject of English had, besides the two professors, only one university-salaried Lecturer. More lectureships could be anticipated and Leavis seemingly had the right qualifications, even though there was a handful of young people already in on the act. He was now also able to offer a lecture course.

In January 1925 Leavis joined the pool of college Lecturers. He gave a course on 'Literature and Society from the Restoration to the Death of Johnson', a natural choice given the subject of his Ph.D. thesis. The lecture-list was ill-provided with eighteenth-century courses: there were only fairly mundane surveys available, from S.C. Roberts (later the Sherlock Holmes *aficionado*) and Attenborough from Emmanuel, soon to leave for a career in university administration. But his departure meant there would be a vacancy for a Director of Studies at Emmanuel. Leavis was clearly thought well of. Bennett was senior in years and experience, but both he and Leavis were interviewed by a fellow in classics to determine whether the 'private tuition' (supervision) should be 'shared between them'. Bennett was appointed as Director of Studies, at £5 a term, with 'Dr Leavis asked to assist'.[1] In October 1925, at the beginning of his first academic year as university teacher, Leavis was allocated the room for teaching on 'K' staircase that had been shared by Attenborough and Bennett, and which he shared with two college fellows. For the start of this year there was a change in the name of Leavis's lecture course. The 'society' element was removed and the period abbreviated, eliminating the period from 1660 to 1700. He was now lecturing simply on 'Eighteenth-century Literature'.

★

The two years following Leavis's graduation (1925–6) saw an unexpected festival of literary criticism in Cambridge English; they were the months of Murry, Eliot and Richards. In February 1925 John Middleton Murry began his series in the Trinity College foundation of Clark Lectures, 'Keats and Shakespeare'. The lectures were both prestigious and remunerative: the fee of £200 rivalled a Lecturer's annual salary. Murry returned in June to speak about criticism and modern poetry to a college society. He nominated T.S. Eliot as his successor, to which Trinity agreed. Eliot gave the first of his series, 'The Metaphysical Poetry of the Seventeenth Century', on 26 January 1926. The lectures were so little Olympian that Eliot ended his first by asking the audience to buy a set book: H.J.C. Grierson's *Metaphysical Lyrics and Poems of the Seventeenth Century from Donne to Butler* (1921). Eliot had written an essay, 'The Metaphysical Poets', as a review of the anthology that appeared too late for his first volume of literary criticism, *The Sacred Wood*. The Clark Lectures gave to a Cambridge audience of opinion-formers, with the new tripos in their charge, the most expansive version to date of Eliot's concept of metaphysical poetry, a concept, also, of his own poetry.* In the same year his own *Selected Poems: 1909–1925* appeared. Richards immediately reviewed it in the *New Statesman and Nation*, reprinting this review as an appendix to the second edition of his *The Principles of Literary Criticism* (1926).

I.A. Richards was not a Cambridge senior; he was younger than Stanley Bennett and only two years older than Leavis. But it was Mansfield Forbes who was the most youthful in spirit of the new Cambridge English. His lecturing style was playful, peppered with neologisms ('savoirfairishness', 'vitaminineous'). He chanted poems (memorably, Blake's 'Hear the Voice of the Bard') and signalled quotation by wiggling his fingers round his ears to represent inverted commas. Forbes managed to enchant his pupils. One of them, Margaret Diggle, wrote a poem about him many years later.

Mansfield Forbes (1889–1936)

The phrase iridescent
The pun whose absurd

---

* 'Eliot had begun a theory based on three metaphysical moments – Dante in Florence in the thirteenth century; Donne in London in the seventeenth century; Laforgue in Paris in the nineteenth century. Implicitly, there was a fourth moment at hand – Eliot in London in the twentieth century', *Clark*, pp. 3–4.

> Inconsequence crescent
> With meaning astounded;
> The quip effervescent
> The fabulous word
> Hydraheaded that rounded
> An acre of meaning;
> Bright sabres of wit
> For the law obsolescent
> The belief overweening –
> Bright words now quiescent
> Yet the sparks that they stirred
> The kindling they lit
> Glow on, incandescent.[2]

Denys Harding described him more soberly:

Forbes's idiosyncrasy was his trustful generosity that allowed him to offer you a share in his thinking and explorations before he had finished with them as a personal adventure and converted them into cautiously qualified statements that he and his hearers might feel safe with. He took us with him into a poem, for instance, while he worked out the most effective rhythms and phrasings, changes of tempo, pitch of voice – all stemming from and adding to one's grasp of what the poem was doing. Of course it took a long time and of course he sometimes exaggerated and of course it wasn't pabulum for hungry examinees; the 'young' people in front of him revealed their prudent middle-age-to-be by smiling and staying away. His interventions in Richards's practical criticism course had similar characteristics, their value depending, of course, not just on their spontaneity and vividness but on the fineness of insight and judgement they conveyed.

I.A. Richards, unlike Forbes, was a theorist. His first considerable piece of work was finished at about the same time as Leavis's. Richards's *The Principles of Literary Criticism* was published in 1924, the year Leavis completed his Ph.D. thesis. Previously he had published a series of articles on psychology and aesthetics, most of which were gathered into his collaboration with C.K. Ogden, *The Meaning of Meaning: A Study of the Influence of Language upon Thought and of the Science of Symbolism* (1923). The title is significant: Richards had devised a new conception of symbolism. For him, 'symbolism' was closer to what many would think to be ordinary language, language committed by its user to make a true record of matter to be transported into statement: that is, referential language. In a paper 'On Talking' (1921, Chapter Ten of *The Meaning of*

Meaning) he distinguished referential language from 'evocative' or 'emotive' language in which the essential concern of the user is the arousal of an *attitude*, by means of 'new, sudden and striking collocations of references for the sake of the compound effects of contrast, conflict, harmony, interinanimation and equilibrium'. He could have been describing the verse of Eliot, a new friend. Or that of John Donne, considering his use of the word 'interinanimation'. In the appendix to the *Principles* (the review of *Selected Poems: 1909–1925*) Richards focused on Eliot's use of emotive language whose logic, in *The Waste Land* published a few months earlier, was not that of a 'coherent intellectual thread'. 'The items are united by the accord, contrast, and interaction of their emotional effects, not by an intellectual scheme that analysis must work out.' By these emotive means 'attitude' is created, the subtleties or velleities wavering yet still forming some sort of whole. It was in such 'wholes' that lay the *value* of emotive or evocative (in short, poetic; but not only metrical) language-use. These wholes were not easily to be understood; the reader must be apt for their apprehension. Moving from his definition of a type of language-use to its value, Richards arrived at a requirement of high competence in the reader (later, *anglicè*, elitism): 'The value lies in the unified response which this interaction creates in the right reader.'[3] The relation of the 'right reader' to other readers (wrong readers and non-readers) was considered in the body of *Principles* in which Richards stated why the 'rightness' of readers mattered:

To bridge the gulf, to bring the level of popular appreciation nearer to the consensus of best qualified opinion, and to defend this opinion against damaging attacks (Tolstoy's is a typical example), a much clearer account than has yet been produced, of why this opinion is right, is essential. These attacks are dangerous, because they appeal to a natural instinct, hatred of 'superior' persons.★

These two factors, the emotive logic of poetry and the desiderated 'right reader', were basic for Leavis. In the same year as he enunciated these factors, Richards also had published his essay 'Gerard Hopkins' in the *Dial*, which elaborated the priority he gave to the *sound* of poetry in his lectures.[4]

In 1926 Richards published a short book, *Science and Poetry*, also basic for Leavis. Richards had a genius for the haunting phrase: in this book it was the *neutralization of nature*. His thesis was that the secular world of

★ On 'superior persons', see this chapter, 'Precarious Terms 1928–1929'.

the twentieth century had experienced the 'neutralization of nature', the
dissolution of the 'Magical View' of nature or of nature as magical. The
natural world was no longer animated by spirit or spirits, neither
possessing supernatural energies, nor possessed by them. His practical
view of nature may have been affected by his experience as an accomplished mountaineer. Had Forbes not offered him teaching for the
English Tripos, he would have become a professional mountain-guide.
Human values were defined by men and women working in social
groups. 'Is this the explanation why the upsetting of the Magical View
had mattered so little?' wrote Leavis in the margin of his copy of *Science
and Poetry*. It therefore fell to the social group, untaught from without,
to create what it valued and recognize distinctions in value not only
between ideas but also between attitudes and emotional states. Richards
thus sharply restated his evaluative sense of consciousness. He had
already proposed one sort of consciousness to be emulated: in Eliot's
poetry he found and had proposed 'a model of the meditative mind'.
Science and Poetry legitimized Leavis's desire to evaluate attitudes.* And
it reminded him of a poem by Thomas Hardy to which he often
returned. Richards said that 'After a Journey' epitomized the 'neutralization of nature'. In the bleak arena of a Cornish sea-haven the slap of
waves is no kind of supernatural speech.

> Hereto I come to view a voiceless ghost;
>   Whither, O whither will its whim now draw me?
> Up the cliff, down, till I'm lonely, lost
>   And the unseen waters' ejaculations awe me.
> Where you will next be there's no knowing,
>   Facing round about me everywhere . . .
>   With your nut-coloured hair,
>   And gray eyes, and rose-flush coming and going.

'You' is not here Pan but Hardy's dead, latterly unloved wife.

Leavis's first full academic year as a teacher for Cambridge English
began in October 1925. In this month three people went up to Cambridge who later were at the core of Leavis's group. Two were to be
editors of *Scrutiny*. Denys Harding went up to Emmanuel and became

---

* As in his dissertation on journalism: see Chapter Two, English at Cambridge,
'Undergraduate and Postgraduate 1919–1924'.

Leavis's pupil. Lionel Knights only met Leavis later as he began postgraduate work, after he had read History at Selwyn. At Girton arrived Queenie Dorothy Roth, who was to be Leavis's most remarkable pupil. And also in October 1925 William Empson, whose poetry and criticism was to exhilarate Leavis, went up to Magdalene.

Queenie Dorothy Roth was the eldest daughter in a North London Jewish family of No. 79, Silver Street, Edmonton; she was born on 7 December 1906. Her father was successively hosier and draper, living over his shop, until some time during Q.D.R.'s time at Cambridge, when they moved up the street to No. 24. Had they not done so, her mother, Jenny Roth, and her sister Ruby Caroline would have escaped death from a parachuted land-mine in December 1940.

Jenny Roth, born 8 September 1876, married Morris Roth when he was twenty-seven years old in July 1903. She was the daughter of Polish immigrants Emelia Motrez and David Krotoszynski (or Davis), a hairdresser of Holywell Street, Shoreditch. Evidently she could not write her name, and only gave a mark in the register rather than a signature. The father of Morris Roth, Aaron, was a 'general dealer', an emigrant from Königsberg first to Glasgow, then Sunderland and finally London. He had two sons: Morris's brother Abraham left England for diamond-mining in South Africa. When he returned to England he suffered from mental instability and died in care; the family believed there was a strain of melancholia in it.

Q.D.R.'s background was that of 'a poor but cultured family hampered by three clever children, two girls and a boy, wanting books, music and college education'.[5] The parents were 'tall, thin, sallow, refined-looking people'. The family was orthodox and the children had a private teacher for Hebrew, from whom Q.D.R. picked up the language by ear when she gave lessons to her brother, the eldest child Leonard. He had an assisted place, as did the other children, at nearby co-educational Latymer School, in Hazelbury Lane. Leonard went on to Clare College, Cambridge, spending some time at Dulwich College before going up. He studied Mathematics and was a Wrangler, or First, in Part Two (1924–6). The two girls also went to Latymer. Ruby Caroline became a schoolteacher in the neighbourhood.[6]

At Girton, Q.D.R. was in the minority of girls who had attended a co-educational school. She did well at sports ('excellent shooting' at netball) and showed from the beginning a gift for writing with extraordinary readability. She wrote poems and stories, some for the school magazine. One of them described vividly a left-wing street speaker, with the red tie and long hair of a socialist, haranguing a tiny crowd from a movable wooden stand. What is interesting about it is that he is seen neither with the awe nor the irony that might be expected of a writer in her teens. There is a romantic element in the depiction of the London street, little crowds capable of materializing out of nowhere as swiftly as in an oriental city. Years later in *Fiction and the Reading Public* Q.D.L. said that the 'racy', 'risk-taking' prose of Elizabethan England is 'oxygenated', a word that suits her own prose, and her personality. A single page of her writing yields a feast of information, discrimination (and recrimination). From one angle she was the *writer* of the two Leavises, lucid as Orwell or Mary McCarthy. Her mind is perhaps 'prosaic': there is nothing – remembering Richards on Eliot – 'meditative' about it, as there is about F.R.L. in full rumination. Q.D.L. is blunt, but in the pertinent clarity with which she projects her enthusiasms there is a crackling idealism. Her enchanted disgust at sloppiness is shown in *Fiction and the Reading Public* when she says that in the good old days before suburbanism and the Baby Austin motorcar, 'No nice girl danced more than twice in one evening with the same man.'

Q.D.R. went up to Girton on a good scholarship. Fellow undergraduates thought she was boastful when she told others in the new intake that her parents 'had waived the emoluments', but students must surely be excused some gaucheness in their freshman weeks. She had a reputation for austerity, was a determined scholar, and she evidently, at least in the first months at Girton, brought some of the ways of an orthodox household to her college life. Sophie Baron, another Jewish girl who went up with her, said that

one extremely cold winter I went into her room early in the morning, having heard her coughing all night. I offered to light her fire for her – her room was icy – and make her a hot drink. She refused vehemently – she refused vehemently – to do work of any kind on the Sabbath was forbidden . . . I reminded her that the Book of Rules expressly allows all rules to be broken in cases of illness if necessary: she snorted and said that she knew that, but a cold and cough, even a severe one like this, was *not* an illness. And she lay in bed until sunset when the Sabbath ends; luckily it was around 4 p.m., without a fire or hot food and drink.

Queenie's brother Leonard arranged with the Girton authorities for her to be out late on Fridays. After the services at the synagogue in

Thompson's Lane, there was usually a guest speaker to be heard in a room above Thurston's Café in St Andrew's Street. Both she and Sophie Baron were members of the Jewish Students' Society and went to a number of its functions. She had weekly parcels from home of kosher food, appreciated because (she later told her daughter) Girton fare was acceptable only to those who had been to boarding-school; it was inedible for the girls who were used to home cooking. It is not known how long she kept up the ways of her religious background. Not long, it seems; and she must have been fully aware of the drastic break that would ensue when she 'married out'. Later there was hardly any consciousness of Jewish heritage in the Leavis family. Their daughter Kate, for example, reminisced that 'I had no idea I was half Jewish until my first year at Oxford, when I was informed accordingly by a contemporary.'

In college Q.D.L. was noted as a book worm, sighted on occasion as a simultaneous walker and reader on the dull half-hour trudge back to Girton from town known as the 'Girton Grind'. She was a member of the exclusive Girton 'secret society' called ODTAA ('One Damn Thing After Another'), to which Virgina Woolf delivered a version of *A Room of One's Own*, after which she promised to send Queenie Roth some pamphlets. She was particularly keen on the novels of Henry James, and journals, taking *The Times Literary Supplement,* the *New Statesman*, the *Spectator* and the more 'feminine' *Time and Tide*. For her English Tripos she chose 'Early Literature and History', under the care of H.M. Chadwick, and was delighted by it and him:

The first thing one noticed about him was how unacademic he was, the refreshing absence of that aura of anecdotes, social values and lack of real interest which is so discouraging to the young. His kindly eyes looked at once innocent and shrewd, he retained his Yorkshire accent, and always wore a Norfolk jacket and bicycling breeches costume.

It was her introduction to the sociology of literature, but that of the ancient world of northern Europe. His capacity for giving a 'unified study' of all kinds of cultural artefacts enthralled her.*

*

* The importance of Chadwick is set aside here for later consideration when describing the period in which interest in him revived. See Chapter Seven, Wartime, 'Old Cambridge 1939–1947'.

Leavis was now living at home with his widowed mother at Chesterton Hall Crescent. By his second academic year (1926/7) the family of Harry Leavis was in decline, but Leavis himself was gaining authority. The music business did not prosper under Ralph Leavis. In 1926 the showroom next to the University Arms Hotel was taken over by a neighbouring dress shop, the Leavis shop confining itself to the former warehouse premises across the road on Downing land. 'Leavis & Son' was now a 'music dealer', not a pianoforte business, perhaps because of the expense of maintaining a stock of large instruments. But Leavis himself prospered. He planned to overhaul his lectures, going over into the modern period. It was announced that he would give a series of lectures each term on 'Modern Poetry', 'Modern Novels' and 'Modern Problems in Criticism', a striking innovation and entry into the field of I.A. Richards, the most popular Lecturer. But at the last minute he changed his mind. He gave only the 'Modern Poetry' course and in the second and third terms Leavis continued to lecture on the eighteenth century.

A curious adventure delayed Leavis's presentation of himself as a modern-ist. During his lectures on the eighteenth century Leavis referred to James Joyce's *Ulysses* (1922). He probably compared the homogeneous reading-public of the eighteenth century to the highbrow versus low-brow divisions of the twentieth century.[7] *Ulysses* had been banned in Britain since December 1922, when a copy was seized at Croydon Aerodrome. From April 1923 Chief Constables were warned by the Home Office to look out for illicit copies. The novel was well known to the intelligentsia. The *Cambridge Mercury* hailed *Ulysses* (with David Garnett's *Lady into Fox*) as indispensable, and *The Granta* reviewed it in 1922, but possession of it was illegal.[8] The suppression of the novel was the indirect cause of Leavis's change of mind about making a début as a modernist.

In the summer of 1926 Leavis got into conversation with his bookseller about the censorship exercised by the American customs authorities. Galloway & Porter was a long-established book business with an intellec-tual bent. Leavis remarked that the situation was the same in England: 'Well, *we* can't talk: there are books you can't get me.' Leavis dictated a letter for Charles P. Porter to send to the Chief Constable of Cambridge, asking if a copy of *Ulysses* could be supplied. A police officer then called at the shop, advising Porter that he needed Home Office permission that could be petitioned through the Chief Constable's office. Porter wrote off a letter (17 July) containing a statement to be sent to the Home Office, saying that Dr Leavis requested a permit to obtain one copy 'which he requires for purposes of illustration and comment in his course "Modern Problems in Criticism". This course is now included in the current lecture list for the English Tripos.' (He must have meant his fiction course, because this one was not yet announced, unless he was writing loosely.) But the bookshop owner went further and also asked if a copy could be supplied, to be placed in a suitable library 'for use of students attending this course only' and asking, alternatively, whether a Home Office representative 'would be in a position to permit us to supply to any student a copy for study'.

This *Ulysses* story was told by Leavis himself in 1963, and accurately, though he omitted one detail, understandably because more than likely he did not know it. Leavis said a copy was requested for himself, but Charles Porter had *also* asked for a library copy, or, indeed, copies that his shop could supply to students. He is to be applauded for his cheek, but he was certainly being disingenuous. His letter presumed that copies could be furnished to 'registered' students, but there was no such category. Anyone could attend Leavis's lectures; many women did so, though still only constitutionally on sufferance at Cambridge. The Home Office was alarmed that they could be exposed to Joyce. Leavis was not lecturing for a designated examination. The sponsor of his lectures was Emmanuel College and paid-up students' fees went to the college, thence to Leavis. If the novel was available to these students, and not merely had passages read from it, then the college would be sponsoring the circulation of an obscene book.

It was not surprising that the Home Office was provoked when it received Porter's request, via the Chief Constable. It was disgusted at the prospect of 'boy and girl undergraduates' reading *Ulysses*, a scheme, surely, of 'a dangerous crank', best interpreted as suitable for a Savoy opera and at worst – goodness knows. Active steps should be taken 'to prevent the lectures taking place'. The Cambridge police investigated, and the Home Office decided that the Director of Public Prosecutions be brought in. Leavis never denied that he challenged the authorities, but it is clear that it was Charles Porter who, having entered the engagement with relish, landed him in trouble by his cheeky additional request. The Chief Constable duly made inquiries, discovering that Leavis did not hold the rank of university Lecturer, though he gave lectures for the English faculty, and that 'he also takes pupils privately'. He discovered that Leavis was planning a course on 'Criticicism' (so spelled), to be attended by both men and women, 'probably 1st and 2nd year'. He assured the Home Office that *Ulysses* was not on sale in Cambridge bookshops – to the private regret of the investigating constabulary – and that Leavis's request was not a hoax.

The inquiry was in keeping with the current political climate. In 1923 the Conservative Party was returned to office; William Joynson-Hicks (or 'Jix') became Home Secretary, enjoying greater popularity with the police force than any other in the century. As an evangelical President of the National Church League, he used his powers to strengthen public morality. The Leavis–Porter initiative was therefore anti-evangelical in the tradition of Harry Leavis. On 31 July the Director of Public Prosecutions wrote to the administrative head of the university, the Vice-Chancellor, Professor A.C. Seward, also Master of Downing College. He asked for action, but 'I am afraid that I am unacquainted with your full authority in the University.' (The remark is a sign of how little, at this date, university offices were understood as part of the apparatus of state.) The 'contemplated inclusion of this book in Dr Leavis's lectures' must be avoided. Of *Ulysses*, 'to use a colloquialism, I am unable to make head or tail'. But he could see that it was obviously gross and indecent, unashamedly so in the last pages, the reminiscences 'as I suppose they may be called, of an Irish chamber-maid'. He offered to dispatch the book to the Vice-Chancellor if he cared to request it.

Professor Seward was not overly impressed. He replied calmly on 5 August that he did not think it necessary for the DPP to send him the book. He promised to interview Leavis, which he did the next day, reporting that Leavis confessed to referring to *Ulysses* in a lecture and now promised not to recommend his students to buy it.* 'He would never think of doing so.' He had only asked Galloway & Porter to acquire a copy for 'illustrations and comment in his lectures'. He added that critiques of the novel had appeared in the *Nation and Athenaeum* and in *The Times Literary Supplement*, 'possibly on March 5 of this year'.[9] The DPP replied with some ferocity. Of course he knew about the reviews of *Ulysses*, but he doubted that reviewers had 'waded through its 732 pages'. He warned the Vice-Chancellor that if possession of the

---

* For the passage actually quoted by Leavis, see Chapter Six, *Scrutiny*: Guarding the Guardians, 'Leaving Richards 1934'.

book came to his notice, he would prosecute, and made it clear 'that if I have to take any such steps, inevitably the source from which knowledge of the book arose will be known, and the publicity will hardly tend to increase the reputation of the university, or the subject matter of its lectures'. At the Home Office this was thought to be 'a model of the way to address Vice-Chancellors'. The DPP also wrote to the Chief Constable in Cambridge, saying that, although it would be difficult for him to get hard evidence of references by Leavis to *Ulysses*, he would be grateful of such reports as could be managed and, if necessary, he would 'address a communication to Dr Leavis personally'. The Vice-Chancellor knew the Leavis family, whose shop was opposite Downing. It is likely that he passed the letter from the DPP across his desk to the young man. Leavis's eye would have caught the sentence, 'I do not pretend to be a critic of what is, as I suppose, literature, but . . .' The word 'critic' was scored out and replaced by 'scrutineer' in handwriting. It was hardly the inspiration for *Scrutiny*, but it was an amusing anticipation of it.[10]

Professor Seward was not distressed by Leavis's actions. Six years later Leavis became Director of Studies in English at Downing College, and a fellow four years after that. Seward clearly did not stand in the way of the appointments and may have encouraged them. It is tempting to make a connection between Leavis and the scientific work of this distinguished botanist: like Leavis, he was preoccupied with organic evolutionary growth. He was also an old Emmanuel man.

The story of Leavis and *Ulysses* acquired some popular resonance. *The Granta* once referred to the 'Leavis Prize for Pornography'. Leavis was thought to be a slightly shocking talker. One undergraduate asked for his opinion of Flecker's *Hassan*, only to be told that 'I think it's a masturbation', even though ladies were present.*

After the experiences of the summer it was not surprising that Leavis proposed a conventional sequence of lectures for the academic year of 1926/7. It was not a year in which to take risks.

Leavis expected reform of Cambridge English when he finished his dissertation, and its reorganization would give him the prospect of proper employment. In 1926 two drastic changes occurred: the university was divided into faculties so that there would now be an English Faculty, staffed by Lecturers with salaries from central funds; and the

---

* 'A masturbation' is a period usage, comparable to 'a nonsense' today.

English Tripos was revised so that henceforth students could take a purely 'modern', that is, a course in literature from Chaucer onwards.

The English Faculty was founded for the academic year beginning October 1926. Twelve Lecturers were appointed, familiar faces from the group who had taught for the tripos since 1919. These new posts were full, tenured lectureships, taking effect from 1 October 1926. The basic stipend for a Lecturer was £200 a year but supplemented by £150 for those who did not have a college fellowship. The standard Lecturer's salary was in the region of £350 a year, though that of a professor was as much as £1,000. Eight of these appointments were relevant for Leavis in that they were for the teaching of 'modern' English literature, and so if one of these appointees ever left Cambridge, they could in theory be replaced by an aspirant like himself. The members of this group have already made an appearance. Q of course retained his chair. There was Manny Forbes, I.A. Richards, the lame Aubrey Attwater and the dapper Downs, and 'Tilly' (as the indefatigable Tillyard was called) and F.L. Lucas of King's. Hilda Murray, who had sponsored Leavis as a Girton supervisor, was appointed, becoming the first female university Lecturer in English, sitting on the Faculty Board and acting as examiner. The most junior appointment was that of Stanley Bennett, who shared English teaching with Leavis at Emmanuel. The appointment of one only just senior to him showed how close to a proper lectureship Leavis was. He and Bennett had been momentarily on a level footing when they were considered for the post of Director of Studies at Emmanuel. The professional gap between them began to widen when Bennett was elevated into one of the new lectureships.

But presently Leavis did make some progress. In January 1927 a second run of appointments was made, this time junior, temporary posts called probationary faculty lectureships. There were six posts and Leavis was offered one of them. The posts were for a limited period and not renewable into permanencies; nor did the posts themselves necessarily survive their holders. The initial contracts were for between one and three years; Leavis's was for two years.

The other five probationers were Joan Bennett, Stanley's wife (with a two-year contract), T.R. Henn and L.J. Potts (three years), Enid Welsford and Basil Willey (one year).[11] It was a family group: for instance, in the Lent term of 1927 Henn, Joan Bennett and Leavis cycled to Girton to lecture to its English Club on the modern spirit in literature. The total group, permanent Lecturers and probationers, with some few subtractions and additions – including Leavis, much later – became the team that dominated Cambridge English for thirty-five years.

The second change of 1926 was that the curriculum was enlarged. There were now to be three sets of examinations, when there had before been only two ('Early' and 'Modern'). The modern set was divided into two, making material for a two-part tripos. Part One was a set of literary history survey papers, with additions, as in the original modern set. From that modern set were removed two of its examinations, on 'Tragedy' and the 'History of Criticism'; they were put into Part Two, where they came to rest alongside new examination papers, the 'English Moralists' (beloved of Q) and a paper 'Passages of Prose and Verse, for Critical Comment'. The third set, 'Early Literature and History', remained much the same. The first diet of examinations for the new English Tripos was set in 1928.

Students could henceforth take a wholly modern course in Parts One and Two or substitute 'Early Literature and History' for one of these. It was rather unlikely that many would choose the harsh, linguistically demanding, older literature; but its master, H.M. Chadwick, did not mind. He wanted enthusiasts, and partly because of this he effected a third change in 1926. He decided he did not want his curriculum to remain within the English Faculty at all. He requested, and was allowed, to take his subject to the Faculty of Archaeology and Anthropology.

To some the new regime was an improvement. Cambridge English, in full strength as an analytical study of the modern British secular scriptures, without recourse to early culture or philology, is sometimes considered to date from 1926 when its tripos was freed from early cultures and linguistic study.

It was significant that Leavis now had a university post, albeit probationary. He was, as we shall see, an intriguing lecturer. But talking from the podium was not the peak of his work. In terms of impact on the student community lecturing was possibly exceeded by Leavis's tutorial work as supervisor. When Peter Greenham talked about the retirement portrait with Leavis and his wife, Q.D.L. said she would like to see him in the sun with pupils around him on a lawn. He was seen like this by many students, and well known as a small-group supervisor from 1925 for Emmanuel, for Newnham and for Girton, the engagement he owed to the don to whom he referred as 'Miss Murray, "daughter of the

Dictionary"'. She also had him set scholarship examinations for Girton, with a cultural studies slant (in the language of the late twentieth century) or (in his) a 'Culture and Environment' element. At the women's colleges Leavis took students for poetry analysis in groups. He gave out typed sheets, usually beginning with a poem by Edmund Blunden (like 'Molecatcher') or by Edward Thomas. 'The excitement came later,' said one student, 'when he told us to buy T.S. Eliot's *Poems 1909–1925*.' Having encouraged phrase-by-phrase commentary on 'A Cooking Egg', he went on to *The Waste Land*. Though Eliot was famous, he was believed to be awesomely highbrow.[12] At Newnham College the Director of Studies hoped that 'young man' would not 'infiltrate' Cambridge. It was still the era of Rupert Brooke, James Elroy Flecker and John Masefield.[13] Leavis saw undergraduates after class individually, for ten minutes, to go through their weekly essays. He disliked students reading essays aloud to him, an Oxford practice, though on occasion he had done this at Emmanuel.[14] He discouraged long essays, asking for only four sides – a Girton pupil purchased large paper. He was tough on jargon, like 'factor', the sort of word, he said, that he used himself in the History Tripos. Some pupils, not expecting a youngish man in a cricket shirt, were taken aback by Leavis's *farouche*, bachelor air. One young woman worried that his dog might get at her essay. Another described him, over cocoa, with hilarity: 'a dirty little man who sits next to you at tables and chases you all around, because he edges close and you edge away'. The former student Gwendolen Freeman, who tells the story of this 'jug' (the Girton word for a coffee or cocoa session), did not go along with the idea that Leavis was 'dirty'. 'With his open shirt and high forehead, [he] gave me rather the impression of cleanliness.'* (Q.D.R. was one of the girls at this 'jug'.)

Supervisions were conducted in scruffy surroundings: the single bulb at Newnham, the army-surplus hut at Girton. They took place after tea, at 5 p.m. Foreign visitors found them bewilderingly informal. An American girl had been accustomed at Bryn Mawr to five lectures a week, systematic note-taking of all the items on the reading-lists and two long papers a semester; she found the weekly class and essay at

---

* Gwendolen Freeman was writing to her mother on 13 October 1926. Her letters, at Girton College, have plenty of out-of-school gossip about, for instance, Stanley Bennett's war disability (a 'cork leg which creaks'), and the rumour that Q was 'a frightful drunkard, and will soon die of it'. Her memoir, *Alma Mater* (1990), published by Girton College, is vivid.

Cambridge refreshing. Sometimes the supervisor did not annotate the essay very intensively. What Leavis liked best was reading poems and taking them apart, 'so that is what we did'. The American wished he would allow her to read the German quotations in *The Waste Land* because she thought he mispronounced them.[15]

Leavis did not only teach the moderns. Pupils admired him on Shelley, and on Grierson's *Metaphysical Lyrics and Poems of the Seventeenth Century from Donne to Butler*, which had been a set-book from the early tripos years, and its status given extra authority by Eliot's recommendation of it in his Clark Lectures. Henri Fluchère, a visiting French student at Gonville and Caius College, found little illumination from the official Lecturer on John Donne and was told that Leavis could help. He visited Leavis, enchanted by the 'luscious apple-trees' at Chesterton Hall Crescent, who took him down to the boat-houses on the nearby river. They went for several tow-path walks. (Leavis once dived dismayingly into the black Cam, emerging into a powerful crawl.)

I was happily surprised at his knowledge of French literature; we could talk fluently of Flaubert, Proust, Baudelaire and so on. He even asked me (but that may have been later) to read aloud one of Baudelaire's poems, just to see what the rhythm and music were like when spoken by someone with a French mouth. He told me of his friendship with André Chevrillon, the academician, who had published enjoyable and still valuable essays on English writers and poets.[16]

Fluchère was most impressed by Leavis's explication of Shelley's 'When the Lamp is Shattered', and the way he was 'brilliantly at ease' with Donne's *Songs and Sonets*. He had Leavis's first long essay published, translated into French by himself.★

Modernism and Lectures 1927–1928

In October 1927, now established at the start of a career, Leavis went ahead with the all-modern course of lectures he had planned. He started the year with 'Twentieth Century Poetry', then two terms of lectures called 'Critics and Critical Problems'. In the following year (1928/9) he

★'La poésie anglaise et le monde moderne: étude de la situation actuelle', *Les Cahiers du Sud* (October 1930). It formed the basis of the first chapter of *New Bearings in English Poetry*.

dropped one of his criticism series, substituting 'Prose, with Passages for Criticism' for a term, a course following the publication of Herbert Read's *English Prose Style* (1928).[17] He gave these lectures for four years, down to the spring of 1931, and this was the programme (contemporary poetry, critical theory, prose analysis) on which his early reputation was founded. In that autumn Leavis took up his part as spokesman on contemporary writing. A certain electricity was created. A student could attend a poetry reading by Edith Sitwell on one day, and on the next hear Leavis speak about her in a lecture. Gwendolen Freeman wrote to her parents that Sitwell was dressed 'queerly with enormous beady things round her neck. She then read some rather mad things perfectly beautifully and explained the wonderful technique of her work.' In his lecture Leavis was not amused. According to Freeman:

Beyond the power of evoking childish memories and translating terms of one sense into another, like 'shrieking light', Edith hadn't much as poet. She had no message, nor had her brothers, and he quite squashed her. We wished Edith had been there.[18]

Leavis excoriated Sir John Squire, 'the model of the philistine that everyone goes on about'. Freeman was charmed by Leavis as a lecturer; he also supervised her. He was

quite an exciting person. He was in the war and had shell-shock frightfully badly, so that when he came out he couldn't speak at all or eat at all for ages. Now, at the most, they say, he can only eat two meals a day and he stammers frightfully at times. He is also going a bit bald, forehead upwards, which makes him, with his other features, look rather like an angelic Puck.[19]

The lectures had a reputation for intensity, and for being inspired by Eliot. In February 1928 an undergraduate paper reviewed one lecture in his series on critical problems. Its opening theme, observed the writer facetiously, was played by the *Sacred Wood*-wind, to be joined on the brass by the 'Credo' of Murry. The lecture was haunted by occasional harping allusions to 'the old-fashioned, emotional Pater nostrum'. The 'Andante' contained the Richards theme. The reviewer scolded Leavis for his awkward delivery 'from manuscript'. But he was respectful, stressing that no one else shared his material or approach.

Dr Leavis's lectures contain a great variety of interesting matter which it is impossible to obtain elsewhere. Moreover, it is not uninteresting to see how modern critical theory may be applied to various problems which have been the source of so much discussion in the past. Dr Leavis is perhaps rather too inclined to fall back on Eliot, Murry or Richards, and to condemn all previous criticism. Nevertheless, it is certainly stimulating to hear the great critics of the past being pulled limb from limb, rather than be obliged to sit and listen to the usual safe method of giving laudatory puffs to anyone who has an established reputation. Dr Leavis's method requires courage and confidence and he does not lack these qualities. One at times feels inclined to rebel against some of his more startling denunciations of such critics as Sainte-Beuve and Lamb, but Dr Leavis does make out a strong case and the fact that his arguments are always founded on the works of the authors themselves makes them unassailable on his own premises.

By 'works' the reviewer must mean examples of the authors' prose, as opposed to their concepts only.[20] In lectures, apparently, Leavis did not stammer, but his delivery was not smooth; he had a 'special voice', with a slight 'rasping quality'.[21]

In the spring of 1927 Leavis attended the Clark Lectures again, delivered that year by E.M. Forster. The lectures were published in October as *Aspects of the Novel*, paving the way to Forster's fellowship at King's. Extremely popular with a largely female audience, which he called 'the intelliganzanettes', Forster was typically modest about his efforts. Leavis, as typically, was 'astonished at the intellectual nullity' of the lectures. His harsh view may have evolved over the years, but there was certainly similar criticism when they were delivered. Ford Madox Ford wrote an essay on them called 'Cambridge on the Caboodle', reproving the brilliant novelist for writing in an amiably middlebrow way about the art of the novel, as if for *Punch*. Leavis himself had one objection to *Aspects of the Novel* understandable in a professional teacher. The book

at once became a nuisance: all the girls' school English mistresses in England seized on the distinction between flat and round characters – which after all was as good as anything the book did yield critically. I speak as one who was largely responsible for the 'English' teaching at Girton and Newnham.[22]

He was irritated by Forster's whimsicality and disappointed by the casual treatment of novelists he admired intensely, like Joseph Conrad and Henry James. Late in life (1974) Leavis thought Forster acquiesced too much in the lectures to Bloomsbury taste. 'To treat the two great living writers, James and Conrad (both of whom had *no* recognition that mattered to them), with that characteristic coterie-stupid and charming ("tolerant") condescension I find I can't forgive – nor would Blake himself have done. Him and Virginia Woolf: the Incomparable Max.'[23] The cloth for the lectures was cut according to Forster's friendships in King's and in Gordon Square. Goldsworthy Lowes Dickinson's fantasy *The Magic Flute* (1920) received unexpected praise, contrary to Forster's private opinion. Forster was anxious that Virginia Woolf should not see the proofs of *Aspects of the Novel* until he had cut 'a criticism of her work which I have modified in the revise!!' In the case of Henry James, Forster used a strategy of criticism that Leavis detested: he praised H.G. Wells's parody in *Boon* of the late Jamesian prose style. Leavis believed Wells read James obtusely. Forster's somewhat conventional approval of parody struck into Leavis's aesthetic. Ordinarily, parody is thought to throw a shaft of light amusingly on a literary style. But Leavis could hardly be expected to think parody was instructive: he believed (as a late Romantic) that the stylistic handwriting of an original writer could not be faked, so parodic imitation that exaggerated mannerisms only showed up on a screen of comedy what was peripheral. Paste jewellery, he would say, bore no relation to the *molecular* structure of the real thing, so parody could teach no real lessons. Leavis could not believe in 'learning by parody', and thought the exercise flattered parodist and reader but demeaned the artist. (Leavis's suspicion of the concept of parody underlay his dislike of Max Beerbohm: he disliked not his gaiety but a smug presumption that parody could capture a real style.)

None the less, Leavis thought that Forster had performed at least one valuable service in his lectures on the novel: the dispatch of George Meredith to literary critical limbo in a passage in which Forster was at his most acute and resolute: 'What with the faking, what with the preaching . . . and what with the home counties posing as the universe, it is no wonder Meredith now lies in the trough.' He did say Meredith was a 'great novelist' – but as the 'finest contriver' or plot-maker in English fiction.

In the spring of 1928 Leavis's first professional disappointment occurred. Because of the imminent retirement of G.G. Coulton and because student numbers had risen, the English Faculty was in May able to appoint three new Lecturers. They were T.R. Henn, L.J. Potts and Enid Welsford – not Leavis.[24] Welsford belonged to the pre-war generation: she was an 'Early and Modern English' scholar of the Chadwick persuasion and a natural replacement for Coulton. Her appointment was part time (called 'part work').[25] But Henn and Potts had been appointed to probationerships at the same time as Leavis and anyway were junior to Leavis, graduates of 1922 and 1923. Potts had gone into a fellowship at Queens'; Henn had taken the road of prizes (Charles Oldham Shakespeare Scholarship, Members' Prize). 'No one,' he said later, 'thought of the Ph.D. as a vital step on the academic ladder.'[26]

Later Leavis was famously bitter about the slow progress of his career, bitterness contested by the suggestion that he had had unrealistic expectations. Were not probationary posts genuinely probationary, carrying no guarantee of promotion? A moment in Tom Henn's memoirs renders this interpretation of events questionable. Recounting the story of his own promotion, he makes an odd slip, dating his recruitment to the English Faculty to 1926 and the 'general mass appointment', that is of twelve Lecturers and six probationers. But Henn was *not* part of the initial faculty establishment: his appointment came later, and was promotion from a probationership (as was Potts's). Henn's error may have been due to a little vanity. More likely, and more understandable, he was conscious of a pool of Lecturers, some senior and some junior, who were expected to join the seniors, with a moral right to do so as they had mostly been doing the day-to-day English teaching before the lectureship system was invented. He did not see two sharply defined grades. Henn's and Potts's promotions illustrated the beginning of a trend towards appointing Lecturers from the pool of probationers. It was not, therefore, unreasonable for Leavis to *expect* that promotion would come before long. The feel of the situation in 1926–8 was that the English Faculty consisted of a block of Lecturers and probationers, the probationers not temporary or in transit but waiting, with fair expectations, in the wings. Leavis waited with two others, Joan Bennett and Basil Willey, and he and Bennett waited an unconscionable time.

Leavis's lack of promotion was not manifestly inequitable at this juncture. It was actually true, if wrong, that doctoral work was not valued highly. Leavis, also, was not a 'pot-hunter' (prize-seeker in Cambridge argot), perhaps because he was a blocked writer. Further, he was unlucky or unshrewd in his choice of academic specialization. He withdrew from eighteenth-century studies, for which there was not much demand, but he did not then offer lectures on one of the periods in which much teaching was needed (like Shakespeare). He went into contemporary poetry, and literary criticism – but he scorned the *history* of literary criticism, as a Tillyardian area (Longinus–Charles

Lamb–Sainte-Beuve: Tillyard's first book on English literature was a short one on Lamb). He dealt with problems, not periods. His choice of field put him alongside Richards, that is, up with the liveliest literary thinker of this time and place. A scientific analogy is relevant: is it surprising that a researcher wants to work with the most brilliant innovator? In this, Leavis was something of a scientist. But, when it came to planning lecture schedules, Leavis could have been thought too close to the specialism of the innovator, and that there could be only one I.A. Richards.

Precarious Terms 1928–1929

Leavis had now a new spur to ambition. At a Girton tea-party, presided over by Stanley Bennett, he met the woman he was to marry, Queenie Dorothy Roth, in the autumn of 1927. The period began in which they were 'gay, good-looking and hopeful', as she put it late in life when she wished there was some memoir to tell their children of the life that had been.

It may be legend that Q.D.R. attracted the attention of Leavis by approaching him after a lecture to ask, 'Dr Leavis, what *is* poetry?' If so, there is a private joke in her book (dedicated to 'F.R.L.') where she remarks that 'the question "What is a poem?" had been settled, in *Principles of Literary Criticism*, to the satisfaction of most of us and the relief of the critic'. The young woman was clearly fascinated by Leavis: some female memories of the period recall, not altogether kindly, the interest Queenie began to take in clothes after Leavis became aware of her. In her third year she became much more sociable with the other Girton students, keen to have people to whom she could talk about the supervisor who possessed, in Muriel Bradbrook's words, a 'cocksure alertness [which was] even to our unpractised eyes a defensive wariness'. Q.D.R. was absorbed too by Leavis's work, which had a special interest for her as a young woman who knew of London (her great-aunt Augusta, sister of Emelia Motrez, sold peanuts in Petticoat Lane) and Edmonton, the satellite country-town, but to whom a provincial city like Cambridge was strange. To a degree, it was an introduction to another England. It was Leavis who taught her to bicycle. His family was not long out of the Fens and, living with his mother in the untidy, garden-surrounded house, just outside the village of Chesterton, Leavis must have still seemed a country person. She could have hardly known what English dissenting 'chapel culture' was. When she was made aware of it, she took to John Bunyan with enthusiasm.* Her own family was, as we saw, Jewish orthodox. (In the other branch her Uncle Abraham had first educated his children into secularism, until he was exasperated by what he called the 'Jimmy Jesus Christianity' of school scripture lessons; then it was henceforth the synagogue for the children.)

If Leavis was another country for Q.D.R. he also could learn from her. Q.D.R. was a writer, and Leavis was not a fluent one. When he met Q.D.R. he had written nothing since his doctoral dissertation, perhaps could not; he eschewed the 'right thing to do', which was to enter for essay prizes. But in November 'he's writing again', Q.D.R. said excitedly to a friend, in the waiting-room off King's Parade that Girton provided for the use of its students between lectures. It was a short review for the *Cambridge Review* of a novel, *The Dark Breed*, by the Irish writer F.R. Higgins, and of Osbert Sitwell's *England Reclaimed*. She knew a good deal of England, from the London end, but came in contact with the provincially rural in Cambridge, and the factor of 'Englishness' that later meant so much to both partners.

Contemporaries say that Q.D.R. fell in love with Leavis during her last year at Girton, an anguished one because Leavis was slow to show his feelings. But by the end of term they came to an understanding. And Q.D.R. graduated with a starred First, many of her examination papers showing marks well above 80 per cent.[27] Leavis urged her to put in for scholarships. She was awarded the Charity Reeves and the Thomas Montefiore Prizes so she could go ahead to do research for a Ph.D., like 'the doctor' as she called him. She registered as a research student to work on a study of popular fiction, indeed, a sequel to Leavis's own dissertation; hers was published in 1932 as *Fiction and the Reading Public*.† She covered the later ground that Leavis omitted from his dissertation when the authorities agreed (after Q's petition) that the scope could be contracted. Q.D.L. was successively supervised by Richards (the second inspiration), by George Rylands and by Forbes.

Leavis continued, in the academic year 1928/9, with his three courses of lectures on poetry, criticism and prose. By now it was clear that the

* Q.D.L. liked reading Damon Runyon's Broadway stories (the origin of *Guys and Dolls*) to her children. Runyon's characterization is not so different from that of Bunyan.
† See Chapter Four, We Were Cambridge, 'Pioneer Performances 1932'.

Faculty was not enthusiastic about him. He dated his unpopularity to this academic year, and to one gaffe in particular. He wrote a piece in the *Cambridge Review* criticizing a member of the English Faculty and fellow of King's, F.L. Lucas.

Lucas's reputation has not lasted, but from the late 1920s he was a prolific and entertaining writer, not a few readers having been introduced to the classics by his anthologies like *Greek Drama for Everyman*. In 1919 J.M. Keynes introduced him to Clive Bell, who called him 'Bloomsbury'. Lucas's word for it was 'hedonist'.[28] The young John Lehmann liked to venture out from Trinity, a comparatively staid college, to King's and the society of Lucas in what he called 'Bloomsbury-by-the-Cam'. Lucas lived opposite King's, across the Backs, with his wife (the novelist E.B.C., or 'Topsy' Jones), where, said Lehmann,

one could talk openly, and listen to talk of passion and wit about modern poetry and modern novels, and (once one had plucked up courage) freely unburden one's heart of all that had choked it, while 'Topsy' uttered a throaty chuckle or a sympathetic comment that showed how exactly she understood what one was going through – even though her Freudian interpretations and pagan suggestions for remedy dismayed on occasion a sensibility still too tender for this bracing air.[29]

This air was not bracing enough for the poetry of T.S. Eliot, to which Lucas was openly hostile. At King's he was Librarian, and it was rumoured that he would not authorize purchases of Eliot.[30] His hostility is simply explained: he was old-fashioned and romantic; Eliot was 'advanced' and classical. It is worth pausing over the nature of this difference, because Lucas represented a large sector of anti-Eliot opinion, the same sector that opposed Leavis: it disliked 'taking literature too seriously'. If this sector is characterized as hedonist rather than intellectual, it could be said that Eliot went eventually over to the hedonists; so the alliance with him for which Leavis longed could never occur.

Why Lucas disliked Eliot is illustrated by what I.A. Richards said of Eliot in a passage quoted earlier about the high demands the poet imposed on his reader, the 'right reader', in which poetry creates a 'unified response'. Richards believed it was the job of literary criticism to bring untutored readers up to the level of 'best qualified opinion' and defend that opinion against anti-intellectualism. Criticism should combat a philistinism that appeals to herd instinct, that hatred of 'superior persons'. Lucas was an anti-intellectual, disliking 'superior persons'.

Strange to find classics don turned English Lecturer as populist? Not really, because for Lucas, Greek and Roman literature was *the* study, genuinely superior. Eliot's subtleties and plagiarisms, always irritating to the classic, expressed refinements of consciousness that had no authority. For Lucas, Homer was archaic, mysterious but eventually accessible by study; Eliot's obscurities were merely recent factitious devisings. Modernist obscurity was parvenu.

In 1928 an anonymous review of Eliot's essays *For Lancelot Andrewes* appeared in the *New Statesman and Nation*. It was certainly by Lucas. The reviewer patronized this 'pleasant little volume written by a man who is evidently fond of reading, generally reads with intelligence, and can always express his opinions with fire and lucidity'. Beta–plus for Eliot. Leavis complained about the review in February 1929 in the *Cambridge Review* in a piece called 'T.S. Eliot: A Reply to the Condescending'. Leavis believed Lucas was its author. Much later he said that his challenge was to 'a contemptuous dismissal [of Eliot] by a Cambridge "English" don in Mr Desmond MacCarthy's *Life and Letters*', a dismissal that was undoubtedly by Lucas.[31] It complained that universities took English studies too seriously: 'I would far rather a young man spent his time reading *The Earthly Paradise* on his back in a punt (I do not say he could not do better) than stewing over the *Criterion*.' In memory, Leavis conflated the two pieces, attributing to Lucas authorship of the review of *For Lancelot Andrewes*.[32] Lucas's *Life and Letters* piece was similar in theme and tone to that of the other. So Leavis thought he was attacking Lucas who was at that time all over the journals: '*Life and Letters* publishes twenty or more pages of F.L. Lucas a month,' wrote Leavis.[33] Having attacked Lucas, he was made 'to realize he had committed a scandalous impropriety'. The editor of the *Cambridge Review* 'was left in no doubt as to the unforgivableness of the offence'. We cannot know whether Lucas was offended and if so whether the offence affected Leavis professionally. But Lucas did subsequently retaliate in 1932 by launching an attack on the whole Leavisian position, choosing as his point of focus Q.D.L.'s *Fiction and the Reading Public*.

The substance of Leavis's 'Reply to the Condescending' dealt with the author's version of a familiar subject, the obscurity of contemporary poetry, and specifically the practice of recondite quotation in Eliot's poetry. Lucas had contended that 'super-literate' poetry was popular only with young people 'whose reading begins with the Edwardians'. Leavis said Lucas condescended to Eliot's allusiveness from the vantage point of a conventional classic, neither understanding that Eliot's learning was used 'dynamically', nor that Eliot's poetry was unique, certainly not that of one obscure modern among many. For Leavis there was 'no other poetry in the least like Mr Eliot's: he is an originator'.[34] The aim of his essay was to disentangle Eliot from other modernisms, including Eliot-like ones.* There was plenty of Eliotism on display in the *Cambridge Review* in the month following, when Leavis reviewed an annual round-up of verse, *Cambridge Poetry 1929*.[35] He singled out two young poets for praise, Richard Eberhart and Richards's pupil at Magdalene, William Empson. A contemporary said, 'Leavis mentions [Empson] in every lecture.'[36]

In February 1929 Leavis became engaged to be married to Queenie Roth. Later she recalled Leavis's gallantry and tenderness, characterizing it by quoting from a poem by Laurence Binyon:

> O world, be nobler for her sake!
> If she but knew thee what thou art,
> What wrongs are borne, what deeds are done
> In thee, beneath thy daily sun.[37]

At the time Leavis was a reader of Housman's *A Shropshire Lad*. During their engagement he wrote to her every day: his delight in her company was noticed by an undergraduate who was sharing a score of César Franck with her, in college over tea, when Leavis turned up.[38] But it was not surprising that Morris and Jenny Roth in Edmonton were shocked that their daughter had decided to 'marry out'. They were proud of their two children at Cambridge, and had even moved house, further up Silver Street, in order to have somewhere better in which to entertain the children's Cambridge friends. Overwhelmed with grief, the parents ceased to take responsibility for their daughter, the breach affirmed with most determination by Q.D.L.'s mother, whose family was more religious than Morris's. It has been said that the family sat *shiva* for her, that is, underwent strict household bereavement observances at the betrayal of their religion. It is not likely that this happened. But contact ceased between Queenie and her parents, except occasionally with Morris Roth. Q.D.R. now had only her Cambridge friends to rely

---

* A couple of months earlier Q.D.R. made the same point about imitators of Eliot more wittily, at the expense of the poems of Sherard Vines, Professor of English at the University College in Hull: 'Those interested in poetry may complain that while Eliot's poems came hot from the blast furnace, [these] are issued by the Mosaics Manufacturing Co.' Her review was called 'Sour Grapes from the Waste Land'.

on. She turned to her research-supervisor, Richards, now a fellow of Magdalene. He and his wife were returning from an honorary degree ceremony to their house in Chesterton Road when they found Q.D.R. waiting for them, sheltering from the pouring rain among the garden shrubs. They were embarrassed to hear all the details of Q.D.R.'s plight and curiously found future contact almost impossible. It is hard to see why they withdrew at this point.[39]

It was not surprising that the Roth family reacted harshly to their daughter's engagement. But neither was it surprising that she chose Leavis. A contemporary at Girton and sensible observer, also Jewish, remarked that Q.D.R. was for Leavis 'a near-perfect mate, who met all the needs, physical, emotional and intellectual and this in the period between the wars known as the Age of the Two Million Surplus Women, on account of the wholesale slaughter of young men in World War I'. It was the era of George Bernard Shaw's 'Life Force', and Bertrand Russell's rationalist ideas about marriage, which appealed to Q.D.R.[40] It is easy to see why Leavis was attracted.

As a married man it became an urgent matter for Leavis to secure a permanent appointment. Q took an interest in his career. He was aware that Leavis was suffering a breakdown, deeply involved as he was in Q.D.R.'s alienation from her family. There was going to be a post vacant at the University of Leeds where the Professor of English, Lascelles Abercrombie, had been appointed to a position in London. At Cambridge inquiries about a possible successor were made through the Vice-Chancellor, and Q wondered whether Richards might allow his name to be put forward. He quizzed him in the (only) Cambridge taxi, discovered he was not interested and weighed up Richards's suggestion that Leavis might be recommended. Q was relieved that Richards wanted to stay in Cambridge, but he was doubtful about Leavis, as he explained in a letter (some of which was quoted above in Chapter Two).

I am really sorry for him, having watched (from a distance) this tragedy coming on 'From a distance' for this reason – I was his supervisor for Ph.D. and no small part of that job was steering him clear of nervous breakdown. Once – I think twice – I got the Board to abbreviate the scope of his thesis and consent to his altering its title. I was extremely anxious about him to the last moment. And then he never even gave me the opportunity of congratulating him – never called, or wrote, – nor have I seen him since he carried away his MS with my prayers for it.

I gather that in your opinion he has since been making good, and I hear that his lectures are well attended. He must, then, have improved. But (frankly) he must have improved quite beyond my old estimate – which is the only one he has allowed me to go upon – before I could recommend him as fit to succeed one of Abercrombie's quality. As I say, I have seen this tragedy coming on: and the root of it is the man's Self-Sufficiency.

Forgive me if my words about him strike you as too hard. I would take a lot of trouble to get Leavis better placed, thankless as that trouble (you know) would be, since no good fortune would easily equal his sense of his deserts.[41]

Richards may have thought well of Leavis, or knew he needed money; or he may have wanted him out of Cambridge: broadly speaking it was the Cambridge way to lead promising graduates into its system. But in this exchange there is no suggestion that either Q or Richards was convinced Cambridge English should keep Leavis at all costs. (None the less, when Richards was asked by Eliot himself who was any good in Cambridge, Leavis was the only Lecturer he specified, 'a good supervisor on literary and general critical matters, but I shouldn't say he was worth coming here under difficulties for'.) Q concluded his letter with a remark about a Jesus man who did poorly in classics in 1928, taking only a Lower Second in English in 1929; he now found he had to 'write about' to find a job for him. The reference to this predicament shows that Q did not feel a need to 'write about' to place Leavis, but this does not mean he thought a permanent lectureship was on the cards. He knew, anyway, there was the possibility of another couple of probationary years. And the two further years for Leavis were granted. In the autumn of 1929 Leavis's contract was extended, as were the contracts of Joan Bennett and Basil Willey. All three were safe until October 1931.

Leavis's progress through marriage and academe differed from that of the Bennetts. It was much more unsteady than that of the comparatively easy-going evolution of the Bennetts: the wealthy parents of Joan Frankau had no difficulty in accepting a modest and charming Stanley Bennett, who had the good fortune to be appointed early and deservedly to a lectureship. But at least Leavis was advancing on the professional path, whereas in 1929 young William Empson, the other British critical genius of the century, was ejected from it. After mathematics, Empson's starred First in Part One of English earned him a junior fellowship at Magdalene. At the end of July it was discovered that he had had a woman in his rooms, and condoms were discovered by a college servant. I.A. Richards would have pleaded his cause in college, but he was away climbing in the Bernese Oberland. 'Struck off the boards',

Empson was forbidden to live within the Cambridge boundaries. He soon entered a twenty-year exile, with some furloughs, in Japan and China. Empson and Leavis were both caught out in free-thinking enterprises, Leavis with the importation of *Ulysses*, Empson in the use of contraceptives.[42] It is possible that the Wykehamist Empson was the more psychologically vulnerable. A mildly bohemian undergraduate but with gentry manners, he was less experienced than Leavis; his fairly conventional upper-class expectations were painfully jolted by the episode.

F.R.L. and Q.D.R. planned to marry before the Michaelmas term. Because of the breach with her parents, Q.D.R. had nowhere to be married from, so she lodged in Leys Road with an acquaintance with whom she had been up at Girton. Dorothy Wooster had also 'married her don', a university demonstrator in crystallography. Leavis bought a little terrace house in Leys Road for about a thousand pounds, a modern estate of terraces to the north-west of the river.[43] Lionel Knights, who got to know Leavis when he went to him for advice about writing a prize essay on contemporary literary criticism, was familiar with Leys Road: his parents had moved there from Grantham. (He had been entranced by the cultural charm of life in the city, after the drab surroundings of his youth: there was no music or painting in small-town Lincolnshire.) Q.D.R. believed in 'trial engagements'. Leavis wrote to her every day until the wedding on 16 September, on which he arrived from his mother's house very early to take her to the Register Office. Bride and groom left after the ceremony for a bicycling and walking holiday in Norfolk. Q.D.L. remembered seeing 'whole haystacks being quanted along on wherries by aged men with side whiskers'.

My husband asked one such if he would like a cup of tea; he replied very slowly and politely, 'No thank 'ee, sir, I'm just going whoom to my beloved, and I'll have a cup of tea with her' . . . My husband's grandfather, Elihu Leavis, lived in a cottage in the village of Denver, near Denver Sluice, roasting his meat on a spit at the open fire, and you could see the stars up the open chimney, and of course he had a well in the garden.[44]

On the train out Leavis read a volume of Tolstoy, including *The Kreutzer Sonata*, slightly alarming the well-read bride. Back home in Leys Road, the couple fitted out their home to be easy to care for, the first in the road to have a type of synthetic-fibre carpeting on the stairs.

The Woosters gave them plants and a Japanese print. Among the 'Gwalias' and the 'Gardenias', the name of the Leavis house was jovially inscribed on a placard: 'The Criticastery'.

The couple now began to entertain modestly, inviting undergraduates and others to regular tea parties at 4 p.m. on Fridays, much appreciated by students from abroad. Later Q.D.L. noted a succession of turbans bobbing along the garden-hedge. An occasional visitor was the philosopher Ludwig Wittgenstein, who had returned to Cambridge in 1929. At one of the Friday teas he was mistaken for an undergraduate, though he was then at least forty.[45] Leavis was perhaps reminded of his own anomalous position: older than a graduate student, in his late thirties, but with hardly more status.

The visits from Wittgenstein began after Leavis met him through his friendship with the elderly philosopher, W.E. Johnson, who supervised Wittgenstein before the war. Leavis had been at the Perse with Johnson's son, Stephen. Johnson and his sister held Sunday afternoon at-homes, and at one of them Leavis encountered Wittgenstein, of whom he then knew nothing.

I ran on and clashed with Wittgenstein. He had just returned to Cambridge (1929), and I didn't know his name. Johnson's innocent myth was that 'Leavis and Wittgenstein fell on one another's necks at first meeting'. Actually, I followed Wittgenstein out and offered to *fall on him*, supposing that my well-earned rebuke would make that natural. To my surprise he put his hand on my shoulder and said: 'We must know one another.' I said (did I?? – anyway, I thought): 'I don't see the necessity', and walked pointedly the other way. But he thereafter, for a year or so, used to call on me pretty frequently. I'm not recessive, and the connection lapsed. *We didn't talk philosophy.*

The reason why Leavis offered to 'fall on' Wittgenstein was comic. He followed him out of the music room to remonstrate because a young visitor, about to sing a Schubert song, politely asked Wittgenstein to correct his German, only to receive the brusque retort, 'How can I? How can I *possibly*?' Loftily departing, an indignant Leavis pursued him. Although Wittgenstein had 'those intensely white and large surrounds to his eyes, that tend to make you uncomfortable', Leavis said his piece. ('I have suffered a lot from holding back.')

With my hand on my collar as if (I later realized) I were about to take my coat off, I said: 'You behaved in a disgraceful way to that young man.' Wittgenstein said [he thought] the youth was foolish. To which I returned, emphatically containing myself: 'You may have done, you may have done, but you had no right to treat anyone like that.' It was to this that Wittgenstein replied, 'We must know one another.'

Once acquainted, they went for walks, mostly at night and down-river, with Wittgenstein restless, agoraphobic (so Leavis believed) and often exhausted by study. In his late memoir 'Memories of Wittgenstein' the Cambridgeshire scene forms a grand setting for Leavis's account of their excursions: the 'Bellevue' boat-house at the end of Mill Lane, steam-organs of the rural Trumpington Feast, the nine-foot furrows of ground by the Granta River opposite Lingay Fen. Leavis said – yarning, it sounds – that they were once 'a resort of mammoths' in which fossils had been found before the war. 'Wittgenstein didn't need telling that coprolites had their use in the manufacture of munitions.'

One recollection in 'Memories of Wittgenstein' throws an oblique light on the critic and the philosopher. Leavis was a popular Lecturer and supervisor; he was chirpy company.* But the chemistry of pedagogy did not always work and one pupil, the 'bearer of a distinguished Victorian name' (that is, Rossetti), proved to be bumptious with the result that there were 'things said', meaning, Leavis decided, 'the relation had come to an end'. One of the things was strange. Rossetti's parting shot to Leavis was, 'You're like Jesus Christ.' Later Rossetti happened to tell Wittgenstein that he idolized his former supervisor. Wittgenstein passed this back to Leavis, who remained impassive. 'I don't really care what Rossetti thinks of me.' 'You *ought* to care,' Wittgenstein exclaimed. Then Leavis retailed Rossetti's remark about being like Christ. Wittgenstein was amazed. 'That's an extraordinary thing to say!' he exclaimed. It was Leavis's turn to be taken aback – at Wittgenstein's capacity for wonder: 'It was a spontaneity of recall, uttering a judgement expressive of the whole being.'[46]

By now Leavis had been a university teacher for five years, some of them freelance. He was beginning to see his pupils succeeding. In 1927, under the influence of Bennett and Leavis, men from Emmanuel took a remarkable five out of the nine Firsts in English. Among the nine there were two non-Emmanuel men sympathetic to Leavis or to become so: Ian Parsons of Trinity (later his publisher) and Ronald Bottrall of

* Geoffrey Walton says he was more 'matey' in those days. 'Chirpy' was a Leavis word; he used it to apologize for his lack of animation when he was terminally ill.

Pembroke, who was to appeal to Leavis for advice about his poetry and for help with publishing it. In the same year Denys Harding at Emmanuel took a First in Part One, and so did Lionel Knights of Selwyn. Both took only one part of the English Tripos, Harding changing to Moral Science (philosophy) and Knights, like Leavis, taking one part of History. He was not supervised by Leavis, but Stanley Bennett put him in touch for advice about the prize essay on which he was working on the future of literary criticism. At his parents' house, just up Leys Road, Knights often saw Leavis leaving 'The Criticastery' with his rucksack. Between 1928 and 1930 Leavis also supervised for St John's, helping Stanley Bennett, whom the college used as a Director of Studies.[47]

The student careers of Harding and Knights illustrate a basic feature of early Cambridge English: it was English-and-another-subject. Harding's transfer to Moral Sciences is interesting because he became one of the closest of Leavis's collaborators. He contributed the first essay to the first issue of *Scrutiny*, 'A Note on Nostalgia', importantly placed in a journal sometimes accused of unthinking commitment to an old order. The Moral Science Tripos was not popular: when Harding was awarded his First in Part Two in 1928, there were only eleven candidates. He took this tripos not for the philosophy, but because it was the only way in which he could study psychology at Cambridge, which interested Harding after reading Richards – and being one of the *Practical Criticism* guinea-pigs. In English, gambolling among the subjectivities of literary criticism, he felt trapped 'in a large plate of porridge'. He wanted to know how personal response to poetry could be articulated with some objective reliability and at that date there was little specific guidance to be had. Richards had said a little on 'value' in *The Principles of Literary Criticism* and had lectured on the subject. But his ideas about literary judgement were not made public until two years later in *Practical Criticism* (1929). William Empson was to write brilliantly on the issue of response and discipline (pages on which Leavis seized), but this was not to be published until 1930, in the last chapter of *Seven Types of Ambiguity*. When Harding changed to philosophy in order to learn psychology, Empson was still studying mathematics. His change of subject also illuminates the informality of the Cambridge system, the model on which Leavis himself operated. Harding vaguely mentioned his doubts about studying English to a graduate student at Emmanuel, R. W. Pickford (later Professor of Psychology at Glasgow), who put him in touch with F. C. Bartlett, later Sir Frederic Bartlett, Professor of

Psychology and author of the classic, *Remembering*. He admitted Harding into Moral Science, but left the teaching of him to Pickford. In this world the influence of the graduate student was potent.[48]

Coincidentally, the experience of the war was beginning at last to be assimilated into English consciousness. In 1929 two books were published about the war which helped many veterans to adjust to their memories through fresh recollection: Richard Aldington's *Death of a Hero* and Robert Graves's *Goodbye to All That*. Leavis read Graves 'with great delight'. He did 'magnificently what Aldington made such a sickening mess of', though Leavis conceded that the 'transcripts of war experience' were good.[49]

At the end of the decade Leavis's mother died. It was the moment he could consider the possibility of a career elsewhere, with his young wife, and indeed look forward to what might become of her career. At this moment, whatever his position, Q.D.L. showed great professional promise. There seemed no question of leaving Cambridge.

Poet-as-Leader, Minority Culture 1931

After his marriage Leavis began to write in earnest on contemporary verse and prose, and on modern culture. He began to link his fields of study, joining the literary sociology of his doctoral dissertation to his literary criticism of new writing. In these months he wrote a long essay on modern poetry and two pamphlets. The *Cambridge Review*, in spite of his reproof of F.L. Lucas, continued to print his reviews, including his excited welcome for Empson's *Seven Types of Ambiguity* in January 1931.

Leavis began his essay on modern poetry in late 1929, as a contribution to Gerald Heard's 'journal of scientific humanism', the *Realist*. Unfortunately, the magazine collapsed in January 1930. 'English Poetry and the Modern World: A Study of the Current Situation' was eventually published in French in October 1930, with the help of Leavis's pupil Henri Fluchère. The essay developed an idea from Richards's *The Principles of Literary Criticism*: that the poet is 'the point at which the growth of the mind shows itself' or, as Leavis puts it, 'the most conscious point of the race in his time'.*

* See Chapter Five, 'To Downing College', 'Incipient Corruption? 1937'.

The potentialities of human experience in any age are realized by only a tiny minority, and the important poet is important because he belongs to this (and has also, of course, the power of communication). Indeed, his capacity for experiencing and his power of communicating are indistinguishable; not merely because we should not know of the one without the other, but because his power of making words express what he feels is indistinguishable from his awareness of what he feels. Almost all of us live by routine, and are not fully aware of what we feel; or, if that seems paradoxical, we do not express to ourselves an account of our possibilities of experience. Our reactions to the shocks and demands of life tend not to be personal, to be merely those which society has taught us to regard as appropriate: we live for the needs of the moment. The poet is unusually sensitive, unusually aware, more sincere and more himself than the ordinary man can be. He knows what he feels and knows what he is interested in. He is a poet because his interest in his experience is not separable from his interest in words; because, that is, of his habit of seeking by the evocative use of words to sharpen his awareness of his ways of feeling, so making these communicable. If we wish to know what is, in our age, the texture of the most subtle human experience, it is to poetry that we must go. Other literary forms can only operate externally, can only talk to us vaguely: poetry moves into the focus of real experiences. If, therefore, poetry loses touch with what the most aware and alert minds of the age feel about the subject of man and his condition, and about the value of life, then the age will be lacking in finer awareness. That this is a really grave danger (as it must be if civilization is something more than comfort, hygiene and material well-being) it is perhaps impossible to bring home to any one who is not already convinced of the importance of poetry. So that it is indeed deplorable that poetry should so widely have ceased to interest the intelligent.[50]

Leavis had dealt with the 'minority' before, the happy few in whom 'the potentialities of human experience are realized'. His doctoral dissertation showed the writer threatened by the market-place, and so the broadening and flattening of his public. Market was set against minority. Now Leavis defined the leader of the minority as the *poet*. Richards had said that the poet could create or enact new attitudes, subtle effects of 'contrast, conflict, harmony, interinanimation and equilibrium'. But poets needed the 'right reader' to understand these effects. Leavis was saying that it was for the poet to educate the minority of 'right readers'.

Leavis was beginning to define the audience for poetry, ever a minority taste, but he also had to think about an audience for his own work. Where and how was he to publish? In this he had a piece of Cambridge luck. Leavis was swept up into a student enterprise that became a real-world enterprise, a process characteristic of the Cambridge arts scene, where amateur theatre ran into professional theatre and the student newspaper into national journalism. Leavis had a pupil at St John's, Gordon Fraser, who started a small publishing outfit for him. 'At the age of nineteen,' he said, 'I was Leavis's student and his publisher: a friendship that was to last fifty years.'

Gordon Fraser's father came from a lower-middle-class clergy family in the Scottish Highlands. He went south when his mother was widowed to seek his fortune. He did so with fairy-tale success. Articled to a Midlands accountancy firm, he was sent on audit to an ailing copper-tubing company in Leeds. He stayed up late with the books and persuaded the Managing Director that the business could be turned around, for which he was offered a post and asked to name his salary: he shrewdly requested an allocation of the then near-worthless shares, resigned from his articles and set about reform, becoming in due course director of a prosperous business. He sent his son Gordon to Oundle, briefly to Leeds University, and then up to Cambridge, where he fell under the spell of Leavis. In his final year Fraser founded a publishing business for Leavisian studies, called – what else? – the Minority Press. St John's College was not pleased to be the editorial address.[51]

Leavis was able to work on the implications of a poetry-led culture in a pamphlet published by Fraser's Minority Press. In *Mass Civilization and Minority Culture* (1930) he explained that it was upon the minority that depended

our power of profiting by the finest human experience of the past; they finally keep alive the subtlest and most perishable parts of tradition. Upon them depend the implicit standards that order the finer living of an age, the sense that this is worth more than that, this rather than that is the direction in which to go, that the centre is here rather than there.

Leavis was staking out for himself a project of *preservation*, he himself working on poetry and Q.D.L. on fiction in the research for her Ph.D. dissertation in which Leavis's account of the history of journalism was married to Richards's theory of culture as needing (and losing) its 'right readers'. Culture high and low was under survey and analysis in the Leavis household. F.R.L. observed how reputations were made among poets; Q.D.L. spent every day in the university library hoovering through volumes of popular fiction. Leavis had Fraser to help him, Q.D.L. had another of his St John's pupils reading up and copying out

passages of data illustrating 'the state of contemporary culture'. Denys
Thompson had taken one year of classics, and was then taught by Leavis
for Parts One and Two of the English Tripos. A clergyman's son from
Darlington, he counted the cheerful visits to 'The Criticastery' among
the most happy of his life. He started a Ph.D. dissertation, 'An Economic
History of English Literature from Scott to the Present Day', but could
not afford to continue and gave it up in 1933.[52] Thompson went on to
teach at Gresham's School in Norfolk, which fed pupils to Leavis, and
he founded the journal *The Use of English* (originally *English in Schools*),
which propagated the Leavisian movement in schools.

In 1930 Gordon Fraser issued *Mass Civilization and Minority Culture*.
By Christmas a further five 'Minority Pamphlets' had been issued: one
by Leavis himself and one by John Middleton Murry, both on D.H.
Lawrence, one by R.P. Blackmur on censorship, a story by T.F. Powys
and a pamphlet about Powys by another St John's pupil, William
Hunter. Fraser was also publishing Henry Fielding's *Shamela*. It was
edited by Brian Downs of Christ's, one of the original 1926 set of
English Faculty Lecturers, the dapper one whom Leavis always liked as
'a gentleman'. Fraser's father did not think the project gentlemanly. He
considered *Shamela* indecent

and came to Cambridge with the intention of having all copies destroyed. I was
a minor. Brian W. Downs had written in his introduction: 'It is undeniably
gross, very gross. But its frankness does what nothing else could do so
effectively.' It was Leavis who persuaded my father of the book's value as a
serious though satiric criticism of Richardson.

Mrs Fraser had a different worry. She told Leavis that 'you had one bad
influence on my son. You did not wear a tie.' Fraser also undertook
longer critical works, like Mark Van Doren's *John Dryden*; Leavis and
Fraser were also sponsoring promising American academics. In view of
his later history, it is not surprising to find Leavis contributing a
pamphlet on D.H. Lawrence to the series; but at the time this was an
excursion into a field to which he did not expect to return. Even in
1933, after the publication of Lawrence's letters (which greatly enhanced
his valuation of the writer), he wrote about his Minority Pamphlet on
Lawrence that 'I shall never again, I suppose, be able to give the body of
his works the prolonged and intensive frequentation that went to the
preparing of that essay, whatever its crudities.'[53]

★

D.H. Lawrence had died on 2 March 1930. In June Leavis was using every spare moment for writing on Lawrence for the May Week issue of the *Cambridge Review*, the basis of the pamphlet for Fraser. He was delighted to read a letter from E.M. Forster to the *Nation and Athenaeum* on the occasion of Lawrence's death, celebrating the importance of the writer who had alienated both 'Mrs Grundy and Aspasia'. 'The greatest imaginative novelist of our generation' could not therefore expect a good obituary press. The following week Eliot wrote in, to say he could not fathom what Forster meant by *greatest, imaginative* (or *novelist*). Forster answered that if he were entangled by Eliot's web 'there are occasions when I would rather feel like a fly than a spider, and the death of D.H. Lawrence is one of them'.

Leavis himself had offended Mrs Grundy and the Home Office in the matter of *Ulysses*: at this stage of his career he acclaimed the Lawrence whom the prudes reviled. He highly esteemed *Lady Chatterley's Lover*, a 'beautifully poised' book in which 'ripe experience is in control'. He contrasted it with *Women in Love*, which bored him and called for 'great determination and a keen diagnostic interest'. Lawrence's wisdom was 'surer' in his late discursive essays (like those reprinted in *Assorted Articles* or the pamphlet *Apropos of Lady Chatterley's Lover*). In the long run Leavis had doubts of the kind typical of Leavisian criticism, concerning the consequences of his judgement. Accept Lawrence wholesale and what would follow? 'If we accepted this, and all it implies, without reserves, what should we be surrendering?' Leavis raised the plain, anti-pluralist issue: taking on board the whole meant surrendering something else. Take Lawrence as a whole and one would have to surrender 'all that Jane Austen stands for'. To accept Lawrence 'as a whole' would implicitly cast doubt (that should not be entertained) on the 'qualities of intelligence and civilization' in Forster's *A Passage to India*. Forster's qualities in a sense *blocked* the path to unqualified allegiance to Lawrence. *A Passage to India* stood in the way of Lawrence, both because of what the novel was (its intelligence, its civilization) and because of what it showed (the portentous experience of Mrs Moore in the Marabar Caves: 'everything exists, nothing has value').

Despite his hesitation, Leavis did not reject either the visionary Lawrence or the Lawrence of 'sexual liberation'. At this date it was not easy to welcome *Lady Chatterley's Lover*. Forster said rightly in his obituary letter that Lawrence had offended 'low-brows whom he scandalized' and 'high-brows whom he bored'. But he scandalized some highbrows too. In 1927 Eliot had deplored that characters in Lawrentian fiction possessed none of the graces which made love 'bearable'.[54] Leavis did not favour these prim doubts about physicality. He thought Lawrence had a genius like William Blake, with 'the same gift of knowing what he was interested in, the same power of distinguishing his own feelings from conventional sentiment, the same "terrifying honesty"', a phrase from Eliot himself. But in the late 1920s Lawrence was not everything for Leavis. In July 1932 he wrote that 'Lawrence is not my prophet, but I know that no front is worth anything that doesn't take account of him.'[55] In 1930 there did not appear to be a front at which justice was being done: Leavis took the protective stance.

Leavis gave prominence to Lawrence's *non*-fictional writings. He promoted *Psychoanalysis and the Unconscious, Fantasia of the Unconscious* and *Apropos of Lady Chatterley's Lover* not quite at the expense of the fiction, though *Sons and Lovers* certainly failed to interest him. Leavis was finding in Lawrence the rebarbative, obdurate observer, he who would not be manipulated, a role Leavis wished to emulate. The manipulation of the public by a complaisant intelligentsia was the theme of Leavis's entry into social criticism. It was the voice of the rank and frank outsider that appealed, the voice also of William Blake or, in the eighteenth century that Leavis admired, the voice of Henry Fielding. But at present Leavis's principal preoccupation was with poetry.

Besides Fraser and Thompson, Leavis became friendly with another young man, a poet with whom he began to correspond in 1930. Leavis met Ronald Bottrall at one of Mansfield Forbes's breakfast parties not long after he became a probationary Lecturer. In September 1929, after graduating from Pembroke, Bottrall took a post as a language teacher in Finland, beginning seriously to write poetry. He sent off four poems to 'The Criticastery'.[56] Leavis was impressed, showing them to 'a critic I respect (my wife, as a matter of fact)', who pronounced that Bottrall was 'Matthew Arnold as a modern', with reference to a poem called 'Antithesis'. 'Not, of course, implying derivativeness,' she added.[57] Leavis wrote that he would like, 'without impertinence', to help Bottrall. He recommended reading: *The Waste Land*, of course, but also Eliot's poem, 'Som de l'Escalina', later to become a section of *Ash-Wednesday*, which had been published in the French journal *Commerce*. Eliot's selection of Ezra Pound's poetry had recently appeared: Leavis found *Hugh Selwyn Mauberley* irresistible. There was also Hopkins, the poems unavailable, though 'a few of him (including one good, long one) are included in Harold Monro's recent *Twentieth Century Poetry* (Phoenix Library, 3s 6d). This anthology is absurd like all the others, but it's worth having.' Leavis told Bottrall he was preparing four printed sheets of Hopkins's poems for his lectures. He recommended Richard Eberhart's 'Bravery of Earth' ('Eberhart's *Prelude*'), except for its 'cosmic gas'. But ultimately he directed Bottrall to experience itself, to essay which, though a platitude, was necessary when there were so few poets on which a young writer could model himself. There was Eliot; but the best tribute to Eliot was to strike out in a new direction and refuse to be hypnotized by him. Leavis was candid. He called one poem ('Why Should I Dream') incomprehensible, a cerebral failure.[58]

In the spring of 1930 Leavis was excited by further batches from Bottrall. 'Frustration' and 'The Thyrsis Retipped' he thought had some promise, as had 'Non Imitabilis Virgo'. Leavis reviewed *Cambridge Poetry 1930* in May, showing he disliked what he considered to be the fake-Eliot of Jacob Bronowski and Michael Redgrave. He wished he could send poems by Bottrall to the *Cambridge Review* to supplement his review: they would show vividly that Bronowski and his cronies, who claimed to be going a step further than Eliot, were posers.[59] Bottrall inquired about where he could publish his work. Leavis recommended the *Criterion*. In June he wrote about the tactics of submitting poems to Eliot, suggesting he omitted 'Over Coffee' (as derivative of Pound's 'Birnbaum' in *Hugh Selwyn Mauberley*), but that 'Frustration', 'The Thyrsis Retipped' and 'Non Imitabilis Virgo' should go in. He thought his technique had improved, but it was still an open question as to what Bottrall would do with his developing skill.[60]

Bottrall sent his poems to the *Criterion* and Eliot wrote encouragingly to Bottrall, but would not publish him straightaway. So Leavis suggested entrepreneurially that Gordon Fraser might do a shilling pamphlet, ideally with an introductory note by Eliot, if all else failed. In the summer Bottrall visited Leavis to discuss publication. Because he felt he had read Bottrall badly before, Leavis was tentative about giving advice, but helped make a selection to submit this time to Chatto & Windus.[61] He was happy to see 'To a Girl on Her Birthday' go, because the lines he liked were used in another poem. He was sorry that 'It is Not Yet Defeat or Victory' was omitted.

In November Bottrall had a rejection from Chatto & Windus, called by Leavis 'one of our least un-intelligent publishing houses'. He therefore took the poems straight round to Gordon Fraser, who said he would make a decision after Christmas, because he was having trouble finding money for a reprint of Van Doren on Dryden. Fraser wistfully wished he had a hundred pounds to spend on printing bills. He was willing to publish Bottrall at Easter and was adamant that Bottrall should not make any contribution to production costs: he certainly did not want to be thought to be a vanity publisher. Leavis was exasperated by Fraser's vagueness, but Fraser had reason to temporize. He could not be sure what would happen to the business once he went down from Cambridge. Leavis assured him that he would see Bottrall's poems through the press himself. He continued to be impressed by the verse. He thought Bottrall could learn from W.H. Auden, sending him 'Charade', though he believed that Bottrall was Auden's superior, unduly obscure.[62]

During the summer Leavis spent an evening reading Bottrall aloud to one of his former pupils, William Hunter, as keen as ever.[63] As always for Leavis, it was the rhythms that mattered, that quality which the lectures of Richards and Forbes helped him to value. He thought 'Arion Anadyomenos' was Bottrall's best, liking in it the contrast between a tense, neurotic passage of febrile hypersensitivity and the concluding affirmative lines.

> Perchance, after all, living within
> And for ourselves, exhaling our entity
> In our perceptions, yet not altogether bent
> With our breaths to petrify and eternize
> Some stony replica, we have tracked
> What song the sirens sang. So may the disjoint
> Time resolve itself and raise up dolphins backed
> Like whales to waft us where a confident sea
> Is ever breaking, never spent.

But Fraser had to leave Cambridge, so it was Leavis who worked with the printers. Soon Bottrall's first volume, *The Loosening and Other Poems* (1931), appeared with the Fraser imprint. Once it was on sale, Leavis made it his business to slip into the bookshops and check it was prominently displayed, and selling. He did so covertly because booksellers were beginning to identify Leavis, not Gordon Fraser, with the Minority Press.

Doing Criticism 1931

In January 1931 Leavis had bad news. Originally six probationers had been appointed to the English Faculty in 1926. Now there were three left, Leavis, Joan Bennett and Basil Willey. Leavis's period of tenure was about to run out, and he was told that there would be no reappointment for the coming October.

Leavis was beginning to have a sense of doom. He had been in trouble over *Ulysses* and the Home Office; he had attacked F.L. Lucas in the *Cambridge Review*. 'Now,' he exclaimed to Bottrall, 'they will starve me out.' He was not *entitled* to a renewal of his probationary lectureship, but reasonable expectations were dashed. He was aware that he had no friend in E.M.W. Tillyard, the main Faculty organizer; relations with Richards cooled after Q.D.L.'s distraught confession before her marriage. In March he and Q.D.L. decided to move from Leys Road back to the old family home at No.6, Chesterton Hall Crescent, even though they could hardly afford the removal expenses. Leavis thought it might impress the Faculty, but 'God knows how long we shall be able to stay in Cambridge.' By now the family business was closed. The main pianoforte shop had gone, and the music shop next to Downing had been taken over by one of the three leading Cambridge piano retailers.

Leavis decided to do some extended writing so as to improve his academic standing by publication. He planned a book called 'Poetry: The Modern World', for the first chapter of which he would use his long essay, still only published in French, 'English Poetry and the Modern World: A Study of the Contemporary Situation'. In the early months of 1931 work went well; in August Leavis approached Chatto & Windus to explain his plans for what was now to be called *New Bearings in English Poetry*. The book would describe how the face of English poetry had been changed by T.S. Eliot and Ezra Pound. The presentation of Pound set him problems: he wanted to play up the importance of *Hugh Selwyn Mauberley*, giving its achievement more weight than Eliot had done. Leavis confided his problems to Bottrall, telling him that he was unsure of where to place discussion of Ezra Pound in his book. He was certain that his stress should be on *Hugh Selwyn Mauberley* rather than on the *Cantos*. Generally, he was insecure about the book, and felt almost impertinent to be deciding which poems and poets would have a fruitful influence on young writers. He was determined to include material about really new poetry, including Bottrall's, which he believed was in some respects exemplary, endorsing the critical argument of the book. In the end he included ten warm pages on it, with Bottrall's permission.[64]

Professional need spurred Leavis to start work on *New Bearings in English Poetry*. There were other events to excite him into authorship. In the summer of Leavis's engagement to be married in 1929, William Empson, having been expelled from Cambridge, used this unexpected hiatus to write his first prose book, an elaborate expansion of an undergraduate essay written for Richards at Magdalene. *Seven Types of Ambiguity* was published by Chatto & Windus in late 1930. Cambridge English had been going for ten years, but it is not too much to say that as yet it had no written model of what literary analysis could be, until the exiled youth spoke out with his book of dazzling detail.* It helped Leavis forward. Having brought Empson the poet into his lectures so often, Leavis now welcomed Empson the critic in a *Cambridge Review* piece called 'Intelligence and Sensibility' in mid-January 1931. Empson was not unknown as a critic: he had done compact reviews as 'The Skipper' in *The Granta*, but they did not compare with the ingenuity, delicacy and fun of his new analyses, a running commentary on much of the material set for the English Tripos and a development of what he had heard a few years before in Eliot's Clark Lectures. Though unemployable in the university, he bequeathed a model to Cambridge English.

'Close reading' or 'detailed verbal analysis' is what Empson is reputed to have established for Cambridge and literary criticism in general. Empson's real value lay in qualities that could be emulated but not simply copied. Leavis's words for them were in his title: 'intelligence' and 'sensibility'. He isolated three particular virtues of *Seven Types of Ambiguity* in a passionate but awkwardly written review.

First, and curiously, Leavis welcomed Empson as an *historian*. *Seven Types of Ambiguity* was a long way from the cause-and-effect, influence-and-indebtedness literary histories of Elton or Courthope. This was a modernist, synchronic history. It was not about how writers used styles, but about the styles themselves and their groupings, or, in Eliot's phrase,

---

* George Rylands's *Words and Poetry* (1928) was not inconsiderable, but had the detail without the analysis. See Chapter Four, We Were Cambridge, '"I'm faced with a void" 1931'.

the 'impressions and experiences' that may 'play quite a negligible part' in the life of the writer but which the writing itself creates.[65] There was, affirmed Leavis, 'more of the history of English poetry in this book than in any other that I know'.

Second, Leavis welcomed Empson the scientist. Not, it should be stressed, that he found in Empson a battery of technical terms, or quasi-scientific facilities, such as seemed to be promised from Cambridge by T.R. Henn later in *The Apple and the Spectroscope* or Tillyard in *Poetry Direct and Oblique*. He did not praise Empson as a literary botanist with powers of categorizing: no one (not even Empson) was completely clear about how the seven types of ambiguity differed from one another. Leavis admired Empson for the tenacity of the scientist. He liked a domain where 'serious standards' obtained – as in science, where decisions had consequences. Empson showed that to be scientific was not to be 'technical' only. It was to show where and how a discovery *made a difference*. What Leavis deplored in ordinary literary criticism was its tendency to work only by accretion: 'this *plus* this *plus* this' is what is said, and any 'this' may be removed according to individual (liberal) preference. In science discoveries ceased to be discoveries; formulae went out of date. When, later, Leavis rejected Richards and much later C.P. Snow, it was for not being scientific enough, not too much. When they left physical or social science behind, they acquiesced in impressionist literary discourse. Empson, on the other hand, appeared a model of rigour.

Thirdly, there was the most important contribution Empson could make to Leavis's thinking, one made by Empson almost at odds with himself. After seven chapters on ambiguity, Empson wrote a final experimental one, on unity. The earlier chapters are ones of discovery: Empson displayed his sixth (or seventh) sense of how much can be read into poetry. He showed himself to be a hedonist of multiplicity. But he was aware that, besides acting as both analyst and annalist of the linguistics of poetry, there were decisions to be made, much to be *done*. He recognized what he ruefully called 'the opposing power', that which makes for unity in a poem, what must be selected, from multiple readings. In the eighth chapter of *Seven Types of Ambiguity* he made a sturdy statement: 'The object of life, after all, is not to understand things, but to maintain one's defences and equilibrium and live as well as one can; it is not only maiden aunts who are placed liked this.' This Leavis particularly admired, and the stamina with which at the end of his book Empson turned round and confronted an opposing self (of his own), unity as against multiplicity.

Empson added a new element to the issue broached by Richards, or (say) he hinted at a solution to a problem posed by him. Richards, following *The Waste Land*, had shown how infinitely subtle and variable an 'attitude' could be. He explained the multiplicity of consciousness, the 'modern mood', which Eliot created in poetry. But multiplicity, the 'exciting strangeness' of the modern world, was also a burden. How was focus possible, or decision? At the end of his book Empson was bold enough to say that it was not only 'maiden aunts' who wanted decision: he believed himself to be under some obligation to depart, even if momentarily, from the divagations of analysis, for some discipline of criticism, to leave practice for *praxis*. In his review Leavis agreed enthusiastically, especially because of Empson's youth: 'It is an event to have the response of a younger generation to the problems envisaged by Mr Eliot and Mr Richards, for Mr Empson is as alive as they to the exciting strangeness of the present phase of human history.' Empson was to acquire a reputation for fancifulness of interpretation; but in 1930, at the end of *Seven Types of Ambiguity*, he proposed a discipline that Leavis cherished, a beacon in an eclectic world.

The Cambridge world was eclectic to a fault, a sophisticate's mall. Its particular brand of 'exciting strangeness' at the end of the decade was well described in a novel by a young member of Cambridge English, A.P. Rossiter:

At this period the Cambridge highbrow inclined himself gracefully before the altar of Mr Eliot, and wrote verses full of bitter reflection on sordid environments, garbled quotations, bones, and rats, all of these being prominent in the works of the slim and dandy Nestor whose sporadic volumes turned the current of highbrow thought whenever a new one appeared. Communists turned Catholic revolutionaries cried for Authority before rushing off unsatisfied to the gospel of the impulses. Today Eliot, yesterday Freud, tomorrow Gide or Lawrence; there was no foretelling the rise of new blind guides, the leading influences in conversation, book reviews, and even examination-papers; and meanwhile the majority of dons, left high and dry, on the shoals of orthodox protestantism, stared with surprise and pain, at the rudderless generation they might have led.[66]

Rossiter described playfully the condition evoked with tragic resonance by E.M. Forster in the scene of Mrs Moore's horrified bewilderment in the Marabar Caves in *A Passage to India*. This scene was Leavis's touchstone account of disintegration (or dis-integration) in the modern world:

The crush and the smells she could forget, but the echo began in some indescribable way to undermine her hold on life. Coming at a moment when she chanced to be fatigued, it had managed to murmur, 'Pathos, poetry, courage – they exist, but are identical. And so is filth. Everything exists, nothing has value.'

In his essay on poetry and the modern world, published in France, Leavis quoted this passage, and commented that 'urban conditions, a sophisticated civilization, rapid change and the mingling of cultures have destroyed the old rhythms and habits, and nothing adequate has taken their place'. It is almost certain that he quoted the same passage in a lecture on modern poetry. Gwendolen Freeman, Leavis's giddy-sounding pupil at Girton, said that he, more than any other Lecturer, 'indoctrinated us with current Cambridge ideas – the jargon of "awareness" and "the modern situation" – and with post-war melancholy. "Everything exists, nothing has value." '[67] A few months later in 1930, when writing up this material for *New Bearings in English Poetry*, he deleted the quotation from *A Passage to India*. It is interesting to speculate why he did so. He may have been aware that there were students like Freeman who identified him with the account of the modern malaise, and he did not want to be typed. He may also have believed that to generalize the modern malaise could be disabling, turning an illness or a tragedy into a metaphor. The horror of Mrs Moore's moment in the caves was grand but static. Leavis was more inclined to action – like Empson in his eighth chapter. However true, the 'Moore'–Forster insight did not help with the business of criticism. Leavis *did* criticism in the spirit of one denying daily that 'Everything exists. Nothing has value.' He liked Empson's propositional energy, his 'scientific' commitment to the next experiment. If there was another role-model, W.H. Auden might be cited. (The idea of these alliances must be entertained despite later estrangements.) At the end of the decade Leavis may have thought the 'Moore'–Forster dilemma was better expressed in some lines he enjoyed from 'Paid on Both Sides' by W.H. Auden, lines both playful and sinister. And the mode appealed: the momentariness or *actualité* of verse, rather than the solemnity of Forster's prose (which when solemn was very much so).

Always following the wind of history
Of others' wisdom makes a buoyant air
Till we come suddenly on pockets where
Is nothing loud but us.

Part Two

STAGE ARMY

1931–1948

CHAPTER FOUR

WE WERE CAMBRIDGE
1931–1932

═══════

And yet, in the light of modern research, it is becoming clear that we may talk about society as an organism, and do more than use a metaphor. And we see the part journalism might play in such an organism.

> – F.R. Leavis, 'The Relationship of Journalism to Literature;
> Studied in the Rise and Earlier Development of the Press
> in England', 1924

'I'm faced with a void' 1931

When the students went back to Cambridge in the autumn of 1931, Leavis, his probationership unrenewed, no longer had an official position as Lecturer. The future was bleak. 'I'm faced with a void,' wrote Leavis to Bottrall. I.A. Richards looked panic-stricken with embarrassment when Leavis encountered him in the street. As a writer, Leavis felt trapped. Pieces sent to the *Cambridge Review* were evidently 'put in the waste-paper basket'. The last to be accepted had been his review of the exiled Empson's *Seven Types of Ambiguity* in January 1931. In March he wrote on W.H. Auden's *Poems* for *The Times Literary Supplement*, but no more books for review arrived.

The failure to retain a lectureship was not the only indicator of disapproval in Cambridge English. Leavis was not invited to act as an examiner for the English Tripos even though probationers were eligible. Basil Willey, always useful for 'The English Moralists' paper, examined in 1929 and Joan Bennett did so in 1930. In March 1931 Leavis suspected that 'they'll put Rylands on the tripos this time to keep me out', and Rylands was indeed appointed as an examiner. George Rylands's star

SECTION TITLE: Leavis used the phrase 'stage army' in a letter to John Gillard Watson (17.11.53) signifying the *Scrutiny* group attesting 'in little place a million'.

rose as Leavis's fell. Just as Leavis had notice that his lectureship would not be renewed, so Rylands was appointed as a probationer. And there was good reason for this. As a theatre-enthusiast, Rylands carried the torch of Rupert Brooke into Cambridge English. He also wrote a successful, interesting fellowship dissertation for King's, which appeared as *Words and Poetry* in 1928. It was a Bloomsbury production, published by 'Leonard and Virginia Woolf at the Hogarth Press', with an Introduction by Lytton Strachey. Rylands's book was an enthusiastic assemblage of verbal effects, a *Seven Types of Ambiguity* without the ambiguity; the only things it lacked were system or criticism, but it was a more substantial display than Leavis had accomplished by its date.

Leavis lost his temporary Faculty post: he also lost his teaching hours at Emmanuel and at St John's, because of a quarrel with Stanley and Joan Bennett. Stanley Bennett, the most junior of the original twelve Lecturers, agreed to take the news to Leavis that his lectureship would not be renewed and that there was no immediate prospect of a post. Academic life has often been insecure, but it was especially so in the early 1930s. Muriel Bradbrook once remarked that the trials of job-hunting were 'agonizing'; in the period in which Leavis was without a lectureship, Bradbrook thought, not jokingly, of going with a Girton friend to become a servant in a large household.[1] When Bennett told him the news, Leavis was angry with the messenger, or exasperated that Bennett should be in and himself out. He jumped to the conclusion that Bennett bore some responsibility for the decision and refused to go on seeing him. Q.D.L. kept in touch, calling at the Bennetts' to deliver periodicals for which they shared subscriptions. However, on one occasion Joan Bennett remarked on how the husbands' misunderstanding could be cleared up. Q.D.L. took exception: anyone who thought F.R.L. did not understand the situation must be 'either stupid or wicked'. No reconciliation was then possible.[2]

Hostilities were confirmed in 1933 when Bennett was elected to a fellowship at Emmanuel. Leavis's own college seemed indifferent to him. In old age he said that

what makes the cessation of the connection so painful a memory to me was the utter blankness of the college to me and my subject. Without a word it appointed a philistine good mixer who was tone-deaf and colour blind so far as literature was concerned and proceeded to procure an Anglo-Saxonist to do the work of an English Fellow. It's a bad memory, without mitigation.[3]

Leavis refers to Bennett as an 'Anglo-Saxonist', though he was a medievalist: but in bitter memory he is associated with the 'Early Literature and History' aspect of Cambridge English. (The 'philistine good mixer' is Fred Attenborough, with whom Leavis was never in competition: he left the college in 1925.) In her old age Q.D.L. saw the breach between the Leavises and the Bennetts in a worse light, even suspecting that Stanley ousted Leavis from college teaching in order to provide supervision hours for his wife, and that during the summer vacation of 1931, when few fellows were in residence, he persuaded the college to take Leavis off the supervision list. When the Leavises called at his teaching room in Emmanuel in September they found 'the room's furnishings turned outside'.[4] This may have happened, but it is unlikely that Leavis was excluded by the simple desire of Bennett to provide employment for his wife. At that stage Bennett was not a fellow of the college and the exercise of nepotism would not have recommended him to the Governing Body. On the other hand, Q.D.L.'s accusation is interesting. But in this matter she may have felt frustrated, not so much at the thought of Joan Bennett having Leavis's supervisions but of her having supervisions at all – and Q.D.L. not teaching. Exactly why Q.D.L. did not take supervision pupils at this stage of her career when so many women academics did is a matter for speculation. One reason may have been that Leavis himself needed all the supervision he could get. Another may have been that she decided to play the part of wife in a full sense: she certainly believed it was the duty of a wife to support her husband unequivocally and disliked the wives of Leavis's pupils who got in the way of their careers. It is also possible that there were simply too many women for the available female supervision – and Joan Bennett was senior to Leavis (she had graduated earlier, even though she was a probationer at the same level).

The estranged couples, Leavis and Bennett, continued to work through the Cambridge system until the 1960s, one amiably accepted, the other rebarbative, even feared. The fortunes of Joan Bennett ran in parallel with those of Leavis.

It was never likely that Emmanuel would prefer Leavis to Bennett, who had served the college well for ten years. On the other hand, it never showed any enthusiasm for Leavis, of the sort shown by Girton towards Q.D.L. It is quite possible that Leavis, an outspoken defender of Eliot, *Ulysses* and the author of *Lady Chatterley's Lover*, looked the wrong sort of young man for a college whose fingers had been burned in a scandal, just before the war, that involved progressive views. In

1909 the Master, William Chawner, read a provocative paper to a college group, the Religious Discussion Society, which resembled the famous university sceptics' club, the Heretics. Chawner was a convert to atheism and in his paper attacked religious orthodoxy. He was enlightened, in favour of working-class admission to Emmanuel – indeed, it was this policy that brought in Stanley Bennett. He sided with Cambridge anti-clerics like F.M. Cornford, who petitioned him to join a protest against the Vice-Chancellor's refusal to allow the university crest to be stamped on a volume of the poems of Swinburne given as a prize. In his paper Chawner foolishly criticized his own college's requirement of twice-daily attendance at chapel. Some indignant fellows believed the Master was in breach of the college constitution; there was even talk of evicting him. The problem was solved when Chawner, seeking relief on the Riviera, died suddenly. Emmanuel fellows who remembered the Chawner affair would be wary of a rebellious literary critic from a well-known Cambridge free-thinking family.[5]

So in the autumn of 1931 Leavis was in a precarious position, though the dangers were not obvious. He was able to find teaching elsewhere, at Downing College (as we shall see). And, though no longer salaried, he was still able to lecture, since the Faculty employed freelance Lecturers. Joan Bennett was in exactly the same situation. Her probationership had not been renewed, but she continued to appear on the lecture list in the coming years. Leavis only lectured up to 1932. His position remained precarious for several years, the period of what he called his 'Six Years War' with the Faculty. Q.D.L., however, was in the ascendant.

In the autumn of 1931 Q.D.L. finished her Ph.D. dissertation and submitted it: 'Fiction and the Reading Public: A Study in Social Anthropology'. Her work was assessed, following convention, by her supervisor, I.A. Richards, and an external examiner, in this case E.M. Forster, 'external' in that he was not a member of the English Faculty. The viva voce examination took place on 8 November 1931. After the interview Forster left the candidate alone with the supervisor, and, according to Leavis, 'a violent passage of arms' ensued. 'She's apt to be terribly drastic, and she exhibited a complete and furious contempt,' presumably because, although the examiners recommended award of the degree, Richards had qualifications about the dissertation and took it away rather unwillingly to mark passages that might be revised for publication.[6] Q.D.L. wanted it published as soon as possible. On 9

November she wrote to Ian Parsons at Chatto & Windus, outlining the contents of the dissertation and promising to send the typescript shortly, because Richards had offered to help with revisions: he and Q.D.L were to thresh out the problems to make a 'fool-proof' book. Richards, however, failed to turn up for the appointed discussion. Q.D.L. sent him a tart note, and he irritably returned the dissertation. She defended herself in a letter, saying that she was disappointed to find that the only markings Richards had made on the typescript were proof corrections. 'Some radical criticism was needed, and that you did not make it I conclude means that you did not think it worth making.' She wanted a quick decision from Chatto & Windus 'in order that it may provide butter for our bread next year in the form of a research fellowship', so she sent the typescript straight off to the publisher. Two days after it had been dispatched, Richards demanded she ask for it to be returned, which she did, telling the publisher that Richards thought the book should be scrutinized for libel, so rude had she been about best-selling authors. In fact, Chatto & Windus were delighted. On 26 November Q.D.L. announced triumphantly to Richards that her publisher believed her work was 'forceful and comprehensive'. 'I suppose they are pretty good judges of the average educated reading capacity?'[7] Richards replied that she had better go ahead, because criticism would have meant extensive rewriting. He thought she was preaching to the converted and wanted her to envisage the objections of an 'incredulous person'. More gravely, 'my further criticisms go much deeper and concern the whole attitude to life that appears in the book. That, however, we could hardly discuss now with advantage.'[8]

Q.D.L. professed bewilderment. She thought Richards had really wanted to go over the problems: now she had merely a swift note from him letting the book go unaltered. In January 1932 Q.D.L. told her publisher that she and Richards differed 'fundamentally about the serious-ness of the changes in our culture of the last two centuries (he now asserts that he is an optimist)'.

Richards was dealing with a young woman in a hurry, one who had made him uneasy when she confessed to him the trials of her engage-ment two years before. The friction was not a matter of temperament: Q.D.L. was adhering to attitudes that *had been* Richards's and that he had rejected. It was Richards in the wake of *The Waste Land* who had promulgated cultural pessimism, deploring the 'arid plain' of a contemporary world in which subtlety of attitude would be lost on mass readership. During the 1920s he became more of a meliorist, less demanding in temperament and as a theorist more optimistic. If he did not believe that the Western mass readerships could be refined, at least he thought that at the basic level of literacy great advances could be made, with the help of 'Basic English', the learning system in which he was absorbed at the time he examined Q.D.L.'s dissertation. This dissertation represented the old Richards. Four years later Leavis finally rejected Richards, his former mentor, by writing an intense critique of his *Coleridge on Imagination*. His argument was intricate, but one fundamental difference was, indeed, over the quality of Richards's new-found 'optimism'.*

The Leavises' friendship with the Bennetts was finished. There was no chance now of cordiality with Richards. Q.D.L.'s assertiveness was amply demonstrated in the exchanges with her former supervisor, made during the moment of maximum tension for an academic (doctoral examination, contract for first book). Even her pleasantries were provocative: when she apologized to Richards for 'curtness', she sent a hand-written letter addressed to 'Mr', not 'Dr' Richards, explaining she had 'abandoned the typewriter and the Litt.D. in order that you should have no excuse for calling this harsh'. The spriteliness may have been lost on Richards.

Q.D.L. told Richards she needed her dissertation published so there could be some butter on the family bread. She was awarded a prestigious university research scholarship, the Amy Mary Preston Read, worth £150 a year, for further study after her Ph.D. dissertation. (She used the scholarship for purposes other than those envisaged by the electors, because during the period of the award she put much of her energy into *Scrutiny*.)† Now Leavis had lost his salary, as well as much college teaching. Q.D.L. was, indeed, the bread-winner and she now played the major part in establishing a comfortable home. Unlike Joan Bennett, she did not teach for a college. The Leavises established a pattern different from that of the Bennetts, who were both active teachers, Stanley the senior. Perhaps the offers did not come, or, as suggested a moment ago,

* See Chapter Six, *Scrutiny*: Guarding the Guardians, 'Leaving Richards 1934'.
† Arguably Leavis owed a debt to Q.D.L. because *Scrutiny* blocked the development of her own career, despite the enthusiasm with which she helped him. For this reason the republication of the journal in the 1960s was important: see Chapter Nine, The Sixties: Orthodoxy of Enlightenment, 'Approaching Retirement 1960–1962'.

she considered that the role of partner meant being a full helper to a husband (including the avoidance of competition). She certainly made a real home of No. 6, Chesterton Hall Crescent.

When the Leavises returned to the family house Q.D.L. set about making it very different from that of Harry Leavis. She decorated cheerfully the maroon walls down the long corridor to the kitchen and dining-room. The glazed outhouse was made into a modern scullery and larder. Better heating was installed; the old bedroom jugs and ewers disappeared, as did the Victorian animal prints. Large reproductions of Gauguin and Van Gogh (two views of the bridge at Arles) went up.[9]

The couple have perennially been associated with puritanism and jokingly associated themselves with it, or Victorianism. A guest could be promised 'plain living and high thinking'. But drabness in daily life could not be expected of the couple who admired Mansfield Forbes (with his experimental and glitzy house, 'Finella') or Gordon Fraser, who was shortly to supervise the building of his modernist bookshop in Portugal Place, designed by the head of the school of architecture, with oak casings, rubber floors and a hot-air circulation system. F.R.L. and Q.D.L. had no money, but they liked clean lines and good materials, and collected, when they could, Cardew pottery. When he took supervision pupils at home they were received in a pleasant room, 'split-level, with modern light-coloured furniture, Leavis looking just like his portrait in pencil (or perhaps a touch of crayon) that hung in the room'. Leavis would ritually make a fuss with the coal-fire, explaining it was 'put out by the sun'. When later he taught at Downing College he took no breaks between departing and arriving pupils, on the go for a stretch of three hours, or more if there was a morning lecture, for which he would depart from one group by bicycle and return for the next. Q.D.L. had a comfortably sized house to run in which she could now keep a table. She chafed at Leavis's bachelor ways, including his dog, a lurcher.[10] Q.D.L. adapted to Leavis's desire for a main meal at mid-day, deriving from, she said, his 'lower-middle-class habits of the Victorian bourgeoisie, with High Tea at six o'clock, a regime I hated and haven't got reconciled to in forty-seven years of married life, but useless to try and change it'.[11]

Leavis's eating habits and what he called his 'dyspepsia' were legendary. Eating after mid-day was difficult for him, but he did for years insist upon a bacon-and-egg breakfast, and porridge in later life.[12] He

had a taste for a relay of cups of milky tea throughout the day. At
Chesterton Hall Crescent the household had a daily help, regarded as
standard necessity even in struggling middle-class homes. Gordon Fraser
had money behind him, but had to live prudently and when married
spent £1 a week on domestic help, out of £4 reserved for living
expenses; 75p went on rent.

After the move to Chesterton Hall Crescent the huge pupil-teas began
or, for some student visitors, 'Real Meals' (Q.D.L.'s phrase) with
provender furnished from the garden.

In the early years of his career Leavis in personal appearance anticipated
the era in which it was hard to distinguish professor from graduate
student: 'one never saw him walking with the other dons'. A small,
slight man, he bicycled majestically, later with infant on child-seat, his
academic gown (necessary for lectures) stuffed in the basket. Most dons
wore suits and waistcoats at that time. Leavis favoured a gingery tweed
jacket and flannels. (Until the war, he always had hand-made shoes and
suits, and silk shirts.[13]) Some people thought he looked the wrong sort:
there was 'something about' Leavis that provoked snobberies (or something about snobs). A literary law student staying in Cambridge for a
term in the late 1930s said he noticed in the street

a smallish man who might have been a gas-fitter save that he wore an academic
gown – a gas-fitter who read Bunyan, be it said, and had graduated from
chapel culture to old-fashioned Labour debating societies, or, perhaps to exchange a social for an artistic image. I would say that he reminded me of Joseph
the Carpenter in Millais's *Christ in the House of His Parents*. This was the great
Leavis who had not yet quite assumed the Gladstonian dignity of a Grand Old
Man.[14]

In winter, fields near Cambridge were flooded to make ice surfaces for
skating, made rough by the frozen leaves. Gordon Fraser's wife, Katie,
was once swept off her skates by Leavis when he came up behind her in
scarlet wool hat, canvas army-coat, socks to the knees and his native fen-
skates ('Whittlesea runners'), with the wide, slightly curved blades.
Leavis waltzed her away, neatly lifting her at the frozen ridges: as fine a
spectacle as George Rylands, who hallooed one winter to the skaters
that he was King of the Ice.

At the end of 1931 Leavis was out of a job. But he was still able to
lecture as a freelance. Somewhat surprisingly he started 1932 with a set

of lectures on quite new material, a survey of English poetry from the metaphysical poets of the seventeenth century up to John Keats. The series was called 'Tradition and Development in English Poetry (with texts)', eventually to be published as *Revaluation* (1936). Leavis had admired Empson's *Seven Types of Ambiguity* as a work of unconventional literary history. It may have contributed to his desire to work on the sequence of poetry before the modern movement in the new lectures, on the eve of publication of *New Bearings in English Poetry* in February 1932, soon to be followed by Q.D.L.'s *Fiction and the Reading Public* in April. Despite the employment situation, 1932 was *annus mirabilis* for the critics at Chesterton Hall Crescent.

Pioneer Performances 1932

Early in 1932 F.R.L. and Q.D.L. published their books, the basis of their careers and core texts for the group that now established itself around them, led by Harding, Knights, Thompson, Bottrall and Fraser.

Leavis began *New Bearings in English Poetry* by proposing to write about significant poetry, not intelligent or serious verse but 'real' poetry. He wanted to demonstrate that poetry had to be redefined after Eliot and Pound, who themselves made it possible to appreciate Gerard Manley Hopkins. These were the central figures of the book; there were adjacent appreciations of Hardy, Yeats, Walter de la Mare and, in a daring finale, William Empson and Ronald Bottrall. Leavis apologized for a certain crispness of presentation: 'necessities of compression have led . . . to effects that might be found ironical'. He appeared in this to be offering a mirror-image of the poetry of compression he was promoting.

Leavis's sense of 'real' poetry went back to T.S. Eliot's seventeenth century, especially John Donne, as described in his Clark Lectures and in *Homage to John Dryden*. All Leavis pupils knew half a dozen lines of Donne from *Satyre Third*, always quoted in seminars and lectures, lines of kinetic poetry, the words like actions or things, contradictory in sound, sometimes labouring, sometimes sudden, trembling between tones.

> On a huge hill,
> Cragged, and steep, Truth stands, and hee that will
> Reach her, about must, and about must goe;
> And what the hills suddenness resists, winne so;

Yet strive so, that before age, deaths twilight,
Thy Soule rest, for none can worke in that night.[15]

This was not the poetry of romanticism, which in the first chapter of
New Bearings in English Poetry Leavis dates from Joseph Warton's *Essay
on the Genius and Writings of Pope* of 1756. Warton perceived Donne as a
man of sense and wit but not a writer of 'pure poetry', an idea of poetry
affirmed many years later in Matthew Arnold's dictum about Dryden
and Pope, that they were not poets because 'genuine poetry is conceived
and composed in the soul'.[16] This idea was sustained in the key anthologies of the Victorian age, Palgrave's *Golden Treasury* (1861) and Q's
Oxford Book of English Verse (1900). The supreme poet of romanticism
was Milton, who was never dismissed by Leavis because he was a great
poet, but one whose genius none the less was antithetical to the initiative
of John Donne. To plead for Donne made a necessity of hesitation about
Milton. He was a 'metaphysical poet' of his own sort: mind and spirit
were never banally separate in his verse-thinking, but his style gave
his successors a warrant for soulfulness. Milton was bard and model
for a romanticism that in the late nineteenth century was spent as a
force that could animate the work of practising poets. After what
Leavis called the 'post-Swinburnian arrest' a modern poet (especially
after Eliot) would no longer serve an apprenticeship in the Miltonic
atelier. When Leavis wrote that Milton had been 'dislodged', he was
stating a plain fact: that 'after two centuries' Milton had ceased to be
a resource for young poets.

A belief in 'soul' as an entity separate from 'thought' could never be
the same after early Eliot, and the tone of 'Portrait of a Lady'. Leavis
argued that in Eliot's 'Gerontion' a seventeenth-century sensibility
became modern, floating free from the first-person speech of the poem.
Both 'Gerontion' and 'Portrait of a Lady' depart from the voices of their
ostensible speakers, one an old man, the other an awkward young one.
In 'Gerontion' impotence and in 'Portrait of a Lady' embarrassment
were pretexts; but 'Gerontion' was more fully removed from its generative situation than 'Portrait of a Lady'. For Leavis it had 'the impersonality of great poetry'.[17]

Some readers were surprised that *New Bearings in English Poetry* had so
little of substance to say about *The Waste Land* in a chapter on Eliot.
Leavis seemed uneasy about the poem. He praised it for its 'vigour': if
the land was dead the mind that made the poem was robust. Its stamina

was evident, Leavis thought, in Eliot's concern for Dante, for austere 'reason', and his preference for a faith of 'an athleticism, a training, of the soul as severe and ascetic as the training of the body of a runner' (remarked in relation to Proust). Leavis, a runner of the ordinary kind, turned intently to 'athleticism' when he commented on *Ash-Wednesday*.

The theme of *The Waste Land* elicited praise: the poem exactly fitted Leavis's conviction that modernity meant alienation from an older, unified world, 'the civilization in touch with the rhythms, sanctioned by nature and time, of rural culture'. Modernity meant 'the perpetuation and multiplication of life as ultimate ends'.[18] Forty years later Leavis translated 'multiplication' into pluralism. The concept of an old world was valuable to Leavis because it was, to a degree, true and also because the idea of that world implied a structure or rationale that could be 'anthropologically' accounted for. The new world *appeared* to be fragmentary, but it had to have a rationale, if obscure. A knowledge of the old world was a training in the discernment of this rationale; it stimulated the observer to see structure underlying modernity's show of multiplicity. Modernity had devised disintegration: bluntly, there were people responsible for it. Leavis found himself in conflict with those of the new world who doubted whether there was ever an old world, an 'organic' one, and preferred to see the fragmentation of modernity as fact, not as creation of its intelligentsia. This was not the view of Eliot, himself a ruralist and readier even than Leavis to find a rationale for fragmentation. The one he found in *After Strange Gods* (never reprinted) was so radically savage that he went his way on soft pads as practising man of letters. After such analysis, what forgiveness?

The Waste Land was consonant with Leavis's sense of the modern world. But he was in his first book more enthusiastic about issues of consciousness than of culture. The plight of being 'too much conscious and conscious of too much' is one he explores with most interest, especially with regard to *Ash-Wednesday*. Leavis was very moved by the prototype sections of the poem that appeared in 1928 in the French journal *Commerce* under Dantesque titles, 'Perch' io non spero' (1928) and 'Som de l'escalina' (1929).[19] Leavis wrote of them as he read them individually, not knowing they would form a sequence. He expressed surprise, even awe, because the poems did not resemble any other work to date by Eliot. Leavis moved carefully, realizing that the poems exposed privacies, following Eliot's injunction that poetry must be taken *as* poetry and recognizing this to be 'highly formal poetry'. To describe them he returned incessantly to the word 'sincerity', seeing them as spiritual exercises in the quelling of self, the recognition of that which is outside self, for which no credit accrues to the 'me' that knows it. The poems were about believing, which may necessarily require exclusions. (Of *The Waste Land*, he said, there were ways in which it is possible to be too conscious.) Leavis's prose lacked the clarity of Eliot's, but he aspired to work in consort with Eliot's total aim: 'He had to achieve a paradoxical precision-in-vagueness; to persuade the elusive intuition to define itself, without any forcing, among the equivocations of "the dreamcrossed twilight".'[20]

New Bearings in English Poetry was well received. Some reviewers, including the anonymous writer in the *New Statesman and Nation*, were flustered by Leavis's intellectuality and attributed it to the influence of Cambridge, and Empson especially. (A Leavis pupil wrote in to explain that Leavis had been lecturing on the same lines when Empson was a first-year undergraduate.) Richard Church in the *Spectator* made a point that was to stick. Leavis, he said, was 'preoccupied with technique'; when he referred to tradition 'he means the tradition of form and expression'. Church attributed this to Leavis's 'apprenticeship to the Cambridge School, which has always tended to emphasize the intellectual side of aesthetics'. Leaving aside technicality (sorting ill with his consideration of belief and sincerity in Eliot) and the attribution of Leavis's interests to the Cambridge School, there remained the presumption that to favour difficult poetry was eccentric in an academic. At this date it was easier to be a philosopher. If Church was right to say that Leavis was 'a poet's critic' (because of his 'technicality'), one poet certainly received him well: Geoffrey Grigson in the *Saturday Review*.

In Cambridge an odd thing happened over the reception of *New Bearings in English Poetry*. The *Cambridge Review* sent it out not to a member of the English Faculty but to Geoffrey Rossetti, the pupil who told Wittgenstein that Leavis was 'like Jesus Christ'. The review was signed 'G.R.', which Q.D.L. thought meant 'George Rylands' (who had supervised her Ph.D. work for a year). The mistake did not promote amity.[21]

New Bearings in English Poetry also started a minor feud with Edith Sitwell, a hare that ran in circles in the coming years. In his survey of the post-war alternatives to Georgian poetry Leavis identified 'Sitwellism' and made his much quoted remark that 'the Sitwells belong to the history of publicity rather than poetry'.* Edith Sitwell had also been stung by Geoffrey Grigson and by Wyndham Lewis in *The Apes of God* (1930). She retaliated in *Aspects of Modern Poetry* (1934), which, despite attacking Leavis, owed more than a little to *New Bearings in English Poetry*. Leavis characterized Victorian poetic taste by an Andrew Lang sonnet ('As one that for a weary space has lain'); so did Sitwell. She appears to have discovered Bottrall from Leavis. For several weeks plagiarism was alleged and rebutted.[22] Sitwell defended herself cavalierly, but she did not disguise the fact that Leavis had been useful, acknowledging some 'finely reasoned' criticism of Eliot; she understood the high valuation Leavis gave to rhythm, but thought this 'puritan' or 'country clergyman' had no 'tactile sense'. And he was uncomprehending on Pound.

In *New Bearings in English Poetry* Leavis was more concerned with consciousness than culture, though he would not have admitted it. The contrast between intelligible old world and the modern waste land of fragments emerged in his doctoral dissertation, was in tune with the early thinking of Richards, was related to Eliot's 'dissociation of sensibility' and it always engaged Leavis. But he dealt with it in terms of myth rather than sociology. His partner, on the other hand, in *Fiction and the Reading Public*, pursued the subject of cultural decline with historical detail and indignant relish. Q.D.L. told the story of how, following the rise of literacy and improved mechanisms of publication, the old British reading-public multiplied into several publics. In the modern section of her book Q.D.L. described the inferior reading capacity of the new publics and the helplessness of the readers who are given, by the masters of publication, what is supposed to suit them. These readers lost the aspiration to understand; they were supplied, in the early twentieth century, with palliatives, low-quality matter that did not urge them

---

* Leavis never commented at length on Edith or Sacheverell. Sitwellism was an upper-middle-class substitute for the avant garde. 'It is hard to overestimate what the Sitwell example meant to me. Their background was not unlike mine: a background of country house security tied in with interludes of Eton and the Brigade of Guards. But they had already shown that it was possible to use just such a background as a springboard, to twist it into fantasy, satire, fresh enterprises of the imagination.' They were easier going than 'stern spirits, such as Wystan Auden, Christopher Isherwood, Stephen Spender, who kept a little aloof and mixed their own blends of medicinal high spirits and rather governessy doctrine'. Alan Pryce-Jones, *The Bonus of Laughter* (1987).

higher on the intellectual scale. Q.D.L. argued the elitist position that in mass civilization only a minority culture was possible. It was the traditional romantic position, of Wordsworth when he attacked 'gross and violent stimulants' of the readership palliatives of his day, or of Coleridge. In her chapter on 'Reading Capacity' Q.D.L. quoted from his *Biographia Literaria*.

It is noticeable, how limited an acquaintance with the master-pieces of art will suffice to form a correct and even a sensitive taste, where none but master-pieces have been seen and admired: while on the other hand, the most correct notions, and the widest experience with the works of excellence of all ages and countries, will not be perfectly secure as against the contagious familiarity with the far more numerous offspring of tastelessness or of a perverted taste. If this be the case . . . with the arts of music and painting, how much more difficult will it be, to avoid the infection of multiplied and daily examples as in the practice of an art, which uses words, and words only, as its instruments.

Q.D.L.'s theme was the 'infection' that prevented people from understanding, or wanting to understand, or even merely respecting, extraordinary art. Her concern was with the feebleness of the material processed for the twentieth-century echelons of print-users.[23] She knew that in the modern world extraordinary art was less accessible to those with the beginnings of literacy than it was in earlier ages, and certainly had been in an age such as Shakespeare's, in which there could be a response to the art of the spoken word by both popular and elite audiences. She claimed that between the periods of Shakespeare and Coleridge a person on the road to reading could eventually, with teaching and determination, arrive at the hard works (Thomas Nashe for Elizabethan; Laurence Sterne in the eighteenth century). 'High' styles were hard of access but not maintained in a different stable from 'low' styles. But in the twentieth century Q.D.L. saw many more markets, hostelries and institutes on the routes between the tabloid newspaper and *To the Lighthouse*. Modern readers must have special qualifications to understand the beauty of construction in a novel by Virginia Woolf, which is more demanding than the stylistic engineering of Fielding's *Tom Jones* or the 'architecture' of Henry James's *The Ambassadors*.[24] *Fiction and the Reading Public* is a story of decline, giving a favourable account of the old forms of social life in which reading was embedded, the re-creations of a lost world contrasted with the de-creations of the present. The old world is frankly idealized, even fantastically so, though it is hard not to be convinced by Q.D.L.'s proposal of what there was to *be* idealized. The book was a passionate one, from a young scholar. Q.D.L. was only twenty-six years old when it appeared, in the third year of her marriage, and technically still a graduate student.

Fiction and the Reading Public was a faithful reproduction of Q.D.L.'s doctoral dissertation but without its subtitle ('A Study in Social Anthropology'). Nor did the book contain the illustrative matter in the original dissertation that Q.D.L. had carefully copied from advertisements. It therefore had a more austerely academic appearance than the dissertation. It was received well and taken seriously even by its critics. The leading authority on popular fiction, Michael Sadleir, noted it drily and authoritatively in the *New Statesman and Nation*. Q.D.L. even became something of a notoriety, famous enough for *Punch* to mention her in a joke poem about the Victorian novelist Rhoda Broughton:

> As a quite unrepentant Victorian,
> I'm viewed with disdain and despair,
> As a species of icthyosaurian
> In Gordon or Bloomsbury Square:
> Yet, though it may prove most unchary,
> To flout MRS LEAVIS, I own
> To a permanent fondness for *Nancy*
> *Belinda* and *Joan*.[25]

Eliot was complimentary in the *Criterion* in July.[26] He endorsed Q.D.L.'s observation of 'the increasing stratification of literature into classes, each of which prefers to ignore the others', those at the bottom ignoring, or despising, the labour of development at the top. One of his sharper sentences could have been by Q.D.L. herself: 'A society which does not recognize the existence of art is barbaric. But a society which pretends that it recognizes art, by tolerating the Royal Academy and patronizing such novelists as Mr Thornton Wilder, Mr Hemingway and Mr Priestley (at best), is decidedly decadent.' Eliot agreed that serious fiction required special efforts from the reader, developing the idea in a way that was prophetic for F.R.L. and Q.D.L. Serious fiction, he said, demanded an understanding 'akin to a poetic appreciation'. He cited *Ulysses* but dated this type of poetic novel to a period earlier than Joyce, further back to the work of James, Conrad and Hawthorne. Here were the beginnings of what F.R.L. later called the 'novel as dramatic poem'.

The Year of Scrutiny 1932

After retirement Leavis looked back to his group of the early 1930s and said 'we were – and knew we were, Cambridge – the essential Cambridge in spite of Cambridge'. A cocky pupil taxed him, reminding Leavis that the neutron was discovered in the Cavendish laboratory in 1932, to which he replied that he was using 'tactical hyperbole'. Leavis was not altogether wrong. *If* the specialism of scientific Cambridge lessened its claim to being 'essential', *if* Cambridge humanities could be identified with Cambridge English, *if* it were agreed that the Leavisian version of Cambridge English commanded the longest attention, then he had a point. In a couple of years when Cambridge English was attacked, *Fiction and the Reading Public* was taken as epitomizing it. And in 1932 the Leavis group began to issue its journal, *Scrutiny: A Quarterly Review*. The journal was created swiftly after some meetings at Chesterton Hall Crescent in late 1931.

Leavis later made fun of heavy-duty academic research, or 'higher navvying'. In the early 1930s he was keen to see research projects. In November 1931 he helped with his undergraduates' research applications, drafted conspiratorially ('I have to disguise my hand'), and planned a 'Researcher's Club', to be run without too much Faculty interference. In the Christmas vacation of 1931, soon after Q.D.L. had her viva voce examination, a group of young men met, with Richards present, at Chesterton Hall Crescent. Richards

came to our house to address the inaugural meeting of the English Research Society. This has been formed by L.C. Knights and half a dozen exceptionally intelligent people who are researching here now. The idea is to get the advantages of organization – exchange, discussion, stimulus, etc. – without the institutional disadvantages: in short, as far as possible to make up for the dearth of intelligent and qualified supervision. Well, Richards offered eagerly to address the first meeting, turned up with his wife and another feminine admirer, and dismissed with an amused superiority that was often close to a snigger every possibility of profitable research in English. It was impossible for me to say anything without endorsing the implication that it was all my little stunt. I think he was partly annoyed at the number of researchers whom I had helped with the formation of subjects and sent round to him in order that he might give them a pass to get by Mr Potts and the [Faculty] Board.

These young graduates exemplified the minority Leavis wanted. All were doing what he called 'anthropologico-literary research', like Q.D.L.

in her thesis now made public, which he proudly called the 'pioneer performance'. The group was held together by its interest in the sociology of literature. These 'anthropologico-literary' young men gave Richards a hard time.

To deal with him on the spot was morally impossible, so half a dozen stalwarts drew up a reply. It's as devastating a document as I've seen. 'Your main contribution seems to us not worth arguing about,' etc. He had dismissed most intelligent kinds of research (my wife's in particular by implication) as involving 'axes to grind'. Is that not merely a way of raising prejudice? Would you, or would you not, say there were no axes to grind in *The Principles of Literary Criticism*, *Science and Poetry*, *Practical Criticism*? But the most drastic effects depend upon close reference to what he had said. The society suggested ironically that he had of course been playing Devil's Advocate, and had meant to provoke this response. On receiving the document, he agreed that of course he had. And he has since been lavish in encouragement.

Leavis was proud of the young men who had gravitated to Chesterton Hall Crescent, doing work along the lines of *Fiction and the Reading Public*, one Ceylon Dutchman working on how English literature was taught in Ceylon, one New Zealander asking whether there was or could be an indigenous literature in New Zealand.[27] In spite of his lack of a lectureship, Leavis was organizing the makings of a research school, though not in conventional English literature. L.C. Knights was working on education, language and society in Jacobean England, a study published in 1937 as *Drama and Society in the Age of Jonson*. Two researchers showed how the Leavisian view was beginning to radiate outwards. Eric H. McCormick was asking why there was no distinctive literature in New Zealand, according to Leavis. Brought up in Christchurch, he took an MA at Victoria College, where he wrote a dissertation on New Zealand literature; most people in Cambridge thought there was none. The dissertation was commended by his external examiner, who helped him to get a postgraduate scholarship at Clare College, where he started to work on the British sixteenth-century compilation *A Mirror for Magistrates*. He attended a variety of lectures and attracted the notice of Forbes and Leavis, who were friendly to the people who stayed behind afterwards. Invitations were issued to 'Finella' and Chesterton Hall Crescent. He became a regular guest at the Leavis teas, where he made friends with Iqbal Singh, Donald Culver and Carlos Peacock, a St John's undergraduate who knew Edmund Blunden and discoursed at length, to McCormick's enlightenment, on John Donne. McCormick had little aptitude for sixteenth-century literature and turned to Leavis for advice,

as the friendliest spirit of his generation. Leavis suggested he continue his
studies of New Zealand literature 'with greater emphasis on cultural and
historical forces', *à la Fiction and the Reading Public*. McCormick agreed
and wrote 'Literature in New Zealand: An Essay in Cultural Criticism'.
He had been supervised by Basil Willey but encouraged by Denys
Harding when he left Cambridge to research in London. His dissertation
cleared the ground for his pioneering *Letters and Art in New Zealand*.[28]

The Ceylon Dutchman was E.F.C. Ludowyk, a Christian-born Eur-
asian whose 'interest in the folk-ways of Sri Lanka was insatiable'. He
took Part Two of the English Tripos at Trinity Hall, and the Charles
Oldham Shakespeare Scholarship in 1931. At the researchers' meeting he
was on the point of returning to Colombo, where he imported the
methods of Cambridge English. Like McCormick, he wanted to experience a national saturation, 'to enter the mainstream of Sri Lankan
culture, rather than nourish the flickering flame of his Burgher inherit-
ance'. He saw the single-poem pedagogy of practical criticism as a
training in specificity that could 'play a part in undoing the authoritarian-
ism of cultures under imperial rule'.

In this group Leavis managed to create the teaching milieu he described
later:

The peculiar nature of the study of English worth pursuing at university level
entails its being in the most essential regards, though a special study, not what
'specialist' suggests. A genuine teacher doesn't find himself holding back his
subtlest insight and his most adventurous thought because they are not suitable
for communication to first- or second-year men . . . What we call 'teaching' is,
if genuine, a matter of enlisting and fostering collaboration . . .[29]

The Chesterton Hall Crescent group was attracted to the idea of a
journal. McCormick and Singh wanted to start one for 'stories, poems
and articles in sympathy with the views of D.H. Lawrence', called 'The
Phoenix'. In November 1931 they had an 'anarchic, chaotic' discussion
with Culver and Peacock and visited printers who were discouraging
about a journal without a circulation of 10,000 and national advertising.
There was another meeting, at which Knights told them he had talked
about 'The Phoenix' to Leavis. He was indeed interested in a magazine
but one of wider scope. Singh and McCormick backed out.

It was Donald Culver who encouraged Leavis to look to America for
a model, and he readily did so. The group was orientated towards the
United States, partly because it furnished a wealth of data and analysis

for Q.D.L. In the introduction to *Fiction and the Reading Public* she
specified a large debt to the sociology of Robert S. and Helen M.
Lynd's *Middletown*. In America mass civilization had arrived; Britain was
not so far into the age of machine communication. This is not to say
that America was an object of despair or superciliousness in the Leavis
group. On the contrary, across the Atlantic the problems had been
addressed in exemplary fashion by the Lynds, or by Stuart Chase,
notably in *Mexico*, which compared the study of a large Mexican village
with the study of Middletown. (Denys Thompson's school pupils were
taken aback to find the first literary text for sixth-form study was
Chase's *Mexico*.) America had forms and levels of social analysis that
were unavailable in Britain, popular and readable but also scrupulously
observant. Its literature supplied allegorical figures, like the American
Mr Polly of Sinclair Lewis's novel *Babbitt*. Leavis's first published essay
on fiction (apart from that of Lawrence and Powys) was on American
literature: John Dos Passos's *Manhattan Transfer, The Forty-Second Parallel*
and *Nineteen-Nineteen*.[30] America supplied models for cultural studies.
When F.R.L. and Q.D.L. set up their homes, there was no source of
dispassionate advice on household purchasing such as was available in
America from Consumers' Research Ltd, another of Stuart Chase's
enterprises.[31] In 1931 there had been talk of a post for Leavis at Harvard,
though this was by then 'the old gossip': 'I doubt whether I could get
there now even if I tried.'[32] The couple would have sorted well with
New Deal intelligentsia.

Leavis knew the American journals, like the *Symposium*, which Culver
introduced from Princeton. His group was keen 'to do the criticism that
is not done in the commercial press, and to focus a "minority" scrutiny
upon contemporary civilization'. '*Scr-r-r-utiny!*' crunched Knights
through his teeth: 'I like that.' Very quickly, a journal was planned for
the spring of 1932 and the plans were realistic. Leavis had some money
in hand from the sale of Leys Road: a start could be made.

At the end of the Lent term Leavis and Q.D.L had a week's holiday in
Paris and at the beginning of May the new journal was launched.
Scrutiny: A Quarterly Review was edited by Knights and Culver, with
Leavis in the background, just as he had been behind Gordon Fraser.
The cover design of *Scrutiny* speaks of one of its models. It was a
homage, by a jobbing Cambridge printer, to the *English Review* under
Ford Madox Ford in the pre-war era. There were other models. Leavis

intensely admired the *Calendar of Modern Letters*, which had a short life
from March 1925 to July 1927; he edited a selection of its prose and
Scrutinies was the name of one of its own compilations of its essays into
book form. The *Calendar* had two features that were important for the
putative *Scrutiny*: it had a lack of awe for established reputation and it
was a journal of creative writing.[33] This last fact may not be obvious
from Leavis's published selection from it, and *Scrutiny* itself had little in
the way of creative writing. But all its criticism was meant to be in the
context of current creation, of advances on the 'creative front'. Another
model, from America, was the *Symposium*, founded in January 1930,
publishing Richards and Murry on the literary side, as well as G. Wilson
Knight and the young Lionel Trilling. It illustrated what was lacking in
Britain. When *Fiction and the Reading Public* came out, the *Symposium*
supplied a magisterial review by J. Cudworth Flint; when Huxley
published his edition of the letters of D.H. Lawrence, there was no
treatment in a British journal as dispassionate as that of William Troy's
in the *Symposium*.[34] Nor was there in Britain an equivalent to the *New
Republic*, or *Experiment*, or *Hound and Horn*.[35] From France, Leavis was
aware of *Commerce*, edited by Paul Valéry, Léon-Paul Fargue and Valéry
Larbaud from 1924. He called it *chic*, though respectfully.

The editors went for a printer to S.G. Marshall in Round Church
Street, a long-established business, in an alley next to the Cambridge
Union Society. Before the first issue they took £40.15 in subscriptions.
They charged 10/– (50p) for four issues, post free. The print outgoings
were about £65. The initial print run was for 500 copies and the first
issue was published on 15 May 1932, with sound commercial success,
especially at W.H. Smith's station bookstall. One hundred copies were
sold in the first week. An additional 250 copies were ordered and sold.
The print run for later issues went up to 1,000 (but never exceeded 1,400).
Leavis seems to have paid in quite substantial sums from his own pocket,
indeed as much as £205 between January and December 1933. Later he
said his early contribution was about £150.[36]

Leavis thought the new journal 'may have considerable success' and it
did, with subscriptions coming in from T.S. Eliot, George Santayana,
R.H. Tawney and Aldous Huxley. The success was partly because
Scrutiny had several publics: Leavis was excited by the idea of 'suitably
intelligent [*sic*] ex-pupils scattered about the world' who would keep the
'lines of communication' open (*Lines of Communication* was, actually, the
name of a former FAU Ambulance Train journal).

For the first two issues Leavis was not an editor, first appearing on the title page of Volume 1, Number 3. We have already seen that he liked to work (in college patois) as 'back-coach'. He was diffident, as in the hesitations voiced to Bottrall when writing *New Bearings in English Poetry*; and he was conspiratorial. He was short of time: he had a career to establish in the writing of books. Temperamentally, he sometimes wanted a scout to go first: he used the idea of reconnaissance fifteen years later when he drew an analogy between critic and 'native tracker' (he was writing an essay on Samuel Johnson).

An analogy: the 'native' tracker owes his skill not to a natural endowment of marvellously good sight, but to analogous anticipations: knowing the kind of thing to look for he is quick to perceive, and being habituated to the significances of the various signs, he is quick to appraise and interpret.[37]

As to staying out of the editorship of the first numbers of *Scrutiny*, it is possible Leavis held back because as an editor it would have been awkward for Denys Harding to contribute a review of *New Bearings in English Poetry* to the first issue. Whatever his position, Leavis wrote copiously for the quarterly from the start, more than he had ever done before.

In the first issues of *Scrutiny* there were several long pieces on education, notably an essay by L.C. Knights about teacher-training colleges, analysing the results of a questionnaire designed and delivered by the *Scrutiny* group. (The questionnaire was a Leavisian device, a tool of 'social anthropology', like Q.D.L's canvassing the opinion, Richards-fashion, of best-selling authors.)

Scrutiny was a success, but a price was paid by Q.D.L. Once the journal got going she did much of the editorial business. She wrote for it and suggested subjects. She did not appear to want to be an editor, or be suspected of being an unofficial one. Once she sent suggestions to Gordon Cox with his draft of a review, emphasizing that she was intervening only because originally she was to have done the review (of books by Edward Upward and Rex Warner): 'I don't normally do anything to contributions beyond correcting the authors' spelling mistakes when typing them, I hope you'll believe. (Frank says I shall be known as Mrs Proudie if it gets round that I have a hand in the editing.)' The joke was partly on Leavis, putting him in the position of Trollope's wife-tormented Bishop of Barsetshire.[38] But a household of literary activity was difficult. In November 1932, just before Leavis became an official editor, he wrote that the strain of the last three years in a hostile Cambridge has come out in my wife, and she's threatened, says the doctor, with a nervous disorder. She's on the edge, and, as the doctor admits, there's nothing to be done since exile and frustration wouldn't improve her. All this because of the petty vanity of A.B. and C. I don't feel indulgent.[39]

'Exile' shows they had thought of leaving Cambridge (and how they regarded the prospect of such a move). None the less, Leavis decided to commit himself to the journal. At the beginning of November Donald Culver moved to Paris, leaving *Scrutiny* to Knights. Thompson was enlisted, but Leavis considered him inexperienced. Douglas Garman and Edgell Rickword were interested, but outsiders. Leavis then became an editor and the Michaelmas term was fraught with the kind of editorial mêlée that became familiar in ensuing years. The history of *Scrutiny* was one of 'improvisations and last-minute salvations', haste making it often 'impossible to consult other editors, whose names stand above what they had no power to correct'.[40] This November they had material: Leavis had written an essay on 'Milton's Verse' and was reading James Joyce's 'Work in Progress' (the first extracts of *Finnegans Wake*), but an editorial piece was necessary, so he wrote an important essay on literary criticism and Marxism ('Under which King, Bezonian . . .?'. There was a bread-and-butter review to be done of an edition of Blake's *Visions of the Daughters of Albion* because the publisher (Dent) was good about supplying books for review, the life-blood of the journal (and a source of cash from the sale of unused copies). Leavis did a page on it. He wanted to rebut the charge that *Scrutiny* was negative, so came up with a review of Aldous Huxley's edition of *The Letters of D.H. Lawrence*, a book he did not want to entrust to his co-editors.[41] Leavis's preferences were being forced into the light. The others were under stress. Knights was preparing the lecture that eventually became a well-known pamphlet, *How Many Children Had Lady Macbeth?*, and

has more than he can do comfortably in the Training College inquiry, and looks alarmingly exhausted (I had to help him). My wife, moreover, is ill. Then at the last moment for press, in spite of wiring and phoning, Rickword fails to send in his long review-article on Eliot and Martin Crusoe's article turning up, proves to be a defence of the Public Schools as training-places for the oligarchy – of course, we can't print it, anyway in the number containing 'Under which King?' So there are a dozen pages (16 is a printer's unit) to be filled. Knights hasn't a sprint in him, and anyway has to go off to his W.E.A. [Workers'

Educational Association] class at Desborough, Culver is in Paris. I had to do the work for the most part. It was very painful.[42]

Leavis's thinking was shaped by *Scrutiny*'s. It was his way to enjoy quickness of response, but to a degree events controlled him. The publication of Lawrence's letters did not block his way, but his sense of what he was doing as a critic himself was seriously changed by them. By provocation he developed. It was also his part, in the first year of *Scrutiny*, to provoke. He continued his career as a pamphleteer, but now in its pages, rather than for the Minority Press.

Precarious in Cambridge, Leavis was becoming known outside it. The editor of the *Bookman*, Hugh Ross Williamson, liked his work ('poor amiable idealist', said Leavis). At Christmas 1931 it was Leavis who surveyed 'Literary Criticism of the Year', applauding (of course) Empson's *Seven Types of Ambiguity* and G. Wilson Knights's *The Imperial Theme*. He was respectful of John Middleton Murry, but said his book on D.H. Lawrence, *Son of Woman*, was not what was needed because it contended that Lawrence was a prophet, not an artist, so literary criticism was what was required, not the pronouncements in which Murry indulged 'as if he had access to Absolute Truth'. In the spring the *Bookman* surveyed 'This Age', an issue opening with a picture of the BBC's Broadcasting House and containing an article by Ronald Knox on 'Broadcast Minds'. The development of broadcasting was a new means of communication: it added a layer to the construction of the intelligentsia. Leavis wrote on this age in literary criticism. In the issue of Christmas 1932 the *Bookman* announced that it had been the year of literary criticism. T.S. Eliot's *Selected Essays* had been published, patronized by the 'wily reviewers' in October. The issues were clear: how were 'the best ideas to gain currency'? In 1932 a frontal attack on mediocrity had been made by Q.D.L. in *Fiction and the Reading Public*. According to Hugh Ross Williamson, the liberal commonplace was that agitation about 'standards' was unnecessary when in a free intellectual market the remarkable work would find its level and following. But Q.D.L. had 'shattered' the argument that there was no difference between universality and popularity: now we knew that popularity was constructed and that part of the work of construction was the denigration of the difficult: the 'highbrow–lowbrow' distinction was a way of blocking the way to the difficult and extraordinary.

Leavis singled out Eliot as the leader of 'This Age', and he clearly would have liked entrance to the court of Eliot, that is, to the contributing panel of Eliot's journal the *Criterion*. It had praised Q.D.L. and engaged Leavisians as contributors (such as L.C. Knights, not to mention James Smith and Empson). Eliot himself encouraged Leavis, but he never gained a foothold, and there was only one moment when realistically he could have done so, in the early months of 1932. Later in the year he had his own journal in *Scrutiny*; apart from ideological considerations he hardly had time to contribute elsewhere.

In late 1931 Leavis hoped for Eliot's favour. Just before Christmas he had an appointment with Eliot in London. He very badly wanted to review T. F. Powys's *Unclay* for the *Criterion*. On the train he read the latest issue of Eliot's journal, which contained a rather enervated round-up review by F.S. Flint of twenty volumes of recent verse. It listed, but did not get round to assessing, the Ronald Bottrall collection, *The Loosening*, which Fraser and Leavis had published. Leavis thought of mentioning this to Eliot in person, but decided against it when they met. Instead, on Christmas Day, he wrote an elaborately urbane letter to the *Criterion* pleading that Bottrall's verse was surely more distinguished than that of Aldous Huxley, which Flint had singled out for (luke-warm) praise.[43] The letter helped the suit of Bottrall, paving the way to his publication by Faber and Faber. For himself, no request to review Powys's *Unclay* was forthcoming. But Eliot did have a suggestion that Leavis should write a companion to *Mass Civilization and Minority Culture*, dealing not with the mass but the minority, with the structure and influence of the intelligentsia. (He was haunted by 'strange gods' of the intelligentsia.) He thought it might be suitable for 'The Criterion Miscellany'. Leavis set to work, but in the end Eliot did not publish the results. However, it gave him material for early issues of *Scrutiny*, about the guardians of the guardians of culture.

Leavis was on the way to becoming a guardian himself, if his presence in London in the *Bookman* was anything to go by. The Christmas issue of 1934 had a full-page line drawing of him by Robert Austin, along with other luminaries, including W.B. Yeats (and A.P. Herbert).[44]

CHAPTER FIVE

'TO DOWNING COLLEGE' ★
1931–1937

Downing are cock-a-hoop. Appointments are always for three years
in the first place. But they, I think, will hardly turn me out after
this surrender. They won't dare.
                    – F.R. Leavis to Ronald Duncan, 1936

This tea-party was also notable for marking the first appearance of
Marius Bewley. He arrived a little late, smiling, diffident, courteous,
in a well-pressed suit of severe East Coast cut made of some
lightweight tweedish cloth, almost black with dark purple flecks.
He had been visiting London and he was greeted by Queenie: 'Ah,
Mr Bewley. How did you enjoy *A London Life*?' He hesitated,
obviously slightly confused, then laughed nervously and said, 'Why,
Mrs Leavis, I thought you meant a London life!'
                    – Patrick Harrison, 'Recollections of Leavis and the
                                        Downing English School'

A New College 1931–1936

In 1931 James Klugmann went up to Trinity College from Gresham's
School, where he had been taught by Denys Thompson. He was to
become an energetic Cambridge communist. Within a few days of
arrival he found a note pushed under his door, addressed to him from
Chesterton Hall Crescent. It said, 'We understand you are an intelligent
[sic]. A group of us meets . . .' Date and hour followed.[1] Schoolmasters
traditionally gave dons advance warning of their pupils' arrival, and
Thompson would have alerted the Leavises to Klugmann so he could be
invited to one of their teas and perhaps join their group. From 1931

★ 'To Downing College' is the dedication to *Revaluation: Tradition and Development in English Poetry* (1936).

Leavis began to base his group in a college new to him, Downing, a quarter of a mile up the road from Emmanuel.*

Q.D.L. was pregnant in the spring of 1933 and the eldest Leavis son was born in January 1934. Ralph Leavis was a difficult child, the first eighteen months of his life taxing. Leavis said that he was more exhausted than he believed possible and afraid that Q.D.L. would break down. He helped out; sometimes he would excuse himself from a supervision at Chesterton Hall Crescent to deal with Ralph's crying.[2] He taught his supervision pupils at home, because he no longer had a college room. After the quarrel with Stanley and Joan Bennett, his connection with Emmanuel ceased. He was no longer a teaching officer of the English Faculty. In spite of *New Bearings in English Poetry*, his pamphlets and the work for *Scrutiny*, he was no more secure than ten years before.

Leavis's probationary lectureship ran out in October 1931. Not until 1936 did he gain a lectureship again, and then only a part-time one. He was kept on 'part work' until 1947, when he was over fifty years old, first facing his 'Six Years War' in the 1930s. Careers were difficult: even the admirable Tillyard was not elected to a fellowship at Jesus until 1933.

Before the 'Six Years War' Leavis had not been friendly with those he admired in Cambridge, young Empson and Richards. Leavis had his group of young contributors, affording floating friendships as they went to what work they could find in the Depression years. Leavis did, however, have one supporter at Emmanuel who proved to be the maker of his career. William L. Cuttle was a year younger than Leavis; he graduated from Emmanuel with Firsts in Classics in 1923. He then went to lecture at Bristol University and be head of a hall of residence. He returned to Emmanuel and became interested in Leavis's work, especially its sociological side, in spite of being a 'classic'. Leavis liked one of Cuttle's few published essays, 'The Story of Suburban London: A Possible Field for Research', an 'anthropologico-literary' title in tune with Leavis's Researcher's Club.[3] Cuttle was elected to a fellowship at Downing College, and there found Leavis some pupils to supervise, to make up for his losses at Emmanuel and St John's.

*

---

* This chapter covers roughly the same period (1931–1936) as the next, 'Guarding the Guardians', in which the focus is principally upon *Scrutiny* and literary journalism, rather than on matters of teaching.

Downing College looks like no other Cambridge college because of the expanse of its court and the fewness of its buildings. In 1931 it consisted of two short, sober terraces each with a classical portico at the end rising to the height of the range. They faced each other across a green at a distance of nearly a hundred metres. One portico was the front of the college Hall, the other of the Master's Lodge. The green, separating two neat rules of building in honey-coloured Ketton stone, resembles a campus in Virginia rather than in Cambridge, England. William Wilkins was the architect, designer of two famous British sites, the National Gallery in London and in Cambridge the Gothic screen that separates King's College from the street. Downing is in Wilkins's Attic style. The college is spacious to this day, although another range joins the original terraces. When Leavis began to take pupils from Downing, there was nothing at each end of the two ranges – the countrified hinterland was never developed by a college that was always short of funds.

In 1931 Downing could not even afford its annual ball.[4] The college was anxious to have more undergraduates and increase its academic reputation. Downing had only a few undergraduates, mostly reading law and medicine. In Cuttle they found a suitable young man, not an academic high-flyer, one who would set up relationships with the schools, care for undergraduates and encourage them to take subjects new to Downing like classics, modern languages, mechanical sciences, mathematics, architecture and the boom subject, English. Cuttle thought English would be good for Downing's diminished reputation. It was an inspired idea that Leavis, the supervisor with strong undergraduate allegiances and excellent results at Emmanuel, should work for Downing.* And Leavis was an athlete – there was college sport to think of. But in this he disappointed Cuttle, whose impressionability amused him: he treated Leavis as though he'd 'won the mile in the 1908 Olympics'.

Cuttle encouraged Downing to use Leavis as a supervisor. He was certainly not elected straightaway to the fellowship, but he was treated with some ceremony. A college Governing Body does not normally note the appointment of a supervisor, but the acquisition of Leavis was so recorded in June 1931. Six months later it was minuted that he had been appointed Director of Studies in English at a termly stipend of five guineas.[5] In May 1932 he was elected to membership of the high table.

---

* See Chapter Three, Exciting Strangeness, 'Precarious Terms 1928–1929', for Leavis's tripos results in 1927.

Shortly before that two scholarships were awarded to young men to read English who became Leavis's Downing lieutenants: R.G. Cox (Gordon Cox) and Geoffrey Walton. Both went on to research.[6] So Leavis had by 1933 his own freshman scholar and exhibitioner.

He remained a reasonably friendly colleague of Cuttle for many years. To him he was to dedicate *Education and the University: A Sketch for an 'English School'* (1943) with the rubric 'Collaboration, a matter of differences as well as agreements'. It was not an easy relationship: Leavis was exasperated by what he understood to be Cuttle's minor public school ways, but he was a reliable friend when Cuttle turned to drink in later years. In letters he was rather scornful of him; in person he was protective. Once a pupil, Tom Birrell, called Leavis on a bad night from a telephone box near the Fitzwilliam Museum to say he was in town and wondered if they could meet. He was surprised to be ordered peremptorily not to stray. Within minutes Leavis appeared through sheets of rain, his black bicycling cape glittering. He was covered with embarrassment to see he had mistaken the sound of 'Birrell' for 'Bill', whom he thought was drunk and stranded.[7] Bill Cuttle remained at Downing until shortly before his death at a Frinton nursing home in 1958.

In 1933 Downing began to use some of its endowment for scholarships and joined one of the federations of colleges that administered scholarship examinations, moving towards the setting of a special scholarship examination in English. The scholarship examination was one mechanism by which Leavis built up his own school of English inside Cambridge English.

The scholarship examination was a key feature of the Cambridge system, as important as a tripos, and possibly even more so. A tripos was related to the undergraduate population; the scholarship examination was a means of communication with the whole school population that had university aspirations. By means of it the colleges communicated with schools. So the scholarship examinations were a commanding presence in the world outside the university. These examination papers were published, thus making public statements of how the colleges defined their academic subjects. Of course, some subjects could not be presented in this form: it was not possible to have a pre-university examination in classical archaeology. But in English the material set at scholarship level and in the tripos was not so very different. The difference was in the level of sophistication and knowledge in the answers.

Each year the scholarship examination papers were published by Cambridge University Press, to be purchased by schoolmasters. Each year eighteen-year-olds travelled to stay in Cambridge for a week of examinations in chilly halls, to be interviewed by dons and shyly meet their peers – after which they waited for telegrams that were dispatched to the successful candidates. Lasting friendships were made during these visits. The scholarship examination was a rite of passage, both academic and social. It was a means by which Leavis could tell schools what he understood by English.

Such consciousness-raising could set problems. Material set in the examinations became available for use in schools. If one of Leavis's favourite exercises was set, then a school student could encounter it again in a Leavis lecture when he went up to Cambridge. It was even possible for a student to see a piece of writing in a scholarship examination, or study a piece at school for practice, from one of the scholarship back-papers, then encounter it again in the 'Criticism and Composition' paper of the English Tripos. The 1937 Downing 'Practical Criticism' paper asked students to compare 'Rise, said the Master', and 'Love Bade Me Welcome' by George Herbert. In 1944, when Leavis was examiner for Part One of the tripos, the same poem turned up in 'Literary Criticism: Passages for Comment', this time to be compared with William Blake's 'The Garden of Love'. In 1939 the scholarship paper gave Robert Browning's 'Meeting at Night', which later appeared in a tripos examination set by Leavis in 1949. During the war, some of the material used in Leavis's lectures appeared successively in the scholarship examination papers. The poems were Wordsworth's 'Surprised by Joy' and 'It is a Beauteous Evening', or Tennyson's 'Tears, Idle Tears', set for comparison with Lawrence's 'Piano'. The question inquired about how these poems handled a 'dangerous' theme, not easy for the candidate who did not know what Leavis (and Richards) thought about sentimentality.* In none of these cases was there the simple problem (or impropriety) of setting material twice, though one colleague (George Rylands) complained to this effect. Leavis replied that the best examples were the best examples. But there was the danger of a closed circuit in this proceeding, a circuit enjoyed by the knowing Downing undergraduates.

*

* See Chapter Two, English at Cambridge, 'Undergraduate and Postgraduate 1919–1924'.

Financially, the scholarship system was important. To go to Oxford or Cambridge cost about £220 a year, about the same as the starting salary of a Lecturer. College awards yielded only between £40 and £100, and free rooms in some colleges, but once awarded the scholar or exhibitioner was eligible for other help in the form of school-leaving scholarships or awards from city guilds. Later the Ministry of Education supplemented college awards. Award-holders thus had funds available outside the Cambridge system.[8]

Several federations of colleges pooled resources for setting and marking the annual diet of scholarship examinations. School students applied to one college, taking an examination common to the group to which the college belonged. In October 1934 Downing started to negotiate entry to the group consisting of Clare, Corpus Christi, King's, Magdalene, Trinity and Trinity Hall. This group did not have a separate English examination.[9] Leavis worried that joining would mean a loss of control over the examining process. He persuaded Downing to hold out for the right to set its own (that is, his) examination in English. In November 1934 the group admitted Downing. The arrangement was to start at the end of 1935.[10] Thenceforth four examinations a year were set: 'Shakespeare', 'English Literature after 1600', 'Practical Criticism' and 'Paraphrase and Comment'. A circular was prepared for inquiring schoolmasters, showing what was expected of candidates. It concluded:

MASTERS directing preparation in English will do well to have read *The Principles of Literary Criticism* and *Practical Criticism*, by I.A. Richards; *Seven Types of Ambiguity*, by W. Empson; *Selected Essays*, by T.S. Eliot; and *Determinations*, edited by F.R. Leavis.

When the first Downing English examinations were published a further means was established by which a Leavisian training could be carried through into the class-room; the booklet was handy for use as teaching material, especially the 'Practical Criticism' and 'Paraphrase and Comment' questions.*

By the end of 1933 Leavis, now Director of Studies at Downing, said he probably did for a living several times more teaching than anyone

---

* The chain of influence was not simply Leavis to schoolmaster to new pupil. Eric Mathieson, later an Anglo-Catholic priest and chaplain to the Royal National Theatre, wrote (12.9.91) that after he went up to Downing, from his tiny country grammar school, Lord William's School, Thame, he corresponded with Patrick Harrison, four years his junior, sending him the Leavis dating sheets.

else in Cambridge English, with the duties of a professor without the status and salary.[11] He still had no university post, but his group was establishing itself. By 1935 Gordon Cox and Geoffrey Walton had come through the system. In June 1935 Downing offered Cox a research studentship and Walton a research scholarship. It also made an award to another undergraduate who would join the *Scrutiny* group, Wilfrid Mellers.[12] After graduating, Gordon Fraser spent some time in Germany and thought of becoming a Cambridge don, but when he wanted to marry an American young woman, Katie Berriman, he realized how little he would earn. He would have noticed the difficulties of the Leavises, whose standard of living was not what he was used to in Leeds. He now had his excellent modern bookshop called 'Gordon Fraser' in Portugal Place, by St John's, backing on to the *Scrutiny* printing works. It was a Leavisian 'Minority Bookshop', with a well-lit picture gallery behind the showroom. Katie Berriman worked in the shop.[13] In April 1936 Lionel Knights took his Ph.D., with the basis of his first book, *Drama and Society in the Age of Jonson*. Leavis still had no salary.

At home there were incessant worries about the health of the infant Ralph; in the spring he was diagnosed as having coeliac disease, which meant that he was unable to digest fats. His weight went right down, and he needed expensive specialized nursing. In April 1935 there had to be journeys to London to hospital in Kennington. A 'massive dietary revolution' was recommended: 'My wife and I are worn out.' Leavis wrote that 'Ralph has had a dietetic revolution inflicted on him, and he has objected. We're finally dumping him in a specialist hospital for observation.' He had to be kept under constant observation and they could not afford a full-time nurse.[14]

In the summer of 1935 there was some hope of an appointment. Aubrey Attwater, near-invalided by the war, died in July, so a vacancy was advertised. It was George Rylands, six years Leavis's junior, who was appointed in December. Understandably so: his *Words and Poetry* was of some importance in Cambridge, and Rylands was an enthusiastic Shakespearean who took on a variety of lecture courses. He became, with F.L. Lucas, the second King's man of the English Faculty. Within a month of this appointment the Faculty lost another Lecturer, the soul of Cambridge English. Mansfield Forbes died on the night of 26 January 1936. He had earlier had a heart attack and was prescribed rest, now living downstairs at 'Finella'. He knew Gordon Fraser and had let out a room in 'Finella' to Katie Berriman, who was working in the bookshop. She returned home to be told by the housekeeper that Forbes had died suddenly. Gordon Fraser took over the arrangements. The next day Leavis arrived at the bookshop to insist that Katie Berriman come to stay at Chesterton Hall Crescent. He was afraid that because Katie was American there could be 'difficulties'.[15] Forbes's death created another vacancy. Leavis believed that Q had promised him the next post.

Forbes's academic field was idiosyncratic: roughly, romanticism and literary criticism, when not Scottish baronial architecture. Possibly it was a tribute to him that the Faculty deemed him directly irreplaceable, and sought a Lecturer who would replace another person who was retiring, Hilda Murray, 'daughter of the *Dictionary*', at Girton. Someone was needed to lecture on Anglo-Saxon and Middle English, so a lectureship for the period '1066 to the Reformation' was advertised. Very surprisingly, the successful applicant was Hugh Sykes Davies of St John's, a 'neo-romantic'. He was an original signatory to the English Surrealist group manifesto and had just appeared in the Faber *Surrealism* (1936) anthology. By 1936 Leavis had come to know Q better, referring his pupils with some wry pride to 'my friend Sir Arthur'.[16] With Q, Leavis allowed himself some indignation, to which Q replied that 'you don't know anything about medieval literature'. 'Neither does Sykes Davies,' replied Leavis. The gossip was that Sykes Davies said he could read it up in the summer vacation. Hilda Murray was thus replaced and the vacancy left by Forbes remained unfilled.

Immediately after the death of Forbes in January, Bill Cuttle tabled a report for the Downing fellows on English studies in the college. It recommended that a college lectureship in English be established and in March 1936 Leavis was offered such a post at £125 a year for three years. His duties were to be similar to those of a Director of Studies. It was made a condition that the post would lapse if he were appointed to a university lectureship. Downing was not keen to fund lectureships. Under the new Faculty system, it thought the provision of Lecturers could be left to the university.[17] However, it was not taking a great risk. Forbes's position was unfilled and Leavis looked a strong candidate. The Governing Body may have reasoned that if Downing demonstrated its support, his chance of a university lectureship was enhanced. Once appointed, Downing could recoup the salary he had been offered.[18]

This was not quite what happened. In May a further English post was advertised – but only for a *part-time* lectureship. Arguably the Faculty was attempting to exclude Leavis, offering little and knowing that he was, for the time being, receiving roughly the same salary (counting supervision fees) as a college Lecturer at Downing.[19] Undeterred, Leavis applied for the post, and, in a memorandum to the English Faculty at Downing, pointed out that under Leavis English students had risen from two to over a dozen each year, with good examination results, and that Leavis had been appointed to a college lectureship. The college observed that it had no wish to set Leavis in opposition to the university, so his lectures would not be available to members of other colleges without the consent of the general board of the Faculty, a touch of diplomatic pressure. Would the university wish to *exclude* students from his lectures?[20]

During this summer Leavis was holidaying near Cromer in Norfolk. He believed Q would be up against Tillyard on the Faculty, whose appointments committee was to meet in the summer. He said he coached Q beforehand in the moves the 'arch-political boss' (E.M.W. Tillyard) would make. Leavis thought his rival was William Empson. 'Tillyard, I learnt to my astonishment, was running Empson: the meaning of the hobnobbing of Empson, Richards and Tillyard over these past eighteen months suddenly came home to me.'[21] On his birthday (14 July) Leavis heard that the meeting adjourned in deadlock:

That's better than I feared; it means the old man stuck to his guns, and at least some educational work will have been done ... They're giving me my money's worth of interest in life. I could do with a modicum of security instead.

Right at the beginning of the autumn term an exceptional meeting of the appointments committee was held, before Q was expected back in Cambridge from his beloved Fowey in Cornwall. Leavis telegrammed the professor, who enjoyed gallant action. As the committee convened, Q entered to say

Good afternoon, gentlemen. I see there is only one item on today's agenda, the appointment of a Lecturer. It's very simple. There is only one man outstandingly qualified: Dr F.R. Leavis. All those in favour? I see we are unanimous.[22]

On 20 October Leavis's appointment as a university Lecturer was announced, with the usual probationary period of three years, after which confirmation was to be expected. The post was to be 'part work'. The following summer Joan Bennett was offered a lectureship on similar terms, so the Forbes vacancy was filled by two part-time posts.[23] For Leavis, the appointment was 'a real finish to the Six Years War'.

The Lectureship is the cheapest thing they've got, but then, it's a footing ...
Downing are cock-a-hoop. Appointments are always for three years in the first
place. But they, I think, will hardly turn me out after this surrender. They
won't dare.[24]

At Christmas 1936 there was cause for celebration. As arranged,
Downing withdrew its lectureship for Leavis and elected him to a
fellowship. This occurred at almost the same time that his pupil Gordon
Cox was elected to a research fellowship, so there would be at Governing
Body meetings a team of three representing English studies (Leavis,
Cuttle and Cox) in a fellowship of only a dozen. There was also to be a
new Master, Admiral Sir Herbert William Richmond, formerly
Harmsworth Professor of Imperial and Naval History, a fellow of Jesus.
Leavis liked Richmond, calling him the 'old sea-dog'.[25]

On 22 December Leavis was admitted to the fellowship, just ahead of
Gordon Cox. Traditionally, the junior fellow handed round coffee after
dinner in hall, a duty falling to Cox, not Leavis, but only just. It
dramatizes Leavis's position to note that if the elections had differed by a
couple of weeks it would have been the other way about: Leavis would
have served his pupil. The new fellow was to receive an annual stipend
of £200 from the college as its Director of Studies, and a room was to
be found for him. The red, yellow and blue fittings were not to the taste
of the man who preferred furnishings from Heal's catalogue: 'Incompat-
ibly patterned curtains and sofa and chair covers. Unspeakable furniture.
Two windows and three doors, all varnished-and-grained.' But

it's all very good news, far better than anything I expected. Cuttle has worked
wonders. It's particularly pleasing to me to know that in my case the work will
be carried on at Downing – when I'm Professor, I mean.[26]

Downing College had reason to be pleased with the acquisition of
Leavis. During his pre-lectureship years he created a community of
students achieving excellent tripos results. In 1938 Downing took four
out of eight Firsts in Part One, noted by the *Observer* as 'a triumph for
what may be called the Downing School of Literature'.[27] In 1939 in Part
Two there were four Downing Firsts out of seven. Part One numbers
had dropped, but Downing took one out of the three Firsts. This did
not necessarily make Leavis popular in the Faculty: there was pressure
from undergraduates to go to him for supervision or from one of his
Downing lieutenants. But he was at last an official member of Cambridge

English. Not until eight months later was Joan Bennett appointed a Lecturer, also on 'part work'.

Downing English 1931–1936

When Leavis was first appointed as Downing supervisor in December 1931, he did all the English teaching. He was not relieved of this until his two pupils, Geoffrey Walton and Gordon Cox, became graduate students and so could take supervisions. Gordon Cox's arrival as an undergraduate was typical. Having taken the scholarship examination, the telegram went to his home in Grantham, he saw the announcement (inaccurate) of his award in *The Times*, and then got a letter from 'a man calling himself W.L. Cuttle' saying 'he is going to be my tutor and won't it be fun'. From Leavis followed 'one of the most badly written letters I have ever seen' with a reading-list that included Richards, Empson and Eliot. Cox hardly knew what hit him, when confronted with what he called this 'clearing-up operation' of critics whose

cool rational analysis deflated all the vague and facile assumptions implicit in much of the critical writing of the day, with its too easy recourse to ideas of inspiration or revelation and its constant entanglement with what Richards called 'bogus entities'.[28]

Up at Downing, Cox observed that Leavis taught daily from 9 a.m. to 1 p.m., and occasionally in the afternoon. He was to be seen dining frequently in hall; he bought a dinner suit for Founder's Feasts. His manner was cheery; Geoffrey Walton remembered him as 'matey'. He enjoyed piquant literary chat, 'chortling' even about Proust's Baron de Charlus. Sometimes Leavis set essays on single poems or groups of them, often using Q's *Oxford Book of English Verse* or ordinary essay topics like the following:[29]

The difficulties facing Milton in writing *Paradise Lost*.
  For what reasons is Donne regarded as important today?
  How does Marvell's *Dialogue between Resolved Soul and Created Pleasure* differ from Milton's *Comus*?
  Without a knowledge of *The Tatler* and *The Spectator* one cannot understand the Eighteenth Century.
  Comic relief in *Hamlet*.
  Chaucer in spirit, taste and technique is composite, both bourgeois and courtly.

Wordsworth's poetry is the reality: his philosophy is the illusion.
Our sage and serious Spenser.
We cannot call a man's work superficial where it is the creation of a world.
Greek tragedy is very different from anything that we mean by drama.[30]

From 1936, with Cox and Walton to help him, Downing English became a group practice, and was known as such to generations of students. Downing English was never simply Leavis, though it may have appeared to be so to those who came into the group tutorials from other colleges. The Downing system meant having Leavis for group work or seminars (Leavis disliked the word), which mainly consisted of Leavis talking, supplemented by weekly supervisions (one or two-to-one) for essay-writing, taken by a young academic, often a graduate student. As a teacher Leavis was always complemented by other supervisors. In the late 1930s Dennis Enright was taught by James Smith as well as Leavis and relished the contrast, one deliberate, one tentative; it is, after all, one style of teaching to be vulnerable. Enright wrote a poem after the death of Gordon Cox that conveys the 'feel' of the college when Cox was a research fellow. The language of the poem is not in code, but some of its words would be wryly the more appreciated by 'Downing men' than others: 'fine distinctions', 'authority' and 'modesty' are Downing English terms. On the other hand, Downing English was a little school of sensibility. It is sometimes said that the Leavisian way was attractive to students because it cut down the reading-list necessary for English studies. A more important attraction was its readiness to encourage sensitiveness of response. The point was once put pejoratively by Peter Ackroyd, who remarked acidly that there was a certain *fin de siècle* delight in sensibility in Leavis. Enright's poem captures the mood of a group of Leavisian greenhorns (doing the characteristic thing: hanging around the quadrangle at a staircase end).

In Memoriam R. G. C.

What (hardly his best) I best remember – not
The essays on The Great Reviews in *Scrutiny*
But the matter of the little bat
That we happened on, hurt and twitching weakly
At the bottom of a staircase in the quad,
Like a creature struck by fine distinctions.

> Someone should put it out of its misery
> As educated people would agree,
> But we were all so bloody tender
> (And I had been reading *Dracula*) –
> Then he came by, for some our supervisor,
> Soon to join the Friends' Ambulance Unit.
>
> Not famous as a friend of Chiroptera
> But famously anxious and kind-hearted,
> Older and wiser, a College officer.
> He pulled a face as we led him to the spot.
>
> One purblind peep, and the bat arose hangdog
> And teetered off. It recognized authority.
> Like Lazarus! we said: which grieved his modesty.[31]

Downing English had its network of social ties. A don's wife was expected to meet 'the men' at least once a year: Q.D.L. did so much more frequently, with Friday afternoon teas at Chesterton Hall Crescent, where undergraduates enjoyed home baking, ample sandwiches, plates of boiled eggs and Players cigarettes passed round, though the hostess warned they could cause infertility. (There was a theory behind Q.D.L.'s lavish provender: she believed that each time there was a world war English housewives took the opportunity to reduce the number and choice of meal-time courses they served.)[32] In college there was the Doughty Society founded in 1934 by Leavis and Cuttle 'to encourage the study of literature in all its branches, classical and modern'. Contrary to later popular belief, Leavis never wanted to narrow his pupils' repertoire of reading: 'Cultivate promiscuity,' he would say.[33] For thirty years the Doughty Society was a platform for Leavisian speakers. At an early meeting L.H. Myers, the novelist favoured by *Scrutiny*, spoke on 'The Function of Literature'. Downing men spoke with (ironical) awe of the elegance of the novelist in his Melton overcoat. Out of college there was a Leavisian presence in literary Cambridge, with Gordon Cox as 'The Skipper' in *The Granta* in 1934. He provided back-up for Leavis, reviewing both *Coleridge on Imagination* and *Determinations*.[34]

Cox and Walton did well in the tripos and went on to research on Leavisian themes. Cox took forward *Fiction and the Reading Public*, working on 'The Great Reviews', the Victorian periodicals mentioned by Enright in his poem, eventually submitting his Ph.D. just before the outbreak of war. Walton wanted to follow through Leavis's interest in the transition from Donne, with its 'mechanism of sensibility' able to assimilate Aquinas and the smell of cooking, to Dryden and after. He worked on Abraham Cowley, who was called by Leavis the 'Aldous Huxley of the seventeenth century'. His doctoral dissertation was on the 'urbane note' in seventeenth-century poetry, issuing in *Metaphysical to Augustan* (1955). Cox was supervised by Q, 'between the two Q's', Leavis said, because Q.D.L. could not resist participation in work on periodicals and readerships. Walton went to Tillyard.* The 'anthropologico-literary' work continued, and also did so at an important but less academically high-flying level among some of the 1930s Downing men. John Spalding Bell went up in 1935 and after war service trained as a coal-face worker, at the same time researching mining folksong, contributing to A.L. Lloyd's *Come All Ye Bold Miners*. Bell, an expert on industrial injury benefit, became a leading member of the General and Municipal Workers' Union. A year after Cox and Walton the group was joined by Wilfrid Mellers, another graduate available as a supervisor; he reviewed for *The Granta* and became *Scrutiny's* main contributor on music. To enable him to continue his studies after English for the Bachelor of Music degree, Cuttle paid his fees; and he became a lodger at Chesterton Hall Crescent. The undergraduates remembered a performance of his 'Homage to Ginger Rogers' at the Doughty Society, and how once, during a supervision, he played a piano piece based on Shelley's *Prometheus Unbound*. 'Here's where they rip out his liver,' he explained.

At this time it was possible for English Tripos candidates to submit an optional dissertation for Part Two. Leavis, disliking three-hour 'stand-and-deliver' examinations, encouraged his pupils to submit work, so most Downing men did one. Walton's work on Cowley began as a dissertation piece. These pieces were also a route into *Scrutiny*, access to which was certainly not only for graduates or post-doctoral students. An important part in Leavis's role was to blur differences of rank. Because he made schoolmasters so aware of what was expected at Downing, his students often came up having already taken the equivalent of a freshman year in the sixth form. And the distinction between undergraduate and graduate was elided. One man who had a Downing training at school

* Cox joined the Friends' Ambulance Unit for the war and spent much of his subsequent career at Manchester University. Walton first taught in Wales, then in Africa after the war.

was Boris Ford, who went up in 1935, having been a pupil of Denys Thompson at Gresham's. He wrote an undergraduate essay on *Wuthering Heights* that was actually published in *Scrutiny* (March 1939) before he took his finals. When he thought of submitting the optional essay for the tripos, Leavis suggested that he put in this essay. Should he type it out again? No, said Leavis, just send in a marked copy of the *Scrutiny* in which it appeared. So two months before the tripos, Ford did so. Dennis Enright's essay on Ben Jonson in *Scrutiny* (December 1940) originated in an essay he wrote for James Smith.

The work of the pupils flowed into *Scrutiny*; Leavis shaped his position by means of them. There was a prominent young American at Downing, perhaps the most important of Leavis's pupils, but, curiously, hardly known as one. Marius Bewley proved to be one of 'the men' closest to Leavis. His book on American fiction, *The Complex Fate*, showed on the title-page that it was 'With an Introduction and Two Interpolations by F.R. Leavis'. Leavis always spoke of Bewley with affection.

Eugene Augustine Marius Bewley went up to Downing in 1937 at the age of twenty-one, having been originally destined for the priesthood. His talk, especially with other Catholics (Bewley had lapsed), was laced with theological and liturgical allusion.[35] Like Eliot, he was from St Louis, Missouri. He was supervised by James Smith, also Catholic. He spent several years in Cambridge, taking a First in Part Two. He left Downing at the outbreak of war, returning in 1949 to write a Ph.D. under Leavis's supervision. *The Complex Fate* (1952) consisted principally of material from *Scrutiny* about James and Hawthorne. Leavis respected Bewley's work. When Empson wrote in to *Scrutiny* to defend *Coleridge on Imagination*, Leavis afforded him only a telegrammatic reply; for Bewley's essays on James and Hawthorne he wrote a careful reply, followed by a rejoinder, and then an introduction to *The Complex Fate*.

Bewley's first contribution to *Scrutiny* was in autumn 1939, a review of a book about poetry and society criticizing the supposed Richards–Leavis idea that civilization depended on a minority 'whose only business was to live finely and preserve it from every vulgar contact'; and he was allowed to publish a 'revaluation' of Coleridge in the following year. On the minority theory, Bewley retorted (of course) that the role of the Leavisian elite was not to withdraw fastidiously but to apply 'relevant and discriminating value judgements'. It could have been said by any young Leavisian. But Bewley was unusual, stylish in manner and in erudition. He did not supervise undergraduates, but gave papers to the

Doughty Society; he socialized and knew some of the Downing men well, especially those of the post-war years, like Patrick Harrison, Karl Miller and David Adams. Bewley was for Adams the Leavisian

of whom I have the tenderest memories. Despite the distinction he had attained, he would treat you as an equal. He didn't just go through the motions. In addition he based himself on something better than the puritanism of the others. To cap it all, in my view he was the only one of Leavis's pupils who could write. He seemed to have taken something from the Baroque writers who were his second love.

Bewley dressed in black, including raincoat in summer and overcoat in winter, with red muffler and broad-brimmed hat, alluding both to the priesthood and the sombrero. A chance encounter with Patrick Harrison in October 1949 led to a walk round the Botanic Garden, where the sight of a large orange pumpkin 'among the sodden autumn wreckage made him feel homesick'. They went on to the Fitzwilliam, where Harrison persisted in explaining late Cézanne in the face of Bewley's reticent dissent, only later learning that Bewley knew as much about painting as he did about John Donne. He had been during the war years the curator at the Guggenheim, and knew Peggy Guggenheim well. Bewley's tact was characteristic. In speech he was 'rhetorical, formal, elaborately wrought' in a way that Harrison thought derived in part from old styles of courtesy still surviving in some regions of America. His delivery was charming and his manner combined 'the rhetoric of W.C. Fields and the suavity of the Hollywood/English movie-actor George Arliss, though late at night there could be screams of rage over God's treatment of cats'. He was alleged to have been Tennessee Williams's secretary.[36] Leavis enjoyed talking to his pupils about him, with mock awe at the memory of Bewley removing bottles by wheelbarrow after a party.

   Detail is liable to make Bewley a 'character', which he was, being glamorous, assured and exotic to post-war Downing. In the United States he was also, to some degree, alienated: a Catholic (and Democrat) member of the East Coast intelligentsia. He was also homosexual, in his own language an 'Athenian', or in that of the time 'not the marrying sort'. He lived with Garry Mackenzie, an illustrator of children's books, and did not involve undergraduates in his love-life. The social oddity of Leavis, his own family not long away from the Fens, could be said to match that of Bewley, though not resemble it. There was an affinity in their unclassifiability. Arguably, it was part of the Leavis mystique (not a consciously constructed part) for his social role to be inexplicable.

Bewley in another sense belonged; he was not an exotic tolerated in the Leavis camp, a Cavalier enlisted on the side of Cromwell. Karl Miller later argued that Bewley was not anomalous but had a proper place among Leavisians, a logical right to be there. He interestingly cited the exaggerated punctilio with which Leavis referred to Tillyard and other Cambridge enemies, always *Dr* Tillyard or *Master* of Jesus's. Leavis was being correct with undergraduates, the polite reference preparing the way for a jibe. Miller suggested that Leavis's mistering and doctoring served to point up his view that Cambridge English was all-too-respectable. The Faculty may have ruled Cambridge English and so in that sense it was the majority party. But it was, of course, in the republic of letters at large a distinct minority, and the proprieties of Leavis's sarcasm showed, according to Miller, 'misters and doctors of a minority culture whose values were to serve as an example and a rebuke'. That Cambridge group, the ruling 'coterie' (Leavisian word), was actually rather *dis*reputable: a class of literary enthusiasts should have no time for professional correctness. How distant was Tillyard from the intelligentsia Leavis wanted, that poet-led intelligentsia I.A. Richards had long since vaunted as a hope for the modern world. Leavis's desired intelligentsia was not one of scholarly amenity and pedagogic decorum. Rather, it should enact the qualities he found in the young Empson: intelligence and sensibility. It should be Shelleyan (if in the vein of Shelley in 'Peter Bell the Third'). In such an intelligentsia Marius Bewley had a rightful place, a more natural place, perhaps, than some familiar Downing types. Miller wrote that 'it was never really all that scandalous, therefore, that one of his pupils should have looked more like some man of letters, about town in the 1890s, than any kind of soldier or devotee of the open air'.

At the centre of the Leavisian group it appeared as if there was always an idiosyncratic figure, often one with a specialism distant from Leavis's. There was Bewley and Wilfrid Mellers; later there was Morris Shapira, and later still Michael Tanner, with whom Leavis in his last years debated about literary criticism and philosophy. In each was the element of eccentricity, distant both from the Tillyardian dignity of the ruling academic minority and the confident 'application of serious standards' of a Denys Thompson. Leavis appears to have had a temperamental need for such people, those who earned more respect than the decent crew of schoolmasters and educational administrators, though the relationship to both sides was variable. Bewley believed Leavis could not resist the flattering orthodoxy of less independent pupils, like Robin Mayhead: 'I think his recent reviews in *Scrutiny* [1951–2] are not only depressingly unoriginal in every respect, but exhibit – rather quietly – some rather unamiable characteristics.'[37] (Mayhead was later embarrassed by his Leavisite phase and did not want some of his reviews in the reprint of *Scrutiny*.) It was not only Bewley's sociable charm that gave him an honoured place in the group; he earned it more by virtue of an eloquent sensitivity much esteemed by Leavis. When Leavis debated with him about James's *What Maisie Knew*, it was about a piece by Bewley imbued with a quality that in *this* case Leavis actually disowned. Here Bewley was the man of sensibility and Leavis the one of sense. Leavis interpreted James matter-of-factly. Bewley expressed shock at what he thought was a spectacle of seeping evil; Leavis expressed only distaste. In this case it was not the master but the pupil who was attracted to 'shift, flow and merge . . . no whither as opposed to a way':

The essence of Mr Leavis's and my disagreement is this: that for me the comedy has something of the infernal about it. I am reluctant to mention a masterpiece like *Maisie* in the same breath with Sartre's *Huis Clos*, and yet the men and women who people Maisie's adult world, parasitically feeding on each other's vices, and trapped in each other's orbits, generate for me that kind of atmosphere with an intensity beyond anything in Sartre's range.

For Bewley, the little heroine Maisie was saved from something more dank and sinister than Leavis saw in the novel. A devious, undulating quality was discerned by Bewley – but this quality would not have been detected *but for* Leavis. Leavis possessed contradictory, appreciative drives, to the undulating and to the sharp-edged: their conflicting claims caused tension (even confusion) at times, for example, in his account of Dickens's *Hard Times*. Miller was surely right that Leavis favoured a 'bohemianism' that was an index of originality; he favoured the outsider, an award of support that had a special edge when his undergraduates lived in a college that could on occasion be terrorized by the Boat Club, which was capable of giving the arty Miller himself a dowsing, or could threaten an anti-Suez political meeting involving Downing English men (Leavis offered a hand, remarking that he could be useful in a rough-house). Leavis stood up for unorthodox pupils, seriously defending one man in the late 1950s who was in danger of being sent down for a 'criminal' (sexual) act. On the other hand, his correct social manners were of a piece with the courtesy many noted in him, not an altogether usual quality in academic life where dons (say, Graham Hough) had the licence to be eccentrically blunt. Leavis looked the bohemian part, but he had a drive to a respectability of his own. Q.D.L. joked that it was all high thinking and plain living at Chesterton Hall Crescent, but, of course, it *was*, and had to be, during two wars ('Six Years War' with the Faculty; the real world war) of family suffering. The Leavises disliked equally the worlds of the Woolfs and Scott Fitzgerald; they pilloried the latter for seeming not to possess a 'sense of even the elementary decencies that one had thought of as making civilized intercourse possible ... There is nothing in his writings to contradict what we know of his life.' This judgement of astonishing severity was made by Leavis in his introduction to *The Complex Fate*. It was a warning shot at Bewley, the man he liked so much. It signalled that Leavis would not cross the frontiers of bohemia – except into the vividly unconventional and evaluative world of the prose of D.H. Lawrence's letters. Bewley affectionately recognized the way that Leavis worked within his barriers. In the 1950s Karl Miller visited Bewley when he was teaching at the Catholic University in Washington. Bewley remarked then that he always thought that 'Leavis was something of an Athenian at heart.' He probably meant by this that Leavis possessed qualities of sensibility and a delicacy of spirit more commonly found in the 'Athenian' world than outside it; for he tended half jokingly to say of any man he really liked that he *must* be an Athenian at heart.*

As Leavis's teaching load grew he began to run larger groups, something between a lecture and a supervision, for Downing men and others, sometimes attended by Q.D.L. In the university English Club, in which Boris Ford was a leading member, there was sharp dissatisfaction with Cambridge English teaching and the curriculum. One group of people wrote a critique of the examinations and proposed that a practical criticism paper be introduced. Another suggested fewer lectures and large-group teaching in 'seminars'. An experimental meeting was mounted in the Downing Music Room, Leavis to lead. He based the

* According to Harrison. Although Bewley was offered a fellowship at King's, he returned to America in 1952 because Garry Mackenzie, as a naturalized American (originally Canadian), would lose his citizenship if he stayed longer. Bewley settled in Staten Island. He taught at Wellesley, Fordham, Connecticut and Rutgers, and joined the editorial board of the *Hudson Review* in 1966. He died in 1973.

class on Isaac Rosenberg's 'Dead Man's Dump', which he rendered broodingly both at the beginning and the end of the session. Boris Ford took the English Club proposal to Tillyard, chairman of the English Faculty. He was curt with it.[38]

Leavis's History 1936

By the time he got his lectureship in 1936 Leavis had published two books, *New Bearings in English Poetry* (1932), which summed up his readings in the poetry in the 1920s, and *Revaluation: Tradition and Development in English Poetry* (1936), which was his 'Downing' book, drawing on the material he used for teaching at Downing from 1931 and from the reviewing he did for *Scrutiny*. When he lost his probationary position he could have gone on giving freelance lectures, but he chose to do so for only the first of his years in the wilderness. He gave one term of his usual course on 'Prose, with Passages for Criticism' and throughout the year his lectures for the Ordinary Degree in literature from 1611 to 1700, an elementary series he had done since 1929. But he also gave a set altogether for one term after Christmas: 'Tradition and Development in English Poetry (with Texts)'. Students were asked to bring Q's *Oxford Book of English Verse* and Grierson's anthology of metaphysical poetry to the first lecture. The lectures given in those two terms were the foundation of *Revaluation*.

Treating the span of English poetry from metaphysical poetry to the Romantics was not at that time associated with Leavis. He was deliberately increasing his range. He had begun his lecturing career as an 'eighteenth-century man', then moving to literary criticism and contemporary poetry. Now he was turning to the historic stream of English poetry, using the lectures to establish new bearings in older English poetry. When his book came out some critics commented on the 'modernity' of *Revaluation*, with its clean design and austere paper bookjacket, a design on it of judicial scales and rust-and-scarlet letterpress, both spiky. (The design looks more like a sextant than scales; it would have been better if it actually was one.) The arrangement of the book was unusual: seven chapters on poetry from Donne to Keats, but each chapter having brief additional sections of verse and prose supplementing the main argument. Originally Leavis called them 'appendices', changing this to 'Notes', as in A.C. Bradley's *Shakespearean Tragedy*, at the publisher's injunction. Leavis said he was 'loath to spoil the tension of the essays by meddling very much', like a lecturer who does not want to interrupt the flow of his discourse with too many slides. The idea of the 'Notes' was consonant with Pound's *How to Read*, which was definitely a modernist propaganda paper with plenty of subheadings. The method of *Revaluation* owes something to Herbert Read's *English Prose Style* (1930), a combination of guide-book and anthology.

In the preface to *New Bearings in English Poetry* Leavis apologized for a certain curtness: 'I notice that in any case the necessities of compression have led sometimes (especially in the second chapter) to effects that might be found ironical.' *Revaluation* is even more compressed, and this was noticed particularly by one of Leavis's readers, René Wellek, a Czech scholar, called by Leavis 'very intelligent', then working at the Cambridge School of Slavonic Studies; he later became a leading historian of literary criticism. Wellek admired the book but was puzzled by it. This highly evaluative work, showing that some modes of poetry could be developed and others were dead ends, had no theory of evaluation and did not explain its criteria of evaluation. Then, also, Leavis did not relate the meaning of poems to the known beliefs of the poet. In his essay on Joyce and the 'revolution of the word' Leavis wanted to make the reader aware of what was 'behind' words. In *Revaluation* he was similarly concerned with what was behind words, but not what was behind a poet, in terms of ideas or beliefs, nor with what was behind *himself* in his critical practice. His aim was for everything to be implied by description but especially by quotation; valuation he wanted to be 'irresistible'. So Leavis evaluated, but did so without explaining his norms. He explained to Wellek in *Scrutiny* that he *could* have explained that he wanted, or was looking for, this or that (say, 'concreteness'). But he believed that spelling out requirements was untrue to what happened between reader and text. Noticing *is* valuing – though for 'noticing' Leavis uses a term with a double-meaning, *realizing*. The reader, by participation, both notices and makes what is real in the text, invited to make it so because of the way in which language is energized.* 'Words in poetry invite us, not to "think about" and judge but to "feel into" or "become" – to realize a complex experience that is given in the words.' Wellek was bewildered. 'As to [my] enumeration

---

* Pound's *How to Read*; see Chapter Six, *Scrutiny*: Guarding the Guardians, 'Guardians: Empson, Pound, Lawrence 1932–1933'.

of your criteria which you consider clumsy and inadequate, they are, of course, absolutely literal quotations from your book, though, I admit, torn out of their context. But to keep their context would have meant transcribing your book.'

To which Leavis replied gnomically in a footnote: 'I must thank Dr Wellek for making my point in so flattering a way.'[39] He meant it. It *was* truly flattering to be read so, when Leavis wanted his criteria to be incarnate in his discourse. His book was not to be about a complex of qualities (of mind in poetry), but to *have* those qualities. Leavis wanted his examples to 'find their bearings with regard to one another' almost of their own accord. The pursuit of economy was not so much literary egotism as its opposite.

Revaluation was dealt with appreciatively by some reviewers. *The Times Literary Supplement* called it 'wise and suggestive' in a feature across three columns whose title cleverly went to the heart of Leavis's argument: 'The Norm of English Poetry: Intelligence and Sincerity in Unity'. Richard Church continued to grumble ('repellent' prose). Low-browism flourished in the *Saturday Review* ('word-mongering'). It may seem strange to record the response of the weeklies: but there were in England few organs for the academic intelligentsia. The situation was not quite Fleet-Street-or-nothing, but close to it. That there was no serious press for such a publication, no 'professional' press, was part of the problem that Leavis defined when he wrote of 'standards' or that Q.D.L. etched dramatically in *Fiction and the Reading Public*. There was no word from Cambridge. But there was considered study from abroad in the form of an admirable essay by Herbert Davis in Canada.[40]

What of Eliot's *Criterion*? That was where criticism mattered to Leavis. In a sense he had enacted in *Revaluation* the work of criticism as Eliot had defined it in 'Tradition and the Individual Talent'. Eliot said that when the new, the really new, work of art arrived, 'the *whole* existing order must be, if ever so slightly, altered'. Leavis wanted to show how the 'existing order', the familiar canon, looked different in 1936, Eliot himself having interjected the 'really new' into the system. *Revaluation* was therefore a tacit tribute to Eliot, 'applied Eliot', as it were. But the treatment it received in the *Criterion* was a bad disappointment. Eliot gave *Revaluation* for review to the twenty-six-year-old Stephen Spender – who ridiculed it. The choice of reviewer looks a little odd. Eliot could have engaged a university man, like Bonamy Dobrée, or Mario Praz, whom he much admired, or even James Smith, whose closeness to the Cambridge scene did not bar him from being reviewer of Empson for the *Criterion*. He could even have reviewed the book himself. Perhaps the fact that he did not do so created an unspoken (and unspeakable) disappointment for Leavis. None the less, Eliot's choice of Spender need not at all be construed as mischievous; there may have been a non-malicious logic in his choice of reviewer. On the face of it Spender could have appeared close to Leavis, a voice from a world of youth; despite the actual disparity of their ages Leavis appeared to be speaking for a young generation. Spender had some Leavisian concerns: he was author of *The Destructive Element* (1935), on modernism from Henry James onwards down to Eliot himself. Eliot may have believed that it was neatly fitting to have a poet review a treatment of poetry that was written from the point of view of contemporary poetry. Leavis was after all trying to show past poetry as it now looked from the vantage point of the 'really new' (or what had been new fifteen years before). Furthermore, Leavis could have been understood by Eliot to be 'humanist'; and Spender was respectably secular, from a Liberal family (which also had Jewish connections): Eliot, a sensitive observer of surfaces, may have felt that in some ways Spender and Leavis were two of a kind.

If Eliot was trying to fit the reviewer to the book, he failed, for in the event Spender's notice was drastically unsympathetic. He dismissed Leavis as politically uninteresting, a 'personal reactions' man who wrote 'dull and cumbrous prose'. He professed himself bewildered by Leavis's analysis of Shelley's 'When the Lamp is Shattered', attacking as 'an incursion into psychology' Leavis's demonstration that Shelley was in this poem 'in love with himself' (or masturbatory, was the implication). Adjudicating Spender on Leavis on Shelley, it is hard not to favour Leavis in the detection of a peculiar shift in the last stanza of 'When the Lamp is Shattered' in which it appears that the poet tenderly sympathizes with a love-lorn woman (if 'the frailest' in the third stanza means woman), but then shades into 'self-pathos'. His argument was only in part that poetic self-pity was embarrassing; mainly he showed distaste at a slide from one type of pity (for someone else) into another (for oneself). He certainly was taking issue with Shelley on moral grounds, but his objection was to an effect created by Shelley's poetics. (And he was not, as Spender implied, making a point about Shelley's sexuality.)

Interestingly, Spender's roughest judgement of *Revaluation* illustrated a common difficulty with Leavis, at the beginning of his career and much later (perhaps lasting to this day): the difficulty of defining

Leavis's place in the republic of letters. Was he an academic? Or a critic? Or a journalist? 'Dr Leavis seems not so much an example of the poet turned critic because he cannot write poetry as of the critic turned Lecturer and don because he cannot write criticism.'[41] Only *The Times Literary Supplement* and René Wellek took the book earnestly: good deeds in a naughty world.[42]

Milton and Shakespeare 1937

In the spring of 1937 Leavis published an essay on Henry James in *Scrutiny*, which has some touches of Q.D.L. in it, giving, for instance, a reading-list at the end. After Spender's *The Destructive Element* there was an obligation to cope with James in *Scrutiny*, but the essay was desultory, connected to indefinite plans for collaborative work on fiction with Q.D.L. During 1937 Leavis went on struggling with 'Authority and Method'.[43] His main work this year was two exhilarated essays, defences or apologias, one of Milton and one of the Shakespearean hero Othello. Now he was a fellow of Downing and a university Lecturer, Leavis was writing rather triumphantly.

Leavis never set himself up as a Shakespeare critic. In 1936 he reacted to the possibility of lecturing on Shakespeare as if it were a cheek: '*Me* – on Shakespeare!' But he did plan (pertinently) an essay on *Timon of Athens*, never written, and now wrote 'Diabolic Intellect, or, the Sentimentalist's *Othello*', the first of several oblique sorties into Shakespeare. A later essay was a vehicle for some of his basic concerns. This was 'Tragedy and the "Medium"', published seven years later; its origins were in 1936 because it was a response to an essay in *Scrutiny* of that year by George Santayana that Leavis had long pondered.*

No other British university had 'Tragedy' in its curriculum, whether in or out of English literature. 'Tragedy' was a Cambridge construct, provoking for English faculty dons, or consoling them if they had started out in the Classical Tripos, like F.L. Lucas or Tillyard. Q had a regular evening seminar on tragedy. Leavis thought the Aristotelian words ('catharsis', 'hamartia') meant either too little or too much. None the less, the subject could not be avoided. 'There's no such thing as

---

* See Chapter Seven, Wartime, 'Language and Tragedy 1944'.

"tragic philosophy", but there is an aura of associations with a dark centre portended by that word "tragic" or we wouldn't use it: a conceptual nebula with a composite nucleus.'

Leavis's essay on *Othello* proved influential, but even during his lifetime it was hardly known that Leavis had ideas about tragedy, except to his pupils. Much of what Leavis said was tentative: that Greek tragedy *cannot* be discussed as achieved, created art; that it *cannot* be translated; that English readers had *no* parallel concepts to place against the Greek. He believed some dramas had been recuperated: Sophocles's *Antigone* could be understood, by means of Hegel. And *Oedipus at Colonus* was clearly 'a most impressive product of European civilization', greater than *Oedipus Rex* ('thrilling drama, a masterpiece in *that* sense'). But it could not stand up to the power of Shakespeare, or to the great novelists, notably George Eliot in her use of the nemesis theme in the story of Mrs Transome in *Felix Holt*.

Greek drama had to be worked on, Leavis said, but much of the work was 'delicately amplifying one's agnosticism about it'. On Shakespeare, he was almost as cautious. Of *King Lear* he was 'not prepared to say anything'. It is something 'so spreading and complex': the 'desperate' Shakespeare is certainly there. The 'glory' of *Antony and Cleopatra* was its problem: it exalts, but how? Yes, the glory *is* 'alcoholic', but 'alcohol is there in life'. 'It's a great force in the world: is the clue in Burns?' In *Antony and Cleopatra* there is no sex, no *passion* or sin, as in *Phèdre*. Yet in Racine there is less sense of gender than in Shakespeare, and so less of love. If the tragedies were really problem plays, a play much vaunted for its problems may be better considered tragic: *Measure for Measure* 'isn't formally tragic, but is really a tragedy. Angelo is a representative figure: he is you or me.'[44] The plays to which Leavis returned frequently were *Macbeth* and *Othello*. *Macbeth* was his prototype of a Shakespearean tragedy, a play 'comparatively simple' but in which the cosmic and the day-to-day knitted 'wonderfully' together. Both protagonists, Macbeth and Othello, were performers of themselves in their own dramas. Leavis's pupils remember his own performance in classes of the death of Othello:

> Set you down *this*.
> And say besides, that in Aleppo once,
> Where a malignant and a turban'd Turk
> Beat a Venetian and traduced the state,

> I took by the throat the circumcised dog
> And smote him *thus!*★

At which Leavis would drive a fist to his lower thorax, his chin jutting. The tutorial performance of Othello was affectionate, not reductive, and the commentary was down to earth. If Othello did smite a circumcised Turk in Aleppo, how did he get away from Syria with his life? Did it ever happen? Or was Othello remembering a part he once *acted*?

Leavis observed, without embarrassment, the subject of *Othello*. Sexual passion consumes the Moor, not the sentiment to which A.C. Bradley, with Edwardian *pudeur*, warmed. Leavis showed that the catastrophe is brought on by sex, not by the intellect of Iago, diabolic or otherwise. But this, however, did not make Leavis see less heroism. On the contrary, the pity was the greater. His essay defended this drama of solitary obsession, and is in some ways similar to the defence he mounted in the same year of Milton, who possessed a character as wilful and solitary as Othello. 'In Defence of Milton' is an apologia for the poet against demeaning scholarship (Tillyard's), as 'Diabolic Intellect' was a defence of Othello against Bradley: the essays protected Shakespeare and Milton from their friends.

Leavis has not been recognized for defending Milton or defending Othello, the figure and the play. It is true that there was a negative element in his accounts, that Milton invented a style that 'denied itself the life of the living language' and that Othello did not die in a state of better knowledge of himself (not having 'learned through suffering'). But in both cases he thought that commentary had invoked unnecessary exculpation: Tillyard explained Milton's style (what he was 'trying to do') and Coleridge excused the passion of the Moor (manipulated by the diabolic Iago). Leavis wanted to show, by contrast, forms of heroism in the poet and the Moor. Milton's nature was, in the last analysis, well understood by tradition as 'a lonely genius, maintaining in his age an aloof and majestic self-sufficiency'. In his last moments Othello may not have known more about himself, but it was no poor thing to be the self he was, simple but magnificent. He died 'belonging to the world of action in which his true nature lay'. This is not to say there is glamour, because the most painful thing in *Othello* is that the play shows what is common to all, *lack* of self-knowledge. 'Its "painfulness is too near to life"'.[45] Self-knowledge may be a good, but it can be ethically greedy to

★ Italics to convey Leavis's stresses.

require it in a fiction; an audience does not have a right to moral afflatus. In the case of both Milton and *Othello*, Leavis took plain views, rejecting what commentators imported to bring the literature up to scratch. Tillyard described a donnish and rather dull Milton who followed seventeenth-century poetic practices, to be appreciated by the student who knows the period. But scholarship, said Leavis, turned Milton into a mundane member of 'his age'.

A.C. Bradley defended the horrors of *Othello* by passing responsibility for Desdemona's death across to Iago. Leavis is blunter: Othello was sexually jealous in the ordinary sense as well as 'cruelly and tragically wronged – a victim of relentless intrigue, and, while remaining noble and heroic, is allowed to recognize the pathos of his own fate'. He was the victim, as 'we have all been', Leavis drily remarked. (His 'Six Years War' may have been in his mind; or Spender.) In seeking extenuation Bradley simplified what Shakespeare showed. By playing down Othello's capacity for self-dramatization, he lost sight of a person (Shakespeare's creation) who was not morally negligible. Othello's 'heroic quality is a real thing, though it is not, as Othello takes it to be, the whole of reality'.

Leavis does not accuse Othello of self-dramatization; he merely demurs, with sympathy, at the absence of a moral quantity that he does not possess. Othello is 'full of himself' and as culpable as any murderer, but not more. It was for his wartime essay 'Tragedy and the "Medium"' that Leavis reserved the subject of emptiness of self.

Incipient Corruption? 1937

It took time for Leavis to get established, a long time. There were administrative reasons for it, but Leavis thought that he was held back, particularly by 'my enemy Tillyard'. He displayed throughout his life what lawyers call a lively sense of grievance, but in passing comment, not so much in print, and then in highly ironized form. There *was* hostility to him. The phenomenon is complex, but a brief comment on Leavisophobia is in order at this point, just when Leavis, evidently, beat the system. Why did he not fit in? Why did he have few supporters in the English Faculty?

The rebarbative element has often been explained anecdotally. Leavis is said to have been ungrateful, 'bit the hand that fed him', a phrase already casting him in the role of dog. Leavis would drily employ the metaphor to himself, remarking once of himself that '*Cet animal est très méchant.*' (He left Buffon's next sentence unsaid: '*Quand on l'attaque, il se défend.*') Apart from temperament, there was in the eyes of Cambridge English something unsettling about Leavis's academic field. He was in his earliest writings much involved with *American* literature, as was *Scrutiny*, something that did not enter the Cambridge English curriculum until after a struggle in the 1960s. Then, Noël Annan once remarked, with more regret than animosity, Leavis was not 'collegial': he was a poor colleague. In one sense he was too collegial, more committed to Downing, to the making of his own group, than to the institution of English in the university. All college fellows who are responsible for an academic subject actively seek the best pupils; tripos results mattered for college prestige. But Leavis needed pupils in a special sense: for an 'English school' within Cambridge English and, quite mundanely, as contributors for *Scrutiny*. He was therefore exceptionally competitive. Further, it is possible that his need for pupils (not disciples, or not primarily so) set up strains in him and in Q.D.L. that were not experienced by other dons or their wives. Breaches occurred between Q.D.L. and former pupils, often after they married, when Q.D.L. thought suddenly that the pupil (for whom her husband had 'done so much') had let himself down. Much was expected of those who were badly needed in what Leavis ruefully called his 'stage army'.

Some light is thrown on Leavisophobia by concentration on a single point of conflict, between Leavis and E.M.W. Tillyard. Tillyard expressed his view of Leavis very cautiously.* It is worth scrutinizing what he said – and what he did not say – because it is symbolic of much hostility to Leavis.

Leavis detested Tillyard ('my enemy', the 'arch ward-boss') and the feeling was reciprocated. Just after the war, an undergraduate at Jesus, Michael Black, was called in by Tillyard, his Director of Studies, before dinner in hall. Black was a *Scrutiny* reader; Tillyard, pink with annoyance, warned him that if he continued to write *Scrutiny*-like essays he would come to no good. Later Black was to become University

---

* 'He had an extraordinary gift for not saying what was in his mind, even while appearing most communicative . . . For example, I now know he had a life-long interest in cricket, but he never once referred to the subject throughout our forty years' friendship (doubtless realizing it would be wasted on me).' Basil Willey, *Proceedings of the British Academy* (1963), p. 404.

Publisher (that is, Editorial Director) at Cambridge University Press.[46]

The two men can be set against each other in literary terms, Tillyard for Milton, Leavis against, but this is misleading. Better to recall the traditional division between Ancients and Moderns. To have studied classics did not make a person 'a classic', but Tillyard was for Leavis the model of a 'classic' possessing a complex of attitudes among which there were two that Leavis distrusted. First, he contested a belief in genre, that there was such a thing as 'epic' or 'tragedy', the words being variable, evolving but real, so presentations of 'this *as* that' could be mounted; like Joseph Conrad's *Nostromo* 'as' epic. Leavis was a Coleridgean, believing that an art-work had within itself the reason why it is so and not otherwise. Second, he contested the view that if English studies were run on the model of classics, they had to supply a compendium of information, 'background' in Cambridge terms, as in Willey's books (like *Seventeenth-century Background*), or Tillyard's, or Theodore Spencer's on Elizabethan England. Q.D.L. pungently called classics a 'plaster of Paris discipline' as commonly practised, actually disqualifying the student for criticism of modern literature because of its faith in antecedents – and its presumption of authority. (On the other hand, *Scrutiny* did play a part in the background of a 'modernist' school of criticism of the Greek and Roman classics: here H.A. Mason and J.P. Sullivan, editor of *Arion*, were pioneers.)

But there was more to the conflict: an ideological conflict (as it was) implies differences over social organization. These are quietly shown in the book Tillyard published in 1958, *The Muse Unchained: An Intimate Account of the Revolution in English Studies at Cambridge*, about the growth of Cambridge English. The book appears dispassionate, but if decoded, Tillyard's distaste can be easily detected. By 1958 Leavis was an international figure, but there were fewer references to him in Tillyard's index than to Aubrey Attwater. He argued that Cambridge English began to decline with an 'incipient corruption' in the 1930s, a phase corresponding with the rise of Leavis.

Tillyard's complaints against Leavis in *The Muse Unchained* were covert, but they show what was felt against him. There were two complaints on grounds of educational principle. First, Tillyard disliked school students starting to do literary criticism before they were 'ready for it'. Second, he disliked the way the scholarship examination provided a direct route to Cambridge English from the secondary school. Leavis clearly favoured both. The significance of the college–scholarship–school

link cannot be exaggerated: a good number of school students went up
to Downing on one ticket and changed to English when they arrived at
Downing. There were also, especially under wartime conditions, people
with all kinds of qualifications, or lack of them. But, roughly, the
college–scholarship–school link was Leavis's lifeline to educational influence, and at this Tillyard shows almost indignation, partly because it
established a 'pure' form of English studies, unsupported by other
disciplines. He may have liked the English Tripos to be post-Renaissance
in scope, but he still wanted the students to have a background subject,
something manifestly 'rigorous' like classics. Further, the college–
scholarship–school link was, he implied, structurally wrong, almost
stealing a march on the system, educating young people *into* English
rather than 'letting them make up their own minds'. This was, and is, a
common objection to Leavis: it is the objection to Leavis as dominator
that may invoke, sometimes self-righteously, the etymology of the word
'education'. It is true that Leavis did, in his use of the scholarship, make a
structural difference to the system, and he did believe young people did
not have to wait to hone their literary critical skills until they arrived at
university. He wanted them capable of going on to other studies at
Cambridge. In this he treated his pupils as adults.

Tillyard applauded Cambridge English for its history-of-ideas course,
'The English Moralists', led by Basil Willey, and he could have mentioned his own *The Elizabethan World Picture*. He approved close analysis
of poetry (Practical Criticism) in the early I.A. Richards phase, believing
it a 'first-rate means of education for the man who has a bent for
literature'. But this was where 'corruption' was 'incipient'. Close analysis
was good in literary enthusiasts joyously immersed in the subjectivities
of English studies after a schooling in austere preliminaries (as the early
graduates of the English Tripos went from classics). It was a different
thing for those who went up to Cambridge pre-trained in English
studies, who did criticism by rote and for whom analysis and evaluation
were routine. These young people had 'a repertory of labels and phrases
to be attached, by cunning, to the proper exhibits', knowing 'the proper
authors to admire or despise'. Tillyard quoted a piece of bouncy student
criticism about some lines by Shelley, an author who had 'acquired a
number of labels of opprobrium' (that they could be learned from
Leavis was unsaid). This person had picked up phrases unsuited for
'schoolboy digestion', probably having taken a scholarship examination
in practical criticism. Tillyard 'always held out against scholarships in

English subjects alone'. In *The Muse Unchained* he argued that the English Tripos spring of the early 1920s turned to the wintry 1930s in which the generosities of liberalism withered in the face of totalitarianism. Despotism, it was felt, had to be opposed with something harsher, when liberty became a burden. It was only one stop down this line of reasoning to *Scrutiny* with its 'authoritarian tone', attracting those 'desirous of being told what they ought to believe'. And with the 1930s came research students. 'Unlike Oxford, we have never made up our minds exactly what we expect of them.' Clearly for Tillyard 'anthropologico-literary' young men need not apply. Close analysis, evaluation, research students and the scholarship examination were Leavisian phenomena. There are some hesitations about William Empson in Tillyard's *The Muse Unchained*, but, as we have seen, Tillyard supported the idea of giving a lectureship to Empson (or so Leavis believed). This is not so surprising. Empson presented no threat to the structural or social organization of Cambridge English. There was a political dimension to at least two essays in *Some Versions of Pastoral* (1935), but only on the larger issues of the class-war. In terms of the politics of education his work was notably untheorized, and in social manner, both personal and in writing, he was credibly donnish. It is Leavis who is the wicked fairy of *The Muse Unchained*. If Tillyard believed in 1937 half of what he wrote in 1958, Leavis was lucky to be appointed at all. It all did hang on Leavis's telegram to Q.[47]

None of this is to say that it was easy to accept Leavis, for those who had not been, as it were, home-reared by him. He did appear to be 'difficult' about T.S. Eliot because to many it seemed that Eliot, who had high cultural prestige, did not need angry defence. Was the editor of the *Criterion* a rebel who needed a defence to a hostile public? However, Leavis's reading of the situation was that much of the public was uncomprehending, and, that while Eliot's work, both poetic and critical, implied and required great changes in literary life, the world seemed to be going about its business much as it had done. Leavis would have been more easily accepted as propagandist for an unappreciated avant garde figure, say, an Ezra Pound. As it stood, he was in the unappealing position of one telling the world to slow down and realize that it hardly understood Eliot if it was not prepared to see through to the consequences of his revolution. Then, it was not altogether clear to the literary public what *kind* of books Leavis wrote, even (or especially) after

Revaluation. Did he do history or criticism? If history, then it was highly subjective, applying a method that Leavis had not separately explained. Leavis was aware of the need to explain his methods. It was for this he planned a book to be called 'Authority and Method', never to be completed.* In it he would have shown what his principles were. It was actually lamentable that it was never written, for he could have presented himself at the level of theory before making forays into regions where there were already vested historical interests. Leavis's *Revaluation* needed 'Authority and Method', and if he had not thought so he would hardly have gone on trying to write it. One concludes it was the running of *Scrutiny* that stopped him. He was to speak sometimes of how he diffused his energies, and how in this he was definitely 'not a genius'. It is possibly his disappointment in himself in this respect that fortified his convictions·about the validity of 'genius'. (He was fascinated by the musical genius of his eldest son, Ralph.)

Although 'Authority and Method' was never finished, we know what Leavis wanted. Three chapters or essays were written, eventually published in *Scrutiny*, and in them can be seen what Leavis wanted for a founding work. The essays were surely in lecture form in the early 1930s. They are called 'Imagery and Movement', 'Reality and Sincerity' and '"Thought" and Emotional Quality', each illustrated by a series of poems. The analyses are intricate, and among Leavis's most remarkable pieces of literary criticism. Indeed, he spoke of them as his best work, along with his analyses of Wordsworth's 'The Ruined Cottage' and Marvell's 'A Dialogue between Soul and Body'.[48] Curiously, although the pieces were little known until after 1945 and not very widely then, they were the discourses best known to his pupils, and were lectured on regularly, the poems appearing frequently on sheets for discussion or in examinations. The choice of pieces was also traditional: in the essays Leavis gave *his* version of the classic Cambridge English analyses, to be found in Richards's and Forbes's lectures. So D.H. Lawrence's 'Piano' was considered, as was Wordsworth's sonnet 'Surprised by Joy', the architectonics of which were analysed by Forbes. 'I owe so much to others,' wrote Leavis while he was preparing 'Authority and Method'. In these essays he moved forward from the others.†

And he moved forward from his own undergraduate experiences.

* See Chapter Six, *Scrutiny*: Guarding the Guardians, 'Leaving Richards 1934'.
† See Chapter Two, English at Cambridge, 'Matters of Feeling: Forbes and Richards'.

When he took the English Tripos one of his tripos questions required (we saw in Chapter Two) a commentary on a ballad by Sir Walter Scott, 'Proud Maisie', to be considered in relation to a passage of prose by Francis Palgrave, the anthologist. In the essay '"Thought" and Emotional Quality', the Scott poem is brought in in relation to Wordsworth's 'A Slumber Did My Spirit Seal' and Tennyson's 'Break, Break, Break'. It is in this triple comparison that Leavis illustrated a long-standing interest, in what he called 'disinterestedness' and 'impersonality'. He was in his essay as respectful of the 'Homeric manner' of 'Proud Maisie' as Palgrave was in the examination quotation (though he did not there refer to Palgrave). He commented:

We never seem to be offered emotions as such; the emotion develops and defines itself as we grasp the dramatic elements the poem does offer – the data is presented (that is the effect) with emotional 'disinterestedness'. For 'disinterestedness' we can substitute 'impersonality' with which term we introduce a critical topic of the 'first importance'.[49]

The essay is a link between Leavis's tripos experience of 1921 and his essay on tragedy of 1944. 'Impersonality' surfaces again and again.

Wild, Untutored Phoenix 1937

When Leavis published his booklet *D.H. Lawrence* in 1930 he did not expect to return to the subject. He was drawn to Lawrence, deeply sympathetic, but some of the main works repelled (or bored) him. It was to the Lawrence that emerged in new publications of his work after his death that Leavis became committed. Lawrence's chosen symbol, the phoenix, was especially apposite for Leavis. A new and richer Lawrence was created in the 1930s with the publication of his letters, edited by Aldous Huxley in 1932, and the publication of a large amount (not all) of his journalism and miscellaneous writing in 1937 under the title of *Phoenix*. Leavis reviewed the letters in *Scrutiny* in December 1932. This significant plea for understanding and learning from the day-to-day informal output of the writer was never prominently reprinted, nor did his review of *Phoenix* (December 1937) become widely known, even though it was a key work of Leavis. It did appear in *The Common Pursuit* (1952) grouped with work on literary criticism; interestingly it is the only essay in the book for which the year of composition is given.

Leavis's review of *Phoenix: The Posthumous Papers of D.H. Lawrence* 'was called ironically "The Wild, Untutored Phoenix"', stress intended on the word 'untutored'. It is partly an essay on Lawrence's education, making the bold claim that

> it seems to me probable that D.H. Lawrence at twenty-one was no less trained intellectually than Mr Eliot at the same age; had, that is, read no less widely (even if lacking Greek), was no less in command of his capacities and resources and of the means of developing further, and had as adequate a sense of tradition and the nature of wisdom.[50]

The volume contains many book reviews, essays on fiction and poetry, some writing on travel and on painting, and the long book-length essay 'The Study of Thomas Hardy', which was, Lawrence himself remarked, not quite fairly, on almost everything except Thomas Hardy. In the face of 'the ruling literary intellectuals', Lawrence is presented as a crucial critic, 'a great literary critic if ever there was one'. It was Lawrence as critic, as writer of non-fiction, though not forgetting his work as novelist (and especially author of 'tales'), who became the model of intelligence for Downing College men. *Phoenix* was the discourse of Downing. For years, when others referred to Lawrence, it was probably to a quite different canon from that known to the Leavisians. This Lawrence became one of the Leavisian guardians, to which we shall turn in the next chapter. A dozen years later it was clear that this prized book had still made no impact on the 'ruling literary intellectuals', a depressing fact of post-war Britain, it seemed. On this ruling class Leavis was to focus in 'Keynes, Lawrence and Cambridge' in 1949.*

---

* See Chapter Eight, No Common Pursuit, 'Bloomsbury Again; Damned Humbug 1949–1951'.

CHAPTER SIX

SCRUTINY: GUARDING THE GUARDIANS
1932–1937

A man's most vivid emotional and sensuous experience is inevitably
bound up with the language that he actually speaks.
– F.R. Leavis, *New Bearings in English Poetry*, 1932

Now it is only in science that perfect communicability is attainable,
and in other words, all that we can profitably say is, in the last
resort, scientific propositions clarified by scientific logic. To the
realm of the Unspeakable, therefore, belong Ethics, Religion, Art,
Artistic Criticism, and many other things.
– Joseph Needham, 'Biology and Mr Huxley', *Scrutiny*, May 1932

Guardians: Empson, Pound, Lawrence 1932–1933

By the time he lost his probationary lectureship, Leavis had established
his own group of regular *Scrutiny* contributors, at the core of which
were Denys Thompson, Lionel Knights and Denys Harding, scraping a
living on the edge of academic life; Thompson as a schoolmaster at
Gresham's was the most settled. Gordon Fraser and his publishing outfit
were on the edge. As Leavis grew in influence at Downing new
members like Gordon Cox and Geoffrey Walton were recruited. Some
new talent turned up from outside Cambridge. In 1934 Harold Mason
took the train from Oxford to Cambridge, to introduce himself and
offer an 'Oxford Letter'. Mason was only twenty-three, having studied
at the University College at Hull, where his father was a customs and
excise officer. He went on to Oriel College, Oxford, where he took a
second in Greats and wrote for *Scrutiny* as a schoolmaster at Stamford
School. (Much later Mason's fortunes intertwined uncomfortably with

Leavis's.)★ Leavis took him on as a reviewer, in which role he used something of Thompson's wincing tone, but with an added bluntness. A handsome Yorkshireman, Mason was the most swaggering of the *Scrutiny* men, starting several flurries of controversy. He was the only contributor to carry through into its pages the anti-censorship convictions Leavis had shown in the *Ulysses* incident. He published a note on deletions from the scenes about sex in the British edition of John Dos Passos's *The Big Money*:

'"You're taking precautions, aren't you?" "Sure thing," said Charley through clenched teeth *and went to his bureau for a condom.*' In the English edition the words in italics are omitted.

Mason's straightforwardness was shown in an admirable review (foreshadowing his later work on Poundian classical translation) of Louis MacNeice's translation of *The Agamemnon of Aeschylus*, which 'keeps reasonably close to the original while using solid, everyday words. (One tends to be pleased merely to see words like "spit" and "guts" in a translation of Aeschylus.)'[1]

By the time Leavis got his lectureship in 1936 the circle of scrutineering guardians was established. *Scrutiny* also had its hero-guardians beyond Chesterton Hall Crescent. Of them Leavis wrote extensively in the first year of *Scrutiny*.

In the autumn of 1931 Leavis had worked on the pamphlet that Eliot had suggested he write, provisionally titled (following Juvenal) 'Quis custodiet ipsos custodes?' *Mass Civilization and Minority Culture* focused on the mass; Leavis now turned to the guardians of culture, asking who kept guard over them. He worried over his pamphlet at Christmas; in the spring vacation he sent it to Eliot and was asked to make 'one or two' changes. Leavis duly made them, but silence followed. *Scrutiny* was now a reality, so Leavis decided to cut his losses, withdraw the pamphlet from *The Criterion Miscellany* and use it for *Scrutiny*. Between May 1932 and March 1933 four essays were published in it that can be given the collective title 'Quis custodiet ipsos custodes?': 'The Literary Mind' (May); 'What's Wrong with Criticism?' (September); 'Under which King, Bezonian?' (December); 'Restatements for Critics' (March 1933). This 'pamphlet' celebrated William Empson, Ezra Pound and D.H. Lawrence.

★ See Chapter Ten, The End of Cambridge, 'Coterie Rejected'.

In 'The Literary Mind' Leavis attacked a no-nonsense exposé of the impotence of literary culture by Max Eastman. He scoffed at the idea that there was one type of literary mind. How could one concept of literariness embrace Edith Sitwell and T.S. Eliot? He refused to endorse any idea of the 'literary mind' that stressed some anti-scientific talent for 'feeling' and 'insight'. Had not Empson demonstrated a model of literary *intelligence* that dissolved the common differentiation between mental (scientific) and affective (literary) powers? Empson had shown a rigour beyond feeling and insight: he 'convicts us again and again of having missed something essential in the passages we thought we knew . . . Was the deficiency in our response one of sensibility or intelligence?' Leavis was addressing the problem posed at the outset by *Scrutiny*. Where was reliable non-scientific thinking to be found? In the first issue Joseph Needham, reviewing Huxley's *Brave New World*, pointed to regions inaccessible to scientific logic and 'perfect communicability'. These were the realms of the 'unspeakable' that could be explored, Empson had shown, as securely and experimentally as a scientist would. The two cultures debate entered Leavis's career early.

The second keeper at the gate of the 'unspeakable' was Ezra Pound, who had described valid literary study plainly in his recent pamphlet, *How to Read* (1931): literary criticism maintained the very cleanliness of the tools, the health of the matter of thought itself. 'The governor and legislator cannot act effectively or frame laws without words, and the solidity and validity of those words is in the care of the damned and despised *literati*.' Lawrence is mentioned in Leavis's first essay, but does not take a leading role as guardian until the last.

Leavis's manner has the cleanliness Pound expected of the literati, a bleaching cleanliness. 'What's Wrong with Criticism?' surveys some worthies of literary London in a manner that would make commissioning editors wary, Eliot included. He had not replied swiftly when he received Leavis's improved pamphlet, but this did not mean he was not sympathetic to the Leavisian position. He had warmly praised *Fiction and the Reading Public* in a review that mocked middlebrow notables like Thornton Wilder, Ernest Hemingway and J.B. Priestley. The creator of Tiresias in *The Waste Land*, fishing upon the shore with arid plain behind, could not fail to sympathize with Q.D.L.'s graphic depiction of cultural waste. But Wilder, Hemingway and Priestley were safe targets for Eliot, Priestley especially so, as he was a deliberate populist basking in the pages of the *Evening Standard*. But Eliot could not be expected to enjoy, or at any rate openly admire, Leavis's insistent, comprehensive contempt for the literary community. The author of *The Waste Land* was employed by Faber and Faber to edit a journal that needed many contributors. He would alienate them if he went in for such crushing surveys as 'What's Wrong with Criticism?' Wry jeering was a speciality of Chesterton Hall Crescent. Denys Thompson, for instance, took to the Q.D.L. manner with relish and exaggerated it, in this specimen of early *Scrutiny* manner:

The [Sir Walter] Scott centenary was a rich seam for the literary racketeers: his reputation bulled, not only because there was money to be had out of superfluous biographies, excerpts and appreciations, but also because your modern novelist-purveyor of soporifics was enabled to link arms with a Sir Walter represented as a good fellow and the finest creator in the history of the novel of the ordinary human kind.

Leavis himself was not so smugly contemptuous: he was always specific about the structure of the literary world. In 'What's Wrong with Criticism?' he traced the interlocking memberships of the Royal Society of Literature and the English Association, and the dependence of the latter for funds on its anthology *Poems of Today*, whose two volumes were found in many school stock-rooms, scarcely containing 'hardly half a dozen good poems' (so young teachers lamented, said Leavis). He was well informed by Q.D.L. He did not have much time for Harold Nicolson, but noted he had written two good books on Swinburne and Tennyson, and that *Some People* was 'a book of a certain distinction'. Only then did he deplore Nicolson's radio talks for 'The Changing World', mounted by the BBC, 'the new organ of culture of which so much is expected'. They were 'notorious for their absurdity, their vulgarity and their sciolism' and Nicolson 'did not have the first qualification for the undertaking'. It was a Leavisian *parti pris* that a cultural commentator or a critic should be 'qualified', but this was not a common assumption in the literary world. His tone was rare in the literary arena, not heard in more than a few paragraphs in the *Bookman* or in the *Calendar of Modern Letters*. Eliot may have seriously thought of publishing Leavis's pamphlet, but its tone would have made him nervous.

The title of the third essay, 'Under which King, Bezonian?', meant 'Marxist or not?' Leavis fielded the challenge with the retort that *Scrutiny*'s job was to engage in 'effective particularity' and that it was anti-Marxist in so far as it put high on its list of priorities an attempt to refine upon the crude Marxian conception of the 'bourgeois'. Marxism had failed if its 'bourgeoisie' included, without differentiation, 'Mr Wells, Mr Hugh Walpole, *Punch, Scrutiny*, Dr Marie Stopes, and the *Outline for Boys and Girls*'. And failed if it allowed Edmund Wilson to group together 'Dostoevsky, Cervantes, Defoe and cummings'. At the core of the essay was an effort to engage with Leon Trotsky's absorbingly heretical version of Marxism.

It was one of his Emmanuel pupils who had interested Leavis in Trotsky's *Literature and Revolution*. John Jenkinson was an 'anthropologico-literary' undergraduate, impressed by *Fiction and the Reading Public*.[2] He became a teacher, educationalist and literary sociologist. Following the penchant of Richards and Q.D.L. for questionnaire-making, he produced a large-scale survey issuing in *What Do Boys and Girls Read?* (1940), the first comprehensive British study of children's reading. Leavis was interested in Trotsky because he was not an orthodox Marxian. Trotsky wrote that he did not envision a proletarian culture purged of bourgeois qualities.

The main task of the proletarian intelligentsia in the immediate future is not the abstract formation of a new culture regardless of the absence of a base for it, but a definite culture-bearing, that is, a systematic, planful, and, of course, critical imparting to the backward masses of the essential elements of the culture which already exists.

Leavis believed Trotsky was correct in seeing that art was not created, explained by or reducible to the Marxian 'methods of production' and agreed with him that it was, none the less, certainly related to communal possessions that were not those of art – that is, 'codes, developed in ages of continuous experience, of relations between man and man, and man and the environment'. And art was related to what Leavis believed to be a 'common' human possession: language.

However, Leavis and Trotsky believed that this relationship between art and its environment was at an end, because industrial modes of production were either damaging to art (the Leavis view) or neutral towards art (the Trotsky view). Industrial systems did, of course, have some positive human effects. In theory, they could release people from work into life in a 'leisure community', in which art could be created. But what productive base was this art connected *to*? Trotsky recognized that 'a class without social functions tends to produce decadent poetry'.

But what was the social function of the poet of the future, as member of a merely leisure community? Leavis agreed with Trotsky that those 'essential elements of the culture which already exist' should be transplanted and developed in a modern culture, one 'independent of any economic, technical or social system', but was dubious about the 'rootless' result. The danger was that it would produce what Leavis called a 'Californian' solution, only slightly more attractive to Leavis than 'Stalin, or the King by Divine Right'. Unlike Trotsky, he was unable to discount the importance of an agricultural base to society, which was rejected by Marxism.[3] For the literary critic the immediate task was unsparing analysis of the 'essential elements' of culture. For this Leavis found a model in the *Criterion* – or rather in Eliot's editorial contributions, which always exhibited the 'uncommon phenomenon of real thinking turned upon the underlying issues'. It was a pity that Eliot's guardianship did not extend to all the pages of his journal, which contained too much of the 'dead, academic kind of abstract "thinking"', often in defence of the usual counters – even if they were ones Leavis himself favoured, like 'intelligence'.

In the last essay of the set, 'Restatements for Critics', D.H. Lawrence is given pride of place. It reflects the impact made upon Leavis by the appearance of Lawrence's letters in Huxley's edition, which Leavis had reviewed three months before in December 1932. The curious title of that review, 'D.H. Lawrence and Professor Irving Babbitt', illustrated the predicament in which Leavis was placed. Babbitt had been Eliot's teacher at Harvard; Eliot had written a respectful but critical essay about Babbitt's humanism in 1928. As Anglo-Catholic and Royalist, Eliot found Babbitt's secular piety unattractive. But Leavis was disappointed that he gave it so much credence. If humanism was an option, there was surely to hand the infinitely more winning and serious humanism of Lawrence. At this point two forces were converging on Leavis. There was the posthumous authority of Lawrence, expanding with the publication of new writings after his death. The letters were available, there was new work to reckon with, work that for Leavis, in some respects, exceeded the rest because it could speak to him directly. He could not emulate Lawrence's fiction or poetry or drama; but his non-fictional means of expression *could* find a way into Leavis's prose. In the letters Leavis could hear a speaker as a pupil heard a teacher. Their week-in-week-out commentary could relate to Leavis's now continuous flow of writings for *Scrutiny*. As letter-writer Lawrence spoke to Leavis's *métier*.

Novels and poems were inimitable; in the letters there was the voice of someone personal but also the voice of a critic, of one 'disinterested'.

The second force was Eliot's hostility to Lawrence. As new publications brought Lawrence into light, Eliot seemed set on edging him back into darkness. A series of damning statements from Eliot emerged sinuously in obscure literary locations. In 1927 he wrote an essay for a French journal on the contemporary English novel, Lawrence appearing as 'un démoniaque', a morbid figure, metaphysically melodramatic, in whose fictions Male and Female appeared in desperate sexual confrontations, stripped of the graces that 'render passion tolerable'. When he wrote in England, Eliot did not express such intense suspicion of physicality, but Lawrence continued to be the focus of his disdain of the secular.* When Lawrence died Eliot had taken pains to reprove E.M. Forster for his respectful assessment. No obituary essay appeared in the *Criterion*, though in July 1931 Eliot reviewed John Middleton Murry's *Son of Woman: The Story of D.H. Lawrence* as if he were obituarizing, depicting again a demonic Lawrence. Eliot speculated that Murry was under a compulsion to expel Lawrence, 'the demon', from himself. He turned on Lawrence's social class and on the Congregationalism (the 'Protestant underworld') of his family that led him eventually into a shocking 'travesty' of the concepts of Christianity. Eliot accused Lawrence of 'ignorance' in a sentence into which Leavis could have read an allusion to himself.

Had Lawrence been sent to a public school and taken honours at a university he would not have been a jot the less ignorant; had he become a don at Cambridge his ignorance might have had frightful consequences for himself and for the world, 'rotten and rotting others'.

Eliot did not mean Leavis. He is suggesting the *kind* of place in which Lawrence could have been a don, like Cambridge with its determined modernism and its English curriculum. But Q.D.L. thought Eliot did mean Leavis and it is easy to see why. Leavis would have sent his Minority Press pamphlet on Lawrence to the *Criterion* for review; there

---

* At the time of 'Restatements for Critics' Leavis had not read Eliot's lectures, published in 1934 as *After Strange Gods*. In this 'primer of modern heresy', Lawrence was portrayed as a danger to the 'sick, debile and confused'. Eliot pointed to 'an alarming strain of cruelty in some modern literature', exemplified in Joyce's *The Dead*, Katherine Mansfield's 'Bliss' and Lawrence's 'The Shadow in the Rose Garden'. The lectures were anti-Semitic and never reprinted

was no other academic in Cambridge articulate in Lawrence's defence. Q.D.L. called the reference 'Eliot's prize piece of defamatory spite'.

When F.R.L. took this up in print, Eliot retreated in the most cowardly way as usual, going about saying to people he thought agreed with us . . . 'it was *most unfortunate* that Dr Leavis took his criticism of Lawrence as applying to himself, when nothing could have been further from his intention' – as though there was any other don at Cambridge or anywhere else then, who had written favourably of Lawrence![4]

Leavis could not take coolly the equation of Lawrence, Cambridge and rottenness. Whatever this meant, he saw in Eliot an offensive against the one writer whom he increasingly believed to be indispensable. Eliot was not only attacking Lawrence directly but failing to block the path of his cruder detractors. The *Criterion* was a fairly broad church journal – except where Lawrence was concerned. In 1955 Leavis described its orientation:

To the Criterionic Right, whether Anglo-Catholic, Neo-Thomist or Social Crediting, [Lawrence] was, of course, no more congenial – the Editor of the *Criterion* could, and did, with large generosity favour the Marxist and Fellow-Travelling poets as well as Joyce and Pound, but never Lawrence. And the spirit of Lawrence's dealings with the relations between men and women recommended itself no more to understanding than it had done in the days of 'Jix' and Lytton Strachey. It was perhaps his supposed attitude in the matter of sex that mainly accounted for the ban on mention of him, maintained by the BBC for nearly twenty years.[5]

At the climax of 'Restatements for Critics' Leavis presented Lawrence as 'the Perfect Critic' (title of a favourite Eliot essay), though it may seem a paradox to say so, for the very function of this essay is to argue that there could be no single authority for criticism: opting for a Lawrence or an Eliot or an Empson was frivolous. Leavis was answering the early critics of *Scrutiny* who then wanted a formula: did it follow Eliot or Lawrence? *Scrutiny* did not go in for gods.

To suggest that one should 'accept' Mr Eliot or D.H. Lawrence is to insult both of them, it might be retorted by gross incomprehension, for, whatever the 'reality' of either may be, it is certainly such that to contemplate 'accepting' it, is to repudiate it.

But Lawrence did have priority for the *Scrutiny* group, as a free spirit.

What Lawrence offers us is not a philosophy or an *œuvre* – a body of literary art – but an experience, or, to fall back on the French again, an *expérience*, for the sense of 'experiment' is needed too. In him the human spirit explored, with unsurpassed courage, resource and endurance, the representative, the radical and central, problems of our time. Of course he went into dangerous places, and laid himself open to reprehension as setting dangerous examples and inciting to dangerous experiments. But if he earned reprehension, we owe him gratitude for earning it.

Leavis implies that the life of Lawrence was greater than his works, as he had stated overtly in the previous issue of *Scrutiny*.

If we find him great, the supreme importance of his books is perhaps that they assure us that he existed. Those of them which are successful as art are in some ways saddening and depressing. The fact of personal existence of which they assure us is perhaps the most cheering and enlivening fact the modern world provides.[6]

Leavis admired some plain qualities in Lawrence: common sense and kindness. When Eliot remarked loftily that Bertrand Russell would have been the better for a classical education, Lawrence simply said that what 'ailed' him was merely the 'inexperience of youth': 'He is, vitally and emotionally, much too inexperienced in personal contact and conflict, for a man of his age and calibre. It isn't that life has been too much for him, but too little.' None the less Eliot was still central for Leavis and *Scrutiny*. When Leavis criticized Richards in 1934 it was because he saw injustice to Eliot in his *Coleridge on Imagination*: Richards had not acknowledged the bounty Eliot bestowed on Leavis's generation. In 1935 Leavis wrote Eliot a fan letter about his essay on Andrew Marvell, and received a graceful reply: Eliot remarked he thought more of such essays than 'the more theoretic' ones.[7] In *Scrutiny* Edgell Rickword said that 'nothing can obscure the value of his example as a literary critic', doing so in the same number as 'Restatements for Critics'. Eliot opined that it was less *boring* to think of sex as evil than 'life-affirming'. None the less, Eliot had his blind side, that chill sobriety in his attitude to D.H. Lawrence. Leavis was not of the 'life-affirmation' party, nor was Lawrence a 1920s hygienist, but he thought perverse Eliot's seeming preference for the idea of damnation to Lawrence's commitment to making 'the sex relation valid and precious, not shameful'. Lawrence was in touch with the ordinary, and possessed some of the straightfor-ward vitalities of William Blake. (Curiously, it had been Eliot himself who, ten years earlier, had given Leavis the cue to bracket Blake with Lawrence.)

Lawrence had always used Christian symbolism, and increasingly did so in his later work ('The Man Who Died', *Apocalypse*). Eliot considered this an offensive issue from the 'Protestant underworld' in which Lawrence was reared. Leavis was not wholly happy with a religiose element in Lawrence. But there was another quality, religious but not summarizable as 'Lawrence's religion'.

To talk of the 'religious sense' that he represents may sound weak, but it should not to those who have read the *Letters*. For many today the essential thing is to meet such a sense in the concrete, dominating ('I am a passionately religious man'), and unmistakably an expression of health, courage and vitality. And we meet it, we find, in Lawrence – in the Lawrence who has the right to exclaim as he does against 'glib reverence', because all his writing exhibits reverence as a fact, a fact of honesty, strength and sensitiveness; the Lawrence who disturbs complacency about 'sex reform' so much more potently than Mr Eliot.

Richards had shown the modern world to be a bazaar of beliefs. As consciousness was 'infinitely plastic' a person could say, 'What kind of mind shall I choose to be?' Leavis liked Lawrence's answer. He said his mind was *not* 'infinitely plastic'. He thanked God that he was *not* free, 'any more than a rooted tree is free'. Both Leavis and Eliot were traditionalists, aware of roots, but Eliot assimilated tradition to a classicism with which he sought to extinguish feared romantic anarchies – or the 'heresies' dismissed in *After Strange Gods*. For Lawrence showed a different way of relating between past, present and future.

While he said also, 'Unless from us the future takes place we are death only,' it was in the past that he was rooted. Indeed, in our time, when the gap in the continuity is almost complete, he may be said to represent, concretely in his living person, the essential human tradition; to represent, in an age that has lost the sense of it, human normality, as only great genius could.

The normality included the 'religious sense'.[8] And the concept of *genius* became a necessity for Leavis, to be reiterated. Eliot and Empson provided Leavis with models of intelligence, and of sensibility. Lawrence provided a model for a *person*: it is Lawrence as person (primarily, at this stage) whom Leavis applauded. He affirmed a way of life (and a way of being a literary critic). To support his conviction that such affirmation was proper, Leavis drew on Eliot himself:

It would appear that 'literary appreciation' is an abstraction and pure poetry a phantom (T.S. Eliot, *Selected Essays*, p. 257): there is hardly any need to illustrate the ways in which judgements of literary value involve extra-literary choices and decisions.[9]

Leavis's 'Quis custodiet?' essays, this 'pamphlet', did not make contact between the writers any easier. In the autumn of 1933 Leavis asked Eliot to review Murry's *William Blake* for *Scrutiny*. Eliot politely declined, excusing himself by saying that he had been 'in the ring' with Murry too often; a younger man might be more suitable. In March 1934 Eliot made a lukewarm remark about contributing to *Scrutiny* himself. In December 1935 he invited Leavis to review a book about higher education in America for the *Criterion*. Nothing came of it.[10]

Attack from Bloomsbury-by-the-Cam 1933

At the end of 'What's Wrong with Criticism?' Leavis considered the view that he was asking in vain for authoritative standards to be used in literary criticism, standards that related to the whole range of society's reading matter. Had there *ever* been consensus about literary matters? Perhaps not, said Leavis, but in the eighteenth century there was such a thing as a scale of quality; people believed that readers could aspire to the high tops of the intellect, and that it was worth making the effort to reach them. In the contemporary Northcliffe era of mass circulation, there was less incentive to leave the shallows of reading. Even intellectuals thought the foothills of literacy were good enough 'in their own way'. At least in the past ordinary people knew there was somewhere to go.

That this was so, and the advantage the ordinary man derived, might be brought out by a study (one is in fact being written) of the memoirs and autobiographies, which exist in considerable numbers, of persons of the humblest origin who raised themselves to intellectual distinction and culture.[11]

The book 'in fact being written' was the latest work of Q.D.L., who was using her research scholarship for a sequel to *Fiction and the Reading Public*, a study of literacy and reading habits in poor households of the past. However, she was also *Scrutiny*'s main office-worker, aiding male contributors, who rarely did the necessary typing, for an unliterary printer. By the end of 1932 she was, said Leavis, 'on the edge of nervous breakdown'. In 1933 she was subjected to a bizarre onslaught from Bloomsbury, or 'Bloomsbury-by-the-Cam' (John Lehmann's name for King's). The attack was on *Fiction and the Reading Public*, but meant for Leavisry at large, written by the English Faculty Lecturer, F.L. Lucas. What Lucas said was wounding; what was worse was the way in which his piece was published.

Lucas attacked Q.D.L.'s 'strange book' in a volume called *University Studies: Cambridge* (1933), a collection of essays on the Cambridge faculties intended for outsiders, especially for prospective undergraduates. Produced at the Cambridge University Printing House, though published by John Stirling, it bore an official demeanour. A series of similar volumes on other universities never materialized. Lucas contributed the chapter on English studies. It would have bewildered the lay person seeking information: instead of simply describing Cambridge English, or even recommending it, Lucas launched an attack on English as a university subject and on two Cambridge figures, his colleague Richards and the very junior Q.D.L., who had no official connection whatever with the Faculty. The very format of *University Studies: Cambridge* made his chapter appear to be an official rebuke of the modernist tendency in Cambridge, an improper one, given the precarious position of Q.D.L.: senior academics do not use quasi-official publications to attack graduate students.

Lucas made fun of Q.D.L.'s enthusiastic account of high art and of the amenities of pre-nineteenth-century literacy. He accused her of sentimentality. The pre-industrial world was nasty, brutish and short for ordinary people. Those who today read *The Sheik* then went to witch-burnings, and surely the 'kinema' was better than the gin-shop? 'To inform one's countrymen that ninety-nine out of a hundred of them are garbage-eating *crétins* may no doubt attract their attention, but who, except literary snobs, is persuaded?'[12] (Lucas mocked Q.D.L.'s assemblage of data by portraying her as having a spinsterly craving for pulp-fiction.) Lucas played the part of the optimist encouraging the student to read for pleasure, warning him against priggish highbrows. The clarity of Lucas's essay masks a confusion that often attends prose driven by epigram. In the section on Richards he averred that Richards would not resent criticism because he had done so much for 'criticism'. The different meanings of 'criticism' ran unhindered into each other. In larger matters Lucas was as careless with his categories. When Q.D.L. claimed there were no emotional orgies in Elizabethan *prose*, Lucas retorted that there were ghastly orgies of torture in the Elizabethan *market-place*, a point made the more tendentious because Lucas's supporting evidence was from a *play*. Lucas did not understand Q.D.L.'s enthusiasm for sophisticated art, treating it as youthful snobbery. He observed that she divided the modern reading-public into highbrow, middlebrow and lowbrow, and then authors into four groups, from highbrow to 'absolute best-seller'. Hardly a complex analysis, but 'the groaning reader may ask why, in the cause of culture, he should be subjected to such language; but, in the cause of culture, let us endure'.[13] Q.D.L. was not ashamed of being highbrow, and wrote movingly of the vigour with which readers handle the demands made by unusual books. The purpose of her analysis was to show that the strata of brows was not imaginary, but observably present in contemporary society in its attitudes to reading, an allowance made for them by the guardians of culture.* The possibility of analysing trends in reading, let alone the interest of Q.D.L.'s particular analyses, was dismissed by Lucas, inevitably so, because his resistance was political. For Lucas's type of reader, schooled in the classics and romantic Hellenism, to advance the theory that the literary world had a structure was too 'sociological' a presumption. Hellenism fostered freedoms of body and spirit seemingly incompatible with systematic social control. To Lucas's take-it-or-leave-it and anti-snobbish spirit it was unacceptable to think that types of writing and publication are designed for market niches. Lucas thought Cambridge English had strayed too far from *belles-lettres*. In a way he was right: Q.D.L.'s 'pioneer performance' did lead to 'anthropologico-literary' studies.

Lucas quizzically dismantled Q.D.L. (and Richards), concluding with a plea for a more old-fashioned English Tripos that would tutor young people in the 'Art of Living', not 'with a lily in buttonhole, but with a sense, too vivid to grow old, of the perpetual oddity, yet beauty of life'.[14] Not a persuasive programme for undergraduates who were to shout 'Stanley Baldwin must be sacked, Join the Franco-Soviet Pact!' in Cambridge streets. The affirmations of Lucas were anachronistic and his negations spiteful. But his essay in *University Studies: Cambridge* was influential. Fifty years later Noël Annan considered his account of Q.D.L. to be authoritative. 'In 1933 [her] travesty of social and literary history was exposed by F.L. Lucas.' At the time Bloomsbury was

* 'Highbrow' had only recently acquired a derogatory inflection. A neutral Americanism before the First World War, it became value-loaded after it, capable of being used with equalitarian intent by highbrows themselves.

convinced: Roger Fry thought that the critique of 'that woman Dr Leak or what's her name is very stimulating'. And that Lucas's essay was 'a brilliant one'.[15]

Lucas proceeded from condescending to Eliot in the *Cambridge Review* to making fun of Q.D.L. in *University Studies: Cambridge*. The attack confirmed the hostility of F.R.L. and Q.D.L. to academic Cambridge English. For Leavis this attacker came to epitomize an undiscriminating spirit, a liberalism that depreciates the new. His inner feelings are demonstrated in annotations he made in the margin of his copy of D.H. Lawrence's *Fantasia of the Unconscious*, next to a passage about what might be called authoritarian benevolence. In 'an ideal of benevolence, we have tried to automatize ourselves into little love-engines always stoked with the sorrows or beauties of other people, so we can get up a stream of charity or righteous wrath.' Against this sentence Leavis wrote the initials: 'F.L.L.'

Lucas's little dart into the Leavis project took effect. Leavis was to be ever more intently and defensively *en garde*.

Leaving Richards 1934

Leavis made one especially interesting mark in his copy of *Psychoanalysis and the Unconscious*. On the title-page, above and below the name of the book, there is this inscription:

I.A.R.

D.H.L.   *T.S.E.*

PSYCHOANALYSIS
AND THE
UNCONSCIOUS

Tom doesn't know as much as you think. He's very clever:
he makes a little go a long way.

It was Richards who said this about 'Tom Eliot'; Leavis often attributed it to him. The place of the quotation matches Richards's name at the head of the page, occupying the peak of a trinity in which Leavis named his masters. Despite a lifetime of doubts, Leavis made repeated rereadings of Eliot up to retirement and beyond; and he was always returning to Lawrence. But in 1934 Leavis set Richards at a distance, though the ferocity of his last references show that he remained an aggravating presence.* The breach is marked by a long review Leavis wrote of Richards's *Coleridge on Imagination*.

As early as 1923 Richards was restless in Cambridge. With the exception of C.K. Ogden and Forbes, he disliked dons and men of letters. He was embarrassed, in 'horrible difficulty', at both being a leading spirit of Cambridge English, conjured in from the Highlands by Forbes, and at being the author of *The Principles of Literary Criticism* (which put the arts 'as the supreme mode of communication, in the forefront of all values'), but also disliking academic life. He believed the poet was paramount, but the way in which he continued to adhere to the belief, with more rhetoric than conviction, was to be at the root of Leavis's quarrel with him ten years later. In November 1923 Richards confided to his fiancée that he had 'half decided to chuck it'.[16] After his marriage in 1927 he spent long periods away from Cambridge. In 1927 from January to October he was in Japan and India; for the academic year of 1929–30 and some of the next he was in China, returning only in December 1930. He then went almost immediately to Harvard for two semesters. He was Q.D.L.'s dissertation supervisor, but his presence was sporadic. When he assessed her dissertation in 1931, and met the 'anthropologico-literary' young men at Chesterton Hall Crescent, he had not been long back in Cambridge and was to be away again, energetic in the promotion of the new world language, 'Basic English', his enthusiasm of the late 1920s. Richards left Cambridge permanently in 1939 for a post in education at Harvard. Like Leavis, he was never to be a professor of English.[17]

Coleridge on Imagination was the result of his preparation for a course of lectures given in 1932/4. 'Lots of things happen to people from having to give a course,' he said. 'I wasn't so much concerned to say what Coleridge had thought as to suggest what might be done to what he had said.'[18] Leavis was interested in Richards's lectures, expecting they would be made into a book – particularly interested because he wanted to anticipate him. He was working on a book of his own on literary critical method, giving examples of how to read poetry. It was to be called 'Authority and Method' and on 'practical criticism', going

---

* For his last words to Richards when he was dying, see Epilogue, 'The End'.

back to Coleridge, who had originally devised the phrase made famous by Richards's *Practical Criticism* of 1929.* There Richards had certainly written significantly about method, but he had not given examples of the practice of criticism. It contained analysis, but analysis of passages of poor literary criticism: a study of pieces done by undergraduates (mainly) for Richards when he asked his lecture audience for commentary on the poems on the printed sheets he distributed. His survey, showing how badly criticism was done by educated young people, did not show good practice. Leavis planned a chapter on Coleridge in 'Authority and Method'. 'I regard him as *the* critic.' He would go further than giving 'model' pieces of criticism. He wanted to 'adjudicate' the balance between 'practice-theory' and 'particular-general', between practice and particularity. This was to be the book that would state *his* position, rebutting those who said he 'got it' all from Richards or Empson. Already Cambridge was popularly supposed by the literary papers to harbour a composite critic, Richards + Leavis + Empson, though one was exiled, one jobless and one thinking of leaving for Harvard. The typical 1930s poet was dubbed 'McSpaunday', comprising MacNeice, Spender, Auden and Day Lewis; the equivalent Cambridge critic could have been 'Lempards': Leavis, Empson and Richards. 'Authority and Method' would have been Leavis's second book conceived as such, as *For Continuity* was a collection of essays. But it was never finished, though he continued to believe it would be. Even in 1946 it appeared in his *Who's Who* entry as forthcoming.[19]

Scrutiny watched Richards with the wariness of the graduate student for senior faculty. He had fashioned the thinking of the *Scrutiny* group, but he was more interested in mountaineering than disciples. The second number had an essay by Michael Oakeshott, 'The New Bentham', a critique of Ogden's claim to have found affinities between the materialist Bentham and the idealist Coleridge. To criticize Ogden was to come close to Richards. It had an essay by Richards himself, and Denys Harding reviewed *Mencius on the Mind* in the same number. Leavis believed that 'we shall never get another article out of Richards – and shan't want it'. But Lionel Knights did persuade him:

'I thought you might like to take the opportunity, sir, to reply to some of Mr Oakeshott's points.' 'That nonsense!' said Richards: 'Mr Ogden relies upon

---

* 'Authority and Method', the absent work in Leavis's *œuvre*, is a crux in his career: see also Chapter Five, 'To Downing College', 'Incipient Corruption? 1937'.

certain documents that Oakeshott can't possibly have seen: he doesn't know what he's talking about.'[20]

But Richards did agree to review Ogden's edition of *Bentham's Theory of Fictions* in the next *Scrutiny*. The same number contained a long critical study of Richards by Denys Harding, commissioned by Leavis, who remembered the occasion as one that was 'the nearest I came to producing an essay to order'. Leavis had Harding speak for him, 'disappointed in hopes for Richards's personal support and [knowing] my admiration of Richards's early work was tempered by a sense of its limitations'.[21] In March 1935 Leavis's review of *Coleridge on Imagination* appeared, called 'Dr Richards, Bentham and Coleridge'.

Leavis's review of *Coleridge on Imagination* is hard reading, but it is a crucial document in his life story. Playing through the prose is a fundamental distrust. Leavis believed that Richards had 'spoiled' Coleridge by annexing him to a cloudy project. Richards, thought Leavis, discouraged readers from absorbing the dazzling specificities of Coleridge's criticism. Richards would argue that he annexed Coleridge *to* theory, revalidating him by claiming that the seemingly scattered and spontaneous insights had a theoretical basis from which moderns could learn. Leavis was not persuaded. He thought the theory in *Coleridge on Imagination* a boast, not a presence. As for the 'feel' of the book, he was exasperated. He wrote to Bottrall that the book was pretentious, its upshot being to elevate its author as having synthesized Coleridge and Bentham, a kind of semiological Einstein. Leavis liked telling his pupils that he kicked *Coleridge on Imagination* across the room: perhaps he wrote this after doing so.[22] His review was intense, knotted. It focused especially on the last chapter.

Coleridge on Imagination concluded with a peroration called 'The Bride of Pegasus'. It dealt with the modern spirit, 'our changing attitudes to Authority in all its forms'. Richards described a mind-frame that either did not exist in the past or for which there was then no means of expression. He called it a modern state, that of 'self-dissolving introspection', a psychological condition expressed in the stream-of-consciousness prose of sophisticated fiction, like that of Katherine Mansfield, Stella Benson and Virginia Woolf. The condition was not only experienced by intense or 'artistic' people; 'the average mind' also knew it. Richards said that it was a feature of the modern age to find value in simply being conscious, *per se*. Only the moderns seemed to value being conscious, rather than being conscious of something. When Defoe's Robinson Crusoe looked out at a sea-shore, his consciousness was full of purpose, practical or moral. A twentieth-century person on a beach was capable of *merely* experiencing 'for the sake of the appearances themselves or the reverberations of their *sensory* qualities in the percipient's mind' – as did Joyce's Stephen Dedalus in *Ulysses*, gazing on Sandymount strand:

The grainy sand had gone from under his feet. His boots trod again a damp crackling mast, razorshells, squeaking pebbles, that on the unnumbered pebbles beats, wood sieved by the shipworm, lost Armada. Unwholesome sandflats waited to suck his treading soles, breathing upward sewage breath, a pocket of seaweed smouldered in seafire under a midden of man's ashes. He coasted them, walking warily. A porterbottle stood up, stogged to its waist, in the cakey sand dough. A sentinel: isle of dreadful thirst. Broken hoops on the shore; at the land a maze of dark cunning nets; farther away chalkscrawled backdoors and on the higher beach a drying line with two crucified shirts. Ringsend: wigwams of brown steersmen and master mariners. Human shells.

Stephen's inner world, said Richards, was 'as phantasmagoric as his outer, being composed of images which shift and flow and merge'. For Richards, it was but a step from consciousness as flux to consciousness as dissolution. It was, he claimed, the fear of dissolution that gave moderns a thirst for order. He was sceptical of fanciful accounts of twentieth-century psychic maladies, 'dramatic pictures of our predicament', in which dreams or heresies or sentiment or Descartes are dragons. None the less, the need for 'some new order' was genuinely felt, in tune with *The Principles of Literary Criticism*. He recommended that moderns turn to poetry for it. Poetry was able to constitute 'an order for our mind' – as he had argued in *The Principles of Literary Criticism*. And Leavis subscribed to the idea of poet as leader: he had given Richards the first word on the subject in *New Bearings in English Poetry*: 'The poet is, as it were, at the most conscious point of the race in his time. "He is the point at which the growth of the mind shows itself," says Mr I.A. Richards.'[23] But now this view was appearing in caricature form, and Leavis found himself in the position of one rejecting not an enemy but a wayward ally. Did not Richards contradict himself? He said order was needed, but then he wondered whether the mind had *ever* been in order. He was dubious about 'picturesque mock-desperate dramatization of our situation'. But it was not clear whether he meant that 'dissolution' was a serious modern ailment that poetry could cure or a contemporary condition, neither good nor bad, to which poetry might make some unspecified difference, 'if freed of a mistaken conception of its limitations, and read more discerningly than heretofore'. Richards said poetry could do *something* 'to remake our minds and with them our world', as had Milton, Blake, Wordsworth, Aristotle and Ben Jonson.[24] What exactly it could do remained obscure.

Leavis shared many of Richards's attitudes. He admired the same passage from *Ulysses*, naturally so with his allegiance to the discourse of 'shift, flow and merge', writing not coarsened by search for 'some singled-out component' with 'no whither as opposed to a way'. Leavis too thought that in the finest modern mode there was 'nowhere to arrive, no final solution'. He shared Richards's judgements: the best modern poetry (Yeats, Eliot, Auden, Empson, Hopkins) differed from that of Rupert Brooke because Brooke's poetry had 'no inside'. 'Lovely though the display may be, it is a display, the reader is visiting an Exhibition of Poetic Products,' said Richards.[25] All this, with which Leavis was in agreement, was in *Coleridge on Imagination*.

But, in the end, poet-as-leader as presented in *Coleridge on Imagination* was a caricature. Did not Richards entertain 'preposterously extravagant' expectations of the poet? The small print of the book distressed Leavis, all the cases where he thought the author must be given the benefit of doubts, all the 'small testings' that sent Leavis into a 'dazed fatigue', after so many of which he was sure 'something had gone badly wrong', like the comparison between Defoe and Joyce. Richards wanted to say that the Joyce passage helped show how the modern world differed from that of the eighteenth century, because 'the nomenclature of the faculties, of the virtues and the vices, of the passions, of the moods, the whole machinery through which self-examination with a view to increased order could be conducted by Defoe, had lapsed'.[26] Leavis examined the obscurity of this sentence in detail. 'Self-examination' and 'order', one facilitating the other, were given as good things, and so was 'machinery'. It *looked* as if they were connected, 'machinery' producing 'self-examination' and that producing 'order'. Those were three things, Richards said, that had 'lapsed'. But what connection did this lapsing have with the early part of the sentence about the 'nomenclature of the faculties, of the virtues and the vices, of the passions, of the moods'? Was it just the names of the faculties that had changed, or had the faculties themselves somehow evaporated? Richards intimated that something grave had happened; Leavis's charge was that he was awfully vague. Richards's evidence for basic changes in national identity (did he mean only

Britain?) could have been spread on the head of a pin: two paragraphs of fiction about sea-shores. They might have been rivers in Macedon and Monmouth. Leavis and Q.D.L. were committed to literary criticism as cultural study, designed to come to reliable if not scientific conclusions. The airiness of Richards was liable to bring their type of study into disrepute. Leavis favoured some types of large-scale vision of the modern world. In his pamphlet on D.H. Lawrence he quoted approvingly Oswald Spengler in *The Decline of the West* on the way in which it appeared that 'Man as civilized, as *intellectual nomad*, is again wholly microcosmic, wholly homeless, as free *intellectually* as hunter and herds-man were free sensually.' He thought Spengler's terminology bloated, but agreed with the idea and believed Spengler at least gave a reason for modern alienation, that is, industrialism.* *Coleridge on Imagination* gave no such reason: Richards's account of the dissolution of consciousness was ahistorical and unpolitical. Without more analysis or indication of where analysis might occur, Richards's diagnostic comparison between the eighteenth and twentieth centuries was to Leavis tendentious.

As time passed, Leavis was becoming more cautious of big statements about modern malaises. He ceased to cite Spengler after 1933. When he adapted his first essay on poetry and the modern world for *New Bearings in English Poetry*, he omitted the passage about Mrs Moore's experience in the Marabar Caves in *A Passage to India*. He had begun to think apocalyptic statements were indulgent; they were grave enough but imprecise – worst of all they were anodyne. The capital letters in *The Decline of the West* bored him. He preferred W.H. Auden's 'simple and often admirable guerrilla vein', and it was to guerrilla work he himself was turning. He approved of Richards's affirmation of the value of poetry, but did not want it portentously underwritten.

Leavis wanted an analysis of modern life to be used to fortify observation of the sophisticated contemporary scene, not siphoned into international schemes like 'Basic English'. It was well to say that con-sciousness could be reordered by poetry, but what difference did this make to the reading of poetry, month by month, in Cambridge and London? If poets had the future in their bones, why did Richards write so infrequently about them? Why, indeed, did he not encourage *Scrutiny* itself, Leavis wondered. The question sounds peevish when it is remem-

* 'Read Frobenius instead of Spengler and some of yr. fog might clear,' wrote Ezra Pound to Leavis.

bered that *Scrutiny* had not been particularly friendly to Richards. (It was a Leavisian failing to believe that people would give up their bad ways if only they realized their weaknesses.) But Leavis had a point: why *was* Richards involved so little in the literary arts of Britain? Leavis surmised the answer: that when Richards vaunted the leader-poet, it was not poetry he was affirming but *language*. Late in *Coleridge on Imagination* poetry was deprived by Richards of its leading role, and language took centre-stage: 'Poetry is the supreme use of language, man's chief co-ordinating instrument in the service of the most integral purposes of life.'[27] The real claim, Leavis thought, was being made for semiology, or, in the terminology of the time, 'not for the poet, but for the semasiologist'. For Richards the development of language study would be a leap 'of the same type as that which took Galileo into the modern world'. The pioneer needed 'theoretical equipment', which former students of language lacked. And this was? Richards was as vague about the 'theoretical equipment' as he had been about the nature of consciousness in its modern state of supposed dissolution. Such geniality towards unspecified 'theoretical equipment' implied rejection of the *existing* skills, of the best contemporary critical practice of the time, including Eliot's.

Leavis suspected that Richards wanted to leave literature. Richards did not actually drop literary criticism or drop Coleridge. (Later, he remarked, with good reason, that he considered that his commentary on, and selection of, Coleridge in 1950 contained some of his best work.)[28] Richards was always capable of darting insights into poetry. But Leavis sensed that Richards's heart was no longer in criticism, the 'science' that he founded and in which he delivered 'Ethics, Religion, Art, Artistic Criticism' into the light, and out of the 'realm of the Unspeakable'. Leavis did not know that Richards was trying to get a post away from Cambridge. *Coleridge on Imagination* gave him reason to fear for the future of Cambridge English. Its early masters were in decline. Forbes was lecturing on Scottish baronial architecture, and in poor health; Richards was committed to Basic English, Q was dutiful but lacked the 'fire in his belly' (which he said Leavis possessed).[29] The senior allies in Cambridge had laid down their arms too soon.

Leavis's review meant the end of commerce with Richards. At the same time he lost Empson, who sprang to Richards's defence in a letter to *Scrutiny* of June 1935. Leavis had been suspicious of Empson since he called at Chesterton Hall Crescent before Christmas: 'He seems no less the clever young man than when he went out, and I'm less patient. I'm earnest, of course, and *Scrutiny*'s earnest (no, I don't mean Empson said so). And *Scrutiny* couldn't have been kept going on the clever young man's interesting ideas, etc.' Leavis was pleased to take for *Scrutiny* 'Proletarian Literature' ('quite a good thing'), but he would not publish Empson's essay on *Alice in Wonderland*. 'He badly wanted us to print his psycho-analytics about *Alice*. Once you've seen the Freudian possibilities in Carroll, you can get some mild amusement in rereading, but who wants the things worked out?' The hostility increased when he read in the *Criterion* a review by Empson of *Coleridge on Imagination*.

No intelligent man has any right to do such a review, however much he liked Richards. Actually, I don't think Empson is very intelligent now, though he was once potentially. He was also dangerously clever, and I think that he's little else now: that terrible capacity for the intellectual game, for getting the ball back over the net, for never being at a loss – that's not thinking. For all its intelligent appearance, that review of Richards, if you know, is downright stupid. [*Coleridge on Imagination*] is as bogus a thing as I've read – and corrupt, through and through. I agree with you about [Empson's] *Letter V*. I still admire very much the poems from *Cambridge Poetry 1929*; but I have never seen any of a later date I was convinced by.[30]

After Leavis's review of *Coleridge on Imagination* Empson wrote to *Scrutiny* to defend it. His letter was written in a style of terse confidence that resembles arrogance. Leavis said it was

written in collusion with Richards, who doesn't propose to expose himself personally. We probably shan't print it. Then the story will go round that Empson wrote a devastating reply which we are afraid to print.[31]

So printed it was, without editorial comment, except cryptically from Leavis: 'No comment on the above seems necessary. Mr Empson is referred back to his texts.' There were private ripples before the letter. Richards wrote to Eliot:

What *is*, indeed, the matter with Leavis? I've not been informed, except through that article. I suppose it was just my turn (as his last friend here in the Faculty!). You mind what you do, it will be your turn before long![32]

Empson was telling a story about the effect of Leavis's review on Eliot. Just after its publication Empson was in Eliot's office at Faber and Faber, seeking a book to review for the *Criterion*. Eliot was looking over his copy of *Scrutiny* and said, 'how *disgusting* the behaviour of Leavis was, what mob oratory his arguments were, couldn't something be done to stop him? – and then, with cold indignation, "Of course, I know it's going to be me next." [33] He echoed Richards's letter. 'Your turn before long' resembles 'going to be me next'. Was Eliot speaking for the benefit of the listening Empson, knowing he was Richards's pupil? He may have been embarrassed by the intensity of praise Leavis bestowed on himself in the review. Eliot may have simulated 'cold indignation', for he was capable of playing the schoolmaster. Later Empson told Leavis himself of the conversation: he 'unguardedly (he's not humanly intelligent) let on about that Russell Square [Faber and Faber] glimpse to me in the 1930s'. (Leavis once said: 'If you want a character study of Empson, go to Iago.') He heard too from Denys Harding (on a summer job at Faber and Faber) that Eliot actually 'agreed with every word' of the review, but 'in talk with the crony-boys, backed the neo-Benthamite against me. "Mob oratory" was Richards's contribution.' [34]

In 1937, two years later, there was a postscript to 'Dr Richards, Bentham and Coleridge'. By that time Empson's intricate analyses in *Seven Types of Ambiguity* were well known and approved in Cambridge. Leavis thought that Cambridge English had become identified with 'ambiguity', especially as Richards eschewed what he called the 'One Proper' or the 'One and Only True Meaning'. Leavis believed that, while analysis should be imaginative, there was a difference between detection of ambiguities and 'a training in sensitive and submissive integrity – and integration – of response'. He made this point when Richards's *The Philosophy of Rhetoric* came out in 1937. Nevertheless, he still praised Richards, remarking that his definition of metaphor in this book was better than that of anyone else. [35]

Primers and Propaganda 1932–1934

Scrutiny had a good audience. The editors wanted the journal to be read by the type of person who read the *Criterion* in Britain or the *Symposium* in America. But *Scrutiny* had a slightly different appeal. One speculates, because a readership survey – exactly what might have been expected from its sociologically conscious editors – was never undertaken. It is likely that the *Scrutiny* reader was a 'practical' intellectual, possibly a schoolteacher who wanted to sift dross from gold. There were urgent claims on the attention of opinion-formers in the early 1930s, especially the claims of politics: if a journal was not political, then a teacher, or his or her friends, would want to know why. There was material hardship among those who had just struggled through into study of the humanities at university: they wanted down-to-earth advice. They wanted a 'line', in good senses as well as bad, whereas the reader of the *Criterion* wanted to explore a library of subtly considered design. When Lucas attacked Q.D.L. he was aware of a new breed of cussed young reader to whom Leavisian impatience was bracing. *Scrutiny* went out of its way to interest teachers and recruit them to 'The *Scrutiny* Movement in Education'. It was militant: the Leavisian mission was to build a public and foster a minority.

But some incongruity was felt between the general aims of the journal and its rather specific activities in wooing schoolteachers. Bottrall did not like the educational side. Leavis defended the *Scrutiny* alliance of literary criticism and education as right in itself (were not the teachers to maintain standards?) and politic. In any case *Scrutiny* needed a professional constituency: it could not rely on simply being a magazine for 'literary people', like the *Calendar of Modern Letters* or the *Symposium* in America.[36] But he was still a little rueful about a circumspect alliance between schools and the broader *Scrutiny* front.

Not that Leavis neglected the schools. In the summer of 1932 he put together, with Denys Thompson ('magnificent propagandist'), a school textbook called *Culture and Environment: The Training of Critical Awareness*.[37] They had so much help from Q.D.L. that it is surprising her name did not appear on the title-page. The book was offered to Dent, an educational publisher, who temporized, so they turned to Chatto & Windus, which published it in early 1933. Teachers were hungry for *Scrutiny*-like material. Lecturers in training colleges wrote in to say they were holding termly seminars on the 'work of the *Scrutiny* group', schoolmasters were organizing summer-schools and the editor of the Workers' Educational Association journal appealed to Leavis to write 'as drastically as possible for it on adult education'.* 'We've all become shameless and adroit at self-advertisement,' said Leavis. Knights promised they would 'attack at other points', like the teaching and examining of English in schools.

---

* W.E. Williams, who later commissioned Boris Ford to prepare *The Pelican Guide to English Literature* for Penguin Books.

There was probably more of Q.D.L. than F.R.L. in *Culture and Environment*. Leavis produced a primer more to his own taste. It was a pamphlet that lay, he said, between 'the literary' and 'education'. In 1931 Ezra Pound published his pungent booklet *How to Read*. Leavis's pamphlet was a reply, written in autumn 1932, first to be called 'A Reply to Ezra Pound', then *How to Teach Reading*. Chatto & Windus did not want it, and suggested Faber and Faber, but it was published by Gordon Fraser.[38] Leavis said he was attempting an 'unprecedented combination' of the educational and the literary. Its tone was one of the least precedented things about it, a deliberate homage to Pound's breezy manner, without a whisper of the academic urbanity used by E.M.W. Tillyard in *Poetry Direct and Oblique* (laborious spin-off from *Seven Types of Ambiguity*). Leavis's other pamphlets had been extended essays. This one was truly polemical.

How to Teach Reading has two parts, 'Critical of Mr Pound' and 'Positive Suggestions', with broadsheet-style headings like 'Mr Pound Rude and Right about "Arts" Courses and Literature' and 'Mr Pound's Perversity'. Leavis thought Mr Pound was right in the dicta that blew away cobwebs ('Great literature is simply language charged with meaning to the utmost possible degree'). He thought he was perverse when he presumed that all languages, and their meanings, were easily accessible. For Leavis literature belonged to *its* language. He thought Pound simplistic in his account of what enabled language to bear the utmost degree of meaning.

For a primer-writer Leavis was daring in that he broached problematic issues of literary aesthetics. Pound defined three forces by which 'language is charged or energized', named Melopoeia, Phanopoeia and Logopoeia: the first relating to 'music', the second to 'picture', the third to 'intellect'. As a former Imagist, the second source of poetic vitality (Phanopoeia, the 'casting of images') was dear to Pound and here Leavis differed, arguing that the language of poetry was not *essentially* pictorial. There was nothing more poetic than the lines with which Lady Macbeth greets Duncan (which he had often heard in the Mummery at the Perse). They are metaphorical, but not pictorial.

> All our service
> In every point twice done, and then done double,
> Were poor and single business, to contend
> Against those honours deep and broad, wherewith
> Your Majesty loads our house.

This is imagery but not visual: not 'vivid' but extraordinarily 'charged and energized':

In 'contend', it will be conceded, we feel an unusual physical force, yet perhaps very few, when challenged, could say offhand how this comes, in what way it is related to the image implicit in 'deep and broad', or what this is. The image is that, felt rather than seen, of a full-flowing and irresistible river, and Shakespeare clearly arrived at it by, characteristically, seizing on and realizing the conventional metaphor of his king's being the 'fount of honour'. But he has controlled his realization to the requisite degree of incipience, so that the image is not felt to quarrel with the following one of 'loads'. And in this marvellously sure and subtle control of realization Shakespeare's genius is manifested as much as in the vividness of his most striking imagery.[39]

Leavis was going to the edge of his academic specialism in this primer. *How to Teach Reading* was reviewed by some distinguished figures, including W.H. Auden, Storm Jameson and Allen Tate. *The Times Literary Supplement* praised its 'skilful economy'. Its bony quality owes something to Pound's prose but also to his poetic lesson in poetic brevity, a work that Leavis intensely admired, *Hugh Selwyn Mauberley*. There was sadly to be no congress with Pound himself. In March 1933 Leavis received two letters from the poet.

The first was twelve pages of monotonously adolescent and re-iterative ejaculation, obscene, of course. The second was four pages ditto. He made not the slightest attempt to deal with anything I said; his most intelligent remark was 'Brit-shit'. I see no point in giving him space in *Scrutiny*. You see, he isn't what one feels he ought to be.

Pound wondered 'why I bother to write this. I don't suppose you want to know anything you don't know already. It wouldn't be professorial of you.' Pound was enraged by Leavis's pert and Eliot-like reminder, in the section called 'The Mind of Europe', that his own pamphlet differed from Pound's because 'the frequentation of other literatures here contemplated aims not at collecting a bag of tricks, but at realizing an order. Mr Pound's advice can lead at best to an elegant and scholarly eclecticism.' Pound went off the deep end.

Again *balls* and *shit*: Bag of tricks, my arse.
All your god damn island has gone on thinking that 30 per cent was 100 per cent and that discrepancy is a great deal more than any question of tricks? Homer and Villon tricks; Dante as trick. *GOD* you ought to live and die in

England. The unspeakable slop that has run the Brit. press during the murky epoch of Murrys, Squires, Gosses, pimps, pewks, Chestertons, etc. exactly in position of art critics who have never seen anything but Royal Academy and won't visit Italian galleries.[40]

He was, of course, far from the truth. Leavis was not a survivor of pre-war literary London. And he was certainly not a 'prof'.

Another piece of striking *Scrutiny* propaganda appeared nine months later. Leavis published a collection of essays from the quarterly as *Determinations* (1934). Leavis thought of calling it 'Cambridge Criticism', having noticed some unexpected behaviour of straws in the Cambridge wind. He was beginning to see Q more frequently and believed he could favour the *Scrutiny* group.* He planned an epigraph for the title page, which was not used until much later.

DETERMINATIONS
IN
LITERARY CRITICISM

Co-operative Labour
'The Common Pursuit of True Judgement'

The contributors were excellent, including Leavis (on Swift), James Smith (on Metaphysical poetry), William Empson (Marvell's 'The Garden', later published in *Some Versions of Pastoral*), Knights (comedy), Denys Harding ('nostalgia') and Michael Oakeshott (on C.K. Ogden), among others. In the introduction Leavis explained that *Scrutiny* was not primarily a literary journal, but one preoccupied with literary criticism because 'literary thinking is the best example of consensus'. Sadly for Leavis there was no personal consensus with Richards, Pound and Eliot. And Lawrence was dead.

Sensuous Experience: Joyce, Milton, Eliot 1933–1936

In 1921 Eliot wrote in *The Times Literary Supplement*:

---

* See Chapter Five, 'To Downing College', 'A New College 1931–1936'.

Tennyson and Browning are poets, and they think; but they do not feel their thought as immediately as the odour of a rose. A thought to Donne was an experience; it modified his sensibility ... The [ordinary man] falls in love, or reads Spinoza, and these two experiences have nothing to do with each other, or with the noise of the typewriter or the smell of cooking; in the mind of the poet these experiences are always forming new wholes.

After Donne this 'mechanism of sensibility', according to Eliot, no longer worked in English poetry. Thought and sense were 'dissociated', a division aggravated by 'the two most powerful poets of the seventeenth century, Milton and Dryden'. This essay, 'The Metaphysical Poets', was reprinted in *Homage to John Dryden* (1924), and the ideas expanded in his Clark Lectures (1926) unpublished until 1993, but attended by Cambridge English *en masse*. Eliot identified Milton especially as architect of a Chinese wall blocking off the sensibility and the styles of the age of Donne. Milton ceased for Leavis to be the fount of English poetry, the great school of language and rhythm. The poet's schoolbook was no longer *Paradise Lost* but the comparatively odd-looking miscellany called *Metaphysical Lyrics and Poems: Donne to Butler*. Having distressed the reputation of Milton in the early 1920s, Eliot continued in 'A Note on the Verse of John Milton' in the literary annual *Essays and Studies* (1936).

The movement against Milton cannot be characterized in a few lines, but its destabilizing effect is obvious. Milton was the author of an English epic, a martial, mythical, religious poem in the navigation of which the classics-educated reader could use Homeric or Virgilian compasses. *Paradise Lost* was a monument, well suited for a curriculum because it required plenty of pedagogy. Donne and Marvell were hard to understand (as Henri Fluchère found), but they could be cracked by analysis. In the late 1920s support for Milton was mustered in Cambridge by the leading organizer of the English Faculty, E.M.W. Tillyard, who assessed what had happened to the poet's 'secure position on an exalted pedestal'. While Leavis was defending Eliot against 'condescension' in the *Cambridge Review*, and Empson was writing *Seven Types of Ambiguity*, Tillyard worked on a solid study of *Milton* (1930). Its 'Epilogue' solemnly trimmed the judicial scales, turning Eliot's notorious digestive metaphor into a literal-minded reproof of Donne, who,

although he devours experience, cannot always digest it. He suffers from surfeits; his mind rejects strange mixtures of food to which he submits it. He does not really know what he wants: or rather he wants everything and cannot harmonize his wants. Hence, with all the eagerness of sensibility, the curious stagnancy of some of Donne's poems.

Tillyard temporized over Donne, attempting to dissolve supposed exclusivity of the Leavisian kind: so he laid out a package of Donne *and* Milton in the same way that there was Donne *and* George Meredith, as was offered by T.R. Henn, whose lectures partnered them in an impossible treaty between Victorian sentiment and Jacobean wit. *Modern Love* was still thought to be devastating on the miseries of love.[41]

A year into *Scrutiny* Leavis turned to Milton, and brought a new figure into debate about Milton: James Joyce.

In July 1933, tired after doing a summer school at Malvern on the industrial revolution and culture, Leavis worked on two essays, on Milton and on Joyce; they were published in September.[42] One was 'Milton's Verse' and the other a review of some Joyceana, including the yet unfinished *Finnegans Wake* called *Our Exagmination Round his Factification for Incamination of Work in Progress* (1929). The review was called 'Joyce and the "Revolution of the Word"'. Leavis's Milton and Joyce pieces built on Eliot's original conception of the thought-feeling flux possessed by Donne and lacked by Milton. It is fairly clear that in this Leavis helped Eliot make new formulations about Milton three years later in 'A Note on the Verse of John Milton' (1936). In that essay Eliot compared Milton's style to that of recent Joyce. Leavis did not make the overt comparison, but his separate essays on Milton and Joyce, back to back in the same issue of *Scrutiny*, implicitly placed the two masters of linguistic innovation together. The two essays formed a single piece of thinking about what is 'behind' the language of poetry. In the Milton essay Leavis took some passages to demonstrate the poet's strengths, one he unequivocally believed to be fine from *Comus* and one less distinguished from *Lycidas*. Leavis quoted from *Comus* the passage in which the Lady is tempted to submit herself to Nature, that is, to the caresses of Comus himself. Nature's bounties made life bounteous

> To deck her Sons, and that no corner might
> Be vacant of her plenty; in her own loins
> She hutch'd th' all-worshipped ore, and precious gems
> To store her children with . . .

This is Milton but not 'Miltonic', claimed Leavis. It had a 'Shakespearean life':

The texture of actual sounds, the run of vowels and consonants, with the variety of action and effort, rich in subtle analogical suggestion, demanded in pronouncing them, plays an essential part, though this is not to be analysed in abstraction from the meaning.

'Beneath' the words was 'a tissue of feelings and perceptions', or so it felt. But in the *Lycidas* lines there was, by contrast, something lacking.

> For so to interpose a little ease,
> Let our frail thoughts dally with false surmise.
> Ay me! Whilst thee the shores, and sounding Seas
> Wash far away, where ere thy bones are hurld,
> Whether beyond the stormy Hebrides,
> Where thou perhaps under the whelming tide
> Visit'st the bottom of the monstrous world. . . .

The poem was one of 'consummate art', but 'personal as it is' the words were cut off from what is 'beneath' or the 'core'.

Though the words are doing so much less work than in Donne, they seem to value themselves more highly – they seem, comparatively, to be occupied with valuing themselves rather than doing anything.

He chose *Lycidas* and *Comus* because it was more interesting to look for a poetic deficiency in a poem where the problem of poetic quality was less obvious than in *Paradise Lost*, a work that was, so to speak, the worse case because it displayed such a manifest lack of 'inwardness'. Its words were *so* often slaves to sound, sometimes unhappy sound at that: the 'foreseen thud', the 'routine thump' that could not be eliminated by artful slidings back and forth of a mid-line pause. In *Paradise Lost* the medium was too rarely sensitized by contact with speech; it was not 'in resonance with the nervous system'. As he had said in *New Bearings in English Poetry*, 'a man's most vivid emotional and sensuous experience is inevitably bound up with the language that he actually speaks'.[43]

In 'James Joyce and the "Revolution of the Word"' Leavis made another suggestion about what is 'beneath' language, again using Shakespeare as an orientation point. In Shakespeare there was

complete subjection – subjugation – of the medium to the uncompromising, complex and delicate need that uses it. Those miraculous intricacies of expression could have come only to one whose medium was for him strictly a medium; an object of interest only as something that, under the creative compulsion, identified itself with what insisted on being expressed: the linguistic audacities are derivative.★

In these cases (*Comus, Lycidas*, Shakespeare) Leavis distinguished between 'surface' and 'core'. Three years later Eliot wrote of Shakespeare and Dante that there was no interruption 'between the surface that these poets present to you and the core'. Eliot continued that Milton and recent Joyce possessed by contrast the 'rhetorical style', in which inner meaning was separated from the surface and tended 'to become something occult'. This pattern of levels, surface and core, is what Leavis discerned, and he also made the value judgement against the 'rhetorical style'. He believed (like Eliot) if 'the future development of the language' was in question, then both Joyce and Milton led down a blind alley. Leavis wanted to show, by quoting the exceptional *Comus* and citing Shakespeare, where there might be a way forward, the possibility of more usable 'work in progress', though progress, he warned, would not be attained by merely *imitating* those styles.

Leavis's essay was a critique of late Joyce, and more. He was confronting an aesthetic exemplified by Joyce, recognized by Joyce's pupils, one of whom was Samuel Beckett. This aesthetic did not admit the differentiation of 'surface' and 'core'. For Beckett (in *Our Exagmination*) 'form *is* content, content *is* form'. The prose of *Work in Progress* was not 'about something; *it is that something itself*' (Beckett's italics). In his copy of the book Leavis marked one passage in particular in Beckett's essay:

Joyce has desophisticated language. And it is worth while remarking that no language is so sophisticated as English. It is abstracted to death. Take the word 'doubt': it gives us hardly any suggestion of hesitancy, of the necessity for choice, of static irresolution. Whereas the German 'Zweifel' does, and, in lesser degree, the Italian 'dubitare'. Mr Joyce recognizes how inadequate 'doubt' is to express a state of extreme uncertainty, and replaces it by 'in the two twiminds'. Nor is he by any means the first to recognize the importance of treating words as something more than mere polite symbols. Shakespeare uses fat, greasy words to express corruption: 'Duller shouldst thou be than the fat weed that rots itself in death on Lethe's wharf.' We hear the ooze squelching all through Dickens's description of the Thames in *Great Expectations*. This writing that you

★ The 'Shakespearean' was a basic Leavisian conception that he wanted to permeate *Scrutiny*. When a pupil in the 1960s revalued *Scrutiny*, Leavis was wounded that he should attack its record of Shakespeare criticism: see Chapter Ten, The End of Cambridge, 'Coterie Rejected'.

find so obscure is a quintessential extraction of language and painting and gesture, with all the inevitable clarity of the old inarticulation. Here is the savage economy of hieroglyphics. Here words are not the polite contortions of C20th century printer's ink. They are alive.

Leavis saw the same qualities in Shakespeare and Dickens; but he would say these qualities did not have to be created *in spite of* the English language. On the contrary, they were sponsored *by* English. Shakespeare, Dickens, Hopkins and Eliot exploited the natural resources of English, a language not in need of 'desophistication'. To a degree Leavis was in tune with supporters of Joyce. In *Our Exagmination* one of them demonstrated that currently Joyce was 'only doing what Shakespeare [had] done in his later plays, such as *The Winter's Tale*'. Leavis was later in close sympathy with Shakespeare's late plays and it is possible that this view urged him towards them. In one of his few essays on Shakespeare he used the same examples, notably from *Cymbeline*.

> Then began
> A stop i' the chaser, a retire; anon
> A rout, confusion-thick: forthwith they fly
> Chickens, the way which they stoop'd eagles; slaves,
> The strides they victors made: and now our cowards,
> Like fragments in hard voyages, became
> The life o' the need.[44]

If English was inherently 'desophisticated' where exactly *was* English? For the 'real' English language, Leavis found evidence in Logan Pearsall Smith's *Words and Idioms*. He found it too in the early 1930s, in the experience of a new friend, the farmer Adrian Bell, who wrote a piece on the English language that Leavis's essay on Joyce was designed to complement. Bell was not a Cambridge man or graduate; his Scottish father believed English universities to be dens of iniquity. Besides being a farmer (introduced to Leavis by Carlos Peacock, Bell's cousin), he wrote novels, of which the best known is *Corduroy* (1930), based on his farming experience, and he also did regular journalism for the *Eastern Daily Press*. In 'English Tradition and Idiom' he argued that in country speech there was 'an intuitive and associative consciousness similar to that of the child', and of a poet. Leavis and Q.D.L. helped him collect material for *Open Air: An Anthology of English Country Life*. Bell and Smith provided Leavis with the linguistic material that fortified his belief that language was in the process of evolution in the English-speaking population. Shakespeare did not come out of a void.[45] English itself was 'work in progress'.

Leavis's interest in country speech belongs especially to the early 1930s. His belief that its powers were on the wane appeared 'nostalgic' to his later critics. He was thought to have averted his eyes from rural hardship, seeming to favour an idyllic world of 'organic' community. The critics said the old world was one of suffering and that its denizens were liberated by industrialism, however harsh the growing pains had been. But Leavis's idea of rural community was designed to illustrate his over-arching conception of organism, not the other way about. If the concept of rural community was vulnerable, the discovery of such weakness did not dispose of the overall conception of organism, or of language.

Poets 1933–1937

While writing on Milton during the summer of 1933, Leavis reviewed a clutch of new books of verse under the sarcastic title 'This Poetical Renascence'. The following June he reviewed another set, this time including Bottrall's two volumes. His criticism of new poetry was confined to the early years of the decade, though he assigned himself major collections by Yeats, Auden and Marianne Moore. He reviewed Hugh McDiarmid, to whose great poem 'The Second Hymn to Lenin' he warmed, claiming it should appear in the 'ideal anthology (which would be a very small one) of contemporary poetry'. He left much poetry reviewing to younger contributors; collections of verse were manageable for beginning critics. Sometimes these reviewers were over-confident of their authority as representatives of a schooled minority, rarely displaying the complexity of tone that Leavis showed in print – the review of *Coleridge on Imagination* was Jamesian – or the hesitancies of his correspondence with Bottrall. Nor did they display Leavis's bursts of enthusiasm, as for Hugh McDiarmid. Leavis sometimes coached his reviewers. A letter to one in 1936, sent with a copy of Robert Frost's *Selected Poems*, illustrates how he advised, on this occasion contesting the current propaganda (so he saw it) for Frost in London. The selection had introductory essays by W.H. Auden and Cecil Day Lewis, among others.

If I may drop a tip (to be picked up or left) the obvious treatment is to bring out his extreme limitations of interest, etc., in contrast to Edward Thomas (to whom he did, as a matter of history, give the decisive impulse). A simple mind (O yes, honest – 'into pity' – and all that) as opposed to a subtle. How it comes out, the contrast, in the rhythms! I can't help thinking that Frost's flatness is just flat. The way the speech movement goes into verse is pointless and monotonous (the Tennysonian weakness where Tennyson offers simple-speech effects). And always the same depressed, reflective, honest plain-Yankee, mood. When you've read one poem you've read the lot. Now if they brought Edward Thomas out with a like army of heralds [i.e., Auden and others] there'd be some point. As it is, no one seems to see anything more in him than the English Robert Frost. Edward Thomas, Robert Frost, and Edmund Blunden were all *London Mercury* poets, 1919–25.[46]

In his first review of a large batch of verse collections, 'This Poetical Renascence', Leavis criticized those who became 'poets of the thirties'. He was interested most in Auden, but depressed by his adoption of an *engagé* left-wing note, as in the poem called 'Song' in *New Verse*:

> I'll get a job in a factory
> I'll live with working boys
> I'll play them at darts in the public house
> I'll share their sorrows and joys
> Not live in a world that has had its day.

Leavis does not quote the ironical opening:

> I have a handsome profile
> I've been to a great public school . . .

But the jokiness of the poem is so unstable that Leavis's observation of a slide into 'something dangerously close to Housemaster–Kipling–Chesterton simplicity' is persuasive. As for the class war, Leavis sighed, 'Ah! those secrets – and that superiority – of the working boys.'

Leavis had taught the poetry of Isaac Rosenberg, particularly stimulating the interest of Denys Harding. There was a brief reference to Rosenberg, as more remarkable than Wilfred Owen, in *New Bearings in English Poetry*.

Rosenberg was out of step with the poetry-reading public. He had been first published two years after Owen in 1922, when war poetry had fallen out of fashion. In the early 1930s he was in danger of being forgotten. Owen was becoming *the* war poet with a new edition in 1931 and strong praise from Day Lewis in *A Hope for Poetry*. In August 1934 Denys Harding visited Rosenberg's sister, Annie Wynick, who showed him her brother's manuscripts. He approached Gordon Fraser with a view to producing an edition.[47] In January 1935 he went to see Rosenberg's pictures, owned by Sir Edward Marsh, and, having conferred with Leavis, decided to go ahead with a full-scale edition of Rosenberg, for which he enlisted the co-operation of Rosenberg's first compiler, Gordon Bottomley, the Georgian poet. Harding contributed the essay 'Aspects of the Poetry of Isaac Rosenberg' to *Scrutiny*, printing six unpublished poems and a prose fragment at its head. Leavis valued the essay highly and used it later in his essay on tragedy.*

Chatto & Windus agreed to publish a collected volume of Rosenberg. Ian Parsons would have liked a preface from Yeats, but he declined; Eliot postponed a discussion because of a cold. In the event Siegfried Sassoon agreed to write an introduction. In June 1937 the *Collected Works* appeared, and on the 22nd of the month a memorial exhibition of Rosenberg's paintings and drawings opened at the Whitechapel Gallery, in east London where Rosenberg grew up. Sir Edward Marsh made a speech and in the evening Leavis gave a lecture on the poetry. One of the organizers, Joseph Leftwich, a man of letters who had been a friend of Rosenberg in his Whitechapel days, was taken aback to hear Leavis claim that it was *Scrutiny* that had made Rosenberg's reputation. He remarked to Harding that there were other 'links in the chain', like inclusion in *Georgian Poets*, a reference by Edith Sitwell in the *New Age* in 1922 and enthusiasm from Graves and Sassoon.[48] Leavis's argument about Rosenberg's reputation was given in his review of the *Collected Works* in September in *Scrutiny*. Rosenberg, he knew, had been noted; but he wished that critics, himself included, had been more persistent. It is one thing 'to feel something strange, original and interesting, and another to recognize its nature and significance'. Although the poet was not unknown, Leavis thought that the recognition of Rosenberg's *genius* dated from Harding's essay, defining in him 'an extraordinarily mature kind of detachment such as is not characteristic of Lawrence'.

Leavis was still interested in Ronald Bottrall, after having arranged publication of *The Loosening*. A poem by Bottrall appeared in the first *Scrutiny*. During 1932 he and Leavis corresponded about an ambitious new poem in four sections to be called *Festivals of Fire*. Leavis gave an extended view on 26 April, in a letter that is a good example of his care for this protégé. He criticized a didactic element in the poem, as if he

* See Chapter Seven, Wartime, 'Language and Tragedy 1944'.

were writing both poem and essay; and the purging of the 'personal' was what *The Waste Land* had, surely, taught his generation. After that knowledge, what forgiveness for manifesto-writing in verse? Bottrall's intellect was at work, at the expense of the rhythms of the poetry. There was also a touch of Pound's *Cantos*. None the less, Leavis was cordial, for once signing himself as 'Frank Leavis'.[49] On 30 May he wrote again, urging once more that Bottrall should go back to Eliot for counsel. He reminded him that Eliot had said in his *Dante* (1929) that 'with Goethe, for instance, I often feel too acutely "this is what Goethe the man believed", instead of merely entering into a world which Goethe has created'. Leavis suggested publishing the first section in *Scrutiny*, with an announcement that Gordon Fraser would bring out the whole ('if he will') in the spring.

Bottrall hoped that Faber and Faber would publish. On 20 July Leavis reported that he had written tactfully to Eliot. He did not want to give Eliot the excuse that there was no need for Faber and Faber to publish *Festivals of Fire* because Fraser would do it anyway. Eliot answered promptly that he had been hoping to print some of *Festivals of Fire* in the coming year, but if there was a chance of the whole being published in the meantime, then publication in part would not deter him. It took months for a decision to be made. Eliot eventually agreed in October 1933 to publish the whole poem as a book.[50] Leavis rejoiced at what appeared a tribute to the *Scrutiny* position.

CHAPTER SEVEN

WARTIME
1938–1948

Upheavals like the war tend to accentuate and speed up drifts and developments that have already set in.
　　　　　　　－ F.R. Leavis, 'Education and the University: Considerations
　　　　　　　　　　　　　　　　at a Critical Time', *Scrutiny*, 1943

Emergency 1938–1944

The autumn term of 1938 approached and Leavis was thinking about writing a new book, 'though the inertia is very great'. During appeasement, he thought the political inertia was also great. War (called by Leavis 'the emergency') was a year away. When it came, few dons were sheltered by virtue of profession or age, but Leavis was peculiarly vulnerable. He was in the position of a person with a business, in his case *Scrutiny*, that did not serve war aims. He could not set aside the quarterly for the time being because this enterprise was tied in with his fullest concept of his own work, and though it may have appeared to be academic (published in Cambridge) with presumed academic support, it was a purely autonomous enterprise. When the war came, it was a struggle for *Scrutiny*: one in which Leavis was defeated.

For the British people the Second World War lasted much longer than the armed conflict; it absorbed the period from appeasement to post-war deprivation, ending for Leavis approximately with the publication of *The Great Tradition* on 4 November 1948.

During these years the Leavis family was established. When war broke out Ralph, a child of Mozartian brightness, able to give instructions from his perambulator, was four and a half years old. He introduced James Smith to Mr Eliot's poems, Smith having settled with his aunt into a house on the corner of Chesterton Hall Crescent.[1] A second child,

Katharine Laura, or Kate, was born in September 1939. The war itself brought more family suffering to Q.D.L. In December 1940 she lost both her mother (aged 64) and her sister, Ruby Caroline (aged 28), in the street in which she had been brought up, which was hit by a German bomb. Morris Roth was buried in the debris for two days. There had previously been talk of a reconciliation with her mother, and when war broke out Morris visited Cambridge, seeing Ralph and Kate. But it was now too late.* The Leavis family in Cambridge had never been friendly; for Q.D.L. there was no chance of recovering her own. A third child, Lawrence Robin, was born in December 1944. Q.D.L.'s pregnancies were difficult. Before the birth of Kate, she was seriously ill and plagued with rheumatism. Before Robin's birth, Kate was ill too, and Q.D.L.'s labour began with a terrifying haemorrhage at home. A month had to be spent in hospital and nursing-home. Leavis was interim 'dietician, cook, nurse and housekeeper'. He thought it 'very funny to see my head on so small an infant'.[2]

The eldest son Ralph continued to develop formidably during the war years, especially his musical talents. By the spring of 1944, aged ten, he had completed a piano concerto. In 1946 his parents sent him to the progressive boarding-school in Devon, Dartington Hall, where his gifts would be, they hoped, looked after by 'an intelligent Polish composer'. At Dartington he was painfully awkward, unable to join two pieces of string without a tangle, but could play Bach keyboard works at any speed required – and dance music, which on occasion made him an unexpected hero when the gramophone broke.[3]

The hardships of wartime were well shown in an exchange of letters between Q.D.L. and the novelist Storm Jameson, an admiring, reliable friend, though at a distance. In November 1948 Jameson sent over from America a box of twelve dozen eggs for the family; they were, according to Q.D.L., 'quite overwhelmed at the sight of so many eggs and all boiling ones' and thought 'the millennium must have come when they can have a boiled egg at breakfast, egg and cress sandwiches at tea, and apple sponge at dinner'. Q.D.L. had been living on soda-water and oranges 'when available' after an exploratory operation. She admitted that suffering in mainland Europe and the likelihood of atomic war should have put the individual British plight in perspective, but

---

* Morris Roth died in 1953 at the age of 78, having lived evidently a solitary life since the war-time tragedy. Q.D.L.'s brother Leonard became a lecturer in mathematics at Imperial College, London. He was killed in a road accident in America in the 1960s.

shortages, illness, high student numbers and *Scrutiny* had taken their toll. 'Frank has had an awful time sustaining the house with one hand and the university English teaching with the other, and, with the worry as well, looks like a skeleton.' Q.D.L. herself was in the poorest of physical conditions. In 1946 cancer was diagnosed; in treatment she suffered radiation burns from which she suffered for years. In 1946 one of her closest friends died, Dorothy O'Malley, the wife of Ralph's moral tutor at Dartington, the Leavisian writer and teacher Raymond O'Malley. Q.D.L. dreamed of a sabbatical, ideally in California: 'we could put Kate in a swell girls' school where Auden teaches English, Ralph could study under Schoenberg and Hindemith, and I should be able to enjoy little Robin before he gets too big to be nursed.'[4] None of this came to pass.

In October 1938 Leavis watched the political scene.

As for the 'emergency', I suppose it will be a gain if Neville [Chamberlain] postpones it for us once more (at what price???). If only there were a lead somewhere, something could be done with the lull. It's preposterously lunatic that we should all be just waiting, when there's so much that *might* be done. One feels the disadvantage of having been un-sociopolitical, sharing no useful connections. For the lines of a programme worth propagandizing with could be fairly easily worked out. Of course, one can't do the work of the Elvins (when they do it at all), but I suppose one ought to have kept in touch with them. An incapacity to do so has been my own disablement, incurred during the last emergency: I wonder if there'll be any profitable stirring in Cambridge next term.[5]

He believed that if anything was to be done, it should follow a resolution from senior members of the university that appeared in the newspapers early in October 1938.[6]

As a literary critic Leavis was involved with two projects that did not come off, his book on criticism, 'Authority and Method', and an essay on Shakespeare's *Timon of Athens*.[7] In the summer of 1938 he wrote a review of Rose Macaulay's book on E.M. Forster, eventually turning it into an essay. Tentative about what he had achieved, Leavis adverted the reader in an initial note to the treatment of Forster by a *Scrutiny* writer Derek Traversi in the April issue of *Arena*. 'It only gradually became clear that I should have to make [it] an article and it became an essay.' He did not think his essay enhanced a good number of *Scrutiny*.[8] A good *Scrutiny* for Leavis was on this occasion one mostly about music (Mellers on Roussel, Rubbra and Busoni) and on European authors (essays on

Baudelaire, Rilke, Rimbaud and Marx). Leavis's 'E.M. Forster' showed his dubieties about Bloomsbury. Q.D.L. attempted to deliver a stake through the heart of Bloomsbury in an attack on Virginia Woolf called 'Caterpillars of the Commonwealth Unite!'*

The war meant shortages for *Scrutiny*. Many contributors left England or Cambridge. James Smith left Chesterton in October 1940 for a British Council post in Venezuela; Gordon Cox left in February 1942, enlisted as a non-combatant. John Speirs was already in Cairo.[9] Derek Traversi left immediately for Italy, to return when it entered the war. Harold Mason was stranded in Basle and became a teacher in a girls' school there for the duration of the war. There was a shortage of skilled workers at the printer, Marshall's. In 1944 the Linotype machine operator was called up.[10] The arrival of contributions was so unreliable that Leavis could not insist on deadlines.

There was a shortage of subscriptions: Leavis still had to dip into his pocket to help out. Occasional contributions of five or ten pounds were acknowledged. The major shortage was of paper. In spring 1940 rationing began. Publishers were allowed 60 per cent of their pre-war output, later reduced to 40 per cent, so a small enterprise would receive little and a large firm like Macmillan a huge allocation (having recently published *Gone with the Wind*). Lord Moberley administered a fund for educational publications, to which *Scrutiny* applied.

On the credit side, the organization of the media of expression in wartime that proved so productive elsewhere (in cinema, for example) brought benefit to *Scrutiny*. The British Council helped. Leavis wrote to Bottrall in 1942 that he believed that over ten years *Scrutiny* had supplied 'a sound critical history of English literature during the period' and that the British Council had been co-operative in exporting the journal abroad (recently twenty copies for Sweden).[11] His gratitude here contrasts with the indignation he felt at the British Council half a dozen years later precisely for failing to distribute *Scrutiny* abroad.† At the end of the war there was a shortage of contributions, though some hope of day-to-day support by the possibility of appointing Harold Mason as an editor.[12] Leavis confided to Cox in 1947 that 'The war, to put it egotistically, was bad luck for us. It means we've not had the succession of recruits we had earned. Things are really desperate.'[13]

* See this chapter, 'Old Cambridge 1939–1947'.
† Chapter Eight, No Common Pursuit, 'Virtue in Our Time 1950'.

Persona Non Grata: Leavis's Occupation 1939–1947

Leavis had been appointed in late 1936 as a Lecturer for three years. This period should not be misunderstood. When he was a probationary Lecturer he was given a set-term appointment that could be extended and was so until 1931. The 1936 appointment was to a straight lectureship. One hesitates to call it a 'full' lectureship, because it was for 'part work'; but a lectureship it was, as opposed to a probationary lectureship. Nor was it an assistant lectureship, the term recently devised for the old probationary lectureship. He could now *expect* his appointment to be confirmed after three years and so it was in 1939 when the provisional period ended. And Joan Bennett, who had been appointed to a lectureship eighteen months after Leavis on the same terms, was also confirmed. But he was still on 'part work', and so was she. This 'part work' status, reducing his salary and his pension contributions, remained in place all the way through the coming war. Joan Bennett was in exactly the same position. (Perhaps Leavis thought that as a married woman she was fortunate; at least both she and Stanley Bennett were earning.)

When Leavis first got his post in December 1936, he told Cox delightedly that he liked the idea of his work being carried on at Downing, 'when I'm Professor, I mean'. Leavis did not become professor and in the years after 1939 became increasingly bitter about his position in Cambridge, a part-time Lecturer still. Leavis later often referred to the harsh treatment meted out to him by Cambridge: it is worth pausing over the justice of his complaint.

It is hard to enter academic life, as hard as the law or the theatre, at least in this time in Cambridge, with English a new subject and a new system of administration (the separate faculties) developing. Leavis was certainly overtaken by younger men like George Rylands and Hugh Sykes Davies, who became a Lecturer just before Leavis, though he had taken the English Tripos only five years before in 1931. With hindsight it does not seem that the Cambridge English Faculty was one of memorable ability. Was Leavis ill-treated by the Cambridge system?

'I was not a full Lecturer till fifty-two,' Leavis said in 1953 and said it often.[14] After 1936 he was part time for ten more years. In longer perspective, there were twenty years between his first appointment as probationer (1927) and his full-time university appointment (1947), and in five of these years he had no university position at all. In 1975 he pointed out that in 1936 he was given half of Mansfield Forbes's post: 'Forbes . . . whose death had made the vacancy, had had a full lectureship, but mine was only "part-time".'[15] The occasion of this statement was a review of the circumstances of Leavis's appointment by Ronald Hayman in a long essay on Leavis's life, first published in the *New Review*, later as a book in 1976.[16] Hayman stated that Leavis became an 'Assistant Lecturer' in 1936. Noël Annan, who had become exasperated by (as it seemed to him) Leavis's exaggeration of his hardships, wrote promptly to *The Times Literary Supplement* to contest Hayman. He said correctly that Leavis's post in 1936 was a full lectureship, and that he merely had to serve the formal three-year probationary period, after which confirmation was virtually automatic. (Leavis himself said in 1974 the post was an assistant lectureship and this is evidently how his family interpreted the position.) He explained too the nature of the probationary lectureship that Leavis originally held, expiring in 1931. Such posts, he said, could not be transmuted into permanencies: two or three years' extension was possible, but essentially these were fixed-term contracts.[17] Thus, although it was tough on Leavis not to be appointed permanently after the expiry of his probationary lectureship, it was not unexpected or unjust. Times were hard and funds low in 1930. Further, when his lectureship came, it was 'probationary' by a technicality: Leavis could have had expectations of a post to retirement.

In neither case was Lord Annan's argument completely persuasive, though he was clearly arguing in good faith. The point about Leavis's lectureship was not that there was a three-year probation, but that it was part time, and went on being so for an unconscionably long period. As to the 'fixed-term' nature of Leavis's original probationary lectureship, here Annan was both right and wrong. He appears to assume that Cambridge English began with the English Faculty of 1926. In fact, as Leavis was quick to point out, both the subject and a group of teachers went back earlier, as far as 1919, and these teachers, after the formation of the Faculty, became either full Lecturers or probationers, and the probationers in turn, with the exception of Leavis and Joan Bennett, became full Lecturers. They were not entitled to it, but it was the custom of this country that they should, a reasonable custom because they had taught the subject successfully when freelance. Annan was right to say that technically the post was fixed term, and so was the post of Assistant Lecturer that replaced that of Probationary Lecturer in 1934.[18] But *traditionally* the posts led to permanencies. The first young probationers could believe they had a claim to permanency, a claim that Faculty practice endorsed. Leavis explained the situation himself:

As a result of the Royal Commission of 1925, the English Faculty got its start in 1927, making possible University status, salaries, security and pension-prospects for the Lecturers who got in. The transition to the new system involved – decency required it – the appointing to Probationary Lectureships of (among others) several persons who had become familiar names in the lecture list. These Probationary Lectureships expired, as Lord Annan records, in 1931. The way was thus clear for the system to be consistently worked by those in a position to control and manage it. Anyone who wasn't persona grata to the managing powers and had no prospect of a fellowship faced a dead wall – and (I can testify) was told so. (I was directed to take a chair in Tasmania – there was no university of the Falkland Islands.)[19]

In the early 1930s there was no established system of assistant lectureships and full lectureships, with various conditions attached to each. The tradition of passage from probation to lectureship was regular between 1927 and 1931 with the result that (so Leavis perceived it) there was an 'atmosphere' of promotion.

Why, incidentally, did Leavis say he had an assistant lectureship? He meant that for himself the probationary lectureship was *like* the assistant lectureship, the post that was defined in 1934. This was on exactly the same terms as the probationary post, except that it was now explicitly stated in the university statutes that the post 'may not be renewed' beyond five years. The change was necessary because it was received thinking that the probationerships were informally renewable. Why was no one else disappointed by non-renewal of a probationership? Because everyone else, with the exception of Leavis and Joan Bennett, had their probationership topped with a permanency!

There are two other questions to be asked, about Leavis's peers. First, why did they not take his part and believe that he was unjustly kept waiting for promotion? I suggest that it was because so few people understood the informal practices of the middle to late 1920s. Leavis's expectations were established in a very short segment of past time – in which most people were not interested. Second, why was Leavis not taken out of 'part work' sooner? A reasonable person cannot attribute his position to spite or conspiracy, though the printed evidence indicates strong dislike on Tillyard's part. Lack of funds is one explanation – enhanced by quotidian inertia. But there was one other factor. Leavis made himself so much a college man, so *frankly* ran a system within the system, that there must have always been a splinter of doubt about having him join the others.

Old Cambridge 1939–1947

The Leavisian position has been often defined in contrast with Bloomsbury. Leavis did indeed define 'us' as the cohort in opposition to Gordon Square, King's and Charleston. The nature of this opposition, and its moment, needs to be detailed.

From the beginning, to be Leavisian was to be against Bloomsbury, merely because Leavis's valuation of Lawrence, and the scale of his valuation of Eliot, was not Bloomsbury's. But there was, besides, a more particular contest worked through by Q.D.L. in the wartime period to be found in a set of *Scrutiny* essays on Cambridge luminaries. The pieces, published between 1939 and 1947, were about A.C. Haddon, Leslie Stephen, Henry Sidgwick and Q.D.L.'s old supervisor, H.M. Chadwick.[20] They represented an Old Cambridge, proposed as preferable to new Cambridge with its Bloomsbury slant. Q.D.L.'s exploration of Old Cambridge went back to her attack on Virginia Woolf in 1937.

When Q.D.L. began writing for *Scrutiny* it was mostly within the convention of the rounded essay, the miniature life-and-works (Gissing, Santayana, Dorothy Sayers, Richard Jefferies). She also did a series of appreciative reviews, belying her reputation for the hatchet job. In these she showed her capacity for defining a type of 'entertainment book' that did not drive a wedge between the reader and more problematic work. An example of such non-authoritarian entertainment was Robert Graves's *Antigua, Penny, Puce.** On the attack, Q.D.L. published in September 1937 a fierce review of Virginia Woolf's non-fictional work *Three Guineas*. This review was the aforementioned 'Caterpillars of the Commonwealth Unite!' Woolf's book, not one of her strongest, is a continuation of *A Room of One's Own* with a tendency to wounded whimsy. Its theme is the victimization of women condemned to use up their energies in attendance on male and family. Q.D.L. took exception not precisely to Woolf's feminism but to a quality of 'femininity' in her conviction that women (or thinking women) were irrevocably impoverished by

---

* Some of the minor books chosen for praise in 1932: H. L. Davis, *Honey in the Horn*; Hugo von Hofmannsthal, *Andreas or The United*; James Farrell, *Studs Lonigan*; Ruth Adam, *I'm Not Complaining*.

marital and household life, and especially child-care. She thought Woolf over-valued 'charm'. Wasn't it, she asked, often the 'uncultivated charm-less woman' who has 'merely' worked hard, who was really more interesting and stimulating than 'exquisite creatures' who had 'to be subsidized as hostesses for the art of social intercourse'? Q.D.L. saw 'no profit in letting our servants live for us'. Woolf said that women had to do their thinking while stirring the pot and rocking the cradle. Q.D.L. retorted that she stirred the pot while writing her review and as for rocking the cradle, 'the daughters of even uneducated men ceased to rock infants at least two generations ago'. She wondered derisively whether 'Mrs Woolf would know which end of the cradle to stir'. Confronting Woolf's position, Q.D.L. argued that there was no solution to the problem by university provision of more 'rooms of their own'. The ill went further back: in primary and secondary schools the rule should be co-education. Women of Woolf's class should not send their children to 'conventual establishments where they never come against masculine standards'.

Q.D.L. erected an ideological defence of the working woman: one mode of life is set against another, and a basic ingredient of her anti-Woolf (and anti-Bloomsbury) position is a view of child-care as positive, not invariably decreative. She championed sharing between the genders. What she set up nakedly against Bloomsbury was the Chesterton Hall Crescent way of life, that of demanding children and difficult careers (and a journal to run). In the background was Q.D.L.'s co-educational life at Latymer school. She detected in Bloomsbury an ideology of somewhat willowy feminism that excluded or degraded her familiar life-activities and their values.

Q.D.L. bluntly set the values of her household against Bloomsbury: her values, she claimed, were actual. During the period she did so she was bringing up children, and life was difficult. Certainly a sense of 'standards' prevailed, but there was also a great deal of jollity in this household. The children were brought up to Bronx, Bowery and Broadway mimicry during high tea readings of Damon Runyon. She enthusiastically devised games, and was keen on dolls' houses: 'Daisies do very well for poached eggs at dolls' tea parties.' The house was light and airy; there were frequent visitors; sometimes permanent non-paying guests, like Wilfrid Mellers.*

---

* Q.D.L.'s letters illustrate her cheerful, headlong interests. Her readings of Runyon are described in one to Brian Worthington, 30 August 1974. She was intrigued by the way

In her essays on Old Cambridge Q.D.L. explained her position, not by further argument based on domestic ethics (the politics of housework was involved) but by reference to a tradition by means of which she established a working mythology or hypothesis. This was done in her set of studies (between 1939 and 1947) about the ancient Cambridge heroes, Henry Sidgwick, A.C. Haddon, H.M. Chadwick, her old professor and, at the head of the table for *Scrutiny*, Woolf's father, Leslie Stephen. Her first essay of caterpillarian endeavour was done 'in the spare time of three days', according to Leavis, who marvelled at her speed.[21]

In 1937 the Leslie Stephen Lecture at Cambridge had been delivered by Desmond MacCarthy, who chose Leslie Stephen himself as his subject. MacCarthy censured Stephen for his defective sense of literary aesthetics. Q.D.L. defended him on several fronts, two of which should be stressed: practicality and honesty. As a literary critic MacCarthy was a descendant of Anatole France of the soul-adventuring-among-master-pieces persuasion. For Q.D.L., on the other hand, literary criticism was 'a process of intelligence', a means of locating 'what is discussable' about a literary work. Q.D.L.'s sense of criticism was unexpectedly more social than MacCarthy's: for her, literary criticism as a form of substitute creation was 'indefensible egotism'. She applauded Leslie Stephen's blunt-ness. His 'sincere record of impressions, however one-sided they may be, is infinitely refreshing, as revealing at least the honesty of the writer'. This was the 'Cambridge' spirit, anticipating and consonant with the libertarianism of the English Tripos, and shown in the plain-spoken questionnaire responses I.A. Richards collected for *Practical Criticism*.

Q.D.L. defined Stephen as a *Cambridge* critic, one who found congenial the 'Evangelical leaning' of the 1850s and an environment that austerely had no such spiritual leaders as Carlyle or Newman. She proceeded in her other essays to present two other Cambridge role-models, the anthropologist A.C. Haddon, and the architect of Cambridge English, H.M. Chadwick. The personal qualities of both were praised, especially their independence, maintained in the case of Haddon in a career resembling Leavis's in some respects. Much of his life was spent as a freelance Lecturer and reviewer. But their academic fields were also

---

his characters spoke always in the present tense: the sign of a first-generation immigrant? She noticed the same in one of her few Cambridge friends, 'Poldy' Gerhard, wife of the composer Roberto Gerhard, even though she was 'very articulate and mixing in the best musical circles'.

Leavis said his father, Harry Leavis, was a 'Victorian radical. There was a fierce, Protestant conscience there, but it was divorced from any religious outlet.' Harry Leavis died in a motorcycle accident during the week of Leavis's final examinations in 1921.

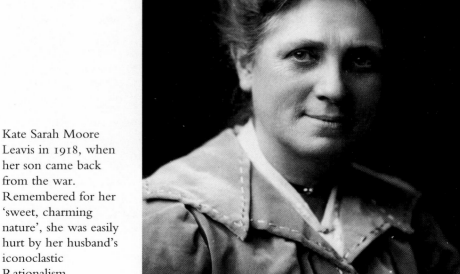

Kate Sarah Moore Leavis in 1918, when her son came back from the war. Remembered for her 'sweet, charming nature', she was easily hurt by her husband's iconoclastic Rationalism.

The Leavis piano business in Regent Street, Cambridge, opposite Downing College, which became Leavis's 'School of English' for thirty years.

Leavis in his grammar school fives' court. This photograph was taken by H. Caldwell Cook, pioneer of theatre teaching at the Perse School; under his direction Leavis played the Gypsy Man in the *Wraggle Taggle Gypsies*.

Leavis as a medical orderly in 1915. 'I joined the Friends' Ambulance Unit. Stinking blankets and lice, and always a job to do that was too much for me. But after the Bloody Somme there could be no question for *anyone* who knew what modern war was like of joining the army.'

Queenie Dorothy Roth in her first term at Cambridge, October 1925. Q.D.L. was a Henry James enthusiast and indefatigable scholar; her first book, *Fiction and the Reading Public*, was well received when it appeared in 1932.

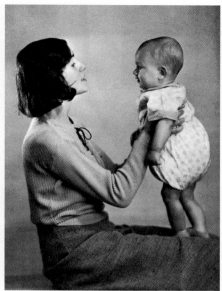

The married couple with their first son, Ralph, in January 1935.

Leavis's childhood home, designed by his father, in Chesterton Hall Crescent. F.R.L. and Q.D.L. returned to it in March 1931 and raised their children there; Leavis also saw his pupils in the house until he obtained a college room in 1936.

I.A. Richards supervised Q.D.L.'s doctoral dissertation on popular fiction and, with E.M. Forster, was one of her examiners. He sent this picture to her in 1929 inscribed 'Since you want it, here it is!'

Morris Shapira shortly before his murder in 1981. He was Leavis's lieutenant in the 1960s at Downing College and intended to be his successor. He was later estranged by the 'Leavis Lectureship' affair.

Q.D.L., Robin and Kate Leavis, with Harold Mason and his son. Mason, a Poundian classicist from Oxford, was *Scrutiny*'s youngest editor.

Marius Bewley, author of *The Eccentric Design*, was one of Leavis's best pupils, despite being an un-Leavisite Leavisian.

The Leavises at Downing College in the summer of 1961.

Leavis in his garden at Bulstrode Gardens, Cambridge, in November 1976. Leavis relished the idea that he possessed a 'hereditary Huguenot-ducal pride or ferocity'.

important for Q.D.L., especially that of Chadwick, who had impressed her so much at Girton.

Q.D.L. was one of the last students to take early literary studies ('Early Literature and History') as part of the English Tripos. In 1926 these studies were removed from the tripos, which some would say improved it. Chadwick himself was happy to leave English behind. The two English parts of the tripos became a coherent sequence, a survey part and specialist part, both modern and medieval, with the international element retained. The Whig view would be that in 1926 an alien element was removed and the muse of English, a study of British secular scriptures, was thenceforth unchained. But the position was not so simple. This view casts Anglo-Saxon as the stranger in the course, which it was, but also presumes it was an enemy to the course, which it was not; many people wanted to study Anglo-Saxon, and they were not in the least anti-modern or in favour of studying early literature just because it supplied hardy grind to a 'novel-reading' tripos. Q.D.L. adored the course. She took pains in her essay on Chadwick to show that his course was not primarily linguistic or philological. Chadwick was a 'linguistic genius', said Q.D.L. 'D'ye knaw, I did a bit of philology meself one time,' he confided once (unreconstructably Yorkshire) to a colleague, minimizing his ability in this field.[22] He launched his students, 'groaning', on languages completely new to them. But he despised mere philology and scornfully remembered hearing Alois Brandl in Berlin lecture for an hour on vowel shifts. The main point about his 'Early Literature and History' was that it aspired to give a total account of ancient cultures, and in so doing it provided a model of study relevant to any period, even the modern. Although the subject matter of Chadwick's 'Early Literature and History' was distant from the reading-publics and communities, the classics and best-sellers and the industry of taste analysed with exuberant distaste by Q.D.L. in *Fiction and the Reading Public*, it was an alien but *usable* model for the 'anthropologico-literary' research that was discussed on the December evening in 1931 at Chesterton Hall Crescent four months before the first *Scrutiny*. Chadwick's tripos, wrote Q.D.L.,

opened for us the doors into archaeology, anthropology, sociology, pre-history, early architecture – all beginnings for future self-education, and he saw to it that these subjects, studied with reference to Scandinavia and England, should also extend to the Celtic and Mediterranean areas, opening fresh vistas.[23]

Chadwick stimulated his students to look into the meaning of all artefacts, including a literature, if there was one. He showed 'how literary studies could be linked up with that school of sociological studies which Cambridge so notoriously lacks'. The relation of this idea of sociology or anthropology to the whole Leavis project is too large a subject to pursue here, though one shard of data might be specified. When the reprint of *Scrutiny* was in preparation in 1968 Leavis tried to persuade Cambridge University Press to bring out a new edition of a classic by a Cambridge scholar of early literature, Dame Bertha Phillpotts's *The Elder Edda*. He always recommended it to his 'Tragedy' pupils.[24]

Leslie Stephen symbolized practicality and honesty; he was little of an aesthete. This is what he brought to the Leavisian 'Cambridge'. Chadwick brought a crucial element, a sociological perspective, an angle of vision more at odds with Bloomsbury than with the moralism of which the Leavises were often accused, and which was supposed to differentiate Bloomsbury from *Scrutiny*. The 'anthropologico-literary' element was more important to *Scrutiny* than moralism, one much at odds with the gallant individualism of Bloomsbury. Bloomsbury really did believe that it was sensibility ('states of mind') from which literary creation flourished; *Scrutiny* believed the literary world was 'constructed'. The difficult part of this belief was its potential application, not only to popular culture but to *all* culture. Bloomsbury itself was not exempt. What was not forgiven was that Bloomsbury could be treated as if *it* were an appropriate field for sociology (or 'homeland anthropology'), like anything else.[25]

Q.D.L. strove to define an alternative world-view to that of Bloomsbury by reference to somewhat objective qualities. Leavis himself dealt with a more intimate conflict of values. On one reckoning it could be suggested that in this he took the female part and Q.D.L. the male.

Education: Ideal and Actual 1940–1943

In *New Bearings in English Poetry* Leavis took the criticism of Eliot up to the 'Ariel' poems and *Ash-Wednesday*. There were greater challenges ahead as the four poems came out that were later called *Four Quartets*. 'Burnt Norton', 'East Coker', 'The Dry Salvages' and 'Little Gidding' are arguably Eliot's most distinctive achievement, though still not widely regarded as such, because the currency of *The Waste Land* is assured by its suitability for educational purposes. Leavis did not find the poems easy. He did not review 'Burnt Norton' in *Scrutiny* when it first appeared. It fell to Denys Harding to cover it in his review in 1936 of Eliot's *Collected Poems, 1909–1935*. 'East Coker' was published in the autumn of 1940, but Leavis told Harding that he had not yet worked up any enthusiasm for it. But he was certainly prepared to defend it fiercely in *The Times Literary Supplement*, where he thought it had been reviewed shoddily; once again, he thought, 'condescension' had been shown to 'the greatest living English poet'.[26] By February 1942 Leavis admired 'East Coker': he reviewed it for the *Cambridge Review*, noting a bleakness closer to 'Journey of the Magi' than anything else of Eliot. By the mid-1940s Leavis became surer of what he valued in these poems, a discovery that coincided with new concerns with the structural planning of higher education. Curiously, the two interests fed into each other.

Leavis's concern for the planning of universities went back to the early 1930s, when he became interested in the work of an American educator, Alexander Meiklejohn. Meiklejohn was a professor at the University of Wisconsin. He had been appointed by his friend Glenn Frank, President of the university and formerly editor of the *Century Magazine*; Meiklejohn had written an essay called 'A New College: Notes on Next Steps in Higher Education' for *Century*, partly based on his experience at Amherst College, of which he had been President. (In *How to Read* Ezra Pound paid tribute to Glenn Frank 'and other starters of ideal universities'.[27]) Frank charged Meiklejohn to set up an experimental programme within the university at Wisconsin. This liberal arts course was to be based on a core of comparative studies between fifth-century Athens and nineteenth-century America; it ran for five years from 1927 and Meiklejohn reported on it to the university, publishing his findings as *The Experimental College*, which Leavis enthusiastically reviewed in *Scrutiny* in December 1932, the first issue for which he was officially editor.

Leavis liked Meiklejohn's American capacity for going back to fundamentals, though he thought his proposals on the literary side did not have enough Empsonian intelligence or sensibility. The Graeco-American comparison was excellent in theory, less so when it took the form of comparison between of *The Oresteia* and *Mourning Becomes Electra*. Leavis was always sceptical of unrooted global eclecticism.★ But

★ See Prologue, 'Being a Critic', mentioning his essay of 1953 for *Commentary*, 'The "Great Books" and a Liberal Education: Must All Free Men Read Them – or be Slaves?'

Meiklejohn did want to start from scratch, with his 'green field' ambitions. Leavis liked to talk about the college he and Q.D.L. could run. On holiday in Norfolk he would look with ironical appraisal at a potential site, a disused priory outside Weybourne. In September 1934 he wrote about Meiklejohn in *Scrutiny*. During the 1930s, while building up Downing English, he often thought about Meiklejohn's scheme, especially when Harold Mason made him aware of the deficiencies of 'Greats' in Oxford as a civilizing and modern course of study.

In August 1940 Leavis was contacted by the BBC about contributing to a series called 'The Writer in the Witness Box'. The producer, C.V. Salmon, visited Chesterton Hall Crescent, where his proposals first received a stony reception, but when Q.D.L. left the room the interest of F.R.L. quickened. He shortly wrote off apologetically to Salmon. 'I know I have the reputation of being a superior person,' he began, with suggestions for a scheme of cultural education. The project fell through in the end, but Leavis's proposals are worth quoting at length because it shows how far he had got towards the general planning that was soon to come in his essays on education and the university.

Leavis began by telling Salmon that making a series on writers meant explaining 'what a *culture* is'.

One might start, by adducing the nineteenth-century, Romantic account of the 'masterpiece' as a product of the inspired individual ('genius'). Then sketch the recent change in critical fashions. Eliot, of course, provides the main *loci critici*, but there is also to be referred to, Arnold's first two essays in the second series [of *Essays in Criticism*]. – Tradition, 'atmosphere' of ideas, and so on: the part of the extra-individual conditions in the work of art. But, one goes on, the conditions to be taken account of aren't to be thought of merely in terms of 'ideas', artistic and literary tradition, and the currency of 'cultural' intercourse.

Consider *language*. '*Language*', of course, is a trickily complex concept. I should now hark back to Shakespeare – certainly an 'inspired genius'. *But*, Shakespeare didn't create the language he used, and the spirit of which he may be said to incarnate. If there hadn't been that English Language there wouldn't have been Shakespeare. This point could be very effectively developed and illustrated – Cultural history and 'practical criticism' together. Everything here would have to be done by the 'talker'. I mean there aren't any obvious books to refer to. If you challenged me I should have to instance this and that odd paragraph of my own that I should develop and illustrate.

But you ought to read L.C. Knights's article, 'Education and the Drama in the Age of Shakespeare', in the *Criterion* for July 1932. Also, very good as far as it goes, there's a little book to recommend: Logan Pearsall Smith: *Words and Idioms* (Constable's Miscellany). I should then go on to Bunyan: he enables one to develop the point about English popular culture.

Topics: the changing relation between popular and sophisticated culture – Shakespeare, seventeenth and eighteenth centuries – Today. We now come to the process of the Industrial Age. I should bring in something of the *Culture and Environment* themes.

Move on to the specifically literary perhaps by way of advertisements, etc. Some 'Practical Criticism' – in particular analysis of elementary type cases – moving on to fiction in some of the *Fiction and the Reading Public* themes: elementary criticism of the novel. Denys Thompson's *Reading and Discrimination* contains a useful collection of exercises, tho' he doesn't do much analysis. (He does suggest further reading.) *Straight and Crooked Thinking* by R.H. Thouless is worth recommending, I'm told (English Universities Press, 3/6). Susan Stebbing did a little book in the Penguin or Pelican series. Biaggini followed up with *Education and Society* (also Hutchinson). Denys Thompson's *Between the Lines* (Frederick Muller Ltd.) could be recommended. (More specifically literary – since you consulted me – did you ever see my counterblast to Pound's *How to Read? – How to Teach Reading: A Primer for Ezra Pound?*)[28]

Although nothing came of these ideas for the BBC, Leavis began to work on his conception for improvements in university education for essays in *Scrutiny*. In September 1940 Leavis published 'Education and the University: A Sketch for an English School', following it in December with 'Education and the University: Criticism and Comment' (an important 'yes–but', never afterwards reprinted). In the spring came another instalment, 'Education and the University: (iii) Literary Studies' (March 1941).

Two years later another and final essay appeared with the subtitle 'Considerations at a Critical Time'. The war had indeed reached a 'critical' point. It was also the time of the Beveridge Report and Butler's Education Bill.[29] These essays, adapted, became *Education and the University* (1943).

Educational reformers do not usually cite recent poetry. Leavis did. His proposals were linked to T.S. Eliot's 'Difficulties of a Statesman', as a timely rendering of the usual approach to social reform:

The first thing to do is to form the committees:
The consultative councils, the standing committees, select committees and sub-
                            committees.
One secretary will do for several committees.[30]

While he was writing on the university for *Scrutiny*, Leavis was simultaneously absorbing Eliot. For Summer 1942 he reviewed 'The Dry Salvages'
in *Scrutiny*. The last instalment of the 'Education and the University'
series appeared in Spring 1943, in the same issue as Denys Harding's
review of 'Little Gidding'. That review was subjected (Summer, 1943)
to criticism by a correspondent in a critique who was in turn answered
at length ('Objections to a Review of "Little Gidding"') not by Harding
but by Leavis himself. When Leavis put together his education articles as
a book for Chatto & Windus in July 1943, he included his review
of 'The Dry Salvages' and made a very warm and pointed reference
('intensely interesting') to Harding's review of 'Little Gidding'.[31] Education, poetry and Eliot were therefore tied closely together, and this is
shown in the shape of *Education and the University*, published in November
1943.

Education and the University shows Leavis to be as anthological as ever.
It is a folio of pieces: three chapters and two appendices, with a preface
and a concluding note consisting of two long quotations from critical
essays by Eliot. The two appendices are Leavis's review of 'The Dry
Salvages' and the whole of his pamphlet *How to Teach Reading*. Literary
criticism and educational theory may sort strangely together; possibly
this was and is the reason why they are rarely brought together. Leavis did
not want it to be thought that his sole concern was with *literary* matters
– which was not the case. A worse charge would have been that Leavis
was cobbling some literary essays to some educationalist ones to make a
book. This was not the case either. Eliot's presence was essential in the
thinking and the structure of the book.

At the beginning of the book Leavis discusses what a university
should be, paying his respects to Meiklejohn. Then in the second chapter
he provides 'A Sketch of an English School'. This chapter does not offer
a course in English literature. What is given is a model of an advanced
interdisciplinary course to which students would come after some other
university course. Leavis has in mind something whose place in student
life would be similar to that of Part Two of the Cambridge English
Tripos. Leavis was therefore proposing a course of senior study. He
envisaged seven examinations, some divided into parts, set out here
(slightly reordered) in paraphrase rather than quotation.

 1. *Practical Criticism*. Meant to examine basic critical competence: several
three-hour papers would be set at the end of the course.

2. *The Seventeenth Century in England.* The focal study, one opened up by Eliot's essays, among other sources. This would be the equivalent of the fifth-century Athenian/nineteenth-century American study in Meiklejohn's experimental scheme. Assessment would be by four or five 'pieces of work'.

3. *The Transition from Seventeenth-Century to Modern England.* One essay required on an aspect of this theme. (Such an essay would be an equivalent to the existing optional tripos dissertation.)

4. *Dante.* 'A general study': one or more papers set at the end of the course.

5. *French Literature.* A 'substantial' essay had to be written during the course.

6. *Book Reviews.* A set had to be written during the course, 'of a number of books which are to be chosen in consultation with authority'. This idea is one of the most surprising, and was perhaps never tried. It was intended to keep the student in touch with the latest understanding.

7. *Oral Examination* at the end of the course.

Participation was 'required in organized discussion- and seminar-work', from which it may be presumed that some examination grading would be done for this work.

Leavis made suggestions about the content of the courses that led to these examinations, but he did not give a syllabus. He gave intense attention, however, to the style of the examinations and to the style of the work that led to them. It is an original feature of his plan that he wanted a relationship established between the work-mode of study (including essay-writing and reading) and the work-mode of assessment techniques.

On the work-mode of study, Leavis was alert to what it felt like to be a student: that is, insecure. He describes the intellectual insecurities of studenthood that would be experienced by those enrolled for the sketched course. But he stressed that these were worries inherent in the condition of a serious student.

The education proposed is necessarily full of incompletenesses and imperfections – the only way in which the required kind of thinking (with which the specialist is frustrated) *can* be carried on. The student is to acquire as a discipline methods and habits that must inevitably be his in subsequent practice if he is to continue using his mind with effect and to the ends desired. The spirit of strict scholarship can be vicious, a mere obstructiveness, a deadness and an excuse for pusillanimity.[32]

It could almost be said that this experience (the survival of the anxieties of imperfection) is described by Leavis not simply to show what taking the course would be like, but that the course was devised *in order to* initiate students into the experience. This, Leavis was saying, is a real mode of study. The student was to be as freely 'personal' as *The Student's Handbook* had required in the 1920s, or as personal as any of the respondents in Richards's *Practical Criticism*. They were also to possess 'intelligence' or 'sensibility' in the Empsonian–Leavisian sense. They would certainly be aware that they knew too little. And none of these things was wrong: they were par for the course. Leavis wanted to set up a new kind of hardness of study, against the conventionally recognized hardnesses of university life to which genuflection was routinely made: the 'grind' of scholarship, the 'athletic endurance' of the week of three-hour tripos papers, the stand-and-deliver process of assessment. Of course the subject matter of the proposed course was important, but so was the 'discipline', in which work was personal but not amateur, 'qualified' but not mechanical or 'dead'. This was the kind of work Leavis asked, courteously, of his pupils – or flatteringly intimated that they were engaged with it. These were the solicitations and intimations that made membership of the 'Downing School' such an honourable matter. Leavis allowed students to experience the pains of seriousness. The usual discipline was characterized by the three-hour examination paper that Leavis contested, not simply on humane grounds but because its rationale was ridden with cliché. It was argued, for instance, that the three-hour paper was gruelling as the real world of deadlines is gruelling. (Formal university examinations are possibly less gruelling than some work in the outside world: there is no telephone in an examination hall.) There are all sorts of training useful for the real world and that world, which pays the piper, may like the idea of seeing them in universities. Leavis was surprised, when his first proposals appeared in *Scrutiny*, to find a correspondent claiming that work in a 'great Government office' needs to be prepared for by intellectual athletics like writing against the clock in the universities. He replied that 'it hadn't occurred to me that I should be called upon to vindicate the idea of liberal education – of education as opposed to special training'.

Education and the University aimed to show university work to be unique *to* universities: they should not be a harbour for other kinds of labour. A 'great Government office' was not the right analogy for work in a university School.

The seven-part scheme for an interdisciplinary course was given in Leavis's second chapter of *Education and the University*. He then proceeded to a chapter on 'Literary Studies', which contained some of his best pieces of poetry analysis, given for the sake of illustration. This was material destined for his still unfinished book, 'Authority and Method'. Apart from appendices, the book ends with pages of literary analysis. That it does so is, perhaps, unfortunate because it is important to remember that 'literary study' was not the climax of *Education and the University*. In the final chapter Leavis set out some qualifications or prerequisites for his course, not its summation. Leavisian students would probably have some of the skills of 'Literary Studies' before they came to university. Those who turned to his course from another subject would need a crash-course in the basics of criticism. 'Literary Studies' were necessary; Leavis believed everyone should have a skill in them. But their presence in his book should not make the reader think that literature, or English literature, was his prime object of promotion. He was not making a bid for English Literature as queen of studies. 'English' was presented as an *exemplum*, a subject in which university thinking is best illustrated. Why 'English' for this role? Partly, and bluntly, because Leavis himself knew it; he always wanted to work from where he was qualified. Then, also, 'English' was manifestly a crossroads subject, signing to routes out and on from itself. Further, 'English' was in the English language.

The chapter on 'Literary Studies' and the 'English School' proposal, though excellent, must be seen as part of an overall plan for post-war reconstruction in which an 'Idea of the University' is revived. The curriculum is a possible interdisciplinary course for senior study, and 'Literary Studies' shows some of the prerequisites the student would need for the course. Unless Leavis's proposals are seen as such, he will appear to be saying what is implausible: that English is the cultural panacea, or saying what he explicitly denied, that students should 'spend their time in a dilettante preoccupation with value'. He added that 'to say that the literary–critical part of the scheme is the crown of the whole, and that the training and testing of judgement on pieces of literature is the ultimate end in view, would be to misrepresent my intention'.[33]

T.S. Eliot was aware that Leavis was thinking about education before *Education and the University* appeared. He remarked on Leavis's first essay at the subject, the sketch for an 'English School', in September 1940, in

the address 'The Christian Conception of Education' at a conference in
Malvern, organized by the Archbishop of York, 'The Life of the Church
and the Order of Society'. Leavis's sketch had been practical, but was
based on certain 'generalities' and on these Eliot unerringly focused. The
basic generality was Leavis's belief that Western civilization appeared to
have lost touch with a definition of an educated class or educated mind.
Civilization had

ceased to find a 'centre' or model of mind, a way of bringing various kinds of
specialist knowledge and training into effective relation with informed general
intelligence, humane culture, social conscience and political will.

Eliot agreed and fastened on the word 'humane', critically following
through its connection with 'humanism'. The poet of disintegration
thought Leavis had seen the problem aright. Perhaps 'humane culture'
could provide integration, a place where specialism and personal consciousness were integrated. But Eliot was suspicious. If 'humane' meant
'humanist', there were many 'humanisms' and some unacceptable ones.

Why should we want humane culture? Why is one conception of humane
culture better than another? What is the sanction for your conception of social
conscience or of political will as against that, for instance, now dominant in
Germany? I do not think that the humanist can give a satisfactory answer.[34]

Eliot turned his gaze on the best version of humanism he knew, the
humanism of Irving Babbitt, which he believed to be a noble eclecticism
embracing Confucius, Buddha, Socrates and Erasmus, but in which
attitudes were cut loose from 'race, place and time'. Babbitt was unreal:
could Leavis do better? Eliot was touching a delicate place. Leavis's father
had been a Liberal republican, an educator at the Chesterton New Institute.
Leavis himself was resolutely non-Christian, always was, and his convictions
did not dim with age. Late in life he remarked to a young admirer who had
sent him a piece on Samuel Johnson, 'Poor Johnson! Not even he was
immune. However hard they try, they won't succeed in assimilating me to
Christianity or The Anscombe.' He was more sceptical than Eliot about
Babbitt-like eclecticism.[35] But he was very far from Eliot's conclusion. For
the taints of varying humanisms were distasteful to Eliot, who concluded
that they were not the proper sanction for education: there was no other
framework for education than Christianity. If Leavis was here rejected, at
least Eliot made his work known. It has been claimed that the printed
version of the Malvern proceedings sold more than a million copies.[36]

As to Eliot's question of what kind of humanism could provide the basis for education, Leavis had given an answer already. Ten years before, in 'Why Universities?', he had considered what was an appropriate model for an 'educated man' and what could be a 'centre' to education. He suggested the problem could be solved by pragmatic avoidance. If a course were fashioned out of the materials already present in the Cambridge English Tripos, would not this form a central core that would command wide assent? Was not this course already far enough away from dubious humanisms? Why not begin by seeing 'if something might not be made of the English Tripos'? He hastened to add that it should not be developed into a course *in* literary criticism, but into a course in which literary criticism would be a prime (but not the only) technique and English literature one (but not the only) fund of material. 'It is literature that gives access to the inherited wisdom of the race, cultural continuity depending, for the most part, on literature and literary tradition.' Why not enlarge what was in hand at Cambridge? Might this not help make a bridge between personal consciousness and specialist knowledge? At this bridge the tolls would be collected neither by Christianity nor humanism.

Although Eliot could not be enlisted into Leavis's project at the time of the first 'Education and the University' essays, Leavis did not diminish Eliot's presence in the book when it appeared. There are frequent references, extracts of prose in the final note to indicate what literary critical writing should be like, and there is, of course, as appendix, Leavis's review of 'The Dry Salvages'. What connection did it have with education or universities? The relevance is made most clear in a reference Leavis makes to Denys Harding and his review, which Leavis constantly invoked, of Eliot's *Collected Poems, 1909–1935*. Leavis's model of university study was not to be of literature only, but was still meant to be literary, and the literary training of language study was to be one of its basic techniques, the combination of objective and personal in miniature. It was Eliot, in his *verse*, as interpreted by Harding, who showed what working with language was like. 'Ordinarily,' wrote Harding,

our abstract ideas are over-comprehensive and include too wide a range of feeling to be of much use by themselves. If our words 'regret' and 'eternity' were exact bits of mosaic with which to build patterns, much of 'Burnt Norton' would not have had to be written. But . . . one could say, perhaps, that the poem takes the place of the ideas of 'regret' and 'eternity'. Where in ordinary speech we should have to use those words, and hope by conversational trial-and-error to obviate the grosser misunderstandings, this poem is a newly created concept, equally abstract but vastly more exact and rich in meaning. It makes no statement.

It illustrates the exploratory use of language to which a university student should be sensitive, a sensitivity that should govern work according to the best idea of a university. But the passage is also, one suspects, commended by Leavis because it validated his own procedure in his account of university education, *his* process of definition, and his better way of doing what 'The English Moralists' did badly. In a sense he 'made no statement' about the ends of his proposed courses. He believed criticism could *be* itself; so he thought there was enough self-evidently valuable in his sketch of specificities.

Eliot's reference to Leavis's *Scrutiny* essay on education and the university was welcome, and not long after the poet and critic himself called on Leavis in Cambridge. He announced to Leavis that he would be up to hear a lecture by E.M. Forster and was invited to Saturday-afternoon tea at Chesterton Hall Crescent. After the slights of the *Criterion* and Eliot's evident complicity with Bloomsbury, Q.D.L. was not best pleased. 'Why do you let that man into the house? You know what he wants,' she warned. What he wanted was, she thought, to have her husband acquiesce in Eliot's neglect of *Scrutiny*. Leavis replied: 'You ought to trust me, my dear. Of course, I know. He won't get it.'[37] In some accounts Leavis shows himself as charmed by Eliot's presence, finding him 'very pleasant'. There was certainly one pleasing interlude, when the young Ralph Leavis came eagerly forward, at first too cowed to speak, as Leavis related.

He has clearly a lofty notion of Eliot's place in the scheme of things.
    Finally, he dashed forward with an open copy of *Commerce*.
    'Look, Mr Eliot, he's spelt your name wrong. Monsieur Jean de Menasce has put in two ts.'
    After that he had a good time. He produced all the texts, and put Eliot through the variant readings. 'You altered that.' (Accusingly.) Eliot explained why. 'H'm! interesting,' says Ralph, 'no punctuation here.' 'That's to show it's to be chanted,' says Eliot. 'H'm! interesting. You haven't finished this. Why didn't you?' 'I couldn't: I'm afraid it will always remain unfinished.' 'H'm! like *Schubert*'s Unfinished Symphony in . . .' – whatever it's in, I don't know, but Ralph does, of course. 'You did this in French, too.' 'No I didn't,' says Eliot. 'Yes, you did. Look.' 'Oh, so I did, I forgot.'

And so on. Looks sharply at Eliot and pointing to the text, '*When* will time flow away?' 'I don't know,' says Eliot. 'What do *you* think?' 'I don't know. But, I think there ought to be as much time as there was before B.C.' 'And how much was that?' 'I don't know,' says Ralph, 'but more than 4,004 years, anyway.'

Ralph then pointed to the first line in *Ash-Wednesday* and the first line of the last section.

'The same, but a little different.' 'As in music,' said Eliot. 'Yes, of course,' said Ralph, and then we had a discourse on first subjects, subjects, modulations and so on.[38]

Ralph left the drawing-room with Q.D.L., and the afternoon drew out, Eliot's cigarette butts copious in the hearth. Later, when Leavis read the last 'quartet', 'Little Gidding', he said he recognized some things said by Eliot that afternoon. An encounter between literary men does, indeed, occur in the poem. In its second 'movement' the poet, at dawn in the London Blitz, accosts (after 'pointed scrutiny') a ghostly figure,

> some dead master
> Whom I had known, forgotten, half recalled
> Both one and many; in the brown baked features
> The eyes of a familiar compound ghost
> Both intimate and unidentifiable.

The master, in the Dantesque *terza rima* lines, is recognizably the great humanist Brunetto Latini. He grimly admonishes the poet, deploring the Dead Sea fruit of a lifetime's aesthetic commitment. 'Let me disclose the gifts reserved for age', and a bleak litany follows, concluding with the awareness in old age

> Of things ill done and done to others' harm
> Which once you took for exercise of virtue.
> Then fools' approval stings, and honour stains.
> From wrong to wrong the exasperated spirit
> Proceeds . . .

'Some of the things in that "Little Gidding" passage he said to me, when – I learnt later – he was writing "Little Gidding". He might have said more if I'd encouraged him. I didn't; merely listened and looked inquiringly at him.'[39]

There were never to be many contacts with Eliot. In 1943 Ronald Bottrall, hoping for further publication of his poetry by Faber and

Faber, accused Eliot of prejudice against him because he had been first published in *Scrutiny*. Eliot replied that he was mistaken. 'I don't think any of my associates know anything about Leavis and *Scrutiny* and as for myself, I have always entertained the most friendly feelings toward him and a genuine admiration and respect for the work he has been doing under great difficulties.' He said that he had tried, from time to time, to assure Leavis of his support in every way possible. Leavis, he said, was given to exaggerated censure and praise. 'My own position at present is that I have been embarrassed by a heavy dose of the latter.'[40]

In his review of 'Little Gidding' Denys Harding paid particular attention to the meeting at dawn with the dour humanist and the chilling narrative of the pains of godless aestheticism. He proposed that

the life presented is one, such as Mr Eliot's own, of effort after clear speech and exact thought, and the passage amounts to a shuddering 'There but for the grace of God go I.' It reveals more clearly than ever the articles in the *Criterion* did, years ago, what it was in 'humanism' that Mr Eliot recoiled from so violently. What the humanist's ghost sees in his life are futility, isolation, and guilt on account of his self-assertive prowess – 'Which once you took for exercise of virtue' – and the measure of aggression against others which that must bring.

Harding believed Eliot had cast into an austere form an account of his own past as literary magister, as editor of the *Criterion*, alluding perhaps to his Olympian manner ('things ill done, and done to others' harm'). It is not altogether clear that he is true to the poem: there are no words that exactly correspond to 'self-assertive prowess' or a 'measure of aggression', though it is certainly true that the poem prays for humility, the opposite of those drives.[41] Harding finds and gives a presence to these Leavis-like qualities in the poem, qualities that are deplored as corrosive by the poet in quest of humility. By so doing Harding was interpreting Eliot to be deploring qualities in Leavis: he is equated with the humanist literary figure. And while Eliot sympathized with Leavis's concern for the civilized, his Christian position obliged him to believe that a godless sense of civilization could be no better than humanist. All humanisms, to the Christian, must be fallible, and, indeed, hard to differentiate in terms of quality, though for Eliot a humanism that espoused D.H. Lawrence must be otiose. Leavis did not like to think of himself as a humanist: he believed that human beings 'did not belong to themselves'. To Eliot this was as bad as godless humanism, and a grim prospect.

When Leavis wrote about 'Little Gidding' in the summer of 1943, he said nothing about the encounter with humanism in the poem. He certainly faced the poem's endeavour for humility, the being taught 'not to care' of *Ash-Wednesday*. In late life he was mocking towards Eliot's humility. But during the time of war he was involved deeply in consideration of how the poem treated the quashing of self and of how it entered this realm, not in religiose or ethical generality but in a myriad of implications in its language. He said he had to read and reread it. He knew it was about 'detachment (distinguished from indifference)' and about how an ending can 'itself lead into the beginning', but

just what corresponding to these phrases one actually grasps is a question that, in the stock-taking with which the reading tries to complete itself, leads one back again and again to a rereading. The poetry and the question – the questions – have to be lived with.[42]

Some of the questions were about a way of addressing the world.

Leavis had been active at Downing from 1931, but it was only at the beginning of 1937 that he was able to act as a member of the fellowship, with voting rights on the Governing Body. So, at the outbreak of war, an increased authority in matters of policy and planning accompanied his work on the principles of university education. Student numbers dropped at the beginning of hostilities, but soon rose. In 1943 Downing had its largest entry yet of students to do English: there were eighteen freshmen and 'these boys need four times as much attention as a normal peace-time lot. They suffer from lack of senior years. Cambridge is very much of a desert. And I myself have to cover the whole ground with them – good for me, but strenuous.'[43] There were new categories of student, for instance, the 'bi-termists' who had to take the first-year examinations after two terms, not three (as he himself had done).[44] Some students went up to Cambridge on armed forces 'short course' (one- or two-year) schemes. There was much teaching and two scholarship examinations a year to run.

After the plans and principles of *Education and the University*, Leavis wanted to experiment in the actual situation at Downing, taking the cue of the English Tripos 'Life, Literature and Thought' courses. Leavis wanted his Downing men to prepare for these papers in a college course

called 'Man, Society and Civilization'. By now he was fairly sure that
his pupils would have had good literary training at school; they could be
trusted to branch out at university. He planned to remove the 'Paraphrase
and Comment' section in the scholarship examination and replace it
with 'England since 1720' to 'promote relations between English and
History, or some exploitation of Life and Thought'.[45] He wanted a
section of the Downing college library to be stocked for 'Man, Society
and Civilization', 'avoiding the term *Sociology*'. It was short of books
and Leavis was not keen on what he called Cuttle's 'enlightened'
acquisitions. (School students who had been taught in the Leavis tradition
were, when up for interview, surprised to notice on Cuttle's study
shelves un-Leavisian works by Humbert Wolfe, John Masefield and
Robert Bridges.) But Leavis maintained good relations with Cuttle,
though he remarked that in conversation the temperature could drop
suddenly, 'till one felt the snow piling up on one's shoulders'.[46] Leavis
thought of 'risking obliquity' by suggesting that Downing alumni
might make donations: 'One's driven to this kind of device: – otherwise
it's waiting for ever. Only the pace must be forced in all these things: it's
now or never.'[47] A large phalanx of students was expected to arrive
when the war ended. 'Cuttle calculates that if all the people who have
had offers made turn up there will be fifty or sixty reading English.'
Having admired American enterprise in the form of Alexander Meiklejohn's activities at Wisconsin, Leavis turned for support to the Rockefeller Foundation, which was interested enough to send representatives to
visit Downing, though not immediately with an open cheque-book.

   Leavis was teaching more nineteenth-century prose, fiction and non-
fiction. The English Tripos had a new special subject for Part One of
the tripos, which stimulated Leavis to devise a plan to help his pupils
master the whole Victorian period. His nineteenth-century plan started
with studies of the essays on Bentham and on Coleridge in John Stuart
Mill's volume of essays, *Dissertations and Discussions* (1859). The recommendation shows how Leavis's concern with the nineteenth century was
not focused only on the novel. With Mill, the student should 'dodge the
technical parts', but note his account of his early contacts with the
Coleridgeans, and with Carlyle, those men who brought home to him
that social data were more difficult to understand and analyse than
Bentham recognized. Next in line was John Ruskin, especially *Unto
This Last*, 'the most respectable, heroically effective anti-the-classical-
political economy' side of Ruskin. Then came Dickens's *Hard Times* – 'a

great book, I think' – which showed at its core, in the marriage of Tom
Gradgrind to Bounderby's daughter, a symbolic union of Utilitarianism
with industrial *arrivisme*. 'I've always meant to write an essay on *Hard
Times*.'[48]

Leavis did not do so yet. What he did do in 1946 was write an essay
called 'Mill, Beatrice Webb and the "English School"', a sequel to
Education and the University. The essay was published in *Scrutiny* in June
1949, and then in 1950 as the preface to a reprint of Mill's essays on
Coleridge and Bentham.[49] It provided a wealth of suggestions for
reading. Leavis draws on Webb's autobiography *My Apprenticeship*
(1926), in which she describes her family life as Beatrice Potter, daughter
of a railway magnate. Webb does indeed give a vivid picture of her
growing social conscience, and desire to become a social investigator.
A revered senior visitor to the Potter household was Herbert Spencer;
he 'taught me to look on all social institutions exactly as if they were
plants or animals – things that could be observed, classified and explained,
and the action of which could to some extent be foretold if one
knew enough about them' (one remembers F.R.L. as Q.D.L.'s mentor,
though Spencer was nearly forty years Potter's senior). Here was a link
with the 'anthropologico-literary' curiosities of Leavis and his original
research group. With the other hand Webb pointed to the novel; when
she set out as a social investigator, 'I had to turn to the novelists and
poets ... for any detailed description of the complexity of human
nature, of the variety and mixture of human motive, of the insurgence
of instinct in the garb of reason, of the multifarious play of the social
environment on the individual ego and the individual ego on the social
environment.'[50]

One wishes that Leavis's writings had been arranged more accessibly,
that, for example, his material on John Stuart Mill and Beatrice Webb
had been reprinted in an enlarged *Education and the University*. But his
writing was done insecurely, and his obligations forced him into a
headlong pace: 'I'm a slow worker, and my position is such (unpaid
unsalaried Editor, ditto-ditto-quasi-Professor, non-titled Bishop, etc.)
that I suffer continual distraction.'[51]

When Leavis was planning a course for Downing, Sir Arthur Quiller-
Couch died, on 12 May 1944. Nearly two years were to elapse before, in
February 1946, there was a new occupant in the King Edward VII Chair
of English Literature, an appointment made on the recommendation of

the Prime Minister. Did Leavis expect an invitation to come? At one
time he thought Bonamy Dobrée was interested; and he heard that T.S.
Eliot was said to have declined.[52] When the appointment was made it
was a disappointment. Leavis was passed over again. Basil Willey was
appointed to the Chair of English. (Ironically, he liked very little about
being a professor.)

In October 1945 the men came back. Some were veterans who had
spent time at university before 1939 then departed to command ships,
fly bombers or lead brigades into battle. Many had families. The college
was thronged, and at Downing supervision in pairs was replaced by
group seminars, twice or more a week. Essays were not urgently
solicited. By February 1947 Leavis had fifty Downing men, and only
some help with the teaching from Wilfrid Mellers, who taught Elizabethan literature to the first year. Leavis was still enthusiastic about an
interdisciplinary course for Downing. In 1948 there was discussion of the
plan in a 'secret enclave', to which he delivered a homily on the ideal of
the college. He addressed the 100th meeting of the Doughty Society on
the same theme in February 1948.[53]

Language and Tragedy 1944

In 1936 *Scrutiny* had published an essay on Shakespeare by George
Santayana. In 1944 Leavis wrote an essay called 'Tragedy and the
"Medium"', in fact answering Santayana, and extending his own
thought about tragedy in 'Diabolic Intellect: The Sentimentalist's *Othello*'. The essay on tragedy is a reunion of ideas, a quintessentially
Leavisian collaborative essay, marshalling from *Scrutiny* Harding and
Traversi and, of course, Santayana himself, Samuel Johnson, Eliot and
Yeats, and Richards to whom there is even a small tribute. Part of the
essay is about Santayana's misunderstanding (as Leavis saw it) of Shakespeare's 'medium'. The more important part is about what 'tragedy'
means, affirming one idea in Santayana but taking it a good deal further
than he did; Leavis also moved forward from an idea in his defence of
Othello in 1937. There, it will be remembered, Leavis said that Othello's
suicide was magnificent, 'mais ce n'est pas tragique'. Othello is, in his
coup de théâtre, like us, with 'an incapacity for tragic experience that
marks the ordinary moments of us all'. Leavis then proceeds to try to
define the exceptional experience that is (he thinks) the tragic. The

definition involves thought about the 'impersonal', a key matter for Leavis. In Leavis, both as writer and teacher, there was such a high level of intimacy, of personally delivered conviction, that it is hardly surprising he was concerned about control and restraint, but also, more generally, about the difference between the private and the personal.

The statement of Santayana that Leavis affirmed and refined in 'Tragedy and the "Medium"' was about Macbeth's 'Tomorrow and tomorrow and tomorrow'. It was, Leavis conceded, a type of Aristotelian *catharsis*: Santayana had said, rather insensitively, that

the rhythms help; the verse struts and bangs, holds our attention suspended, obliges our thoughts to become rhetorical, and brings our declamation round handsomely to a grand finale. We should hardly have found courage in ourselves for so much passion and theatricality; but we bless Shakespeare for enabling us still to indulge in such emotions, and to relieve ourselves of a weight that we hardly knew we were carrying.

We are relieved (the cathartic purgation) of something we did not know we had. As the words go through our heads, we let ourselves into an excess of theatricality that we daren't or can't normally indulge. The catharsis is a way of declamation. Leavis wanted to go further: yes, the tragic *is* a way of using language, but not at all this one. For one thing, the tragic is not theatrical if that means lingeringly or boisterously noble: whatever it is, tragic discourse is not 'full of itself', and certainly distant from the spirit of one of the highly popular essays of the early twentieth century, Bertrand Russell's 'A Free Man's Worship' (1903), which was both about tragedy and written in a self-consciously tragic vein. The tragic sense was not one of what Russell called 'the bitter beauty of the universe and the frail human pride that confronts it for a moment undismayed', one of Leavis's favourite quotations for ironic delivery. The tragic state of mind is *not* that: egotism is alien to it. It establishes 'below' the level of psychological assertion an

impersonality in which experience matters, not because it is mine – because it is to me it belongs or happens, or because it subserves, or issues in, purpose or will, but because it is what it is, the 'mine' mattering only in so far as the individual sentience is the indispensable focus of experience.

Is the 'tragic' here something felt or something said? It is surely some form of expression, indeed, the 'tragic' appears to be the attainment of a form of expression, and that form of expression cannot exist under certain conditions. The form of the expression was attained, argues Leavis, by Isaac Rosenberg, at least as described by Denys Harding. The effect of tragedy, the effect of its continence, is to make available what is being experienced to the observer: because non-egotistic, the tragic invites participation. Leavis quoted W.B. Yeats: 'I saw plainly what should have been plain from the first line I had written, that tragedy must always be a drowning, a breaking of the dykes that separate man from man.' For the tragic, language-use must be exploratory, the speaker cannot know what is coming next. He seems to be relieved of the tamperings of the will, but he is not Nietzschean: if there is a 'tragic calm' – Leavis is obviously unhappy with the idea of calm here, but puts up with it – it is 'not in the least the calm of the tensed and self-approving will'. Throughout the essay Leavis did not disguise that he was struggling, qualifying more than usual, resorting to his authorities here and there. At the end it is clear that, besides being concerned with his familiar theme 'impersonality', he was attempting to overtake the thought not only of Santayana but also of his old guide, Richards. Richards introduced him to 'impersonality' in *The Principles of Literary Criticism*, whose pages on tragedy contained 'some of the most valuably suggestive things in the book'. Richards proposed there was a 'joy' in an encounter with the 'full tragic experience'. But Leavis could not accept that this joy registered that 'all is right here and now in the nervous system'. Richards shied away into an unsatisfactory, materialist conclusion. If he was dealing with 'the most valuable experience in the arts', is this all it was? A poise or harmony in the 'nervous system', one that can be imparted 'by a carpet or a pot or a gesture as unmistakably as by the Parthenon'. To call an experience of art 'tragic' presupposes passion and transcendence. The experiencer achieves, the observer is awed; he or she is spared, but also has a sense of sharing. He or she does not feel simply better organized internally. Leavis favoured something closer to Yeats's 'breaking of the dykes' than Richards's reliance on impulses and nervous system that was a descent into 'the utilitarian calculus – with its water-tight unit self, confined, for all self-transcendence, to external transactions with other selves'. Leavis's wartime essay on tragedy established his conviction about the connection between extraordinary literary experience and 'self-transcendence'. Literature shows, as it were, where the self stops.

New Bearings on English Fiction 1945–1948

Many of the men came back in 1946 to icy Cambridge terms. It was the worst winter in recent memory; there were power cuts, snow and floods. Leavis took to wearing what a pupil called 'an extraordinary sort of Red Indian duffle coat, the gift of an American admirer'.[54] There was now a Special Subject on George Eliot for Part Two of the English Tripos, which stimulated Leavis to prepare a course in nineteenth-century studies, eventually issuing in his guiding text, *Mill on Bentham and Coleridge*. It also pushed him towards the writing of a much better-known book, *The Great Tradition: George Eliot, Henry James, Joseph Conrad* (1948), the first also behind which may be felt the presence of Q.D.L., whose field was the novel. The book consisted of chapters on each of these authors, and a final chapter on Charles Dickens (but only on *Hard Times*). There was an introductory chapter, 'The Great Tradition', which gave the rationale of Leavis's selection, and introduced two other writers in the tradition, Jane Austen and D.H. Lawrence. It is evident that the book in hand was to have a companion, a promise partly fulfilled by *D.H. Lawrence: Novelist* (1955). But Q.D.L.'s essays on Austen, silently assumed to cover the first member of the line, did not appear in separate book form. The book concluded with an appendix: a full reprint of Henry James's essay of 1876 about George Eliot's *Daniel Deronda*, an exceptionally elegant piece, a dialogue between two ladies and a gentleman. The penultimate words of *The Great Tradition* are notably feminine.

PULCHERIA (to the little dog): We are silenced, darling, but we are not convinced, are we? (The pug begins to bark.) No, we are not even silenced. It's a young woman with two bandboxes.
THEODORA: Oh, it must be our muslins!
CONSTANTIUS (rising to go): I see what you mean!

The Great Tradition was a timely work. There was in 1948 no argumentatively discriminating book about the late Victorian and Edwardian novel. The standard 1950s books, by Walter Allen, Arnold Kettle and Dorothy Van Ghent, had not appeared and were less tight in focus, except for V.S. Pritchett's *The Living Novel*. There were some pre-war books, of which Percy Lubbock's *The Craft of Fiction* (1921) and Forster's *Aspects of the Novel* (1927) were the best known. There was J.B.

Priestley, and ubiquitously Q. Closer to Leavis, there was a book by
Ford Madox Ford. Provocatively, there was David Cecil's *Early Victorian
Novelists: Essays in Revaluation* (1934), which, though everything Leavis
disliked, had a thesis and shouted for substitution. *The Great Tradition*
answers *Early Victorian Novelists* in several respects, not least in its
attempt to erect an alternative view of art (and of entertainment).★

The Great Tradition possesses the Leavisian compression, the 'ideogrammatic' method, applied for the first time to a study of prose. There are
interesting divisions in the book that may be highlighted by noting its
genesis in the summer of 1946. Leavis wrote then to Gordon Cox that
he was working on 'Authority and Method' (now called 'Judgement
and Analysis'), and

I wanted to get it done in this Long Vacation, but when I'd at last finished the
last and monstrous instalment of George Eliot for the December number, I
found that I had a book written. So I devoted the rest of the vacation to putting
that together – *The Great Tradition: George Eliot, James and Conrad*. I had to
write a long opening chapter justifying the title, and making the book a kind of
'New Bearings on English Fiction'.[55]

'New bearings' *on*, not *in*, is interesting: would 'New Bearings *on*
English Poetry' have been better for the earlier book? There was a
difference from *New Bearings in English Poetry* that Leavis appeared not
to recognize. That book was written for the sake of new shoots of life in
poetry itself, as was its historical companion, *Revaluation*. The pair were
intended to show what contemporary poetry issued from and where it
could go: it was meant to be about yesterday, today and tomorrow.
This was not true of *The Great Tradition* in which tradition, bluntly,
appears to be over – except in the recent case (to which attention is
promised) of D.H. Lawrence. He occupied a special position: he had
been dead fifteen years, but, of course, he was 'living', especially so
when vilified by the intelligentsia (or Bloomsbury). Lack of recognition
required support from Leavis of an intensity that conferred on Lawrence
honorary status as a 'contemporary'. The book differs from *New Bearings
in English Poetry* because the reference to Lawrence is the nearest it comes

★ It was reviewed (S, March 1935) by Frank Chapman: 'George Eliot receives full
recognition for her intellectual superiority, but Lord David Cecil, though realizing it to
be her chief asset, seems to be repelled by it and finds her inferior to Dickens in "creative
imagination".' One of Leavis's problems in *The Great Tradition* was to define an
alternative 'creativity'.

to the contemporary – even in the provocative footnotes to the first chapter, though there are mentions of T.F. Powys and L.H. Myers (said to be 'not primarily a novelist', though the author of one 'very remarkable novel', *The Root and the Flower*).

Leavis's account of the origins of *The Great Tradition* is intriguing in one respect. He told Gordon Cox that, having finished his 'monstrous' instalment of a series on George Eliot, he found he had virtually written a book, if he added in essays already done on Conrad and James. Actually, he had not done much on them. Five years earlier Leavis had published two essays on Conrad, but on James he had done little. There was only one essay, nearly ten years old, not substantially about James's novels at all, but about R.P. Blackmur's collection of James's prefaces to the New York edition of the novels.[56] This piece, 'Henry James', was to become a chapter of *The Great Tradition* ('The Later James'), possibly a rather unhappy piece of self-borrowing because the essay is about James's attitudes in his late, complicated period, but does not explore the novels. Leavis had charmingly debunked the reverence afforded to James's later styles in *Scrutiny* in 1937. He used a long anecdote, in a footnote, about losing the way with Edith Wharton in Windsor, having motored from Rye, during which James could not bring himself to ask a straight question. (In the 1930s there was a snobbish mystique of the enjoyment of the late James, elevating *The Ambassadors* at the expense of *What Maisie Knew*.) There was also a reading-list of James's shorter fiction slapped on at the end of the essay, and rightly dropped for the book. But the Windsor anecdote, though excellent as literary journalism, is retained and is disarming as part of the whole book's invitation to basic reorientation. And another anecdote is introduced: a snobbish and patronizing reminiscence in which Leavis recalls a comment from Q that James 'didn't know the right people', that is, spent more time with plutocrats than the serious middle class, 'e.g. the milieu of Henry Sidgwick'. In this the Leavisian delight in respectable Old Cambridge gets out of hand. (Henry Sidgwick could not have written – or admired – *What Maisie Knew*.)

Authors often underestimate how long it takes to get a book ready. In the coming months, from the summer of 1946, Leavis was slow to produce more James material, if one judges that work on James went into *Scrutiny* as soon as it was ready. Essays on *Roderick Hudson* and *What Maisie Knew* appeared respectively in Autumn 1947 and Summer 1948, and too late for the book. When he got down to it, Leavis was working back to back with Q.D.L. Her review of a collection of James stories and his review of Matthiessen's *Henry James: The Major Phase* both appeared in *Scrutiny* (Spring 1947).

There was an oddity in the preparation of the book and the finished product. Leavis wanted to make James central, one of his triumvirate, but he had said little before about him. And at the same time, he was writing on the novel under the heading of 'The Novel as Dramatic Poem', giving Dickens great significance – but Dickens was to be excluded from *The Great Tradition* and material about him only inserted at a late stage. This is not very peculiar: the point of Leavis's method was discipline, getting the *main* thing said; Dickens was not the thing that called for attention. It is interesting, however, that if Leavis's scheme for *The Great Tradition* did not fit exactly his own history, it did match the interests of Q.D.L. She was a James enthusiast from her early years, 'fabulous days of the sixpennies and sevenpennies', when there were excellent reprints, such as the Nelson series, that 'lay around the house when I was a child'.[57] The negative case, with respect to Dickens, was true too. Up to 1946 Q.D.L. had little time for Dickens. He is compared, in *Fiction and the Reading Public*, very unfavourably to eighteenth-century novelists, as 'emotionally not only uneducated but also immature'. In *The Great Tradition* Leavis used insights from George Santayana on Dickens's strengths. Q.D.L. contributed an essay on Santayana to *Scrutiny* (December 1935) and from him F.R.L. chose to quote a passage of devastating criticism of Dickens that runs to almost two pages.[58] (She does say Santayana recognizes the 'unique merits' of Dickens, but her preference is clearly for the 'placing' attack.)

It could, therefore, be said that the schema of *The Great Tradition* was dear to the heart of Q.D.L. F.R.L. had a greater concern than she, at this stage, for Dickens, but he is marginal to the book, and so far he had shown less interest in James. The question of Q.D.L.'s contribution can be further explored. On several occasions she made claims to have played a larger than collaborative–inspirational role in the composition of Leavis's books. When *The Great Tradition* appeared she referred, in a letter to Storm Jameson, to 'my husband's, or rather our book on the novel'. After Leavis's death she wrote to Boris Ford about 'having been pushed out of *The Great Tradition*, which was my undertaking, and great parts of which, besides all the first chapter and all the footnotes, I wrote personally'. 'The whole subject,' she said, 'of our careers and work is too painful for me to review at present.'[59] She talked about this difficult subject with less anguish to the former pupil who became a friend, Nora Crook. Chatting about how they worked together ('we shared everything, we were always feeding each other ideas'), she described the composition of The Great Tradition, during which she was always ready with suggested footnotes. The crisp footnotes in the finished book do have her touch. Q.D.L. was, indeed, an enthusiastic footnote composer for her own Fiction and the Reading Public and for F.R.L., as the surviving manuscripts show.* Apart from this, it is understandable that she should have thought, at times, of The Great Tradition as 'my undertaking' because the book is so much in tune with her frame of reference, and not decisively within that of Leavis himself at this stage.

A 'sharing' of the subject may explain a certain tension in The Great Tradition, particularly noticeable in the relationship between the first general chapter and the last, on Hard Times.

In the first chapter, with determined economy, Leavis seeks reorientation of the novel, displaying his triangulation points. His hostages to fortune, or 'line', are Austen, Eliot, James and Conrad. There is an oddity because no section on Austen follows. Q.D.L. had written on her in Scrutiny but the (footnote) reference is perfunctory. If Austen is invisible in the body of the book, Lawrence is not mentioned in the first line-up of authors, said to stop 'at a safe point in history', though several pages are devoted to him at the end of the chapter, 'The Great Tradition'. In the course of it occurs the notorious exclusion of Dickens from the tradition: 'That Dickens was a great genius and is permanently among the classics is certain. But the genius was that of a great entertainer . . . The adult mind doesn't as a rule find in Dickens a challenge to an unusual and sustained seriousness,' a very Q.D.L. view. This does not square with the presence of the final chapter on Hard Times, though it is said in the first chapter that this novel is the one in which genius 'is controlled throughout to a unifying and organizing significance'. It could be said that Hard Times is adduced because it has special 'un-Dickensian' qualities, but this does not work out. Later, in 1970 when F.R.L. and Q.D.L.

---

* Nora Crook, 'Taking Tea with Mrs Leavis' in The Leavises, p. 129. Crook adds that in twenty years of friendship with Q.D.L., she never suggested rivalry or plagiarism in the partnership, discounting the claims made by John Sutherland in The Times Literary Supplement (9 April 1982). The manuscripts of D.H. Lawrence: Novelist at the Harry Ransom Humanities Research Center, University of Texas at Austin, illustrate the collaborative process.

published *Dickens the Novelist* under both their names, it was often remarked that Leavis had recanted, simply changed his mind about the earlier estimate of the Dickens *œuvre* and refused to say so. The touch of contradiction within *The Great Tradition* itself and its period of composition shows his relationship was complex (or slightly confused).

The straightforward view of Leavis's early treatment of Dickens would work if he had simply advanced the view that the novelist was a chaotic entertainer, but with one neatly organized 'moral fable' (*Hard Times*) to his credit, a view often attributed to Leavis. But his position is not so sharp. Despite the dismissal of most Dickens as non-'adult' in the first chapter, he is called a 'classic', and in the *Hard Times* chapter compared to Shakespeare, and not on a vague criterion of scale: Dickens is said to show possibilities of 'concentration and flexibility in the interpretation of life such as we associate with Shakespearean drama', challenging common definitions of the novel. Later, in this chapter it is said there is no greater master of English except Shakespeare. 'This comes back to saying that Dickens is a great poet.'* It appears that Leavis has fewer qualifications about Dickens than he sometimes intimates; and this may be felt the more strongly if the *material* for *The Great Tradition* is considered, that is, the writings in *Scrutiny* that eventually went into the book.

The *Hard Times* chapter, the fifth of *The Great Tradition*, was published first in *Scrutiny* (Spring 1947), but certainly not as 'An Analytic Note'. On the contrary, it appeared with more of a fanfare, initiating a new series to be called 'The Novel as Dramatic Poem'. The second in the series was an essay by G.D. Klingopulos on *Wuthering Heights*. All the subsequent ones were by Leavis himself, on James's *The Europeans*, and on two novels and a novella by D.H. Lawrence (*St Mawr*, *Women in Love*, *The Rainbow*). The *Hard Times* essay, therefore, appeared, as the *beginning* of a book on the novel-as-poem, a book about Dickens, James and Lawrence, not as the *end* of one about Eliot, James and Conrad. So the essay can be seen in two different types of continuum, its surroundings affecting its meaning. Consider, for example, the initial selection of *Hard Times* from the *œuvre* said to represent Dickens's genius, 'together with a strength no other of [his novels] can show – that of a completely

---

* The idea that Dickens was a 'poet' was not unusual. It had been the peak claim of David Cecil in *Early Victorian Novelists*, and because of its presence there it was a hard claim to make for Leavis, who was dissociating himself, and the English novel, from David Cecil.

serious work of art'. As a journal-essay of 1947 this could be read as the beginnings of a rehabilitation of Dickens. As a concluding chapter (a 'note') to a book of 1948 on three other writers, whose initial chapter excludes Dickens from the file, it could be read (and was) as a rejection of Dickens.

Whether read in *Scrutiny* or *The Great Tradition*, Leavis stresses that *Hard Times* is a moral fable, as is James's *The Europeans* and George Eliot's *Silas Marner*. But the point is made by Leavis with a certain instability. He obviously wants to revive interest in these novels, believing they had been ignored because they were not 'novel-like', lacking 'lots of "life"', a created world. He argues for another type of novel, the fable type about moral issues, which has plenty of wit and point, where 'the intention is peculiarly insistent, so that the representative significance of everything in the fable . . . is immediately apparent as we read'. This is meant to be a type of fiction, an unregarded type; it is not meant to be the whole of good (or 'great tradition') fiction. But Leavis does not allow the idea of 'moral fable' to exhaust the interest of *Hard Times*. He only says that it is neater than other Dickens, so not 'Dickensian', and unappreciated as a result: the neatness kept it from the front rank. But – importantly – it seems that moral-fable quality is not *necessarily* connected to the 'novel as a dramatic poem'.

It was not, after all, 'a peculiarly insistent intention' that made a poem remarkable for Leavis: his prime faith was in organic form. When Leavis first published in *Scrutiny* the essay on *Hard Times* that concluded *The Great Tradition*, the general series title at its head, 'The Novel as Dramatic Poem', was completely at odds with 'insistent intention' or 'moral fabulation'. In his first three paragraphs on *Hard Times* the word 'insistent' is used four times, to indicate what had been off-putting about the novel, not to show what is splendid about it. In the next paragraph, having got away from why it is unregarded and on to why it is splendid, Leavis says something to enforce what has gone before, but which is in fact quite contrary, suggesting a slide in reasoning.* He claims that in *Hard Times* 'the creative exuberance is controlled by a profound inspiration'. So far he has posited 'insistent intention' for the novel but definitely not 'profound inspiration'. He could (one suspects,

* There is some evidence that the original *Hard Times* essay was hastily written because in the first couple of pages there were some slight alterations for book publication. One alteration is unfortunate, that of 'the grim clinch of the title, *Hard Times*' to 'the title, *Hard Times*'.

would) retort that 'insistent intention' is surface movement, activated deep within the structure, wave marks on the shore, traceable to the ocean swell. But clearly the two do not necessarily go together. 'Profound inspiration' must surely be capable of creating surface effects other than 'insistent' evidence of intention. 'Moral fable' appears to be what makes *Hard Times* unloved. By 'profound inspiration' Leavis surely means something other and larger, a secret of art beyond moral fabulation. He proceeds to show what the other and larger thing is. It is not too much to say that 'moral fabulation' and 'insistent intention' are soon discarded, false hares in an essay that is cumulatively interested in the 'poetic'. When Leavis returns to generalize about what makes a good novel, he actually excludes 'insistent intention' and 'moral fabulation'. What matters, he says, are 'possibilities of concentration and flexibility in the interpretation of life, such as we associate with Shakespearean drama'. In one sector of his mind Dickens was still paramount; no wonder he did not believe he had been guilty of a *volte face* over Dickens. None the less, he had been unclear.

Leavis had his plan for *The Great Tradition* in the summer of 1946, a plan that fitted the ultimate form of the book that appeared in November 1948. However, the book took some time to get into print: more had to be written than he thought, and the James part was slowest coming. There were delays through 1947. It seems as if Leavis was not happy working on James, on whom his best work, on *The Europeans* and *What Maisie Knew*, appeared after *The Great Tradition*. Within *The Great Tradition* some old material was not very appropriately reused, and there was some padding. Was reproduction of the James essay on George Eliot really indispensable? It is almost as if Leavis were waiting for contributions from Q.D.L., so this could become a joint book. The completed book certainly had room for her contributions, on, for example, James's stories about literary life. It is understandable that Q.D.L. occasionally said she was 'pushed out'. On the other hand, at one stage it looks as if the same could be said of Leavis himself. Only at the very last moment did his essay on *Hard Times* get included. He petitioned Parsons for its inclusion on grounds that 'several colleagues' had requested it, a reason that sounds contrived. Parsons was very glad indeed to have the essay, believing that it would strengthen the whole book 'out of all proportion to the size of the note'. And it was he who chose to have it in the climactic position.[60]

With *The Great Tradition* Leavis became known primarily as a critic of the novel. Of course he had begun with work on fiction in his doctoral thesis, but it is clear that his career was powered by his experience of the feel of a handful of post-war poems. Certainly he went on writing about poetry (especially Eliot), but there was to be none of the engagement with it of the early 1930s. It seems not quite coincidental that in the period of *The Great Tradition* Leavis gave up all relations with Ronald Bottrall, with whom he had corresponded so ardently in the early *Scrutiny* period. In •1942 *Scrutiny* published, in the Summer and Winter issues, a series of poems by Bottrall about marital anguish. 'Having so strenuously resisted his constant (and utterly unscrupulous) pressure to say privately and publicly about his poems what he asks for, I've been anxious to take every opportunity to show I wasn't biased against him (and the Bloomsbury boycott *has* been unfair).' It was the last poetry the journal published. Bottrall was soon to regret the appearance of the poems. He wanted to appease his wife with a sequel, but Leavis would not publish any more. He became increasingly irritable with Bottrall, partly because he had hoped that his position in the British Council would enable *Scrutiny* to become better known: Leavis resented the fact that Bottrall did not even take out a subscription for himself. (Five years before he had been grateful to the British Council for distributing *Scrutiny* abroad.*) In 1947 a request came directly from an official of the British Council to forward some *Scrutiny* material because Bottrall wanted it 'for basic research'. Leavis wrote angrily to Bottrall, who retaliated and took the letter to show Denys Harding at Birkbeck College, as evidence of Leavis's excessive intransigence. Harding found the episode 'horrible'; though he was not impressed by Bottrall, he felt Leavis had exposed himself unwisely. Leavis explained his rage to Harding:

Several things had determined me to hit him hard (and he's one of the major pachyderms). James Smith, after five years' magnificent work for the British Council in Venezuela, was disgustingly treated by them (he's not a B. C. type – too genuine and for all his foibles, portentously qualified). I mentioned the case in replying to one of Bottrall's requests for a good review. Bottrall immediately took the official B. C. line and the official tone. Reported this way it mightn't sound much, but it was very nasty. Again he tried to bribe me to give him the review he wanted. In a letter which started by . . . saying that this time he'd like a fair review, he went on to talk (as never before) solicitously about *Scrutiny* –

* See Chapter Seven, Wartime, 'Persona Non Grata: Leavis's Occupations 1939–1947'.

to say he would contribute £10 if we were in straits. (In a P. S. he added: 'I'll see Geoffrey Walton gets a good post in Italy'.)[61]

Leavis said he had snubbed Bottrall 'for a dozen years, and told him, with variations, that *Scrutiny* sets up to be the enemy of the kind of sophistication he and Empson stand for'. None the less, before the 'dozen years', at the dawn of *Scrutiny* and the publishing activities of Gordon Fraser, Leavis had worked enthusiastically with Bottrall. Such an engagement did not occur again.

Part Three

AFTER THE WAR

1949–1963

CHAPTER EIGHT

NO COMMON PURSUIT
1949–1960

... I can't go into it all much – but the rough sense of it is that I believe only in absolutely independent, individual and lonely virtue, and in the serenely unsociable (if need be at a pinch sulky and sullen) practice of the same; the observation of a lifetime having convinced me that no fruit ripens but under that temporarily graceless rigour, and that the associational process for bringing it on is but a bright and hollow artifice, all vain and delusive.

    – Henry James to John Bailley, 1912, when declining membership
    of the English Association (epigraph for *The Common Pursuit*, 1952)

Function of Criticism 1949–1952

In 1949 there was some comfort in the lives of F.R.L. and Q.D.L. Leavis wrote an optimistic New Year letter to his publisher about his book on criticism 'Authority and Method' and about one by Q.D.L. on Jane Austen. They had their first peace-time seaside holiday in 1949, at a less stark resort than Aldeburgh, which they had favoured. They went a few miles further north to a 'pleasant, narrow-fronted Georgian house' in Southwold 'superimposed (it would seem) on fishermen's cottages. It's much too tastefully furnished (from antique shops) to have children happily.'[1]

The major change was that Leavis was to have a permanent assistant at Downing. At last relief came. He managed to persuade the college, by 'unwilling but triumphant politicking', to appoint Harold Mason as his assistant. Leavis said, 'The difference for me will be immeasurable.'[2] Mason had a gift for encouraging pupils more intimately than Leavis. He could see 'where an undergraduate was', remembered one of them.

The acquisition of Mason was facilitated by American money. It was first planned that he should be full-time assistant to Leavis, doing college supervision and assisting in the management of *Scrutiny*, at a salary of £1,000 a year, of which the Rockefeller Foundation would supply two thirds, the remaining third to come from supervision fees and revenue from *Scrutiny*; he was allowed free dinners at high table. His title was to be 'Additional Director of Studies in English'. The offer was improved to provide a salary with supplementary supervision fees, to which the college might contribute £100. The post was for three years, ending in August 1952, and pensionable. He was not to be a fellow, nor, of course, a university Lecturer. Mason accepted the college offer on condition that suitable accommodation was available. Downing purchased a house (No. 1, Park Parade, on Leavis's bicycle route to college), which was allowed him rent-free. Mason had an Oxford degree, but the college wanted him to have a Cambridge MA taken by incorporation and waived the registration fee. In November 1949 the college asked Leavis to pay £84 of the £3,500 that Mason's rented house cost.[3] In 1951 the post was extended. The Rockefeller Foundation agreed to fund the appointment up to August 1955.

Mason was a strong influence at Downing between October 1949 and August 1955. He then departed for the University College of the South-West, which was in the process of becoming the University of Exeter. He joined John Speirs, the *Scrutiny* medievalist, who went there to lecture for some years after his wartime spell in Cairo. Ten years later Mason was to return to Cambridge with sad consequences.

The college had some reservations about Mason. In July 1951, just before the post was renewed, the Governing Body hoped he 'would apply himself to producing a book within the next two or three years'. There may have been reservations nearer home. Q.D.L. was setting her Jane Austen material into order for a book, and realizing how far she was from the career her qualifications promised. Mason had found an enviable, though not permanent, place in Cambridge, rather as Joan Bennett had done before the war. On the face of it the unpublished man with a Second from Oxford in 'Greats' had established himself in Cambridge more centrally than the brilliant Girtonian, nationally known for *Fiction and the Reading Public*.

In 1949 neither 'Authority and Method' nor Q.D.L.'s book on Jane Austen were dispatched to Chatto & Windus. Leavis's next publications were to be *The Common Pursuit* (1952) and *D.H. Lawrence: Novelist*

(1955), two of his best-known books, which established post-war knowledge of him. *D.H. Lawrence: Novelist* was a strange book but a masterpiece; *The Common Pursuit* became possibly Leavis's most used book, but is disappointing in some respects. Although it contains important essays, the overall project appears disorganized. The essays could have been phased, perhaps with a 'Shakespeare' section or one on seventeenth-century literature. The attitude of Leavis dominates in a way that the reader does not experience in *Revaluation*, which was confident but less aggressive. The 'common pursuit' of the title was offered as an ideal, and it was one in which Leavis believed, but Leavis's complaints, when accumulated, out of the context of *Scrutiny* in which the essays originally appeared, gave the title a sour taste of irony. It would not, however, have been a Leavis book if its plan had followed a conventional template (a bit on this and a bit on that). The book contains two dozen excellent essays, but Leavis did not have to produce a *book* of this kind. That he did so may be explained by the stresses of the time in which it was conceived.

The Common Pursuit appeared early in 1952. It did not consist of new material, so it could be produced quickly. Actually, its origins went back two years. In April 1949 Leavis was wondering whether he could 'ease some problems by getting a volume of my essays out'. He had much *Scrutiny* material that could be collected. He was also impelled by his response to Eliot's writing and wanted to put his critique of Eliot's position into a more solid form than journal writing. Eliot had recently pronounced on Milton in a lecture to the British Academy; he now looked much more favourably on Milton and dissolved his earlier critique, the one that had, arguably, been shaped by Leavis's ideas. Eliot appeared to be saying what anyone could say – or could *have* said – before the First World War. So this leader of the modern movement was not, in his role as literary critic, writing as a modernist on Milton. Thoughts of Eliot influenced Leavis so much that he thought of calling his new book *Mr Eliot and Milton and Other Essays*. But, at Chatto & Windus, Parsons did not like the idea, so Leavis settled on *The Common Pursuit*, a phrase that nodded to Eliot, who had used it to describe literary criticism ('the common pursuit of true judgement') in an early essay. To follow the nod in the title Leavis decided to open the collection with essays on Milton, first on Eliot's attitude to him, then the contemptuous essay, largely about Tillyard's *Milton*, which Leavis wrote for *Scrutiny* once his lectureship was secure. Leavis felt he was at the end of the road with Eliot. A young American pupil, Seymour Betsky, had written a huge book about his work and Eliot had expressed some interest in writing a preface to it. Leavis was adamant: Betsky must not pursue the matter. Eliot learned of his attitude from Parsons and interpreted it, surely correctly:

I have always had considerable respect for Leavis and *Scrutiny*, and have more than once gone out of my way to call upon him in Cambridge; but I know he feels I ought to have come actively to his defence in the *Criterion* days, and that somehow my support at that stage might have made all the difference. So it seemed to me possible that he had objected to my writing a preface, for reasons arising out of this reproach.[4]

The Common Pursuit enacted the reproach.

Further, Leavis had intimate reasons to make himself better known as an academic. It now appeared that Basil Willey, Q's successor in the chair, was at the peak of Cambridge English. Leavis had to fight on to get himself known; and fight with serious worries at home. Q.D.L. had been gravely ill, was down to six stone in weight, though she was working hard, reading, writing, aiding *Scrutiny* and looking after the children, including the 'prodigiously intelligent' Ralph. She was, Leavis said, 'very much the mother of the modern Mozart'. And he was as protective as ever of her. He understated the case to an old pupil: 'She's fighting for her life and this makes her impatient at times.' By now Q.D.L. resented the editorial treadmill: she was tired of 'drudging for my husband and *Scrutiny*' and sought 'the time in future for my own purposes'.[5] She wanted a reprint of *Fiction and the Reading Public* with the addition of several recent essays. Parsons, her publisher, thought the whole body of the text should be updated, and Q.D.L., understandably, believed this was impossible. Parsons suggested, after consulting F.R.L., that Chatto & Windus should publish a straight reprint without revisions. Q.D.L. agreed, but the edition did not materialize.

Leavis was fifty-five years old, and worried about how much money he would have on retirement. He had school fees to consider, and probably the prospect of medical expenses for Q.D.L. He may have wondered whether Q.D.L. could survive him, despite the gap in their ages. He had the further worry of moving house, finally away from the home in which he had been brought up. In the autumn term of 1951 the family moved from Chesterton Hall Crescent to a more grand address. The house was not better, nor much larger, but it was in a leafy area of villas just off a main road (the A10, London Road, a continuation of Trumpington Street) out of Cambridge; it was certainly in a professorial area. No. 16, Newton Road was semi-detached but substantial, originally on the site of an arboretum, with a good lawn; Leavis liked to scythe. He remarked wryly its Victorian gothic castellation, which put him in mind of Miles and Flora in James's *The Turn of the Screw*, about which he argued with Marius Bewley. But it was not a gloomy house, though the garden needed a lot of work. Adrian Bell wrote in his diary that 'they intend to wrest the big garden of the late Victorian house in Newton Road back from nature. Already F.R.L. has laboured in it – despite his protestations that he has no time.' Soon after they moved in they were amiable hosts. Bell was relieved that he and his wife could share a bedroom, and 'discovered through Mrs Leavis that Leavis refuses to sleep separately from her'.[6]

The pressures of the last months of the wartime decade affected Leavis's decision to publish his essays, as well as the desire to make a public, if coded, reproach to Eliot in the very title of his book. *The Common Pursuit* was conceived in exasperation; Leavis need not have made it his next project: quite apart from his nearly defunct 'Authority and Method', his central, self-imposed task was the sequel to *The Great Tradition*, on D.H. Lawrence.

There was also a new factor in Leavis's life that affected his desire to have his work in hard covers. During 1949 Leavis believed the 'convention of my non-existence' was dwindling. He was becoming well known. *The Great Tradition* was selling well. When the BBC approached him for a talk on D.H. Lawrence, this time he accepted. A new edition of *New Bearings in English Poetry* was to be published, for which he wrote an epilogue over Christmas, finishing it in January 1950. But, in spite of these successes, he believed there was a new danger, that of plagiarism. The threat erupted in early 1950, no doubt affecting his decision to publish his essays in book form, where they would be less easy to plunder than from the pages of *Scrutiny*. Had not Edith Sitwell used him before, and admitted it? The fear of plagiarism was aroused in January when he was finishing the epilogue for *New Bearings in English Poetry*; it set his sights to a new angle.

In the *Radio Times*, the BBC listings paper, Leavis read that Geoffrey Grigson was giving a series of talks on the English novel. Leavis believed this would be 'clearly plagiarism' of *The Great Tradition*, an offence compounded by the neglect of *Education and the University*. Leavis was quick to take offence at the mere announcement of talks seemingly on the broadest of literary themes. Both he and Q.D.L. were sensitive to the idea of plagiarism: she even sought the permission of Denys Harding to publish an essay on Jane Austen in *Scrutiny* because he had done so earlier. Leavis was inexperienced in institutional life outside college, and he was intemperately observant of slights. But his reaction was not absurd. The broadcast talk was a somewhat Olympian mode of discourse, one also so brief that the courtesies of acknowledgement could be neglected. While Leavis did not invent the 'English novel', he had certainly put it on the agenda of discussion. He and Q.D.L. may not have been wise to act on all signals detected by their antennae. It may have been hard for them to diffuse or de-fuse these signals in the way it is done by many people: in gossip. But they could not but be sensitive to 'their' themes being advertised across the air-waves from Broadcasting House.

Having learned of Grigson's radio programmes, Leavis contacted Chatto & Windus (by telegram) to demand legal action, taking the pretty worldly line that, even if there were no damages, there was the 'publicity value of a row'. Believing that Basil Willey (now King Edward VII Professor of English Literature) had been consulted about the radio talks, Leavis wrote to him, complaining of the supposed plagiarism. Had not Willey himself mentioned *Education and the University* in his inaugural lecture without proper acknowledgement? Leavis threatened to approach the PEN Club about violation of his rights, and even enlist Eliot's help: 'He's desperately anxious to make amends for the past, and I shall let it be known that his coming round to see me as he does, talking well of me behind the scenes, is not enough.'

Almost immediately after seeing the Grigson issue of *Radio Times* Leavis sent off material to Chatto & Windus. But the book was slow to come out. Page-proofs were not ready until a year later; there were delays while Leavis expunged references to *Scrutiny* (of the 'elsewhere in these pages kind'). *The Common Pursuit* eventually appeared in January 1952. Within days it sold 2,000 copies. Reviewers commented on its acerbity, but there was warm praise from Edwin Muir and Vivian de Sola Pinto, Professor of English at the University of Nottingham who, without personal contact, fashioned a Leavisian historical–critical school of English.* There were 'querulity' (querulousness?) and complaint of

---

* Leavis was delighted when Pinto asked if an extract from *Revaluation* could be used in his edition of poems by John Wilmot, Earl of Rochester, because the Muses' Library was

prose 'coke-like in its roughness and chill' from *The Times Literary Supplement*. But there was non-obsequious praise from voices closer to the Leavisian world, ones as disparate as Tom Birrell and Thom Gunn. But from this world too came an American voice, that of Marius Bewley, who asked some pertinent questions in private about the consequences for his pupils of Leavis's aggression.

Leavis will never learn, and there *is* something irritating about a person who won't. I think the people who have studied with him have some right to resent his intractability that has destroyed an influence that he, for the sake of those same people, ought to have safeguarded and enlarged. His undergraduates have expended years, energy, and money, to study with him, and enlarge his reputation. The least he could have done would have been not to cultivate a position in the academic world that wouldn't have made an association with him a positive liability when it came time for those people to make their living. That he should have failed to understand this point is a really shocking weakness.

Later in the year Bewley said, with regard to their debate by correspondence over *The Great Gatsby*, 'the only reason I get irritated is because I like him so much I hate to see him wrong'.[7]

Virtue in Our Time 1950

In 1950 there was an event that changed Leavis's attitude to *The Times Literary Supplement*, perhaps to 'the system' as a whole. He did something that showed a new orientation.

The 'literary supplement' of *The Times* started in 1905. It declined during the Second World War, when it courted popularity by shorter articles and pictures. After the war, under Stanley Morison, sobriety was restored and circulation had increased to 30,000 by 1948. Leavis was broadly in favour of *The Times Literary Supplement*: in 1946 he called it 'on the whole a credit to English critical journalism'. But in 1948 Alan Pryce-Jones became editor. He was a Sitwellian, at home with Nancy Cunard and Maurice Bowra. His first post had been as Sir John Squire's assistant on the *London Mercury*, after he had been sent down from Oxford. The British Council helped Pryce-Jones seek talent abroad, in the era of currency restrictions. He began a series of special issues.

'a scholarly series'. He believed that the Nottingham English school was based on *Education and the University*.

Pryce-Jones was energetically open to the post-war world. With a Sitwellian past and an eclectic present he was hardly Leavisian. But he did seek contributors from the civic universities, indeed, inviting on Leavis's advice, when he was still assistant editor in 1947, Leavis's pupil Gordon Cox, then at Manchester University, to review for the paper. He did so regularly, becoming for a time the principal contributor on literary criticism (including Leavis's own).[8]

Early in 1950 Pryce-Jones visited Cambridge to give a lecture to the English Club. At Harold Mason's suggestion David Matthews, a Downing man who was on the Club committee, asked Pryce-Jones over the pre-lecture sherry why *The Times Literary Supplement* did not review *Scrutiny*. Pryce-Jones replied that 'we consider it well enough known among its subscribers'.[9] A couple of weeks later he gave a radio talk on little magazines: the *London Magazine*, the *Criterion*, *New Verse* and so on were all mentioned, but there was no reference to *Scrutiny*. Leavis remarked on this in a letter to C.P. Snow, who had written to him to commiserate.[10] Not long after the new edition of *New Bearings in English Poetry* was published, with its additional 'Retrospect'. *The Times Literary Supplement* only noticed it under 'Books Received' in May, mentioning that Leavis found the course of English poetry since 1932 'depressing in the extreme'. The reference was cursory.[11] In August the paper published a long survey of British writing for overseas readers, giving the briefest of references to *Scrutiny* and no reference at all in the four-column 'Literary Periodicals' section. However, the 'Literary Criticism' section suggested that one option for the critic was to follow 'the Cambridge Critics centred on the periodical *Scrutiny*', which attempted 'to establish scientific criteria of excellence'. The reference was pretty ill-informed, for 'Cambridge' certainly did not support *Scrutiny*, and not many of its contributors were there. A complaint came from Cambridge in the form of a letter from Maurice Hussey, one of Leavis's former pupils, published in the issue of 5 September. The editors of *Scrutiny* were not behind Hussey's letter, according to Leavis. An editorial comment said that the supplement on contemporary writing was meant to be about creative writing, so *Scrutiny* was excluded, adding that a full-scale assessment of *Scrutiny* was in train. After Hussey's letter appeared, Leavis dispatched one of his own. He scored some substantial points (for instance, that the survey had included non-creative-writing journals). He was slightly disingenuous when he refuted the remark about 'scientific' criticism by saying that one major contributor was a priest, head of a Roman Catholic college. He widened Hussey's charge, complaining that Pryce-Jones did not mention *Scrutiny* in his Third Programme talk about 'little reviews', which actually included the *Criterion*. This letter was not published, and in this surely Pryce-Jones committed an error of judgement. Although Leavis's attack on Pryce-Jones in his non-editorial capacity (as broadcaster) was slightly improper, Pryce-Jones replied airily, disclaiming 'persecution'. Leavis then returned an obviously not-for-publication letter, which Pryce-Jones rebuffed abruptly, remarking it was not suitable for publication, when it was clearly not meant to be. 'I decline to be involved in so silly a discussion,' he concluded.

Leavis's replies are not pleasing reading. But to be pleasing is an easy attainment in these circumstances. In the end, he was simply right in that *Scrutiny* had been excluded. And the exclusion was serious, for the special issue in which it might have featured was designed for the foreign readers *Scrutiny* desperately needed. Business, not only taste, was at issue.★

Leavis's next move was of a new kind for him. He had the exchange of letters with Pryce-Jones typed up and cyclostyled on ten sheets. He gave this *feuilleton* the title 'Literary Periodicals and *The Times Literary Supplement*' and dispatched it to as many people as he could think of. One copy was lodged with the London Library. He titled some copies by hand, 'Virtue in Our Time'. Gordon Cox was sent the 'dossier', as Leavis called it, in September and asked to 'pass it round his Common Room'. Leavis told him Pryce-Jones had written a final 'carefully insolent letter', saying *Scrutiny* had an admirer on the Gold Coast.[12] The dossier continued to circulate. In public Leavis took issue with Pryce-Jones in *Scrutiny* in early 1952 in a review of his contribution on 'Literary Periodicals' to *The Year's Work in Literature, 1950*, published by the British Council. Leavis was beginning his post-war years with guerrilla activities, spiking the establishment where he could. He was developing a taste for pamphleteering, seeing himself as not unlike the Ruskin of *Unto This Last* or the Arnold of *Friendship's Garland*. (Although his first writings were pamphlets, they were not pamphlet-polemics.) He may have realized that new means of promotion were necessary because *Scrutiny* was ailing.

★ Did Leavis have an inflated sense of his own importance, consistent with persecution fantasy? He made an ironical remark in a letter to David Holbrook (14 April 1951), which suggests the contrary: 'A very great man, said E.M. Forster in New York recently (and compared with Rylands or Lucas – I *am*). It's a pity he isn't a little more human.'

Bloomsbury Again: Damned Humbug 1949–1951

I am damned critical – for it's the only thing to be, and all else
damned humbug.   .
                          – Henry James, epigraph to 'Keynes, Spender and
                                       Currency-Values', *Scrutiny*, 1951

Leavis laid his plans in *Education and the University* for a contribution to
reconstruction of the post-war world. He was never sanguine about
cultural change, but in the immediate post-war years his optimism for
planning diminished. The cultural 'ruling class' (Leavis's phrase in 'The
Wild, Untutored Phoenix') looked the same; indeed, it was if anything
more powerful, for the institutions of culture that had been established
in wartime could now be operated suavely, he thought, by this class.
Leavis considered Maynard Keynes to be 'the most formidable promoter
of the coterie-spirit that modern England has known'. The significant
issue was not simply one of Keynes's power but his taste. Bloomsbury
scorned the Leavisian concern for 'standards' before the war. During and
after it Keynes deftly promoted the arts, notably as chairman of the
Council for the Encouragement of Music and the Arts (CEMA),
founded in the early years of the war to become in 1946 the Arts
Council of Great Britain. He also promoted the middlebrow, especially
in the theatre, by the support he gave to Hugh Beaumont, the managing
director of H.M. Tennent Ltd, who ingeniously discovered that the
Finance Act of 1916 could be interpreted so as to gain exemption from
entertainment tax for theatre companies, so long as the management set
up a subsidiary non-profit firm. Beaumont did so by founding Tennent
Plays Ltd (with the same Board as H.M. Tennent Ltd) for relatively arty
productions, confirming a hold over London theatre from the West End
that would outdo the interests of specialist companies. CEMA and later
the Arts Council played a key role in authorizing claims for tax
exemption to Customs and Excise, which administered the Act: it is
now clear that Keynes always supported Beaumont, whose exploitation
of government policy ended in 1950 when the Arts Council realized it
was endorsing the growth of Shaftesbury Avenue matinée culture.
Leavis was as sceptical of Keynes as the theatre director Tyrone Guthrie:

Lord Keynes, great man though he was, was a 'sucker' for glamour. Lewis Casson was now Drama Director of the Arts Council and as such subject to Keynes as his chairman. Keynes, a complete amateur, kept overriding the advice of his more experienced subordinate and leaned more and more heavily in the direction of Tennent Plays.

Leavis's instinct for (or sociological observation of) the effect of the Keynes taste on post-war Britain was shrewd.[13]

The publication of several Bloomsbury works triggered an outburst of pessimism in Leavis: Keynes's essay 'My Early Beliefs', published posthumously in *Two Memoirs* (1949), Stephen Spender's autobiography *World Within World* and Roy Harrod's life of Keynes, both of 1951. On these Leavis wrote two essays, 'Keynes, Lawrence and Cambridge' and 'Keynes, Spender and Currency-Values' (1951).[14] It was 'My Early Beliefs' that focused Leavis's hostility to Bloomsbury. His critique of Keynes was based on a conviction about the way in which a social nexus or milieu could foster and favour a writer's sensibility. The theory behind the conviction was expounded in two immediately post-war essays, 'Literature and Society' and 'Sociology and Literature'.

Keynes wrote 'My Early Beliefs' to supplement a piece by David Garnett, which had been read to the Bloomsbury 'memoir club', informal gatherings in which memories were revived by the delivery of one or two papers, often in the great drawing-room at No. 46, Gordon Square. Garnett had spoken about Lawrence's hatred of his Bloomsbury and Cambridge circle, so intense that it led to the breakdown of contact between the two friends. Lawrence thought they were 'done for forever':

I feel I should go mad when I think of your set, Duncan Grant, Keynes and Birrell ... Keynes I am not sure ... when I saw Keynes that morning in Cambridge it was one of the crises of my life. It sent me mad with misery and rage.[15]

'That morning' was 6 March 1915. At that time Bertrand Russell and Lawrence were delighted with each other's company and intended to collaborate on a series of revolutionary lectures in London on social reconstruction. Russell invited Lawrence up to Cambridge, where he dined him in Trinity. In hall Lawrence sat next to G.E. Moore, who could think of nothing to say, but later Lawrence evidently enjoyed talking to G.H. Hardy. Next morning, at late breakfast in his rooms in King's, Keynes entered and he and Russell talked 'at' each other for

Lawrence's benefit, so it seemed. Keynes, in his pyjamas, was 'hard, intellectual, insincere', recalled Russell, believing (wishfully) that Lawrence liked him, but could not get on with him: 'I get on with him, but dislike him. Lawrence has the same feeling against sodomy as I have. All examples I know confirm me in thinking it sterilizing.' Lawrence wrote to Garnett of Cambridge society that 'I cannot bear its smell of rottenness, marsh-stagnancy.'[16] From his own and Russell's account it seems that a subtle combination of cerebration and sexuality disgusted Lawrence.

Keynes's essay did not take the part of Garnett in the conflict or attempt to rebut Lawrence. On the contrary, the purpose of the essay was to suggest that there was something to be said for Lawrence's reaction. Perhaps he had instinctively grasped something significant about the mental and psychological universe of Cambridge Bloomsbury life. 'Although it was silly to take it, or to estimate it, at its face value, did the way of responding to life which lay behind it lack something important?' 'My Early Life' is a meditation on what Keynes calls the 'religion' of his group in Cambridge of the years before the First World War, the passionate conviction (inspired by G.E. Moore) that

nothing mattered except states of mind, our own and other people's of course, but chiefly our own. These states of mind were not associated with action or achievement or with consequences. They consisted in timeless, passionate states of contemplation and communion, largely unattached to 'before' and 'after'.

The essay is a remarkable one, an unpretentious, lucid and humble piece of autobiography. According to Garnett, it was one of only two unpublished pieces that Keynes wanted to be printed after his death. It was designed for the Bloomsbury 'memoir club' with serious but slightly impish intent. The club papers were more often than not about personal relations. Keynes proposed to speak on 'for once mental or spiritual, instead of sexual adventures' and recall the 'youthful religion' of 'the dozen years before the war'. He set out, in an urbane and patient fashion, a critique of Bloomsbury. His conclusion was that its 'youthful religion' had degenerated; over the years some falsity had entered its 'view of man's heart'; there had been some falling away into sexual intrigue, 'from the purity of the original doctrine'. He believed that in the old days they had 'got round' the rich variety of experience by bringing much too much under the heading of 'aesthetic experience'. 'We would deal, for example, with all branches of the tragic emotion under this head.' And when Lawrence denounced Bloomsbury perhaps he should have been paid more attention. Indeed, he had been 'very unfair to poor, silly, well-meaning us'. But 'this is why I say that there may have been just a grain of truth when Lawrence said in 1914 that we were "done for"'.[17]

Keynes admitted 'a grain of truth' from Lawrence, the outsider. But he did not wish to go further, certainly not as far as saying that insiders should leave the fold. He also still believed that Lawrence had looked on Cambridge with 'ignorant, jealous, irritable' eyes. He believed Lawrence was jealous of Cambridge 'civilization'. It was the imputation of 'jealousy' that Leavis attacked.

Leavis knew that Lawrence was shaken by the incident; it 'was one of the crises of my life', he said. But was he jealous? Eastwood and Nottingham were not Eton and King's, but Lawrence was, Leavis argued in 'Keynes, Lawrence and Cambridge', a highly educated man growing up with smart, widely read young people. When Ford Madox Ford, the novelist and man of letters who 'discovered' Lawrence, visited Eastwood around 1910, he braced himself for a mining-town out of Zola, only to be astonished by the sophistication and knowledge of Lawrence's peers, with their talk of Nietzsche, Wagner, Leopardi, Flaubert and Marx. 'Those young people knew the things my generation in the great English schools hardly even chattered about.' Keynes never said that his Cambridge was the be-all of culture; it was, he noted carefully, *one* culture, *a* civilization. But Leavis thought Keynes should have recognized that Lawrence came from as civilized a milieu as Keynes's own, and, indeed, that the originating milieu of both had some affinities with Leavis's. Lawrence's Eastwood was a mining village; the Leavis family had not been long away from the Fens.[18] But all three families shared some of the qualities of British Nonconformism. It was part of Leavis's quarrel with Bloomsbury that it set a wedge between Walker Street, Harvey Road and Chesterton Hall Crescent, the early Eastwood and Cambridge homes of Lawrence, Keynes and Leavis, a quarrel further agitated by the *déraciné* Eliot whose snobbish denigration of Lawrence fixed the wedge more securely. Keynes, however, could not be bothered with modern Nonconformism. 'Serious culture' depressed him. In Henry Sidgwick he was wearied by a lack of 'intimacy', 'clear-cut boldness'. The quickness of observation that Keynes admired he found elsewhere, even in the prose of Lytton Strachey, which (said Leavis) Keynes could not resist, imitating him in some of the glittering parts of *The Economic Consequences of the Peace* (1919), in which Lloyd George, Wilson and Clemenceau are paraded, in a definitely 'clear-cut' fashion, like eminent peacemakers *à la* Strachey:

The President, the Tiger, and the Welsh witch were shut up in a room together for six months and the Treaty was what came out. Yes, the Welsh *witch* – for the British Prime Minister contributed the female element to this triangular intrigue. I have called Mr Wilson a non-conformist clergyman. Let the reader figure Mr Lloyd George as a *femme fatale*.

About this Leavis agreed with Sir Charles Kingsley Webster, himself a member of the 'serious' oligarchy: 'The political caricatures of the *Economic Consequences* did as much harm as the economic insight did good.'[19]

Leavis was surely wrong to expect from Keynes a concern for Nonconformist 'serious' culture. He was after all a campaigner for the Bohemian wing of the upper middle class. He had a reasonably high opinion of Lawrence's abilities and was not obliged to add to this a genuflection to the vitality of provincial culture. For Leavis to expect from Keynes a paean to Eastwood was to expect too much. But something else could have been expected in 1938, when Keynes looked back to Lawrence in wartime Cambridge. He could have shown a greater knowledge of Lawrence as artist and thinker. It was hardly excusable for Keynes (and Bloomsbury) to look at Lawrence and see so little. In this case it was Bloomsbury that lacked generosity of understanding, marginalizing Lawrence into a maverick motivated, in his dislike of Cambridge, by nothing more than jealousy, not by the elaborate point of view that might not have been evident in 1915 but was certainly to be seen in 1938, when almost the whole Lawrence *œuvre* was available, including uncollected essays and Huxley's edition of the letters. Of all this, Keynes's retrospect is surprisingly incurious.

There is a coda to Leavis's critique of Keynes and defence of the Lawrentian social class. After the war the subject set for the university Le Bas Prize was the Leavisian hero Leslie Stephen. The winning dissertation was by Noël Annan, who had returned to a fellowship at King's after his war service in the Cabinet Office and military intelligence. Annan was a King's man who had graduated in 1939. Back at Cambridge he joined the Faculty of Economics, for which he taught politics, and later became Provost (Master) of King's in 1956. Annan was to be a leading member of the liberal intelligentsia. His Le Bas dissertation was published in 1952 as *Leslie Stephen: The Godless Victorian*.[20] In his conclusion Annan assessed twentieth-century reaction to Stephen, noting Desmond MacCarthy's lecture on Stephen in Cambridge in 1937 in which his lack of aesthetic sense was castigated. MacCarthy had been reproved for this lecture by Q.D.L. in 1939. Stephen's straightforward readiness to state his preferences in criticism was given legendary status in her essay 'Cambridge Critic'.* Annan noticed that MacCarthy was virtually attacking literary criticism itself. MacCarthy's Bloomsbury was led by artists; its study of art was appreciative, not judgemental. Its faith was that criticism should be the homage paid by the uncreative to the real artists, a branch of *belles-lettres* in which the civilized mind cleans the painting of genius. Annan suggested that actually Cambridge recognized this and despite its judgemental and scientific aura ('wily Tillyard spun theories about poetry direct and oblique'), it was little interested in value, even in the case of I.A. Richards. It was Eliot who was concerned with 'right judgement', Eliot who excited 'the Leavises' (and Edgell Rickword and Geoffrey Grigson). But their use of literary *criticism*, judgemental criticism, was less meaningful than Eliot's, because he, as an Anglo-Catholic, possessed a 'citadel of belief', whereas the Leavises were evangelical and merely serious about moral problems. Annan sounded satirical when he characterized the Leavises' concern for judgement, but he admitted they had a point. If literary criticism was not (following MacCarthy) to make judgements, then it was different from every other branch of study: scholars had to distinguish between what was valid and what was not: to follow MacCarthy's road was 'to deny that critical concepts had any meaning not only for literature but for all the humanities.'[21]

On the other hand, about Q.D.L. a 'niggling doubt' seemed to remain. He made a clutch of criticisms of the Leavises' (he soon generalized from Q.D.L.) and Stephen's handling of the relation of society and the writer. Whatever his faults, said Annan, Stephen at least related literature to society, unlike the Leavises, who contended that 'the character of a writer exists only in his book'. Annan mistook the heuristic emphasis of Leavis, that the book is the first thing to examine (the thing to be related *to* society), for a lack of sociological interest. His assertion was entirely inconsistent with Leavis's writing on the

* See Chapter Seven, Wartime, 'Old Cambridge 1939–1947'.

connection between cultural milieu and literature, as delivered in the essays 'Literature and Sociology', 1943 and 1945, of which Annan seemed unaware. (Annan also said that Leavis thought 'characters in novels were only illustrations of the moral qualities which sustain the novel', a travesty of his conception of 'the novel as dramatic poem'.) However, continued Annan, if F.R.L. and Q.D.L. failed to see the social and artistic rapports of literature, this was not unlike Stephen, who made a claim to do so but was not a success at it. *English Literature and Society in the Eighteenth Century* (1904), the late book much admired by Leavisians, lacked scholarship, he said, and so did Q.D.L. in *Fiction and the Reading Public*, which was bold enough and industrious but not knowledgeable, because it rested its theory of reading on the untenable hypothesis that there was once a Golden Age in which 'standards' of writing were maintained, before the complexities of crowd-pleasing created under industrialism. The Leavis position was equated with a travesty of Q.D.L.'s book. The specific charge was unfair. Q.D.L. may have idealized past reading conditions, but she also drove vigorously into sociological observation of late nineteenth- and early twentieth-century reading conditions. She did find data and did attempt a sociology of present literature, however much her picture of pre-Victorian Britain glowed. Annan, with a King's College preference for Bloomsbury individualism and writerliness, looked away from her modern studies. And with him began the trend of neutralizing all the historical and sociological concerns of Leavis and Q.D.L. by fastening on their vision of 'the world we have lost', the 'idyllic picture' (Annan's phrase) or the 'organic societies' (theirs). There is some evidence such societies existed. But even if they did not, even if the idylls or the organisms never were, there are such concepts as myths of origin whose explanatory validity remains. To argue there was never an organic society did not mean that the Leavises' analysis of the management of the modern literary taste was invalidated. Annan's charges were very like those of F.L. Lucas in 1933: King's would not forgive the Leavises their modern sociology.

In the 1960s the line between the liberal Annan and the sceptical Leavis was to be sharply drawn. The antagonism was classic: it is those with much in common who fight most fiercely. At this date it was really *only* Annan and the Leavises who had taken an interest in the significance of Leslie Stephen, and Annan after his book on Stephen continued to pursue some of the subject matter that especially concerned

Q.D.L.: the making of the middle-class intelligentsia; his essay 'The Intellectual Aristocracy' in 1955 was standard work in her field.

There was another side to Leavis's critique of Bloomsbury in the post-war years. It is shown in a tart but not sour passage, in his review of the biography of Keynes by Roy Harrod. Harrod explained that Keynes had to speculate on the financial markets to maintain his independence: 'He had many things to tell the nation. And he wanted a sufficiency. He must be able to take stalls at the Russian ballet whenever he wished.'[22] Keynes detested the prospect of a relapse into 'salaried drudgery', to become what he was in his earliest life, a don and university Lecturer. Leavis certainly mocked the sophisticated patron of the arts, but, more drastically, he was shocked at the lack of respect ('drudgery') given by Keynes to the vocation of university teacher. Perhaps Keynes's 'harvest of speculation' was beneficent, but by implication he degraded a profession. Leavis wanted respect to be retained for the teaching intelligentsia. (His dislike of Keynes on this point was possibly prophetic of changes that were to occur a quarter of a century later when public respect for the profession of teaching declined.)

The End of Scrutiny 1949–1953

In 1949 matters with *Scrutiny* were difficult. The spring issue was 'desperately improvised'. Then the supply of material improved: in June 1950 Marshall the printer was 'well-loaded up'.[23] In 1951 Leavis received a visit from his old pupil Boris Ford, at that time Chief Editor at the Bureau of Current Affairs. The director of the bureau was W.E. Williams, an adviser to Allen Lane of Penguin Books. Lane wanted to publish a history of English literature, and Williams asked Ford to sketch one, which he did, after reading and consulting three friends. He planned a seven-volume series and went to Leavis to explain it: for it would draw on *Scrutiny* contributors, indeed on the whole Leavisian idea. Leavis was cautious about the project, doubting that there were enough contributors available: he thought the best people 'wouldn't want, or be able, to do that kind of writing'. Ford was a little dashed by his response: subsequent events and the publication of the first volume of his *Pelican Guide to English Literature* would show why Leavis made it. In principle the *Guide* was not exactly in conflict with the Leavisian idea: it could have resembled a printed version of the scheme Leavis proposed to the BBC in 1940.[24] However, in daily use study guides usually become reference books, and this was quite contrary to *Scrutiny*'s ambition for nimble, opportunistic response to the present. Of course, there was room for a guide and *Scrutiny*. But what if the same contributors were to be engaged for both?

The end of *Scrutiny* came not long after, and very suddenly. The fourth number of *Scrutiny*'s nineteenth volume was due for October 1953. There were delays with setting up copy in type. Leavis was about to stage a row with the printer when he heard that three contributions were not coming. He had nothing in reserve, he said; so he retrieved the bundle of material from Marshall's to make pages in a dummy issue in which to publish a 'Valediction'. The whole enterprise, Leavis said, was a 'piece of foolish quixotry and self-importance' and at an end: for once the 'stage army' could not swell a progress.[25]

Leavis had nothing in reserve. Not quite: he had nothing in reserve that he wanted to use, at that point, but there was one contribution that had got as far as galley proof, a very long essay by Harold Mason called 'The Perfect Critic or Pope on Empson'.[26] The essay, in tune with Leavis's doubts dating back to the rejected essay on *Alice in Wonderland*, dealt with Empson's verbal misreadings.[27] But it was about an unusual subject, Alexander Pope's *Essay on Criticism*, in which Mason endeavoured successfully to revive interest by critical and imaginative use of early eighteenth-century criticism. His title, 'The Perfect Critic', was an allusion to Eliot's essay of that name of 1917; he was making a plea for works to be read as wholes (Pope's moral too). The way that Mason started reconsideration of a poem from scratch, a study far out of the usual *Scrutiny* parameters, shows why he appealed so much to the new generation of Downing men. To some of the best he gave something new to do. 'Research' had a new lease of life at Downing. The pupils were frequenting the university library, the 'UL', rather than the Faculty library, their former resort.

It might be thought that Mason's 'The Perfect Critic' was deviously persuading *Scrutiny* readers to look afresh at Eliot's essay in search of inspiration for a quarterly that was by now mildly sclerotic. Why did it not appear? Possibly because Pope's *Essay on Criticism* was so far off the board of *Scrutiny* interests of the time that it could not be countenanced – and because Leavis himself was engaged in *Scrutiny* in a debate about criticism and historical understanding with the Oxford don and editor of the journal *Essays in Criticism*, F.W. Bateson. At the heart of this debate was an argument about what it was necessary to know about poems of past eras in order to understand them. The debate focused on a poem by Andrew Marvell, 'A Dialogue between the Soul and Body', with Bateson proposing that Marvell was showing the unshowable by means of silent reference to the way the soul was portrayed in seventeenth-century emblem books in which the letterpress was accompanied by illustration. This was in the same field as Mason's work on Empson. But Leavis did not use 'The Perfect Critic'; there seemed to be not enough material, so *Scrutiny* had to stop.

He blamed himself for not being able to keep his contributors together, and, not too bitterly, blamed them for failing to make *Scrutiny* the first call on their time. He recognized that contributions to this journal were not necessarily helpful on a curriculum vitae. The *Scrutiny* circle was not more prosperous after the war. Leavis knew his group, now with families, needed to earn money and establish careers. Its members had often sought needed payment: *Scrutiny* would not even have had Denys Harding's 'Regulated Hatred' on Jane Austen in 1939 if an American journal had not turned it down. Ford's *Pelican Guide* was able to drain off potential contributors: it was the *coup de grâce* – as Leavis 'unaggressively told him'. Apart from disagreeing with the principle of such a guide, Leavis thought that

we couldn't afford to lose *one* essay a year. Our people do their *Scrutiny* work in a very narrow margin of time and energy; and Ford's gain (sometimes he didn't want the result of the writers' labours when it was done) was *Scrutiny*'s loss. He approached my main people. I'm not accusing with animus; I'm just stating facts.[28]

Leavis had always felt uneasy in the presence of Ford's rather upper-middle-class imperturbability; he now bitterly called it 'Napoleonic conceit'.[29]

When readers saw that they had in their hands the last *Scrutiny*, there was response from many quarters. The *Spectator* commented that 'our government machinery for encouraging culture was unable to keep our best critical review alive'. There were letters to the press, from Ceylon, from Uganda, and one from South Africa, which led to a plan that eventually brought about the reprinting of the whole run of *Scrutiny* in the 1960s.[30] There was a letter of sympathy from C.P. Snow.

The end of *Scrutiny* gave Leavis a sense of termination, a prelude of retirement, ten years before it was due. It came exactly ten years after

Education and the University, to which he felt there had been no response. It confirmed his

life-long exclusion from any say in the English School. When I am retired (on the pension of one who wrested a part-time lectureship from the Faculty at forty-two), and a full-time lectureship (at fifty-two) all that I have worked for at Cambridge peters out ... The lack of recognition at Cambridge has been fatal.

He began to think about *Scrutiny* in terms of 'suppression'. It should not be thought that Leavis expected literary criticism to be universally Leavisian. He truly believed he was a necessary opposition:

A real critical organ exists largely to be differed from, criticism being essentially a collaborative matter: one can't be Criticism oneself. The desperate thing about the present situation is that one can't start a real critical exchange.

Briefly, he considered the idea of an annual *Scrutiny*. After the end of *Scrutiny* he readied his essays on D.H. Lawrence for publication, but wrote nearly nothing new for three years. In the year of the end of *Scrutiny* Morris Roth, the father of Q.D.L., died.

One event compounded the bitterness. In November the Director of the BBC Third Programme, P.H. Newby, wrote to Leavis, offering *carte blanche* to give a talk or talks on the radio. Leavis replied suspiciously, saying that the BBC had been no friend to him, having broadcast a talk hostile to John Speirs's *Chaucer* that he construed as an attack on himself. The only talk he could give, he said, would be 'sociological' and critical, about the effect of 'recent developments of civilization' (Welfare State, etc.). Newby replied cordially and followed up with advance notice to Leavis that a young Lecturer at Reading University, Frank Kermode, was going to give a talk on the end of *Scrutiny*. He was actually engaged on a series of talks on unfamiliar poems that could be enlivened by reference to their historical background. This theme fitted the argument between Leavis and F.W. Bateson that was going on in *Scrutiny* about poetry and historical understanding; Kermode was indeed a contributor to *Essays in Criticism*. He was to adapt his last talk to comment on *Scrutiny*.

Kermode's radio talk was, on the face of it, innocuous. His manner was that of one walking round a grand Victorian edifice in wonder, with piety just on the edge of sarcasm. It is almost possible to miss the force of statements that nearly slip by: '*Scrutiny* has never materially changed its view of any important writer, past or present.' On the matter of the dispute about criticism and historical knowledge, between Leavis and Bateson, Kermode if anything favoured Leavis, but hinted another view altogether may be taken. He complimented Leavis by considering him to 'be' *Scrutiny*, the 'real' voice. But, of course, in doing this he invalidated the communal project of *Scrutiny*, and had little to say about the sequences of studies of which the quarterly was rightly proud. The only reference to a contributor other than to Leavis was to a clumsy (and self-righteous) piece by a young pupil on David Jones's *Anathemata* in the last year. In short, Kermode patronized. Leavis asked if he could see the script and after he had read and heard the talk he returned an angry letter.[31] Newby tried to explain and offered Leavis the chance to attend the Third Programme Monday afternoon talks committee.

My attending one of your committees could neither undo the past, nor throw any light on the relevant inner history of the Talks Department. The damage has been done, and the BBC had a major part in it. It is obviously not for me to be implicated in any suggestion of a reformed policy – even if there could be one, at this date, that could make any difference to the causes that have suffered such injury.[32]

It was painful to Leavis to have a judicial summing-up from a very junior person; it was as if his ease with young people had turned round on him. The same kind of injury came from another source. The editor of the *London Magazine*, John Lehmann, wrote to Leavis deploring the end of *Scrutiny*, offering him space, perhaps on Conrad or Lawrence. Leavis replied that he was working on books; he was, indeed, getting ready his material on Lawrence for publication. In March 1954 Lehmann was approached by Laurence Lerner, a young extramural Lecturer at Queen's University, Belfast, who wanted to contribute an assessment of *Scrutiny*, especially as he was 'the sort of person to whom *Scrutiny* was addressed'. It contained much of the best criticism of the past twenty years, 'but its faults stick out a mile'. Lehmann did indeed publish 'The Life and Death of *Scrutiny*' in January 1955, only then to receive a complaint from Leavis. Lehmann offered him 1,800 words, at which Leavis protested. He was exasperated, he said, to be called a genius ('poor young man'). He asked for more words and was given them, for the March issue.[33]

The death of *Scrutiny* was one of the bitterest times. But there are several witnesses to a moment of refreshment in this black period. In October 1952 John Farrelly, a wealthy American, friend of Marius Bewley and formerly a journalist on the *New Republic,* came to take the tripos at Downing. Like Bewley he had been a Catholic, was from St Louis, drank (more than Bewley) and wore good suits from Pratt Manning in Trinity Street. He rented summer houses, often in France, and in 1952 the Leavis family accompanied him, with his wife and child, to Dinard. Leavis enjoyed the red wine, to Farrelly's surprise. Q.D.L. dogmatized about the merriment of beach life for children and sometimes Ralph let himself go at an old piano, playing wild bebop. During this holiday he remarked that 'my wife is the embodiment of passionate will'. Farrelly later told Patrick Harrison that once Leavis drew his attention to Q.D.L. sitting beside the sea: 'just like some young girl'.[34]

Lawrence 1949–1955

At the beginning of the autumn term 1955 Leavis published *D.H. Lawrence: Novelist.* Some reviewers considered the book momentous. A. Alvarez called it Leavis's 'critical *summa*' showing his genius for conveying 'what it feels like to read an author'. In *Encounter* the novelist Angus Wilson's review had a political dimension. This, he said, was the study for which readers had been waiting, by the great critic whom 'liberal culture' rejected and about the greatest novelist of our time 'who saw and set down the failure of the liberal intelligentsia' of the 1920s and 1930s. Leavis too distrusted that liberal intelligentsia, like Lawrence, who said he was *glad* the 'Bloomsbury highbrows' hated his *St Mawr.*[35] Wilson dissented on one matter. Leavis saw Lawrence, according to Wilson, as an arbiter of normative truth about sex, but did not recognize what Wilson located as Lawrence's bisexuality. In this he went to a central issue. From this point on there was some coincidence of activity between Angus Wilson and Leavis; Wilson was about to begin a revaluation of Dickens, though not one Leavis would recognize.*

It had not been obvious that Leavis would focus next on Lawrence. Some pupils of the early 1950s said they were taken aback to find him

---

* See Chapter Nine, The Sixties: Orthodoxy of Enlightenment, 'Against Snow 1962–1963'.

working on Lawrence, an example (they thought) of how you could not tell which way Leavis would jump. His career had begun, of course, with Lawrence, but he had said that he would not return, and there had been no extensive treatment in *Scrutiny*. This was noticed by a Leavisian enthusiast, Harry Coombes, in a letter to the journal in March 1949. Coombes liked to keep cuttings and sent in a collection of typical anti-Lawrence statements that had been printed elsewhere; he regretted that 'a full article on Lawrence' had never appeared in *Scrutiny*. This was true, even though Leavis's enthusiasm for Lawrence had grown, especially in the course of reviewing the *Letters* (1932) and *Phoenix: The Posthumous Papers of D.H. Lawrence* (1936). Replying to Coombes, Leavis promised in an editorial note that he would see what could be done. In a sense, *D.H. Lawrence: Novelist* was written to request.

Just as *Scrutiny* had not published much on Lawrence, there was no proliferation of Lawrentian commentary elsewhere. In America there was Harry T. Moore, a faithful scholar, critic and biographer of Lawrence, who attested to Lawrence's neglect, calling him 'the great unread' in 1940, reiterating this in 1952 in the *New York Times*. Moore had published a life-and-works in 1951, reissued as *The Intelligent Heart* (1954) a year before *D.H. Lawrence: Novelist*.* Leavis was entitled to consider himself among the pioneers, and alarmed that his own work might be upstaged.[36] He was suspicious of work in train from the Cambridge English Faculty by Graham Hough.

Coombes's letter to *Scrutiny* and Leavis's editorial endorsement of it was noticed at the BBC by the radio producer R.C. Keen. This seemed to be an occasion for a radio talk on Lawrence, so Keen solicited one from Leavis. On holiday in Southwold he agreed and started work immediately, though 'I never undertook a more difficult job than in trying to say anything at all about D.H. Lawrence in that space.'[37] His spurt of composition coincided exactly with the publication of J.M. Keynes's memoir about D.H. Lawrence, which Leavis had reviewed in September 1949. Leavis was now the more determined to protect and explain Lawrence. He wanted to show that he was not 'Lawrentian', a

---

* Moore was something of an academic maverick, like Leavis himself, though to Leavis he appeared a member of the establishment. *D.H. Lawrence: Novelist* did not acknowledge Moore; and when Moore's edition of Lawrence's letters appeared, Leavis derided 'Lawrence scholarship' as 'the accumulation of impertinences'. The review, in the *Sewanee Review* (January 1963), later published in *Anna Karenina and Other Essays*, is persuasive.

producer of 'turgid prophetic lava'.[38] He concentrated on the long short-story called *St Mawr*, which he compared to *The Waste Land*, taking pains to establish that Lawrence was not 'obsessed with sex'. Wasn't Eliot, he asked, open to the same charge?

Leavis was now back with Lawrence. A torrent of essays began, coinciding with the last months of *Scrutiny*. There were two in 1950, five in 1951, two in 1952, and one more in the last issue of *Scrutiny* (October 1953). Leavis also published the essay 'Lawrence and Class' in the *Sewanee Review* in 1953. He wrote with the conscious plan for a book. After a lecture in March 1951 on Lawrence, sponsored by the admirable Vivian de Sola Pinto at Nottingham University, the book seemed to be taking shape.[39] He wrote furiously in the summer of 1954, sometimes with exhilarated confidence. He told Parsons he had been Lawrence's main supporter for twenty-five years and that one day a triangular relationship would become a fact of literary history: Lawrence–Eliot–Leavis, himself the mediator, standing for a form of vitality that he believed to be absent in Eliot. A couple of days later he apologized to Parsons for his pretensions. Leavis was increasingly aware of books on Lawrence in the offing. There was Harry T. Moore, and he heard in January 1954 of Graham Hough's progress with what was going to be *The Dark Sun: A Study of D.H. Lawrence* (1956), which he viewed irritably, remarking unreasonably that he had been reading Lawrence before Hough was born. Leavis had a sense there was a race on for Lawrence.[40] The book was delivered to the publisher on 23 October 1954.

During the editing process at Chatto & Windus a serious problem arose. Leavis's typescript contained extraordinarily long quotations from Lawrence. Just when corrected proofs were ready for the printer, someone in the office noticed that there was a blank in the space in which acknowledgements were normally made to copyright holders of quoted material. The rights were handled by Laurence Pollinger, who acted for Lawrence's widow, Frieda Lawrence Ravagli. As soon as this came to Parsons's attention he telephoned A.S. Frere, Chairman of Heinemann, who held the British publishing rights in all Lawrence's work. He responded decisively. 'Who is this bloody Cambridge don who thinks he can ride roughshod over the laws of copyright by quoting vast quantities of Lawrence's work without permission?'

The ejaculation was relayed by Parsons back to Leavis, who replied to Frere that he knew 'many Cambridge dons *were* absolutely bloody – but

I am one of the exceptions'. Leavis was distraught. He went to a Downing graduate student, David Craig, to see if he would help distribute the quotations for his book around Cambridge in cyclostyled form. Leavis then remembered he had a former pupil working at Heinemann. He telephoned Tony Beal despondently: 'My life's work is in jeopardy.' Would he try to negotiate? Obviously Leavis and Frere both had Lawrence's interests at heart. Beal himself had just completed making a selection of Lawrence's literary criticism for Heinemann. Beal talked to Frere, an appointment was made, and Leavis met Beal for a briefing in a Bloomsbury tea-shop. Then they both went up to Frere's office in Great Russell Street. Fortunately, the two men immediately took to each other and quotation rights were granted, provided that a copyright notice appeared at the front of the book. The agreement over the 'bloodiness' of dons seems to have done the trick.[41]

D.H. Lawrence: Novelist was published on 29 October 1955, ahead of Graham Hough's The Dark Sun.[42] Hough had accomplished a survey of Lawrence, covering novels, stories and poetry, with a long final section on 'the doctrine' that was mainly about the non-fiction. It was a straightforward professional job and illustrated exactly what Leavis did not attempt; the reader looking for an overall guide in D.H. Lawrence: Novelist would have been disappointed. Leavis had little on the non-fiction, nothing on the poetry and did not bother to cover all the fiction. The book weighed heavily towards the tales and long readings of two central novels, The Rainbow and Women in Love. These were at the core of the book, in which there is recantation of his earlier view of Women in Love (and of his enthusiasm for Lady Chatterley's Lover). 'I have not always thought Women in Love one of the most striking works of creative originality that fiction has to show.' In the last moments of writing Leavis insisted that a footnote 'to which I attach much value' should appear at the end of the chapter on The Rainbow. It quotes Lawrence's own valuation of his work: he thought The Rainbow the real beginning of his art.

The only copy of my books I ever keep is my copy of Methuen's Rainbow because the American editions have all been mutilated. And this is almost my favourite among my novels: this, and Women in Love. And I should really be best pleased if it were never reprinted at all, and only those blue, condemned volumes should remain.

Familiar novels are hardly mentioned: Sons and Lovers receives less attention than *Aaron's Rod*. Leavis's book differs also from Hough's because it is combative, though Hough was, indeed, making a case for Lawrence and recognized that he was ill appreciated: the snippets of Lawrence vilification that Harry Coombes sent in to *Scrutiny* were not imaginary. In Lawrence, Hough showed a bracing art for which readers familiar with realist fiction may have been ill prepared, specially for the 'violent oppositions, the abrupt changes of front' that are more disconcerting 'to the amateur of conventional fiction than they are to the observer of life as it is lived'.[43] Leavis, likewise, wanted to persuade but somewhat differently: it was not that Lawrence was more true to all the violent distresses of life, but that he used a new kind of art. Leavis proceeded from *The Great Tradition* by showing not that the English novel succeeded artlessly, but that it had a special *type* of art, a 'Shakespearean' art and that of the 'dramatic poem'. His defence of Lawrence, therefore, had a different basis from Hough's and unsurprisingly it was conducted more assertively: it was part of Leavis's definition of this art that it could not be understood by the British ruling idea of art, locked into its Bloomsburyism. In his book aesthetic and polemic were intricately melded; Hough was the more stately commentator.

Some of Leavis's ways as a literary critic can be illustrated by comparing the detail of his prose with that of Hough. In the following passages both describe the climax of the tale called *The Woman Who Rode Away*, a moment in which the protagonist is set for human sacrifice by Mexican Indians. Hough has a lucid digest.

The sacrifice is to take place away from the village, on a bleak wintry day. The long procession files out to a cave among the hills. There the woman is placed upon an altar. The mouth of the cave is overhung with a great column of ice. When the red setting sun sends a ray through the pendent icicle, the old chief is to 'strike, and strike home, accomplish the sacrifice and achieve the power. The mastery that man must hold and that passes from race to race.'

The prose of Leavis is richer, with an almost parodic excess that dramatizes the scene and (more important) has implications about the type of tale that includes it.

The rites, the ceremonies, the colours, all the strangeness of the Indian world, are evoked with irresistible actuality, and with them the quiet certitude of the Indians, and the hypnotic effect produced upon the woman. It is for her a vivid dream actuality; she knows what is going to happen to her, feels a kind of unrealizing agony of despair, but no impulse of resistance. The winter days shorten towards the shortest day, when the ceremonial procession of dancers escorts the litter up through the high frozen world to the cave in the rock-face. The tense barbaric tableau within the cave, all eyes fixed on the fang of ice hanging at the entrance (the last red beam of the sun will in a moment strike it and strike through) makes a perfect close.[44]

The Leavisian rendition is rapt: the style of Lawrence here becomes woven with his, some of his words – 'irresistible actuality', 'vivid dream actuality' – point to something more and less than reality, to what is real in a trance: and trance-like art is what Leavis believes *The Woman Who Rode Away* to be. He calls it a 'feat' of imagination, that is, a *tour de force*. A contrast is offered briefly with another feat, Coleridge's *The Ancient Mariner*.

The Woman Who Rode Away is a highly 'Lawrentian' work. Part of Leavis's purpose is to highlight neglected qualities, like Lawrence's capacity for different types of comedy. He cites a moment in *St Mawr* in which the bold, cynical American mother, Mrs Witt, tells her daughter Lou how much she enjoys watching funerals.

These exchanges, intimately *tête-à-tête*, between Lou and her mother are marvellous in their range and suppleness, their harmonic richness, and the sureness of their inflexion, which, since the surface, belonging to the conversational everyday world, is always kept in touch with the depths, can blend in one utterance the hard-boiled sardonic with the poignant. It is astonishing what Lawrence can do, in dialogue, with complete convincingness; dialogue that starts from, and, when it likes, lapses back into slangy colloquialism, yet, invoking the essential resources of poetic expression, can hazard the most intense emotional and imaginative heightening. One would have said that the kind of thing hadn't been done, and couldn't be done, outside Shakespearean dramatic poetry – which has the advantage of the formal, and explicitly poetic, verse mode.

Leavis's praise here is remarkably close to his praise, years before, of Eliot's 'Portrait of a Lady' with its 'delicate play of shifting tone that is essential to the theme and communication of the poem'. The setting of the conversation in *St Mawr*, mother and daughter watching the descent of an unusually long coffin, was to Leavis's liking: he favoured scenes with juice, comedy that was a few degrees from the grotesque. Poise mattered but not the poise of 'impersonality'. He illustrated the quality in a commentary on the tale called 'The Daughters of the Vicar', about a mining parish that did not want its vicar and his family. They are not humbled by the experience, but become self-sufficient and coldly superior. The clergyman consciously hates the majority and unconciously hates himself. Leavis comments that 'the superiority that exacts this terrible price is shown to us in all its nothingness. The uglinesses bred in the clinging to it appear repellently for what they are.' The subject looks like one for satire (grotesque, derisive or pitying), but Lawrence, says Leavis, while not stinting on the stony selves of the family, also shows there is 'something heroic about it – something almost tragic'. He quotes:

The children grew up healthy, but unwarmed and rather rigid. Their father and mother educated them at home, made them very proud and very genteel, put them definitely and cruelly in the upper classes, apart from the vulgar around them. So they lived quite isolated. They were good-looking, and had that curiously clean, semi-transparent look of the genteel, isolated poor.

The family is not pinioned. After the quotation there is a difficult passage of Leavis, rather choked, and ending in indignation that this writer could be thought 'an uncouth and arrogant genius brought up in cultural barbarism'. Some of his strongest positive words are used ('incorruptible', 'clairvoyant' and others), almost too relentlessly to touch the desired mark; they pile up at the net. But it is clear that Leavis was trying *not* to say something. He wanted to communicate the concept of 'reverence' but without tender-mindedness, or idealization, or sentimentality. On the side of temperateness, simple 'respect' will not quite do for the attention Lawrence gives to a family that is in many respects 'ugly'. Leavis wanted to define some momentary magic: 'They were good-looking, and had that curiously clean, semi-transparent look of the genteel, isolated poor.'[45]

D.H. Lawrence: Novelist had the usual mixed press, interesting praise given as above by A. Alvarez and Angus Wilson. As usual, there was no comment in the British literary-critical or English-studies journals, like *Essays in Criticism* or the *Review of English Studies*. It was reviewed in the *Cambridge Review*, edited at that time by Michael Black, by the gifted Cambridge Leavisian Andor Gomme. As usual the rounded commentaries, not necessarily favourable but judicious, came from America, for instance in the *Hudson Review* and the *Yale Review*. There was a partly unfavourable but careful review from the new school of Lawrence studies, by Eliseo Vivas in the *Sewanee Review*. *The Times Literary Supplement* chose John Middleton Murry for its anonymous review. He thought Lawrence did not sit well in Leavis's 'great tradition'. The same view was expressed by another who knew Lawrence, but with much greater sympathy for Leavis. Lawrence's widow, Frieda Lawrence Ravagli, liked the book and took trouble over trying to write a suitable letter to Leavis, but, dissatisfied with the result, it was never sent. One draft, written in May 1956 from El Prado, New Mexico, is as follows:

I read your book. I was interested in your reaction to Lawrence. Your defence of L is very convincing. But I think you take T.S. Eliot too seriously. I argued with Aldous Huxley about him, finally Aldous said: 'The poor man's wife went mad.' 'There you are,' I cried, 'no real man lets his wife go mad.'

It would never have occurred to me to compare Lawrence with George Eliot. So I read *Adam Bede* again. It is very real, all that life, but I got so furious, with that Dinah Morris and her smug holiness and frozen sympathy for her fellow man, especially the so pretty Hetty Sorrell. How differently Lawrence would have felt about the pretty Hetty! To Lawrence as to me a genuine physical attraction is a sacred and god-given thing. It seems so inevitable that Arthur should fall in love with Hetty! And that is the depth of sin! No, I can't see any connection between George Eliot and Lawrence.

If you read again in *The Rainbow* about the child Ursula's relation with her father you will see that it is not a mother and son relationship, but a father and daughter one. It was *mine with my father*, but in actuality it was asparagus not potatoes.

You mention *Anna Karenina*. Soon after Lawrence and I were together I read this book again. Anna I thought made a mess of her marriage with Vronsky because she could not take the social condemnation. I would not let that happen to me.[46]

The issue of social defiance was to arise in the 1960s. After the publication of *D.H. Lawrence: Novelist* in 1955 the forces gathered that determined the last act of Leavis's Cambridge drama.

Helpers 1955–1960

From 1949 to 1955 Harold Mason assisted Leavis at Downing, taking the largest share of the teaching. Mason had been very useful indeed on *Scrutiny*, a copious contributor whose best work was on the French literary scene and its fiction; but he was never slow to come out fighting on cultural issues and contemporary poetry. In person, Mason's manner contrasted with the amused self-containment and social alertness of Leavis, whose manners were so often praised. Mason was closer to the stereotype of a newspaper-man, amiable, discursive, mock-horrified at a *double entendre*. He did not have the self-dramatization of an anecdotalist as did Leavis. He was, in Leavis's terms, a 'classic', a refugee from Greats at Oxford, but also a disciple of Ezra Pound and his 'Make It New' principle, that is, of creation and re-creation by means of the freest type of translation. (Mason, as we have seen, had a considerable influence on the school of classical studies represented by J.P. Sullivan and his journal *Arion* in the 1960s.) He was also a bookman, curious about textual variation and more interested in the scholarly world than Leavis. He had a trick of keeping open questions that seemed closed to Leavis pupils. Tennyson, for instance, was to be investigated from his beginnings. Mason was a refreshment to Downing men because he simply gave them so much to do. For his pupils, Leavis pared down literary study to the astonishing critical moment. Mason enabled them to see the succession of works from an author's hand as evolutionary. He brought in a plain (rather Yorkshire) geniality, and with it some garrulousness. Mason enjoyed investigative study into the documents of literature and ancillary writing. During his Cambridge period he set to work on sixteenth-century literature. He became fascinated by a commonplace book compiled by Richard Hill, preserved at Balliol in Oxford, comprising a miscellaneous collection of literary pieces and household oddments, including recipes. Mason used it to illuminate the poems of Sir Thomas Wyatt that survive in the so-called 'Devonshire' manuscript.[47]

When Mason moved from Downing to Exeter in 1955 he embarked on an elaborate series of undergraduate lectures on Sir Philip Sidney's *Apologie for Poetry* and Alexander Pope's *Essay on Criticism* (which were circulated in manuscript by Downing men back at Cambridge). Both texts were rather old-fashioned classics in the history of literary criticism, neither the kind of work that, in Leavis's view, would actually help a student become a literary critic. (At that time the Exeter syllabus was determined by the University of London, so Mason had to teach what it required.) Mason went back to these texts afresh, carefully reconstructing what and who Sidney and Pope were speaking for. There was shortage of praise for Leavis in his explorations, though Leavisians found Mason's manner at odds with his mentor. Marius Bewley had said before that Mason supported Leavis with 'a great good will', but 'made such a Gilbert and Sullivan performance out of it that it supplied its own inverted commas'.[48] Mason significantly restored an incentive to historical studies among Leavisians, varied and disinterested historical studies, not merely of the 'background–determines–foreground' type. He set about organizing projects that had only been ideas for Leavis, like seminars on Dante.

In Exeter, Mason set about his first book, *Humanism and Poetry in the Early Tudor Period*, a study notably about Sir Thomas Wyatt, Sir Thomas More, Erasmus and Ben Jonson; it considered European Renaissance humanism in the perspective of Matthew Arnold's desire that English scholarship should be informed by a 'central, truly human point of view'. Mason wanted to bring to the Leavisian platform some of Arnold's qualities, those that Arnold saw in Montaigne. He wanted to be *ondoyant et divers*, supple and various; and also urbane, which he was to a fault, some Leavisians thought. But his post was not renewable and all the stimulus was taken away to Exeter. Not surprisingly, the Downing pupils, when they went on to graduate work, looked to Mason as head of a government in exile.

After Mason left there were changes at Downing. There was a shortage of supervision for third-year Downing men; a subtle, temporary, college move away from Leavis and English began, coinciding, it seemed, with the death of the Master, Sir Lionel Whitby, in November 1956. Among the possible candidates for the Lodge one commended himself to Leavis, and he was eventually elected Master. W.K.C. Guthrie was a gentle historian of classical philosophy. Leavis did not think that any

tyrannical pressure of creative intellectual interests will get in the way. Yet he can be used to create the cultural climate of the college. I considered his election a great triumph. (I discovered diplomatic and persuasive powers – in the face of our great majority of scientists – I'd hardly supposed I had.)[49]

In 1958 Leavis's old sparring-partner, Bill Cuttle, was sinking, removed from the Evelyn Nursing Home next to the Leavis house to the seaside town of Frinton, 'where he'll fade out . . . a macabre tragedy . . . Poor Cuttle! I've shed much of his blood in the past, but think of him now only with pity. He's conscious enough to know what he has done to himself.'[50]

Apart from Downing, there was much difficulty at home.

In July 1954 Ralph Leavis took a First at Oxford, but there was uncertainty about what he should do. 'He wasn't destined to be a mere musicologist.' Leavis thought that at only twenty he was 'peculiarly unfit to look after himself'.[51] In all the talk about decisions for his future there was a quarrel between the eldest son and Q.D.L., and all relations between them ceased. Leavis would visit Ralph in Oxford, where he continued to live. Going there was easier after Leavis retired from Cambridge, when he travelled to give visiting events around England. Kate Leavis was to go up to Oxford in October 1958. The youngest son, Robin Lawrence, was coming up for entry to Leavis's old school, the Perse.

Most drastic was the fact that Q.D.L. had been suffering from radium burn that had not healed after her treatment for cancer. The condition came to a crisis in May 1957, when she was taken into Addenbrooke's Hospital. At the end of July she was discharged to see if a holiday at Aldeburgh would help, rest perhaps dispersing the antibiotic-immune streptococcus that was infecting the ulcer. She could hardly walk two steps. After the holiday she returned to hospital: the specialist was alarmed and would only operate if a thoracic bone-specialist was present. In the event, it was this specialist who did most of the work, involving a long operation to remove quantities of necrotic bone. Q.D.L. convalesced at the Evelyn Nursing home, 'where the food is eatable'. Back at home in Newton Road she could slip through the side gate of the Evelyn for her dressings. 'It will take months before she's restored.' Later, it was decided she should go to hospital in Norwich for skin-graft treatment. Leavis travelled there frequently by train, reading, among much else, Shakespeare's sonnets on the train.[52] When convalescing, she was acutely anxious about not being able to continue to run the house.

Mason had gone, but there were at Downing graduates, or near-graduates, who could take his place in assisting Leavis. Three were particularly important: Morris Shapira, John Newton and Ian Robinson. Shapira belonged to the generation of men who were pupils when Leavis was writing on D.H. Lawrence. Newton and Robinson were of the Mason generation, both of whom went on to graduate studies with Mason-like subjects, the history of English teaching in universities (Newton) and the metrics of Chaucer and medieval poetry (Robinson). Newton and Shapira were influential on Leavis's life in the early 1960s; Robinson intervened in the early 1970s.

Morris Shapira had taken English and Modern and Medieval Languages at Downing, then left for Harvard, where he had scholarships for three years. He returned to Downing in 1957 to the Graham Robertson Research Fellowship, so was thenceforth installed in college rooms. Leavis appointed him as Director of Studies, and he became Leavis's companion on the governing body. He became the most constant visitor to Leavis and Q.D.L. Like Mason he had a gift for languages; unlike him, and more like the Leavis family, he had a strong visual sense. He was Jewish, a pleasing and useful bachelor friend for Q.D.L., alert to Cambridge domestic necessities; they shared cleaning-ladies and recipes. His students were dazed by Shapira's flair for music, painting and interior design, by his disorientating allusions and by his laugh – of all Leavisians of this period, it was only Shapira who was much given to loud mirth. Shapira was closest to Leavis in admiration of D.H. Lawrence, especially the free-wheeling, instinctive style of Lawrence's literary criticism. For his research at Downing he planned two books, on 'Englishness' and on 'Frenchness' in literature. Like Leavis, he needed to be in the sun.[53]

John Newton was the less Lawrentian and more Victorian figure, though the younger by five years, with a sturdy, quiet seriousness in the mould of the idealist T.H. Green. For his supervision pupils he had a gift for meticulous essay-reading and listening, seemingly unworried by a pupil's silence. Quietness is a rare resource among teachers, though Newton's patience could create anxiety. Newton's doctoral studies followed Mason's historical initiatives by recovering, in a very un-Leavisian way, merits in the early masters of the university English schools, like Walter Raleigh. Little respectable work had been done on the past of 'English'. Newton was capable of submitting himself to alien documents. He remarked at the beginning of his thesis that it did not shake 'many of the ideas I began with', but to 'enter the minds of those past teachers' makes present ideas 'a little fresher and subtler'. He had a commitment to detail, which made him an exceptional Leavisian controversialist.[54] Unlike Shapira, he was a reviewer of contemporary poetry and a fluently indignant writer.

Newton took a First in Part Two of the English Tripos in 1957, as did a friend from Newnham, Jean Charlton; from the same college Ann Hogben took an upper Second and shortly married Newton. In 1959 Richard Gooder, on a scholarship from Columbia to Clare, took Part Two and married Jean Charlton; both registered as research students, Gooder working on a subject inspired by Mason, the sixteenth-century humanist Juan Luis Vives, and Jean Charlton on a Leavisian one, Henry James. (At Clare, up on the same scholarship as Gooder, was André Schiffrin, later Leavis's American publisher.)

From 1959 much of the college English teaching at Downing, Newnham and Clare colleges was done by Newton, Richard and Jean Gooder, as well as Shapira. Newton and Gooder were to become fellows of Clare, and Jean Gooder a fellow of Newnham. A tight group formed, meeting regularly at Shapira's rooms for lunch on Saturdays. With the exception of those from relatively prosperous families (Shapira and Jean Gooder), the graduate supervisors were down-at-heel in the ordinary 1950s way, living in tiny terrace houses, often married with babies. Most had several part-time jobs.

The graduate studies of Newton and of Jean Gooder were supervised by Leavis himself. He had other doctoral students in sympathy with his work, taking on also D.F. McKenzie for a short time, Richard Drain (working on D.H. Lawrence), Roger Gard (1959, on James) and Simon Gray (1962, on Dickens). There is nothing unusual in a senior academic having six graduate students in his care. But this was a change in pattern for Leavis. Strangely he only ever had, throughout the whole of his Cambridge career from 1925, twelve research students of his own.[55] Even Cox and Walton in the 1930s had been supervised by others. It seemed as if he was achieving what he had wanted in the old days: a group like the 'Researchers' Club' of 1931. Some members of the group had their eyes on Exeter, hoping Mason would return: for Leavis was to retire in 1962. The anxieties in which *The Common Pursuit* was conceived were over. Leavis now had more of a group about him than had really existed since the early 1930s. His pupils were staying behind in Cambridge. They were domestically present in a cheerful way. The foundations were laid for a good deal of the calling in that happened later: Shapira's college rooms to hand in Downing, the Gooders' pleasant house near the Botanical Gardens on Leavis's way from Newton Road into college. A little society was forming, though not quite yet a writing society. Only Newton was the writer – and probably only Newton was much committed to thinking about poetry as it came out. (Mason, never a thinker about the new, did not stimulate a taste for current creative writing in his pupils.) Newton was curiously close – even down to being the only athlete in the group – to the Leavis of the English research group of 1931. If in Newton a promising shoot could be seen, it was one that some years later cracked Leavis's autumnal vessel.

During the later 1950s there was some momentary peace for Leavis. He was involved in day-to-day university matters in a fresh way. Some of his specialized concerns as an academic spiralled into show for a public beyond Cambridge.

In the late 1950s English Faculty members were worried about the place of literary criticism in the curriculum, and about a perennial problem for English departments. The flow of English literature itself runs on unabated: how, bluntly, can or should student and syllabus keep pace with it? For Leavis the problem appeared artificial: was not literary criticism there to filter the flow? In the summer of 1957 he delivered a memorandum to the English Faculty on the subject. He remarked that by the year 2,000, much of 'what passes for English literature' would have disappeared, if literary criticism did its job.

We obviously cannot think of English literature as a field canonically and finally delimited – as something determinate and fixed, demanding deferential acceptance and appreciation on established 'correct' lines . . . We have to think of the stretch of literature that happens to be in question as something waiting to be discovered and explored, and have to think of the discovery and determination as involving an effort that is formative and creative.

But literary criticism had to come from somewhere. The curriculum should stimulate it. Texts of literary criticism should not be set to form an extra subject, one more field to master on top of the literature,

an added burden of work promoting skill in a kind of gymnastic at which a man may be an adept who shows, when tested, that he has no judgement, no literary perception, and no power at all of dealing intelligently with actual works of literature.

Literary criticism should be functional: the set-books should show students 'how to criticize', in Q's old phrase of the 1920s. So Leavis opposed setting such texts as Aristotle's *Poetics*. This honoured and enigmatic work was supposed to ask 'all the right questions'. It did not show what it was like to be involved with handling the demands of recent, extraordinary literary art, those extremities of bewilderment and exhilaration. The *Poetics* was a conventional Cambridge classic, on which Q had given his weekly ceremonial seminars and on which F.L. Lucas based his lectures on tragedy. Aristotle, for Leavis, dealt only with the externals of tragedy. Leavis's attempt to think about tragedy from the inside was shown in 'Tragedy and the "Medium"'.

In practical terms the problem of criticism arose in the first-year examinations for the English Tripos (the Preliminary Examination). It had a set paper on criticism in two parts, one of passages for comment, one requiring answers on classics of criticism like the *Poetics*. Leavis wanted more texts that were models of practice for the student. The opposing view was that the classics of criticism were safer, or that Leavis wanted to give students too much direction. C.S. Lewis thought so, favouring less directed tutoring in criticism and more freedom. 'Freedom to be unintelligent?' asked Leavis. 'We have not only to face the rapidly and insidiously developing threat with something better than the kind of journalistic "literary mind" we might reasonably be charged with offering as our representative product.'[56] The problem of the syllabus interested Leavis enough for him to consider publishing a book on criticism to be called 'The Critical Function', including what he had done on Johnson, Coleridge and Arnold, with chapters added on Eliot and Lawrence. He wanted a concentrated work that would present 'an Idea, and (in my way) not an abstract one'.[57] But other concerns intervened.

In 1960 this seemingly parochial problem became quite well known: not widely bruited, but mentioned in national weekly magazines with enough intensity to show prophetically that Leavis was becoming more ready to argue Faculty matters outside Cambridge. This was an early warning to journalists that Cambridge English could provide good copy. A controversy began in a tiny Cambridge magazine publishing mostly verse called *Delta: Poetry and Criticism*.

Delta was edited by two Trinity men, Andrew Roberts and Simon Gray, later the playwright, who had a Downing orientation. Before Cambridge, Gray taught in France, where he met Geoffrey Strickland, who introduced him to Leavis and Lawrence.[58] As an undergraduate at Trinity, Theodore Redpath sent Gray to Leavis's seminars. He became aware of Downing men, including Newton, who was publishing Leavisian reviews in the *Cambridge Review*, as was Shapira. Gray disliked Newton, satirizing him and Shapira in the novel *Little Portia*. But he was an addictive reader, anti-authoritarian and liked a fight. In February 1960 he published a rude piece in *Delta* on Cambridge student-journalism. He accepted for *Delta* an article by Newton that was savagely critical of a recent book by Dorothea Krook, much of the contents of which had been delivered as lectures for the English Faculty. *Delta* was beginning to represent Leavisian bite in the small world of Cambridge letters. About the same time C.S. Lewis heard an undergraduate read a paper at Magdalene on Jane Austen that irritated him so much that he wrote a note about unlettered students for the cyclostyled listings paper

Broadsheet. Gray organized a whole issue of *Delta* on the remoteness of the English Faculty from its students, using Lewis's polemic as a springboard. Newton offered a centre-piece on the tripos, but when it did not arrive in time for publication Gray did the piece himself, calling it 'Professor C.S. Lewis and the English Faculty', which appeared anonymously. The article was so blunt that Donald Davie, the magazine's Senior Treasurer, resigned.[59] Gray wanted total revision of the tripos,

with intelligence, with imagination, and above all with honesty, if English at Cambridge is to be prevented from degenerating into an academic game, on the one hand, or a purveyor of slick and uncentred cultural 'manner' on the other.

The debate moved into the *Listener*, which published an editorial in October 1960 on *Delta*'s impudence, noting the usual conflict between the old (classics, Q and history) and the new ('Dr Leavis, psychology, sociology and practical criticism'). The *Listener* gravely rebuked *Delta* for the *lèse majesté* of being unimpressed by Aristotle as guide to the twentieth-century novel.[60] *Delta* replied that the *Poetics* came from another world. It wanted literary critical set texts that gave insight into

the *act* of criticism [. . .] especially in the first year, classic examples of actual criticism (we lay emphasis on Johnson, Arnold, Lawrence and Eliot) would be more relevant than the *Poetics*, which is irrelevant (here, and here only, do we apply the word) to such a purpose. In saying this we are not 'sneering' at Aristotle; we are only suggesting that the *Poetics* raises theoretical issues so remote from the context of the English student's main concerns, that it would be as well to omit it as a prescribed text.[61]

Having had his name taken to represent something of a distortion of his position, Leavis joined the dispute ('my attention has been drawn', a phrase he often used in the 1960s).[62] Specialized academic worries were getting public ventilation.

At last on the Faculty Board, Leavis was now taking advantage of his new position. He became more involved with English Faculty practicalities than hitherto. It is likely he was appointed to the Faculty Board as a result of some pressure from the Shakespearean critic A.P. Rossiter. From 1956 onwards he was to serve on the Board in all for fourteen years.[63] Professionally, Leavis was dignified with the title of Reader in English in May 1959. As usual, the honour was belated. Over ten years earlier both Stanley Bennett of Emmanuel and Leavis's old foe at King's, F.L. Lucas, had both been awarded readerships by a slightly different procedure from that used for Leavis.[64] During the year of his readership Leavis was Chairman of the Part Two Tripos examinations, probably setting 'Criticism and Composition', with a hand in the 'Tragedy' paper.

By the late 1950s Leavis's books were bringing him an income: the annual royalties had steadily risen, paying over £700.[65] He was becoming much better known, but at this time he for once lacked a long-term writing project. His publications were not desultory, but by the end of the decade seven years had passed without Leavis enjoying (or suffering) his natural medium, *Scrutiny*. He published more often in American journals, where he was allowed respectfully ample space; but what he wrote there did not get well known in Britain, where his name was becoming associated with controversy (as in the matter of *Delta* and criticism). He was acutely aware that retirement would come in 1962. One particular concern of this period was with Joseph Conrad. He wrote a short piece, 'Polish Master of English Prose', for *The Times* in 1957, and a long essay for the *Sewanee Review* in the following year. The key work for him now was *The Shadow-Line*, with its beautiful evocation of the commitment of a captain to the ship of his command. It was also, Leavis recognized, a tale about nightmare and loneliness.

CHAPTER NINE

THE SIXTIES: ORTHODOXY OF ENLIGHTENMENT
1960–1963

═══════

There are things that everyone knows but at the same time has agreed to unknow. For the everyone of that world I both exist (to the extent of obsession) and don't exist.

> – F.R. Leavis to Ian Parsons, 1962

Approaching Retirement 1960–1962

Leavis was due to leave his university and college posts before the autumn term of 1962. His retirement was officially due at the end of September. However, consciousness of retirement usually reaches back many months before the event itself. The retirement of an academic is different from other professions because scholarship or criticism need not stop, nor, indeed, at Cambridge need part-time teaching be given up. Retirement affords opportunities to the academic for travel and invitation lectures. None the less, the academic does in late career encounter a wave of students with whom at last he or she too will be leaving the university.

Leavis spoke of retirement as early as 1954.[1] Later in the 1950s he had intimations of departure, some focused on fears about how, or whether, his work would continue at Downing College. Morris Shapira was an ideal manager of the college English teaching, but he only had a limited-term research fellowship that ran out in 1960. When the college prepared to elect a replacement, Leavis hoped for a permanency for Shapira. In October 1960 Leavis addressed the Governing Body on the future of English in the college. The beginning of his 'retirement phase' can be said to date from then.[2]

The retirement phase did not really end until four years later, when

Leavis, for various reasons, put Cambridge behind him much more decisively than he had ever envisaged. In 1965 he took a visiting chair at the new University of York, taking care to arrange his weekly visits around Cambridge English Faculty Board meetings. But by October 1966 he had resigned from the Board and his honorary fellowship at Downing; he had also repudiated the charitable trust founded to commemorate and continue his work. Thenceforth he considered his place to be at York. The retirement phase was then over.

When Leavis went to Trinity to give the Clark Lectures in 1967 he returned as an outsider. He gave up Cambridge for York, entering rather incongruously the world of the new universities, eating in refectories and taking seminars. He was invited to formal occasions with his 'partner'. He was remarkably happy at York, at the beginning.

During the six-year retirement phase (1960–1966) Leavis struggled in Cambridge with faculty and college; indeed, he did so too on the national stage. The focal point was the lecture he delivered in the retirement year of 1962 on C.P. Snow and the Two Cultures, the scientific disciplines versus the humanities. Leavis entered public debate in a way still unusual for a don. Later in the 1960s there were to be academic interventionists of whom Noam Chomsky was the most celebrated in the United States; Raymond Williams and E.P. Thompson were to become British cultural commentators. The role was hardly written in the early 1960s.

Retirement brings honours. A college fellowship expires at retirement, and Leavis was elected to an honorary fellowship. Downing College commissioned the portrait from Peter Greenham, to be ready for the Royal Academy exhibition of May 1962.[3] One honour was not available. He did not hold a chair, so he could not be elected Professor Emeritus. Having never, therefore, given an inaugural lecture, some of his retirement addresses may be seen as surrogately professorial, late opportunities for expressing beliefs for which he had no earlier institutional platform. As for other honours, there was an attempt to produce a *Festschrift*, the complimentary collection of essays 'presented' to a venerable academic. It came to nothing. The triumphant publishing event of the retirement phase was the reissue by Cambridge University Press of the whole of *Scrutiny*, with an elaborate if incomplete index and a 'Retrospect' by Leavis. The establishment of a post in Cambridge by the F.R. Leavis Lectureship Trust, financed partly by donations from pupils, was intended as a tribute. Unfortunately, the consequences were bitter for all concerned. The usual genialities of retirement did not occur for the literary critic who in 1962 added the following epigraph to a new edition of *The Common Pursuit:*

The Norwegian Society of Authors gave him a loving cup, but he asked them to scratch off the inscription and give it to somebody else (obituary notice of Knut Hamsun).[4]

However, there was one honour from a rather modest source in college that proved momentous.

There was nothing harsh or difficult about Leavis's behaviour with undergraduates. He saw his pupils frequently, four one-hour seminars a week, and entertained them to tea when Q.D.L.'s health permitted. One pupil complained that George Eliot's *Daniel Deronda* was out of print: Leavis arrived at his room before breakfast with his own marked copy, apologizing for the binding. He supported Downing productions of Shakespeare in the fellows' garden. Like all colleges, Downing has an association for alumni, with a distinguished college man as honorary president. Leavis was invited to preside, and declined. Having done so, he thought it would be churlish to refuse another college invitation from the undergraduates, who asked him to give the annual Richmond Lecture, which is in the gift of the junior common-room, or 'Amalgamation Club'. In January 1962 he was trying to get this written, 'a foundation, or memorial, lecture for a month (no! 3 weeks): couldn't escape'.[5] For his subject he chose another Cambridge lecture, C.P. Snow's Rede Lecture of 1959, 'The Two Cultures and the Scientific Revolution'.

No stronger terminal address could be imagined than Leavis's Richmond Lecture. It brought unprecedented publicity, and even derision. Pupils and sympathizers were now called a 'hidden network of Leavisites'.[6] Leavis took the opportunity to promulgate some of his dearest conceptions, notably those in the neglected *Education and the University.* The Richmond Lecture can be seen as the professorial inaugural lecture that he never had the chance to give. It certainly inaugurated new forms of expression for him. After it, he embarked on a series of lectures, later published, which he conceived as a series of Arnoldian or Ruskinian pamphlets. In the 1950s, after the demise of *Scrutiny,* Leavis had been short of places to publish his work. The Richmond Lecture helped solve the problem. In it he staked out the ground on which he was to fight the campaigns of his retirement phase, and later. It was the first full-scale version of a series of passionately cautionary memoranda, designed to slow down the progressive intelligentsia and teach it what he called, in a later piece about the triumphalism of the pro-Europe lobby in 1971, a sense of 'complication'. 'The industrialist, economist, and politician debaters, and primers of debate decline to spoil the effective simplicity of their criteria by recognizing complications.' In the retirement phase Leavis's scepticism was directed at several targets, but its underlying object in this period was the rhetoric of 'economic growth treated as an end in itself'.[7]

At the beginning of the retirement phase Leavis had no intention whatever of leaving his Cambridge mission. On the contrary, having recently been elected to the Faculty Board, and with pupils to hand who wanted academic careers, he was optimistic. In 1961 he recommended that one, Ian Robinson, risk taking a research fellowship at Churchill College. He did not want an old pupil's career jeopardized, but he thought there were openings in Cambridge under the new quinquennial planning system. There were to be new posts available, and some members of the English Faculty were, anyway, on the point of taking new posts, whether temporary or permanent. He also had hopes of an ideal successor at Downing in the person of Morris Shapira.[8]

Lady Chatterley *and History* 1960–1962

Leavis continued to work for Lawrence. He had been supervising the Ph.D. thesis of his new graduate student, Richard Drain, one among the group of research students who had come in the late 1950s. In *D.H. Lawrence: Novelist* Leavis had protected Lawrence, once again, from the condescending. In 1960 there was a curious event in which Lawrence was swept up into the literary establishment and Leavis was invited to join the procession. The novelist, and the liberal establishment, were put on unprecedented display when Penguin Books was tried at the Old Bailey for publishing *Lady Chatterley's Lover*.

Leavis declined to be a witness for the defence. After the event he spoke out to defend Lawrence, so to speak, from his friends, from modern, unprejudiced opinion or the 'orthodoxy of enlightenment', perhaps Leavis's phrase for 'The Sixties'. The literary intelligentsia affirmed the value of *Lady Chatterley's Lover* – a spectacle out of Gilbert and Sullivan, thought Leavis. To Court Number One at the Old Bailey proceeded the great and the good, from Noël Annan to a recent Newnham graduate ('educated at the Convent of Our Lady of Sion in Bayswater'). Leavis stood by with a *non serviam* and a new critique of the novel he had so much liked in 1930, before his revaluation of *Women in Love*. The literary critic who was increasingly absorbed by Dickens was unimpressed by the consensus generated by 'the end of the Chatterley ban', as Philip Larkin called it. It was a very different consensus from that of the 1920s when Leavis was in trouble with the Home Office for attempting to import *Ulysses*. The consensus was effective and Penguin Books acquitted.

'The trial of Lady Chatterley' (inevitably so called) took place because in 1960 Penguin, having published most of the major works of Lawrence in paperback, decided to mark the thirtieth anniversary of his death with some new issues. One was *Women in Love*, another *Lady Chatterley's Lover*. As much to the point was the fact that the Obscene Publications Act (1959) appeared to offer relaxation of the law on obscene libel.

Sir Allen Lane of Penguin Books had published much of Lawrence, beginning with *The Prussian Officer* and *Sons and Lovers* (1945–8). If the publication record of Penguin is examined, it looks as if a good many other twentieth-century authors preceded Lawrence into paperback, but it must be remembered that rights were not easily available. In 1935 Heinemann had bought a 45-year option on the works for an advance of £7,000 and was protective of its copyright. But Heinemann was not a significant paperback house, and so in the 1950s Penguin was allowed to make up for lost time. W.E. Williams, who initiated *The Pelican Guide to English Literature*, directed the Lawrence publishing programme. He hoped to publish virtually all the works for the anniversary in 1960, speculating that after the new Obscene Publications Act it would be safe to issue an unexpurgated *Lady Chatterley's Lover*. Mercenary motives were later attributed to Lane and Penguin, and a reasonable profit was expected from sales of the unexpurgated novel. But there is no sign that the firm provoked prosecution in order to reap rewards from the publicity if it was acquitted. Evidently, no legal advice was taken, though on publication sample copies were lodged with the Director of Public Prosecutions. After acquittal, a good profit was indeed made: Penguin announced the figure of £112,000 for the novel when it issued its prospectus prior to becoming a public company in 1961.[9]

After the acquittal Sir Allen Lane brought out an account of the event,

The Trial of Lady Chatterley, with a specially bound edition as a Christmas gift for friends and associates. The trial, and this record of it, alerted Leavis to a new raft of agreement among the intelligentsia. He addressed this phenomenon in a review of *The Trial of Lady Chatterley* in the *Spectator* in February 1961 in an essay called 'The New Orthodoxy' and later 'The Orthodoxy of Enlightenment'.

In 'The New Orthodoxy' Leavis attacked the trial's defence argument that *Lady Chatterley's Lover* was, if not great, then essential to understanding Lawrence's art.[10] Leavis argued that actually the novel offended against Lawrence's own principle that art should be made in a fashion independent of will, expressed in a dictum Leavis much admired: 'Never trust the artist; trust the tale.' He said that *Lady Chatterley's Lover* was damaged by didacticism, which sanctioned the moral cruelty and artistic crudity of putting the husband of Connie Chatterley in a grossly symbolic wheelchair. He wanted to say that liberal applause should not drown out criticism of the novel, to echo Henry James once again and call out 'Humbug!' His main criticism was directed at Lawrence's rendering of the lover, Mellors.

Leavis and the Defence concurred that Mellors's four-letter words and sexual specificities were central to *Lady Chatterley's Lover*. But he believed the novel was mostly tract, devised to enlarge the repertoire of human behaviour by putting certain forms of colloquial speech into written currency. That was Lawrence's 'hygienic' purpose, which Leavis regarded as a disaster. Once in print the taboo words had two different kinds of presence. First there was the pioneering usage intended by Lawrence to be 'non-obscene' or 'undefiant'. Then there was the familiar usage, the way of things as they stood in 1928. The four-letter words were, of course, common in real speech. In *Lady Chatterley's Lover* 'fuck' was used in two ways, in the ordinary speech of Sir Clifford's entourage, and then also as part of the liberating or redeemed discourse of Mellors. The artistic problem, argued Leavis, was that Lawrence had to find a new register for Mellors's words, distinguishing a 'tender' use of 'fuck' from the ordinary usage of the free-talking intelligentsia. To make Mellors's language seem 'pure', more humane than the speech of the smart set to which Connie belonged, Lawrence (said Leavis) embroidered his use of four-letter words into a Nottinghamshire brogue. Mellors was given a dialect by the novelist to wash down, so to speak, and make homespun the rough intimacies of an idealized sexuality. Mellors as a dialect-speaker *had to* be working class, or rather be a dialect *character* when it suited the purpose of the novel – but not consistently. Leavis pointed out that he was, after all, an intellectual, had held an army commission and was irretrievably and securely (according to Leavis) a 'gentleman'.

For Leavis the four-letter words were a questionable feature of the book, preventing it from being 'a good novel . . . a decent work of art, or a convincing piece of didacticism'. He did not want Lawrence to become 'the author of *Lady Chatterley's Lover*' by means of this paperback publication. He focused less on a moral weakness in the book than on its artistic failure. He was concerned also with one matter of social class and the issues that had arisen in his earlier analysis of Bloomsbury and Keynes's attitude to Lawrence. His argument here was also related to Lawrence's use of dialect in the novel. Leavis believed that Mellors was endowed with a Nottinghamshire brogue partly because Lawrence himself was embarrassed at the use of crude words. This embarrassment was buried beneath defiance and his 'hygienic' purposes, but none the less there and rooted in the modesties of his own social origins in Eastwood. Such a view was more often given negatively, by saying that Lawrence could not escape being locked into lower-middle-class gentility. Leavis, though, wanted to pay tribute to this gentility, or the 'finely civilized upbringing in a Victorian working-class home'. Its linguistic environment was *not* a handicap but a fountain. Lawrence, he claimed, learned the delicacies of an artist from the decorous speech of that home. The modesties of Eastwood were therefore a training in sensibility.

This *pudeur* became in the developed and mature Lawrence the exquisitely sensitive human delicacy of the great artist – something so patently manifested in his novels and tales that we don't need the extraneous evidence we have that he didn't like 'emancipation'.

Leavis claimed that the 'embarrassment' of the four-letter words that failed to integrate was a sign of Lawrence betraying his origins. To propose (fictively) that it was *this* language (four-letter words, the brogue) that showed a humane way forward rather than *that* language (the discreet language of Eastwood, with its *pudeur*) cast a slur on the latter. Leavis did not want in *Lady Chatterley's Lover* an elegy for Eastwood. He did not want to see a book made famous that said farewell to Lawrence's class and time, and made famous by the very personages who had formerly denigrated that class and that time. Leavis's refusal to participate in the 'Chatterley event' was an implicit defence of his idea of civilization, an idea that did not reject the values of the 'Victorian working-class home'. It was a bold defence on the threshold of the 'The Sixties' – bold too in its implication that literature is made out of the discourse of actual social intercourse, and that a strong strand in Lawrentian discourse came from the ethos of the 'Victorian working-class home'.

For Leavis civilization was not classless, or upper class, or dependent on rejection of lower-class life: the Bloomsbury view, and an uncomfortable one given its laudable egalitarian aspirations. In his review of *The Trial of Lady Chatterley* he made his point again that civilization and art are not *in* languages, but *are* languages, continuous with usage. But was not the language of Lawrence's Eastwood a thing of the past, simply over? Perhaps: but was history over?

At this time Leavis was aware of his own past, hoping that his protégé at Downing, Morris Shapira, might escape the same insecurity he had experienced in the 1930s, and reminded too of his own past by his younger son, now at the Perse and its cross-country running champion as he had been. Robin was not an academic high-flyer, or rather not thought to be so by Q.D.L. On one occasion she interviewed his schoolmaster and explained that he was not as gifted as his brother and sister. Alone with the young teacher, as he showed him out, Leavis explained that he believed his son was 'all right' in English.

He looked at me very straight and tapped his chest lightly. 'He has the strength here.' Then he turned to make quite sure he would not be overheard through the open door of the sitting-room, and added, 'My wife is a very remarkable woman, you know.' He sounded both proud and daunted.

In fact, Robin Leavis won a scholarship (an Exhibition) to Clare College. The parents were delighted and Q.D.L. full of cheer at his success.[11]

Leavis was exhilarated by his work on *Lady Chatterley's Lover*. He thought he could write 'a good deal more' on it. He wondered where he might publish. 'The *Cambridge Review*, I'm sure, won't print me at all: it's wrong to affront the Provost of King's, Mrs Bennett and Mr Hough.'[12] It is curious to think of the literary critic, now in his prime, considering this local journal as his first port of call. Ten years after *Scrutiny* Leavis was uncertain of where to find a platform. He was possibly not aware how much better known he would become as a result, ironically, of the interest Penguin Books had taken in his own work. The firm brought out a new edition of *The Common Pursuit* as one of its first Peregrine Books, a series of paperbacks produced to a higher level of quality than Penguins. Copies were sent to Leavis at the beginning of 1962, with the traditional extra one that Sir Allen Lane liked to have signed for his collection of memorialized Penguins. Leavis sent this copy back unmarked, with the note 'I do not think that Sir Allen Lane did a service to literature, civilization or Lawrence in the business of *Lady Chatterley's Lover*.'[13]

The problem of finding a platform was solved unexpectedly in a year's time when Leavis returned to attack the 'orthodoxy of enlightenment' from a new angle in his Richmond Lecture for the undergraduates at Downing on the Two Cultures. He was now concerned with 'science', as he had been exercised over language and class in *Lady Chatterley's Lover*. The concern with history remained. In a practical way he now approached his own history, as focused on *Scrutiny*.

Leavis's belief in the 'finely civilized upbringing in a Victorian working-class home' recalled the readings from Dickens by Harry Leavis during his own childhood. It invoked too Q.D.L.'s never-accomplished plan to write a book on the lives of the poor. In the winter of 1961 Leavis set in motion a plan to recover some of his more recent past. He wrote to R.J.L. Kingsford, the Secretary of Cambridge University Press, to say he had had an offer from another publisher to reprint the whole run of *Scrutiny* for sale at £45. He inquired whether the Press would be interested in issuing such a reprint itself, as *Scrutiny* belonged so obviously to Cambridge.

Leavis was referring to a plan proposed some two years earlier. In 1959 R.T. Jones, a pupil then a Lecturer at the University of Natal, Pietermaritzburg, wrote to the university publications committee to ask it to consider reprinting *Scrutiny*, in view of its importance and the half-inch file of requests for back numbers evidently languishing at one Cambridge bookseller. The librarian wrote back promptly from Durban, having set up in type some sample pages.[14] Jones informed Leavis, but he was hesitant about the project. What part would the other former editors play? He was on poor terms with D.W. Harding and L.C. Knights. The question was 'difficult, delicate, paralysing'. He himself was 'high-handed' (he '*had* to be'); Knights, in whom Leavis saw an Eliot-like Christian gentleness, shrank from his 'aggression'. They had never genuinely collaborated, he said, so how could they do so now? He had to consider the effect of the idea on Q.D.L., 'my indispensable and only effective collaborator'. He had 'funked and funked' mentioning it, because 'her emotional intensity, when there's reason, is portentous'. Anyway, how would royalties be arranged?[15]

Leavis hung fire, then decided to contact Kingsford at Cambridge University Press. On 8 April 1961 he sent in a list showing the relative lengths of the volumes. Michael Black, editor of the English list, was enthusiastic, but R.W. David, manager of the London office, therefore Sales Director, was cautious. The Syndics (the Board) knew that to date the total reprint of a journal was unprecedented. And the proposal was something of a trap. If the Syndics declined, David believed that 'Leavis would take it as one more snub from official Cambridge. If they accept the proposal it will be taken as indicating that official Cambridge now acknowledges Leavis's work to have been of some importance.' But, in June, Kingsford told Leavis that the reprint would be done. Leavis informed Jones that the Natal plan would have to be dropped, and in September a contract for publication of the whole of *Scrutiny* was agreed. Leavis promised an introduction, which in the event became a long essay called 'A Retrospect', printed in a final volume. It was also agreed that Leavis should edit a selection of pieces from the journal.

In fact, a selection from *Scrutiny* had been published in 1948 in an American paperback edition, edited by Eric Bentley and published by the Grove Press. Bentley's *The Importance of Scrutiny* was produced five years before the end of *Scrutiny*. It remains an excellent book, divided into sensible sections, with an appendix on Leavis's relation to the *Calendar of Modern Letters*, a full list of the contents of *Scrutiny* to date and of books consisting of mainly *Scrutiny* material. This paperback, considered a rather exotic item, was usually on sale in Cambridge at Galloway & Porter. It should be remembered that in the early 1960s the British production of high-quality paper-bound academic books was in its infancy. There were many scholarly Penguins, but when Leavis negotiated with Cambridge University Press there were few larger format, sewn volumes on the American pattern, like Penguin's new Peregrines. When invited to make his own selection of *Scrutiny* essays, Leavis remarked that he would make his choice with 'a malicious eye' on Eric Bentley, whose selection Leavis had insisted should only appear in America. 'I'm angry – but have done nothing – about the paperback invasion of England by "his" book.'[16] After *The Trial of Lady Chatterley* Leavis was unenthusiastic about the proposal for a Penguin selection from *Scrutiny*.[17]

The plan to launch a Cambridge reprint of *Scrutiny* was a success.

Another scheme, a slightly more frivolous one, came to nothing. In January 1961 Leavis allowed himself to be nominated for the Chair of Poetry at Oxford. There were four candidates: Leavis, Robert Graves, Enid Starkie and Helen Gardner; the statutes were altered to allow women candidates for the first time. Leavis was not successful, polling only 116 votes against Graves's 329. But he did well, notwithstanding: his total was only one vote less than Gardner's, the leading Oxford scholar of Eliot.[18] Leavis must have been mildly attracted to the delivery of a series of lectures, as Matthew Arnold had from this chair. He was to have other opportunities.

Before the Richmond Lecture 1959–1961

Leavis – so he said – was now considered to be a figure of some gravity. In Cambridge 'my status now is archiepiscopal (in formal treatment), but I'm a complete outsider'. At Downing 'judging by the way they treat me, I'm now formidable with a Gladstonian grandeur'.[19] His concern for English currently took up whole half-hours of Governing Body time in Downing.

Leavis hardly ever spoke of modern fiction, so his pupils were interested to note an inclination to mention the novels of C.P. Snow. He mischievously remarked that the Master (W.K.C. Guthrie) enjoyed them. Evidently in the summer of 1961 Leavis purchased a copy of Snow's *The Two Cultures and the Scientific Revolution* (1959), paying out three shillings and sixpence at the Cambridge University Press showroom in Trumpington Street. He was curious because the Science versus Humanities issue came up so often in sixth-formers' answers in the Downing scholarship examination papers. At about the same time two things happened that quickened Leavis's interest in Snow. One occurred in the *New York Times* and the other in the little Cambridge magazine, *Delta*, which under Simon Gray was imperturbably supercilious about the Cambridge English establishment.

Leavis defended *Delta* when the *Spectator* reproved it in November 1960. At that time it characterized *Delta* as 'Leavisite' and therefore pro literary criticism and anti history. What, inquired Leavis, was the difference?

How does one get access to the 'historical past'? – that, surely, is the great problem. But to you [the *Spectator*] it is *no* problem: you see (it appears) no relation between it and that delicate cultivation of perception, sensibility and intelligence you refer to as 'practical criticism'.[20]

In the summer of 1961 *Delta* had a very Leavisian issue, reviewing Yvor Winters (applause) and George Steiner (disdain) and concluding with a mocking parody of the *Critical Quarterly* by John Newton. There was also a very long essay by Morris Shapira, Leavis's lieutenant at Downing, reviewing a collection of essays by Frank Kermode, *Puzzles and Epiphanies: Essays and Reviews 1956–1961*. In it he used a word prominent in Leavis's critique of *Lady Chatterley's Lover*: 'hateful'. The review interestingly shows the route to Leavis's Richmond Lecture and shows what the Leavisian mode was like, at a point close to the master.

Frank Kermode was the young academic who had wounded Leavis by his patronizing valediction to *Scrutiny* in a radio talk for the BBC. Shapira's essay was called 'Critical Twiddle-Twaddle', a quotation with no source given but familiar to *Delta* readers from D.H. Lawrence's definition of literary criticism in his essay 'John Galsworthy'. Leavis was actually never mentioned in Shapira's essay, but it was a statement intensely committed to him and especially to the Leavis who distrusted Eliot's idea of 'impersonality', his belief that there is a separation between the man that suffers and the mind that creates. Leavis, of course, did not believe art was cut free from its maker; it may be 'disinterested' but not private. Kermode in *Puzzles and Epiphanies*, on the contrary, celebrated 'impersonality', that art which is created by an artist's surrendering of himself. He quoted Paul Valéry – to be an artist 'I must be essentially inhuman'. Kermode was an aesthete, close to Art for Art's Sake, but sensibly not prepared to say that there was no human relevance in the work of the impersonal artist. In Eliot, even in Valéry, we are aware, he said (quoting Wallace Stevens), of the 'thing that is incessantly overlooked: the artist, the presence of the determining personality'. But Kermode certainly applauded art that was beyond moral judgement, that was consummately out of nature, like the clockwork bird in W.B. Yeats's 'Sailing to Byzantium'. This art enraptured the reader who experienced it by the egotistic accomplishment of its own doing. One of his examples of 'total technical control' was William Golding, in whose work 'every kind of beastliness and depravity is given the virtue of form'.

A Leavisian was unlikely to enlist with aestheticism. But the commitment to high art was so full blooded in *Puzzles and Epiphanies*, even at times so light-hearted – Kermode promised 'new-found methods' and 'compounds strange' – that it is surprising that Shapira took the trouble to attack the book and make himself unpopular by the attack: he could hardly expect golden opinions after saying that a respected literary academic was 'hateful'. But he was emboldened by two particular challenges. One was dislike of the company in which Kermode placed Eliot. Then there was the alternative he offered to high art, the aesthetic on the other side of the fence (from Golding or Valéry, Joyce or Beckett), the aesthetic to which he gave some appreciative attention and one in which he silently implicated Leavis.

Shapira disliked the way in which Kermode associated Eliot with other aesthetes, making him only one version of aestheticism among others in late Romanticism. One form of aestheticism that clearly intrigued Kermode was the performance art of the *fin de siècle* dancer Loie Fuller, which Shapira thought hopelessly arty. Eliot's belief in 'impersonality' surely did not belong to *that* world? Leavis was in many respects unsympathetic to 'Tradition and the Individual Talent', but respected it and knew (Shapira implied) that Eliot's conception of impersonality was a momentous one, upon which he had called in handling some of his dearest subjects, like tragedy or Isaac Rosenberg. The disinterestedness he found in Lawrence was a revision of Eliot. He admired Lawrence, not for a spontaneity contrasting with the prim mode of Eliot, but because he had *another* mode of impersonality. If Eliot was wrong (for Leavis) in his use of the idea, he was at least formidably wrong. Shapira wanted to say that Kermode trivialized the idea of impersonality by association, in lauding its more trivial manifestations.

What Shapira protested against most vigorously was Kermode's handling of the alternative to high art, the realist mode, because in that Kermode brought his exposition to an account of C.P. Snow (polar opposite to the Golding–Valéry aesthetic), at which point he brushed up against Leavis – or against what Leavis was supposed to be. On one side, Kermode admired high art, out of nature, with 'total technical control', the art of Golding, Beckett or Joyce. This was Symbolist art, transcending ordinary perception. Then, there was the alternative, the other mode: art committed to observation and realism. This is where the novels of C.P. Snow come in. Kermode made no reference to Leavis, but it was the realist tradition with which Leavis was associated at that date, the tradition of art that was candidly referential, art whose method was ordinary perception advanced to high tops of detail and stamina.

In *Puzzles and Epiphanies* Snow showed up as a contemporary representative of Leavisian art, a 1960s member of the 'great tradition'. Of course, the art of the 'great tradition' was very far from Snow's, but it had the *reputation* of plain sobriety. There was a danger of Leavis and Snow being merged into a single 'complex'. Shapira showed Leavis that Snow was a figure from whom he had to dissociate himself.

Against Snow 1962–1963

Sir Charles Snow was a novelist, a science administrator and influential civil servant. He was also a playwright and had a regular literary column in the *Financial Times*. His lecture *The Two Cultures and the Scientific Revolution* was in its ninth impression. Snow was ten years Leavis's junior. In 1956 in the *New Statesman and Nation* he first sketched the notion that the scientific mind was socially progressive and the literary mind reactionary. A physicist by training, Snow had specialized in infrared spectroscopy after a Ph.D. at the Cavendish Laboratory in Cambridge in 1928. He took his first degrees in science at University College, Leicester. He became a fellow of Christ's in 1930, just as Leavis lost his lectureship and his connection with Emmanuel; he was a tutor of Christ's from 1935 to 1945. Snow found his *métier* as a manager, rather than as a practitioner, in the world of science, with a particular gift for the appointment of personnel. He was also a lucid popularizer. Just before the war he used his explaining skills as editor of the journal *Discovery*, much read in sixth forms. Early on he showed a flair for narrating the romance of scientific work in *The Search* (1934), which was partly based on his experiences at the Cavendish.

Snow had a good war. In 1942 he came into his own as Director of Technical Personnel at the Ministry of Labour. From 1945 he was Civil Service Commissioner in charge of recruiting scientists, for which he was knighted in 1957. Two years later he retired for the sake of full-time writing and consultancy, principally as a director of English Electric. By 1961 Snow had written eight novels in a saga of post-war technocrats, whom he called the 'new men', starting with *Strangers and Brothers* (1940). Three more were in the pipeline. Snow's stilted novels, which resemble those of his Leicester contemporary, William Cooper, but are less lively, have a sombre, dreamy quality that is not unattractive. Kermode commented well on a pleasing innocence in them: 'I notice that when somebody does something unexpected . . . Eliot [the peripatetic observer in Snow's novels] is always more surprised than I am.'

The Two Cultures and the Scientific Revolution was the Sir Robert Rede Lecture at Cambridge of 1959. It is sometimes thought that the lecture was about scientific method, or the logic of science set against the logic of art. Actually, it was not about science but about scientists and their politics, compared to the social thinking of literary artists, or 'literary people' in general. Here a problem arose: it was never really clear whether Snow was writing about scientists or about people who vaguely favour science and a 'scientific approach' to human affairs. Two Cultures is unlike the studies of scientific method of the time, notably Thomas H. Kuhn's The Structure of Scientific Revolutions (1956) or Karl H. Popper's The Logic of Scientific Discovery (1959). Nor was the Rede Lecture in the tradition of such post-war works of popularization as C.H. Waddington's The Scientific Attitude (1948). One interesting difference between Snow and philosophers of science (Kuhn and Popper) and practitioner–popularizers (Waddington) was that Snow displayed actual hostility to the non-scientific culture. The theorists of science and the popularizers seemed to have nothing against literature, but Snow, though a man of letters, was dubious (if cautiously and sorrowfully so) about literature, both literature of the British tradition of radical dissent (Ruskin, Morris, Dickens and Lawrence) and the modernists like Ezra Pound and Wyndham Lewis. He reported approvingly the view of a 'scientist of distinction': 'weren't they not only politically silly, but politically wicked? Didn't they bring Auschwitz that much nearer?'[21] (Snow made a minor exception of W.B. Yeats, for his 'singular magnanimity'.[22])

If not about scientific method, the Rede Lecture was certainly about the 'scientific revolution' and the technology that ensued from it. Snow put on display the plain human benefits of material advance and satirized the frivolity of the traditional literary culture of 'intellectual persons'. In the nineteenth century they were the ones who shuddered at 'the hideous back-streets, the smoking chimneys', blind as Luddites to the benefits that would follow the first traumas (admittedly grievous) of industrialization. The Industrial Revolution had its horrors, but so did the ancient transition from the life of hunting and food-gathering to that of agricultural economies. Snow accused the British of snobbery about science and industry. It fell to Mond and Siemens in Germany to learn applied chemistry and electrical engineering and then make their fortunes (and create employment) in Britain. 'Industrialization,' he concluded, 'is the only hope of the poor.'

At one level the message was irresistible, and international. The scientific revolution could be carried out in 'India, Africa, South-East Asia, Latin America, the Middle East, within fifty years'. Snow was himself a lesson in internationalism. *The Affair* (1960) was to sell 100,000 copies in the Soviet Union.[23] Snow dismissed national and ethnic differences. He recounted that when Sir John Cockcroft was asked in the 1930s what Soviet skilled workers were like, he replied tersely they were '"Just about the same as the ones at Metrovick." Well, he has never been a man to waste words. A fact is a fact is a fact.'[24] Of course, language other than that of fact can, to a degree, be discounted in the culture of science (or some science), but it can never be discounted in literary culture: it is the *point* of literary culture; but this issue was never raised by Snow. Nor can language be discounted in non-scientific discourse, that is, in 'culture' itself. Snow observed that educated people could be fastidiously unwilling to understand the many different industrial planes on which material progress was made and he was probably right. But he was on shaky ground to say that a literature-based culture of 'intellectual persons' was responsible for this unwillingness. Nor did he recognize any of the values of *speech*. A part of the body to which his sense of welfare did not extend was the tongue.

On the face of it, Snow adjudicated between 'Two Cultures' that he pretended to be equal in status, deploring one for clipping the wings of the other. But the undertow of his lecture told another story. His real message was that literary culture had little value, or only 'personal' value. *Time* magazine succinctly observed that Snow was really lecturing not on a threat to science from art but on 'the tendency of technology to suffocate humanities'.[25] If this was not readily noticed in Britain, it was because it seemed implausible that such a man-of-letters could be carrying the assassin's pillow.

Leavis was in touch with the repute of Snow, partly through Shapira's reference to him in *Delta*. In the summer of 1961 something else happened to make him curious.

In July there was an essay by the novelist Angus Wilson in the *New York Times*, linking Leavis's name to that of Snow. And his face: Leavis and Snow were paired as allies in neighbouring photographs. Wilson identified Leavis as the literary-critical counterpart of Snow, promoting a concerned realism in fiction, suspicious of fantasy. Wilson's essay interestingly showed his own evolution away from realism, from *The Middle Age of Mrs Eliot* (1958) to the blend of fantasy and realism, bordering on the grotesque, in *The Old Men at the Zoo* (1961) – a novel as much about academic succession as Snow's *The Masters* (1951). When he wrote, Wilson could not have predicted Leavis's revival of interest in Dickens in the 1960s, a move that interestingly he shared. Wilson showed a plain, dry Leavis, not one Leavis himself would recognize. Leavis had always been called a puritan, and he was quite proud of the label. But in the early 1960s his supposed puritanism became not a mild slur (which Leavis did not mind) but a formidable fact, defined with admiration by, for example, Martin Green in *A Mirror for Anglo-Saxons* (1960), which paid tribute to a 'decent' Leavis who was honest, English and Orwellian. In 1961 an old admirer, S. Gorley Putt, published a study on similar lines, exasperatingly linking the critic with Q – and also with Snow.[26] Leavis disliked being summed up. The circumstances were ready for him to show how unlike Snow he was. He also wanted to show how much his world – the university – differed from the version of this world Snow had put on display. Snow had described the academic world, especially Cambridge, for a wide public, and a very mundane account he gave, remote from Leavis's collegiate life, either real or ideal. *The Masters* had sold over 20,000 copies in the 1950s. *The Affair* was also popular, and in 1962 was to do excellent business on the West End stage. Cambridge or the academic world was in danger of becoming Snow's fictional Cambridge in the public mind.

Late in 1961 Leavis received the invitation from the Downing College junior common-room to deliver the Richmond Lecture. This lecture was normally given not by an academic but by a public figure. Leavis decided to speak on C.P. Snow, whom he knew would be well known in Downing, with its now strong scientific orientation. His *Two Cultures and the Scientific Revolution* was much taught in sixth forms. Leavis tuned his subject to the undergraduate moment. It turned out somewhat differently.

The Richmond Lecture was advertised for 28 February 1962. Leavis started work after Christmas and on 14 January he was writing 'fast'. A week before the event, on 23 February, the BBC made an approach for permission to record and broadcast the lecture. Leavis was obdurate. 'There can be no question of recording my lecture, or using it for any BBC purpose.'[27] It was to be a parish event, a lecture about Snow, late of Christ's, where Hough ran English and L.C. Knights had his research fellowship and where the Master was the ever-respected Brian Downs, who always sent Leavis pupils when he was Director of Studies in English. The lecture commemorated Admiral Sir Herbert Richmond, whose naval bluntness was unlike the plain-man certainty of Snow, who was not always unable to resist the tone of a pundit.

On the evening of 28 February, Leavis faced a packed dining-hall at Downing, some of his listeners perching in alcoves. The Downing English men came early to give support on the benches near the front. Many had to stand, including Snow's old friend from Christ's and his Leicester days, the historian J.H. Plumb. Leavis stood between the Master and the President of the junior common-room. As a Lecturer, Leavis usually began with austere deliberation, and he did so that night.

If confidence in oneself as a master-mind, qualified by capacity, insight and knowledge to pronounce authoritatively on the frightening problems of our civilization, is genius, then there can be no doubt about Sir Charles Snow's. He has no hesitations.

In the pause that followed some of the audience must have been wondering whether they could believe their ears. Leavis continued: 'Yet Snow is, in fact, portentously ignorant.' Half a minute later there was a rustle.

Leavis believed his lecture possessed a certain musical organization. It was, indeed, carefully paced, its initial solemnity followed by attack, then some skirmishing, some of it appropriate to a college club supper. (There was a joke about Snow's novels being created by an 'electronic brain called Charlie'.) Soon Leavis discoursed himself into the heart of his argument: Snow was not wrong, but he said and saw too little; of course, the 'accelerating movement of civilization' should not be defied, but the acceleration could not have as its goal merely material assurance – or *jam*, as Snow put it in his notorious formulation: 'Jam today, and men aren't at their most exciting: jam tomorrow, and one often sees them at their noblest.'[28] Snow frequently stressed the speed with which today turns into tomorrow; Leavis called for pause and claimed that if the brakes were applied Snow showed little to look at.

The advance of science and technology means a human future of change so rapid and of such kinds of tests and challenges so unprecedented, of decisions and possible non-decisions so momentous and insidious in their consequences, that mankind – this is surely clear – will need to be in full intelligent possession of its full humanity (and 'possession' here means, not confident ownership of that which belongs to *us* – our property, but a basic living deference towards that to which, opening as it does into the unknown and itself unknowable, we know we belong). I haven't chosen to say that mankind will need all its traditional wisdom; that might suggest a kind of conservatism that, so far as I am concerned, is the enemy. What we need, and shall continue to need not less, is something with the livingness of the deepest vital instinct; such as intelligence, a power – rooted, strong in experience, and supremely human – of creative response to the new challenges of time; something that is alien to either of Snow's cultures.[29]

How can the 'fully' human be distinguished from the 'less' human? How are levels of distinction to be defined? Snow hardly went into the matter, a difficult one; but *some* account could have been possible, a fuller idea (than 'jam') could have been given of human ambitions. Because Snow was so proudly reductive, there was plenty of room for Leavis's plea for 'fulness'. Snow's conception of human behaviour was empty of spirituality, on the grounds that the stomach must be full before the soul can sing. He did not recognize that souls vary, whether bodies are newly or long-fed. There was, Leavis argued, more to survival and growth than 'abundant jam, salvation and lasting felicity to all mankind'.[30] The omission of 'quality of life' (that more recent phrase) in the Rede Lecture was understandable because of the urgency of Snow's concern: 'We have very little time. So little I dare not guess at it.' But he left little room for such considerations. Leavis, at one point, sketched what there is besides jam by rapid allusions to Conrad's *The Shadow-Line* and Lawrence's *The Rainbow*, both used to illustrate deference to the unknowable. The illustrations were only as tendentious as any account of human need that goes beyond the materialistic. Leavis did, however, seize on one subject that Snow ignored and about which there could be no controversy, that is, language.

Snow wrote as if there were two great edifices, the scientific and literary, with optional entry to either (or both, by turns). Leavis believed that the methods of literature related to the individual quite differently from the methods of science, because the language of literature was in some sense the language of the individual – not in an obvious sense but at least in a *more* obvious sense than the language of science. The phrase 'language of science' in itself illustrated the way in which the discourses of literature and science are not parallel entities, for besides there being many languages of science, there was division between discourses *of* science and *about* science. The discourses of and about literature need not be inherently alien to the discourse of individuals; discourse about science need not be alien either; but the discourse *of* science certainly is. For Leavis, neither the physical universe nor the discourse of its notation was possessed by observers in the way in which literature could be possessed by its readers; or by its writers – because he would claim that literature and literary culture was constructed not from words learned but from intercourse. Language was inherently incomplete, speech-acts soliciting other acts, marking out the space between people, the space in which their shapes, as individuals, are defined. Leavis had always worked from a theory of society, society being this space shaped by discourse, neither private nor public. He drew his diagram of literary criticism. It works by the inquiry 'This is so, isn't it?' that invites the reply 'Yes, but . . .' Of course this was appropriate for literary dealings, but Leavis was here not offering only a technique for pedagogy or a way of conducting a class about a poem. Question-and-answer was typical of human intercourse at large.[31] Between the question and the answer was the specifically human thing. In his lecture Leavis called it the 'Third Realm'.

These ideas about language had been adumbrated in *Education and the University*. In the Richmond Lecture they were revived, with this new term, 'Third Realm', for the space shaped by discourses (or 'society').

It is in the study of literature, the literature of one's own language in the first place, that one comes to recognize the nature and priority of the third realm . . . the realm of that which is neither merely private and personal nor public in the sense that it can be brought into the laboratory and pointed to. You cannot point to the poem; it is 'there' only in the re-creative response of individual minds to the black marks on the page. But – a necessary faith – it is something in which minds can meet.[32]

A difference between Leavis and Snow is that Snow was more concerned with feeding than with meeting. For a novelist he was strangely uncon-cerned with society. In good faith, and decently shocked by the scale of international deprivation, Snow believed only in individuals, as I.A. Richards, influenced by C.K. Ogden, thought only of individuals nearly thirty years before. Leavis's analysis of Snow was a re-run of his analysis of Richards's *Coleridge on Imagination*. In that book Richards gave in to Bentham, Leavis argued. The Richmond Lecture initiated a decade of attacks on modern Benthamism, what was henceforth to be called by Leavis the 'Technologico-Benthamite' world. In the Richmond Lecture, as also in his old critique of Richards, Leavis was distressed by an absence of history and a tendency to Messianic pronouncement about civilization. What Richards displayed in *Coleridge on Imagination*, Leavis found in Snow's *Two Cultures*.

The BBC expected in the Richmond Lecture an event of moment. After its delivery the press responded quickly. Leavis believed a *Times* stringer alerted the newspaper, because a report appeared in that paper on 1 March and two days later in the *Sunday Times*.[33] Snow wrote on 5 March to Leavis for a copy of the lecture, but steps had already been taken for it to be published. Leavis spoke on the telephone to Iain Hamilton, literary editor of the *Spectator*, and in its issue of Saturday, 2 March, it was announced that the full text would appear the following week. Hamilton realized there might be defamatory statements in the lecture, calling Snow's scientific ability into doubt. Leavis had speculated as to whether he understood the abstruse 'Contradiction of Parity', so the *Spectator* sought legal opinion. It was advised that there were passages '*prima facie* highly defamatory' and 'serious professional libels'. The lawyers did not recommend publication, unless there was a written indemnity from Snow himself.[34] Hamilton sought Snow's approval. The only person at the *Spectator* who knew Snow personally was the assistant editor, Cyril Ray, a well-known essayist whom Snow had sponsored for membership of the Athenaeum. Ray was duly dispatched to Snow's flat in Cromwell Road, where he admired the Sidney Nolans and handed over the text. Snow was suffering from a detached retina, so the manuscript was read to him by his wife, Pamela Hansford Johnson. He was 'nettled by some and amused by some', but declared straight off that 'we must print it exactly as it stood'. Lady Snow showed more anger at Leavis than Snow.[35]

The *Spectator* published the lecture on 9 March. The shock with which it was received was undoubtedly affected by the irreverent illustration Hamilton chose for his magazine cover, a witty double head of Snow sketched by Quentin Blake, a former Downing pupil. (The lecture itself was embellished by other wobbly heads of Snow. There was one sketch of Leavis at his most athletic: it was later used on the cover of a Swedish edition of his essays.) The text was preceded by a note from Leavis.

The lecture was private and representatives of the press who inquired were informed that there was no admission and that no reporting was to be permitted. The appearance in the newspapers of garbled reports has made it desirable that the lecture should appear in full.

Snow himself was convinced that Leavis had planned publicity for his lecture. He said later that news of a coming onslaught reached him in the middle of February. He believed that Leavis himself belied his claim that the lecture was 'private'.[36] Did he not say in the lecture that Snow had to be dealt with in an 'insistent public way'? But Leavis did have his own conception of insistence and the public. The Downing men were, after all, his public. 'Sixth-form masters were making their bright boys read Snow,' he said, and the hall at Downing had been full of 'bright boys' not long out of school, many of whom would go back and teach others.[37] There had certainly been Downing talk about the Master enjoying Snow's novels, and Leavis was not above giving discomfort in his retirement period. But it is unlikely that he orchestrated publicity, or had the means to do so.

Publicity there certainly was. The lecture had been blunt: Leavis called Snow 'portentously ignorant', meaning that his ignorance of history (especially the 'human history of the Industrial Revolution') was a portent, but with Matthew Arnold or John Ruskin in memory, let alone eighteenth-century pamphleteering, the lecture appears only a good contribution to robust debate. But it proved to be shocking. In the *Spectator* for two weeks there were pages of indignation. (Among the unexpected private supporters was Ivy Compton-Burnett, who was seen 'chuckling' over the Richmond Lecture.)[38] And there was some encouragement in Cambridge. Brian Downs, Master of Christ's (Snow's college), congratulated Leavis: 'Yes, you *were* rude. But *I* shan't cut *you*,' he said. So did a former Master of Christ's, the retired Canon Professor Raven, who wrote a 'courtly letter', thanking Leavis for having had the 'courage to say what some of us ought to have said long ago'. (Raven had been livid about the prospect of a novel about Christ's, which became *The Masters*.)[39] Chatto & Windus received some letters of praise.[40]

How did Snow react? After publication he opted for silence. He spoke at a *Yorkshire Post* literary luncheon of the dying virtue of magnanimity.[41] But he was distressed, and evidently astonished. To a friend he wrote of a 'man putting arsenic in another man's beer with the expressed intention of killing him'.[42] He was believed to say later that Leavis had obstructed his chance of the Nobel Prize.[43] He regretted having so easily agreed to allow publication of the lecture, and Leavis regretted he had too, considering that Snow had been given the opportunity to 'let him off'. Snow's acquaintances and friends rallied. William Gerhardie, whose novels Snow admired, wrote a long letter of complaint to the *Spectator*. J.H. Plumb at Christ's was redoubtable. He supplied material for a reply to Leavis, enabling Snow to contradict his reading of the Industrial Revolution. Plumb urged him to tackle 'Raymond Williams, Hoggart and Leavis as a group on this subject [hostility to industrialism] – These are the dangerous descendants of the craft socialists.'[44] Graham Hough promised to 'publish a short pamphlet on Leavis's shortcomings – his ignorance, lack of scholarship, obtuseness, etc.' It never appeared.

Once it was public, Leavis wanted to see the Richmond Lecture in book form, preferably, like the Rede Lecture, under the imprint of Cambridge University Press, as befitted his 'deep piety towards Cambridge'. The Press was unwilling. It considered that Snow might take legal action, not being aware that he had promised not to. It also thought that too much 'amplification' was necessary: it believed some of the novels cited should be subjected to analysis. It was not clear whether it meant Snow's novels, or those by Conrad and Lawrence that related to Leavis's thesis. Leavis replied that he was not surprised at the Syndics' decision, but he adamantly refused to make changes. The lecture was

addressed to the occasion: its point and edge and 'attack' are inseparable from that functional quality. There would be no point in my trying to 'explain' to the classics who are the resisters . . . If one had to concede that the lecture didn't explain itself, then there would have been no point in trying to do the educational work with less than a volume – or a set of volumes. You can't educate Public Orators – or Syndics.

I've looked through the lecture again and am bound to say that I've done better than I should have thought possible. I can't help saying, modestly, that it will be a classic.[45]

He went next, naturally, to Chatto & Windus. Leavis considered writing a postscript or afterword. In the end he opted for printing the lecture, together with a supplementary essay that he had liked in the *Cambridge Review* by Michael Yudkin, a young biochemist.[46] Yudkin enlisted the help of Simon Gray to polish it. Chatto & Windus was approached by Richard Gooder's friend André Schiffrin, who had been at Clare, to ask if he could have his firm, Pantheon Books, publish the lecture in the United States. Leavis agreed and supplied an explanatory essay.

There remained the question of how Snow would regard yet more attention. Chatto & Windus had bought the copyright of the lecture from the *Spectator*. Snow was unenthusiastic about Leavis's appearance between hard covers. He told Ian Parsons that before magazine publication he had been willing for it to appear, but with no comment on the lecture and no suggestion in the *Spectator* that there would be publication elsewhere:

You are now asking me, as I understand it, to give the same agreement to a publication in a different form, as a pamphlet or small book. This I am not ready to do. Let me be quite clear. I am not interested in the legal aspect. You need not worry about me on that account, as I think you know. There is nothing to prevent your going ahead. But this affair, in my judgement, has had a long enough run for the time being, and I am not prepared to say that I approve.[47]

He also could not permit additions to the lecture. Parsons replied that no statement would appear indicating Snow approved of hardback publication. Curiously, although Parsons mentioned (with studied off-handedness) the contribution of Yudkin, it was ignored by Snow and the piece was never submitted for vetting.[48]

One complaint Leavis had against Snow was that he distorted the history of the Industrial Revolution. But it was urged he himself said little of this history. The lecture came in a period in which Leavis's publications were scattered, and the debate about the lecture would have improved if one of these pieces had been better known. In it Leavis presented some of the evidence of the human impact of industrialism. The essay was on *Dombey and Son* and it had appeared in the *Sewanee Review*; it was not widely known until it appeared in *Dickens the Novelist* (1970). In it Leavis was hardly a Luddite, for he showed Dickens's capacity for an affirmative depiction of the Industrial Revolution. He demonstrated how the presentation of the Toodle family showed the earthquake effect of railway construction, whose 'energy and promise' Dickens exalted. Contrary to Snow's view that Victorian novelists were unprogressive, Leavis shows how Dickens believed in

the railway as the triumphant manifestation of beneficent energy. And, characteristically, the beneficence that he acclaims manifests itself in terms of immediate human betterment. It is figured directly and representatively in Toodle himself – Toodle and his family. 'Where have you worked all your life?' Mr Dombey asks him at the first interview.

'Mostly underground, Sir, till I got married. I come to the level then. I'm a going on one of these here railroads when they comes into full play.'

The prosperity and happiness of the Toodle family are associated with the 'coming into full play' of the railways – and seen as a representative accompaniment.[49]

It was wrong to depict the conflict between Snow and Leavis as one between the scientific and the literary. It was a conflict over history, in which Leavis was increasingly interested in the 1960s. The interest emerged also in his review in the spring of 1963 of the long-awaited edition of Lawrence's letters by Harry T. Moore.

Retirement 1962–1963

The Richmond Lecture was in the middle of Leavis's retirement year and was its most conspicuous performance. There was also his final lecture as a full member of the faculty. He completed his last lecture course in Cambridge in March, at the usual podium in Mill Lane. He spoke of the 'common pursuit', about the way in which literary evaluation happened in the relation between readers and writers, and of how criticism was never accomplished by the application of absolute standards: there were no standards to dictate response. He quoted a favourite saying of George Santayana on moral absolutism, to the effect that to believe that something is good in itself is like believing that whisky 'stands dead drunk in the bottle'. Typically the don who praised the undergraduate Empson in his 1928 lectures, Leavis mentioned *Delta*. In conclusion he said, 'This is the end, the end ...', switching off the lectern light, murmuring a reference to one of his favourite displays, Othello's 'Put out the light.' At Cambridge a round of applause was customary at the end of a course of undergraduate lectures. This time it was rousing, appropriately led by a Downing pupil.[50]

The reference to *Othello* had resonance. In the spring of 1964 the tragedy was produced by John Dexter for the embryo National Theatre. Leavis's essay on the play had been given to Dexter by Kenneth Tynan and he enthusiastically communicated it to Laurence Olivier, who made the interpretation a key to his reading of the part. Olivier's view of his performance is relevant to Leavis's rendering of the final speech: 'I stretched the elastic of their tolerance to a huge degree, pushed them further and further away from me, and then at the very, very end, well into the death scene, I pulled their emotions right back into loving him with an intensity they otherwise would never have felt.'[51]

Leavis's retirement year (October 1961 to September 1962) turned out to be bleak.[52] Q.D.L. was gravely ill. Just after the Richmond Lecture she went to hospital in Norwich for three months, where she suffered badly. Leavis visited constantly, leaving Cambridge at about eleven o'clock and returning by the 4.30 train. The house in Newton Road had served its usefulness, so Leavis set about finding somewhere smaller. Money was a problem. At Chatto & Windus, Ian Parsons considered appointing Leavis an adviser, to protect him if retirement brought a drop in income. Leavis declined, confident that he could manage. 'Anyway, I'm not afraid.'[53]

There was the issue of who would succeed Leavis at Downing and here there was a hopeful sign. Newton, Richard and Jean Gooder and Shapira always regretted that Harold Mason was no longer in Cambridge. Newton especially relied upon him, and kept Leavisians supplied with cyclostyled scripts of his Exeter lectures. He recommended his pupils to seek junior posts in Exeter, or consult him about research projects. Leavis too was sorry about Mason's absence. He remarked in 1961 that Exeter was 'lucky to have Mason, who, of course, ought to be in Cambridge. But how to manage the re-acquisition?' and, separately, that 'No pupil of mine has ever been appointed' – in Cambridge, he meant.[54] Newton wanted to unite the statements and get Mason to Cambridge, even though he was not quite a pupil, but something close. He also believed, as did the Gooders, Shapira and some other Leavisians in posts outside Cambridge (notably Geoffrey Strickland at Reading and Roy Littlewood at Bristol), that a journal should be started in succession to Scrutiny but less aggressive. Several titles were mooted, including 'The Stourbridge Review', after the great medieval fair held at Cambridge, or 'Wrangler's Corner', a crossroads near Cambridge. Eventually they founded the Cambridge Quarterly.

Newton decided that it would be worth making an appeal to all Leavis's pupils, reminding them that Leavis had said no pupil of his had a lectureship at Cambridge. Could not funds be raised to endow a lectureship, or at least finance a series of visiting Lecturers in sympathy with Leavis's work? That the lectureship, in whatever form, was to be in

Cambridge was always a condition of the scheme. Newton was showing a spirit similar to that in which *Scrutiny* was started in the 1930s. In April 1962 Newton approached the Master of Downing, to tell him that an F.R. Leavis Lectureship was being planned. Downing was interested in the possibility of Mason coming to Cambridge, and in June it resolved that, should he be appointed to a university lectureship, Mason would be elected to the fellowship. The fellows must have considered that appointment to a university lectureship was the condition of election. It is impossible to say whether they considered the condition would be met if Mason occupied a privately funded lectureship; they may have presumed that such a lectureship could be adopted by the university. In the autumn of 1962 the Master kept Newton in touch with the attitude of the Governing Body to the proposed lectureship.[55]

During the autumn term (1962/3) Leavis continued to lecture even though he was no longer on the Faculty list; he gave a series for the English Club on Dickens. There was a small charge. At the beginning of term, on the afternoon of Sunday, 7 October, a group of trustees for the F.R. Leavis Lectureship Trust met at Newton's house off Chesterton Road, two minutes from the former Leavis home in Chesterton Hall Crescent. Newton was Secretary and the Chairman was Denys Thompson. The other trustees were Jean Gooder, Boris Ford, Roy Littlewood, Raymond O'Malley, W.W. Robson, Geoffrey Strickland and William Walsh. Several sympathizers resident abroad were appointed as 'consultants': Seymour Betsky, Reuben Brower, Dennis Enright, D.F. McKenzie, T.B. Tomlinson and Yvor Winters. In March 1963 the Trust was officially registered as a charity.[56] Some time after this October meeting and February 1963 there was another Sunday meeting of the trustees at which the name of Mason was proposed as the Lecturer by Geoffrey Strickland. There had been various suggestions from the trustees, but Strickland was aware of Newton's enthusiasm and shared it. At tea he suggested to Newton that Mason be proposed, which he did when the meeting was reconvened. The result was that Mason became the Trust's candidate.

The day before this meeting there was an uncomfortable incident. Strickland was up for the whole weekend, and he turned up with Shapira at the Leavises on Shapira's motorcycle. Q.D.L. had been out shopping, and she remarked how many old Leavisian acquaintances were to be seen that day. Leavis distracted her attention by fussing over a kettle. It occurred to Strickland that Q.D.L. was in the dark about the

Trust and the meeting for which the trustees had come. He asked Shapira if she knew about it. 'No,' he replied on their way back to his flat. 'And she's not supposed to.'[57]

For the time being there was every promise in the plans of the Trust. It looked as if a succession would be happily accomplished.

The most important public event of Leavis's retirement year had been the Richmond Lecture. It illustrated Leavis's tendency to seize an opportunity. Snow's original lecture was richly symbolic material, both subject matter and author, his and its circumstances, a former Cambridge figure from a particular college; there was much to be exploited in a retirement discourse. Leavis's lecture initiated a phase of new concerns, and even a new phase of writing, that of 'higher pamphleteering' – if the essays that flowed from the Richmond Lecture were 'higher pamphleteering'. This did not mean that Leavis underrated their creative quality.

I remember having told someone myself that the Richmond Lecture is a poem. 'Musically organized' is what I've also said about my lectures – the necessity of making each of which self-contained helped me to conceive the book – helped me to solve the greater writing (*thinking*) problem.[58]

During 1962 Leavis sought a new house, smaller, modern and easier to run than Newton Road. At Christmas a move was made to No. 12, Bulstrode Gardens. Cambridge has a mile-wide gracious strip of land between the Backs of the colleges and the country, on the road to Bedford. Within this strip lie college playing-fields, college residences (Clare and Corpus new courts) and the massive 1930s university library. The strip is bounded by Grange Road, beyond which are Edwardian villas. A little further out of town are avenues and crescents of plain post-war housing, built not for Trevelyans and Rothschilds but for wartime professors wanting easy properties, enjoying proximity to the library. Bulstrode Gardens was such a little road. No. 12 was a compact detached house. F.R.L. and Q.D.L. moved in just after Christmas 1962, to be immediately inconvenienced by a small fire, though Q.D.L. was thrilled to satisfy an ambition to call out the fire-brigade. The house had to be refitted; kitchen units were ordered from Remploy. The Cambridge shops seemed no good for the purpose, 'except Primavera which we can't afford'.[59] Q.D.L. cheered up the house. Plain cream walls, a Guy Rogers Manhattan sofa, rush-bottomed chairs and a Jimson ladder-back chair were set off by her taste for bright colours: vermilion-stained cupboard, Morris loose-covers in rust and yellow, patchwork of her own making. There was a large photographic blow-up of Antonello's 'St Jerome in His Study' over the fireplace, unglazed and unframed; certainly not a Medici print.[60] As well as being in a new house, there were structural changes in the Leavis family. Ralph Leavis, continuing to live in Oxford, was no longer a visitor, after the estrangement with his mother. Kate and Robin Leavis were in or approaching their university years, Kate at Oxford and Robin going up to Clare College, where he was to be a pupil of John Newton. As for Leavis's intellectual family in Cambridge, some of its young members were, as we have seen, on the edge of founding a new journal, the *Cambridge Quarterly*, which would consign *Scrutiny* to history. It was one situation to have *Scrutiny* lost, quite another for it to be replaced by a new generation.

In December 1964 J.P. Brockbank, the Professor of English at the new University of York, began negotiations that enabled Leavis to become a Visiting Professor at York. At last, in 1965 at the age of seventy, Leavis was to have the best title in a completely new institution. The promising familial initiatives did not turn out well.

Part Four

NEW SHIPS

1963–1975

CHAPTER TEN

The End of Cambridge
1963–1965

═══

The animated, experienced things that share our lives are coming to
an end and cannot be replaced.
– Rainer Maria Rilke, quoted by Leavis in *English Literature in
Our Time and the University*, 1969

University Expansion 1963–1964

Ever since his private 'English Research Society' of the early 1930s,
Leavis had envisaged a university within the university. His idea became
actuality at Downing and in *Scrutiny*. In the 1960s the university
structure of Britain changed, Cambridge included, and to the theory and
practice of the changes Leavis addressed himself. He was aware that in
the era of new universities and five-year planning there would be new
posts; now, perhaps, Leavisians would have their chance. 'There will be
a number of Faculty posts going this five years (quinquennium they call
it)', Leavis wrote in 1961 in the new language of planning. There were
new Lecturers at Cambridge: a middle generation was becoming established, younger than the old English Faculty that went back to the
1920s. There was Graham Hough and Ian Jack. At the junior end there
was John Holloway, who had broadcast critically about Leavisry in 'The
"New Establishment" in Criticism'. Leavis had good pupils coming up
– and he had Morris Shapira now installed in a research fellowship at
Downing. He anticipated more growth, as he saw in Cambridge signs of
the national expansion of higher education.

After the war university education in Britain was shaped by the

SECTION TITLE: 'New Ships' is a quotation from T.S. Eliot's 'Marina' (1930), called by
Leavis 'that lovely poem (a limiting description) with the epigraph from Seneca' in
Scrutiny (Summer 1942).

findings of the Barlow Report, *Scientific Manpower* (1946).[1] The brave new world was, indeed, to be that of C.P. Snow. Barlow stimulated investigation into the financing of higher education by the University Grants Committee, which secured huge new subventions from the government. In 1953 it predicted there would be a need in 1966 for 135,000 student places, to cope with a need for training and a birth-rate bulge. In 1960 the figure was revised upwards to 150,000. It became 200,000 for 1973.

After the death of *Scrutiny* there was prodigious growth. Before 1950 the English civic universities (Bristol, Manchester, Hull, Durham, Sheffield, Birmingham and Leeds) were supplemented by 'university colleges', outposts of London University. In 1950 the completely new university of Keele in North Staffordshire opened, after which independence from London was granted to the university colleges (Nottingham, Hull, Leicester, Southampton and Exeter). In 1956 Jimmy Porter in *Look Back in Anger* mocked the 'white-tile' universities (compared to 'redbrick'). New universities were created, with Sussex first approved in 1958. The University Grants Committee considered twenty-eight submissions and approved six: York and East Anglia (1963), Essex and Lancaster (1964), Kent and Warwick (1965). All had distinctive English departments. A plan was announced in 1963 for a 'University of the Air' to teach by means of television, radio and correspondence; this was to be the Open University.

The organization of university admission changed. In 1961 the Universities Central Council on Admissions (UCCA) was set up. Sixth-formers could now make a standardized application for entry to universities of their choice. They were no longer tied to traditional alliances between school and university, or to a tradition of studying near home. This did not immediately affect Oxford and Cambridge, which only joined the scheme very much later, but it was a step towards bringing them into a system in line with 'ordinary' universities, edging them away from their elitist status. In the 1950s it was possible for a British student to receive funding twice over for a first degree, once as a student at a 'redbrick' (or 'white-tile'), with a grant from his or her town hall, and then again (if a scholarship was won while studying at a 'redbrick') as an Oxbridge undergraduate.

Oxbridge lost its dominant position. After the war there were more students outside Oxbridge than within, but in the decade from 1955 this total increased from about one and a half to two and a half times as many students.

A new style of professional academic became recognizable, the 'Lecturer' rather than the 'don', based in a department rather than a college. John Holloway and Kingsley Amis were both young Lecturers of the period, both from Oxford, with first posts in Aberdeen and Swansea respectively. In the early 1960s Holloway went to Queens' College and Amis to Peterhouse. Leavis was to refer, scurrilously, to Amis as a 'pornographer': Amis wrote on his relish for the James Bond novels of Ian Fleming, and even published one himself after Fleming's death. What mattered most to Leavis was Amis's irreverence about universities in *Lucky Jim* (1954): a lack of respect that could not be forgiven, as with J.M. Keynes.* Leavis did not like to see the academic personage derided. At Peterhouse, Amis was in the same position as Morris Shapira at Downing, though more secure; Shapira only had a research fellowship of fixed term and Amis, a professional academic from one of the civic universities, had a full fellowship. Leavis (ever suspicious of Noël Annan) suspected that there was a plot to have Amis appointed to a university lectureship.[2]

In 1963, when Amis went to Peterhouse, an important event occurred in the world of higher education. The new universities were approved, if not all open, by that year, but a question was still to be answered: whether there should be a change in the *pattern* of higher education. In 1963 the Robbins Report was published; *Higher Education* was 'one of the great state papers of the century, perhaps the last of its line'.[3] Its purpose was not primarily to deal with numbers of universities or students, but to examine the total structure of higher education. It scrutinized the very concept of a university. Robbins recommended that some other institutions (colleges of advanced technology) should be given the same name. It affirmed that modern universities should have new methods. It expressed doubt about traditional ways, such as the intimacy and informality of contact between pupil and teacher in small-group classes. It asked whether students were best served by the intensity of one-to-one contact of Oxbridge tutorials or supervisions. Robbins prepared for the academic the world satirized in Malcolm Bradbury's novel *The History Man* (1975). Bradbury, an accomplished sociologist of literature, observed there how university-as-community (*Gemeinschaft*) had given way to university-as-corporation (*Gesellschaft*). Of course, as

---

* See Chapter Eight, No Common Pursuit, 'Bloomsbury Again: Damned Humbug 1949–1951'.

well as the question of principle, there was the question of numbers, of both under- and postgraduates.

Leavis addressed the question of student numbers from the graduate rather than the undergraduate end. Shortly before the book publication of his Richmond Lecture in 1962, he gave an address about graduate research at Birmingham University. The following summer, believing his arguments about Cambridge English were 'more conveniently fought' in the press, he took up the subject again in *The Times Literary Supplement*, which had published a series of articles about literary criticism by varied worthies.[4] Leavis did not contribute, but sent in a letter that was published as the article 'Research in English'. For once Leavis supported the *The Times Literary Supplement*. It had started a hare by publishing a middle-page review of a book about American magazine verse of the late nineteenth century, a piece of heavy-duty scholarship, 'a quantitative survey' that dumped, loaded and analysed shoals of doggerel.[5] The reviewer made fun of the pretensions of publish-or-perish scholarship, and expressed fears for the survival of the old-style scholar–critics who had a 'burning desire to pass on to their juniors the joy they have themselves experienced from an informed reading not of "the poet, but of individual poets", not of "social comment" but of individual novelists'.

The Times Literary Supplement congratulated its reviewer for discerning a trend: its leader writer reminisced about pompous European scholarship; he even suggested the pedants responsible for it were easy game for the Nazis. Thank goodness in Britain a thesis could still make a decent book. Was literary study safe from the influence of American doctorate factories? 'As in science,' it lamented, 'so in the humanities.'

Letters followed, even one from I.A. Richards; there was one from a Leavis pupil, Philip Hobsbaum, who reasonably called for a definition of 'literary research'. So far *The Times Literary Supplement* had only mocked quantitative literary studies from a standpoint of non-academic common sense. The tabulation of Victorian doggerel may be a joyless enterprise, but was it beneath the notice of scholarship? The relationship of the analysis of cultural data to a larger academic enterprise, like the sociology of literature, could have been mentioned. Leavis entered the debate, though not to posit such a relationship, in spite of his early 'anthropologico-literary' interests. But he did show himself to be concerned with some relationships between individual research projects and the overall world of study they inhabited. He said that if research was to be defined, then at least a connection should be shown between it and the way literature is studied at large in a university. Research should not be orbital, related only geographically to the principles of an English School. He sketched out the ideal position of a graduate student in the academic community. He or she should have 'an essential liaison function', acting as an intermediary between seniors and undergraduates. But graduate students should be capable of working on their own, and hardly need training. Graduate researchers preferred, he thought, not being regimented and they 'evade the campaigning and self-proffering helpers as much as they dare'. He was not in favour of 'classes in research'.[6]

Over a dozen years, Leavis said, he had been dismayed at a drive in Cambridge towards a new-style Ph.D. in English with a preparatory or training element. He evoked the old days of the 'English Research Society' at Chesterton Hall Crescent in 1931, when the relationship between tripos work and research was clear, or 'organic'. Now, in 1963, professionalism was sought, fuelled by university expansion, with greater numbers of graduate students to be schooled and processed in a manner very different from the intimate way of the 1930s. Leavis ventured several unsayables. One was that expansion was dangerous and that it might be humbug 'realistically' to proclaim it noble (duty-based) and necessary. Perhaps some universities should *not* shape up to training hordes for the Ph.D., if many of the new students could hardly put up a fair show for the BA. He did not, unlike *The Times Literary Supplement*, take an anti-scientific stance. On the contrary,

work in the scientific departments must be in close touch with the experimental-creative front. In the same way, for the university English School there is a creative front with which, in its function and nature, the School must be in the closest relation.

Why should Cambridge English be different from Cambridge science, which did not alter its courses to suit the clientele? New duties or alleged ones should not persuade Cambridge to abrogate its standards. What no one questioned about science was true also of English. Trouble was stirred.

A week later there were letters from the Cambridge English Faculty. One was signed jointly by Graham Hough and Muriel Bradbrook; one was from Ian Jack. Neither attempted to define literary research. Both dealt only with numbers. Leavis had made fun of the progressives, who gave 'a polite bow' to the old, independent researching graduate, then rallied to realism: 'The university has a new duty, we are told: there is a besieging host.' Hough, Bradbrook and Jack all took the progressive line, proclaiming that the universities had a 'responsibility to transmit the incomparable wisdom for living that English literature can supply.' 'Wisdom for living' was probably meant to be an ironical reference to what Leavis was supposed to believe in. None the less, they thought the new entrants would be difficult; they would not be among 'the happy few who are capable of looking after themselves and inspiring their teachers [and who] provide a refreshment that an overworked Faculty is likely to welcome'. Hough and Bradbrook were referring in code to what they supposed to be Leavis's relation to his pupils ('happy few'). Ian Jack took the offensive more bluntly. He attacked what he clearly thought were Leavis's sentimentalities about the 'superannuated ideal' of a research student who knew what he or she wanted to do, with 'exceptional enterprise and self-reliance'. Jack retorted that such students never existed. *All* research students were initially fallible and needed help; they should be coached through a 'propaedeutic year', a course in research method. He (almost audibly) snapped that the research students who admired Leavis were especially fallible, even downright incompetent: when, as examiner or publisher's reader, he saw their work, it was 'without exception' flawed, 'more or less seriously, by culpable ignorance of what had been written on the subject by other scholars'. This was not a wise sally. Who did he mean?

Leavis now had quick-witted graduate aides, one of whom, John Newton, had recently submitted a Ph.D. thesis himself. Was he then one of those of 'culpable ignorance'? Newton swiftly noted Ian Jack's impropriety. He wrote to *The Times Literary Supplement*, inviting Jack to name names. Of course Jack could not. Leavis himself was very angry. He complained to two members of the Degree Committee of the English Faculty that Jack had called him incompetent in public. He received, he said, no satisfactory answer, so he wrote to the Chairman of the Board giving his resignation from all graduate supervision. It could hardly be fair to his pupils if it was believed that he did not maintain proper standards. The resignation was not minuted by the Faculty meeting, so he then wrote to the Secretary of the university Board of Research Studies, with a newspaper cutting of Jack's letter to show why

I cannot supervise any research in English, the replies received from the two senior members of the Committee having made it plain that I must not count on any vigilance on the part of the Committee to ensure that the students for whom I was responsible should not be examined by Dr Jack – or someone else who saw nothing unexceptionable in his letter.

This incident – 'the smear' Leavis later called it – was the first of a series of resignations that took place in the period in which Leavis shed his Cambridge connections.

There were happier events during this period. Preparations began for the issue of the reprint of *Scrutiny* by Cambridge University Press. The publication date was set for 25 October 1963. As it approached, Cambridge University Press sought publicity. The manager of the London office wrote to T.S. Eliot, hoping he would write a puff, but he was unwilling.

In its earlier stages it did great credit to the University, but I should, however, feel rather embarrassed to state my opinions frankly and I should not wish on the other hand to dissimulate them; so I would, with regret, prefer to keep silence as I so strongly disagreed with Dr Leavis during the last stages of the magazine and objected to his attacks and innuendoes about people I knew and respected. I think it is a pity he became so intemperate in his views and was extravagant in his admirations, as I had, in the earlier stages of the magazine, felt great sympathy for its editor.[7]

The publisher began to consider spin-offs. There was talk in the New York office of an essay prize to be judged by Alan Pryce-Jones. Fortunately Leavis did not hear of it.

Interest grew in further work from both F.R.L. and Q.D.L. Michael Black at the Press inquired whether Leavis was really planning a book on Dickens. He had moved in that direction in his essay on *Dombey and Son*, to which he added work on *Little Dorrit* when in March 1964 he was invited by John Sparrow to give the Chichele Lectures at All Souls College in Oxford.[8] To Black's inquiry in 1964 he replied that he would only publish on Dickens if Q.D.L. did not, and that she was open to an offer. He thought it would be worth negotiating for her long-awaited book on Jane Austen.

I've for years been painfully anxious for her to complete the book she alone could write. Those pieces are fragments of a concerted work, wholly original, and much preyed upon by parasites. The non-completion belongs to the whole painful history of my notorious life of 'persecution-mania'. Very delicate – I'm afraid to raise the matter ... I'm too sad about the whole history, understand her attitude too well: I'm no mediator.

A letter of reference from Ian Watt strongly supported the idea. Leavis himself was momentarily tempted by the proposal from Black of editing a 'Cambridge Book of English Verse'.[9]

Succession Crisis 1964–1965

The battle for Cambridge English against the new professionalism, which Leavis believed had to be won, was fought in the weeklies. It was also fought within Downing College.

In the disputes of the early 1960s there were vivid ostensible matters at issue, like the principles of *Scrutiny* or what research in the humanities was supposed to be. The issues went down to matters of personal relations within scholarship and criticism in the institution. When Leavis referred to what study had once been, he meant study in the specific circumstances of a group, or within a college. The question of the graduate researcher for Leavis came down to the place of the graduate, between seniors and juniors, with the capacity also for independence. There was another question that came down to personal relations, that of the examinations system. Leavis never liked the 'First Class' man or woman, who played the system and was advantaged by the impersonal methods of the three-hour ('stand-and-deliver') examination. In 1964 the 'First Class' man appeared to be in the ascendant. If numbers increased there would be mass examinations; examination systems of the conventional kind, though seemingly rigorous, were notoriously naïve in not rewarding the tentative writer or the late-developing intellectual with stamina. The home of genuine thinking and research was the college, and it looked as if this would hardly survive. Hugh Trevor-Roper wrote sceptically about the new ideals of university planning in the *Sunday Times*; Leavis supported him, with a comment on the supposed 'First Class' man.[10] It was the college, said Leavis, in which intimate teaching took place:

It is an essential truth that, except as conscious and active members of an informal intellectual-social community, a man can't hope to arrive at any solution to the problem of making his studies a real education such as a university is supposed to offer.

This could only be done in person, not through a 'University of the Air':

I won't lend myself in any way to the suggestion that university education is, or could be, a matter of being lectured to – of taking notes from an informative authority and following up his reading suggestions.

What was the hope for a college after Snow? Leavis was alluding, not kindly, to his own college, Downing, which he believed to be run by scientists. But, most of all, the threat was outside, a threat (he concluded with sombre irony) that the 'Faculty – the university – should take over all teaching, and eliminate the licentious and injurious irregularity represented by the part (the major part) the College has up till now played.' The threat was actual in a Cambridge that was intensely debating whether many of the functions of the college should be taken over by the university. Graham Hough believed that more time and energy should be spent on the primary functions of the university, unimpeded by the colleges, even though they may be 'admirable youth hostels, sporting organizations, dining clubs, and old people's homes'.[11] The sarcasm might be expected from the Faculty side, but Leavis's sense of the college was also under pressure from within his own college itself.

With the publication of *Scrutiny* Leavis was able to make an affirmation about his and 'our' Cambridge. In the spring of 1964, after the Chichele Lectures on Dickens, a piece of good fortune occurred, but one that turned into what Morris Shapira came to call 'the Downing mess'.

In retirement Leavis continued to have classes for Downing men, naturally invited to do so by Shapira, now the Director of Studies. Shapira was still precariously placed, but there were inviting prospects. Universities were being founded or growing fast, so there were to be more posts available all over Britain, and in Cambridge too.[12] In March 1964 one of these posts fell to a Leavisian. John Newton was appointed to a university assistant lectureship.

Leavis believed Newton's appointment was the result of his own determined influence, especially his lobbying of Tom Henn, which Leavis believed had exacerbated Henn's nervous stammer.[13] After the appointment was made, the traditional offer came from Newton's own college, Downing, of a fellowship in April. After a couple of weeks' consideration, he turned it down. This was not surprising, because to accept it would have been to displace Shapira.[14] He had, anyway, the chance of a fellowship at Clare College. Leavis hinted that, with a pupil at Clare, Downing should be left to Shapira: if Shapira were established, Leavis would have two colleges in his domain. Downing, however, was taken aback by Newton's refusal, though it was not so uncomfortable as to offer a full fellowship to Shapira. He had, after all, no university post, and had not even finished a Ph.D. thesis. So Downing took soundings, without success, elsewhere. It was too late: all the recently appointed Lecturers in English had found college places.

At the end of May W.K.C. Guthrie, the Master and a man whose ascetic fair-mindedness was to be tried in the coming months, invited a young man, Brian Vickers, a research fellow of Churchill College, to dine in Downing to see if he would be interested in a fellowship. Vickers, originally from Trinity, was, like Newton, a newly appointed university Assistant Lecturer, and so an eligible man to whom suit might be paid.[15] A cheerful and industrious scholar, Vickers was to Downing eyes refreshingly unaggressive, displaying none of the edgy personal persistence of Newton or the odd boldness of Shapira. He was a Shakespearean and what could be more 'normal' than a Shakespeare specialist? Vickers discussed the offer with his former supervisor at Trinity, Theodore Redpath, and with Tom Henn.[16] He decided to accept, even though he had been at Churchill only a short while. (A fellowship, even a research fellowship, was not to be baldly resigned.[17]) On 22 July Vickers was elected to a fellowship at Downing, to begin in October. Shapira was invited to continue directing English for a further year, assisted by Vickers. So Vickers could 'get to know the college' (and work on his Ph.D.). This arrangement meant also that Shapira would be in office when the new students came in the coming term, students to whom awards had been made in the last round of scholarship examinations and who would be expecting to be taught by Leavis or a Leavisian.[18]

Guthrie immediately wrote by college mail to tell Leavis about Vickers's appointment – at which Leavis promptly resigned his fellowship. He insisted that his name be removed from the college books forthwith: 'I am especially anxious that there shall be no misleading entry in the new residence list, or the various official places.'[19]

A few days later Vickers received a Saturday morning telephone call from Theodore Redpath. He read out part of a letter from Leavis in which he claimed that Vickers's appointment was a way of ousting Shapira and therefore a form of persecution against himself. According to Vickers, Leavis wrote that the new fellow would 'be the liquidator of Downing English, and that his name would go down in history as the destroyer of a thirty-year-old tradition'.[20] Vickers went straight to see Redpath, who telephoned Leavis, suggesting he meet the young and rather nervous pretender. Leavis demurred. He was afraid he might actually like Vickers, and considered the issue one of principle, not of persons. Vickers reported on his conversations with Redpath to Guthrie: 'I find myself resisting his threats and intimidations, and the view of literature and teaching he so passionately proclaims.' Vickers was prepared to face the difficulties, but was uneasy because he knew Leavis to be 'a dedicated and fairly unscrupulous controversialist'.[21] The pressure was certainly on Vickers. In the event, he decided that he would withdraw from the fellowship. He wrote accordingly to Guthrie, who urged him to reconsider: had not Leavis weakened his position by refusing to see Vickers? He would surely have done so if a principle truly was at stake. He realized there would be 'unpleasantness' for Vickers, but pledged unanimous support from the Governing Body, which would take a poor view of Leavis intimidating Vickers. Guthrie echoed the word 'intimidation' that had been used by Vickers. It resounded in the coming months.

But Vickers stuck to his guns: he insisted on withdrawing. He was rewarded by a letter from Leavis, in the spirit of Jacques's farewell to Arden in *As You Like It*: 'Hereafter in a better world than this, I shall desire more love and knowledge of you.' Leavis thanked him and said he was wise to avoid an embarrassing incident on the threshold of his career. Downing, he said flatteringly, might well turn out to be the loser, for there were 'nullities' who could be appointed at the instance of 'the Houghs, Jacks and Watsons'. He explained he had never been on the Faculty appointments committee and that no pupil of his had been appointed a Lecturer, except Newton. He concluded that he was obliged to resign, but that there was no animus, indeed, he hoped he would meet Vickers one day, wishing for a 'co-operative alliance'. He said he believed Churchill was a good place for a young academic, in spite of the fact that George Steiner, whom he disliked, was there. There was no sign that Shapira would be established at Downing and Leavis's resignation stood, awaiting confirmation by the fellows when they returned from the Long Vacation.

In the early days of September Leavis and Guthrie exchanged letters about Redpath's intervention. Leavis was convinced that Redpath never meant to recommend Vickers to a full fellowship at Downing, however suitable he thought he was for a research fellowship at Churchill.[22] A month before term began (4 September) Leavis wrote to Guthrie more fully about his resignation in a letter that surveyed his disillusion with Downing's attitude to English. He asked for the letter to be tabled for the Governing Body. Leavis pointed to the relative inexperience of Vickers, but emphasized that his main objection to the appointment was that the schools approached sent pupils to Downing for a Leavisian education. Leavis wrote that the schools were watching the situation: they *expected* their students to receive a Leavisian education at Downing, and were confident of Shapira's capacity to supply it. Schoolmasters were in touch with Cambridge politics, he believed; certainly any who visited would hear dark intimations about the Faculty affairs. Leavis accused the college of disguising the nature of the appointment by not announcing in the press which subject the fellowship was for. He referred to a Faculty cabal, claiming it had directed Vickers to Downing. But broadly he was convinced that Downing was 'blankly complaisant about national expansion of university education'.

Leavis also pointed to the analogy that must have always been in his mind when supporting Shapira, the analogy between Shapira in the 1960s and himself in the 1930s when Downing (Bill Cuttle, especially) rescued him from penury. Why could the college not have acted as it had done twenty-seven years ago? (Because Shapira was not the author of books equivalent to *New Bearings in English Poetry* and *Revaluation*, and was not the editor of a journal equivalent to *Scrutiny*.)[23]

When term began in October 1964 the fellows of Downing received Leavis's resignation. They recognized they were in an awkward position: there were no Assistant Lecturers in English left whom they could engage by means of an offered fellowship. If Shapira was not replaced, there would be no one to direct English in the college in twelve months' time.[24]

All was not conflict, however, for Leavis. Newton, Shapira, Jean and Richard Gooder were encouragingly to hand. In November Leavis gave a talk to the Clare College Modern Languages Society, 'The Aims of the English Tripos'. Harold Mason, up from Exeter, was present. After the lecture, when a core group remained, Leavis and Mason conducted a long public conversation: Leavis reminisced affectionately about the fresh-faced young Empson ('ruined by Richards'), Mason confided about Eliot, with rather typical melodrama, 'I couldn't say this in public, of course, but what does he know about man and woman? Only what he read in Ovid.' The next day Mason gave a paper on Shakespeare at the Doughty Society in Downing.[25] On the face of it there was no obvious conflict between the Leavisian avant garde and the lesson of the master. John Newton was lecturing on the importance of eighteenth-century literary criticism, a seemingly innocuous theme; but his point was that there were insights in Samuel Johnson not to be found in, say, Scrutiny's leading Shakespeare critic, Derek Traversi. It should be remembered that while Leavis himself had great respect for Johnson, it was central to his literary aesthetic that Johnson did not grasp the 'creative-exploratory' (that is, Shakespearean) use of language. Newton was playing with the heart of Leavis's convictions. In other spheres he was revaluing Leavis, on Hopkins, on Dickens and on Henry James. He lectured critically on The Portrait of a Lady and stimulated at least one Leavisian undergraduate to attempt a fifty-page defence, to be quoted by Newton in a lecture, but its position rejected. Within the Leavis world there was some ferment. It was a moment of excitement. Leavis had said there was only one way to live: dangerously. A lecture on Hopkins, an essay on James: Leavisian sports did not seem life-threatening or (pace Q.D.L.) oxygenic to outsiders, but these gentle initiatives led to catastrophe for the Leavises and the group.

Back at Downing, some were disturbed to see one of its most famous figures on the rack. Clive Parry, Professor of International Law, went up to Downing to read English in the 1930s, but had changed to law. He was one of the few to enjoy Shapira's company. Leavis's resignation distressed him. 'I should hate to see him hurt in any measure beyond what the self-infliction of wounds must produce.' He wondered if it was too 'specious and legalistic' to tell Leavis that an honorary position could not be resigned.[26] Guthrie was dubious: although Leavis had acted in haste in the summer, there was his long letter of justification in September. He had thwarted the college decision by an insupportable use of 'pressure'. After all, Leavis had had his chance of a Leavisian being installed: the offer only went to Vickers after the withdrawal of Newton.[27]

So far the mess was confined to Downing. At the end of October it became public property. Every year a directory of university personnel, *The Resident Members List*, is published in Cambridge. This term its readers were surprised to find the well-known fellow of Downing to have his college listed as 'Emmanuel'. On 25 October *The Times* announced that 'Dr Leavis Resigns Fellowship', with a statement from the Master. Even the *Daily Express* joined in two days later. *The Times* followed up with a report that Leavis believed the Master's statement misrepresented his position. Once the news was public a number of complaints came in to Downing.

There was another Leavisian resignation in October. Michael Tanner, the Moral Sciences fellow at Corpus Christi College, having run English for the college for some years, as well as philosophy, his own field, announced he was giving up as Director of Studies in English in exasperation at the college's failure to provide a full-time incumbent for the post. In the press there appeared to be some connection between Tanner's and Leavis's resignations. There was none but for a thread. The F.R. Leavis Lectureship Trust believed there was a chance of a fellowship for Mason at Corpus, and he was considered.[28] Had Mason been elected, he would have handled English for the college and Tanner need not have made his gesture.

In Downing, Guthrie duly brought the question of Leavis's resignation and English in the college to the assembled fellows in the Governing Body at the end of October. He reported events leading up to the resignation and the withdrawal of Vickers. Most of the fellows were indignant at Leavis and at the pretensions of English. Four critical decisions were made: no reappointment of Shapira as Director of Studies; permission for tutors to reduce the number of places for English; permission for them to make their own arrangements for directing the undergraduates' study of English (that is, sending them to directors at other colleges); discouragement of the organizers of the F.R. Leavis Lectureship Trust, if it petitioned the college to adopt its Lecturer. Even the Leavisian past was to be fumigated. There were old agreements to elect either Mason or Klingopulos to the fellowship, if either had a university lectureship; these were rescinded. None the less, it was agreed that a fellow in English should still be sought. Shapira was informed again that he should not suppose Vickers's withdrawal meant he could go on as Director of Studies after September 1965.[29]

When Guthrie reported what occurred at the Governing Body meeting to Leavis he made a remark, almost in passing, of great significance.

Leavis always hoped that somehow the college could persuade the English Faculty to appoint 'its' candidate to a university lectureship (that is, Shapira). Guthrie said that a fellow had remarked it was not proper or possible for a college to bring pressure to bear on a Faculty's appointing policy, and that this had 'not happened twenty-seven years ago'.[30] The allusion was to Leavis's appointment to his lectureship in 1936. Leavis probably believed that pressure *had* then been brought to bear on the Faculty to appoint him. If then, why not now? Could not the college use some influence to have Shapira appointed to a lectureship? He may have been right about 1936, when the college announcement of his position was a challenge to the Faculty, but his assessment of the situation in 1964 was unrealistic.★

During the autumn Shapira was dealt with abruptly in the college and saw Leavis treated as if he had terrorized Vickers. He protested to Guthrie, who replied after Christmas that surely Leavis *had* intimidated Vickers. Shapira sent him a long letter, both melancholy and impudent, saying that Leavis's opinion should have been sought before Vickers was elected – or Mason's (though he had no particular standing at Downing, other than that of having been Leavis's assistant ten years before). If Leavis had intimidated Vickers, this meant Leavis was 'a liar or unscrupulous'. For the first time Shapira introduced the idea of 'lying' into the dispute, an idea that had drastic consequences for him and for the F.R. Leavis Lectureship Trust group in two years' time. Guthrie told Shapira that he might have had a chance of permanency at the college if he had got on with his research. He would have done best to 'give priority to original work or he should have sought a post elsewhere'. Shapira replied that 'I took part in several fellowship elections; I don't remember capacity for productive scholarship as a determining factor in any of them.' He displayed a belief, contrary to the university codes of the 1960s, that a don should be first a teacher and college man, rather than a publishing critic. There is no doubt of Shapira's sincerity in describing his 'original work' as spending 'thirty to forty hours a week trying to eradicate conventionalities and clichés of thought to allow the growth of a vigorous, fresh, individual idea of literature'.[31]

Leavis himself addressed the issue of 'intimidation'. On 18 January he issued a typed statement about it to the Master and fellows. In early February Guthrie appealed to Vickers to reconsider his position; he

★ See Chapter Five, 'To Downing College', 'Downing English 1931–1936'.

declined.[32] On 14 March Leavis defended himself again, at which point there was a new development. Clive Parry had been in touch with Leavis and with Newton. The fact that no one was going to be responsible for English at Downing seemed an opportunity for the lectureship group. Could not Downing elect Mason to a fellowship? The Trust had funds enough to appoint its first Lecturer. If Downing had Mason he could organize its English studies, and even though he would not be a university Lecturer, his endowed post would have some authority. The Trust was promoting its Lecturer as Leavis had been promoted by Downing in the 1930s, and as he had promoted Mason in the 1950s. Mason would be happy with such an arrangement, though he would not want to be, or appear to be, the successor to a still-alienated Leavis. Parry was able to tell Guthrie that Leavis was prepared to abandon the idea of Shapira succeeding him; there seemed little hope, as Shapira himself recognized.[33] Parry told Guthrie that Leavis was 'profoundly unhappy'. Was not this 'more important than our corporate feelings'? Leavis's letter of 18 January had still not been considered by the Governing Body, so the issue could be revived. He gently (and authoritatively) reminded the Master that a special meeting of the Governing Body could be called. At the same time there was strong pro-Leavis feeling among the undergraduates, who thought of changing the name of the Doughty Society to the Leavis Society. At the end of November the Master received a letter from eighteen undergraduates doing English, complaining about the way Shapira had been treated.[34]

In the early spring of 1965 Guthrie agreed to put the issues before the Governing Body again. On 19 March he summarized them for the fellowship. He said the college had been divided, pro and anti Leavis. He lamented the fact that he had not consulted Leavis about the appointment of Vickers. A new factor had emerged in the intervention of the Lectureship Trust. It had, after all, been the wish of the college to honour Leavis. It had agreed to accept Mason – if he became a university Lecturer. The college had confidence in the Secretary of the Trust (Newton), to the extent of having offered him a fellowship. Since the series of anti-English resolutions (of 19 February) it had become clear that the college was hardly being responsible in its teaching of the humanities. Would not all this be solved by (at the least) appointing Mason as Director of Studies in English?[35] (He did not suggest his election as a fellow.)

Guthrie's equitable proposal did not command majority support, in spite of a loud protest by Parry at the end of the meeting. Guthrie bore the news to Leavis, and to Newton; the latter wrote back politely, saying that some arrangement for Mason's future seemed possible. That Mason was to become the F.R. Leavis Lecturer was now known to the *Sunday Times*.

Guthrie had made a reasonable attempt at a treaty, but the college rejected it. There was nothing he could do to reassure Leavis, who now considered the college to be a lost cause. He told Guthrie that the college itself was in shock after the appointment of Vickers. He himself was experiencing the effects of an impersonal disaster, the destruction of a school of studies built over thirty years. The college seemed blank to the catastrophe. In the ensuing period of pamphleteering Leavis frequently resorted to the concept of 'blankness'. For Leavis, the college was discredited, and had perhaps ruined the career of Shapira, who, he believed, had something of a genius for the office of college teacher, sensitive to his pupils but not soft, and indefatigably generous: more generous than the college.[36]

By June a solution to the college problem had been found. Vickers himself had withdrawn, but never actually resigned because he had not reached the stage of being 'accepted' into the fellowship. The college was persuaded in the end to revoke the withdrawal. It was announced that Vickers would resume his fellowship so there would be no break in English teaching in the college.[37] Several letters of complaint followed.[38] With the tribute to Shapira, Leavis turned away from Downing. As he had written to the Master of Downing in September 1964: 'My resignation was inevitable, clear-eyed and to me bitter. I am in my seventieth year, and an end of this kind is indeed an end.'

Leavis had, fortunately, a new place to seek 'collaborative loyalty', in the University of York. Six months earlier, in December 1964, J.P. Brockbank, the new Professor of English, visited Leavis in Cambridge to work out the details of his taking a visiting post at York in the academic year 1965/6. A professorial position had been arranged for the much respected Perse School master Douglas Brown. Besides school teaching, Brown published on literature, and was a Cambridge supervisor in the circle of colleges Leavis favoured, like Corpus. After his retirement from schoolmastering, Brown lectured for a short time at the University of Reading, where it was hoped he would join the York team, several members of whom had come from Reading. Brown died prematurely and so Brockbank could make an offer to Leavis. He was interested, but in late 1964 he still believed in the fight for Cambridge and insisted that his periods in York should not keep him away from Faculty Board meetings.[39] He had no official place in Cambridge, though he still supervised groups in a room in Corpus on loan from Michael Tanner. In 1965 he gave a series of lectures for the undergraduate English Club, on Dickens. By the summer of 1965 the fight for Cambridge may have seemed lost. But there was another fight to come, a bizarre one, before the end of his retirement phase and the possibilities of Cambridge were put away.

Coterie Rejected

In the spring of 1965 Newton had told Guthrie at Downing that the F.R. Leavis Lectureship Trust could set up its lectureship immediately, with Mason as a permanent Lecturer. The Trust appeared to be one of the graces attendant on Leavis's retirement. But there were, within its structure and history, seeds of discord that were soon to grow into visible life. The Trust group in Cambridge became for Leavis, with frightening speed, a hated 'coterie'. There had been an intimation of discord two years earlier when the newly formed Trust met in Cambridge and embarrassingly it emerged that Q.D.L. had no idea of its existence – and was not supposed to. What had been concealed broke open at Christmas 1965. The early months of 1966 were gravely shocking for the Cambridge Leavisians in the Trust group.

There was potential for danger within the financial arrangements made by the Trust. It had raised money from Leavis's pupils, and from admirers all over the world; Muriel Bradbrook was the first contributor and Mary McCarthy was an early donor from America. It had been exasperating that there was not enough money to endow a lectureship at the moment Downing appeared ready to elect a Leavisian fellow. However, relief had come from one quarter in the Trust group. Jean and Richard Gooder were aware of a family trust with funds for educational projects. Its secretary, W.B. Hall, a Hull businessman, took a lively interest in the plan for a Cambridge lectureship in tribute to Leavis. The Newby Trust considered the plans and made a substantial donation to the Trust (exceeding half of what had already been collected), with Hall himself prepared to act as its financial adviser. The intervention of the

Newby Trust was a piece of good fortune. The Trust now could afford a proper English lectureship in Cambridge. The Cambridge group (John Newton, Richard and Jean Gooder, Morris Shapira) had always hoped for Harold Mason's return from exile in Exeter and that now seemed possible. There were funds enough too for occasional lectures by distinguished speakers. The only trouble was that prosperity, if it did not change the character of the Trust, meant that the Trust could be perceived differently by Leavis himself. It was no longer a fund garnered from individual Leavisian enthusiasts out in the field, so to speak, or from public bodies. Funds had been raised, but not exactly from the constituency Leavis envisaged. The Trust group exercised some delicacy in avoiding an outright declaration to Leavis that his name had raised relatively little cash from admirers and (admittedly impecunious) pupils. The aid of the Newby Trust meant that it had a 'majority shareholding' relating to, though certainly not controlled by, two members of the Cambridge group, Richard and Jean Gooder. Another problem was also in the air. The Trust had ceased to be a pious hope, regarded with gloomy sympathy by Leavis, its best probable outcome being the occasional series of lectures; now funded, it could appoint a fully pensioned Lecturer. This Lecturer could be Mason, the man favoured by Leavis's closest Cambridge confederates. But there was a difficulty. Q.D.L. thoroughly detested Harold Mason. Or at least once Mason became a prosperous presence in Cambridge, close to the Gooders, Shapira and Newton, no longer in one of the dependent roles he had formerly played, Mason would be a candidate for hatred.

In March 1965 the trustees mounted their first public event, the lecture 'English as a University Subject' by W.W. Robson. They secured Sir Edward Boyle, the former Tory Minister for Education and Science, now in Opposition, to introduce it.[40] He wanted it known that his presence should not be construed as 'part of the Opposition campaign against the new Ministry of Technology', in which C.P. Snow was prominent.

In the summer of 1965 Harold Mason sold his Exeter property to a building developer: he claimed, wryly, that he had become the largest private landowner within the boundaries of the city of Exeter. He therefore had funds to supplement the Trust's lectureship. He moved to Cambridge, taking a rented house in Sylvester Road, near the university library, quite near the Leavis house in Bulstrode Gardens.[41] At the beginning of the autumn term the *Cambridge University Reporter* announced that Mason was to be the F.R. Leavis Lecturer, his college given as Downing. The Faculty Board had difficulty deciding where, and if, the announcement should be printed. L.C. Knights said, sensibly, that a typographical line could be put between it and the Faculty lectures.

In his first term, the Michaelmas term of 1965/6, Mason lectured on Shakespeare's *Antony and Cleopatra* and gave a series in the second term on Tennyson. He ran informal classes on Dante in his home. Newton was lecturing for 'The English Moralists' on Plato and Aristotle, on Arnold, Johnson, the metaphysical poets and recent novels (notably David Storey's), with follow-up classes. One purpose of Newton's lectures was to find insight into literature outside Leavisian orthodoxy. The Leavisian presence was strong in October 1965. L.C. Knights was now King Edward VII Professor of English. Mason and Newton were lecturing and supervising; Shapira continued to supervise. And the Trust group (though not the Trust itself) was about to publish the first issue of its journal, the *Cambridge Quarterly*. It was to contain an essay by Leavis himself, on Tolstoy's *Anna Karenina*. Remarkably in the middle 1960s the Leavisian pieces could be said to hold the centre of the board in Cambridge: with the Trust's lectureship; with the *Cambridge Quarterly*; and with three pupils in influential positions, that is, Shapira precariously at Downing, Newton in a university lectureship and Jean Gooder, whose Ph.D. work was supervised by Leavis, Director of Studies and a fellow at Newnham. Also that autumn Q.D.L. was taking an active part in teaching affairs in Cambridge. She was doing some supervising for Churchill College and for Gonville and Caius, where Jeremy Prynne had a high regard for her. The quality of her supervisions was known to undergraduates. Rupert Christiansen at King's petitioned her to supervise him and persisted – even after he was initially told at the Bulstrode Gardens front door that he was a hopeless case. Disappointed in English studies at King's, he said he thought it was time he actually learned something. Q.D.L. took on Christiansen, and corresponded warmly with him in later years. Most of all, Jean Gooder encouraged Q.D.L. to teach for Newnham, where she also helped with marking the scholarship examination scripts. For once Q.D.L. was working as a 'normal' academic. Jean Gooder would often drive her back to Bulstrode Gardens, listening to her machine-gun expostulations about literary culture and Cambridge English. (Leavis also liked to chat to the Gooders, stopping at their house on his way to collect and dispatch mail at

Downing; he would mention Q.D.L., her electricity: 'You can feel it coming through the wall.') It was almost and at last a late Leavis idyll, the new generation making its way in very Leavisian terms, through college work and journal editing. However, sociable idylls do not work for men who preface a book with such an epigraph as that for *The Common Pursuit* about Knut Hamsun: 'The Norwegian Society of Authors gave him a loving cup, but he asked them to scratch off the inscription and give it to somebody else.' Much later the novelist Howard Jacobson, a Downing man, remarked on the suicidal strand in Leavisian ideology.

During the autumn of 1965 Leavis may not have been particularly alert to Cambridge affairs. In the last week of September he visited Finland to lecture, Q.D.L. teaching seminars. They spent time at Helsinki and at the two universities, Swedish- and Finnish-speaking, in Abo. The British Council, which arranged the visit, was concerned that all should go well, given Leavis's strictures about its ambassadorial role. They were charm itself and said 'all the right things in praising the appearance of Abo'. Q.D.L. had always been enthusiastic about Finnish design.[42] On his return, Leavis began commuting to the University of York. One afternoon in Cambridge, Leavis was on his way home to Bulstrode Gardens from a Faculty Board meeting to collect his suitcase and a taxi for the station, when he met Mason in Sylvester Road. Leavis thought he behaved oddly, so oddly he wondered if he was drunk. He concluded later that Mason was in an agony of embarrassment, having realized that Leavis did not know that the Trust lectureship was permanent. Leavis appeared to think that Mason was only a temporary visitor. Ominously, Mason's inaugurating lecture was arranged for a day on which Leavis would be in York and Leavis was not invited to preside. Leavis's younger son, Robin, was now an undergraduate at Clare. He attended the lecture and was embarrassed to hear Mason announce how times had changed from the Leavis era.

In December tension mounted between Leavis and the representatives of the Trust that bore his name. Q.D.L. was known to be working on *Wuthering Heights*. Shapira, the Leavises' most frequent visitor, asked if the *Cambridge Quarterly* could have an essay from her on the subject. Q.D.L. objected that while 'one likes to be useful, to be made use of is another matter'.[43] She told Shapira that neither of them liked 'being manoeuvred'. At Christmas Jean and Richard Gooder noticed nothing wrong, dispatching as always a modest present (for Leavis a bottle of favoured port, a brown 'Arabia' teapot for Q.D.L.).

But immediately after Boxing Day there was an explosion. Q.D.L. had been sent some books to review for the *Cambridge Quarterly*. Shapira received back, by post, the cost of them, though not the books themselves. He protested that he had torn up the cheque. Q.D.L. replied that the Trust and the *Cambridge Quarterly* group (the same thing) had 'duped and exploited' the Leavises.[44] It is hard to detect the precise moment of alienation. During the Christmas vacation Leavis spoke harshly to Shapira about Newton, Robin Leavis's supervisor at Clare. He asked for a meeting with Mason, Newton and Shapira all present, but this was refused. Robin Leavis had evidently expostulated to his parents about Newton, though it is not clear exactly what had been said.[45] Ironically, for the second time and this time more shockingly (because a son and pupil were involved), the conflict penetrated into relations within the institution Leavis valued most, the college.

Newton was currently pursuing a course of drastic revision of Leavisian thinking, which had begun in public with lectures on Plato; in these Mason was not altogether playfully called a successor to Socrates. They were attended by Robin Leavis. Newton had already given his critical lecture on Henry James's *The Portrait of a Lady*, to be published as 'Henry James's Spiritual Disease'. Shapira wrote to Leavis to say that the doors between them could close if he quarrelled with Newton, though they had not yet done so. Leavis replied in conciliatory manner on 1 January: 'I think you oughtn't to have answered me in that way.' He did not want doors shut or locked. What he had said about Newton was not cruel. He wanted to show Shapira the difficulty of his son's position, caught between parents and teachers. He concluded his letter by saying how attached he was to Shapira, and that he would not cease to want to help him.

A week later he wrote to Shapira that the situation was 'monstrous and heartbreaking – my loyalty and delicacy have been exploited'. He charged Shapira with explaining to 'them' (Newton, Richard and Jean Gooder and Mason himself) the reason for 'my and my wife's contumely'. He was ready to be approached by either Mason or Newton, 'though not at my house or either of theirs (in Newton's case, out of concern for his [Newton's] wife)'.[46] Q.D.L. was most intensely wounded.[47] It seems (so Leavis said) that she only realized the truth from an announcement in *The Times* read on the flight to Helsinki. During this term Robin Leavis was likely to have brought home reports of Mason's lectures. It may have become clear for the first time that Mason was actually taking up a permanent post, a job for life. Some rancour may, especially, have been felt when Mason moved into a very large house indeed, grandly situated on the Huntingdon Road, and familiar to any Girtonian like Q.D.L. Possibly the position of Richard and Jean Gooder created some inner bitterness. Their position mirrored that of the Leavises thirty years before: a young couple, one of them settled into the Cambridge world from outside (Q.D.L., and Richard Gooder, from Cincinnati), living a teaching life of college supervision and running a journal. There was a difference. The circumstances of the Gooders paralleled in two respects those of Stanley and Joan Bennett. Jean Gooder and Joan Bennett came from relatively well-off families and from 'good schools' (Bedales and Wycombe Abbey School respectively). And both the Bennetts, unlike the Leavises in the early 1930s, had strong college support, from Emmanuel and Girton; the Gooders were well appreciated at Newnham and Clare. If there could be a cause for retrospective envy it might have derived from the fact that both Bennetts and Gooders had jointly prospering careers, with rewarding, not ultimately draining, family lives. The Gooders had two young sons and Jean Gooder was pregnant with her first daughter, 'the little bun in the oven', Q.D.L. remarked to Jean Gooder, attributing the phrase to Jane Austen.

It is certain that Q.D.L. thought she was being exploited. It is possible that Leavis knew she would object to the arrival of Mason as a permanency and so kept the facts from her. It is possible he knew Mason's Trust-funded post was permanent. The main event in the transition from vague approval (if that is what it was, on his part) to a sense of being 'duped and exploited' was the publication of the first number of the *Cambridge Quarterly*.

This first number does not look very aggravating. It contained, indeed, Leavis's own essay on *Anna Karenina*, and on English literature there was only W.W. Robson on *Measure for Measure* and Newton on Philip Larkin's *The Whitsun Weddings*. However, on the subscription page, facing Leavis's contribution, was an announcement of a forthcoming essay by Newton on '*Scrutiny*'s Failure with Shakespeare'. This was not a tactful initiative. Leavis had, to be sure, seen versions of this essay before, but the advertisement gave Newton's defence of A.C. Bradley (against, mainly, the *Scrutiny* Shakespearean, Derek Traversi) a new meaning: the essay promised to reject *Scrutiny* from within the Leavisian world. How could it be known how much or how little Leavis favoured the revision? Further, the essay promised to cast doubt on the whole *Scrutiny* endeavour as a journal, the endeavour to which Q.D.L. gave so much energy. For Leavis and many others *Scrutiny* was an institution, now under threat.

The first issue of the *Cambridge Quarterly* also had a section of notes, one of which was a comment on Robson's lecture for the Trust on 'English as a University Subject', anonymous but obviously by Mason, who made a plea for reintegrating the Greek and Roman classics into the English curriculum.[48] 'Would the terms used to define the claims of English also be unacceptable to those who have come to see things as they really are and as they ideally might be?' This was hardly promising for one who had burned for Cambridge English. Mason was making a plea for the classics in the spirit of Pound's 'Make It New'. But how could he appear other than as 'a classic' to Leavis? How, anyway, could Newton's ungainly sounding essay do other than tell the enemy that the Leavisians were seriously disappointed? Newton was the boldest junior. If he rejected *Scrutiny*, what was there to save?

In January 1966 Leavis's indignation grew. He wrote round immediately to the Trustees who were not in the *Cambridge Quarterly* group. He told William Walsh in Leeds he had been pressurized into associating with the quarterly.[49] He sent Walsh an 'indictment', saying the 'outside' Trustees were victims: 'I trust you, Denys Thompson and Littlewood completely.'[50] The 'indictment' expressed the accumulated resentment of the autumn term, especially at the reports of Mason's lectures provided by 'the undergraduate son of the man whose name had provided the lectureship'. He was astonished, according to Leavis, by their 'insolent and unscrupulous tone and content'. In the 'indictment' Leavis attacked the Trust, past and present. No formal acknowledgement to Leavis had been made at Mason's first lecture. The Trust had been secret: he heard 'nothing whatever from them before seeing the name of the appointed Lecturer in the Press'. He denounced the demolition of his principles by the 'coterie' in Mason and Newton's lectures and in the *Cambridge Quarterly*.

It is very clear that my name has been exploited in their own interests by a coterie, with the unconscious connivance of the Trustees. I am not honoured but dishonoured and insulted by the results. In these circumstances I am surely justified in requesting that a full meeting of the Trustees should be called as soon as possible, with myself present, to discuss what can be done, since not only will I not lend my name to this cause but I have a conscience about the money subscribed by my old pupils and those grateful for the work of *Scrutiny*, money which is plainly being used for a purpose they would never have sanctioned.

Leavis announced in *The Times Literary Supplement* that the presence of his essay on *Anna Karenina* in the *Quarterly* meant only that he had responded to 'urgent requests for permission to print a lecture'. It was certainly 'not a first contribution by a member of the connection. I can make that quite plain by saying that it will be found to be my last.'[51]

In Cambridge, Leavis went to see one of his oldest Downing allies, the Downing lawyer Hyde Whalley-Tooker. He agreed that Leavis had a right to address a meeting attended by Mason: 'I've nothing to hide from Mason. No!' A meeting was arranged. Leavis wanted to attend accompanied by Gordon Fraser, now an extremely successful business-man. He reassured Whalley-Tooker, who was afraid of libel, that he would play down his 'typed page of statements'. The strain was palpable: 'I had, in succession, a rich black eye, and an arterial-red white in the other.' He was glad the Trustees promised that his turn to speak would be before Newton, secretary of the Trust.[52]

The meeting took place in early March at Leo Salingar's room in Trinity, appropriately neutral ground. Before going in, Newton said to Strickland that he wanted to call out to Leavis, 'Liar! liar!' Someone else said this might kill Leavis. 'Yes,' replied Newton, 'but at least he'd die in the truth.'[53] At the meeting Whalley-Tooker presided. Leavis spoke, as he insisted, before Newton took the floor. Mason was not present, nor was Jean Gooder, at that time expecting her daughter. Leavis, 'addressing no one in particular' (according to Geoffrey Strickland), stated that he had been exploited and had not been told that Mason was to be the Trust's Lecturer. He was shown a letter, evidently by himself written to Roy Littlewood, that appeared to show approval of Mason's permanent appointment.* Leavis said he wanted no more money raised in his name; he agreed not to make further public comments about the Trust. Leavis attributed to Jean Gooder, who made the Cambridge Leavisians aware of the Newby Trust, a leading part in establishing the lectureship Trust that 'exploited' his name. The ire, shockingly unexpected from one so

---

* The letter cannot be found.

normally gallant, embarrassed the group, especially Denys Thompson who said that such accusations were intolerable. Leavis then left the meeting 'looking in no way shaken', according to Strickland. During this period there were some hopes that Q.D.L. might be accepted for a college post at Newnham, and, indeed, a university lectureship, which in both cases would have been imaginative appointments for one of her age, though she could hardly be expected to work reliably with others. In the period of 'exploitation' she more than once took out her anger on Newnham pupils. But neither college nor university post materialized. Both Q.D.L. and F.R.L. were in arms against what he called 'the coterie'. In coming months, indeed years, Leavis spared no opportunity of vilifying the Trust group to his correspondents in contemptuous, actionably satirical language.

The academic year of 1965/6 was a dreadful one for all concerned: the loving cup had gone back. What caused the crisis? Leavis did not appear to be an enemy of Mason. He relied on him as a *Scrutiny* editor and assistant at Downing. In 1961 he actually wrote that it was a pity Mason could not be brought back to Cambridge. The Trustees believed that they had Leavis's approval and that he repudiated it, after the intervention of Q.D.L. Newton believed that Shapira had asked Leavis in person whether he approved the choice of Mason, and he had said he did. Leavis admitted that he favoured Mason as a candidate for a fellowship at Corpus. As a result the Trustees may have imputed a greater degree of enthusiasm to Leavis.[54]

It seems that Mason was approved and that the Trustees' way of handling matters, one of 'informal trustfulness', was one that Leavis accepted. For Mason to be a fellow at Corpus (or a successor to Shapira at Downing) almost certainly implied, though not quite, that Mason would be a full-time, salaried Cambridge fixture. Leavis was dealing with a trusted group. Newton was a star pupil, and a steady one, who was also the supervisor of his son. Leavis was a regular visitor at the house of Jean and Richard Gooder. Jean Gooder had taken great pains in an unsuccessful attempt to have Q.D.L. elected to a fellowship at Newnham. She relied on Q.D.L. for a substantial amount of supervision of Newnham undergraduates. It would seem as if 'informal trustfulness' could flourish. But some useful formalities were certainly missing. There appears to have been no written statement to Leavis that Mason was to be offered a full-time appointment. Nor was there an unequivocal statement from Leavis to the Trustees of his approval of Mason's appointment. He was shown a letter of his to Roy Littlewood at the meeting in Trinity, but if anything this shows the lack of documentary evidence the Trust had to support its position. Littlewood was not the Secretary.

There is one reason to believe that the Trust was short of written proof that Leavis knew of Mason's impending elevation. Shapira sent a letter to Newton, intended clearly to be an *aide-mémoire*, written in the month of the Trinity meeting, to provide Newton with ammunition so that he could explain how positive Leavis's attitude to Mason had been. Shapira gave a digest of what was known to him of Leavis's attitude. If the Trust *did* have a clearly written statement by Leavis that he approved of appointing Mason as a permanent Lecturer, then Shapira need never have done this.

Shapira made five main points in his letter to Newton. (1) In 1960, when the scheme for a lectureship was broached, Leavis said he thought it was impracticable, but it appealed to his sense of adventure: he liked the Trust's welcome but 'madcap' demonstration. (2) In 1962 Leavis visited Mason at Shapira's flat to tell him it was his duty to accept Downing's offer if he received a university lectureship. (3) In 1965 Leavis was pleased at Newton's handling of Trust affairs, reporting to Shapira that Q.D.L. thought Mason's book on Tudor literature was distinguished. But he added that Mason should not be mentioned in front of his wife. (4) In 1965 Leavis told Clive Parry at Downing that the best way to restore his confidence in Downing would be to elect Mason as a fellow. (5) Once, Shapira reported to Leavis that Mason said contact with Leavis was one of the attractions of the lectureship: he hoped he could meet him often. Apparently Leavis said there would be no difficulty on this score. Shapira knew Leavis did not like Mason's sociable manner, and there had been a piece of unspecified tactlessness in 1949; but he thought he fully appreciated that Newton was really working for Mason as the only serious candidate. On the question of whether Leavis understood that a full-time, permanent lectureship was envisaged, Shapira believed Leavis accepted this because he sympathized with Q.D.L.'s view that schoolmasters could ill afford giving money to pay for merely occasional lectures.[55]

The whole matter was delicate. If Leavis did not say anything very definite about the prospect of Mason's appointment, it is not surprising. The Trust planned to honour him and he may have considered it immodest to inquire too closely about the arrangements. It is, anyway, most likely that Leavis never really believed in the plans: how could he have anticipated the financial coup from Jean Gooder that turned a pipe-dream into reality? This is what Leavis said much later, in 1974:

In the course of discussing the lectureship project I had replied to Newton that there were two prohibitive objections: (i) it was ridiculous to suppose that there could be any hope of finding the necessary supporting college and (ii) it was a fantastic dream that money enough could be raised. This constituted my firm but delicately put no. Newton later remarked to me: 'Mrs Gooder says it's remarkable how easy it is to raise money.' Since I hadn't given him a direct no, Newton and the Gooders ... chose to take it that they had the green light. Gordon Fraser told me quite recently of the financial reality: Mrs Gooder ... contributed 'on loan' enough from her own resources.[56]

There is no strong evidence that Leavis supported Mason for a full-time lectureship. If there had been, Shapira would not have needed to write to Newton as he did, gathering all the scraps of favour he could find that Leavis showed for Mason. It is most likely that the trustees, or the core-members who were long-standing enthusiasts for Mason, had heard from Leavis what they wanted to hear. And he was always courteously, or cannily, unspecific.*

Leaving Cambridge

Henceforth Leavis was libellously scathing about the Trust. His reaction raises a matter frequently invoked: that of 'paranoia'. Observers could cite half a dozen examples of behaviour that might be described as 'paranoid' in Leavis. Two earlier ones, of 1950, were indignation that the mere advertisement of radio talks about the English novel did not acknowledge *The Great Tradition*, and his distribution of copies of his correspondence with Alan Pryce-Jones about the neglect of *Scrutiny* by *The Times Literary Supplement*.† It is certainly important to understand the structure of Leavis's anger, but this probably cannot be done in the context of the word 'paranoia', a term that in recent years has been valuably subject to deconstruction. Not long before his death Denys Harding, Leavis's old pupil and long-standing contributor to *Scrutiny*,

* Mason later became a fellow of Clare Hall, Cambridge. He died on 25 November 1993.
† See Chapter Eight, No Common Pursuit, 'Virtue in Our Time 1950' and 'Function of Criticism 1949–1952'.

both a literary critic and a Professor of Psychology, sent me a reference to a paper in the *British Journal of Medical Psychology*, published in 1992, on delusion and the concept of 'paranoia'. He suggested that the author, David J. Harper, was right to observe that even within the psychiatric profession (and perhaps possibly especially there) the concepts of 'paranoia' and 'delusion' were too unstable to be useful clinically. Part of the 'official' definition of delusion, from the American Psychiatric Association, is 'a false personal belief based on incorrect inference about external reality' – which reads, as Harper notes, 'as if the notions of truth and falsity, or personal knowing and of belief were unproblematic', and that 'belief' is used in 'an equally unclear manner'. Harper quotes John Stuart Mill:

The tendency has always been strong to believe that whatever received a name must be an entity or being, having an existence of its own. And if no entity answering to the name could be found, men did not for that reason suppose that none existed, but imagined that it was something peculiarly abstruse and mysterious.[57]

As to the structure of Leavis's angry retaliation, in such a case as the Lectureship affair, one suggestion might be made, intended to integrate his response with his chosen role as critic (though certainly not to say that the response was premeditated application of a principle). Despite his formidable individuality, Leavis as literary entrepreneur favoured the invisible, advisory role. We saw that when, in late 1931, he gathered a group of disgruntled graduate students at his Chesterton Hall Crescent, for the inaugural meeting of (his) proposed English Research Society, he was delighted that they treated I.A. Richards with scant respect, as he wished to himself, but he could not do 'without endorsing the implication that it was all my little stunt' – as indeed it *was*. It was Leavis's way to play the invisible trainer or, in Cambridge sporting terms, the 'back-coach'. But it was a matter of anguish if the trainer were disregarded, his influence not transparent but invisible. It is joyless to be an ignored conspirator.

In coming months Leavis lost no opportunity to vilify the Lectureship group. The saddest result was for Morris Shapira.

He spent a good deal of time with Richard and Jean Gooder, and with Newton, and he respected and was amused by Mason. He thought the Trust had a reasonable chance of furthering Leavis's interests, but he was less passionate in his belief in Mason than the others. He only just belonged to the group, and very soon gave up having anything to do with the *Cambridge Quarterly*. The group itself folded itself into Cambridge and Shapira soon left for a post at the new University of Kent at Canterbury. Leavis, until the breach, admired and cared for him. Even at the end of January, the time of the 'indictment', Leavis could write to him, exceptionally, as 'Dear Morris', ending 'F.R.L.'.[58]

But by the end of March, when '*Scrutiny*'s Failure with Shakespeare had appeared, he believed Shapira had deceived him about the orientation of the *Cambridge Quarterly*. He now believed he had backed Shapira blindly, and Newton too, who repaid the support with an attack (so it seemed) on the central enterprise, *Scrutiny*, which had cost the Leavises so much.[59] Shapira answered back with remarkable courage. Leavis had mentioned a pupil in his letter, one who was in straits, referring to him, with a very Leavisian inflection, as 'Poor X'. Shapira fastened on the phrase:

'Poor [X] whom you like and respect.' You mean 'poor F.R.L.'. I never liked it when it was 'poor Shapira' or 'poor Mrs Gooder' or 'poor Mason' . . . Why should you assume that I should be loyal to people who were less my friends than you – whom I saw, normally, less than you, and whose opinions I share, usually, very little. I was loyal to a working ideal and to a man – who now seems to be dead. Professor Leavis is not merely a glamorous man of intellect who dominates all companies. He is (as we all have been) cruelly and tragically wronged – a victim of restless intrigue, and, while remaining noble and heroic, is allowed to appreciate the pathos of his own fate. Who does not, in some moments, readily see himself as the hero of a *coup de théâtre*?

What strikes me as utterly contemptible is the effect that all this poppycock has on your wife's reputation. So long as you are overcome by the pathos of yourself as the noble dupe and count, effectively, on the affection, trust and respect that F.R. Leavis has created, those who care for you are bound to ask what it is forces this noble intelligent being so far from what anybody outside the charmed family circle recognizes as truth.

It's all part of the general effect of your denial of responsibility for our 'craft' and your lack of a spirit of captaincy. You let down the whole nation and are shocking in the way that that old captain was. If our craft wasn't yours, it now never will be. Like Conrad's captain [in *The Shadow-Line*] you've got your eyes only on your own ego. You'll kill yourself if you persist in 'remaining lucid about essentials' which seems to mean, keeping up a remarkable structure of loosely interlocking lies by force of will.[60]

Leavis replied only with 'Dear Shapira'.

Few of us are without vanity and I have known you to show obvious aplomb, from time to time, in offering to tickle what you saw of it in me. But the question is – 'responsible'. The word in your context has clearly such different forces for writer and reader.

I've myself written to [X], saying, what I could helpfully say. He will, no doubt, as I suggested, pass this letter on to you with his comments. That, I think, will have been a good economy, responsible as far as I am concerned.

There would be no point in my reciprocating with a diagnosis. My recognition of that explains my resolving, after the last letter of yours I made reply to, to read no further communication from you.[61]

The end of Leavis's friendship with Shapira was marked by a reference to Joseph Conrad. In 1966 Leavis was thinking of the novelist and especially the novella *The Secret Sharer* on which he lectured at York. At the close of the story a deliberate and terrifying risk is taken by the young captain to save the fugitive he has concealed and befriended. The captain's seeming irresponsibility is, Leavis argues, a response to 'his profoundest ethical sense': the 'good ship' cannot be created without such conditions. 'Conditions and circumstances tell, of course, but creative action makes it, and creative action, collaborative though it must be, depends upon creative individuals and creative will.' Here the individual will takes precedence, just, over collaborative action. Leavis had always asserted that the individual was the focus of response and decision. But it is possible that the dreadful breach with Shapira marked a change in his sense of the creative. Perhaps his sense of collaboration diminished. The end of things with Shapira concluded the retirement phase.[62]

CHAPTER ELEVEN

New Universities
1965–1975

I'm no journalist, but I'm inexhaustible.
— F.R. Leavis, letter to Ian Robinson, 1971

It was expediency, not faith, that he served. His passing over to the Tory camp needs no defence; but as a controversialist he must plead guilty to unscrupulous opportunism. If a weapon, or a method, of attack promised to be damaging, that was enough for Swift: he did not allow truth and justice to hamper his onslaught.
— F.R. Leavis, 'The Relation of Journalism to Literature', 1924

York and Elsewhere 1965–1970

In 1965 Leavis went to the University of York as Visiting Professor. He was paid £500 a year, not quite twice the amount E.M. Forster received for his Clark Lectures in 1926.[1] The university had one of the most pleasant of the 1960s campuses, built around Heslington Hall, lawns and lakes separating white colleges, with the medieval city within bicycling distance. Leavis described warmly the 'beautifully landscaped site' as evidence of 'modern skill, modern and humane architectural intelligence' seeming 'to grow in its modernity out of the old Hall'.* The York architects convinced him that his idea of the university 'isn't merely mine'. The founding Professor of English, J.P. Brockbank, was a post-war graduate from Cambridge (Trinity); he was a shrewd Shakespearean scholar, committed to literary criticism. At York studies were interdisciplinary. Leavis was attached to a Department of English and Related Studies. The department was, and continued to be, strong in French studies.

---

* But later he said to Patrick Harrison: 'No pubs, no cafés, no people. Quite a trail to get into York. Most of them [students] have never been away from home before. There's no proper college life. No town around them. They're lost and unsupported. Prey, easy prey, to the committed political activists.'

In his seventies there was no shortage of invitations to lecture and travel, but the way of life that followed the York appointment was not that of an elder statesman. The later years of a distinguished academic are embellished with advisory visits, *Festschriften*, external examining and service as 'chairman of many committees' (*pace* Eliot's 'East Coker'). Leavis's role was much more like that of his own recent graduates, settling in the new universities. The man who believed in the 'ancient university', and knew nothing hitherto but that, moved into the world of the Robbins Report as a participant, listening to discussion of syllabuses, eating in refectories. He embarked in 1966 on a decade of new audiences at York, and other universities around the United Kingdom and abroad, sometimes offering what he called a formal 'score' to large audiences, or 'seminars', a term for which he continued to use quotation marks. In them he was not confined to one hour (as in Cambridge) so talk, usually his, stretched out. 'What can you get done in an hour, particularly since it is very important that [students], too, should be forced to articulate?'[2] According to the university Registrar at York, John West-Taylor, who had known Leavisian Cambridge in the 1940s, he was 'happy for the first time in his life'. He would travel up on a Tuesday night after the Cambridge Faculty Board and stay until Friday. York was organized into colleges so Leavis felt its system was sympathetic to him, showing an understanding of the principle that a university is 'not a mere convocation of specialist departments'. He liked the York examination system, a 'diversity of methods – of considerations and tests', he called it, providing more types of student assessment than the three-hour paper, 'the real iniquity of the Oxford and Cambridge system, staking everything at the end on examinations against the clock. It is wicked and it penalizes the good people in English.' His self-esteem was enhanced. 'Yes,' he wrote to Denys Harding,

retirement is arduous, but I won't pretend that the ardours don't go with a great measure of satisfaction. My business at York (I'll risk the self-importance of saying this) has been to keep the university conscious of its better intentions, and I'm expected to spend no time on routine. I do what I think best. I sincerely wish you no worse retirement.[3]

The student troubles (of 1968) were later to distress him.[4]

In 1967 Leavis returned to Cambridge public life to deliver judgement on English and the university. He was invited not by the English Faculty but by Trinity College to give the Clark Lectures. It is probable that the Master, R.A. Butler, was instrumental in effecting the invitation. (Trinity was patricianly neutral about Cambridge English, for many years having no English don and a broad agreement among the fellows that English hardly existed as a subject. Theodore Redpath, lawyer and philosopher and editor of a much used edition of John Donne's *Songs and Sonets*, 'looked after' the English men.) Leavis's six lectures were published as *English Literature in Our Time and the University* (1969) and showed the results of his seminars on literature at York, and his observations from a distance on Cambridge English.

The lectures were dedicated, ominously, to H.M. Chadwick and Mansfield Forbes, the informing spirits of the original Cambridge English, both fellows of Clare College, like John Newton and Richard Gooder, in Leavis's eyes the now-disgraced leaders of the Trust coterie. The range of the lectures was wide, almost as wide in scope as the Richmond Lecture. In his summing-up Leavis quoted from an article by Lord Radcliffe in the *Spectator*, 'The Dissolving Society', which concluded that 'We must, I think, get back quickly to the active realization of our identity.' Leavis respected Lord Radcliffe, but was disappointed, because his concept of national identity appeared no more than 'the nation-state as we know it'. For Leavis 'our' business was to foster the past through to the present, 'to maintain the continuity of life and consciousness that a cultural tradition is, and not to lose anything essential from our heritage – the heritage that is kept alive by creative renewal (which means change) in every present'.[5] He dwelled on his old theme of 'continuity', engaging with it in several down-to-earth ways, one of which was the plain difficulty for students of getting through the reading necessary for a course in English studies. He meant especially the reading of novels, that 'highest form of human expression so far attained', as he quoted from D.H. Lawrence.

The theme of the lectures was the 'monstrous unrealism' of planning by numbers. Leavis kept close to one thing he knew intimately, the Cambridge English curriculum in which he saw one example of 'monstrous unrealism' that may appear surprising, the presence of an English Tripos examination on 'The Novel'. Given his commitment to the 'novel as dramatic poem', to what Lawrence called 'the one bright book of life', Leavis's opposition to this Faculty plan appears capricious. What was his objection? 'The Novel' would be one among, say, five examined courses and to be meaningful study for them it should be organized. He believed that 'The Novel' simply threw a chaos of names at the student. More planning was necessary than a policy of catholic inclusiveness, mentions of novelists multiplying to make up a global list. Leavis remembered at one Faculty discussion one 'zealous collaborator' piping in with Sir Philip Sidney's *Arcadia* for the list of texts. Leavis was hard on the planning processes of the English Faculty, but the simple liberalism of laying on authors for a course, leaving choice to the student, was and is typical of British university English departments. The freedom of the original Cambridge English had turned into (he thought) systematic indecisiveness as to what English (or 'literature') entailed. Leavis, of course, believed 'the achievement of the novel in the English language is one of the great creative chapters in the human record', but there had to be 'living sense, regarding the amount of reading an undergraduate can be expected to get done [and of] the considerations that should determine what reading is worth doing'. To ignore the *conditions* of study was what he meant by 'monstrous unrealism'. He extended his account of the local liberalism to late 1960s social planning at large.[6]

It was Eliot and Lawrence who provided Leavis with model ideas of tradition in the Clark Lectures, Eliot for the diagram in 'Tradition and the Individual Talent' and Lawrence for his practice. At this time Lawrence was a model practitioner in an unusual place, his travel book *Twilight in Italy*, which contains a chapter called 'The Theatre'. In it Lawrence described some provincial performances of Ibsen's *Ghosts* and Shakespeare's *Hamlet* by a touring company: an affectionate account of itinerant players moves into a wide-arched consideration of matters of civilization and soul from the Renaissance to the present. Leavis had never written about *Hamlet*, but it was a special case for him for several reasons. First, it was a work that drove a wedge between him and Eliot. Eliot had claimed the play was extraordinary but 'an artistic failure'. Hamlet himself experienced 'emotion in excess of the facts'; there was no 'objective correlative' to his expressed feelings: the play ultimately lacked 'impersonality'; it remained fascinating, private, ultimately incoherent. Leavis's view was that Eliot read incoherence into the play, because it mirrored guilts of his own, to be expressed (or the repression theatricalized) in his own Hamlet-like play, *The Family Reunion*. Leavis believed that Eliot foundered over the intimate drama of *Hamlet*, its 'tentacular roots' reaching down to intimate fears and desires that made it uninterpretable for him. For Leavis there was no barrier to interpretation: he had the aid of Gilbert Murray ('Hamlet and Orestes') and Bertha Phillpotts (*The Elder Edda*), which enabled him to see the *Hamlet* story in a long and legendary perspective, perceiving a drama fashioned by Shakespeare in the modernism of the Renaissance, using his knowledge of Montaigne's 'Apologie for Raimond Sebond' (a source to which Eliot himself had pointed). Lawrence did not think the Prince of Denmark was 'neurotic', but saw in his struggles a philosophical drama about the nature of being. This, not suicide, was the resonance of 'To be, or not to be'. Leavis's conception of *Hamlet* (and a dislike of the prince himself) was dyed with Lawrence's reading. Leavis believed that some imputed emotional disablement in Eliot made him see in *Hamlet* only a personal drama, not the mythological one of Lawrence and Murray and Phillpotts, whose long-range anthropological interpretation was very Cambridge English in the Chadwickian sense. Eliot had given Leavis so much of a sense of tradition, but this form of 'continuity' he ignored. There may have been a personal pressure to explain Leavis's interest at all in Shakespeare's *Hamlet* and Eliot's. The matter of fatherhood could hardly have been a more living issue for him, as father to his pupils and as real father to his son, always explained as 'a genius' or 'a genius (alas!)' with gifts worthy of any in Wittenberg.[7]

Hamlet and Lawrence was one of Leavis's York preoccupations; and there too he became increasingly interested, for the first time since the late 1920s, in Lawrence's non-fiction, notably *Fantasia of the Unconscious* and 'The Study of Thomas Hardy'.*

For the printed version of his Clark Lectures at Trinity Leavis supplied three appendices: his essay in *The Times Literary Supplement*, 'Research in English', a quotation from Rainer Maria Rilke on 'vacuity' and a provocative letter by himself to *The Times* called 'The Function of the University', which threw out a challenge. By now Leavis had a bouquet of symbolic names, like 'Snow' and 'Plumb', enabling him to litanize the ills of materialism. 'The Function of the University' was a reply to a letter of Lord Annan's in *The Times* (19. 1. 68). In it Leavis reminded the reader 'how brutally political, practical and menacing the realities are that present themselves as enlightenment and dedicated zeal for that

---

* One of the Lecturers Leavis found most congenial at York was the educationalist J.V. Davies. He was instrumental in having Heinemann publish an edition of Lawrence on *Hardy and Painting* (1973), edited by Davies.

basic matter: reform in the field of education'. Readers might have been surprised to think that Leavis intended to refer to the mild and meliorist former Provost of King's, Noël Annan. He was now Provost of University College, London, and shortly to become Vice-Chancellor of London University.

Dickens 1970

The centenary of the death of Charles Dickens fell in 1970. For that year Leavis and Q.D.L. produced *Dickens the Novelist*. It will be, wrote Leavis to his publisher in 1968, '*the* book for the centenary'; it was published in October 1970.

For some time both F.R.L. and Q.D.L. had had a book on Dickens in view. Back in 1963 Michael Black at Cambridge University Press had asked Leavis if he was working on a Dickens book. No offer came from Cambridge. Two years later it was under discussion with Chatto & Windus and in July 1968 *Dickens the Novelist* was contracted. 'The wind and tide are good and strong, and we are taking them,' Q.D.L. wrote cheerfully in 1969 to an old Girton friend. Both were busy and she reported that 'at seventy-four he thrives on this kind of life'.[8] Leavis was making an Italian tour (Naples, Rome, Padua, Bologna and Milan). He had been commuting weekly to Bangor and Aberystwyth as Visiting Professor at the University of Wales for a term. The Clark Lectures had been published, as had an edition of the Victorian novel *Miss Marjoribanks* by Margaret Oliphant, with an introduction by Q.D.L. It was an old favourite of hers for which she had campaigned for publication. She was typing up their work on Dickens. Leavis was 'brooding' on a book on *Four Quartets*, on Blake (for an essay) and possibly one on *Hamlet*. He was still thinking of completing 'Authority and Method'. These were more immediate prospects even than the Dickens book, in the sense that Leavis believed that his part in it was already done: he had published on *Hard Times*, on *Dombey and Son*, and had finished his manuscript on *Little Dorrit* for the Chichele Lectures at All Souls in Oxford. He was 'suggesting' to Q.D.L. that she do the rest, including 'the other supreme work, *Great Expectations*'. Publication was therefore a means of gaining authorship for Q.D.L., who would provide four out of the seven chapters. This is not quite how Leavis explained it, however. He wanted the work to be 'a book', with chapters, not a collection of essays.

(Oddly, he considered that as 'a book' it should have no index.) It was to be the one possible collaborative book.

Our minds (as I've told her again and again through the years) are very different, but we were – knew, without discussion, we were – of one mind about what had to be done. Without controversy the six great novels divided themselves. It's my judgement that the book is really a book, though there was no *ad hoc* consultation – we just, each of us, got down to work.[9]

When they began Leavis may have expected to do more work than in the event he did. Although he said in July 1968 that he had his *Hard Times* essay to hand, perhaps for revision, in December he asked Parsons at Chatto if he could merely reprint it in the book. Parsons recognized some oddity in the request because the piece was not simply an essay but a chapter, albeit called 'an analytic note', of *The Great Tradition*. (Parsons suggested reasonably that if Leavis did this the chapter should be removed from future editions of *The Great Tradition*.) When it was agreed that the chapter be included, there was little for Leavis himself to do. But there was one especially interesting thing he did for the book.

In *Dombey and Son* the love of the harsh shipping magnate of the title is focused upon his delicate son, Paul, at the expense of his daughter, Florence. For the new book Leavis used his essay on the novel *Dombey and Son*, published in America in 1962, but he added several pages on the ailing Paul Dombey.[10] He retained a reference to what was 'disconcertingly Victorian in the pathos of the dying Paul', but modified it by saying that in the rendering of Paul there was more than simple melodrama, and no sentimentality. 'Nowhere is the poet–novelist's genius more apparent than there.' He gave intense attention to a passage describing Paul warming his hands by the fire:

And he went on warming his hands again, and thinking about them, like an old man or a young goblin. Mr Dombey was so astonished, and so uncomfortable, and so perfectly at a loss how to pursue the conversation, that he could only sit looking at his son by the light of the fire, with his hand resting on his back, as if he were detained there by some magnetic attraction. Once he advanced his other hand, and turned the contemplative face towards his own for a moment. But it sought the fire again as soon as he released it; and remained, addressed towards the flickering blaze, until the nurse appeared, to summon him to bed.

'I want Florence to come for me,' said Paul.

'Won't you come with your poor nurse, Wickham, Master Paul?' inquired the attendant, with great pathos.

'No, I won't,' replied Paul, composing himself in his armchair again, like the master of the house.

Leavis added to his original essay a comment on this passage:

The emotional situation presented here has a complexity that positively disclaims anything like a sentimental purpose. Paul himself isn't the ideally sympathique child-victim. He is a victim, right enough, but that doesn't make certain of the characterizing traits the less disconcerting. It isn't Wickham (not yet in the room) or Mrs Pipchin and Mrs Blimber who here see Paul as 'like an old man or a young goblin', but we ourselves and (for we take the suggestion) Dombey. Of course, these traits are very largely the products of the substitute for love that Dombey, with the devoted co-operation of his friends and allies, makes the formative spirit of the child's upbringing. But in this passage itself we have the intimation that the child is the son of his father:

'No, I won't,' replied Paul, composing himself in his armchair again, like the master of the house.

Florence does take the boy away, carrying Paul up the 'great, wide vacant staircase', singing, Paul's head 'lying on her shoulder, one of his arms thrown negligently round her neck'. Thus borne, Paul's goblin 'slyness' has gone, Leavis observes. His praise of the passage is rallied further into making a distinction between the 'disinterested love' of Florence (and Dickens) and the evocation of the whole 'absorbed spontaneity of childhood'. 'The spontaneity is the flowing of life, emotional and imaginative.'

Leavis's addition to his essay enabled the chapter to concentrate more closely on the idea of childhood, a basic term in his definition of 'creativity', the development of which is the inner purpose of his contributions to Dickens the Novelist. The 'image of childhood', the title of a book much admired by both F.R.L. and Q.D.L., was also basic to Leavis's own instincts and responsibilities.[11] There was his son Ralph, who had perhaps been treated harshly, whom he visited alone as often as he could in Oxford, and of whom he talked as he travelled all around the country on what he called 'evangelical forays' to universities, where he may not have lost hope of finding Ralph employment. There was also Q.D.L. herself, never less than energetic, always frail, to be cared for.[12]

After the Dickens chapters had been sent off, Leavis was (according to

Q.D.L.) 'writing *all the time*' on Wordsworth and on Blake, as he had planned: she wanted to discourage him from contributing to the 'saturated' Blake market.[13] Then, soon after Christmas 1969, when *Dickens the Novelist* was with the printer, there was a shock. 'Over my head, the waters have met,' said Leavis, quoting Swinburne. Q.D.L. suddenly fell ill and Leavis was told that her cancer might have returned, showing signs through her whole system; pneumonia followed, but responded to treatment. She knew she was dying – but then, against all expectation, began to recover: 'I suddenly felt the sap begin to rise,' wrote Leavis. Q.D.L. spent six weeks in hospital, then at home she was confined to the ground floor. 'The intensity that makes her "difficult" is the vitality that for years made the doctors marvel.' The couple were therefore able to see the publication of *Dickens the Novelist*, Leavis's way of having the name of Q.D.L. on the cover of a book for the first time since 1932. Their collaboration was advertised in a dedication.

We dedicate this book to each other as proof, along with *Scrutiny* (of which for twenty-one years we sustained the main burden and the responsibility), of forty years and more of daily collaboration in living, university teaching, discussion of literature and the social and cultural context from which literature is born, and above all, devotion to the fostering of that true respect for creative writing, creative minds and, English literature being in question, the English tradition, without which literary criticism can have no validity and no life.

The word 'English' is used twice in a dedication very un-English in its boldness. Leavis was evidently the author of the dedication, but wrote to John Tasker that he was somewhat dubious about it, though he thought, in the end, the testimony was right, a kind of consolation for Q.D.L., considering the way, he believed, she had been badly treated by her college and by the literary world.[14] Ian Robinson planned a review of *Dickens the Novelist* and sent a draft to Leavis. He replied that he hoped there would be not even a hint of the banal valuation, which he found repellent, that Q.D.L. was not such a great critic as her husband. 'She has rare gifts; and she paid for her efforts on her contribution to *Dickens the Novelist* with terrible illness.' Even so, the book was a limited effort, not at all what they had hoped to do.[15]

The work on *Dickens the Novelist* was, indeed, gruelling for Q.D.L. In the making of the book the couple built a barrier round their project, living in the present with a ferocious tenacity. Leavis remarked to Parsons in 1965 that he would like to make some changes to *The Great*

Tradition because 'in the last twenty years I've been changing my view of Dickens, and am now (have been for years) his "vindicator". I contend that *he* created the modern novel. He did.'[16]

But the nature of the change was not chronicled. The two writers set out no relationship to their own past. Jointly in the 'Preface' they trounced the view that Dickens's 'line was entertainment'. In Leavis's chapter on 'Dickens and Blake: *Little Dorrit*' he rejected the valuation of Dickens as 'great entertainer' as 'misleading' (though 'indisputable'). This view flies barefacedly, it appears, against *The Great Tradition*: 'That Dickens was a great genius and is permanently among the classics is certain. But the genius was that of a great entertainer, and he had for the most part no profounder responsibility as a creative artist than this description suggests.'[17] Other commentators were trivialized, the unfortunate Philip Collins anonymously pilloried as one who performed, at public readings, 'assorted "Dickens characters" with histrionic gusto'. (He did so, but he was also an admirable Dickens scholar.) American criticism, from Edmund Wilson onwards, was said to be 'essentially ignorant and misdirecting'. The drawbridge was up against all comers.

Yet *Dickens the Novelist* was an extraordinary book, written in two diverging hands. On one side there was Q.D.L.'s electrically explanatory manner (almost with a screech of the blackboard), full of observant listings, notably good on Dickens's illustrations. On the other, there was F.R.L.'s circuitous and literally eccentric discourse, in, for example, the newest long piece of writing about Dickens and William Blake – which does not mention a single work by Blake. Leavis's references to what he calls 'the mythical works' of Blake give, perhaps, a clue to the strangeness of his procedure, works with 'complexities, ambiguities and shifting "symbolic" values that defy the diagrammatizing interpreter'. Was Leavis writing of himself? His chapter was 'mythical' work, repeating and revolving. The chapter on *Little Dorrit* was Blake-like because also 'prophetic' with attack, incorporated into the literary analysis, on the 'technologico-Benthamite' age, of which the elevated peons on this occasion are Harold Wilson and Lord Snow. 'Technologico-Benthamism' was identified with the 'nothingness of the Dorrit–Gowan–Barnacle human world'. Against that world is set Dickens's portrayal of the Alps in which is set the Great St Bernard Convent, through which the Dorrit family pass in the novel. That 'daunting Alpine transcendence', Dickens's evocation of 'time, eternity, the non-human universe, the de-realizing lights and vapours, and death' is set against the 'social impertinences of the recent decade with its orthodoxies of enlightenment'. For Leavis to bring into conjunction the St Gotthard Pass and the *New Statesman* was extraordinary, and vulnerable to criticism. The question inevitably arises of whether social commentary can admit such visionary experience. The answer is that it cannot – until the use of vision is remembered. Is the social ethic that *excludes* the sights of the seer, or eschews understanding of its own fragility, ultimately entitled to absolute confidence in the proclamation of practicality? Leavis pressed his symbol against the world. The difficulty for the reader of 'Dickens and Blake: *Little Dorrit*' is that its discourse was unusual for mid-twentieth-century prose. Leavis's desire was to put Eliot of 'East Coker' (and Milton) into his own literary-social critique:

> O dark dark dark. They all go into the dark,
> The vacant interstellar spaces, the vacant into the vacant,
> The captains, merchant bankers, eminent men of letters,
> The generous patrons of art, the statesmen and the rulers . . .

For Leavis it was now 'Mr Harold Wilson' and 'Lord Snow' who led the hordes into 'vacancy'.

Field-performances 1969–1971

In the early 1960s, before the *Cambridge Quarterly* group became 'the coterie', Richard and Jean Gooder invited Leavis to dinner to meet Richard Crossman, a neighbour of Jean Gooder's family in Sussex. Leavis was not a Labour voter. He supported the Liberal Party to the extent of acting as sponsor for the local Liberal candidate.[18] But Crossman had once written a book on Plato, mildly favoured by Leavis; there was perhaps hope that some Leavisian influence might prevail if and when Labour was returned to power. However, Leavis did not care for Crossman. He asked him about the need to maintain the 'real university', and what part Labour could play in fashioning it – or rather respecting the ideal, for it was not bricks and mortar that Leavis was concerned with. Crossman replied that 'we'll smash the oligarchy!' – 'lifting a rhetorical fist': Leavis said he could only return, 'There are oligarchies everywhere.'

During the years from 1963 Leavis spoke out against a number of blunt practical reformers, having begun with C.P. Snow (as Matthew

Arnold had attacked Liberals) in his phase of 'higher pamphleteering', of which the Richmond Lecture was the first in a 'six-lecture series'.[19] The Richmond Lecture was followed in 1966 by 'Luddites? Or There is Only One Culture' given at Harvard. The remaining 'field-perform-ances' were lectures in Wales and at Bristol and York, and there was one piece in a journal started by Ian Robinson in Swansea – [20] '"English": Unrest and Continuity', '"Literarism" versus "Scientism": The Misconception and the Menace', 'Pluralism, Compassion and Social Hope', 'Elites, Oligarchies and an Educated Public'.

Leavis told Parsons at Chatto & Windus he was keen to bring these pieces out as a book, with a challenging title. He wondered about 'Nor Shall My Sword' in December 1970, but Q.D.L. disliked the title. 'Hatred of the enlightened' made him feel like Blake. 'They can't – cannot – forgive the questioning, or dismissal, of the orthodox postulates and assumptions.' But 'don't suppose I hope to build Jerusalem'.[21] The 'pamphlets' received wide publicity. Two appeared in *The Times Literary Supplement*, the Wales lecture (1969) and '"Literarism" versus "Scientism"' (1970). Leavis was famous enough for *The Times* to use his name in an advertising slogan: 'What have Monty and Dr Leavis got in common?' (they were *Times* readers). He had hoped to hitch 'tin-cans to Robbins's and Annan's trousers' seats'; the rattle was indeed heard in the corridors of power.

Many years before, with the publication of Denys Thompson's *Reading and Discrimination* (1934), a literary criticism primer, an issue arose that was quickly noted by the *Bookman*, a paper with strong Leavisian sympathies. The editor picked out one sentence: 'The reading of literature is the best means now of improving one's capacity for living.' 'Utter and unforgivable nonsense,' he exclaimed, glad it was not Leavis but Thompson who wrote this. But Thompson's dogmatism, certainly from the Leavisian camp, did give the editor an insight into 'Leavisphobia'.[22] Down the years the idea of literature as the one thing needful for right living did become associated with Leavis, though he never voiced it. It hit him with particular force in the 1960s when George Steiner asked how the humanities could justify themselves, given that the least humane people of the century, officials at Dachau and Buchenwald, often did not lack artistic cultivation. Leavis was aware of this issue in 1969 when, at the last minute, he scrawled '"English": Unrest and Continuity' for a colloquium on 'English' at the University of Wales conference centre at

Gregynog. Leavis hurried straight from a lecture at Newcastle-on-Tyne to deliver it. 'It was an opportunity – a hazard – taken in the field: *c'est la guerre.*'[23]

In this lecture Leavis stated the contemporary problems brusquely: 'violence, wanton destructiveness, the drug menace, adolescent promiscuity, permissiveness, the enlightened praise of the young for their "candour" about "sex", and "student revolt"'; and he stated equally sharply his belief in the university: 'Society's only conceivable organ for such an effort is the university, conceived as a creative centre of civilization.'[24] The first point of his lecture was that by 'university' he did not mean a place with a dominant English department and cultured people (like the 'finely cultured persons' who countenanced Dachau). By university Leavis meant, as before, a community whose conduct was well or best illustrated by the relationships that ideally occur in English studies. The essay was therefore on university-as-community and to establish his ideal Leavis attacked what he now called the 'bi-categorists' who saw the double category of arts and science, the arts on one side providing the 'higher amenities' and the dignifying graces of life, but still a 'soft' option. Leavis obviously wanted a definition of 'English' that would show how it might command respect for its own discipline of intelligence when set against science. But he was more concerned with another 'bi-categorism': the conventional division between teaching and research.

If one's concern is essentially with teaching one doesn't think of oneself as 'teaching'. One thinks of oneself as engaged with one's students in the business of criticism – which, of its nature, is collaborative.

The lecture was hardly decorous; it made an amusing stab at the novelist Margaret Drabble, who had been reported as saying that she took a First in English at Cambridge without doing much work. He also tolled out modern offensiveness in a list that gave Noël Annan understandable irritation. The lecture reiterated the theme of *Education and the University*, much of it keeping close to the lesson of T.S. Eliot. But there was a concluding peroration that spoke to the particular moment. On one side of the Atlantic he observed American demoralization: it was only in September 1969 that Richard Nixon announced the gradual withdrawal of American troops from Vietnam. Britain was in as much confusion, preoccupied with the certainty of its decline as a world-power. In January 1968 the Prime Minister (Harold Wilson) announced the evacuation of all British military bases east of Suez by 1971. In Britain there was a distinct and righteous anti-Americanism among young people. Leavis concluded roundly that 'the hope of salvation in America depends on our success in the creative battle here. When I ask what hope there is for humanity in Russia, I turn cold.' The creative effort was '*our* business', which would receive heartening welcome across the Atlantic. When the lecture was published there was support from America, including one letter from a recent expatriate, the critic and poet Donald Davie, formerly from the University of Essex, the most troubled campus of the 1960s. He was surprised at how positive Leavis was, at the 'stubbornness' of his belief of what could be done in Britain.[25]

In December 1969 Leavis was still 'tormented' by what he called the Mason–Shapira–Robson–Gooder, conspiracy. He did not like rereading his Clark Lectures, but decided to publish them. He was still commuting to Wales, and he had his last public lecture for Bristol coming up after Christmas.[26] He had the clue for a subject in an article in *The Times Literary Supplement* of 1 January on computers. He delivered it and was invited to print it in the same paper.

The lecture, called '"Literarism" versus "Scientism": The Misconception and the Menace', is remarkable in the sequence of 'field-performances' because of its simplicity: it neither substantiates the case by reference to literary studies (thereby risking the inference that literature is everything), nor does it rehearse the relatively arcane definition of creativity to which Leavis resorted in the later stages of his polemic against mechanization. He circled two topics in particular, a chance remark from a philosopher that computers could write poems, and the claims made by *The Times Literary Supplement* writer for computerized teaching methods. On this occasion Leavis was most concerned with letting cliché be felt. He used the term 'organic', but metaphorically to describe processes, rather than to locate an historical 'organic society'. The opposite of 'organic' is here 'structural': the computer 'will control all structured tasks', but, Leavis asked, what were the 'structured tasks' in his subject? The 'world's finest teaching systems' would be made available to those in reach of a 'communications system':

The use of the word 're-structure' is profoundly significant: 'education' is to be re-structured, society is to be re-structured, life is to be re-structured. The sense that 'organic' means something is out of date; it has been left behind . . . The organic isn't congenial to statistical treatment, and therefore it doesn't matter; it can be forgotten, and is.

A specific target is Noël Annan, 'who edited a selection of Matthew

Arnold's prose for the World's Classics'; Leavis thought he endorsed the idea that a university could be an industrial plant, ever-humming, ever training a youthful clientele for admission (even those who left school voluntarily at the age of fifteen). Perhaps because, on this occasion, 'English' did not figure so large in the discourse there was noticeable affirmative response to the lecture when it was published in *The Times Literary Supplement* on 23 April. *The Times* had a news report on 'Dr Leavis's Fears for Education: Running Universities as Industrial Plant'. This received very approving attention in *The Times*'s first leader. But there was another, less agreeable message at its headquarters in Printing House Square.

On the day before publication of '"Scientism" versus "Literarism"' there appeared in *The Times* an advertisement from its sister publication, *The Times Literary Supplement*, announcing that the next day 'Dr Leavis is here to tell you that the pen is mightier than the print-out', promising certainly a reply from Annan and 'possibly one from C.P. Snow'. Thick with cliché, the puff promised action, cudgels being 'taken up' and 'a few swings of the club' from Leavis at Snow. Four readers from Bristol University, including Christopher Ricks and Henry Gifford, protested and inquired whether Leavis had been told he was to be so publicized. Annan did, indeed, reply to Leavis in the essay 'The University and the Intellect: The Miasma and the Menace'; he was annoyed to be associated with student unrest and the other ills of the late 1960s. He was bewildered too, believing rightly that he had addressed the problem of national educational need. Annan focused on a simple ideal: the sovereignty of the 'intellect'. The difficulty was that he did not go further than this word, and that Leavis wanted to reach into what words meant – but Leavis's efforts did not impress Annan, so established was the conviction that to use 'organic' must mean he desired to revert to a folk-community, and that he was a unitary thinker, believing 'in one set of values'. These values seemed to him simply and self-evidently 'puritan'; they bore little relation to Leavis's struggles over Eliot and Lawrence. Annan said he favoured 'the morality of pluralism and compassion'. *The Times Literary Supplement* called for correspondence and plenty followed, some of it common sense, proffered helpfully, righteously or ruefully, about computers and about education. On education, the debate went into basics, but not into essentials, that is, learning and training. 'Creativity' and its relation to education, if any, was not discussed. The main reply was that of Annan, and Leavis directed another piece at it, for Annan was a close combatant, even a quarry for Leavis. Leavis considered him a key member of the establishment. Indeed, his position was confirmed as such within three years of this debate, when he was chosen to head the government investigation into the future of broadcasting, which, consistent with his place in the debate, recommended greater 'pluralism' in the control of media of entertainment and education.★ Like Snow, he was a Cambridge figure, and like him too chosen by Leavis with almost a novelist's instinct for a symbolic 'character'. Leavis chose 'Snow' for his novel (so to speak) of the 1960s and 'Annan' for his novels of the 1970s. Annan was central for a man who knew his Cambridge, but also for what Leavis perceived was obscure to the world at large. Annan was to his mind a successor to Matthew Arnold, and not necessarily a worthy one. He was not an Inspector of Schools like Arnold, but he had been and was the administrator of two great educational institutions. It must be remembered that before he became Vice-Chancellor of London University in 1978 he was Provost of University College, London, for the ten preceding years, an emblematic location for the nineteenth-century intelligentsia: it was, indeed, a home of the rationalist persuasion to which Harry Leavis adhered. (Symbolically, it is also 'Bloomsbury', adjacent to Gordon Square.) Annan was expert in the world of the old masters and decencies, the Sidgwicks and the Stephens. He was author of a genuinely seminal essay, 'The Intellectual Aristocracy', on late nineteenth-century Britain. Like Leavis, he was an historian. There was even a certain temperamental affinity, at least in the way he perceived problems, if not in his solution of them. He said in his reply to '"Literarism" versus "Scientism"' that he suspected Grand Designs and gave his own version of Leavis's 'yes, but' without discerning a connection with Leavis. He said that the art of 'actuality' lay in

holding the essentials of the scheme in one's mind, and, like an architect, giving here an inch where he has to to the planning authority, and there an inch to his client ... but sustaining the essence of the scheme against all these legitimate pressures.

★ The *Report of the Committee on the Future of Broadcasting* (1977), Cmnd 6753, known as the 'Annan Report'. As to *Lady Chatterley's Lover*, Annan did not see Leavis's struggle with the novel, only what seemed like hypocrisy: moderate praise for the novel in *D.H. Lawrence: Novelist* and hostility at the time of the trial. His quotations from Leavis on this matter are slightly selective.

This is not so far from one of Leavis's favourite conversational analogies: literary criticism as carpet-laying; get it right in one corner, only to find an exasperating swelling out in another. Leavis's criticism, in which receptivity and implicit comparison mattered so much, liked to hang in with all the variations.

Leavis turned to Annan's 'pluralism' and 'compassion' in a lecture at York in October 1970. There he dealt with these value terms of liberalism in 'Pluralism, Compassion and Social Hope', a title that combined Snow ('social hope') and Annan ('pluralism', 'compassion'). The lecture was fairly general, about the use of language itself, contesting Annan's presumption that his value words were self-evidently meaningful. Leavis wanted to say radically (and insultingly) that they were literally out of currency: 'In our time it is very necessary to insist that the most important words . . . are incapable of definition.' He concluded his exordium: 'The defence of humanity entails their reclamation for genuine thought.' Leavis's position was to be strengthened when he published his own meditations on 'thought' – but this was to be five years away in the future, in *The Living Principle*.[27]

Leavis presumed that 'Pluralism, Compassion and Social Hope' would appear in *The Times Literary Supplement*. However, the editor (Arthur Crook: 'an elevated prater', according to Leavis) sent it back. Leavis therefore turned to the relatively obscure journal the *Human World*, edited by his old pupil Ian Robinson, with which he became associated up to its demise in 1974. The lecture was published in it in February 1971.[28]

In these late lectures Leavis used anecdote more freely than before. Incidents that might have been previously mentioned as asides in teaching were worked upon. There is Leavis hurrying through Cambridge on successive days, by a route that took him during Christian Aid Week past half a dozen churches: outside each there was 'the legend that invited my attention': 'Hunger is an unnecessary evil.' There was the 'student-politician' who held the floor about Mexican poverty at a York meeting about the future of universities, 'on which Leavis interposed and stopped him. He was very angry. "Dr Leavis's tears," he told the assembly, "are crocodile tears."' Annan had made the same complaint less bluntly: Leavis was 'disqualifyingly callous – patently incapable of the compassion that no decent person is without'. 'Compassion' was the latest ingredient of the orthodoxy of enlightenment. 'It confers confident superiority, and it costs nothing.' It is too often merely 'righteous' or 'malignly righteous'. Anecdotes, however, only gave points of focus and the lectures can hardly be called garrulous.

There were three strands that substantiated Leavis's anti-progressivist rhetoric. First, he contested 'distraction', calling for universities to attend to their proper business. The function of the tough and angry elder is to demand realism, and responsibility: he or she is there to tell the junior ruling class that it *can* act, and shrug off bland slogans (such as 'Politics is the art of the possible').

The second and third strands were more important. There was only a glimpse of the second, a flash of colour in the pattern, but without it the Leavis position lacked identity. On 'compassion', a presumably impregnable virtue, Leavis remarked that 'the pretension to sympathetic disinterestedness' masked 'self-indulgence'. Then: 'I am not thinking primarily of the point Lawrence makes when he observes that the compassion of "social hope" is self-pity.' Leavis was touching on the ethic of love as benevolence, and especially the critique of it by D.H. Lawrence.★ With this ethic he identified Bloomsbury, and, if only passingly in 'Pluralism, Compassion and Social Hope', he brought Lawrence up against Bloomsbury, represented here by Annan.

The third strand, as vividly coloured, is an evocation of the artist, here symbolically William Blake. It was axiomatic of Snow's 'Two Cultures' that the individual condition was tragic, but that there was 'social hope'. The core dispute was about enlightenment's differentiation of individual and social, and Leavis found the means of uniting the two (as he had done since the 1920s) in an idea of the artist, whose 'creativity' was the best idea of a condition that is neither social nor individual. Blake, and his concept of identity, became the Leavisian emblem for this necessary paradoxical state in 'Pluralism, Compassion and Social Hope'. 'Creativity' was bound into 'responsibility': 'The Blakean sense of human responsibility is as much the antithesis of the defiant Byronic hubris as it is of the hubris of "technologico-positivist" enlightenment.'

Blake was Leavis's embodiment of creativity on a grand scale; closer to ordinary conduct was the figure of Daniel Doyce, 'engineer and inventor', in Dickens's *Little Dorrit*. Dickens was introduced at the

★ In his copy of Lawrence's *Fantasia of the Unconscious* Leavis marked this passage: 'Whereas, in an idea of love and benevolence, we have always tried to automatize ourselves into little love-engines always stoked with the sorrows or beauties of other people, so that we can get up steam of charity or righteous wrath.'

climax of this lecture, an allusion made for several reasons, one of which was to reiterate that there was no old world or idealizable harmony in pre-twentieth-century Britain, but that there was none the less then a wealth of possibility for the adaptation of industrial innovation. On this occasion Dickens was his model for anti-Utopianism.

To this lecture a reply came from Annan, dealing with individuals rather than with the concept of the individual. He censured Leavis for attacking himself and other public figures, and for herding these figures into a block. In particular he pointed out that he had himself taken the unpopular course of defending elite universities in the mid-1960s. He reproved Leavis for his tactics, noting as especially odious the way he could blackguard other commentators on Dickens, especially Americans, including Edmund Wilson and Lionel Trilling, when they had led the way towards an appreciation of Dickens, while he had lagged behind, making *Hard Times* the centre of Dickensian gravity. It is certainly true that *The Great Tradition* did not open the subject of Dickens for Leavisians, however much Leavis himself believed (and with good faith) that the *Hard Times* chapter was an earnest of 'deferred commitment'. No Leavis pupils or students were working on Dickens (in Ph.D. dissertations, for instance) between 1948 and 1958. Leavis was ready for the subject to be opened only in the summer of 1962, when the signal went up from Leavis's essay on *Dombey and Son* in the *Sewanee Review*. Only then did Simon Gray begin his Ph.D. dissertation on Dickens.

Annan's reply presumed that the case against Leavis was easily made: the central subjects, like the high valuation given to the artist in social thinking by Leavis, were not debated. Very few of Snow's defenders went into the question of what status to give the thinking of artists in socio-cultural study, or into what the thoughts of artists were, or what the nature of their thinking was like. The key matter for Leavis was the transfer of art into thought and this was left largely unaddressed. Annan's reply to 'Pluralism, Compassion and Social Hope' appeared almost on the tenth anniversary of the Richmond Lecture. There had been few contributions above the Snow line that showed the thinking of artists (or 'art-speech', in Lawrence's phrase) was other than Luddite, or not capable of assimilation into the consideration of public policy.

In 1971 Leavis gave another 'field-performance' at York, a lecture called 'Elites, Oligarchies and an Educated Public'. It dealt partly with what

Leavis calls 'blankness', or again 'monstrous unrealism', that is, the intelligentsia's capacity (he claimed) for self-hypnosis by phrase-making. In the course of the lecture he told the story of talk about the First World War in an Oxford common-room, involving a young American, of research-student status, 'inquiring and obviously nice'.

Concluding that I was old enough to have been contemporary with the 1914 war, he asked me some questions about the moral impact on the country, and referred in due course to the Somme. I replied that, yes, I supposed the country *had* been profoundly disturbed; speaking as one who had found himself trying to tot up from the casualty-lists in the papers, and the odd reports, the sum of school-fellows dead in the morning, I didn't see how it could be otherwise. I added, still dwelling on a recalled particular sense of the general realization of disaster that shook the country, and not meaning in the least to imply irony – certainly not prepared for the response I drew, that those innumerable boy-subalterns who figured in the appalling Roll of Honour as 'Fallen Officers' had climbed out and gone forward, playing their part in the attacking wave, to be mown down with the swathes that fell to the uneliminated machine-guns. The comment, quietly sure of its matter-of-fact felicity, was: 'The death-wish!' My point is that I didn't know what to say. What actually came out was, 'They didn't *want* to die.' I felt I couldn't stop there, but how to go on. 'They were brave' – that came to me as a faint prompting, but no; it didn't begin to express my positive intention; it didn't even lead towards it. I gave up; there was nothing else to do.

That the phrase-maker here was 'inquiring and obviously nice' (and 'American': no disqualification this for respect from Leavis) did not damage Leavis's point. He was saying that some things were becoming unintelligible, 'values and possibilities that for reductive enlightenment don't exist'. 'Higher Education' may be counted on to 'confirm the reductive habit'.[29]

The essay in which this passage appeared was published with the other 'field-performances' in *Nor Shall My Sword* (1972). But Leavis deleted the whole passage about the boy-subalterns. Later the philosopher Michael Tanner wrote to him that he thought the passage one of the finest he had written. Leavis replied that he was very glad 'you feel as I do about that excised passage'. But

I was afraid it might lead some readers to suppose I was talking about myself. So in the end I cut it out. I'd listened [e.g. in the Somme salient] to the barrages, tormented by concern for the men on *both* sides.[30]

Liaison 1970–1974

In the winter of 1966/7 Leavis still regarded the Trust bitterly, his enmity directed principally at Shapira, the Gooders, John Newton and Harold Mason. He wrote a piece for the *Oxford Review*, unpublished, that he used to stake out his case against Mason, calling him, amidst much abuse, 'a classic', hardly for Leavis the innocent word it seems.[31] The day before the first of his Clark Lectures, Leavis wrote to Walsh, hoping that the *Oxford Review* piece would frighten Mason into cutting his losses, 'decamp before things get worse, or he sinks further into the morass'.[32] Time passed and Leavis referred less frequently to the Trust, though it was still an irritant that sometimes flared into angry life.

Since 1931 Leavis had enjoyed a stable relationship with Ian Parsons of Chatto & Windus – even though the firm published Tillyard. However, the Trust affair damaged the friendship. Chatto & Windus published Harold Mason's second book, *Shakespeare's Tragedies of Love*. Leavis was indignant to see Mason described as 'F.R. Leavis Lecturer' on the back of the book-jacket.[33] Parsons instructed his editorial staff to exclude all references to Mason as Leavis Lecturer (or even editor of *Scrutiny*) on Leavis book-jackets.[34] The memory of Allum and McKenzie's bibliographical *Check-List* (of the writings of F.R.L. and Q.D.L.) haunted Leavis, poisoning communication with Parsons. In 1973 he was angered by the fact that the revised edition of *Dickens the Novelist* went on sale at a higher price, but with no higher payment per copy for the Leavises. Parsons explained that they would not lose by the arrangement, and was very upset by the accusation of 'sharp' dealing. It was a charge relating to the *Check-List* that wounded him most, so deeply that he felt unable to make an immediate reply. Leavis alluded more cuttingly than usual to the 'scandal' that this publication (which, he said, he had never authorized) was used to raise money for the lectureship, something stated in the preface but which was against his own wishes. But, after discussion with Parsons, Leavis acknowledged that he had misinterpreted. He apologized, explaining that, while he had been 'mildly glad' that Allum and McKenzie would work together, having been introduced to them by Shapira ('indispensable Mosca'), he realized that there were connections with John Newton that made him shy away from the whole subject. 'The emotional field was insufferably horrible to me and my intensities therefore very selective.' He had believed that the *Check-*

List would be published only in Wellington, New Zealand. Leavis's apology to Parsons was less concerned with his own intensities than with Q.D.L.'s. He explained that he had long formed a habit of sparing her from whatever would touch off 'dangerous emotional intensities – hers are intense indeed. Vigilance can't be marked off from cowardice.' He explained how he kept his problems to himself. (On one occasion, travelling between Cambridge, Belfast and Cambridge, he had blacked out, having not eaten enough, and found himself in a pool of blood, after walking into a wall and being knocked unconscious. He failed to tell Q.D.L.) Leavis was miserable about having wounded Parsons.

In the early 1970s Mason approached retirement age. He decided to resign his Trust-sponsored position. He had the opportunity of a fellow-ship at the new graduate college, Clare Hall. There could be no question of a successor for him in the lectureship. Apart from Leavis's hostility, there was less than £30,000 in the fund, and commitment to a loan. In 1974 the question of disbursement of the fund arose. Only about £10,000 remained. Leavis was asked to a meeting, which he attended. He insisted on the appointment of some new trustees: Ian Robinson; Harry Coombes, a loyal Leavisian from Cheltenham who, on Leavis's recommendation, edited a large collection of criticism of D.H. Lawrence for Penguin Books; and John Tasker, the editor of *Letters in Criticism*.[35]

Leavis did, however, have support he valued from another quarter. In August 1972 wrote to Ian Robinson, his old pupil, then a Lecturer at Swansea, that 'my *liaison* idea *could* be actualized only at *this* statistically negligible point and *that*; and that Swansea could represent such a point would make a very significant difference'.[36] Leavis thought that a few souls were rallying, and that an excellent focal point would be Robinson, who had founded, edited and was managing the *Human World*.

Robinson was one of the most interesting of Leavis's pupils. He graduated in 1958, so he was of the *Cambridge Quarterly* generation. He researched in Cambridge, working on a Mason-related topic (pre-Shake-spearean verse), though he originally wanted a more Leavisian one (T.F. Powys). Quieter even than Newton but also shy, he was one of the poor scholars who supervised for Downing (in a farm-house, where students, muddy from their cycle ride, would help with its water-pump). He briefly had a research fellowship at Churchill, then took a permanent post in the University of Wales at Swansea.[37] He mixed with members of the philosophy department who were much engaged with Wittgen-stein studies. Robinson wrote freely and readably, with two books in the 1960s published by Cambridge University Press on Middle English literature and prosody; he also published essays on language, in *The Survival of English: Essays in Criticism of Language* (1973) acting as the linguistic observer of the 'orthodoxy of enlightenment'. In 1961 the New English Bible version of the New Testament appeared, and Robinson scrutinized its language in a brilliant essay for the *Cambridge Quarterly* called 'Religious English'. He specialized in remorselessly detailed observation, for instance, in one charting 'The Vulgarization of *The Times*'. Robinson was a natural pamphleteer, a common-sense Anglican, educated at Swansea into Wittgenstein and observant of case-law. In the spring of 1970 Robinson told Leavis that, having acquired an old printing-press, he and some friends had decided to sink some savings in a journal.

The *Human World* was, like the *Cambridge Quarterly*, meant to be more than literary, but the Cambridge journal had difficulty in finding non-literary articles: its only copious contributors were Mason and Newton, neither of whom dealt with the political and ethical issues that were meat and drink to Robinson. Also, unlike the *Cambridge Quarterly*, Robinson was sympathetic towards publishing creative writing. In these senses he was closer to the original *Scrutiny* ideals. He was prepared to write much of the journal himself (and set its type by hand). He also, again unlike the *Quarterly* editors, was prepared to pay contributors, a difficult but dignified decision. Robinson thought of calling the journal 'The Third Realm' (the area between private and public apostrophized by Leavis in the Richmond Lecture), but decided this was too obscure. He settled on the *Human World*, a reference to another passage in the lecture. Snow had proposed the intricacy of scientific knowledge as the 'most beautiful and wonderful collective work of man'. Leavis said there was another, prior work: 'the creation of the human world, including language'.[38] It was a good title. The journal began with a fierce attack on contraception and defence of chastity by the Roman Catholic philosopher G.E. Anscombe. This was the liberation era of (for instance) *The Little Red School Book* – which was caustically reviewed in the *Human World* by Andor and Susan Gomme.

Leavis supported Robinson. He believed that for a journal 'you need to generate and hold a public and be a feared, pervasive, haunting menace'.[39] He became a regular contributor. When Arthur Crook sent back Leavis's 'Pluralism, Compassion and Social Hope', it was Robinson's gain. A series of Leavis pieces then appeared in the *Human World* up to its demise.

Leavis had three other potential agents of liaison. One was Philip Dossé, editor and proprietor of *Books and Bookmen* and a string of other arts titles (*Plays and Players,* and so on). Leavis regarding him as somewhat naïve, rather in the same way as he looked upon Hugh Ross Williamson, editor of the *Bookman* and a Leavis fan of the 1930s. Leavis was slightly bemused by Dossé's enthusiasm. (Both F.R.L. and Q.D.L. had a penchant for 'real' journals, that is, journals without academic affiliations: the *New Review* might conceivably have counted, had it not had Arts Council backing.) The second supporter increased Leavis's reputation for affray, by editing his uncollected letters to the press, *Letters in Criticism* (1974). John Tasker, a Leavis enthusiast from Manchester University, had been so delighted with the Richmond Lecture that he offered to edit the collection of Leavis's letters, a scheme that Leavis approved only in 1973, therefore ensuring support from Chatto & Windus, which was cautious about Tasker's zeal. The collection contained useful material, but also a good deal of sniper-fire.[40]

The third 'liaison-officer' was a resourceful figure who had Tasker's indignation on behalf of Leavis, and some of his aggression, but also more experience of socio-literary cultural research. Garry Watson was a Sussex University graduate who had sent to Leavis a study of the reception (hostile) of his works. Its first title was 'A More Important Society: Situating the Leavises'. It was finally called *The Leavises, the 'Social' and the Left* (1977). Leavis was more delighted with the book than he had been with the interventions of Dossé, Tasker and even Robinson (whose care for 'philosophy' and Anglicanism unnerved him). He said it was a 'very intelligent book, incredibly fully documented (by an old *Left-Review* leftist) arguing the case for justice to "the Leavises"'.[41] The book was, indeed, important, but it was only published with difficulty. Chatto & Windus were dubious of it, claiming they were overloaded, and recommended Watson to try Cambridge University Press, where the book was applauded by Michael Black, 'but we can't do it'. Frank Kermode received thorough criticism from Watson, and he was on the board of management (the Syndics) of the Press. How could Black say to Kermode, 'Oh, look Frank, here's this excellent book, and of course he's pretty devastating about you, but you don't mind *really* do you?' Black very much disliked taking this part, saying it made him feel 'poltroonish'. He petitioned Dennis Enright at Chatto & Windus to reconsider publication. Enright was not so inclined, partly because 'it rakes up old quarrels in a manner inopportune (I feel) to what Leavis calls the "volte-face" in his favour – I cannot believe it would help that.'

The actual number of people who joined in with Leavis as 'liaison-workers' was extremely small. There were many more people, as deeply implicated in his criticism, who did not join his campaigns for various reasons. One reason was that the cultural problems adumbrated by Leavis had built into them an element of despairing unsolvableness. Leavis also solicited recognition of problems whose existence was manifestly clear: there was no point in following the Leavisian route to them when they were known. Also, many who acknowledged (and disliked) 'technologico-Benthamism' had to deal with it through the material or the techniques of their own academic disciplines – but Leavis, at this stage, did not recognize the significance (or existence) of such material and such disciplines. It was perfectly possible to agree with the visionary, but less easy to work within his own terms. At this stage of a career a collection or collections of essays by pupils are sometimes published, pushing forward the 'lesson of the master'. Some such books were mooted, but came to naught, largely because Leavis was unwilling to sanction contributions from those outside his immediate circle of 'liaison-officers'. After the Trust affair, it was understandable that he might feel he wanted to associate with only those of his friends who were closest to him in conviction and terminology. It was probably better that these projects did not get off the ground. The most constructive consideration of Leavis and tribute to him came not in book form but in a journal, *New Universities Quarterly*, edited now by Boris Ford. Its issue of December 1975 had several good essays, especially one from Michael Tanner that provoked a response by Leavis.

In early 1974 Robinson was sure the *Human World* could not survive: Q.D.L. deplored news that it was sinking. ('Praise from *her*!!!' ejaculated Leavis: the exclamation points are almost unique in his correspondence.) In August Leavis congratulated Robinson on having managed at least four years: 'a great achievement. The supreme tribute comes from Q.D.L. – most formidably and unrelentingly feminine of critical voices.' She said:

'Why couldn't the *Human World* have carried on? Now there's nothing to read – nothing to publish in.' She won't listen to my accounts of the advantages we enjoyed in Cambridge – and by a start in the 1930s.[42]

The *Human World* was an enclave in which Leavis could publish what mattered to him, unhampered by what he called the need to 'keep the royalty flow going'. The publishing world was, none the less, not at all uniformly hostile. In 1973 Heinemann Educational Books brought out an edition of *Lawrence on Hardy and Painting*, edited by J.V. Davies, whom Leavis had met and encouraged at York; he had urged Anthony Beal at Heinemann that Lawrence's book-length essay on Thomas Hardy should be in print. He congratulated Beal and Heinemann:

The appalling 'educational' output of the contemporary heavy industry is now a byword in the universities in routine cynical currency ... The Lawrence reprint won't be a best-seller, but the fact that Heinemann have made these pieces available will have been registered by that minority which still matters in education, and so to publishers (above all to the publishers of D.H.L.) [meaning Penguin]. I, though not advertised, am widely known as the Enemy of the industrialists, and as such have an influence that surprises me. I shall use the [Heinemann Educational Books] reprint at York in the coming academic year. Of course, I am impelled to make the most of *Phoenix*, but that volume must necessarily remain too costly for general use. But many of the *crème de la crème* I work with (largely young Lecturers from many places at home and abroad) will carry away tips and propaganda. I *had* thought of writing a commentary on those two pieces, and shall certainly be *talking* one next academic year. I may very well *write* it, but when (as I tell Chatto's about so many projects) I can't say: I have books on the stocks, (tho' I'm not old) have just turned 78.[43]

Thought and Memory: Wittgenstein, Montale 1973–1975

Since the late 1950s there had been estrangement from Leavis's eldest son, Ralph, who lived in Oxford. Leavis visited him alone, more frequently in the course of his post-retirement lecturing forays. In 1973, at the age of seventy-seven, Leavis's anxiety was intensified 'to push on with the retrieval of Ralph', who, he believed, had been damaged by his experiences as an undergraduate at Oxford, and at Dartington Hall, the progressive boarding-school in Devon. He 'never came back from Oxford', where he was befriended and helped by the Miss Denike sisters, well known in Oxford musical circles. One Miss Denike was now dead. Leavis believed that at length a connection was being made for which he had hoped for twenty years.[44]

In 1972–3 Leavis was engaged in some retrospective considerations. He was in the life-period of reminiscence; he turned his recollections to typical effect. The phase can be dated back to the spring of 1969, when he went to Italy to lecture and had Eliot on his mind for the sake of lectures or seminars at York.

Yes, I *have* some drastic limitations to urge *re* Eliot's 'reality'; – not merely some 'Yes buts', but some Noes. Limited? – it's starved, and there's too much 'Baudelaire at any rate believed in damnation' about it.[45]

'Baudelaire' is a telegrammatic reference to Leavis's dislike of Eliot's belief in the sanity of believing in damnation (greater sanity than in Lawrence's desire to make 'the sex relation valid and precious, not shameful'). In Milan Leavis met the great Italian poet Eugenio Montale, almost an exact contemporary. They discovered together they could recite from memory tracts of Valéry's *Le Cimetière marin* which Leavis associated with a memory of Eliot quoting Thibaudet in 1924 praising the 'reticence' of Mallarmé, his rejection of personality. 'To reduce one's disorderly and mostly silly personality to the gravity of a *jeu de quilles* [game of skittles] would be to do an excellent thing.'[46] Montale's poetry appeared to provide an antidote to Eliot, to be austere but personal, spontaneously natural with the 'wiry bounding line' of Blake. At York *Le Cimetière marin* became the work by means of which Leavis demonstrated the 'Noes' about Eliot he had been formulating. He was still alive to his history of criticism of (and disappointment with) Eliot, as well as distrusting what he believed to be Eliot's factitious impersonality.

I recoil from Eliotic Christianity, and hope to make it plain some time that, as I see it, what 'tech-B' [i.e. technologico-Benthamite] spiritual Benthamism calls for is not *his* kind of answer. But (apart from writing his poetry) he was the *enemy* of creativity all his life . . . I must try and find courage and tact to come out with the full commentary I've *contained* on the terza rima passage in 'Little Gidding' . . . Some of the things in that 'Little Gidding' passage he said to me, when – I learnt later – he was writing 'Little Gidding'. He might have said more if I'd encouraged him. I didn't; merely listened and looked inquiringly at him.[47]

It is clear that Leavis had to return to Eliot after his 'field-performances' against 1960s pluralism and materialism. Could not Eliot be thought to provide in *Four Quartets* a gateway to the spiritual? It would seem to posit an idea of society *as* spiritual, not as a 'universe of little things', as Coleridge called it. Leavis wanted, however, to block off Eliot as a source. This procedure was accomplished, though, with intense sympathy in his York lectures, which appeared in 1975 as the third part of a new book, *The Living Principle: 'English' as a Discipline of Thought*; the third part consisted of a long close-reading of *Four Quartets*. In 'Thought, Language and Objectivity' (the first section of *The Living Principle*) Leavis mustered new resources for an account of the spiritual, positive alternatives to 'technologico-Benthamism'. It should not be thought that there was plain rejection of Eliot, for there was much of him in at least one of the two words upon which Leavis relied for his current definition of the spiritual, terms that became a signature of his writing of the 1970s. One word was English, 'nisus'; the other German, *Ahnung*.[48] *Ahnung* was used for (approximately) 'instinct'. 'Nisus' was close to 'will' of a special sort and related to Eliot because

I first found that I needed the word 'nisus' in discussing *Ash-Wednesday*. The problem is to define the sense in which Eliot has become religious. He will not affirm because he cannot . . . 'Nisus' is irreplaceable. In explaining its necessity one has to invoke something like Blake's distinction. 'Effort' doesn't suffice; it implies conscious, explicitly realized, and deliberate purpose, and these tend to imply what Lawrence points to diagnostically with the triad, 'ego, will and idea'. The need for a word that eliminates this suggestion is implicit in Blake's 'I know that it is not mine'.

And it was implicit in *Ash-Wednesday* because while Eliot could there not affirm merely with the will, after the nihilism of *The Hollow Men* and *The Waste Land*, he found within himself a drive, a 'will-not-willed', which (said Leavis, without hostility) was 'a Christian nisus'.

As for the other term, *Ahnung*, it was 'intimately related', but something with which Eliot could give no help.

Ahnung is unnaturalized German that must clearly remain unnaturalized . . . I found no English substitute. Lawrence, in the 'Study of Thomas Hardy', I noticed, uses 'inkling' – uses it more than once. But, pondering the kind of argument for which I should want it, I decided that it hadn't enough weight – hadn't a grave enough charge of suggestiveness. 'Inkling' can translate 'Ahnung' as used in some German contexts, but it can hardly suggest anticipatory anticipation that carries the weight implicit in 'foreboding' which is often the right rendering of 'Ahnung'.

Leavis added a reference to one of his new sources:

You can hardly read [Michael] Polanyi without perceiving that *he* requires such a word. I haven't time to remind myself what word he actually uses. I don't derive from philosophers: I merely *use* them tactically. – D.H.L. has many Laurentian ways of responding to this need.[49]

Leavis opposed Snow's 'Benthamism' with his 'Third Realm', the collaborative space between discourses, and to define it he drew on several discursive thinkers or philosophers. He now recommended four books to his York students: Marjorie Grene's *The Knower and the Known*, Michael Polanyi's *Knowing and Being* (a collection of his essays edited by Grene), R.G. Collingwood's classic, *The Idea of Nature*, and, at a lighter level, J. Andreski's *Social Sciences as Sorcery*, blasting pseudo-science and 'the advanced stage of cretinization which our civilization has reached under the impact of the mass media'.[50] Leavis, debonair, said that he happened across the work of Marjorie Grene in Heffer's old bookshop in Petty Cury, 'poking round the philosophy shelves'. But it could be said that Polanyi and Collingwood were lying in wait for him. Polanyi spoke out in 1959 on the occasion of Snow's lecture on the Two Cultures, calling for the biological sciences, including psychology, to be 'emancipated from the scourge of physicalism'. It appeared in *Knowing and Being* and Leavis could have remembered its original appearance in *Encounter*. As for Collingwood, it is evident from Leavis's chapter on 'Burnt Norton' in *The Living Principle* that he had known *The Idea of Nature* for some years. The major part of *The Idea of Nature* for Leavis was its conclusion, an attack on Alfred North Whitehead. He had known about Whitehead from the excellent essay of 1934 in *Scrutiny* by James Smith, giving a critique as remorseless as Collingwood's of Whitehead's concept of nature as endless flux, exciting 'novelty', suitable for enthusiasts forever seeking 'a keener thrill':

It is necessary only to consider with whom, and against whom, he ranges himself. On his side and speaking his language are the group Movement, the Scout Movement, the Rotary Movement, the cinema poster; opposed to him are Plato, Aristotle, and all those who stand in the main tradition of European thought.[51]

Polanyi was for Leavis in the main tradition of European thought, seeking (Marjorie Grene showed) what Meno sought of Socrates, the kind of knowledge of the unscientifically, non-objectively shadowy: 'Why, on what lines will you look, Socrates, for a thing of whose nature you know nothing at all?' Leavis's allies were unhappy at his terminologies and new abstractions, although he was as emphatic as ever that philosophy as normally practised did not interest him. Ian Robinson thought he belaboured Eliot with jargon.[52] Michael Tanner took him to task for being impressed by 'an insignificant work of philosophy which he had chanced upon in Heffer's', to which Leavis replied with manifest sincerity that he did, indeed, have limitations, and

I'm not being modest when I say I'm very slow. There is such a lot of literature, and so little help in dealing with it. And who can draw a line round the Study of English Literature (*Life and Thought!*)? . . . What I'm avowing is that I'm not philosophical in the innocent sense (now archaic) of the word. I'm 'engaged' and embattled – and terrified.[53]

The remarks may not seem directly related to the charge of taking too seriously thinkers (Grene, Polanyi, Collingwood) who did not impress Tanner. If there was such a lot of literature, could these thinkers help? No, surely, was the answer: but they could ring it against an enemy that denied the viability of the 'Third Realm', that realm epitomized by 'English'. For 'English' was not a syllabus or curriculum, but a cipher for a spiritual condition. Leavis remarked, in the context of an account of his current ideas by P.N. Furbank, that it was a mistake to believe that 'my assigning a central place to English is to be understood in terms of formal institutionality'.[54]

Although Tanner could not get interested in Leavis's play with the humanistic biologists, he was seriously hopeful of engaging Leavis in some cross-relationship with philosophy. Leavis perpetually claimed not to be a philosopher, but Tanner assured him that 'the problems with which you are dealing when considering such things as the autonomy of the human world and how we should see our relations to it *are* philosophical questions'.[55] It seems that Robinson, and possibly Tanner, considered persuading Leavis to take an interest in Wittgenstein and he was not unwilling to do so from Christmas 1971, thickly and antipathetically annotating the margins of David Pears's short 'Modern Masters' book about Wittgenstein.[56] He spoke of writing on Wittgenstein in late 1970. In the summer of 1972, staying in a Cheltenham vicarage ('I refused to undertake marriages or christenings or services, but was ready to give spiritual advice'), he did not make any progress, but sent Robinson a piece on William Blake for the *Human World*. He was nervous of work on Wittgenstein ('delicate and difficult'): 'I *had* to touch on my "philosophical" (damn philosophy!) disagreement with Wittgenstein, but knew I mustn't get philosophically *involved*.'[57] At the end of August he managed to get something written, sent it to Robinson and invited him to revise it if necessary. He was anxious to avoid the 'possible suggestion of anything in the nature of name-dropping – and I've nothing of philosophic interest to offer'.[58] Having read David Pears, he wanted to show Wittgenstein was humanly subtle and that in his presence there may be a clue as to liaison between 'poetic' and conceptual thinking.

It's dreadful to be supposed that Pears fairly represents – or at all – Wittgenstein, who was a genius and very subtle. Nor do I suppose that 'philosophers' are no good – any more than I'd say that about Englishers. About both categories we know – what we know about human arrangements and human nature, even academic. I've really meant what I've said about the necessity of 'co-presence', and, even if I had not read any patch of Wittgenstein's later work I should have known that he could provide the right education for a Moral Science elite. My liaison idea could be actualized only at this statistically negligible point and that Swansea could represent such a point would make a very significant difference. Hope must depend on 'small things'.[59]

Part of the Leavis legend was that he was concerned only with 'words on the page', scorning the involvement of personalities in criticism. This was true, to a degree, though it could hardly be fully so, given Leavis's reiterated conviction that literature came from the way that language was used in real communities. The legend also made Leavis's own methods sound more austere than they were; scraps of reminiscence surfaced in his prose, like his allusion to the World's Classics volume of Milton he carried through the war or to the issue of *Commerce* in which he read the beginnings of *Ash-Wednesday*. In the early 1970s there were two pieces more or less dependent on memories, the essays on Wittgenstein and on Montale. Of Wittgenstein Leavis wrote a detailed reminiscence of the occasions on which the men met in company, or alone at Chesterton Hall Crescent or on long walks; Leavis does not appear to have visited Wittgenstein in his lodging in Frostlake Cottage, Malting House Lane, on the edge of Newnham by the Granta river-inlets. Wittgenstein 'began a practice of dropping in from time to time for a couple of years'. We saw earlier some of what Leavis had to say about his own valiant defence of a young man snubbed by Wittgenstein, at a Sunday afternoon tea at the house of W.E. Johnson and his sister, Miss Fanny, where philosophers young and old gathered.★

★ See Chapter Three, Exciting Strangeness, 'Precarious Terms 1928–1929'.

The essay is an extraordinary narrative, with moments of wry comedy.

'Memories of Wittgenstein' contains two grand set-pieces. One is the account of the occasion on which Wittgenstein turned up after lunch, his visit running into one of the customary Friday teas. During the gathering Wittgenstein drew attention to himself ('ensuring full general attention') by picking up a volume of Proust that topped the pile by his chair. Printed large on the torn NRF cover was the title: *Sodome et Gomorrhe.* 'With quiet diagrammatic intensity', Wittgenstein seemed to address the room at large. 'This is the world!' he said. Then, after the guests had gone, he was unwilling to part; Leavis eventually accompanied him to give a paper to the Moral Science Club. Then there is Leavis's rendering, in Hardyesque fashion, of a nocturnal expedition up-river, during which Wittgenstein wanted to explore Trumpington Feast, evident from a glow in the sky and the thump of steam-engines. Leavis persuaded him to return – because the canoe-attendant had to wait for them to go home.

'Memories of Wittgenstein' was full of messages, though rigid inter-pretation would be inadvisable. It could be argued that Leavis 'saw himself' in Wittgenstein, especially in the passage in which he described him as a teacher, a role in which he did not particularly admire the philosopher for reasons that were later advanced for not admiring Leavis: an exclusiveness of effect. Leavis remarked that he believed (heard from W.E. Johnson) that once a pupil went to Wittgenstein, he would henceforth have little time for other teachers, and didn't necessar-ily come away from Wittgenstein with ability enhanced. Then, Leavis dealt with Wittgenstein as an exponent of 'yes, but' – one who was all 'yes' and little 'but'. The same was said of Leavis. Discussion was carried on *by*, not *with* Wittgenstein. The value of his presence was in watching 'the sustained spontaneous effort of intellectual genius wrestling with its self-proposed problems'. Leavis took pains to say that he did not have a chance to hear Wittgenstein talking with his peers, nor was he qualified to engage with him as a philosopher. All he wanted to show was that there were certain contacts, certain 'memories' (with quotation marks persistently included by Leavis) that made him see an absence of two-way communication, but *none the less* rare distinction in the presence of the thinker. One could, passingly, say that the account points to Leavis's own intellectual demeanour (though he presents himself in the essay amusingly as a straight-man feed to Wittgenstein). What the essay brings into focus is further thought about the 'Third Realm'.

There are two other implications in 'Memories of Wittgenstein'. On one occasion Wittgenstein simply arrived to exclaim to Leavis *'tout court'*, 'Give up literary criticism!' Nothing else is recorded by Leavis on this subject. He does describe a conversation in which he tutored Wittgenstein in Empson's poem 'Legal Fiction', though the explication fizzled out because it was plain that Wittgenstein could do literary analysis perfectly well unaided. 'He went through the poem, explaining the analogical structure that I should have explained myself, if he had allowed me.' But it is not in connection with this incident that Wittgenstein said, 'Give up literary criticism!' It was, indeed, said *tout court*. It is unlikely that Wittgenstein was saying that Leavis should give up his *own* style of literary criticism, which hardly existed, legibly, in 1929. He must have been referring to Cambridge literariness (perhaps George Rylands or F.L. Lucas at King's). Certainly Leavis presumed he meant Bloomsbury for 'frequenting the Bloomsbury milieu . . . he couldn't in any case imagine that literary criticism might matter intellectually'.[60] Leavis knew that literary criticism at that date as yet hardly existed: it is almost certain that the exchange took place before *Seven Types of Ambiguity*, and it must not be forgotten how little hard evidence of exacting literary criticism there was before its publication in 1930. There were numerous exciting initiatives, but not so much practice, from Cambridge at any rate. Richards had written. But how many pages on actual poems? Leavis understood Wittgenstein to be exclaiming in negatively prophetic fashion, implying there was no such thing yet as respectable literary criticism. But

Even at that time I had an opposing conviction: it was, as it is, that the fullest use of language is to be found in creative literature, and that a great creative work is a work of original thought.

'Give up literary criticism!' did not mean 'Stop writing, Leavis!' (One would like it to have meant 'Become a philosopher!') The tough judgement was of something else. His expostulation may even have referred to I.A. Richards for whom (according to Leavis) Wittgenstein had little time. In the 'Memories' he recalled complying with Wittgenstein's desire for an explanation of 'Basic English'. Leavis 'told him'. Wittgenstein only said: 'Would he do *that*!' Once, Wittgenstein called at Chesterton Hall Crescent and scrutinized a snapshot of Richards 'my wife had put on our drawing-room mantel-piece'. He looked up to remark, 'Hm! you can see that he has a mildewed soul.'[61]

In April 1973, after 'Memories of Wittgenstein' was published, Leavis recounted to Robinson that 'an elderly don', stopping him outside King's, said he knew the Bloomsbury ethos and disliked J.M. Keynes. It is puzzling that the old gentleman fastened on the presence of Keynes in 'Memories of Wittgenstein' – for he is hardly given an appearance. On the other hand, it is hard not to believe that Leavis was consciously erecting Wittgenstein into a monument of an intellectual type more distinguished (he thought) than Keynes. Keynes and King's went together for Leavis, and went with homosexuality. Leavis found in Wittgenstein a distinction, perhaps a 'purity', though he does not use the word himself. He may have been unaware of Wittgenstein's homosexuality; he acknowledged him to be 'tortured'. In a letter written in 1976, unusual in criticizing Wittgenstein, and in its frankness, Leavis commented that

Wittgenstein, for my liking, was too much at home in Bloomsbury–King's. But I saw no signs in him of the Bloomsbury–King's cult. But he was a formidable personality, and, if he were known to be anti-buggery, would strike the most brazen King's-normal as 'innocent'.[62]

It is clear that Leavis thought that in some respect Keynes was *defined* by his sexuality. One function of 'Memories of Wittgenstein' was to make the model of one type, an ineffable one, of twentieth-century distinction, human as well as intellectual. And the richness of the setting, accomplished with novelist's flair, achieved one expressive function: Wittgenstein was cast into honorary membership of Old Cambridge, a statue along with Sidgwick, Haddon and Chadwick.

Leavis's meeting with Montale in Milan in 1969 had more consequence than to put him in mind of Valéry's Le Cimetière marin and Eliot's hunger for control. Montale was born within a few months of Leavis, and by the 1960s he was established as a modern classic in Italy, indeed, internationally. In 1963 he suffered the loss of his wife. The Italian literary world was astonished when in his mid-seventies he published three new, substantial collections of verse, including a series of poems about the loss of his wife, 'Xenia I' and 'Xenia II'. In 1971 Leavis published an essay, 'Eugenio Montale's "Xenia"'. He dismissed it as a 'bluff': 'I'm not qualified to be a critic of Italian', saying – he may have pretended diffidence – that he felt coerced into writing this piece, which was to be translated for an Italian collection. Recently an Indian Professor

of Italian literature from Queen's University, Belfast, Ghan Shyam
Singh, had made himself known to Leavis and taken great pains to
introduce his work into Italy, including arranging the visit to Milan. He
was translating Montale, and Leavis, liking Singh, an enthusiastic *littéra-
teur* with perfect manners, felt some obligation to him. 'He's a Rajput,
high caste, very intelligent and disinterested as aristocrats sometimes
are.'[63] (Singh joined the group of semi-foreigners – Marius Bewley
included, though in this case there was actual collaboration – with
whom, over the years, Leavis felt at ease.) In the end he agreed to write
on Montale because the poet 'himself might not have believed that I'd
declined out of genuine modesty'.[64]

Leavis had long admired Thomas Hardy's sequence of poems of
1912–13 written after the death of his wife. The analysis of 'Hereto I
come to view a voiceless ghost' was included in the never published
'Authority and Method', the poem quietly recited to Peter Greenham in
Downing College Hall when sitting for his portrait. In Montale's poems
Leavis found something that, in some respects, exceeded Hardy – and
Eliot. The poems were limpid, austere, but lacked the tightening of
Eliot's controls. They were as personal as Hardy's, but there was no
straining in them to fight against Victorian 'poetic diction', no effort *not*
to be eloquent in poems that were more plainly speakable in a modern
language (Italian) than Hardy's. 'Montale is immensely more subtle,
more supple and more diverse than Hardy. The fact is apparent at once
in the texture of the verse (hardly a felicitous metaphor – but what
better is there?).' Although Leavis wanted to say that Montale exceeded
Eliot, lacking his studied 'reticence', it was as if Leavis was again
discovering what it was in Eliot that first generated his passion for
poetry in 'Portrait of a Lady'. Most of all Leavis appeared to enjoy the
sense of a person in the poems, that is, Mosca, the late wife of Montale.
The relations of husband and wife were evoked, he said, 'in representative
particularity', with a 'day-to-day ordinariness'. Leavis himself had his
'reticences' or 'matter-of-factness' (as found in Isaac Rosenberg).* Into

---

* On Rosenberg and 'matter-of-factness', see Chapter One, Origins, 'War 1915–1919'. It
is interesting to compare the 'Xenia' poems with Shelley's 'When the Lamp is Shattered'
and Leavis's accounts of them (of the Shelley, in *Revaluation*, pp. 216–20). Leavis's
distaste for Shelley's poem and applause for Montale derive from the same source in
him. See Chapter Five, 'To Downing College', 'Downing English 1931–1936', which
mentions Stephen Spender's strictures about Leavis's reading of 'When the Lamp is
Shattered'.

his admiration of these love poems of a widower it is hard not to read Leavis's losses, and what may have been a fearful, and must have been a vivid, anticipation of loss in his experience of the frailty of Q.D.L. He quoted several examples of Montale's own 'matter-of-factness': 'There is no nuance here of cynicism or doubting hesitance in the face of contemplated reality.' One extract is:

E strano che a comprenderti
siano riucite solo persone inverosimili.

Strange that only
Improbable persons could understand you.

Part Five

EPILOGUE

1975–1978

You see, I know that it's difficult to think well about 'certainty', 'probability', 'perception', etc. But it is, if possible, still more difficult to think, or *try* to think, really honestly about your life and other people's lives. And the trouble is that thinking about these things is *not thrilling* but often downright nasty. And when it's nasty then it's most important.

— Ludwig Wittgenstein in George Malcolm's *Memoir of Wittgenstein*, quoted by Leavis in 'Mutually Necessary', *New Universities Quarterly*, 1976

Still Writing

Leavis's eightieth birthday fell on 14 July 1975. It was widely noticed, notably in a radio programme produced by Philip French called 'Leavis at Eighty: What Has His Influence Been?' John Tasker had wanted a *Festschrift* on the theme of the 'Two Cultures'. Chatto & Windus were relieved when Leavis withdrew his support. Tasker had edited *Letters in Criticism*, the collection of Leavis's letters to the press, in 1974; it was planned as early as 1966 and supported by Leavis, but had a bumpy ride at Chatto & Windus, where both Parsons and Dennis Enright were embarrassed by the 'us-or-them' tone of its apparatus. Leavis's hackles were not raised by Enright. It often happened that an ally or pupil survived in favour if he practised a discipline outside English literature; Enright was a German scholar and a poet, and, in any case, a decent man. 'He had to make his way in the world as it is. I, *puritano frenetico*, have survived against that world, after a very hard life in which my highly gifted wife has suffered worse than myself.'[1] (Leavis much enjoyed the phrase *puritano frenetico*, which had been used of him in a newspaper when he visited Italy and met Montale.)

At the age of eighty questions arose about a biography. In the summer of 1974 Chatto & Windus commissioned a study of Leavis, with minimal biographical material, by William Walsh, former pupil, then Professor of Education at Leeds University; it appeared in 1980. In October 1975 a long biographical essay 'Leavis at Eighty: A Biography' appeared in the *New Review* with a striking photograph of the schoolboy Leavis on the cover. A year later it was published by Heinemann Educational Books, managed by a former pupil, Anthony Beal. The book was a brief but a well-researched and enthusiastic study, drawing on useful reminiscences. Leavis 'leafed it over loosely' to decide it was no good: he was committed to disdain by its provenance: the *New Review* was funded by the Arts Council, that Keynesian body, and its editor, Ian Hamilton, was tarred by friendship with John Gross, former editor of *The Times Literary Supplement*, but principally an object of offence as author of *The Rise and Fall of the Man of Letters: English Literary Life since 1800*. This was a lively trespass upon the field of Q.D.L. and addressed the issue of varying roles for literary students (mainly academe versus literary journalism, with Leavis seated uneasily between). Gross's book was fairly favourably reviewed by R.G. Cox in the little Cambridge magazine *Delta*, Leavis's sympathy for Cox then cooling. Leavis himself began to consider autobiography, but not for long. In January 1973 he wrote to John Tasker that he had been urged to write his memoirs; but there was no time. The distress and excitement to Q.D.L., if the subject of his career was being aired while writing about it, would endanger her health. He vowed that the story of Tillyard's domination over the English Faculty, and his use of Potts and Henn to keep him out, would remain untold, or that no more would be told than in his introduction to the Clark Lectures.[2] He continued to believe, or at least say to Q.D.L., perhaps in order to side-step the subject, that a woman might be able to tell the story of the intimate professional wounding, but that he could not. That he should not want such an account to be part of his *œuvre* hardly needs explaining. Q.D.L. planned to put the facts on record after Leavis's death, but her memoir was never written.[3]

An offshoot of Hayman's *Leavis* was consideration of the publication processes of Leavis's work in the publishing world. Beal at Heinemann rather drily, as one publisher to another, drew Ian Parsons's attention to Hayman's remarks about the apparent casualness with which the material in *The Common Pursuit* was presented. Parsons (and Leavis himself) became aware of the uncollected material that might still be published. Leavis had some favourite essays like 'The "Great Books" and a Liberal

Education', a review written for the American journal *Commentary* about the *Encyclopaedia Britannica* culture-library with complementary 'Synopticon'. He considered reprinting his landmark rejection of Richards, 'Dr Richards, Bentham and Coleridge', but 'chivalry is in the way of my reprinting it now. I.A.R. (CH) is an old man and decayed.'[4] (Richards had been given one of the highest British civil honours, Companion of Honour.) Leavis did want to see in print 'one of the best things I've done', a lecture given at Bristol University in 1970, 'Wordsworth: The Creative Conditions', which had only appeared in America. In his last years Leavis was preoccupied with Wordsworth, the artist who made the late start, and in whom springs of creative energy dried early. He especially wanted to put on record his lifetime appreciation of 'The Ruined Cottage', a poem of devastation. He began to consider Wordsworth's best poems as epitomizing the type of 'perfect poem' in the creation of which individuality is transformed unanimity, and in the reading of which minds may meet. His 'Notes on Wordsworth' were first published after his death in *Valuation in Criticism* (1986).

Leavis was still writing. He wanted to add a third book to his recent two, making a 'triad'.[5] *The Living Principle* (1975) was essentially an 'Eliot book' in which the long reading of *Four Quartets* supported the initial general section. It was matched by the 'Lawrence book', *Thought, Words and Creativity: Art and Thought in Lawrence* (1976). He planned a third that he may have wished to call *The Critic as Anti-Philosopher*. A book of that name appeared after his death containing a range of mostly late essays. It is not altogether certain whether it is what Leavis intended (or, indeed, whether he had a sharply defined intention). Possibly he meant to write something less anthological, as is suggested by the 'headings' (his term) that he planned, quoted by Singh, the editor of the volume (and one of his literary executors).[6] Some of this thinking was provoked by contributions that appeared in an eightieth birthday celebration issue of *New Universities Quarterly*, mentioned above, especially an essay by the young philosopher, Michael Tanner, who had been a good aide to Leavis. His 'Literature and Philosophy' evoked a reply from Leavis early in 1976, forty-five pages of handwriting called 'Mutually Necessary' that he dispatched rather grudgingly to the journal.[7] Leavis had never been fond of the editor, Boris Ford, partly because he believed that Ford's *Pelican Guide to English Literature* was one factor that caused the demise of *Scrutiny*: it had used up the time and energies of potential contributors.

'Anti-philosophy' was certainly a Leavisian term, meaning unwilling-ness to define criteria of literary judgement explicitly; it also referred to the philosopher's way of handling words with less absorption than the literary critic. 'Mutually Necessary' had a section in which Leavis went again over the arguments with which, many years earlier, he had taxed René Wellek, who had been puzzled about the basis and authority of Leavis's judgements.* However, if 'anti-philosophy' was really intended to be in the title of a third book of a 'triad', Leavis was misleading himself and his readers, for his argument with Tanner was that literary criticism and philosophy *were* mutually necessary. There was no question of giving literary criticism primacy. Leavis, in old age, was now giving special emphasis to the thinking of literature, the means by which it could be taken seriously *as* thinking: the word 'thought' ought to appear almost redundant, but is not, for lack of agreement in the points Leavis was trying to establish. His reply to Tanner shows yearning for a link with philosophy, 'one of the necessary intellectual disciplines'. Indeed, it was more than *a* discipline, given the degree to which literature was shaped by philosophy. But where was the time-pressed student to go to become even slightly qualified in philosophy? Clearly not Russell's *History of Western Philosophy* and not, perhaps, Marjorie Grene and Michael Polanyi, whom Tanner believed to be marginal. Tanner himself did not quite come close to satisfying his need. As it turned out, almost the opposite of what Leavis wanted became current: hostility to philoso-phy was conveyed by the phrase 'anti-philosophy'. *The Critic as Anti-Philosopher* congealed a reputation as a pragmatist and moralist.† The title hardly did justice to his yearning for 'thought'.

The End

In the summer of 1977 Leavis was going downhill. He was liable to blackouts, sometimes confused about the time of day, with numerous physical ailments.[8] But he wrote on. In April a well-wisher in India wrote in to Chatto & Windus for news of the book he had heard Leavis was writing. The publisher could not help, nor was Q.D.L. able to find

* See Chapter Five, 'To Downing College', 'Leavis's History 1936'.
†What Leavis meant by 'philosophy' was not necessarily 'theory' – nor was his 'theory' the 'Critical Theory' of the 1970s and after.

a manuscript in his study, clearance of which, she said, would be a herculean task.

In the summer Leavis had the strength (or provocation) to correspond briefly with David Holbrook. Holbrook had detected a reference to himself in *Thought, Words and Creativity*, published the previous summer. In the chapter 'The Captain's Doll' Leavis mentioned two commentators on his use of the word 'life'. Neither was named. One was Roger Poole, an English Lecturer at Nottingham University, with a strong philosophical training, and the other, whom Leavis identified only as 'a well-known indefatigible publicist on the themes of pornography', was Holbrook, who was understandably hurt. He wrote to Leavis that to reprove a man who was actually his ally was inappropriate, indeed, 'jealous' or even 'wicked'.[9] Leavis replied promptly, in an exceptionally shaky hand but with no intellectual hesitation. Leavis told Holbrook that he always had a low opinion of him, and 'now you come out with your "wicked", it's the time to let you have it'. Holbrook did not know how ill Leavis was. Despite its savagery, Leavis ended his letter with a caveat; Holbrook was, after all, a pupil. 'Don't be silly. But you have energy and ambition.'[10]

Q.D.L. was caring for Leavis alone, with occasional weekend help from Kate Leavis, who looked after the house, garden and her parents as much as she could. Leavis had begun to show his age: he could be irritable and dictatorial. He seemed not to take in what was said, but his hearing could be painfully sharp, once his ears had been syringed. He had an intermittent speech defect that obliged him to repeat phrases, to the embarassment of Q.D.L. when there were visitors. He was grateful for the warmth of Q.D.L. and Kate. 'That is very *reassuring*,' he would say, the word frequently used. (He was 'reassured' when Q.D.L. had a large electric clock put in his room.) His appetite varied; on one occasion straight after dinner he went to the kitchen, saying, 'Didn't I hear some mention of breakfast?' He dozed and slept in the daytime, but at night would escape vigilance, and, after being seen to bed, might go out in dressing-gown and slippers for a night walk, returning cold and wet. Q.D.L. appealed to the former pupil and schoolmaster Brian Worthington to find a medical friend who could explain Leavis's moods; she herself was reminded of *King Lear*. In 1977 some of the illnesses of old age were less common knowledge than, say, fifteen years later.

In the autumn of 1977 Brian Worthington noticed how his frailty contrasted with the substantial meals set out by Q.D.L. for such a visitor as himself. As usual, he hardly ate but quite frequently took a little brandy. Worthington sat at his bedside one evening. Leavis said to him that people thought him happy, but this could not be further from the truth. There is no reason to believe that he was speaking of the present. The next day he was helped outside to catch the sun, moving restlessly from cane armchair to folding aluminium one. Worthington saved him when he stumbled, snagging a hand, which he held up for Q.D.L. to bring elastoplast. Later, when settled and Q.D.L. was indoors, he still showed signs that he was both alarmed by and protective of Q.D.L.'s buoyancy.[11]

Nothing would occupy him. Worthington suggested buying a tortoise to Q.D.L., knowing his love of the garden and creatures. Outdoors, he imagined things, including butterflies. He thought he saw Red Admirals, but could not see the Painted Ladies he expected. Q.D.L. told him they were everywhere, blending with the leaves.

At times it seemed unlikely Leavis could last long. None the less, though Q.D.L. believed he was suffering from 'chronic brain syndrome', Leavis was in basic good health and she believed the present condition would continue indefinitely. He said he longed for oblivion.[12] She was afraid of what would happen if she had a heart attack, especially when she was dealing with Leavis's night-time departures. The doctor persuaded Leavis to sign a power of attorney so that Q.D.L. could handle the bank account, something that had always been in his control. He agreed; Q.D.L. was surprised to find £17,000 'wasted' in a current account. She was able now to get a home-help for two hours, once a week; not more because Leavis was not strictly bed-ridden. A former pupil and monk, Dom Hilary Steuart, from Downside School, called and Q.D.L. was taken aback when he asked if he might gently urge Leavis to think of salvation. She unwillingly agreed, but understood Dom Hilary's professional obligation. She was uneasy to see him troubling one who was 'not really compos', the son of a Victorian Rationalist. The solicitations distressed Leavis; Q.D.L. paid the price of a very bad night.[13]

By the end of 1977 Leavis was often confused. He puzzled Q.D.L. by associating ideas and feelings with objects. On one occasion, he held her hand urgently, and said, gazing at her in anguish, that he was troubled by a problem. It was the problem of decency, he said, something that had become increasingly urgent to him. He pointed to a tea-cup, which met his eye as he came into the room; he murmured that it represented the problem.[14]

Before Christmas Q.D.L. wrote to Ralph Leavis, asking him to come; he replied that he was too busy. An old friend of the family, Etain Kabraji, who had been at school with Ralph at Dartington Hall and later at Newnham, found a photograph of Ralph at the age of about twelve in the school orchestra, with someone helping him to tune his violin. Q.D.L. had an enlargement of it framed. Leavis cherished it and was ill at ease if it were out of his line of sight in his bedroom.[15]

After Christmas there was good news. Leavis was named in the New Year's Honours List as a Companion of Honour, 'for services to the study of English Literature'. He was honoured by the Labour Government, a recommendation of the Prime Minister, James Callaghan, to the Crown. The other Companion of Honour was Jack Jones, General Secretary of the Transport & General Workers' Union, who the previous year had declined a peerage and advocated the abolition of the House of Lords. The pairing of two such resolute figures did not pass unnoticed. The Times devoted a leading article to them. The honour came too late: 'Dead Sea Fruit,' said Q.D.L.[16]

At the end of January 1978 Leavis received a letter of congratulation from I.A. Richards. Richards had wondered whether such a letter would be in order, but his wife persuaded him to write. He was right to hesitate, because an insulting one-sentence reply was returned. More than likely Q.D.L. guided Leavis's hand, for by this stage he was not writing. She addressed the envelope.

Obviously Leavis could not receive the medal for the CH in person. Nor could Q.D.L., so she arranged for it to be posted. At first Leavis was pleased, but soon did not want it shown to visitors.[17] Q.D.L. said that 'sometimes he seems to think I am his mother, very natural, I suppose, as I have to treat him as a child'. She was exhausted by nursing: in March she looked ahead to the summer and planned a week for Leavis in a nursing-home in June so she could take a holiday with her daughter.[18] By the middle of March he would take no solid food and two weeks later no liquids. In April, in addition to all else, he developed shingles.

In 1978 the spring was late. Leavis once joked that 'spring comes very fast up Bulstrode Gardens'. On 13 April John Speirs called; he was to be Leavis's last visitor. Speirs (whose son Leavis taught at Downing) was for many years the Scrutiny writer on Scots literature, but especially on

medieval literature and Chaucer. Leavis always made a point of acknowledging the supremacy of Chaucer, partly to distance himself from Eliot's
alliance with Dante: 'I can't for the life of me see why Dante should be
exalted above Chaucer; the civilization that produced Chaucer is the one
I much prefer.'[19]

Leavis died on Friday, 14 April 1978.

Immediately after Leavis's death Q.D.L. received many letters of
condolence and appreciation from all over the world, Moscow, Saudi
Arabia ('Arabia Petrolea', Leavis called it), India, Australia and America.
She was astonished to receive letters from Labour politicians Shirley
Williams and Denis Healey. There were no letters from Cambridge
professors, except one from the Secretary of the English Faculty, John
Stevens of Magdalene College, saying that some of his colleagues had
asked him to write. It is likely he took the initiative: Leavis had
regularly asked Stevens to supervise Downing men in medieval literature.
Q.D.L. was naturally distressed by most of the press coverage. There
were extensive surveys of opinion in the literary pages, notably the *New
Statesman and Nation*, the *Sunday Times* and the *Observer*. The tributes
were respectful but also down to earth. With a professional eye the
Bookseller noticed that the news of Leavis's death was known in time for
the London *Evening Standard* to publish it in its lunchtime edition on
Monday, 17 April, and some dailies had long pieces on Tuesday morning,
but it appeared 'beyond the wit and competence of *The Times Literary
Supplement* to produce something in time for a paper on the streets on
the Friday'.[20]

Q.D.L. did like the tribute by John Casey in the *Cambridge Review*,
which attempted a presentation of Leavis's importance for the 'educated
reader'. He explained Leavis's conviction that language was not inert, a
collocation of items, but is made in the collaboration (literally) of
minds.[21] Casey was a fellow of Gonville and Caius College, colleague
there of Jeremy Prynne, who also had a high regard for Leavis.

After his death Q.D.L. had a photograph taken of Leavis, then
bearded, which she kept in her bedroom-study in the months following:
a picture of a Leavis known so well to her during the nursing but one
unknown to the world. Leavis's funeral was at the Cambridge cremato-
rium on Huntingdon Road, a couple of miles further on from Girton
College. It was attended by Q.D.L., Robin and Kate Leavis. Nora
Wooster, with whom Q.D.L. lodged in Leys Road before her wedding,
noticed the announcement in the local newspaper and attended. She and

two Japanese visitors were the only outsiders. One of them went up to Q.D.L., but she said she could not speak to foreigners at that time. She felt she had 'mostly died with him, after half a century of looking after him'.[22] She burned most of the letters he wrote to her, unable to bear other eyes seeing them. He had written to her every day during their engagement to be married and whenever she was in hospital. It was heart-breaking, she said, to destroy the evidence of so much passion, tenderness, devotion and gratitude. But she felt so ill she could not risk keeping them.

In the summer there was a distressing clash with the BBC. An advertisement appeared in the *New Statesman and Nation* making an appeal for material to be used in a biographical film about Leavis's life. Q.D.L. protested in letters to the journal and to *The Times Literary Supplement*. The producer, Will Wyatt, replied that he would not give in to her opposition, but that he would consider her case. Q.D.L. urged many friends and former pupils to complain to the Director-General of the BBC and the 'fell project' was dropped.[23] She herself died on 17 March 1981.

ACKNOWLEDGEMENTS

═══

I am in the debt of individuals who have furnished me with permission to reproduce material written by F.R. Leavis, Q.D. Leavis or other writers (whose names are given in brackets below). These individuals in many cases also supplied me with valuable information, ideas and hospitality. They are Anthea Bell (Adrian Bell); Margaret Bottrall; John Bourne; Marjorie Cox (R.G. Cox); David Craig; Martin Dilly (D.W. Harding); Jane Dowling (Peter Greenham); Boris Ford; Andor Gomme; David Holbrook; R.T. Jones; Richard Luckett (I.A. Richards); S. Gorley Putt; Ian Robinson; Philip Snow (Sir Charles Snow); Geoffrey Strickland; Guy Symondson (Sir Arthur Quiller-Couch); Michael Tanner; John Tasker; Etain Todds (Kabraji); William Walsh; Geoffrey Walton; John Gillard Watson and Brian Worthington.

Many other people have written to me with reminiscences of Leavis or other kinds of record. I am indebted to David Adams; Lord Annan; J.E. Baines; Sophie Baron; Michael Baxandall; Anthony Beal; the late Muriel Bradbrook; Graham Chainey; Margaret Diggle; George Greenfield; Norman Guilding; Patrick Harrison ('Recollections of Downing and the Cambridge English School'); David Holbrook; Father P.C. Hunting; G.D. Klingopulos; Richard Luckett; David Matthews; Eric McCormick; Neil Roberts; Stephen Sedley; Frank Whitehead (for his tape-recorded interviews of Elsie Duncan-Jones and Wilfrid Mellers); Charles Winder (for his transcription of Leavis lectures); Dorothy Wooster.

Permission to quote from manuscripts has been granted by the University of Bristol; the British Broadcasting Corporation, Libraries and Archives; Cambridge University Press; the estate of F.R. and Q.D. Leavis; the Brotherton Library, University of Leeds, the Master and Fellows of Clare College; the Chatto & Windus Archive at the University of Reading; the Master and Fellows of Downing College; the Master and Fellows of Emmanuel College; Faber & Faber Ltd (poetry and prose by T.S. Eliot, Ezra Pound and lines by W.H. Auden from *Collected Poems*, edited by Edward Mendelson); the Harry Ransom Humanities Research Center, the University of Texas at Austin; Laurence Pollinger Ltd and the Estate of Frieda Lawrence Ravagli.

Permission has been given for the reproduction of pictures by the following: Sarah Betsky-Zweig; Cambridgeshire Collection, Cambridgeshire Libraries and Heritage Service; Alistair Cooke; Peter Dewes; Jane Dowling; Master and Fellows of Downing College; Mistress and Fellows of Girton College; Kate Leavis; Peter Sharrock; Robert Fothergill; John Cleave and Times Newspapers Ltd; the National Portrait Gallery.

ABBREVIATIONS

═══

AK	*Anna Karenina and Other Essays* (Leavis)
B	Ronald Bottrall papers (HRC)
BBC WAC	BBC Written Archives Centre, Caversham Park
Bristol	Bristol University Library
Brower	*I.A. Richards: Essays in His Honour* (Reuben Brower, Helen Vendler, John Hollander, eds., 1973)
C	R.G. Cox
CAP	*The Critic as Anti-Philosopher: Essays and Papers* (Leavis)
Chatto	Chatto & Windus Publishing Archive, University of Reading
CI	*Coleridge on Imagination* (I.A. Richards, 1934)
Clare	Clare College, Cambridge
Clark	*Varieties of Metaphysical Poetry* (T.S. Eliot's Clark Lectures)
CP	*The Common Pursuit* (Leavis)
CR	*Cambridge Review*
CUR	*Cambridge University Reporter*
DFP	Downing College: Fellowship Papers
DGB	Downing College: Governing Body Minutes
DHLN	*D.H. Lawrence: Novelist*
DN	*Dickens the Novelist* (F.R.L. and Q.D.L.)
ECM	*Emmanuel College Magazine*
ELT	*English Literature in Our Time and the University* (Leavis)
EU	*Education and the University*
FRP	*Fiction and the Reading Public* (Q.D.L.)
Girton	Girton College, Cambridge
HRC	Harry Ransom Humanities Research Center, University of Texas at Austin
L	*The Leavises: Recollections and Impressions* (Denys Thompson, ed., 1984)

LA	*Lectures in America* (F.R.L. and Q.D.L.)
LP	*The Living Principle: 'English' as a Discipline of Thought* (Leavis)
MCMC	*Mass Civilization and Minority Culture* (Leavis)
MU	*The Muse Unchained* (E.M.W. Tillyard, 1958)
NBEP	*New Bearings in English Poetry* (Leavis)
PC	*Practical Criticism* (I.A. Richards, 1929)
Principles	*Principles of Literary Criticism* (I.A. Richards, 1924)
R	Ian Robinson
R	*Revaluation* (Leavis)
Reading	Reading University
Russo	*I.A. Richards: His Life and Work* (J.P. Russo, 1989)
S	Morris Shapira
S	*Scrutiny*
SW	*The Sacred Wood and Other Essays* (T.S. Eliot, 1920)
T	Transcript of letters by Leavis made by John Tasker
TC	*Two Cultures and the Scientific Revolution* (C.P. Snow, 1959)
TCSS	*Two Cultures? The Significance of C.P. Snow* (Leavis)
THES	*The Times Higher Education Supplement*
TLS	*The Times Literary Supplement*
TM	*Two Memoirs* (J.M. Keynes, 1949)
Trinity	Wren Library, Trinity College, Cambridge
VC	*Valuation in Criticism and Other Essays* (Leavis)
W	Geoffrey Walton

NOTES

═══

Many references to manuscript material give a name or an abbreviated name and a date in brackets. The material is therefore either by Leavis, the name or the abbreviated name indicating the recipient, or the material is by the named person, from a communication sent to the present author. It is evident from the context which is which. So 'Baxandall (17.10.93)' means material in a letter to Ian MacKillop. On occasion more information is given, in this order: location, author of material, recipient. So 'Chatto: Parsons–Stewart (10.2.48)' means a letter in the Chatto archive from Ian Parsons to G.W. Stewart. In some cases a collection is specified in brackets, so 'Clare (Shapira)' means the Shapira items at Clare College. The full names of those who have supplied information are given in the list of Acknowledgements, which shows, for example, that 'Baxandall' is Michael Baxandall. Other names are in the list of Abbreviations.

Prologue 1961

1. C (12.11.61); T (8.2.72).
2. R (18.5.62).
3. Greenham ('February, 1992'). The first paragraph of this letter is as follows:

   The Roth family: I am pretty sure that I met only one, Queenie's sister, at Leslie Horwood's home in New Cross; though Leslie used to tell me about Queenie's mother. I suppose it must have been Leslie who first told me about *Fiction and the Reading Public*. I liked it enough to write a letter to the *Sunday Referee*, which had attacked it, I think for being too lofty. I said (as far as I remember) that far from being lofty (I'm sure that wasn't the word and 'élitist' hadn't come in) it gave ordinary people a standard and an ally. There was another connection, as well as Leslie; and that was Derek Traversi, who also lived in Dulwich. There was also Walter Todds, who much later became a friend of the Leavises, through teaching Ralph [Leavis's elder son] at Dartington Hall. When *Scrutiny* came out, we all took it, and indeed Tom Butcher, who was a few years younger than Leslie [Roth] and me, still has the complete set. Leavis once told me that a set was worth £100, but that was in 1963. Now and again I look at it in the Oxford Union Library, and it still seems to me to contain the best literary criticism, though the accusation that it let you off reading Spenser and Thackeray and even Milton would have to be answered, I suppose.

4. Crook, *L*, pp. 129, 131; W (17.5.78).
5. Letter only survives in transcription by Bradbrook, *L*, p. 29.
6. W (25.7.75). F.R.L.'s Clark Lectures were published as *English Literature in Our Time and the University* (1969).
7. W (30.5.72).
8. W (30.5.72; 25.7.75).
9. W (25.7.75); see also T (20.1.73).
10. It could be called 'My Struggle with Cambridge', said Williams who declined to write a 'life and works' of Leavis in the 1960s (*THES*, 5 June 1978). Leavis told his publisher in 1973 he believed the basic facts to be the triumph over E.M.W. Tillyard after the English Faculty was founded in 1926, Tillyard's appointment of L.J. Potts and T.R. Henn to keep Leavis out and the intimidation of a bookseller into not stocking *Scrutiny*.
11. Baxandall (5.7.91).
12. Clare (Shapira): Holbrook–Shapira (12.11.61).
13. 'Johnson as Critic', *S* (Summer 1944).
14. *S* (December 1947); *SW*, p. 15.

Part One
Culture and Environment 1895–1931

CHAPTER ONE
ORIGINS 1895–1919

1. Todds (3.7.74).
2. The Huguenot Society (2.11.92) has no record of Leavis or Lévis. For ancestry see May Hudnutt Leavis, *The Leavis Family: 1660–1954* (n.d., privately printed, in Cambridge City Library), p. 9; C.R. Busby (9.4.91).
3. Graham Chainey, 'The Other Leavises', *CR* (January 1985).
4. May Hudnutt Leavis, p. 7.
5. Graham Chainey, 'The Other Leavises: A Postscript', *CR* (March 1985).
6. One is owned by Quentin Skinner, the philosopher. See also *Cambridge Evening News* (18.4.92).
7. Cambridge County Record Office (1.7.92).

8. Chainey (1985), p. 8.

9. T (17.9.73); Sir Harry Godwin, *Cambridge and Clare* (1985), pp. 40–41.

10. Pitter, *L*, pp. 18–19.

11. 'Leavis at School', *L*, p. 185.

12. Roberts (20.9.90).

13. *FRP*, p. 288; Chainey (January 1985), p. 9.

14. 'Yeats: The Problem and the Challenge', *LA*, p. 61.

15. Pitter, *L*, p. 18.

16. S.J.D. Mitchell, *Perse: A History of the Perse School 1615–1976* (1976).

17. Black (16.8.94). *Annual Reports of the Headmaster and Examiners to the Governors of the School*; obituary of F.R.L. in *The Old Persean Society Chronicle* (October 1978).

18. *Perse Playbooks: No. 3, Plays and Poems by Boys of the Perse School, Cambridge* (1913), with preface by W.H.D. Rouse and essay, 'Playwrights or Playwriters?', by H. Caldwell Cook; *Cambridge Daily News* (31.3.13).

19. *DHLN*, p. 292.

20. John Clinton-Hewson (20.11.73).

21. Patrick Harrison, CBE, was born in 1928 and successively an administrative Civil Servant in Scotland and Secretary of the Royal Institute of British Architects (1968–87).

22. Harrison, pp. 125–6. He continues:

   I found these remarks so mysterious (they were as bald as I have stated) that I mentioned the incident to Peter Lienhardt. He had no explanation to offer . . . but thought it might have something to do with the treatment of conscientious objectors in the early stages of the Great War. Apparently there had at first been considerable popular support for such draconian measures as pushing them into the front line, until church leaders and other influential national figures had combined to insist that more responsible measures prevail. Peter thought that York might possibly have been a mustering point for conscientious objectors during this early phase and therefore a painful and anxious episode that F.R.L. wished to forget.

23. Letter to Tanner (n.d. but *c.* 1977), *L*, pp. 138–9.

24. T (n.d., letter 142). 'In Defence of Milton', *CP*, p. 43.

25. *Friend* (21.8.14).

26. C (no full date: 24.12.?; 7.9.40). He added: 'I hope you're not being too much worried by the hospital-bitches, who permanently lowered my notion of female human nature.' 'In Defence of Milton', *CP*, p. 43.

27. Hunting (24.6.91); Harding (13.8.91).

28. Meaburn Tatham and James E. Miles (eds.), *The Friends' Ambulance Unit: A Record* (Swarthmore Press, n.d.), pp. 134–41.

29. Roberts (20.9.90).

30. *Lines of Communication: A Souvenir Volume, being pages from the Train Magazines* (n.d.), p. 75. Leavis's movements are logged in the FAU Register.

31. *Friend* (23.3.17).
32. W (4.11.71); Winder, p. 24.
33. Watson (8.4.52). For the ambulance train service, see *Friend* (22.3.18). Unfortunately many train journals do not survive: these included *Lines of Communication*, the *Bully* and the *Platform* (AT 17), the *Orderly Review* (AT 16), the *Fourgon* (AT 11). See *Friend* (14.7.16); Tatham and Miles, pp. 140–41.
34. Tatham and Miles, pp. 160–63; Lyn Macdonald, *They Called It Passchendaele: The Story of the Third Battle of Ypres and of the Men Who Fought in It* (1978), p. 87.
35. See Reuben Brower and others (eds.), *I.A. Richards: Essays in His Honour* (1973), p. 22; I.A. Richards, *Complementarities: Uncollected Essays*, ed. by J.P. Russo (1976), p. 255.
36. T (26.1.74).
37. 'The Loneliness of the Long Distance Runner', *Guardian* (8.4.60); the letter to John Bourne is undated.
38. F.R.L. quotes from Rosenberg's letters and values their unedited spelling and punctuation. Considering F.R.L.'s praise of Rosenberg as 'matter-of-fact', it seems that a certain stylistic coolness was in vogue in the early 1930s. Denys Harding refers to 'the movement which is rediscovering the value of taking pains, being intelligible, and avoiding intellectual and emotional fixation' in a review of Robert Graves.
39. Especially *Cymbeline*, V. iii: see *CP*, p. 178.
40. Letter to George A. Panichas (12.1.67), quoted in his review of Lord Avon's *Another World 1897–1917* in *Modern Age* (Summer 1978).
41. Harrison, pp. 126–7; Chainey (January 1985), p. 7.

CHAPTER TWO
ENGLISH AT CAMBRIDGE 1919–1924

1. Walton (22.12.40).
2. Sir Harry Godwin, *Cambridge and Clare* (1985), pp. 2–14.
3. *Athenaeum* (5.12.19).
4. *LA*, pp. 33–4.
5. 'Milton's Verse', *S* (September 1933).
6. 'Three Essays on Modern Poetry', *Chapbook* (1920); F.R.L., 'The Recognition of Isaac Rosenberg', *S* (September 1937).
7. *ELT*, p. 14.
8. *On the Art of Reading* (1920), introductory lecture (25.10.16).
9. Given from October 1927.
10. *Student's Handbook* (1919), pp. 404–5. Titles of examinations are taken from papers themselves and reordered. In place of 'Criticism' and '1789–1870' papers could be taken on '1066–1350' and history of the language.

11. *The Granta* (2.3.23).
12. F.L. Lucas, 'English' in *University Studies: Cambridge* and E.M.W. Tillyard in *MU*.
13. This is applied to students who were preparing for English while doing another Tripos, but the statement goes with the idea that English is a 'private reading' course.
14. *ELT*, p. 13.
15. Gwendolen Freeman, *Alma Mater* (1990), p. 124.
16. Margaret Diggle, 'Mansfield Forbes on the Romantic Revival', and letter by Knox Cunningham, *Cambridge Quarterly* 6 (1973); Godwin, pp. 99–106.
17. Empson's view: Russo quotes *Magdalene College Magazine and Record* (1978–9), pp. 1–6.
18. F.L. Attenborough was the director of studies at Emmanuel. A mature student, he had taken Firsts in the English sections of the Modern and Medieval Languages Tripos. He was a protégé of Chadwick, who set him to work on the Anglo-Saxon legal system. He had been a non-combatant because of a football injury. He went straight from graduation in 1918 to an Emmanuel fellowship in 1919. Attenborough left in 1925 for a career in university administration. He was father of David and Richard Attenborough. D.S. Brewer says that in 1920 he was known as 'Assistant University Lecturer in the Faculty of English', questionable as the Faculty did not yet exist: *ECM* (1971–2).
19. *The Times* (8.7.72); *ECM* (1977–8); D.S. Brewer, *A List of His Writings, Presented to H.S. Bennett* (1960); *ECM* (1972). An unpublished memoir by Stanley Bennett is very valuable: 'Journey from Obscurity', with appendix, 'By Chance We Met' by Joan Bennett. The typescript is owned by Liz Eccleshare.
20. 'Bunyan through Modern Eyes', *S* (April 1938), owes something to Owst, as does the choice of the long quotation from Sir Walter Raleigh on the language of Chaucer in 'Sociology and Literature', *CP*, pp. 196–7.
21. Basil Willey, author of Tillyard's obituary in *Proceedings of the British Academy* (1963).
22. 4th Royal Lancashire Regiment (Territorial Forces); France (1915–16), Salonika (1916–19), OBE; three mentions in dispatches.
23. 7th Royal West Kent Regiment and Intelligence Corps, wounded in 1916, gassed in 1917.
24. *MU*, p. 40, quotes A.C. Benson's diary (11.7.14): 'Rupert Brooke told me he had offered to help Quiller-Couch in English next term.'
25. Journal entry of 1926: see *Clark*, p. 12.
26. Bill Willey, *Spots of Time: A Retrospect of the Years 1897–1920* (1965), p. 9.
27. Though blazer-wearing was thought snobbishly to be lower middle class in

later years, this was not the case in 1920s Cambridge, but simply sporting and informal – not to be worn for dinner in Hall.

28. *CUR* (1920–21), p. 998.
29. *Cambridge Independent Press* (27.5.21).
30. Emmanuel (F.R.L.): Q–Attenborough (16.7.21).
31. Clare (Forbes): F.R.L.–Forbes (22.7.21).
32. Magdalene (Richards): Q–Richards (17.6.29).
33. *Men of Letters and the English Public in the XVIIIth Century, 1660–1744: Dryden, Addison, Pope* (1949), translated by E.O. Lorimer and edited by Bonamy Dobrée, became a Downing College classic.
34. Renate Simpson, *How the Ph.D. Came to Britain: A Century of Struggle for Postgraduate Education* (1983), p. 155.
35. T (5.10.73).
36. Russo, p. 535, quotes Richards's journal (8.3.72).
37. John Constable (ed.), *Selected Letters of I.A. Richards* (1990), pp. 36–7.
38. *PC*, p. 79 (without author's italics).
39. *PC*, pp. 78, 83–4, 113. F.R.L. told Tasker (21.10.73) 'I detect myself' in these notes, and identifies Forbes's 'overworked, but very witty and effective commentaries'. See also *ELT*, pp. 15–16.
40. Margaret Diggle, 'Mansfield Forbes on the Romantic Revival', *Cambridge Quarterly* 6 (1973), p. 111, from notes taken at Forbes's 1924/5 lectures.
41. 'Gerard Hopkins', *Complementarities*, pp. 139–47; *ELT*, p. 17.
42. *LA*, pp. 35–7.

CHAPTER THREE
EXCITING STRANGENESS 1925–1931

1. Emmanuel: Education Board Minute Book, 1910– (28.4.25; 12.5.25).
2. Margaret Diggle's poem is in *A Telescope of Years*, Westgate Chapel and One World Centre, High Street, Lewes, East Sussex; Harding (11.6.91).
3. *Principles*, pp. 226, 231.
4. *New Statesman* (20.2.26); Hopkins, *Dial* 81 (1926).
5. W (n.d., but 1976).
6. Information about Q.D.R. comes from Freeman and Bradbrook, *L*, pp. 2–16 and 29–43, and M.C. Bradbrook, 'Queenie Leavis: The Dynamics of Rejection', *CR* (20.11.81). The pieces by Bradbrook are packed with detail, but possibly unreliable and oddly patronizing; see also Baron (10.7.91).
   My account of the Roth family owes much to a paper by Marjorie Glick, 'The Early Life of Mrs Q.D. Leavis', given to the Jewish Research Group of the Edmonton Hundred Historical Society on 14 December 1994 and to a conversation with Leslie Horwood, Q.D.R.'s first cousin, son of Jane Roth's sister, who remembers visiting the 'clever cousins in the country'. I

am indebted to suggestions by Leslie Horwood and Kate Leavis. For Q.D.R.'s 'A Street Orator', see *Latymer Magazine* (February 1921). Her school magazine pieces are available from Edmonton Green Library in London and are listed under 'Juvenilia' in Kinch, Baker and Kimber's Leavis bibliography.

7. Deduced from the Vice-Chancellor's letter that the allusion was in a lecture, but it could have been in a supervision.

8. 'The English Novel in 1923', *Cambridge Mercury* (28.2.24); *The Granta* reviewed *Ulysses* (1.12.22) in the Egoist Press 'New Edition'.

9. The essay on *Ulysses* was by Murry.

10. Home Office HO144/20071 148870. See A.D. Harvey, 'Leavis, *Ulysses* and the Home Office', *CR* (October 1993) and Alistair McCleery, 'Naughty Old Leavis', *The Times Higher Education Supplement* (13.9.91). Harrison reports the *Hassan* story, told to E.A. Morley. 'Usually, only the hardy attended throughout his [lecture] courses but apparently the lecture hall was packed with keen students that day, hoping to hear something "dirty".' The story was told in connection with Leavis's promotion in the 1930s. Some undergraduates in the 1930s believed Leavis was threatened with non-promotion if he lectured on *Ulysses*, but he did do so. Greenfield (12.6.91).

11. The appointments were all to 30 September, so F.R.L.'s was actually for two and a half years and the other terms correspondingly longer or shorter.

12. Margaret Flower (7.5.91).

13. T.R. Henn, *Five Arches*, p. 51.

14. C.G. Hutchinson (1.7.92).

15. Gwendolen Freeman, *Alma Mater* (1990) and letters at Girton College; Elsie Duncan-Jones (interview with Frank Whitehead); Margaret Flower (6.6.91).

16. Fluchère, *TLS* (9.1.76). On Shelley, F.R.L. recommended Chevrillon, *La Nature dans la poésie de Shelley* (1921) and Koszul, *La Jeunesse de Shelley* (1910).

17. Richards reviewed it: *Criterion* (December 1928).

18. Freeman, p. 44.

19. Freeman, p. 33.

20. 'Lecture Criticism: Dr Leavis, of Emmanuel. A Symphony in E', *Gownsman* (18.2.28).

21. H.L. Elvin (28.4.92).

22. Oliver Stallybrass, 'Editor's Introduction', *Aspects of the Novel* (1974), 'Abinger Edition'.

23. R (17.7.71).

24. *CUR* (1927–8), pp. 753, 946.

25. At £120 a year: an important author on the English masque and the 'Fool' in legend and literature.

26. T.R. Henn, p. 88.
27. *FRP*, p. 213; John Holloway (28.4.92) recalled the high percentages when L.J. Potts, one of Q.D.R.'s examiners, showed him her examination scripts many years later.
28. Clive Bell, *Old Friends: Personal Recollections* (1956), pp. 131–3.
29. John Lehmann, *The Whispering Gallery: Autobiography I* (1955), pp. 138–9.
30. *Clark*, p. 12.
31. In 'Retrospect 1950', *NBEP*, p. 219.
32. 'Criticism', *Life and Letters* (November 1929); *New Statesman* (29.12.28); *CR* (8.2.29); *NBEP*, p. 219. Richards asked Eliot himself if he had seen it.

I was much amused by F.L. Lucas's attack on you. I thought it very smart. I can see him grinning away and licking his chops as he did it. Pity that people with such gifts should have no idea or wisdom! Do you know M.D. Forbes's celebrated lecture-room description of F.L. Lucas across the way in *his* lecture-room in King's? Sowing the puffed wheat of scholarship.

John Constable (ed.), *Selected Letters of I.A. Richards* (1990), p. 56 (13.7.30).
33. B (15.1.30).
34. *VC*, p. 11.
35. *CR* (1.3.29).
36. Richard Luckett and R. Hyam, 'Empson and the Engines of Love', *Magdalene College Magazine and Record*, n.s. 35 (1990–91).
37. See '"What for – What Ultimately for": The Leavises in the Sixties and Seventies', *Cambridge Quarterly* 17, 1 (1988).
38. C.G. Hutchinson (1.7.92).
39. Story mentioned by John Constable, editor of Richards's *Selected Letters*; see also Luckett (12.8.92).
40. Baron (14.8.91).
41. Magdalene (Richards): Q–Richards (17.6.29).
42. Empson expulsion: Richard Luckett and R. Hyam, above.
43. Wooster (28.2.91).
44. Crook, *L*, p. 128.
45. 'Memories of Wittgenstein', *Human World* (1973) are reprinted in *CAP*.
46. T (November 1970), and see *CAP*, p. 132. F.R.L.'s account is mentioned in a private paper, 'A Day with Dr Leavis' (January 1971), by D.F. Rowe, a Downing man of 1938, who returned after the war.
47. St John's College Council Minute (M 1283/16).
48. Harding (9.8.91).
49. B (15.1.30). Review of Aldington, *CR* (25.10.29).
50. *Cahiers du Sud* (October 1930), p. 600, translated by M.B. and Peggy Kinch, 'F.R. Leavis's "English Poetry and the Modern World"', *English Studies* (February 1988). The same passage was used in *NBEP* but with some sentences omitted.

51. Peter Guy (3.8.91), supplying a brief undated paper by Fraser himself about Leavis. 'Mass Civilization and Minority Culture', *For Continuity* (1933), p. 15.

52. Cambridge University Board of Graduate Studies (7.3.94).

53. *For Continuity* (1933), p. 2.

54. The essay is in French. My reference to 'graces' relates to Eliot's 'les aménités, raffinements et grâces', developed over centuries to make 'l'amour supportable': *La Nouvelle Revue Française* (May 1927). See also *DHLN*, pp. 23–4.

55. B (13.7.32). And Harding: 'I know that Leavis in those early days viewed Lawrence with moderate respect but with a clear sense of his limitations and aberrations, certainly without giving him anything like the importance he gave him later.' Harding (9.8.91). Rosenberg: review of *Complete Works, S* (September 1937).

56. *TLS* (24.10.80); B (15.1.30).

57. B (15.1.30).

58. B (15.1.30).

59. B (12.5.30).

60. B (7.6.30).

61. B (5.9.31).

62. B (5.1.31).

63. B (14.7.31).

64. B (23.3.31, 23.7.31); *NBEP*, pp. 207–8. Not all Leavisians went the whole way on Bottrall. Harding thought Eliot was capable of the 'positive energy', which F.R.L. believed was beyond his compass, but within Bottrall's (*S*, May 1932).

65. 'Tradition and the Individual Talent', *SW*, p. 20.

66. A.P. Rossiter, *Poor Scholars: A Novel* (1932), p. 201.

67. 'La Poésie Anglaise', *Cahiers du Sud*, pp. 606–7. This is the passage that F.R.L. quotes at length in his first account of the 'modern world', which he gave in the draft for the chapter 'The Situation at the End of World War I' in *NBEP*. (The passage is not in the book.) Freeman, p. 34.

Part Two
Stage Army 1931–1948

CHAPTER FOUR
WE WERE CAMBRIDGE 1931–1932

1. Bradbrook described the situation in a talk at Girton in 1987 and in a tape-recording of reminiscences. Perry (2.3.94). 'I read from curiosity and

delight *and* from a dread of the dole queues amongst pre-war graduates.'
Klingopulos (19.6.91).

2. Margaret Diggle (1.1.93; 10.6.94) was told the story of Stanley Bennett's
visit to Leavis by Joan Bennett. She said ruefully that 'this was the only
faulty judgement she had known her husband make!'

3. Emmanuel (Gray) (25.7.75). In 1978 the Master of Emmanuel asked Q.D.L.
if the college might congratulate F.R.L. on his appointment as Companion
of Honour. '*No*,' she replied.

> In my opinion, the attempt to do so, and to claim for the College a share in his
> distinction, shows a mixture of effrontery, bad taste and poor judgement, and adds
> insult to injury. His achievement was in spite of your College, and, let me add, that
> the only reason my husband did not take his name off the College books was that
> he would then have been unable to use the University Library. I hope you will
> circulate this letter among the body of your fellows.

Emmanuel (F.R.L.): Q.D.L.–Brewer (10.1.78).

4. Q.D.L., 'In the Great Tradition: A Rebuttal', *Encounter* (July 1979).

5. *ECM* (1970/71), pp. 5–11.

6. B (11.10.31; 21.10.31).

7. Magdalene (Richards): Q.D.L.–Richards (26.11.31). The letter on curtness
is only dated 'Friday'.

8. John Constable (ed.), *Selected Letters of I.A. Richards* (1990), p. 63.

9. Pitter, *L*, p. 20.

10. 'Rumpus', illustrated in *L*, was a neighbour's dog.

11. W (28.2.77).

12. Diggle (17.9.91).

13. W (11.6.78).

14. Derek Stanford, *Inside the Forties: Literary Memoirs 1937–1957* (1977), p. 45,
remembering autumn 1939. Interestingly, the allusion to a Christ picture is
made by someone absolutely out of sympathy with F.R.L.

15. 'Milton's Verse', *R*, p. 55.

16. *NBEP*, pp. 7–9.

17. *NBEP*, p. 83.

18. *NBEP*, p. 93.

19. *Commerce* published several pieces on age and asceticism, including Hardy's
last poem, 'Felling a Tree', translated by Paul Valéry (1927), and Valéry's
interesting essay on Montesquieu, 'Au sujet des *Lettres Persanes*' (1926).

20. *NBEP*, p. 119.

21. Q.D.L., *Critic* (Winter/Spring, 1948).

22. G.W. Stonier first noticed plagiarism, reviewing *Aspects of Modern Poetry* in
the *New Statesman* (24.11.34). Correspondence followed in the *TLS* after
reviews of *Aspects* by John Sparrow and in the *Listener*, notably by Bonamy
Dobrée (28.11.34). Victoria Glendinning, *Edith Sitwell: A Unicorn Among
Lions* (1981), pp. 186–7 and Geoffrey Elborn, *Edith Sitwell: A Biography*
(1981), pp. 112–15.

23. Q.D.L. was intensely respectful of the best art, but a remarkable feature of her temperament was a bracing sense of quality in relatively minor work; *Biographia Literaria*, xxii.

24. *FRP*, pp. 221–6.

25. *Punch* (17.8.32), p. 178, referring to Q.D.L., 'Bestsellers of Yesterday: (1) Rhoda Broughton', *Listener* (3.8.32), pp. 158–9.

26. In America the *Symposium* bracketed the book with Trotsky's history of the Revolution as one of the most important of 1932.

27. B (13.7.32).

28. E.H. McCormick, 'My Association with F.R. and Q.D. Leavis' (11.11.91). McCormick influenced the decision of Maria Tibbetts, biographer of the Canadian painter Emily Carr, to work on Canadian culture.

29. Alan Filreis, *Wallace Stevens and the Actual World* (1991), pp. 174–7. Like McCormick, Ludowyk was a cultural historian as well as literary critic, as in *Modern History of Ceylon* (1966). On his teaching principles, see *Marginal Comments* (1945).

30. *ELT*, p. 66.

31. 'A Serious Artist', S (September 1932).

32. Q.D.L., 'A Middleman of Ideas', S (May 1932).

33. B (27.3.31).

34. *Symposium* (October and January 1933).

35. F.W. Bateson, 'The Alternative to Scrutiny', *Essays in Criticism* (January 1964).

36. Figures based on pages of a ledger (owned by Keith and Nora Crook) and L.C. Knights's contribution, see *L*, pp. 72–3. Possibly sums paid in by F.R.L. were on behalf of another. He gave the sum of £150 in a letter to Harding (Emmanuel) (20.7.47). Payment of £80 has 'R O'M' (Raymond O'Malley) against his initials. Print run figures based on records in this ledger of copies sent to Deighton, Bell, bookseller and subscription agent. *Scrutiny* was printed on a press now in the Cambridge Museum of Technology.

37. 'Johnson as Critic', S (Summer 1944).

38. Marjorie Cox (25.8.92), quoting Q.D.L. to R.G. Cox.

39. Emmanuel: F.R.L.–Harding (22.5.41).

40. B (4.11.32).

41. B (1.3.32).

42. B (30.1.32).

43. *Criterion* (January–April 1932).

44. *Bookman* (1934), p. 142. The frontispiece of this book.

CHAPTER FIVE
'TO DOWNING COLLEGE' 1931–1937

1. Sedley (18.5.91).
2. HRC (Putt) (21.4.35).
3. *Universities Review* (October 1931), pp. 21–7; S (September 1932).
4. DGB (12.8.31).
5. DGB (13.6.31; 22.2.32).
6. DGB (28.5.32).
7. T.A.B. Birrell (24.5.91).
8. At one time it was possible for a school-leaver with local authority funds to take a degree at a university other than Oxbridge and then win an Oxbridge scholarship that could be topped up by a state grant. So a second undergraduate degree could be taken and six years' funding study received.
9. DGB (17.10.34).
10. DGB (26.1.34; 17.10.34; 17.11.34; 10.1.35; 4.5.35; 30.1.35; 4.5.35).
11. *TLS* (19.12.75).
12. DGB (7.6.35; 22.7.35; 24.6.35).
13. 'Gordon Fraser' in Britain signifies greeting cards. They originated from Katie Fraser. After her marriage she disliked the available cards for her first Christmas in England, so she commissioned some designs. The result was a prosperous business.
14. Walton (7.4.35); C (4.4.35).
15. *CUR* obituaries: Attwater (11.7.35); Forbes (26.1.36).
16. Geoffrey Walton (15.3.91). Q said to Walton about F.R.L., 'He's got the fire in his belly.'
17. DGB (23.5.27): on college lectureships.
18. DGB (31.1.36; 17.3.36).
19. *CUR* (19.5.36) advertised a part-time vacancy, evidence that it was not by choice F.R.L. became a 'part work' Lecturer, because, for instance, of the volume of his Downing teaching or his *Scrutiny* work.
20. DFP: F.R.L. Anonymous typescript (19.6.36). I suggest this is the draft of a reference, perhaps to be sent above the signature of the Master.
21. B (5.12.36).
22. Chatto: Parsons (July 1936, 14.7.36); Greenfield (12.6.91) in a private paper, 'Notes on F.R. Leavis'. Greenfield was a Downing freshman (1936/7) who went to Q's *soirées*. My account of the appointments committee is based on Greenfield's recollection of Q's talk, and what he heard from his Downing contemporary, Frank Bradbrook, brother of Muriel Bradbrook.
23. *CUR* (8.6.37).
24. C (3.11.36).
25. Admiral Richmond may have had some influence on Leavis's election, only

installed at Downing as Master after it. A.L. Rowse (7.5.92) believed that 'Q backed F.R.L. for the job at Downing with his friend Admiral Richmond.'

26. Walton (30.7.37).

27. *Observer* (19.6.38). That is, half the Firsts given went to Downing. For one college to take half the Firsts was rare. It happened in 1936 for St Catharine's, a strong English college, with T.R. Henn and supervision by Arthur Humphreys; and under the influence of Bennett and F.R.L., Emmanuel took an extraordinary five out of nine Firsts in 1927. And two of the non-Emmanuel Firsts on this occasion were, in different senses, Leavisian: Ronald Bottrall (Pembroke) and Ian Parsons (Trinity).

28. Cox's recollections come from a letter to Norman Shrapnel, in possession of Mrs Marjorie Cox. See his review of Brower, *Sewanee Review* (Fall 1974).

29. Especially poems 255, 356, 357, 526, 607, 614, 617, 647, 711 and 802.

30. Preserved in the undergraduate essays of R.G. Cox. On Gray, Cox wrote that he knew poetry was more than just sentiment. F.R.L. commented: '"Knowing" in *general* is nothing.'

31. *London Review of Books* (17.9.90).

32. Tanner, *L*, p. 135.

33. Tanner, *L*, p. 133.

34. *The Granta* (23.1.35; 10.10.34). Another Leavisian, Frank Chapman, preceded him.

35. My account of Bewley is much indebted to Patrick Harrison.

36. Bewley's widowed mother had to attend to the family garage, so Bewley was brought up by another widow, the wife of Frank James, brother to Jesse James, the bank-robber. As for his manner of speaking, Bewley was given to the declamatory 'Why' as in 'Why, Peter, do you think we could persuade Talog to come to the Fort St George for a few beers!'

37. Adams (31.12.91). Karl Miller, *Doubles: Studies in Literary History* (1987), pp. 383–7; Harrison, pp. 54, 58.

38. See 'Report of a Committee of Inquiry into the Problems of Teaching in the English Faculty, Cambridge (February–April 1937)', a TS in Cambridge University Library (Cam.a. 937.2).

39. *S* (September 1937).

40. 'Criticism from Oxford and Cambridge', *University of Toronto Quarterly* (January 1937).

41. *Criterion* (January 1937), pp. 350–53. Spender himself later had no interpretation of Eliot's choice of reviewer. He remarked that 'my reasons for being hostile to Leavis were perhaps that he had from the publication of my *Poems* (1933) onwards been completely contemptuous of my poetry in *Scrutiny*.' He believed that he 'unscrupulously' exploited 'his position as editor-cum-university teacher': Spender (1.7.94).

42. F.W. Bateson of Oxford also contributed to the debate. Wellek's critique of *R* had in its vicinity discussion of the same themes in *S* by Bateson. A dossier of argument in *S* about literary history and *R* could be compiled: F.W. Bateson, *English Poetry and the English Language* (1935) reviewed by Leavis (June 1935), replies by Bateson and rejoinder from Leavis (September 1935), *R* (October 1936), reply by Wellek, 'Literary Criticism and Philosophy' (March 1937), answer by Leavis as 'Literary Criticism and Philosophy: A Reply' (June 1937), rejoinder by Wellek (September 1937). (Wellek's interventions were long letters to Leavis, the publication of which he authorized.) Such an exchange of views was unique in the British academic literary world of the time, not to be found even in the *CR*. For a parallel, see, for example, the exchanges of views in the American *Critical Inquiry* in the 1980s.

43. Harding (12.4.37; 5.4.37).

44. In his essay on the play of January 1942, F.R.L. refers to a recent Cambridge production of *Measure for Measure* in which Angelo was played as a study in neurosis, 'strained and twitching from his first appearance'. This was the Marlowe Society–Amateur Dramatic Club (4.3.41), with George Rylands as Angelo.

45. Remarks on *Othello* are from Winder's notes.

46. Black, *L*, p. 87.

47. Tillyard, *MU*, pp. 124–38.

48. T (21.11.68).

49. *S* (Spring 1945).

50. *S* (December 1937).

CHAPTER SIX
SCRUTINY: GUARDING THE GUARDIANS 1932–1937

1. *S* (March 1937).

2. Augustus John Jenkinson (1908–1992): *ECM* (1992); Dobson (20.9.91).

3. The argument about the 'leisure community' is made with reference to A.L. Morton, *Criterion* (October 1932) and to agriculturalism mentioned by Eliot in the *Criterion* (October 1931).

4. W (20.3.78).

5. *DHLN*, pp. 20–21.

6. *S* (March 1933; September 1932).

7. HRC (Eliot) (16.12.35).

8. *S* (September 1932).

9. *S* (March 1933). F.R.L. dissociated Lawrence from surrealism, discussed in the same issue by Fluchère.

10. HRC (Eliot) (16.3.34; 16.12.35).

11. *S* (September 1932).

12. *University Studies: Cambridge*, edited by Harold Wright, pp. 283–4.
13. *University Studies: Cambridge*, p. 278.
14. *University Studies: Cambridge*, p. 293.
15. *Listener* (21.10.82); Fry to Helen Anrep (21.6.33), *Letters of Roger Fry*, edited by Denys Sutton (1972), p. 678.
16. Russo. p. 764: letter (19.11.23) to Dorothea Richards.
17. Russo, p. 796.
18. Russo, p. 762; Brower, p. 33.
19. HRC (Putt) (2.10.33) for 'Authority and Method' and Harding (12.4.39) for F.R.L.'s work on it just before the Second World War.
20. Harding (18.8.32; 4.11.32).
21. Harding, L, p. 197.
22. B (19.1.35). The kicking anecdote: John Constable (ed.), *Selected Letters of I.A. Richards* (1990), p. xli. F.R.L. often referred to kicking (presumably fictitious and mentioned with fiery self-deprecation) when exasperated.
23. *NBEP*, p. 13.
24. *CI*, p. 229.
25. *CI*, pp. 213–15.
26. *S* (March 1935).
27. *CI*, p. 230.
28. Russo, p. 360.
29. Walton (15.3.91).
30. B (19.1.75; 26.3.35).
31. C (4.4.35).
32. Richards, *Selected Letters*, p. xli. An extract is quoted by the editor, but the undated letter not reproduced in full.
33. Brower, pp. 74–5.
34. Hunting (24.6.91); T (15.9.74).
35. *S* (September 1937).
36. B (4.11.32).
37. B (20.7.32).
38. *How to Teach Reading* is, I think, an extraordinary work that was neglected (as were some others) because of Leavis's unusual modes of publication. It disappeared as a pamphlet, surfacing as an appendix to *EU* (1943), a book that itself, in turn, submerged.
39. *EU*, p. 116.
40. B (19.3.33). HRC (Pound): to F.R.L. (2.3.33); *EU*, pp. 135–6.
41. Leavis enjoyed telling a story about Henn grimly admonishing a pupil: 'Go down on your knees, Mr X, and pray that you may never understand *Modern Love.*'
42. HRC (Putt) (29.7.33).
43. *NBEP*, p. 82.
44. *Exagmination*, p. 88; *Cymbeline*, V, iii.

45. *Open Air* preparation: Bell (5.3.92).
46. Walton (18.12.36).
47. Joseph Cohen, *Journey to the Trenches: The Life of Isaac Rosenberg* (1975), pp. 180–83.
48. Bristol (Rosenberg): Leftwich (28.6.37) replying to Harding (25.6.37).
49. B (26.4.32).
50. B (29.10.33).

CHAPTER SEVEN
WARTIME 1938–1948

1. C (4.4.38).
2. C (24.12.39; 14.1.45).
3. Raymond O'Malley to Boris Ford (16.12.92); C (28.4.44).
4. *Journey from the North: Autobiography of Storm Jameson*, vol. 2, p. 235.
5. C (16.9.38).
6. HRC (Putt) (1.10.38).
7. W (25.4.38; 15.12.38).
8. C (16.9.38).
9. C (14.2.42).
10. W (23.4.44).
11. B (n.d.: spring 1942).
12. Emmanuel (Harding): (25.6.47).
13. C (14.7.47).
14. Watson (17.12.53).
15. *TLS* (12.12.75; 19.12.75).
16. *New Review* (October 1975).
17. Lord Annan (16.1.92) consulted Joan Bennett and M.C. Bradbrook about the procedures.
18. *CUR* (1.10.34).
19. *TLS* (3.3.74). See also 'The Cambridge English Faculty, which kept him from having a Lectureship until he was turned 50 ...' Q.D.L.–Ford (22.3.78); and Robin Leavis to Denys Thompson: 'In 1936 my father had only an *Assistant* Lectureship in the English Faculty; this was quite another thing from the full Lectureship attributed by Harvey.' Emmanuel: F.R.L. (25.9.82).
20. All in *S*: 'Academic Case-history' (review) on A.C. Haddon (Summer 1943); 'Leslie Stephen: Cambridge Critic' (March 1939); 'Henry Sidgwick's Cambridge' (December 1947); 'Professor Chadwick and English Studies' (Spring 1947).
21. Harding (12.4.39).
22. *MU*, p. 41.
23. 'Professor Chadwick and English Studies', pp. 206–7. The other inspiration

for Q.D.L.'s literary sociology was F.R.L. himself, in person and in his Ph.D. thesis. Both Oxford and Cambridge produced compelling sagas of old Britain. J.R.R. Tolkien's *The Lord of the Rings* might be said to be typical of Oxford English and T.H. White's *The Once and Future King* of Cambridge English. White's annotations to his copy of Richards's *Practical Criticism* are in HRC.

24. Phillpotts, Mistress of Girton (1922–5), could be counted as a member of the Old Cambridge. She was the only woman member of the statutory commission on the University of Cambridge, 1923–7. F.R.L. wrote to Michael Black of Cambridge University Press in 1966: 'I'm shocked to find that Bertha Phillpotts's *The Elder Edda* – CUP which I want to present at Harvard and get into the library at York – is out of print. Is there any chance of it being issued as a paperback? I and my wife are always pushing it (Tragedy, background of Shakespeare; why Eliot is absurd about Hamlet; Racine's inferiority; etc. etc.).' Trinity (CUP): Black (17.10.66).

25. Note Q.D.L.'s application of 'sociology' to university 'Eng. Lit.' in 'The Discipline of Letters' in *S* (Winter 1943), especially on the conformities of seeming mavericks C.S. Lewis and A.E. Housman.

26. Harding (24.9.40), *TLS* (21.9.40).

27. *How to Read* (1931), p. 20.

28. BBC WAC (8.9.40).

29. See Paul Addison, *The Road to 1945* (1975).

30. Quoted at the beginning of 'Education and the University: Considerations at a Critical Time', *S* (Spring 1943). Not in the book version.

31. C (17.8.43); *EU*, p. 104.

32. *EU*, p. 59.

33. See 'Education and the University: Criticism and Comment' (*S*, December 1940, not the book version), an essay containing long quotations from critical correspondents and 'Yes (and No), buts' from Leavis.

34. *Malvern 1941: The Life of the Church and the Order of Society* (1941), pp. 201–13.

35. The admirer was Michael Tanner (*L*, p. 33), and 'The Anscombe', G.E.M. Anscombe, the Catholic philosopher, then professor at Cambridge.

36. Addison, p. 187.

37. R (30.8.74).

38. Walton (18.7.41).

39. T (3.3.69).

40. B: Eliot (24.3.43).

41. Harding's review: *S* (Spring 1943). During the war Harding was interested, as a social psychologist, in the distinction between assertive ('integrative') behaviour and aggression ('The Custom of War and the Notion of Peace', *S*, December 1940). It is hard to believe that this was not related to his personal knowledge of Leavis, who both thought about and experienced varieties of aggression and assertion.

42. From F.R.L.'s 'Reflections on the Above, i.e. "Objections to a Review of 'Little Gidding' by Harding"': *S* (Summer 1943) by R.I. Higginbotham.
43. C (17.8.43).
44. Baines (23.6.91).
45. C (28.4.44)
46. Guilding (7.8.91).
47. Walton (17.7.44)
48. C (3.6.46).
49. A letter to Ian Parsons, Chatto (10.7.49), explains that this essay lay in a drawer for three years before it was published in *S* in 1949, when he was desperate for material.
50. *S* (June 1949).
51. Chatto (1.8.49).
52. W (11.2.45); C (14.1.45).
53. W (27.2.48); Guilding (7.8.91).
54. Beal, 'My First Acquaintance with F.R.L.' (with memoir of the publication of his *D.H. Lawrence: Selected Literary Criticism* and Morris Shapira's *Henry James, Selected Literary Criticism*) private paper (13.1.92).
55. C (n.d. 1946).
56. *S* (June, October 1941; March 1937).
57. *S* (Spring 1947).
58. *FRP*, p. 157.
59. *The Times*, 'Mrs Q.D. Leavis' (26.3.81). The letter quoted by Ford is lost.
60. Chatto: Parsons–G.W. Stewart (10.2.48) and Parsons (25.1.48).
61. Emmanuel (Harding) (29.7.47).

Part Three
After the War 1949–1963

CHAPTER EIGHT
NO COMMON PURSUIT 1949–1960

1. C (7.8.49).
2. C (5.4.49).
3. DGB (7.8.48; 23.4.51; 31.5.51; 15.6.51; 27.7.51; 12.10.51).
4. Chatto: Eliot–Parsons (4.8.51).
5. Ford, *L*, p. 109.
6. Bell's journal entry (15.6.52). Bell's journal is in the possession of Anthea Bell, who well describes the Leavis hospitality for children (23.1.92).
7. Matthews (21.8.52; 21.11.52).
8. *S* (December 1946); C (21.11.47).

9. Matthews (24.9.91).
10. HRC (Snow) (31.3.50).
11. *TLS* (25.5.50); C (31.8.50).
12. C (29.9.50).
13. Tyrone Guthrie, *A Life in the Theatre* (1959), pp. 201–2. For Keynes, Beaumont, CEMA and the Arts Council, see Charles Landstone, *Off-Stage: A Personal Record of the First Twelve Years of State Sponsored Drama in Great Britain* (1953), pp. 66–81. Keynes, Rylands and Beaumont could be seen as belonging to a King's nexus.
14. 'Keynes, Lawrence and Cambridge', 'Keynes, Spender and Currency-Values', *S* (March 1949; June 1951). Also relevant is 'Poetry Prizes for the Festival of Britain: 1951', *S* (Winter 1949).
15. *TM*, p. 77.
16. Ronald W. Clark, *The Life of Bertrand Russell* (1975), p. 261.
17. *TM*, pp. 101–2; Garnett, editing *TM*, makes it clear that for '1914' Keynes should have put '1915'.
18. For Keynes's Nonconformist background, see 'Ancestors' in Geoffrey Keynes's *The Gates of Memory* (1981).
19. *S* (June 1951). Webster (1886–1961), historian of diplomatic relations, knew the peace negotiations at first-hand, having been attached to the Foreign Office in 1919. He was author of *The Congress of Vienna* (1919).
20. A completely revised edition appeared in 1984; this is used here.
21. *Leslie Stephen: The Godless Victorian* (1984), pp. 328, 322–38.
22. *Studies in Social History: A Tribute to G.M. Trevelyan*, edited by J.H. Plumb (1955); *S* (June 1951).
23. C (5.4.49; 5.6.50).
24. Boris Ford organized the questionnaire about teaching in Cambridge in 1937 and had thought about critico-reference guides to literature, having reviewed the *Concise Cambridge History of English Literature* for *S*. The friends he consulted were L.C. Knights, Leo Salingar and G.D. Klingopulos.
25. Watson (17.11.53).
26. In lecture form at the Institute of Contemporary Arts.
27. Empson evidently made disparaging remarks about F.R.L., who referred to 'a mean and nasty "smear" at my expense about which I protested, fruitlessly, to Ransom of the *Kenyon* [Review]. Ransom replied that he regarded Empson as a kind of saint. Empson is a great power in America – very much more so than Richards.' C (4.4.51).
28. Holbrook (3.12.53).
29. Holbrook (22.3.57).
30. *Spectator* (11.12.53 and after).
31. BBC WAC: Newby (28.11.53; 25.1.54); Holbrook (24.12.53).
32. BBC WAC (26.2.54). Kermode's talk is in the same archive, transmitted on 18.2.54.

33. HRC (Lehmann): Lerner (9.3.54); (12.1.55); F.R.L. (16.1.55).

34. Harrison, 'Recollections', pp. 71–2, 132, 115–16; Karl Miller, *Rebecca's Vest: A Memoir* (1993), p. 142; Joseph M. Robertson (13.1.94).

35. Quoted as from a letter 'a year later' than 13.7.26 in *Thought, Words and Creativity*, p. 32.

36. Chatto: F.R.L.–Parsons (17.2.55).

37. BBC WAC: Keen (2.9.49).

38. 'D.H. Lawrence: The Novelist', BBC WAC, radio script (15.9.49).

39. Chatto: F.R.L.–Parsons (18.3.51).

40. Chatto: F.R.L.–Parsons (26.1.54).

41. Beal (14.7.92).

42. F.R.L. told his pupils that when Hough left his book at the F.R.L. house it was returned unopened.

43. *Dark Sun*, pp. 174–5.

44. *Dark Sun*, p. 144; *DHLN*, p. 275.

45. *DHLN*, p. 75.

46. HRC (Frieda Lawrence). Two letters were drafted, obviously near in time and very similar in subject. One is dated '22.5.56'; it is the other letter that is quoted here.

47. *Humanism and Poetry in the Early Tudor Period: An Essay* (1959), p. 146.

48. Matthews (21.8.52).

49. Emmanuel (F.R.L.): Matthews (6.5.57).

50. Holbrook (25.10.58; 9.11.58).

51. Holbrook (23.7.58; 5.7.54).

52. DFP (F.R.L.): Whalley–Tooker–Guthrie (6.8.57); C (20.10.57); Holbrook (12.7.59).

53. The 'feel' of Shapira's teaching is given in a draft essay designed to introduce a book of Lawrence's art criticism, with plates, intended for collaboration with a pupil (Peter Sharrock) and published after Shapira's death in the *Cambridge Quarterly* (1982).

54. See his review of George Watson, *The Literary Critics* in *Delta* (Summer 1964): 'Readers of *Delta* will recognize the indebtedness of my general argument to Mr Mason's ideas about translation as well as to Mr Eliot's account of the historical sense.'

55. Cambridge University: Board of Graduate Studies (16.6.92).

56. Shapira, 'The Study of Criticism for the Preliminary' (July 1957) and 'Further Notes re Criticism' (February 1958), both typescripts, dated in Shapira's hand. There is a third paper, 'Criticism, the Preliminary and the Tripos' (August 1957).

57. Chatto: F.R.L.–Parsons (3.12.59).

58. See 'My Cambridge', *An Unnatural Pursuit and Other Pieces* (1985), pp. 220–21; also contains 'The Pursuit of F.R. Leavis'.

59. University journals run by undergraduates were required to have a senior

financial supervisor. Without a Senior Treasurer, the journal had to close. This one survived by passing into the care of graduates.

60. The *Listener* had a respected literary section: its first editor was J.R. Ackerley and it was later edited by Leavis's pupil Karl Miller. It had a much wider circulation than many cultural weeklies because, published by the BBC, its prime function was to print radio talks.

61. *Delta* (2.60 and 10.60); *Broadsheet* (9.3.60); *Spectator* (27.10.60).

62. *Listener* (3.11.60).

63. In December he was elected on to the Board for four years, and then elected for another four years at the end of this term, taking him up to the end of 1963. On that occasion he was not re-elected, and John Holloway defeated him in December 1963. There was a certain amount of protest from the undergraduates. Then he was re-elected, which would have taken him to the end of 1968. He was then off it for one year to return for 1965, elected for a further four years; he then resigned, prematurely, in the summer of 1966.

64. *CUR* (27.5.59; 17.7.47).

65. Chatto: F.R.L.–Parsons (2.4.59).

CHAPTER NINE
THE SIXTIES: ORTHODOXY OF ENLIGHTENMENT
1960–1963

1. For example, in the letter to C.P. Snow (1.1.54).

2. DGB (26.2.60; 21.10.60).

3. DGB (13.1.60): choice of painter.

4. 'Obituary notice of Knut Hamsun', epigraph to *CP*, edition of 1962.

5. Black (14.1.62); Chatto: F.R.L.–Parsons (7.2.62).

6. *Observer* (11.3.62).

7. *The Times* (2.11.71).

8. R (2.8.62). 'X' is Morris Shapira.

9. Hans Schmoller, *The Times* (6.1.78; the date of Schmoller's letter); Alan Hill, *In Pursuit of Publishing* (1988), pp. 67–8.

10. C.H. Rolph, *The Trial of Lady Chatterley: Regina v. Penguin Books Limited* (1961).

11. The teacher was Christopher Parry; his unpublished paper, 'The Leavises and Young Life', is quoted, on the Leavis family and their son's education at the Perse.

12. Emmanuel (F.R.L.): F.R.L.–Gray (21.2.61).

13. Bristol (Penguin Books): (12.1.62).

14. Jones (27.6.59); Perry (20.7.59).

15. Jones: F.R.L. (8.10.59).

16. Trinity (CUP) (30.8.61; 24.11.64). He did not know that the New York

office of Cambridge University Press once considered reprinting Bentley's selection. Trinity: Mansbridge (31.5.63).

17. Trinity (CUP) (26.11.63; 30.8.61).
18. *The Times* (17.2.61).
19. C (19.8.61).
20. *Spectator* (3.11.60).
21. TC, p. 7.
22. He was more dubious still in *A Second Look* (pp. 96–7). Could anyone who wanted human welfare really 'participate without qualification' in the literature of the avant-garde?
23. Philip Snow, *Stranger and Brother: A Portrait of C.P. Snow* (1982), p. 122.
24. TC, p. 45.
25. *Time* (20.4.62).
26. 'Technique and Culture: Three Cambridge Portraits', *Essays and Studies* 14 (1961).
27. BBC WAC: Keen (23.2.62); F.R.L. (27.2.62).
28. TC, p. 44.
29. TCSS, p. 27.
30. TCSS, p. 25.
31. It is usually presumed that F.R.L.'s 'This is so, isn't it?' means what is said by one person to another. It can also refer to what a critic says to himself.
32. TCSS, p. 28.
33. He surmised that the connection was L.P. Wilkinson, King's College, the University Public Orator. Wilkinson was an obituary editor of *The Times* and its Cambridge correspondent. He attended the lecture by invitation and whoever sent the invitation must have been aware of his Fleet Street roles. A young journalist, Bruce Kemble (a recent Downing English graduate), also kept the newspapers in the picture.
34. The legal opinion, from Oswald, Hickson, Collier & Co., is given in a statement in the Chatto archive. Evidently the *Spectator* forwarded it to Chatto when negotiations for book publication began.
35. HRC (Snow): Ray–Snow (11.4.70)
36. HRC (Snow): Snow–Putt (20.11.63); TCSS, p. 10.
37. TCSS, p. 11.
38. Hilary Spurling, *Secrets of a Woman's Heart: The Later Life of Ivy Compton-Burnett 1920–1968* (1984), p. 221.
39. HRC (Snow): Snow (3.12.47).
40. T (15.12.68); R (9.11.70).
41. Chatto: F.R.L.–Parsons (10.3.62; 2.7.62); Ray in the *Spectator* (16.3.62).
42. HRC: Snow–Putt (20.11.63), who published 'The Snow–Leavis Rumpus', *Antioch Review* 23 (1963), from the point of view of F.R.L.'s pupil and Snow's friend.

43. Philip Snow, p. 130.

44. HRC (Snow): Snow–Plumb (1.7.62). In Snow's Afterword, 'The Two Cultures: A Second Look'. Notes 43 to 45 owe much to Plumb. To Plumb (3.9.63) Snow refers to 'the quotation you wrote down for me'.

45. Trinity (CUP): Black (28.4.62; and 16.8.94 on the Press's doubts about publishing the lecture); F.R.L. (1.5.62).

46. 'I saw it would go with mine beautifully' Trinity (CUP): Black (24.8.62).

47. HRC (Snow): Snow–Parsons (27.7.62). The draft of this letter makes it clear that the last two sentences were devised by Snow's editor, Lovat Dickson at Macmillan.

48. One of the most dispassionate accounts of the dispute was 'The Snow Affair' by Mary S. Simpson, *Bulletin of the Atomic Scientists* (April 1963).

49. *Sewanee Review* (April–June, 1962), p. 190.

50. Norman Henfrey, later editor of a selection of writings by George Santayana. The account of the lecture is based on Henfrey's recollections and John Harvey, 'F.R. Leavis: An Appreciation' with Q.D.L.'s correction, *Encounter* (May–July 1979). The lecture was 'reviewed' by George Steiner in *Encounter* (May 1962), appearing influentially in *Language and Silence: Essays 1958–1966* (1967).

51. Anthony Holden, *Olivier* (1988), p. 380; Tarquin Olivier, *My Father Laurence Olivier* (1993), p. 247.

52. A 'very bad' year, F.R.L. wrote to Black: Trinity (CUP) (15.5.62).

53. Chatto: F.R.L.–Parsons (10.3.62).

54. Holbrook (7.9.61; 28.8.61).

55. DGB (26.10.62; 9.11.62).

56. Registered charity number: 313516.

57. Strickland (9.7.92).

58. R (27.3.71; 14.7.71).

59. S (2.1.63).

60. The house is beautifully described by Nora Crook in 'Taking Tea with Mrs Leavis' in L.

Part Four
New Ships 1963–1975

CHAPTER TEN
THE END OF CAMBRIDGE 1963–1965

1. Cmnd 6842.

2. Clare (Shapira): Shapira–Holbrook (12.11.61). Holbrook wrote that he thought F.R.L. was obsessed with a plot to have Amis elected to the

Faculty Board. It is more likely that he meant a lectureship. Snow supported Amis when he was attacked by Somerset Maugham: Philip Snow, *Stranger and Brother: A Portrait of C.P. Snow* (1982).

3. Cmnd 2154. On the grandeur of the report, Noël Annan quotes the committee assessor, John Carswell, in *Our Age* (1990), p. 502.
4. R (27.8.63).
5. Robert H. Walker, *The Poet and the Gilded Age* (1962).
6. 'Research in English', *TLS* (26.7.63), quoted from *ELT*, p. 193.
7. Trinity (CUP): Eliot (25.7.63); copy sent to Black.
8. He gave two only (because the notice was short) in May 1964: *DN*, p. xii.
9. Trinity (CUP): Mansbridge and Watt (14.4.63; 1.5.63); Trinity (CUP), undated reply to Black letter of 4.6.63 and on the 'Cambridge Book of English Verse' (5.9.64).
10. 'Questions of Degree', supported in 'A Degree of Judgement', *Sunday Times* (2.8.64; 9.8.64). F.R.L. is quoted from the latter.
11. *CUR* (1962), pp. 1841–2, discussion of 'Report on the Syndicate on the Relationship between the University and the Colleges' (13.3.62). Hough had dealt with the issue of numbers earlier in the year in 'Are the Dons Out of Touch: Crisis in Literary Education', *Sunday Times* (17.3.63). See also David Cecil, 'Wisdom through Delight', 'Bearding the Dons'; Denis Donoghue, 'It's a Battlefield', reviewing a reprint of *NBEP*.
12. DFP (F.R.L.): Whalley–Tooker–Guthrie (25.5.64).
13. R (21.3.64).
14. DFP: Guthrie–F.R.L. (27.4.64): on offering fellowship to Newton.
15. DFP (Vickers): Vickers–Guthrie (29.5.64).
16. Henn's advice is in a letter to Vickers (27.7.64) in Vickers's possession.
17. DFP (Vickers): Vickers–Guthrie (6.7.64).
18. DGB (29.5.64; 22.7.64); Wild–Shapira (24.7.64).
19. DFP: F.R.L.–Guthrie (22.7.64).
20. Vickers: personal paper, written May 1965, in his possession.
21. DFP: Vickers–Guthrie (26.7.64).
22. DFP: F.R.L.–Guthrie (5.9.64; 8.9.64), Guthrie–F.R.L. (7.9.64).
23. DGB: F.R.L.–Guthrie (4.9.64).
24. DFP: Gay–Guthrie (10.9.64).
25. The lecture at Clare College was on 27 November: Neil Roberts in a private paper, 'Leavisite Cambridge 1964–70' (1992); and Roberts (20.9.90).
26. DFP: Parry–Guthrie (14.10.64).
27. DFP: Guthrie–Parry (15.10.64).
28. W (24.3.64?). '1964' is almost illegible.
29. DFP: Guthrie–Shapira (29.10.64).
30. DFP: Guthrie–F.R.L. (n.d.: 29.10.64?), replying to F.R.L. (10.10.64).
31. Clare (Shapira): Shapira–Guthrie (5.1.65).
32. DFP (Vickers): Vickers–Guthrie (24.2.65).

33. It is important to note that Shapira ceded his claim (even though it was hopeless). His doing so shows how he did submit to the overall plan of the Lectureship Trust. Parry said: 'I may add that, though these are not wholly relevant matters, F.R.L. and Shapira both realize that any proposal that a College office should be given to the latter would be unwelcome and unacceptable by the college.'

34. DFP (F.R.L.): various to Guthrie (29.11.64).

35. DFP (F.R.L.): Guthrie's notes (19.3.65).

36. DFP (F.R.L.) (5.5.65), replying to Guthrie (25.4.65).

37. DFP (F.R.L.): press release (25.6.65).

38. E.H. Freitag, a young Swiss fellow in engineering who was friendly with Shapira and would run, cordially, with Leavis, wrote forcefully on the situation to Guthrie: DFP (F.R.L.): Freitag (22.7.65).

39. R (8.12.64).

40. Published by CUP (1965).

41. R (n.d.).

42. Enkvist (27.8.91); L, p. 127.

43. S (10.12.65).

44. S (28.12.65; 8.1.66, marked '65').

45. To be inferred from F.R.L.'s letter to Shapira (7.1.66) in which he says that 'he [Robin Leavis] didn't go to him *ad hoc*' to complain about supervision: 'it came up'.

46. S (7.1.65).

47. W (2.3.66). The text has a mistake in it, marked here in square brackets: In late January 'my wife and I, [after] 3 or 4 weeks ago, broke out volcanically.'

48. By Mason because, apart from the style, he invariably referred to 'Mr Leavis' in his signed writings, except for 'Professor' in his lecture on *Antony and Cleopatra* published later. Newton used the usual 'Dr' and Robson 'Leavis'.

49. W (24.1.66).

50. W (1.2.66).

51. *TLS* (17.2.66).

52. W (9.3.66).

53. Strickland (9.7.92).

54. W (24.3.66).

55. S (4.3.66).

56. R (30.4.74).

57. David J. Harper, 'Defining Delusion and the Serving of Professional Interests: The Case of Paranoia', *British Journal of Medical Psychology* (1992). Harper takes the remark by J.S. Mill from S.J. Gould, *The Mismeasure of Man* (1981).

58. S (27.1.66).

59. S (31.3.66).
60. S (1.4.66).
61. S (6.4.66).
62. Shapira was murdered in a random act of violence in 1981.

CHAPTER ELEVEN
NEW UNIVERSITIES 1965–1975

1. Q.D.L.–Worthington (10.8.77).
2. Inglis (27.6.71).
3. Brian MacArthur, *Manchester Guardian Weekly* (23.6.66); Emmanuel
   (F.R.L.): F.R.L.–Harding (8.10.67).
4. R (7.2.72).
5. *ELT*, p. 184; *Spectator* (13.5.66).
6. He was also dubious of a let-in-all-comers 'Novel' course because fifteen
   years before he planned a 'well-defined, compact and manageable' course
   on the American novel (Fenimore Cooper, Nathaniel Hawthorne, Herman
   Melville, Henry James). See his Introduction to Bewley's *The Complex Fate*
   (1952).
7. *ELT*, p. 164.
8. Chatto: (16.7.68); Diggle (15.9.91).
9. T (8.8.70).
10. 'Dombey and Son', *Sewanee Review* (1962). The additions are from p. 13
    ('We may recall') to p. 24 ('with Mr Dombey').
11. Peter Coveney's *Poor Monkey* (1957) was revised as *The Image of Childhood*
    and published with an introduction by Leavis in 1967.
12. 'Evangelical forays': Chatto: F.R.L.–Smallwood (17.3.69).
13. Chatto: Parsons–Q.D.L. (15.11.70).
14. T (8.8.70), Diggle (15.9.91).
15. R (7.9.71).
16. Chatto: F.R.L.–Parsons (n.d.).
17. *GT*, p. 19.
18. He signed the Liberal candidate's nomination paper and subscribed to the
    Liberal election fund: letter to *Sunday Times* (1.11.64).
19. T (17.11.70); R (2.11.70).
20. R (23.3.71; 2.11.70).
21. Holbrook (23.12.70).
22. *Bookman* (April 1934).
23. T (19.6.69).
24. He quotes his letter to *The Times* (8.10.68).
25. *TLS* (3.7.69).
26. T (13.12.69).
27. T (3.3.69).

28. T (17.11.70); R (2.11.70; 27.3.71; 14.7.71).

29. Annan's reply to 'Pluralism, Compassion and Social Hope': *Human World* (February and August 1971). 'Introductory' to *Nor Shall My Sword* is also quoted.

30. *Human World* (August 1971), p. 18. The letter to Tanner is quoted from his contribution to *L*, pp. 138–9.

31. W (16.1.67).

32. W (19.2.67).

33. Chatto: F.R.L.–Parsons (25.2.72).

34. Chatto: Parsons, office memorandum (2.3.72).

35. At the last meeting of the Trust (12.7.75) its assets were transferred to the University of York.

36. R (28.8.72).

37. R (11.4.63).

38. R (15.4.70); the concept was used in 1966 to define 'culture' in 'Luddites? Or There is Only One Culture', *LA* (1969), p. 15.

39. Tasker (19.6.69).

40. Chatto (17.4.75).

41. Chatto: Enright (14.12.75).

42. R (10.2.74; 30.8.74).

43. Beal (1.8.73).

44. Holbrook (18.2.73); T (20.1.73). F.R.L. spoke freely and wrote about family matters and was evidently anxious to give versions of them to professional contacts.

45. T (3.3.69).

46. *CAP*, p. 147.

47. T (3.3.69). Eliot's spirituality is associated by F.R.L. with Dante. He writes in the same letter that the third poem in *Ash-Wednesday*

> when I read it (as a separate poem, with French translation *en regard*) first was entitled 'Som de l'escalina' – from the Provençal passage spoken by Arnaut Daniel in *Purgatorio* xxvi. Of course, Eliot doesn't take over Dante's purgatorial steps, but the idea of a disciplined advance by stages is there – as disciplined (humble! – ah) advance ('I made this') is the essential offer in *Four Quartets*. It's pretty plain that Eliot associates 'La Figlia' memory/episode with Dante's childhood encounter with Beatrice. I dislike his Dante essay.

Was not *Ash-Wednesday* crucial for F.R.L.? 'Yes, but':

> My habit of saying that Chaucer is the great neglected poet goes back to decades before your Downing years. And I had long ago formed the sense of Eliot that made me say, with an eye on him: I can't for the life of me see why Dante should be exalted above Chaucer; the civilization that produced Chaucer is the one I much prefer (R 18.12.71).

48. The origin of 'nisus' is Latin (*niti*, to endeavour), but the *OED* gives seventeenth- and eighteenth–century English usages.

49. Holbrook (16.12.74).

50. *LP*, p. 25.
51. 'Alfred North Whitehead', *S* (June 1934).
52. In 'Anarchy and Criticism', *The Survival of English: Essays in Criticism and Language* (1973): possibly the best response to late Leavis.
53. *L*, p. 138; 'Life and Thought' refers to the titles of English Tripos examinations.
54. R (10.1.73) referring to Furbank, 'What Leavis Wants', *Listener* (30.10.75).
55. Quoted from 'a philosopher who had written to tell me that he and his friends had been for some time interested in my work', *LP*, p. 16.
56. R (2.8.72).
57. R (22.8.72).
58. R (29.3.71; 15.12.70; 25.7.71).
59. Still seeking for a nucleus such as that of the *Scrutiny* group. At this moment he counted Robinson and Tanner as possibilities; also John Tasker and the admirable Philip Dossé, editor of *Books and Bookmen*. Swansea refers to the University of Wales at which Robinson taught, and at which Wittgenstein had stayed. This letter to Robinson was written on 28 August 1972.
60. Quotations from 'Memories of Wittgenstein' from *CAP*.
61. T (24.11.41).
62. R (2.4.73); Tasker (8.2.76).
63. T (5.10.73).
64. R (25.4.71); first published in *Nuova Antologia* (1971).

Part Five
Epilogue 1975–1978

1. Chatto: Parsons (19.4.75).
2. T (20.1.73).
3. *VC*, p. 5.
4. Chatto: Parsons (5.12.76).
5. Chatto: Parsons (19.11.76).
6. *CAP*, p. x.
7. Chatto: Parsons (27.1.76).
8. Worthington (1.8.77).
9. *Thought, Words and Creativity*, p. 92.
10. Holbrook (22.6.77).
11. Worthington (5.9.77).
12. Harrison (21.5.75).
13. W (28.2.77; 25.11.77).

14. Worthington (25.11.77).
15. Worthington (10.11.77).
16. *The Times* (31.12.77); Collingwood (22.1.78).
17. Magdalene (Richards). The letter is dated 'January 20 1978' and reproduced in John Constable (ed.), *Selected Letters of I.A. Richards* (1990), p. 67; Worthington (20.3.78).
18. Worthington (20.3.78).
19. R (18.12.71; 21.3.64).
20. *Bookseller* (29.4.78).
21. *CR* (2.6.78).
22. Harrison (21.5.78).
23. *New Statesman* (7.7.78; 4.8.78); *TLS* (4.8.78); W (17.9.78).

BOOKS AND PAMPHLETS BY F.R. LEAVIS

―――

Mass Civilization and Minority Culture (1930)

D.H. Lawrence (1930)

New Bearings in English Poetry: A Study of the Contemporary Situation (1932)

How to Teach Reading: A Primer for Ezra Pound (1932)

For Continuity (1933)

Revaluation: Tradition and Development in English Poetry (1936)

Education and the University: A Sketch for an 'English School' (1943)

The Great Tradition: George Eliot, Henry James, Joseph Conrad (1948)

The Common Pursuit (1952)

D.H. Lawrence: Novelist (1955)

Two Cultures: The Significance of C.P. Snow (1962)

'Anna Karenina' and Other Essays (1967)

English Literature in Our Time and the University, The Clark Lectures (1969)

Lectures in America (1969). With Q.D.L.

Dickens the Novelist (1970). With Q.D.L.

Gerard Manley Hopkins: Reflections After Fifty Years (1971)

Nor Shall My Sword: Discourses on Pluralism (1972)

The Living Principle: 'English' as a Discipline of Thought (1975)

Thought, Words and Creativity: Art and Thought in Lawrence (1976)

'Reading Out Poetry' and 'Eugenio Montale: A Tribute' (1979)

Leavis wrote over 120 pieces for *Scrutiny: A Quarterly Review* from 1932 to 1953, many but not all collected into book form. The journal was reprinted in its entirety by Cambridge University Press (1963) along with *Scrutiny: A Retrospect* by Leavis, published with the Index and as a pamphlet. Leavis edited several collections of work by himself and collaborators, the most important *A Selection from 'Scrutiny'* (1968) in two volumes: Leavis's correspondence with Cambridge University Press shows that the work represents a carefully conscious act of selection from the enterprise, *Scrutiny*, the totality of which he considered his major achievement to date. His other main editorial works, or books to which he contributed prefaces, are: *Towards Standards of Criticism: Selections from 'The Calendar of Modern Letters' 1925–1927* (1933), *Mill on Bentham and Coleridge* (1951), Twain's *Pudd'nhead Wilson: A Tale* (1955), Conrad's *Nostromo* (1960), Eliot's *Adam Bede* (1961) and *Felix Holt* (1967), James's *Selected Literary Criticism* (1963) and Bunyan's *The Pilgrim's Progress* (1964). Uncollected essays appear in posthumous volumes edited by G.S. Singh: *The Critic as Anti-Philosopher: Essays and Papers* (1982) and *Valuation in Criticism and Other Essays* (1986).

INDEX

Leavis taught many students at Cambridge and elsewhere. Some of these were specifically his undergraduate pupils at Emmanuel or Downing colleges. The names of his pupils mentioned in this book are marked with asterisks in the Index.